Eleanor
of Castile

Eleanor of Castile

Queen and Society in Thirteenth-Century England

John Carmi Parsons

St. Martin's Press
New York

ELEANOR OF CASTILE
Copyright © 1995 by John Carmi Parsons
All rights reserved. Printed in the United States of America.
No part of this book may be used or reproduced in any
manner whatsoever without written permission except
in the case of brief quotations embodied in critical articles
or reviews. For information, address St. Martin's Press,
Scholarly and Reference Division, 175 Fifth Avenue,
New York, N.Y. 10010

ISBN 0-312-08649-0

Library of Congress Cataloging-in-Publication Data

Parsons, John Carmi, 1947-
    Eleanor of Castile : queen and society in thirteenth-century
England / John Carmi Parsons.
        p. cm.
    Includes bibliographical references and index.
    ISBN 0-312-08649-0
    1. Eleanor, Queen, consort of Edward I, King of England, d. 1290.
2. Great Britain—History—Edward I, 1272-1307. 3. England—Social
life and customs—1066-1485. 4. Queens—Great Britain—Biography.
I. Title.
DA229.P37 1994
942.03'5'092—dc20
    [B]   94-31086
                                                           CIP

First Edition March 1995:
10 9 8 7 6 5 4 3 2 1

†M. M. S.

❀ Contents ❀

List of Illustrations

❧ Preface ❧

This is not the book I intended to write when I set out, years ago, to research Eleanor of Castile's life. I expected to produce a straightforward biography, but while the book retains some vestiges of that form it has also pursued other paths. The change in direction grew in part from the tensions between Eleanor's contrasting images in contemporary sources and in later writings about her; in part, it was imposed by the amount and nature of the original source material. The result is a study not only of a queen's life but also of the formation of her reputation, both in her own day and as she has been represented over the seven centuries since her death. Far better regarded in death than in life, she is an historical and an historiographical enigma whose career has taken longer to unravel than I could have anticipated. The tale has grown in the telling but is, I hope, the better for it.

Of the instructors, colleagues and friends whose encouragement and advice contributed to this book, I must mention Leonard Boyle OP, J. Ambrose Raftis CSB, Brian Stock, Jim Reilly, Anne Hutchinson, and James P. Carley; at the University of Toronto's Centre for Medieval Studies, John Leyerle, Roberta Frank, Walter Goffart, David Townsend, A. George Rigg, David Klausner, Cynthia Martin, Grace Desa, and Jean Mutrie; at Victoria University's Centre for Reformation and Renaissance Studies, Germaine Warkentin, Konrad Eisenbichler, David Galbreath, and Joe Black. I am particularly grateful to those who read and commented on portions of the manuscript in various forms: E. A. R. Brown, Paul Strohm, Janet Nelson, Margaret Howell, János Bak, Pauline Stafford, Michael Prestwich, Paul Brand, Phillip Lindley, Nicola Coldstream, and Paul Binski, though of course none bears responsibility for the conclusions I have advanced. David Parsons arranged a commemorative conference on Queen Eleanor in 1990 and his generous invitation to speak there allowed me to focus many aspects of the work in progress. In Toronto, my thanks are due the Reverend Donald Finlay CSB and his staff including Sister Wilma Fitzgerald, Mary English, Nancy Kovacs, Carolyn Suma, and the late Mrs. Lorraine Egsgard. Randall Rosenfeld designed the genealogical tables. Among the many friends who have offered encouragement, I must regretfully limit myself to recognizing Bonnie Wheeler and Jeremy Adams, John Sommerfeldt, Anne and Ed DeWindt, Susan Stuard, Phyllis Pobst, and Louise Fradenburg. I marvel at the patience of a mother and sister who endured explanations about Eleanor that were sometimes solicited and sometimes not. This book would not have been possible without the assistance of staff at the Public Record Office, the Reading Room and the Students' Manuscript Room at the British Library, Ms. Anne Oakley at the Dean and chapter library, Canterbury, and Mr. F. S. McMichael MA, keeper of the muniments at Westminster Abbey. At St. Martin's Press, I gladly recognize the patience of Mr. Simon Winder, Ms. Laura Heymann, and Ms. Nancy Hirsch.

The fine and gentle scholar to whom this book is dedicated shepherded me through the material's first manifestation a decade and a half ago, and more recently gave me the benefit of his discreet counsel and encouragement as I reworked it. It is a cause of profound regret to me that he did not live to see it completed.

Centre for Reformation and Renaissance Studies
Victoria University in the University of Toronto
March 1994

❋ Abbreviations ❋

Standard abbreviations are used for pre-1974 English counties and months of the year. In dates, 1241 X 1290 means between 1241 and 1290. To distinguish the king's officials from the queen's, the former are capitalized (Treasurer); the latter are not (treasurer). All dates are in modern form.

abp	archbishop
acct	account(-ed),(-ing),(-ant)
ackn.	acknowledge(d),(-ment)
acq.	acquire(d), acquisition
admin.	administration; administer(-ed); administrative
adv.	advowson
agst	against
als	*alias*
anct	ancient
appt(d)	appoint(-ed)
appurt., appurts	appurtenant(-ces)
appx	appendix
arr.	arrange(d)
ascr.	ascribe(d)(-ing)
assoc.	associate(d)
atty	attorney
b.	born
bef.	before
bf	bailiff
bis	twice
bk	book
bldg	building
bp	bishop
br.	brother
bur.	buried
ca.	circa
ch.	church
chap., chaps	chapter(s)
cl.	claim(ed), (-ing)
clk(s)	clerk(s)
coh.	coheir
col.	column
commn(s)	commission(s)

commr	commissioner
conf.	confirm(ed), confirmation
cons.	consideration
ctss	countess
d.	died
dau., daus	daughter(s)
dcn	deacon
depr.	deprive(d)
disp.	dispense, dispensation
distr.	distraint
doct	document
e.	earl
Exch.	Exchequer
exch.	exchange
ed(s)., edn	editor(s), edition
esp.	especially
exor	executor
expn(s)	expense(s)
f.	founded
fl.	flourished
fol., fols	folio(s)
gt(d)	grant(ed)
h.	heir(s)
idem	the same
ident.	identical, identify(-ied)
incl.	include(d), (-ing)
inq.	inquest
insp.	*inspeximus*
intr.	introduction
jr	junior
K	king
knt(d)	knight(-ed)
kpr	keeper
marr.	marriage
m.	membrane
m.	marry (married)
Mich.	Michaelmas
mr	master
MS	manuscript
no., nos	number(s)
nom.	nominate(d)
n.p.	no place of publication/publisher given
occ.	occurs

oct.	octave (one week after)
OFM	Order of Friars Minor (Franciscans)
OP	Order of Preachers (Dominicans)
OSB	Order of St Benedict (Benedictines)
parlt	parliament
pl.	plate
pr.	prove(d)
preb.	prebendary
pres.	present(ed), (-ation)
prob.	probably
Q	queen
qu.	querent
quinz.	quinzaine (two weeks after)
qy	query
r.	reigned
recd	received
ref.	reference
res.	resigned
recogn.	recognize, recognition
rpt	reprint
s.	son
s.a.	no year given
s.d.	no date given
sher.	sheriff
sjty	serjeanty
s.n.	no volume number given
s.p.	without children
sr	senior
subord.	subordinate
s.v.	see under the word
svt(s)	servant(s)
temp.	in the time of
ten.	tenure; tenement
ter	thrice
trans.	translation, translated
vct	viscount
witn.	witness(ed)
yr	younger

TITLE ABBREVIATIONS

Manuscript sources

BL	London, British Library
BN	Paris, Bibliothèque Nationale
AHN	Madrid, Archivio Histórico Nacionál
PRO	London, Public Record Office
Westm. Abbey muniments	London, Westminster Abbey

PRO classifications cited: *

C 47/	Chancery Miscellany
C 62/	Chancery *liberate* rolls
D.L.	Ancient Deeds, Duchy of Lancaster
E 9/	Exchequer of the Jews, Plea rolls
E 13/	Exchequer of Pleas, Plea rolls
E 36/	Exchequer, Treasury of receipt, Miscellaneous books
E 40/	Exchequer, Treasury of Receipt, Ancient Deeds (series A)
E 101/	Exchequer, Accounts various
E 159/	Exchequer, King's (Queen's) remembrancer, Memoranda rolls
E 327/	Exchequer, Augmentation Office, Ancient Deeds (series B)
E 372/	Pipe rolls
E 403/	Exchequer *liberate* rolls
JUST 1/	Justices Itinerant
K.B. 1/	*Coram rege* rolls
S.C. 1/	Ancient Correspondence of the Chancery and Exchequer
S.C. 6/	Ministers' Accounts

Published Sources and Authorities

Abingdon	*Chron. Monasterii de Abingdon*, ed. J. Stevenson. RS 2 (1858)
Ann.	Annales
Ann. Paulini	*Annales Paulini*, ed. W. Stubbs in *Chrons. of the Reigns of Edward I and Edward II*. RS 76.ii (1883)
Barnwell	*Liber Memorandorum Ecclesiae de Bernewelle*, ed. J. W. Clark (Cambridge, 1907)
BEC	*Bibliothèque de l'École des Chartes*
BF	*The Book of Fees (Testa de Neville)*, 3 vols. (PRO, 1921–1931)
BIHR	*Bulletin of the Institute of Historical Research*
BJRL	*Bulletin of the John Rylands Library*
Bliss	*Entries in the Papal Registers Relating to Great Britain and Ireland*, ed. W. H. Bliss *et al.* (PRO, 1894f)

*For these records, M = Michaelmas term, H = Hilary term, E = Easter term, T = Trinity term.

Br. Chronology	Fryde, E. B., *et al.*, eds. *Handbook of British Chronology*. Royal Historical Society Guides and Handbooks, no. 2, 3rd edn (London, 1986)
Burton	*Annales Monasterii de Burton*, ed. H. R. Luard in *Ann. Monastici.* RS 36.i (1864)
Bury	*The Chron. of Bury St Edmunds*, ed. A. Gransden (London, 1964)
Cal.	Calendar(s)
CChR	*Cal. of Charter Rolls* (PRO, 1903f)
CChyV	*Cal. of Chancery Rolls Various, 1277–1326* (PRO, London, 1912)
CChyW	*Cal. of Chancery Warrants* (PRO, London, 1927)
CDI	*Cal. of Documents relating to Ireland*, 5 vols. (PRO, 1875–86)
CHEC	J. C. Parsons, ed., *The Court and Household of Eleanor of Castile in 1290* (Toronto, 1977)
Chester	*Annales Cestrienses*, ed. R. C. Christie. Lancashire and Cheshire Record Society. (1887)
Chron.	Chronicle (chronicon, chronica)
ClR, CClR	*Close Rolls* (PRO, 1902–75); *Cal. of Close Rolls* (PRO, 1902f)**
CFR	*Cal. of Fine Rolls* (PRO, 1911f)
CIM	*Cal. of Inquisitions Miscellaneous* (PRO, 1916f)
CIPM	*Cal. of Inquisitions Post Mortem* (PRO, 1904f)
CLR	*Cal. of Liberate Rolls* (PRO, 1917f)
cont. Gervase of Canterbury	Continuator of Gervase of Canterbury, in *The Historical-Works of Gervase of Canterbury*, ed. W. Stubbs. RS 73.ii (1880)
Cotton	*Bartholomaei de Cotton Historia Anglicana*, ed. H. R. Luard. RS 16 (1859)
CPR	*Cal. of Patent Rolls* (PRO, 1901f)
CRR	*Curia regis rolls* (PRO, 1923f)
CYS	Canterbury and York Society
DC	*Descriptive Catalogue of Ancient Deeds* (PRO, 1894f)
DNB	*Dictionary of National Biography*
Domesday	*Liber Censualis vocatus Domesday-Book*. 4 vols. (London, Record Commission, 1783–1816)
Dunstable	*Annales Prioratus de Dunstaplia*, ed. H. R. Luard in *Ann. Monastici*. RS 36.iii (1866)
EFF	*Feet of Fines for Essex*, ed. R. E. G. Kirk *et al.*, 4 vols (Colchester, 1899–1964)
EHR	*English Historical Review*
Fasti 1066–1300	J. le Neve, *Fasti Ecclesiae Anglicanae 1066–1300*, new ed., Institute of Historical Research, 4 vols. (London, 1968f)

**Full Latin texts of the *Close Rolls* are published for the reign of Henry III; for the reigns of Edward I and later sovereigns, the rolls are published in English calendar form.

Fasti 1300–1541	J. le Neve, *Fasti Ecclesiae Anglicanae 1300–1541*, new ed., Institute of Historical Research, 12 vols. (London, 1962–67)
Foedera	T. Rymer, ed., *Foedera, Conventiones, Literae et Cujuscunque generalis Acta Publica.* . . . 4 vols. (London, Record Commission, 1816–69)
GEC	G. E. Cokayne, *The Complete Peerage*, 2nd ed., 13 vols. (London, 1910–40)
Glastonbury	J. P. Carley, ed., D. Townsend, trans., *The Chronicle of Glastonbury Abbey* (Woodbridge, 1985)
Guisborough	*The Chron. of Walter of Guisborough*, ed. H. Rothwell. Camden Soc. 3rd ser. 89 (1957)
Howden	*Chron. Rogeri de Hoveden*, ed. W. Stubbs. RS 51 (1868–70)
JMH	*Journal of Medieval History*
Kalendars	F. Palgrave, *Antient Kalendars and Inventories of the Treasury of His Majesty's Exchequer*, 3 vols. (London, Record Commission, 1836)
KW	H. M. Colvin, R. A. Brown, and A. J. Taylor, *The History of the King's Works: The Middle Ages*, 2 vols. (London, 1963)
Lanercost	*The Chron. of Lanercost Priory*, ed. J. Stevenson (Edinburgh, 1839)
Lehmann-Brockhaus	O. Lehmann-Brockhaus, *Lateinische Schriftquellen zur Kunst in England, Wales und Schottland (901–1307)*, 5 vols. (Munich, 1955–60)
Liber Quotidianus	Society of Antiquaries of London, *Liber quotidianus contrarotulatoris garderobae Anno regni Regis Edwardi primi vicesimo octavo. A.D. MCCIX et MCCC* (London, 1787)
London	*Annales Londonienses*, ed. W. Stubbs in *Chrons. of the Reigns of Edward I and Edward II.* RS 76.i (1862)
MA	W. Dugdale, *Monasticon Anglicanum*, 2nd ed., 6 vols. in 7 (London, 1846)
Manners	B. Botfield and T. Turner, eds., *Manners and Household Expenses of England in the Thirteenth and Fifteenth Centuries* (London, 1841)
MGH	*Monumenta Germaniae Historica* (SS = Scriptores)
Moor, *Knights*	C. Moor, *Knights of Edward I*, 5 vols. Harleian Society, 80–84. (London, 1929–32)
Osney	*Annales Monasterii de Oseneia*, ed. H. R. Luard in *Ann. Monastici.* RS 36.iv (1869)
Oxenden	*Chron. Johannis de Oxenedes*, ed. H. Ellis. RS 13 (1859)
PA	*Placitorum Abbreviatio, Richard I-Edward II.* Record Commission (London, 1811)
Paris, *CM*	Matthew Paris, *Chronica Majora*, ed. R. R. Luard, 7 vols. RS 57 (London, 1872–84)
Peterborough	*Chron. Petroburgense*, ed. Th. Stapleton. Camden Soc. 47 (1849)
PL	J.-P. Migne, ed., *Patrologia cursus completus, series Latina*, 221 vols (Paris, 1844–64)

PRS	Pipe Roll Society
PW	F. Palgrave, ed., *Parliamentary Writs and Writs of Military Summons*, 2 vols. (London, 1827–34)
Ramsey	*Chron. Abbatiae Rameseiensis*, ed. W. D. Macray. RS 83 (1886)
Records 1285–86	*Records of the Wardrobe and Household, 1285–1286*, ed. B. F. and C. R. Byerly (PRO, 1977)
Records 1286–89	*Records of the Wardrobe and Household, 1286–1289*, ed. B. F. and C. R. Byerly (PRO, 1986)
Reg.	Register, Registrum, Registra
RG	*Rôles gascons*, ed. M. Francisque-Michel, Ch. Bémont, 4 vols. (Paris, 1896–1906)
RH	*Rotuli Hundredorum*, 2 vols. (London, Record Commission, 1812–1818)
RHF	*Recueil des historiens de Gaule et de la France*, ed. D. Bouquet et al., 24 vols. (Paris, 1869–1904)
Rishanger	*Chron. Willelmi Rishanger*, ed. H. T. Riley in *Chron. Monasterii Sancti Albani*. RS 28.ii (1865)
RO	*Rotuli Originalium in Curia Scaccarii Abbreviatio, Henry III-Edward III*, 2 vols. (London, Record Commission, 1805–1810)
RP	*Rotuli Parliamentorum: the Rolls of Parliament*, 7 vols. (London, 1783–1832)
RRAN	*Regesta Regum Anglo-Normannorum*, ed. H. W. C. Davis et al., 3 vols. (Oxford, 1913–1968)
RS	Rolls Series
Stafford, *QCD*	P. Stafford, *Queens, Concubines and Dowagers. The King's Wife in the Early Middle Ages* (Athens GA, 1983)
Stagg, *CNFD*	D. J. Stagg, ed., *A Calendar of New Forest Documents, 1244–1334* (Hampshire County Council, Record Series 3, 1979)
Tewkesbury	*Annales de Theokesberia*, ed. H. R. Luard in *Ann. Monastici*. RS 36.i (1864)
TJHSE	*Transactions of the Jewish Historical Society of England*
Tout, *Chapters*	T. F. Tout, *Chapters in the Administrative History of Medieval England*, 6 vols. (Manchester, 1920–33)
TRHS	*Transactions of the Royal Historical Society*
VCH	*Victoria County History*
Waverley	*Annales Monasterii de Waverleia*, ed. H. R. Luard in *Ann. Monastici*. RS 36.ii (1865)
Winchester	*Annales Monasterii de Wintonia*, ed. H. R. Luard in *Ann. Monastici*. RS 36.ii (1865)
Worcester	*Annales Monasterii de Wigornia*, ed. H. R. Luard in *Ann. Monastici*. RS 36.iv (1869)
Wykes	*Chron. Thomae Wykes*, ed. H. R. Luard in *Ann. Monastici*. RS 36.iv (1869)

CHAPTER

1

Theme and Context

More than forty years have passed since Vivian Galbraith dealt in an important article with the survival of notions about good and bad kings in the medieval history of England. Decrying the Victorian proclivity for sweeping pictures of "great," "weak," or "evil" kings alternating upon the throne, Galbraith voiced an "instinctive distrust of these all-embracing moral verdicts." That his words were taken to heart is shown by the flood of scholarship that has appeared since 1945, dealing not only with the kings themselves but with a broad spectrum of questions surrounding their reigns. But while interest in women's history in general, and in the lives of royal women in particular, has been observed to increase when England has a reigning queen, the ladies who shared the lives of English kings have not benefited from the same historiographical trends that have advanced understanding of their husbands' reigns. Relegated to an insignificant political role, queens are little noticed by scholars toiling over the kings' doings, nor have the strategies the consorts adopted to meet the particular challenges they faced as the wives of powerful men become areas of interest in their own right. Documented studies of individual queens through which the intricacies of queenship might be examined are lacking;

the few that have appeared do not incorporate the advances seen in studies on kings.[1] In the popular tradition founded by Agnes Strickland, biogra-
phies of medieval queens still magnify to excess the virtues and vices handed
down in anecdote and legend, reducing queens to a moral puppet show com-
plementing "great," "weak," or "evil" kings.

The Victorian rhetoric regretted by Galbraith could not have found a
more congenial backdrop than the royal couples so brightly painted by
Strickland and her heirs. Edith-Matilda, descendant of Anglo-Saxon kings,
is a gentle intercessor tempering Henry I's Norman harshness. Stephen's
energetic wife, Matilda of Boulogne, is a welcome contrast to his ineptness.
Vacillating and treacherous, Henry III is paired with the meddlesome
Eleanor of Provence, and Edward II gets his just desserts from Isabella, the
she-wolf of France. Philippa of Hainaut, amiable and gracious, fits perfectly
beside Edward III, victor of Crécy and Poitiers. Amid this Tussaudian
gallery Edward I, the English Justinian, conqueror of Wales and Hammer
of the Scots, is flawlessly complemented by the Castilian Eleanor,
Strickland's "virtuous woman and excellent queen" who, "foreigner as she
was . . . won the love and good will of her subjects." Modern readers most
frequently encounter Eleanor of Castile in this gracious incarnation, epito-
mized for the twentieth century in the popularizing works of Thomas
Costain, and recognizable in the pages of reputable historians.[2]

Even before she put down her pen, however, the seeds of Miss Strickland's
undoing were sown and ripening. Since the eighteenth century, in fact,
there has crept into print a slow trickle of material suggesting that Strickland's
portrait of Eleanor of Castile embodies exactly the sort of moral verdict to
which Galbraith objected. Petitions in parliaments from the reigns of her
husband and son, in print from 1783, reveal that her administration had
scant respect for the rights of those whose lands lay near hers. The Hundred
Rolls, printed in 1812, show that misconduct by the queen's ministers was
official knowledge, and her executors' accounts, edited in 1841, record
damages paid to those who had proved wrongdoing by her officials. Walter
of Guisborough's chronicle, first published in 1848, preserves a doggerel
critical of Eleanor's appetite for new estates ("The king desires to get our
gold / The queen, our manors fair to hold"), echoed in 1866 when the Rolls
Series brought out the Dunstable annals' epitaph for the queen, "by birth
a Castilian, who acquired many fine manors." Letters from Archbishop
John Pecham of Canterbury, edited in the 1880s, show the Primate taking
Eleanor to task for obtaining those new estates through Jewish usurers, for
exactions that were reducing her tenants to indigence, and warning her that
she was blamed for the strictness of the king's rule. The rolls of Chancery

and the Exchequer of the Jews, calendared in this century, have added many untidy details to the picture suggested by the earlier edited sources.[3] Since Strickland and her imitators somehow managed to overlook all this evidence, there are obvious contradictions to be resolved between the accounts deriving from Strickland's glowing report and the less attractive picture that emerges from sources contemporary with Eleanor. By themselves these discrepancies speak loudly enough to demand attention, but later historians' unquestioning acceptance of Agnes Strickland's Eleanor raises new questions as to why two markedly different traditions about one woman should exist and why the more engaging of the two should have been the one to achieve prominence.

If these anomalies are the starting point for an investigation of Eleanor of Castile's career, the next step is naturally to seek out what biographical data the sources can provide. The materials for such a study are greater in bulk than for any earlier English queen, but are unevenly dispersed from year to year and are of widely varying quality. A single paragraph would suffice to state the year of her birth and all that is known of her life in Castile, but pages are needed for the negotiations preceding her marriage in 1254, and the sources thereafter fall silent again until Edward's accession in 1272. As queen, Eleanor appears often in Chancery and Exchequer records, which are of value chiefly for her administrative activity, but evidence for her personal life is less plentiful: only one of her forty-seven extant letters concerns anything other than administrative business, a note of thanks to the abbot of Cerne for sending her a book she had asked to borrow. The wardrobe accounts for the thirteenth century, which are the chief source for the personal lives of English medieval kings and their wives, survive only in limited numbers.

Contemporary chroniclers have little to say about Eleanor. They remark her without elaboration as the wife who accompanied Edward on great occasions, as the mother of his children, as heiress to the French county of Ponthieu at her mother's death in 1279, and when she herself died in 1290. So bland is their profile of Eleanor that the Guisborough and Dunstable texts come as a welcome relief, and the few further exceptions are so valuable as to claim almost disproportionate attention. The St. Albans *Gesta Abbatum* describe a dramatic encounter between queen and townspeople there in 1275; the Barnwell chronicle notes her acquisition of that priory's advowson in 1280. The Worcester annals record that in 1290 Eleanor wrote to the cathedral chapter there to support a plan by Bishop Godfrey Giffard to annex churches in his patronage to prebends in the church of Westbury. According to Nicholas Trevet's Latin and Anglo-Norman chronicles, the

latter written for Eleanor's daughter Mary, the queen opposed Mary's early
religious enclosure but acceded to her mother-in-law's demands.[4] Apart
from the Guisborough and Dunstable comments on the queen's land hunger,
however, the chroniclers writing in Eleanor's lifetime penned no estimates
of her character, not a word on her piety nor on the wifely devotion that is
a byword in later writings about her; nor do they give the slightest hint that
she was suspected of influencing the king to rule harshly.

The chroniclers' silences on Eleanor of Castile contrast with the often
lengthy discussions of royal women and their influence in historical writings
from earlier centuries, when ideas of politics and the relationships between
gender and power were only slowly coming into focus. It might be supposed
that by the thirteenth century, acceptance of the desirability of orderly customs of succession, the development of bureaucratic administration, and
changing ideas on women's fitness for, and access to, power had so limited
an English queen's official role as to justify the chroniclers' failure to mention Eleanor of Castile. The ramifications of their silence, however, are
more complex than such generalization would allow. Despite changes in
society and government, the queen remained the closest of the king's subjects to the center of authority; her exalted position exposed her to scrutiny
and made her a focal point for both praise and criticism. Thus thirteenth-
century English chroniclers still fulminated at length on Eleanor of
Provence's influence with Henry III and on the discord she was thought to
have sown between husband and son in the early 1260s. As much of this
criticism centered on Eleanor of Provence's behavior in years of political crisis, it may be noted that in the first eighteen years of Edward I's reign, years
during which Eleanor of Castile was alive, no such crises arose in which the
the chroniclers might focus such charges as they penned against Eleanor of
Provence. But their evidently slight interest in Eleanor of Castile must be
compared, too, with twelfth-century chroniclers' silence on Henry II's wife,
now understood to reflect the political limbo to which Henry relegated
Eleanor of Aquitaine.[5] Whether it is ascribed to an absence of political crisis or to Edward's decision to allow his queen no part in official life, chroniclers' indifference to Eleanor of Castile could mean that she was not as
widely believed to wield such overt influence as Pecham's letter suggests:

> My lady, the saints teach us that women are naturally greater in
> pity and more devout than men are, and scripture therefore says,
> "He that has no wife will wander about mourning." And because
> God has given you greater honor than to others of your lordship,
> it is right that your pity should surpass the pity of all men and
> women in your lordship. Wherefore we ask you for God's sake and
> our Lady's, that you will incline the heart of our lord the king

towards our dear brother, the bishop of Winchester. . . . My lady, we require you for God's sake that you will so do in this matter that those who say that you cause the king to use severity may see and know the contrary. . . . My lady, for God's sake, let pity overcome you, and our Lord keep you, body and soul, forever. . . .[6]

Arising not in later writings about Eleanor but within contemporary sources, this anomaly re-emphasizes the chroniclers' failure to remark the suspicions reported by Pecham and raises questions about the real nature of the influence she was thought to exert on her husband.

The chroniclers' lack of comment on Eleanor thus highlights relationships between their silences and the record evidence as a fundamental element in unraveling the formation of Eleanor's reputation (or reputations, as the case would seem to be). It also directs attention to the distinction that much of the record evidence was created within Eleanor's immediate circle and conveys information about her that was perhaps restricted to that circle, while most chroniclers worked outside the court's orbit and, when they did mention the queen, were likely to record a less rarefied view of her. It remains to be seen whether it is possible to reconcile the often divergent views of the woman afforded by sources of such dissimilar origin. While the dearth of witnesses to contemporary opinion about Eleanor thus suggests limitations to a study of her life, it also extends its scope by soliciting consideration of the wide variety of factors that underlay formation of the perceptions of which record does exist.

Criticism of the sort implied by Pecham's warning was likely to focus on such perceived departures from expectations as Eleanor's behavior evidently represented to contemporaries. That modern interest too is readily drawn to such points of departure is suggested by that handful of medieval queens most often discussed by scholars, women whose anomalous prominence sets them apart: regents like Blanche of Castile, great heiresses or divorcées like Eleanor of Aquitaine, reigning queens like the two Joans of Naples, politically influential women like Edward II's wife Isabella of France or Henry VI's Margaret of Anjou. These women were not typical of the majority of their sisters. Certain themes are common to the lives of royal women throughout the Middle Ages, but the lives of any two queens were more likely to be markedly different than similar, the variables almost beyond counting. One might marry a strong king, one a weak king. One might live in a time of peace and plenty, another amid want or war—her husband perhaps victorious and perhaps not. Many queens enjoyed social prominence bolstered by a prestigious share in ceremony and ritual; others, like the Plantagenet third wife of the Emperor Frederick II, vanished into an almost Oriental seclusion. Second wives, stepmothers and not mothers of heirs, had to conciliate stepsons while looking to their own interests and those of their children, who might be left dependent on an older half-brother's goodwill.

This diversity highlights the need to explore the variants in queenly experience as well as the similarities, to identify points at which the lives of these women correspond and diverge, and to see what might be inferred from difference as well as resemblance. The object here is not to present Eleanor as a "typical" queen, but rather to define her against the common backgrounds she shared with most of her sisters. The process may reveal new points of contact among the lives of medieval queens, imply new ways of looking at royal women to focus future research, or shed new light on certain aspects of Edward I's reign. It will be obvious by now that answers to the questions raised by the sources just discussed will not be found in a narrow search for Eleanor of Castile's role in the politics of Edward I's reign. Some chronological narrative is essential to describe any life, but given the problems posed by the surviving sources, it will be necessary to take a broad approach to the formation of popular perceptions of Eleanor by examining theme and context within the intricate relationships between queen and realm. The sources must ultimately be turned to the reconstruction of thirteenth-century English society's experience of Eleanor, both as woman and as queen.

BIRTH, MARRIAGE, AND FIRST YEARS IN ENGLAND (1241–1272)

That a thirteenth-century Castilian king's daughter became queen of England was by no means out of the ordinary in an age when sovereign power was conceived as patrimony and a political system organized around male roles was supported by matrimonial alliances among its reigning houses. The society that regarded women as commodities to be exchanged in the interests of that system prescribed their compliant acceptance of diplomatic marriages; but if such unions transcended individual hopes (or less politely, ignored them), they also afforded their female partners dignity, wealth, and opportunities for power that could encourage a diplomatic bride's personal ambitions. The initiatives royal wives took up are, however, precisely that aspect of their careers most seldom witnessed by the chronicles and documents created by men for a male audience. These records concern themselves with power relationships among male rulers, not with the unofficial means by which medieval royal wives pursued power, and since a queen's career depended in great measure on the relevance and strength of the official relationships that determined and were reinforced by her marriage, queenly initiatives must yield first priority to that diplomatic aspect when any queen's life is investigated.

It is entirely typical of the factors that shaped such alliances that the background to Eleanor of Castile's 1254 marriage to the future Edward I of England must be traced not in England, but in a network of inheritance and alliance linking that kingdom with France and the duchy of Aquitaine as well as Castile. And it is not going too far to say that the course of events leading to the marriage was set as early as the year 1152, when Eleanor of Aquitaine's second marriage, to the future Henry II of England, added her vast duchy to the Plantagenet domains. For the next century and a half, the kings of England followed matrimonial policies largely shaped by the southwestern inheritance, selecting wives from, and marrying daughters into, houses ruling on or near Aquitaine's borders. The first of these unions, in 1170, coupled Henry II's daughter Eleanor with Alphonso VIII of Castile, who later claimed that to secure Eleanor's dowry Henry pledged Gascony, Aquitaine's southernmost region. Though it is most unlikely any such promise was made, Alphonso claimed the dowry was never fully paid and used Henry's supposed pledge as the pretext for an invasion of Gascony in 1204. This was just after Eleanor of Aquitaine's death, at a time when King John was preoccupied by Capetian advances against Anjou and Normandy, and Alphonso most probably fabricated Henry's promise to legitimize the easy territorial gains he hoped for at a particularly fragile moment of transition within the Plantagenet domains. He soon abandoned the Gascon invasion but never formally renounced his ephemeral claims.[7]

Alphonso's turn to the North was no more than a brief distraction from medieval Castilian kingship's primary goal. The recovery of Muslim lands in the South of Spain, initiated by Ferdinand I in the eleventh century, had been pursued with varying determination by his successors, though as an ideal the Reconquest sufficed to establish and reinforce a strongly militaristic ethos in Castilian society and its monarchy. Defeated by Muslim forces at Alarcos in 1196, Alphonso VIII regrouped, gathered troops from other realms inspired by papal designation of the undertaking as a crusade, and decisively routed the caliph of Morocco at las Navas de Tolosa (1212). The pace slackened again in the brief and troubled reign of his son Henry I (1214–17) and in the early reign of Ferdinand III (1217–52), son of Alphonso's daughter Berengaria and Alphonso IX of León. But as Ferdinand matured, and especially after his father's death in 1230 united León and Castile in his hands, he continued his grandfather's campaigns and a succession of victories spread his reputation as a valiant crusader throughout Europe.[8]

Amid these conflicts, Eleanor of Castile was born to Ferdinand III and his second wife, a marriage with its own interest as an example of medieval matrimonial diplomacy. Ferdinand's first wife, the Hohenstaufen Beatrice of Swabia, died in November 1235. As she was survived by seven sons, there was no urgent need for him to remarry, but his formidable mother, Berengaria, was concerned lest he contract liaisons unbecoming his dignity and decided to find him a new wife. In her search, it is very likely that she turned to her sister Blanche, the redoubtable regent of France, who as it happened knew of a suitable candidate in need of a husband whose lordship posed no threat to Capetian interests. In the year of Queen Beatrice's death, a marriage had been negotiated between the bachelor Henry III of England and Jeanne, daughter and heir of Countess Marie Talvas of Ponthieu and her husband Simon, cadet of the house of Dammartin. The marriage would have brought Henry Jeanne's small but well-located inheritance, straddling the Somme estuary and bordering on Normandy, to which Henry still laid claim though Philip Augustus of France had seized it from Henry's father John in 1204. When the Anglo-Ponthevin scheme came to their attention, Blanche and her son Louis IX soon quashed it. Twenty years earlier, Count Simon had joined a league of French nobles who supported John against Philip Augustus; the league was defeated at Bouvines in 1214, and as part of the price of reconciliation with the French Crown in 1231, Simon swore on pain of forfeiting his estates not to marry his two elder daughters without the French king's approval. When Louis IX invoked that clause to threaten Simon and Marie with the loss of Ponthieu, Jeanne's betrothal was terminated. Henry soon married Eleanor of Provence, sister of Louis' queen and a niece of Henry's prominent Aquitanian vassal, the viscount of Béarn; but Jeanne was left without a husband.[9]

Jeanne's marriage to the English king was a political liability for the Capetians, but in the nobility of her descent she was still a highly eligible candidate for matrimony. (Countess Marie's mother was a daughter of Louis VII by his second wife, Constance of Castile.) Queen Blanche and her son could, moreover, regard Ferdinand III as an eminently suitable husband for Jeanne: her kinship to Louis would preserve links between the two kings, Ferdinand's many surviving sons by Beatrice virtually assured that Ponthieu would not be united to a foreign Crown, and Jeanne's absence in Castile might allow for some opportune strengthening of Capetian influence in Ponthieu. She was accordingly betrothed to Ferdinand in the summer of 1237; they married that October. She was rather younger than he and was thought a great beauty—a potentially dangerous combination, but she became by all indications a dutiful wife, accompanying Ferdinand to Andalucía in 1244 despite a perilous military situation and living in his camp at the siege of Seville in 1248. And she bore him five children, of whom three survived infancy. Her son Ferdinand was born a year or so after her marriage; probably after the king's return early in 1241 from a thirteen-month campaign in the South, Jeanne conceived again and late that year bore her only daughter, whom the king—as his Chancellor later remembered—named Eleanor after his grandmother, Alphonso VIII's Plantagenet queen. Jeanne's third child, Louis, arrived before the end of March 1243.[10]

Little is known of the early years of Jeanne's children. It is, however, unlikely that Eleanor was raised like her half-brothers, in spartan conditions far from the court's luxuries. She was born in the North, in Old Castile; her parents presumably took their family to the South some time after Ferdinand III permanently moved his operations to Andalucía in 1244. Eleanor is said to have been at his deathbed in Seville in May 1252 and seems to have lived there with her mother until her marriage in 1254.[11] The shadows of her early life are partly dispelled by considering aspects of her adult behavior that suggest traces left by her years in Castile. She may have carried to England a liking for chivalric culture nourished by a militaristic society and the knightly ethos that informed the rituals of its kingship. It was only after Eleanor left Castile that her half-brother Alphonso X codified his ideas on the education of royal women in his vast law code, the *Siete Partidas*; but the Dominican writings on which his ideas evidently rested were known in Castile during Eleanor's childhood, and clearly they influenced Alphonso's vision of royal women as tractable and pious creatures occupied with their psalters or with duties suitable to their rank, so as to avoid anger, "the one thing which most quickly leads women to sin." As Eleanor later promoted the Dominicans at the English court, where they probably taught her children, she herself may have been instructed by the friars who were fixtures at the Castilian court in her early years. But it is likely, too, that as she absorbed the assertively literary atmosphere at the cosmopolitan court of her father and brother, she developed a command of the written word that went beyond the decorative or pious accomplishment it is often said to have been for medieval women of rank. Her sophisticated literary activity in adulthood leaves scant room for doubt that her early training well prepared her as an agent of cultural exchange: an evident ease with historical writings and her deployment of focused vernacular literary expression, which included at least one translation from a classical work, echo the ardent interest in historical writing at the Castilian court, her father's promotion of the vernacular for administrative purposes, and the many translations he and his sons sponsored.[12]

As Eleanor grew up, whatever enmity lingered between England and Castile after Alphonso VIII's Gascon invasion was receding. Anglo-Castilian relations resumed as King Ferdinand's campaigns against the Muslims won the admiration of his colleagues including his cousin Henry III of England, and from the 1230s the two kings enjoyed increasingly frequent and evidently friendly diplomatic contacts. Nothing is known of the matters their envoys discussed though signs point, not surprisingly, to crusading fervor as a theme in Anglo-Castilian relations at this period. But despite their improving ties in the 1240s, it does not appear that the two kings considered a marriage between their children. True, Jeanne's aborted betrothal to Henry was dredged up in 1249, when Pope Innocent IV commissioned an inquest into the betrothal's possible consequences for the validity of Henry's 1236 marriage to Eleanor of Provence. The commission's sentence, published in 1251, affirmed that the betrothal had not created a valid bond of matrimony; Henry and Jeanne had been free to marry elsewhere. But it is extremely doubtful whether any connection existed between the inquest and a dispensation Innocent IV granted on 5 August 1250, allowing "the noble damsel Lionors," daughter of King Ferdinand of Castile, to contract matrimony with "any noble man" to whom she was related in the fourth degree of consanguinity; still less whether there was a connection between either inquest or dispensation and the negotiations for Eleanor's marriage, begun by Henry III in the spring of 1253. Nothing but a coincidence in time connects inquest and dispensation as signs that Eleanor's marriage to Henry III's son Edward might have been conceived during the 1249–51 inquest; nothing links the inquest to the 1253–54 negotiations save that Bishop Peter d'Aigueblanche of Hereford, a kinsman of Henry III's wife, appropriately but most probably coincidentally served on the inquest and was among Henry's envoys to Castile in 1253–54. (For one thing, Jeanne's obdurate refusal, despite repeated peremptory citations, to appear at the inquest personally or by proxy would hardly have allowed the bishop to initiate the contacts that would have to be assumed, were there any real progression from the commission of 1249 to the dispensation of 1250 and the negotiations of 1253–54.)[13]

The dispensation's anonymity, and the fact that Edward, born in 1239, was not the only man to whom it might apply, indicate that Ferdinand III (who must have requested it) could have been considering a number of potential husbands for Eleanor. The German ties opened by his first marriage would be reaffirmed if she married Albert, heir of Otto I of Brunswick, or Henry of

Swabia, son of Emperor Frederick II; given Ferdinand's crusading interest, links to the East created when his sister wed John de Brienne, titular king of Jerusalem, might be extended by Eleanor's marriage to Hugh, son of Henry I of Cyprus. And as will be seen, Alphonso X in the summer of 1253 was pursuing a fifth candidate ardently enough to delay the negotiations for his sister's English marriage. Henry III had launched one matrimonial venture for Edward, a 1247 embassy to Brabant remarked by the well-informed chronicler Matthew Paris. If Henry was considering a Castilian bride for Edward in 1250, Matthew almost certainly would have known of it; but he never mentioned such a project, even when he described a 1251 embassy from Ferdinand III urging Henry to accompany him on crusade. Indeed, when Anglo-Castilian marriage talks were undertaken in May 1253, Matthew was as bewildered as any other English chronicler as to whether the bride would be the Castilian king's daughter or sister, and his perplexity surely means that despite his access to much privileged information, he had heard nothing about a Castilian marriage for Edward before 1253.[14]

It was only after Ferdinand III's death that the Gascon factor again came to bedevil Anglo-Castilian relations and made a marriage between the two royal houses a desideratum. After Philip Augustus' successes against King John in Normandy, Anjou, and Poitou, Aquitaine from 1206 remained the only Plantagenet continental possession, its ties to England rather less dependent on political loyalties than on its wine trade. Castilian claims to Gascony, dormant under Ferdinand III, might have been discussed by the Anglo-Castilian envoys in the 1230s and 1240s but if so, they were not resolved by treaty; the potential for discord remained, and it was not the only menace to Plantagenet dominion in Gascony. The kings of Navarre made frequent raids into the Adour valley and found support among the nobles there; Thibaut I had battled with the English seneschal of Gascony as recently as 1244, and continued to aid and abet his Gascon cronies. Aragon had attempted no encroachment in Gascony, but Anglo-Aragonese relations were remote and the English never ignored the possibility of intervention from that quarter. Gascony's unstable southern frontier only heightened the uncertainty of the king-duke's relationship with the French Crown, never defined by treaty; peaceful Anglo-French relations over Gascony were extended by a series of truces, periodically renewed. This brittle situation was further troubled as Henry III's unsuccessful attempts to reform the duchy's administration from England confounded relations between his officials and the inhabitants. He entrusted the duchy to a succession of lieutenants, who served at pleasure but rarely enjoyed his active support or attentive supervision; the appointee in 1248 was Henry's brother-in-law

Simon de Montfort, whose energetic performance by 1252 provoked wide-spread ill-will among Aquitanian nobles and townspeople alike.[15]

At roughly the same moment, the death of Ferdinand III (May 1252) brought to the Castilian throne Eleanor's thirty-year-old half-brother, Alphonso X. If Ferdinand had sought friendly relations with England, Alphonso's behavior at the outset of his reign suggests that, after a long apprenticeship, he was eager to impose new priorities. It is unclear whether the Aquitanians provoked by Montfort's vigorous administration first approached Alphonso, or he them, but certainly he now recalled his great-grandfather's claims to Gascony and, like Alphonso VIII, looked northward at a time of political uncertainty there. It has been suggested that Alphonso X intervened in Gascony with the sole object of obtaining an English alliance sealed by Eleanor's marriage to Edward, but given the steady improvement in Anglo-Castilian relations over the preceding decades, it is an untenable idea that Alphonso could find no better way to attract Henry III's attention than by resurrecting claims to Gascony.[16] The signs are that Alphonso, who often demonstrated a proclivity for pursuing vague hereditary rights, was very much in earnest when he renewed his great-grandfather's Gascon pretensions. Every obstacle that delayed the marriage negotiations of 1253–54 was in fact thrown up by Alphonso himself, probably because (as will be seen) his Gascon venture connected handily with another long-standing element of Castilian policy—also based on an antique hereditary claim—to make a different marriage for his sister more attractive to him.

Alphonso X's formal documents began late in 1252 to proclaim Aquitanian nobles as his vassals—the viscount of Béarn prominent among them—and the Gascon wine merchants began to seek out new markets in Castile, closer to home. It was thus a warning from Bordeaux, center of the English wine trade, that informed Henry III of Alphonso's actions early in 1253. As Henry saw it, Alphonso was out to vindicate his ancestral claims—and as Alphonso presented himself as the heir of John's ill-fated nephew Arthur, a claimant to the English throne recognized by Philip Augustus as duke of Aquitaine, Alphonso X's ultimate ambitions might reach far beyond Gascony: Henry was to claim at one point during the crisis that Alphonso planned to invade England itself.[17] At a parliament in April 1253, Henry announced he would go to Aquitaine to deal personally with the situation; and since "friendship between princes can be obtained in no more fitting manner than by the link of conjugal troth," the king on 15 May 1253 accredited his secretary John Maunsel and the bishop of Bath and Wells to seek a marriage between the two houses. English chroniclers understood the object to be a Castilian bride for Henry's son Edward, but were unsure whether she would be Alphonso's daughter or sister.[18] The frequent Anglo-Castilian contacts in the 1240s, however, had surely informed Henry III about the members of the Castilian royal house, and he was probably well aware of Eleanor's existence. The chroniclers' confusion most likely reflects their ignorance of the fact that in the spring of 1253 Alphonso's wife was awaiting the birth of their first child; his half-sister, now rising twelve, was the only possible Castilian bride for the English heir.

Eleanor of Castile's name first appears in English records on 24 May 1253, when Henry told his envoys to arrange Edward's marriage to her, but any hopes for an early end to the crisis were dashed by a combination of factors of the kind that often muddled medieval marriage negotiations.[19] Notions of royal dignity developed extraordinary sensitivities when two monarchs resolved confrontation and allied; it was inevitable that both gave ground, one no more than the other, but Alphonso's response to the English proposals suggests that he was out to assure himself the greater honor. Castilian kings greatly valued the prestige they derived from knighting noble youths, and Alphonso now asked that Edward come to Castile to be knighted before the wedding. Henry declined, lest he deliver the perfect hostage. Significance attaches too to Henry's first offer of a thousand marks' dower for Eleanor. A fragile aspect of any diplomatic marriage, provision for the bride from her husband's domains was seen by Alphonso as tacit acknowledgement of the nobility of Castilian royal women and as proof of his solicitude for them. The strict attention he was to give Eleanor's dower, and the larger assignment he finally obtained, strongly imply that the initial offer was rejected as demeaning.[20]

Other indications suggest that Alphonso's wish to knight Edward and his attentiveness to Eleanor's dower served the double purpose of delaying but not ending the English talks while he pursued another project for her marriage. Almost certainly he was hoping at this time to marry her to Thibaut II of Navarre, over whose Pyrenean realm the kings of Castile had claimed feudal supremacy since García VI of Navarre swore homage to Alphonso VII of Castile in 1134. Alphonso's resuscitation of this alleged supremacy upon the death of young Thibaut's father Thibaut I, in July 1253, was doubly motivated, for control of Navarre promised access to the Pyrenean passes into Gascony where, as noted earlier, Thibaut I had his own designs. Any hopes for the Navarrese marriage evaporated in August 1253, however, when the widowed Queen Margaret of Navarre evaded Castilian control by submitting herself and her son to the king of Aragon's protection with an explicit promise that Thibaut would "never, at any time in his life, marry the sister of the Lord Alphonso, king of Castile, daughter of the Lord King Ferdinand and the Lady Queen Jeanne." The framers of the document left the sister unnamed but identified her clearly enough, and it is unlikely that Margaret's promise would have been so exactly phrased had not Alphonso recently been urging Eleanor's marriage to Thibaut. And probably he was not the first to have done so: as the two were related in the fourth degree, Ferdinand III (who had also asserted Castilian supremacy over Navarre) very likely intended the marriage dispensation of August 1250 to expedite Eleanor's marriage to Thibaut.[21]

Henry III landed in Aquitaine three weeks after the queen of Navarre's agreement with Aragon, and within six months he reduced the Gascon crisis by diplomacy and military action. Nothing is heard of Anglo-Castilian contacts during these months, but as Henry's position in Gascony improved, Alphonso's weakened: he had been unable to compel Navarrese submission even in the matter of Eleanor's marriage, and his nobles' support for the Gascon venture, never strong, eroded steadily with Henry's successes. Early in 1254, moreover, Alphonso's brother Henry, claiming that Alphonso was denying him lands their father had meant him to have, rose in rebellion and soon allied himself with a group of noble families estranged from the royal house.[22] These developments favored renewed contacts with Henry III; it is unclear which side made the first move, but on 8 February 1254 Henry nominated the bishop of Hereford and John Maunsel to treat with Alphonso on the matter of Gascony and to arrange a marriage between Edward and Eleanor. Given the breakdown in negotiations the previous summer, a significant clause in the new envoys' instructions was a promise that Edward would have lands worth £10,000 yearly and that Eleanor would be dowered as fully as any queen of England ever had been. That the dower remained a critical point is shown by Alphonso's demand in the summer of 1254 that the charters recording Henry's grants of land to Edward should be sent to Castile for inspection. When they arrived, Alphonso noticed they did not bear Henry's great seal; Henry explained that it was still in England, but promised that the charters would be reissued with it as soon as possible. Alphonso's exacting attitude as to dower highlights a complete silence on the matter of dowry: there is no sign that he offered a sum of money with Eleanor, or that Henry expected it. The terms of the Anglo-Castilian treaty agreed upon in March 1254 imply rather that Henry saw as sufficient achievement the restoration of order in Gascony, Edward's marriage, and the resulting new alliance. He was borne out by its consequences for English diplomacy.[23]

The treaty established an alliance both offensive and defensive. The kings of Castile and England became allies against all enemies, saving their allegiance to the Christian faith. Edward was to be knighted by Alphonso on or before the next feast of the Assumption, marry Eleanor, and help to impose Castilian supremacy over Navarre; Henry III agreed to seek commutation of his crusading vow and assist Alphonso with an invasion of North Africa. Alphonso renounced all claims to Gascony based on Henry II's promises to Alphonso VIII, or upon alleged recognitions by Richard I and John. Henry III would restore losses suffered by Gascons who supported Alphonso, and at Alphonso's mandate the Gascons would restore to Henry any lands seized in the troubles. Henry further agreed to marry his daughter Beatrice to one of Alphonso's brothers, the choice among whom was left to the Castilian king. Alphonso on 1 April issued Edward a safe-conduct, and on 22 April ordered the Gascons to return to their allegiance to King Henry. It was now further agreed that when Alphonso made peace with Navarre, Henry would recover all Gascon lands seized by the kings of Navarre, a guarantee clearly meant to encourage the English to keep their promise to help in Navarre; with a like intent, Alphonso promised Henry half the lands conquered in the African expedition.[24]

Alphonso thus gave up his Gascon claims in return for English promises of support for his Navarrese designs and the African crusade, and the privilege of knighting a king's son. Henry III turned the crisis to better account: his son had a royal bride—a touchstone of dynastic prestige—and some stability was restored in Gascony, its southern frontier strengthened with an important ally beyond the Pyrenees. Louis IX was sufficiently concerned at the recovery in Anglo-Castilian relations to approach Alphonso with the idea of a double marriage alliance between them, and Henry's improved position in the South led to negotiations with Louis that produced the Treaty of Paris in 1259 and the formalization of Henry's rights in Aquitaine. Dowry or no, Henry probably got more from the Castilian treaty than he or Edward ever had to give.[25]

A final round of negotiations began with Henry's promise on 18 July that his son would marry Eleanor within five weeks after Michaelmas. (Henry hoped the wedding would take place on the feast of his patron Edward the Confessor, on 13 October.) On 20 July Edward assigned her dower lands worth £1000 yearly, with 500 marks in English lands to be added when she became queen, and on 23 July named John Maunsel to conclude by proxy the marriage between himself and Eleanor, "whose beauty and prudence we have heard by general report."[26] A Castilian embassy headed by Eleanor's *ayo* García Martínez arrived in Gascony in August to accept the dower assignment. Henry now reassured Alphonso as to the use of the Great Seal on his grants to Edward and promised that Eleanor's dower would be assigned as promised; if Alphonso questioned the location of the lands assigned, others would be substituted elsewhere in England. Maunsel and Martínez were appointed Henry's proctors for any further arrangements; Martínez was to treat with Castilian bishops—presumably to ensure that the principals were of age and that the consanguinity between them was canonically dispensed—and with Eleanor's mother.[27] The mothers of royal brides were not excluded from their daughters' marriage negotiations, as is often supposed, but this is the only indication that Jeanne was consulted about Eleanor's marriage. That she does not appear more frequently in the proceedings was presumably the result of her eroding position at the Castilian court. Her relations with Alphonso X, never warm, had congealed after he refused her the exercise of seigniorial rights in certain estates Ferdinand III left her; Alphonso may have withheld other lands from her, as his brother Henry claimed he was denied his due. Jeanne made common cause with her rebellious stepson, and as the warmth of her support for Henry kindled rumors about the nature of their relationship, her rift with Alphonso widened into scandal. The rumors were unfounded, but Jeanne's actions were ill-advised, especially her probable attendance at one secret council Henry held with his confederates at Burgos. Whether to withdraw from an ominously defamatory situation or to signify her displeasure at Alphonso's treatment of her—in either case with the convenient excuse of assuming her inheritance after her mother's death—Jeanne did not remain in Castile for Eleanor's wedding. On 16 July Henry III issued safe-conducts for her and her son Ferdinand to cross Aquitaine on their way north; they were at Bordeaux with Henry and Edward in August, and Jeanne entered Abbeville, the principal town of Ponthieu, on 31 October.[28]

No chronicler recorded the date of Eleanor's wedding. The Bury chronicle states that Edward reached Burgos on 13 October, but he was at Bayonne as late as 9 October, and a Castilian chronicle more reliably puts his Burgos entry on 18 October. Alphonso then knighted Edward and some English companions, as he had insisted on doing from the outset of negotiations. The wedding all but certainly followed on 1 November, the date of Alphonso's renunciation of his Gascon claims in Edward's favor, and most likely at the Cistercian convent of las Huelgas near Burgos, the burial place of its founders, Eleanor's great-grandparents Alphonso VIII and his Plantagenet queen.[29]

The couple reached Gascony in late November, to spend a year there while Edward learned the business of governing the duchy, but the year's records do little to dispel the obscurity surrounding his young wife. The immediate consummation demanded by the circumstances of their mar-

riage was permissible as both partners were of canonical age; at Bordeaux
in May 1255, seven months after her wedding, Eleanor may have borne a
daughter who soon died. By September 1255 her wardrobe had been set up
under her mother-in-law's clerk John de Loundres, and William de Cheney
was seconded from the king's household as her steward. As early as July
1255, Henry III was planning for her entry to London, which he meant to
coincide with the feast of Edward the Confessor on 13 October; but she
landed at Dover in such poor array that Henry had to send 100 marks to
buy what was needed for a proper show. Her London entry was delayed
until 17 October, but was none the less splendidly celebrated, and culmi-
nated with Eleanor's rich offerings at St. Edward's shrine.[30]

Like many medieval wives of rank, Eleanor was now faced with the
business of adapting to a strange country, a potentially treacherous passage—the *Magna Vita* of St. Hugh of Lincoln recounts that in Paris the
bishop once was summoned to console a weeping Blanche of Castile, twelve
years old, recently wed to the Capetian heir and, it would seem, miserably
homesick. The few extant details about Eleanor's first years in England are
less intimate, though as her mother was French, she was probably fluent in
the language of the English court and was spared the isolation of a newcomer unable to converse with her associates. But Blanche of Castile's
grandniece likely did experience some frustrations as she contended with
new customs. An Anglo-Norman life of Edward the Confessor either presented to her or acquired by her at the time of her arrival, for example, introduced her to the cult of the Plantagenet royal tutelary; but Castilian kingship
knew no such patron nor—as Alphonso X derided notions of regal thau-
maturgy—would Eleanor's early years have prepared her for the spectacle
of King Henry touching for the "king's evil." How Eleanor went about the
pivotal business of assimilating cultural differences can only be guessed.[31]
No records survive from Edward's wardrobe before 1272, and what little
was remarked about his wife between 1255 and 1260 is soon told. She
went on a pilgrimage with Eleanor of Provence to St. Albans in October
1257, and in September 1258 attended the consecration of Salisbury
Cathedral. At Mortlake on 1 January 1259 she received a knight from the
viscount of Béarn; her mother-in-law provided the two sapphire rings she
gave him and one for Eleanor's attendant Albreda.[32] Eleanor probably went
with the king and queen to France in January 1260 for their daughter's
wedding to the Breton heir; they met there with Eleanor's brother
Ferdinand and probably her mother Jeanne, who obtained privileges for
Ponthevin merchants in England. Later that year Eleanor was pardoned for
taking stags from the king's park without license, but then, between

November 1260 and July 1262, her name disappears from surviving English records.[33]

If the shadows around Eleanor are difficult to penetrate in these years, it is clear that treacherous undercurrents swirled beneath the glossy sheen of ceremony and the intricacies of alliance formation. She had been preceded to London by a Castilian embassy headed by her half-brother Sancho, the elect of Toledo; the English found the Castilians ostentatious and vulgar, and greeted with derision the sight of Eleanor's apartments, which Henry furnished on Sancho's advice in Castilian fashion, with carpets on the floor. At a time when Henry's resources were already strained by his liberality to aliens, his gesture gave the English a fresh reminder of his weakness for all things outlandish, and sober Englishmen feared a new wave of interlopers as Eleanor's countrymen sought out Henry's purse. For a time, this must have appeared to be exactly what was happening. The king had promised land and money to García Martínez and English benefices to both García's son John and Eleanor's half-brother Philip. Eleanor's maternal relatives began to enter the English royal households within weeks after her marriage, and in August 1256 the turbulent Henry of Castile came to England in the hope that Henry III and Edward could reconcile him with Alphonso X; he stayed for three years, during which he lived entirely out of the king's pocket.[34] An already delicate situation was aggravated by ongoing tensions in Anglo-Castilian relations: Henry III was lax in fulfilling his obligations to Alphonso under the 1254 treaties, and Alphonso continued to intervene in Gascony to demand equitable treatment of those who supported him in 1253. In July 1256 Henry informed Alphonso that papal refusal to absolve him from his crusading vow forced him to withdraw from his commitment to pursue the African crusade. A month later, to Alphonso's extreme irritation, Henry received the errant Henry of Castile. And early in 1257, Alphonso—pursuing another vague hereditary claim, through his Hohenstaufen mother—became a candidate for a German royal election in which his chief rival was King Henry's brother, Earl Richard of Cornwall; Henry insisted he knew nothing of Richard's candidacy beforehand and hoped the disputed result would not disturb their relations, but Alphonso accused him of faithlessness and refused to recognize Richard's election.[35]

Then, in June 1258, the project to marry King Henry's daughter Beatrice to one of Eleanor's brothers collapsed when Henry learned that Emmanuel, the brother designated for the honor, had married another; Henry politely asked if Alphonso wished to substitute another brother, but no more is heard of it. The project had, in fact, hung fire since 1254 while Henry vainly asked Alphonso to specify the lands he intended to give Emmanuel and to guarantee Beatrice's dower. In January 1256, however, Henry sounded a new note by demanding that Emmanuel be guaranteed tenure of his lands lest Alphonso later seize them, as he had done to others.[36] Given the objections Alphonso raised over Eleanor's dower in 1253–54, it is tempting to think that Henry was merely paying him out in his own coin, but almost certainly the concern Henry voiced in January 1256 was roused by Alphonso's 1253 seizure of Henry of Castile's lands. As Henry III surely had known of that episode for some time, however, it is odd that he used it only in 1256, and intriguing questions are raised by the possibility that Henry of Castile was now in contact with his English cousins. He reached England in August 1256 but was certainly seeking a refuge well before that. His revolt collapsed in October 1255 with his defeat at Morón, and his hopes of an alliance with Aragon vanished as Jaime I, whose oldest daughter was Alphonso X's queen, now refused Henry her younger sister (though Henry swore he had exchanged promises of marriage with her while he was disguised as her servant). Henry then fled to France, where Louis IX refused to have anything do with him.[37]

Henry of Castile's arrival in England in the summer of 1256 is thus a puzzling development. True, the English court was a likely refuge; according to Matthew Paris, Henry of Castile hoped that Henry III and Edward could reconcile him with Alphonso since Edward had recently married their sister. But however favorable to foreigners Henry III was, however remiss in his obligations to Alphonso X, he must have understood, as Louis IX did, that Henry of Castile's presence in his realm would anger Alphonso. His reasons for welcoming the exiles remain obscure. Matthew Paris saw an active role only for the males of the family, but by mentioning the sister (whom he left unnamed, like those who framed the dowager queen of Navarre's promises to the king of Aragon in 1253), he touched on the classic role of royal women as go-betweens, which may have been significant in this case. Recently arrived in England and perhaps pleased at the prospect of a fraternal visit, Eleanor would seem a natural link from brother to husband and father-in-law. But it would be startling to find her, at fourteen, boldly risking Alphonso's wrath by assisting Henry of Castile, let alone inviting him to England. But there was another woman to whom Henry of Castile could appeal, one with links to the English court: Eleanor's mother Jeanne, now living in Ponthieu just across the Channel. As Henry of Castile must have been in France for some time before he went to England, obviously not as Louis IX's guest, he could well have been with Jeanne in Ponthieu by the early months of 1256. Her rift with Alphonso, it will be recalled, originated when he deprived her of rights and perhaps land, just as he had denied land to Henry of Castile; and Jeanne had espoused her defiant stepson's cause once before. If she had not given Henry III her version of events at Bordeaux in 1254, she perhaps did so now, late in 1255, to prepare Henry of Castile's arrival in England while he wandered in Aragon and France—and in the process worried Henry III for Beatrice's future. As Jeanne in later years was ready to use her influence at the English court to help those who asked, it could well have been she who legitimized Henry of Castile's advent in England by hinting that Henry III might reconcile the brothers. By putting matters in that light, she could lead Eleanor, unseasoned but clearly already aware of her role as a peaceweaver, to imagine a positive result to her brother's visit, one Alphonso might welcome. With that understanding, perhaps Eleanor did ask Henry III and Edward to receive the exile. It is not likely that Jeanne and Henry of Castile were out to muddy the waters between England and Castile but as things turned out, Henry's visit did prove calamitous for Anglo-Castilian relations. The resulting intensified contacts between Henry III and Alphonso X may, however, have given Jeanne's daughter an opportunity to shape a worthier role for herself on the diplomatic stage.[38]

The degree to which Eleanor's early years in England were affected by popular misgivings or diplomatic crises is not easily judged. Youth as well could have impeded her escape from obscurity, as might the fact that her rank was defined by no recent precedent:[39] since 1066, only the sons of Stephen and Henry II had married in their fathers' lifetimes. Both wed French kings' daughters, critical alliances when the Plantagenets still held Normandy and Anjou, and though both marriages suffered from political strains the English acknowledged the brides' importance. Eleanor's connections were less vital; King Henry might plume himself on ending the Gascon crisis, but Aquitaine was a distant unreality to most of his subjects and the diplomatic nuances to Edward's marriage hard to appreciate.[40] Eleanor's claims to deference on these grounds were slight, and in the 1250s she likely lacked the experience to turn them to her advantage; they could even have been damaged if Alphonso X took offense at any assistance she may have given Henry of Castile. Apart from the daughter perhaps born in 1255, moreover, Eleanor is not known to have had another child until after 1260; the absence of an heir could have weakened her status, though an apparent lack of concern for her fertility is puzzling. Like her daughter-in-law, Eleanor of Provence married when nearly thirteen, and after three years of barren marriage it was feared that she would prove sterile. That no such worries are found in Eleanor of Castile's case suggests that given her youth at marriage, and considering the possible loss of a child in 1255, her parents-in-law chose to wait before allowing the couple to begin regular conjugal relations. (In 1282, the two Queens Eleanor, both probably remembering their experiences as adolescent brides, convinced Edward I that his thirteen-year-old daughter was too young for marriage.)[41]

Immaturity, childlessness, and an ill-defined official rank could have kept Eleanor from finding her depth amid the endemic jockeying for position at court among the extended families of King Henry and his wife. The king's unpopular Poitevin siblings, the Lusignans, enjoyed his unstinting generosity after they came to England in 1247. Eleanor of Provence's Savoyard relatives, better behaved and less odious to the realm at large, had arrived in the late 1230s and managed to entrench themselves in a court party more cohesive than the Lusignans', and as it was Eleanor of Provence who supervised Edward's education, her kin and their supporters grew used to their influence over him. For medieval royal or noble heirs, however, marriage meant emancipation, and their weddings often initiated periods of tension between aging fathers and restless eldest sons. The diplomatic success sealed by Eleanor's marriage was one thing; to have her in England, at Edward's side, was another matter. His wife must eventually emerge as an important figure in his life, but the court veterans were perhaps not anxious for this to happen too soon, lest a youth known to be impetuous prematurely assert his independence. Eleanor of Provence's supporters might now have come to regard Edward's wife with some apprehension, particularly as her relatives began to descend on England. With regard to Jeanne's plausible role in preparing Henry of Castile's arrival, it is significant that all the other kinsmen Eleanor had with her in the 1250s were her mother's Picard cousins, through whom Jeanne —well versed in court intrigue—might have been supporting her daughter. If Eleanor's youthful inexperience was enough to impede her deployment of these cousins to create a power base at court in the 1250s, the imprudent Henry of Castile was mature and ambitious.[42] The potential for a new Picard or Castilian faction at court could have been as troubling for the court veterans as for the realm at large. All things considered, there is unambiguous meaning in the appointments to the young couple's households in the first years of their marriage: chosen from the establishments of Edward's parents or with their approval, these attendants came from the older court party under whose tutelage Edward was unlikely to challenge authority.[43]

But after two years of increasing friction between the king and his son, Edward broke with the Savoyards in the spring of 1258 and aligned himself with the Lusignan uncles with whom his prior relations had been distant. Since the Savoyards backed the reforms demanded at a parliament in April 1258, Edward opposed them, to support his uncles whose exile was among the demands. Henry and Edward were obliged to accept reform at the Oxford parliament that June; the Lusignans were expelled, but Edward began to recruit new supporters with ties to the Poitevins. It can never be known whether Eleanor had encouraged Edward's actions, but it is in the wake of his shift in allegiance that the first signs of her influence and methods surface. The Lusignan uncle highest in Edward's favor was Geoffrey, whom he tried in 1258 to name his seneschal in Gascony; and just around 1260, Geoffrey wed Eleanor's cousin Jeanne, daughter of her aunt the viscountess of Châtelleraut in Poitou—apparently the first occasion on which Eleanor involved herself in a cousin's marriage, a favorite tactic in later life. Edward's alignment with his uncles was thus reinforced, and Eleanor may have advanced herself in other ways, for the king cannot have been displeased: following the Treaty of Paris in 1259, the marriage could strengthen a Plantagenet presence on Aquitaine's northern frontier.[44]

Eleanor's January 1259 meeting with the viscount of Béarn's envoy again relates her activities at this time to the southwest. Edward saw his position in Aquitaine threatened by the negotiations that led to the Treaty of Paris, and in March and October 1259 he was aligning himself with those in England whom he thought likely to obstruct the treaty. Eleanor's audience with the viscount's knight might suggest that she was supporting Edward on that front, were it not that Eleanor of Provence's provision of gifts for the envoy argues that the meeting had that lady's approval and hence was presumably not related to Edward's dislike of the treaty. A more plausible explanation for a January 1259 meeting that involved the two Eleanors and the viscount would weigh the harm to Anglo-Castilian relations done by Henry of Castile's stay in England. It was even feared that Alphonso X was considering a new Gascon intervention, and in July 1258 Henry III appealed for support to Gascon notables including the viscount, still Alphonso's client though he had returned to his English allegiance. As Béarn was also Eleanor of Provence's uncle, a meeting with her approval that put him in touch with Alphonso's sister suggests that with her mother-in-law and the viscount (with whom she had other contacts in these years), the young woman was taking part in diplomacy to resolve the crisis.

On his way to serve as a mercenary with the king of Tunis, Henry of Castile left England in July 1259, after swearing not to attack Alphonso.[45] Of course the expulsion of aliens from the court was very much in the air, as witness the Lusignans' exile at just the same moment, but the chroniclers do not indicate that his departure was in any way associated with the

Poitevins' ouster. Neither does it appear that the realm was widely ill-disposed toward him; though Henry III clearly favored him, he never really obtained as strong an influence with the king as the Lusignans enjoyed and his impact on English affairs was confined to the diplomatic crisis he caused. That his sister took part in negotiations preceding his departure can only be theorized, but the point is worth pondering from the standpoint of royal women's role in such maneuvers, how Eleanor weighed them and the benefits she might win. Assuming she had urged Henry's arrival, the circumstances of his leaving must have been unpleasant for her, and as there were likely those at court glad to see the back of him, his departure could have been embarrassing for her. But as with her cousin's marriage, Eleanor would have helped both Henry III and Edward by turning her ability to induce him to leave into a gateway to enter the negotiations. And again assuming she had connived at his advent, to Alphonso X's displeasure, her labors to prepare the exile's departure could restore her standing with the Castilian king. Whatever their personal feelings, royal women had to be ready to exploit such prospects for personal initiative amid the ceaseless turmoil of international relations.

The absence of Eleanor's name from English records between November 1260 and July 1262 implies that she shared Edward's "exile" in those years, after the inglorious collapse of his first foray into political life; he spent much of that period on the Continent, extending his control over the administration of Aquitaine and traveling to tournaments as far afield as Savoy. The couple was in England in June 1262 and in the next month traveled to France with King Henry and his wife. Henry returned to England in the fall, but Edward stayed in France, taking part in tournaments, until Henry's sharp letter early in 1263 bade him abandon boyish wantonness and return to shoulder his responsibilities.[46] Following papal absolution in 1261 from his oath to keep the 1258 Provisions of Oxford, Henry had failed to reform his government, and events were moving rapidly toward an open rupture between king and barons. It is unnecessary to rehearse here the events of 1263–65, save insofar as they directly touched Eleanor. The contest was nonetheless a crucial passage for her as Edward came to personal and political maturity; her future depended on his command of affairs if he lived to reign, and the lessons he learned in crisis would inevitably affect her later career.

After his father's caustic summons, Edward returned to England late in February 1263 and, in deepening crisis, strengthened the garrison at Windsor with foreign mercenaries. Eleanor most probably had a hand in this, for the imported troops included archers whose names—de Abbeville, de Neel—show they came from her mother's county across the Channel.

Consistent with her prior support for Edward, such actions were likely to create the perception that she upheld his position, and this may well have had repercussions upon her in the following months.[47] As the crisis deepened, Windsor remained her stronghold; it was on the pretext of visiting her there that Edward locked himself up in the castle after an October parliament ended in confusion.[48] A month after the king's army was defeated at Lewes in May 1264, however, Windsor was stripped of its garrison, and on 17 June, Eleanor was ordered to leave the castle and join Henry with her infant daughter Katherine and her household. Henry's promise to excuse her to Edward for leaving implies that he had told her to stay there no matter what happened, but no reason for the king's order was given. After the garrison left, of course, he and Edward would naturally have been anxious for her safety, especially as another child was expected. But the decision to remove her was more likely the barons' response to rumors that the mercenaries Eleanor of Provence was recruiting in France included Castilians, "as Edward had taken to wife the sister of the king of that land." The "sister" was again unnamed, as Matthew Paris left her anonymous in 1256, but the reference to her in 1264 again begs consideration of her role. Ponthevins were among Edward's hired troops in 1263; rumors that Castilians would now follow suggest that Eleanor was again intriguing, or that her earlier support for Edward at least persuaded the barons that she was plotting with Alphonso and her mother-in-law. Whether such scheming was real or imagined, from the barons' standpoint it was prudent to remove her from Windsor to some place where her activities might be more attentively supervised.[49]

The following grim months saw Edward in captivity, the queen in France, King Henry taken wherever Montfort needed him. Eleanor was in isolation, her future clouded by political crisis, by the chance of Edward's death in prison or battle, and by her repeated failure to produce a son. (Katherine died in September 1264; the child born in January 1265 was another girl, Joan.) The king met her expenses in November 1264 and provided medicines at Joan's birth, but before 15 April 1265 Eleanor had to borrow £40 for expenses from Hugh Despenser, the justiciar appointed by the barons; the lack of money may have followed the seizure by the earl of Gloucester and others of three manors in Eleanor's custody that were restored to her only in March 1265.[50] After Edward made his escape in May 1265, his swift marshaling of the Marcher lords greatly weakened Montfort's position, and on 4 August the royal army defeated Simon at Evesham. King Henry was restored to administrative control, and Edward's role in preparing the victory won him a wider share in the affairs of the realm than he was previously allowed. Eleanor now celebrated a triumph of her own with the birth of a son, John, on the night of 13–14 July 1266. Those who carried the news were well rewarded, the Londoners cannily marked their reconciliation with the king by celebrating his grandson's birth with holiday and procession, and Henry seized the chance to exploit dynastic implications: John was born at Windsor, but Eleanor was churched at St. Edward's Westminster shrine.[51]

John's birth a year after Evesham conveniently marks a point from which to review Eleanor's first ten years in England. She arrived an inexperienced girl in a court dominated by faction, an outsider in a kingdom increasingly resentful of the alien presence around its king. The quick arrival of several of her relatives after her marriage and Henry of Castile's ill-advised visit to England cannot have done much to paper over Eleanor's foreignness. It may well have been that Jeanne hoped for some influence in English affairs through Eleanor and, at a distance, promoted her daughter's taste for court intrigue. But as Eleanor matured and perhaps as her mother-in-law, at closer quarters, acquired the greater influence with her, the picture changes. If under her mother-in-law's guidance Eleanor helped to end Henry of Castile's residence in England and Alphonso X's displeasure thereat, it was perhaps a hard lesson but one she had to learn. That it was learned is implied by the evidence for her behavior as crisis developed in England, as she gave all her support to the husband on whom her future depended: the Lusignan marriage, her sharing of his "exile," Picard mercenaries in 1263 and (perhaps) Castilians in 1264. Such methods reflect the hard fact that Eleanor's family, whose ranks provided both bride and mercenaries, remained virtually the only resource she could command at this time. It is unlikely she could have appealed to supporters outside her household or Edward's,[52] and the fact that Eleanor of Provence supplied the gifts for the Gascon envoy might mean that Edward was unable to provide his wife with adequate revenue. Eleanor of Castile's quick rise to prominence in 1265 can be divorced neither from Edward's political emergence nor her long-delayed status as the mother of a son, but the range of activities in which she so suddenly appears in official records in the months after Evesham implies that her concerns and methods were indeed defined by recent firsthand experience of inadequate resources and a lack of supporters. As her actions in the late 1260s point directly to significant areas of her later endeavors, the evidence for this period is best considered in relation to those areas: her revenue, its sources, and those who administered it.

The relationship between Edward's finances and his wife's before 1272 is not documented, but beyond question it was, on Eleanor's part, dependent. She brought no wealth to the marriage, and since thirteenth-century English royal wives did not enter dower lands during their husbands' lifetimes, her sole source of funds was Edward's coffers. It can only be guessed that the £1000 promised as her dower in 1254 corresponded to a yearly sum allowed for her expenses; even if such conjecture is accurate, Edward's revenue in the 1250s never reached the £10,000 projected in 1254 and Eleanor's income most likely suffered too. Unable to grant away his lands, moreover, Edward could not augment her revenue by assigning her any estates; it was at his request that Henry III granted her Ashford in 1264, and only from 1266 did he make grants to Eleanor from his own lands.[53]

That Eleanor's resources were seen to be inadequate is evident from the fresh sources of income opened up to her in the later 1260s. Around the time of John's birth, Edward granted her the issues and profits of the New Forest, and Henry early in 1268 provided that as Edward was lord of Ireland, his wife should enjoy there the perquisite known as queen-gold: an additional tenth on the amount of any voluntary fine above ten marks. In April 1268 came the first grant to Eleanor of a Christian knight's debts to a Jewish moneylender, the first in a series that would have major consequences for her finances and her reputation.[54] These sources of revenue, closely linked to the prerogatives of the Crown, affirmed Eleanor's rank as well as her need for a suitable income. Financial pressures were reflected too in the additions to her estates: the terms of Henry's grants to her in the late 1260s show they were to provide for her maintenance. But cash gifts from the king were still needed, and her expenses remained a problem in the 1260s.[55]

There is no better guide to the extent and sophistication of Eleanor's endeavors at this period than a letter she sent in September 1265 to her clerk John de Loundres, containing instructions for replacement of a manor granted her earlier that month but then mistakenly regranted to another. The letter shows Eleanor taking an active role in the acquisition of her lands and her awareness that her actions would affect opinion about her: Loundres is twice told to handle matters so that her wish to replace the manor will not be put down to greed. Her links to royal officials were already informed and useful; she had access to Chancery through John de Kirkby, and her intimate knowledge of the king's official circle allowed her to suggest how certain individuals might be induced to favor her request. Before she left on Crusade in 1270 a series of grants and exchanges systematically increased her lands, and by 1270 the management of her estates and income was flourishing. Of her officials, Walter de Kancia was well established by the autumn of 1265, and probably by that time Loundres had been replaced in her wardrobe by William de Yattenden, who had family ties to Edward's household.[56]

Figure 1.1. Illuminated initial S from the "Douce" Apocalypse, showing (top) the Lord Edward and Eleanor of Castille holding shields of their arms as they kneel before the Trinity (The Bodleian Library, Oxford, MS Douce 180 fol. 1).

As Eleanor's retinue grew to impressive size by 1269, the ties among her household and those of King Henry and his wife, imposed on her in the 1250s, did not weaken. Henry's archers above twenty years, the Senches, entered her household after assisting her Ponthevin archers in 1263; the

Ferrés, Gascons long favored by Henry and his wife, were with Eleanor of Castile by 1266.[57] But it is clear that Eleanor was now beginning to select her own attendants. The married couples typical of her household as queen were already present: William Charles, her knight in 1264, married her damsel Joan "de Valle Viridi" around 1262, and John de Weston, her steward in 1264, was probably married to Hawise, Eleanor of Provence's damsel. Robert de Haustede, indebted to Eleanor of Castile for reconciling him with the king in 1266, around 1270 wed a woman named Margerie, later Eleanor's most trusted woman attendant.[58] The presence of Castilians and Picards in Eleanor's household suggests that her background influenced her choice of workers, and her origins were reflected as well in the privileges she obtained in the later 1260s for Castilian and Ponthevin merchants trading in England. These, together with the pardons and respites she secured for such petitioners as the Haustedes, show that she had grasped the value of publicly exploiting the influence she now enjoyed with King Henry.[59]

That influence could only have been bolstered by the births of a second son, Henry, in May 1268, and a daughter, Eleanor, in June 1269. The king now had chambers built for his daughter-in-law at several royal manors, but the best evidence for her standing at this period is his order at Christmas 1268 that she and her retinue should have robes identical to those of the queen and her household. There is otherwise little to report of her before August 1270, when she and Edward left England for the Crusade. Edward visited Castile for the November 1269 wedding of his cousin Blanche, Louis IX's daughter, to King Alphonso's eldest son Ferdinand, but while Eleanor was likely with him, no proof is to be found. Later in the winter of 1269–70, she visited Faringdon with the king, the queen, and Edward. She continued to watch over her cousins' interests.[60] Alphonso X perhaps sent to England a copy of his 1264 French version of the Arabic *Ladder of Mohammed*, and possibly other manuscripts as well.[61]

Recent attention given to the Crusade of 1270–72 is to some extent out of keeping with its modest successes.[62] The daughter of a king whose campaigns against the Moors won him an international reputation as a crusader, Eleanor apparently never doubted that she would accompany Edward, as her mother had accompanied Ferdinand III. She assisted personally with some preparations in France and must have assented to Edward's decision to send their infant son Henry to Louis IX as a pledge for Edward's promise to accompany Louis on the expedition. No authority earlier than William Camden, however, asserts that Eleanor justified her decision to accompany Edward with the edifying remark that "Nothing must part them whom God has joined, and the way to heaven is as near in the holy land (if not nearer) as in England or Spain." Nor do the sources suggest that Eleanor was as keen on a second Crusade as her husband professed to be; the only later indication that her travels made an impression on her are the goods she purchased from merchants active in the Holy Land.[63] After Edward committed their three children to the care of his uncle Richard of Cornwall, the couple left England in August 1270. Their route was planned to include a visit to northern Spain and a meeting with Alphonso X, but as contrary winds kept them in England two weeks beyond their intended departure, that part of their itinerary may have been abandoned. After reaching Tunis only to realize that Louis IX's death had robbed the expedition of its impetus, the couple wintered in Sicily and reached Acre in May 1271. Eleanor's activities during her sixteen months in Palestine are scantily documented apart from the births at Acre of two daughters; only the second, Joan, survived. While in Acre, Eleanor had one of her clerks, a mr Richard, prepare an Anglo-Norman version of Vegetius' *De Re Militari*, the medieval bible of chivalry; as mr Richard personalized the text with a reference to a skirmish Edward won at Kenilworth a few days before Evesham, Eleanor probably intended the work for her husband, whose military skill was a major element in his reputation.[64]

The most frequently recounted incident from the Crusade of 1270 is the attempt on Edward's life at Acre on 17 June 1272, recorded by most English chroniclers and at least one English writer of Latin verse. According to the circumstantial account in Walter of Guisborough's chronicle, Edward was stabbed in the arm with a poisoned dagger and his life was despaired of until a surgeon cut inflamed flesh from the wound; before this was done, Eleanor had to be led away, weeping and lamenting, by Edward's brother Edmund and John de Vescy. In its details Guisborough's account is not free from difficulty — Edmund appears to have left Acre a month earlier[65] — but it clearly supersedes in contemporaneity and sheer plausibility the later legend that Eleanor saved Edward's life by sucking his wounds. Despite its fantastic nature, this story has influenced popular opinion into the present century, and some attention must be given to it here. The tale first appears in the *Historia Ecclesiastica* written in the 1320s by an Italian Dominican, Bartolomeo Fiadoni (Ptolemy of Lucca), who reported it only as a popular tradition; he omitted it from his shorter *Annales*. After recounting essentially the same sequence of events given by Guisborough, Fiadoni's *Historia* continues:

> They say, however [*Tradunt autem*], that at that time his wife, a Spaniard and the sister of the king of Castile, showed her husband great faithfulness; for with her tongue she licked his open wounds

all the day, and sucked out the humour, and thus by her virtue
drew out all the poisonous material; whereby, when the scars of his
wounds were formed, he felt himself fully cured.[66]

This version of events seems to have been unknown in England until
Camden published it in *Britannia* in 1586; as late as 1577 Holinshed's
Chronicles note the attack but give Eleanor no part in its aftermath.[67] The legend's genesis is also clouded by a still later version assigning the hero's role
to Edward's Savoyard companion Otho de Grandison, who supposedly
led a charmed life and had no qualms about sucking the festered wounds.
A possible clue to solve the riddles is offered by the tale's appearance in an
Italian Dominican chronicle. As they returned from the Holy Land in the
spring of 1273, Edward and Eleanor traveled northward through Italy,
where their progress created a tremendous stir. During that journey Edward
became ill, possibly from the wounds he had suffered at Acre (which were
also blamed for an illness he had in England the next year). Fiadoni's report
perhaps grew from local Italian traditions based on Edward's illness there,
rather than on the events at Acre; that a Dominican writer noted a report
of which he was clearly uncertain might be ascribed to Eleanor's support of
that order, whose members long cherished her memory.[68]

After Edward's recovery and the birth of his and Eleanor's daughter
Joan, the English party left Palestine in the third week of September 1272
and reached Trapani on 4 November. At the court of his uncle Charles of
Anjou, an active exponent of the ancestral Charlemagne cult initiated by his
grandfather Philip Augustus of France, Edward made his only known
attempt at literary patronage, lending Rustichello da Pisa a large volume of
romance from which he asked the Italian writer to create a new work. The
result, an Arthurian prose romance now known as *Meliadus*, is no outstanding example of its kind, but its creation hints at Edward's interest in
chivalric culture, awakened or encouraged by the Vegetius translation
Eleanor sponsored at Acre, and possibly at his desire to emulate Charles'
energetic exploitation of a royal ancestral cult.[69] For her part, Eleanor
endeavored in Sicily to secure the release of her brother Henry of Castile,
imprisoned by his former patron Charles after Henry turned his coat and
supported the Sicilian claims of his Hohenstaufen kinsman Conradin.[70]
While still in Sicily, probably early in 1273, Edward and Eleanor learned
of Henry III's death in England (16 November 1272). The new king and
queen passed through Rome on 5 February and two days later reached the
papal court in Orvieto, where Eleanor secured dispensations for her chief
clerk to hold multiple benefices. After they left Orvieto, their progress was

slowed by Edward's illness; they reached Bologna only in May, and descended from the Mont-Cenis pass on 7 June. After visiting Edward's cousins in Savoy, they entered France through Burgundy.[71] When Edward arrived at Paris on 26 or 27 July 1273, Eleanor was not with him. The usual explanation, that she now visited Castile, rests upon a letter to Edward from Alphonso X as printed in Rymer's *Foedera,* with the date 23 June 1273. The original is in fact dated 18 June 1282 and in no way implies that Eleanor had visited her brother; Alphonso merely asked Edward to listen to her on matters she would discuss with him.[72] Chronology alone shatters the myth that she went to Castile in the spring of 1273: then in the fourth or fifth month of pregnancy, she would have had to travel at blinding speed from the Mont-Cenis on 7 June to reach Seville by 23 June and then race north at once, since on 26 July she passed southward through Limoges on her way to Aquitaine for the birth of her child. Eleanor must have remained with Edward until just before he reached Paris, when to avoid travel later in pregnancy she left him to go into Aquitaine; in fact, a letter to England from an anonymous member of Edward's retinue says as much. During the summer of 1273 she urged Alphonso to visit her, and he journeyed to Bayonne in November for the baptism of his new nephew and godson, whom he lifted from the font and who, exceptionally for the son of a reigning English king, was given his maternal uncle's distinctive name, Alphonso. Eleanor's roles as royal wife and mother thus assembled the males of her family—husband and brother at her son's cradle—to raise her diplomatic profile. She also showed a sure instinct for turning such moments to her benefit by inducing Alphonso (whose interest in such matters was surely known to her) to ask that Edward increase her dower assignment.[73]

Eleanor was already conducting official business at long distance between Gascony and England. That she often sent to England to ask about her children's health comes as no surprise; she had lost five and of the four living, Eleanor and Henry were sickly. They were doubtless on her mind as treaties were concluded in October 1273 for young Eleanor's marriage to the Aragonese heir, and in November for Henry's to the heiress of Navarre, alliances that promised expanded diplomatic horizons for a Castilian-born queen of England.[74] Despite papal pleas that Edward delay his coronation to attend the general council at Lyon, the investiture was fixed for 19 August, though royal progress toward England was leisurely. In Ponthieu in June, Edward agreed that their infant daughter Joan should be raised there by Eleanor's mother. After a four-year absence, the king and queen landed at Dover on 2 August 1274.[75] Eleanor had been

honored as queen from the time of Edward's accession, and in that sense
the coronation only confirmed her ascent to the office. But while it accorded
her dignity not authority, the rite—celebrated amid rich splendor and great
pomp—must have been a highly charged experience for her: Castilian
kings were rarely anointed or crowned, their wives hardly ever.[76]

Such are the outlines of Eleanor of Castile's life before the full light of
queenship begins to reveal her actions in greater detail. Generalization is
risky from the fragments concerning her before 1274, but it is clear that well
before Edward's accession she had escaped the obscurity of her first years
in England. The parameters of her life as queen were already fixed: supportive wife, attentive mother, prudent patroness of her relatives, astute
manager of estates and money, a figure of some consequence in relations
with Castile, Gascony, and Ponthieu, and a woman of varied literary interests. As queen she could operate on a wider scale by reason of her new rank
and the increased resources at her disposal; official records more consistently note certain aspects of her activities, but will not support a discussion
of her years as queen in a narrative context. The problems involved in
attempting this with small amounts of evidence will have become obvious.
Uneven distribution of the admittedly far more copious sources for Eleanor's
life after 1272 means that a narrative account would be a mere rehearsal of
the events of the reign with an occasional remark of her presence on some
great occasion, or a digression on administrative appointments or the acquisition of one manor or another. Such an approach would shed no light on
the questions that lie at the heart of this work. Eleanor's administration and
the complex tangle of her land gathering will be dealt with in succeeding
chapters, as required by the amount and the nature of the sources that
bear on them. The questions raised at the outset of this chapter will be more
fully investigated as the themes suggested by Eleanor's early life are now
examined in the contexts of her career as queen.

YEARS AS QUEEN (1272–1290)

The salient characteristic of Eleanor's life as queen was the court's constant
movement from one residence to another. While the Edwardian court's
carefully planned displacements contrast favorably with the unpredictable
relocations of Henry II so eloquently bewailed by Peter of Blois a century
earlier, endless travel was on occasion an irritant. Early in 1286 Eleanor's
women had to do without their pages when the king and queen visited the
queen-mother at Marlborough, which could not contain three royal households. Eleanor's carts never managed to hold all her baggage; the larger cof-

fer for her chapel furnishings was often left behind unless an extra cart was hired. There were accidents, some more serious than others, and fire was a constant menace: the couple barely escaped when their chamber at Hope Castle burned at night in August 1283, not the only time Edward's life was endangered by flames.[77] But for all its drawbacks, travel was a vital tool of kingship: the arrivals of king and queen at town or abbey provided opportunities for encounters between monarchs and community against a rich backdrop of royal pageantry. The queen enjoyed her own place of honor at such moments, received separately by local notables in a second procession that followed the king's, and she was shown every reverence at her destination even when not traveling with him.[78]

The extent to which Eleanor's life was influenced by frequent relocation can be observed at the intersection between travel and childbirth, which can hardly be left out of consideration since she had as many as sixteen children. Before 1270 most of them were born at Windsor, but as queen she could not plan such things as she pleased; from 1275 her children came into the world at royal manors across England, the last of them in a newly built shelter on the site of Caernarvon Castle. Regardless of location, childbirth did not impede really important matters: Eleanor traveled and transacted business within a week before a birth and afterward resumed her travels as soon as possible.[79] Her confinement at Woodstock in 1279 was probably more disturbed than usual, but typifies the problems that could arise at any moment. Mary was born on 11 or 12 March; five days later the death of Eleanor's mother made her countess of Ponthieu, involving her directly in complex administrative and diplomatic maneuvering. Within two weeks of the birth, Eleanor obtained the wardship of some East Anglian lands that lay near manors she already held, the kind of neat arrangement that is an immediately recognizable characteristic of her land gathering; as her bailiffs informed her on the availability of property in their neighborhood, and as she consulted both her council and the king's when seeking a grant from him, she was probably active in securing the 1279 grant. And on 9 April an inquest by the bishop of Worcester at Eleanor's chamber found that one of her damsels had exchanged promises of marriage with one of the king's marshals while the court was traveling to Woodstock in January.[80]

That Eleanor so involved herself in the lives of her attendants suggests that her household offered a nucleus of friends and associates to balance the lack of a settled residence. As her records do little more than identify those in her service, however, details of household makeup will be postponed until they can be treated from an administrative standpoint; only general observations on her personnel will be offered here. That her knights and women were of modest English knightly origin—Haustedes, Bruyns, Westons, le Bretons—represents both continuity and contrast. Most of Eleanor of Provence's women were from modest English families,[81] but Eleanor of Castile's retinue harbored no aliens as prominent by birth or in counsel as was Peter of Savoy in the older woman's household.[82] The absence of well-born aliens in Eleanor of Castile's retinue, consistent with other aspects of her behavior implying her awareness of attitudes toward conduct in royal circles, also suggests an effort to avoid faction in the queen's household, as had come about under Henry III and would happen again in Edward II's reign. The absence of ranking English nobles is no less easily explained. The itinerant court had not yet evolved into a fixed cultural or social center brilliant enough to attract regular noble attendance; the royal couple's travels around the realm, and their knightly attendants' export to the shires of the customs they observed at court, were the means by which the royal establishment broadcast its way of life to the kingdom at large. Nor had kings tumbled to the idea that their dignity could be enhanced by service from the great; magnates and their wives rendered personal duties to king or queen only on great occasions, when they claimed hereditary offices that testified to exalted descent.[83]

The familial aspect of the households was strengthened by the presence, encouraged by both the king and queen, of married couples and their children, intertwined with the generations of the royal family. (It was Edward's idea that Eleanor's damsel Joan "de Valle Viridi" wed her knight William Charles; her executors rewarded Benedict de Blakenham who "married at the queen's will," but as Edmund de Hemmegrave and Eleanor de Ewelle discovered, royal matchmaking was not resisted with impunity.)[84] But despite the great favor otherwise shown curial marriage, Eleanor's attendants seemingly did not aim for a court oligarchy: the daughters of William and Iseut le Bruyn married Hampshire husbands whose lands were near those granted their parents by the king and queen, and a Kentish marriage Edward granted Robert and Margerie de Haustede provided a husband for their granddaughter. Using their children's marriages to protect new local interests was a prudent choice, for while their service was properly rewarded, none of these families became as wealthy as Hubert de Burgh or the Despensers, and local concerns remained critical to their future.[85]

Outside the household, Eleanor's closest associates were John de Vescy and his wife (the queen's cousin Isabella de Beaumont), Earl Henry de Lacy of Lincoln and his wife Margaret Longespee the countess of Salisbury, and Otho de Grandison.[86] The queen's ties to members of the Beauchamp, Tybotot, and Giffard families also witness the strength of family links within her circle. Walter Beauchamp, the earl of Warwick's brother, was a knight of Edward's household and in 1289 became his steward. His wife Alice was a daughter of Petronilla de Toeny, whom Eleanor favored; the queen, who evidently sponsored a number of her courtiers' daughters, was likely godmother to the Beauchamps' daughter Eleanor.[87] The Giffards of Boyton were the offspring of Edward's childhood guardian Hugh Giffard and his wife Sybil de Cormeilles, midwife at the king's birth; Eleanor was friendly with their sons, Archbishop Walter of York and Bishop Godfrey of Worcester, whose niece Sybil le Poer was one of her women.[88] Robert Tybotot, Edward's ally before 1270, was an executor of the will Edward drew up at Acre, and was the only individual outside the court to be urgently notified of Eleanor's last illness in November 1290; his wife, Eve, was probably a sister of the queen's chaplain Payn de Chaworth.[89]

The prevalence among Eleanor's friends of close family connections to the court parallels the marriages she promoted within her household and echoes her reliance on her own kindred during her early years in England, a reminder that queens' family connections were a major impetus to their share in politics and diplomacy.[90] Eleanor's behavior in the context of her family connections may, then, be examined in the expectation that some insights will emerge about her public role and popular cognizance of it. If prudence alone argued that a queen sustained relationships with her relatives, the vigor with which Eleanor advanced her kin is among the more remarkable facets of her career, especially as she attracted markedly less criticism than her parents-in-law in the same arena. This was evidently the result of judicious choice, for apart from two bastard nephews and an obscure cousin Rotheric, she settled no Castilian kin in England.[91] It was not that distance weakened Eleanor's ties to Castile. She upheld the waning fortunes of Alphonso X, was attentive to the plight of her nephew Ferdinand's widow and sons, and kept in touch with the imprisoned Henry of Castile to the end of her days; but contact with Castile depended on embassies and the exchange of literary works or other gifts.[92] Most of the relatives Eleanor brought to England were thus maternal kin from Picard houses with long-established ties to England, and her relations with them reveal a careful approach in her patronage. She arranged no marriages between wealthy English heiresses and her male cousins, as Henry III and his wife had done, to the English magnates' fury. Eleanor instead married female cousins to English husbands; the rare exceptions involved heiresses of modest substance married not to the heads of foreign lineages but to cadets who settled in England.[93] Such cautious tactics recall Eleanor's concern in 1265 to avoid any suspicion of greed as she sought a new manor from Henry III and suggest her awareness of attitudes toward royal conduct. English chroniclers in general have little to say about Eleanor of Castile, but given baronial anger at the matrimonial maneuverings of Henry III and Eleanor of Provence, the chroniclers' silence on their daughter-in-law's activities in the same area would almost suggest that shrewd planning allowed her to avoid controversy.

Eleanor arranged these marriages in a businesslike manner, insisting on guarantees that the husbands' lands would be preserved intact and on promises of indemnification should the marriage prove barren.[94] Her aim clearly was to assure a new generation of loyal kin, an echo of her curial marriages that so often produced the next generation's attendants, and a reminder that a queen might urgently need supporters in adversity. Through centuries of genealogical bad luck and marrying daughters to foreign rulers, moreover, English kings had never produced those "lords of the blood royal" whom later centuries saw as the Crown's natural advisors and supporters. Until Edward I's Lancastrian nephews and his Clare and Bohun grandchildren grew up, the only kin English kings could boast in England were bastard offshoots or the issue of kinsmen imported by their queens.[95] Eleanor's matrimonial ventures, then, shared in a venerable and not invaluable tradition in English queenship, albeit one rather tarnished by her parents-in-law.

The queen's cousins could assist her outside England as well, for the Plantagenets needed connections to the Continent and their wives' families were a handy supply. A royal consort could thus widen her diplomatic role by cultivating sib and kin, and Eleanor corresponded steadily, receiving messages and responding with messages and gifts.[96] In this context, the choice of envoys between the French and English courts is revealing. Edward's proctors at the Paris *Parlement* in July 1280 were his Poitevin cousin Maurice de Craon and Geoffrey de Geneville or Joinville, half-brother of Louis IX's biographer and by marriage lord of half of Meath; Philip IV's emissaries at an English parliament in February 1286 were Craon and Eleanor's cousin John de Brienne. As a relative of the English king and an important French lord, Craon was well suited to missions of this kind. Geneville, connected to Edward through the Savoyards, was a former justiciar of Ireland who had carried out Eleanor's business in Ponthieu. John de Brienne was stepfather to Edward's brother-in-law Alexander III of Scotland, and shortly before John was sent to England in February 1286, his granddaughter Margaret de Fiennes was married by the queen to Edmund Mortimer.[97] These men cannot have been haphazardly selected as envoys between England and France; Eleanor had openly shown her benevolence toward the Briennes, and the French agents' ties to both her and Edward imply they were chosen for their ability to enlist her influence with him.

If it was advisable that a queen maintained ties with relatives abroad, it was vital that she interacted positively with her husband's family too; at the nexus of family and power, a royal consort's role could be a damaging one. In an earlier age of spreading royal kindreds, dynastic conflicts frequently centered around wives, each of whom hoped to secure her future by seeing her children provided for and their rights protected, as witness the Brunhild- Fredegund feud in Merovingian France, the aftermath of Louis the Pious' second marriage, or Ethelwulf of Wessex's deposition by sons who feared displacement by a child of his second wife.[98] Margaret of Anjou and Elizabeth Woodville are later examples of the familial contentions that could surround queens, and it will be recalled that Eleanor of Provence and her Savoyard kinsmen favored the exile of Henry III's Lusignan brothers in 1258. Eleanor of Castile's actions echo none of these cases; Edward I could rely on his male collaterals' loyalty, and his wife did not disturb peaceful relations. She had frequent and evidently friendly contacts with the king's brother Edmund of Lancaster and his wife, the dowager queen of Navarre.[99] Edward's wealthy and pious cousin Edmund of Cornwall appears rarely in Eleanor's records, but despite financial complications between them, she mediated his dispute with the bishop of Exeter in 1280 and, with his countess, secured episcopal confirmation of a grant to the nuns of Ivinghoe.[100] (Edward's sisters, Queen Margaret of Scotland and Beatrice, wife of the Breton heir, both died early in his reign.)

Far more than cousins or brother, the royal circle in England was defined by the presence of Edward's mother, and while Eleanor of Provence's influence with her son lessened over time, he was lucky—unlike Louis IX—in that his wife and mother were respectful of each other.[101] Traceable from 1259, their cooperation continued virtually unruffled to the end of their lives. Eleanor of Castile in 1276 secured from Edward a grant for Tarrant Abbey, committed to his mother by the bishop of Durham in 1236 and always much favored by her; after a grandson's death in 1274, Eleanor of Provence founded in his memory not a Franciscan house, in keeping with her own inclinations, but a Dominican priory, as favored by the boy's mother.[102] The queen-dowager's 1290 warning that a stay in the North would threaten another grandson's health supports impressions that the younger woman's children were a field of mutual concern; in June 1282 the two women together convinced Edward that his eldest daughter, then thirteen, was too young for marriage, rare proof of community of feeling among medieval noblewomen and evidence that they did not acquiesce in silence to their male relatives' matrimonial control. But the children could elicit conflict too, as when the two queens in 1285 disagreed over enclosure of the king's daughter Mary.[103] Their 1282 collaboration was, however, surely grounded in memories of their own early marriages, and a 1287 incident offers some confirmation for the idea that the two women shared an understanding of queenship's role in their lives. The queen-dowager held the town of Southampton in dower from 1273. In 1276 Eleanor of Castile was given custody of the castle and the king's houses there, and to repair them Edward in 1286 granted murage for four years. The townspeople refused to pay, and to reach Edward's ear they appealed to the dowager, who duly sent him a message that the payment would impoverish the town. When that letter reached Edward in Gascony, his wife sent a sharp order to his lieutenant in England to sort out matters—unleashing her wrath not at the mother-in-law who had responded to a petition as was expected of her, but at the townspeople who had presumed to appeal to the dowager.[104]

At the convergence of queenship and family, a queen's office inevitably marked relations with her children, potentially a critical resource for her. In centuries when succession patterns were undefined, a royal widow could best protect herself by bringing a son to the throne and securing her influence over him. The gradual acceptance of stable patterns of succession thus cost many queens an important area of political activity; in another sense, it afforded them greater security as the mothers of acknowledged heirs to the throne. After the deaths of several sons, Edward I in 1290 faced candidly the possibility that a daughter might succeed him and took steps to protect his eldest daughter's rights before the second daughter wed the powerful earl of Gloucester, confirming that his daughters were potential heirs to the throne and assuring Eleanor that all her children's rights would be respected.[105] A queen of England was therefore well advised to cultivate relationships with sons and daughters alike, but despite their importance to her Eleanor rarely saw her children while they were young. Until they grew old enough to tolerate the court's incessant travels, they stayed at Windsor, Woodstock, or Langley, joining their parents only on great occasions; they were gradually introduced to itinerant life from about the age of seven. In 1289–90 Eleanor's three oldest daughters, then twenty, eighteen and fifteen, traveled with the court most of the time; the youngest children, aged eight and six, visited now and again.[106]

Separation did not mean that Eleanor was inattentive to her children's welfare. As noted earlier during her absence between 1270 and 1274, she often sent to ask after their health,[107] and her protests against Mary's enclosure in 1285 convincingly echo her objections to young Eleanor's marriage in 1282. Both parents were mindful of the hazards that faced their children; alms were offered, prayers sought for their health, and grants made to religious houses for the souls of those who died.[108] An apocryphal story of Edward's fortitude when he learned of a son's death has led to the idea that he was unmoved at the deaths of his children.[109] That the Plantagenets were no strangers to parental feelings, however, is shown by Eleanor of Provence's letter to Edward asking that the mother of a royal ward might visit her son — "I know well the longing of a mother to see a child from whom she has long been parted." Edward liked to speak of his children, and his scolding letter to Margerie de Haustede, who forgot to send him news of his children by his second wife, is not the message of a careless father.[110] Still, it is hard to find testimony of the parents' reactions to the loss of so many children, and impossible to identify their feelings very closely with the conventional terms in which the chroniclers describe their grief at the deaths of three of their sons. Though it might be thought that the death of an infant daughter was not a great blow to royal parents, the only trace left on extant records by one of Eleanor's tiny daughters, probably her firstborn, shows that the queen did remember and commemorate her thirty years or more after the child's death.[111] But the most convincing evidence for the parents' sense of loss at the death of a child comes with the passing of Alphonso (1273–84), who alone of those who died young lived long enough to give his parents some idea of a developing personality. Archbishop Pecham's moving letter to Edward upon the boy's death shows the loss was a severe blow, and of all her children Eleanor had only Alphonso's heart reserved for burial with her own.[112]

If the parents were not inattentive to their children's welfare, evidence suggests that the children related with difficulty to absentee parents. During her parents' Crusade, young Eleanor (1269–98) evidently became close to her grandmother Eleanor of Provence, with whom she and her brother Henry lived after the deaths in 1272 of Richard of Cornwall and Henry III. In 1277–78, when the girl was just beginning to travel with her parents, she visited her grandmother at Marlborough or Clarendon whenever she left court to rest from itinerant life; during the Welsh war of 1282–84, the second daughter, Joan, went to Wales with her parents, but young Eleanor again stayed with the dowager.[113] As much the same relationship can be assumed for young Henry, it was perhaps better that in October 1274 the dying boy was supported by the grandmother he knew intimately, not the mother he had met for the first time in his memory only some ten weeks earlier.[114]

The next daughter, Joan "of Acre" (1272–1307), was separated from her parents for four years (1274–78) while she lived with her maternal grandmother in Ponthieu. Joan is best known for her clandestine second marriage in 1297, but other examples of willful behavior are not lacking. While her parents were in Gascony in the 1280s, she quarreled with a wardrobe clerk from whom she thereafter refused to accept money for her expenses, and Edward had to pay her debts when he returned to England. Nine days before her 1290 wedding to the earl of Gloucester, it was noticed that Joan had two yeomen fewer than her sisters; the wardrobe did not specify who it was that went about counting up the servants, but that two yeomen were hired in for the nine days implies that whoever made the discovery, Joan's reaction was unfavorable. She and the earl left court soon after their wedding, to Edward's displeasure, though Joan did return for the Clipstone parliament that autumn, possibly to announce her pregnancy. In 1305 she learned that her brother Edward, out of favor with the king, was deprived of his seal, and sent him her own with an offer to put all her goods at his disposal.[115] Joan clearly stood in no awe of her parents, and it is tempting to ascribe this to the fact that her relationships with them developed only after she arrived in England at the age of six, perhaps thoroughly spoiled by an indulgent grandmother.

Figure 1.2. Miniature from a manuscript written and illuminated in England ca. 1300 of Aegidius Colonna's *Government of Princes*, showing a king and queen with their children. Their gestures indicate they are discussing their daughter (Baltimore, The Walters Art Gallery, MS 10.144 fol. 41).

The four-year absence on Crusade made young Eleanor and Henry closer to their grandmother, and Joan's four years in Ponthieu interrupted and perhaps deeply marked her relationships with her parents. In the same way, the queen's stay in Gascony from May 1286 to August 1289 must have impeded the formation of bonds with Elizabeth (1282–1316) and Edward (1284–1327). By the time she returned to England, Eleanor was already fatally ill, and in the months before her death little contact with these two is recorded. The queen's relations with Margaret (1275–ca. 1333) are poorly documented; the most shadowy of the lot, she is remarkable only for her haughty rejection of jewels prepared for her journey to Brabant in 1297, seven years after she wed its duke.[116] Mary (1279–1332) was effectively separated from the king and queen when she was enclosed at Amesbury in 1285, but she enjoyed a generous income and rich gifts from them and later from her brother and nephew Edward III. Veiled in 1291, Mary visited court often, gambling whenever there on what would have been a ruinous scale had not her father and brother paid her losses. Little credit attaches, however, to the earl of Surrey's 1344 claim of a sexual liaison with Mary; he was estranged from his wife—young Eleanor's daughter—and alleging premarital fornication with her only maiden aunt (conveniently deceased) was but one tactic he adopted in the effort to shed an unwanted consort.[117]

As adults Eleanor's daughters gave proof of attachment to their father; Elizabeth seems to have become his favorite, the one he kept with him most consistently, and Mary once asked that for the ease of her heart Edward must send her news of himself by every messenger.[118] But when young, the children seem to have had difficulties in bridging the figurative and literal distances that separated them from their parents, and it was important that the queen found other ways to sustain her presence in their lives. Their education offered such means. Any queen's supervision of her son's training was critical to her establishment of her influence with him for the future; consideration of relationships among royal mothers and daughters suggests that the alliances among husbands, brothers, and sons, celebrated in chronicle and treaty, concealed and subordinated parallel alliances that naturally formed among the daughters and sisters left unnamed by chroniclers and clerks—a resource no wise queen would fail to develop by attentively preparing her daughters for the careers she knew awaited them.[119] Eleanor's interest in her children's training shows her not indifferent to the need to prepare them for the lives their rank would thrust upon them. As she made many appointments to their households, there is more than passing interest to the fact that in 1290 she sent her scribe Philip to Woodstock, where six-year-old Edward was then living. The king's wardrobe book in the same year reveals the presence of Dominican friars in the boy's household, another echo of the queen's interests that suggests young Edward was better educated than has been supposed. The strongest sign of her influence is evidence that young Eleanor was literate, reflecting the queen's ardent literary tastes; a response may be detected too in the Anglo-Norman chronicle Nicholas Trevet dedicated to Mary.[120]

Figure 1.3. Early fourteenth-century panel painting of a king from the Westminster Abbey sedilia, thought to represent Edward I (National Monuments Record).

The most intimate and critical relationship in Queen Eleanor's life was naturally that between wife and husband. It is a commonplace for biographers of Edward I to represent Eleanor as a restraining influence on him, her death as the loss of a potential check on the bad temper of his later years. This was the role urged upon royal wives by the Church, and the flow of petitions to the thirteenth-century queens shows that society expected them to mediate with their husbands. The contemporary evidence, however, does not allow the relationship between Edward and Eleanor to be reduced to such simple terms. Not that there is much: after their return to England in 1274, the couple were rarely separated for any length of time save when Eleanor was in childbed, at times during the Welsh wars of 1277 and 1284, when Edward went to Aragon in 1288, or when the queen visited an ailing lady attendant in 1289. As there was scant need for letters between husband and wife, no first hand evidence survives for the interaction of their personalities.[121]

The testimony of third parties, however, implies that those who knew the couple were wary of Eleanor and feared she might turn Edward against any who crossed her. Archbishop Pecham warned her that some in the realm suspected she caused the king to rule harshly; deeper misgivings surface in his 1279 letter to the nuns of Hedingham, who refused to admit a lady whose vocation the queen supported—the Primate bluntly told the nuns that if they knew what was good for them, they would submit.[122] Bishop Godfrey Giffard of Worcester in May 1283 advised the prior of Deerhurst to present the queen's chaplain to a church to which the prior had already presented another: Giffard had received letters from Eleanor and the Chancellor, and warned against incurring royal wrath. As Pecham also warned the bishop of Winchester of the dangers of inciting the king's indignation in a very similar case involving presentation of Eleanor's Spanish physician to the church of Crondall in the early 1280s, it does appear to have been suspected (or known) that she was quick to anger when crossed and that the consequences for whomever she identified as the culprit might be grave. In fact, the Crondall dispute probably gave rise to the letter from Pecham quoted earlier, reminding Eleanor of her duty to be merciful and referring to Edward's treatment of the bishop of Winchester; in that context, the letter implies that Pecham attributed the king's behavior to her rancor at her physician's inconvenience in obtaining the church.[123] Fear of her anger appears too in a letter from Count Esquivat of Bigorre, who around 1278 heard that she held him in contempt after he could not assist Alphonso X in Navarre; he begged Edward to excuse him to her.[124]

Eleanor may have fostered such apprehensions by wielding her access to Edward as a threat, as when she commanded Edmund of Cornwall to take order with the men of Southampton in 1287.[125] But Edward was capable of overruling his wife if her behavior exceeded proper bounds. In 1283 she was granted the wardship of the lands of Patrick de Chaworth, whose widow soon married Hugh Despenser without license; Eleanor then exacted from Hugh a fine of 1000 marks. Despite the efforts of supporters, including the king's uncle William de Valence, Hugh had to acknowledge the debt, and only direct appeal to Edward elicited an order that Eleanor relax her demands.[126] In 1287 Eleanor heard that a manor near her estates in Northamptonshire was to be conveyed against the Statute of Mortmain to Peterborough Abbey; with the all-but-certain intent that he should grant her custody of it, she energetically insisted that Edward take the manor into his hand, but he would do nothing contrary to right.[127]

Revealing evidence for the official relationship between king and queen is found in a letter of June 1290 from the Chancellor, Robert Burnell, to that same Bishop Giffard of Worcester who alerted the prior of Deerhurst in 1283 to the dangers of provoking royal wrath. Burnell wrote Giffard on that earlier occasion too, perhaps to advise him (as Pecham warned the nuns at Hedingham in 1279) that it was wiser to let the woman have what she wanted. Giffard in 1290 faced prosecution for 350 marks Eleanor claimed he owed her, and he turned to Burnell for advice. The Chancellor assured Giffard that no estreat had issued despite the queen's insistence that it had; but for the moment, Giffard should acknowledge the debt and ask to pay by installments. Burnell's last suggestion is the more telling: "We believe, however, that when you have had speech with our said lady queen, the matter will find a happier end if we are present."[128] Clearly Burnell was aware of Eleanor's tendency to demand and pursue, and he felt himself well enough acquainted with her to assure Giffard that he could maneuver her. As Edward's most trusted advisor, Burnell must have known well the king's views on behavior proper to the queen, and it can be supposed that he never would have opened his mind to Giffard on so delicate a matter had he not known that this was exactly what Edward expected of him.[129]

The chroniclers' silence on Eleanor of Castile's official role now begins to come into sharper focus. It is often implied that Edward's powerful regal personality overshadowed those around him; to an extent he perhaps cast even his wife into the shade. The evidence just presented, however, suggests a deliberation in Edward's actions that requires attention. As noted earlier, the absence of aliens from Eleanor's retinue and her desire in 1265 to avoid giving any impression of greed suggest that she was aware of popular reactions to behavior in high places. A like sensibility on Edward's part is implied by his awareness of the strong feelings aroused by perceptions of

Eleanor of Provence's partisan political activity—as shown by his attempt at Lewes to avenge the July 1263 attack upon her in London.[130] The limits Edward placed on his wife's actions—and the degree to which it appears she accepted his decisions (perhaps keeping her own mother's behavior in mind)—might, then, be ascribed to a mutual desire to protect themselves from controversy. They succeeded to the extent that there was never a physical attack on Eleanor of Castile; but notwithstanding the scant attention the chroniclers paid her, it must be kept in mind that other evidence strongly suggests that she did attract a certain amount of rumbling if not eruptive criticism.

Revealing though it is as regards their personal relationship, Edward's restraint of Eleanor's behavior should be associated with certain more widely pervasive factors in English kingship and queenship. An English king's children were his expected heirs, but—as shown by Edward's marriage agreement with the earl of Gloucester in 1290—an uneasy balance survived between the ideal of hereditary succession and the historical reality that the throne could be seized by almost anyone powerful or adroit enough to make his claim prevail. That a woman could succeed to the English throne implied other prospects for the disruption of royal succession, including the possibility that a widowed queen (or, if she remarried, her new husband) might use the regency to seize power. Thus no dowager queen of England was ever formally acknowledged as regent; Eleanor in 1270 was excluded from Edward's provisions for the guardianship of their children and the regency of the realm should he die during the Crusade, and the will he made following the 1272 attempt on his life at Acre confirmed her isolation from such bases of political leverage, guaranteeing her dower but naming her neither regent nor legal guardian of their children.[131] Edward's later watchfulness over Eleanor's conduct should be understood within the context of this tendency to restrict a queen's access to official dominion, and its ramifications can be seen in Eleanor's role in politics and diplomacy.

Pecham's 1283 letter apart, there is really no convincing evidence that Eleanor's political role troubled her contemporaries. She did mediate in a number of disputes between prominent individuals—most notably the simmering rivalry between the earls of Hereford and Gloucester—and conveyed petitions to the king or his officials;[132] such incidents may imply some regard for her judgment, but can hardly have fostered such suspicions of political meddling as plagued Eleanor of Provence. The intercessory role, indeed, could carry very positive implications for a queen's office. The king's attention to such requests affirmed her prominence and encouraged others to seek her patronage, allowing her to forge valuable networks of influence. It was inevitable, moreover, that Marian overtones would attach to a queen's intercession, enhancing the dignity of her office as she assumed the intercessor's ideally submissive posture—benign, gracious, and prudently secluded from the king's authority even as she helped reveal that authority as just and merciful. Given the anomalies noted earlier between Pecham's warnings of improper influence and Eleanor's intercessory activity, however, the last word on her behavior in this respect is better postponed until more material is digested.[133]

The share Edward did allow Eleanor in the exercise of his authority was a not-insignificant role in the process, critical to effective royal lordship, of distributing wealth through wardships and marriages. He granted her many of these, and she purchased almost as many for herself; some she used for her cousins, and others for families long attached to the court, constructing (or perpetuating) networks of curial families indebted to her for their continued prosperity. Given the political overtones already identified in the queen's matchmaking it is clear that she was pursuing an important area of activity, though one in which she was never altogether independent, for in all cases Edward's authority clearly underlay her actions.[134]

A similar pattern emerges in Eleanor's diplomatic role, which generally must be inferred, not documented, as with her 1259 meeting with Gaston of Béarn's envoy, the Lusignan-Châtelleraut marriage at around the same time, and Henry of Castile's departure from England in 1259. The records of Edward's negotiations with other princes rarely refer to his wife, save to inform them that she was in good health. There are thus few overt signs of her activity other than those occasions on which Edward supplied her with plate to give to visiting notables or envoys—much of it in the form of silver-gilt cups, an intriguing echo of the image of the lord's wife as cup-bearer and bringer of peace.[135] In other cases noted in wardrobe accounts, Eleanor's activities suggest the domestic, as in Gascony in 1288 when the king was negotiating the prince of Salerno's release by the king of Aragon: she prepared the prince's lodgings and sent his wife news of the negotiations.[136] As implied by her support of Edward in the crisis of 1259–64, by Alphonso X's 1273 visit to Bayonne, and by the Anglo-French envoys in the 1280s, however, Eleanor most easily entered the diplomatic arena through her family connections, though her role often becomes clear only when thorough familiarity with the situation is developed. Edward's appointment of a royal clerk, John de Montibus, to negotiate with his cousin the count of Savoy and the marquis of Montferrat in 1282, for example, takes on its full meaning only when it is realized that Montibus, a Savoyard, was one of Eleanor's clerks, evidently introduced to her service by the Grandison bishop of

Verdun, and that the marquis of Montferrat was the widower of her niece, Beatrice of Castile. A letter from the count of Savoy shows that Eleanor was indeed involved in the business handled by the 1282 envoys. (It was not unknown for a queen to promote marriages to further her own international objectives, but it is unclear if Eleanor encouraged her niece's 1271 Montferrat marriage to provide herself a contact through which to participate in Edward's relations with his relatives in Savoy.)[137] Similarly, the records for the 1284 negotiations for the marriage of Eleanor's daughter Elizabeth to the count of Holland's son identify John de Lovetot, a justice, among Edward's envoys to Holland; a year later, Lovetot mediated between Holland and Eleanor's cousin the count of Gueldres. But only records for the administration of her estates reveal that Lovetot was also the auditor of her accounts and that she rewarded him and his family for his services.[138] As it was likely in just such discreet ways that royal women claimed a share in their husbands' diplomacy, only close scrutiny is likely to retrieve their participation from obscurity. Their contributions may have been greater than is otherwise apparent, especially in the area of the matrimonial diplomacy in which they were so intimately experienced.

There is an obvious familial context, too, in Eleanor's main contribution to Plantagenet diplomacy, her succession to Ponthieu in 1279. The tiny county would never be so weighty an inheritance as Aquitaine, but it heightened her profile with regard to France and gave her a base comparable to Angoulême, where John's widow had chosen to preside rather than lead a dowager's life in England (as Eleanor's mother had preferred Ponthieu to Castile). Apart from her years as guardian of her granddaughter Joan, Jeanne appears rarely in English records after Edward's accession, usually only when asking him to deal favorably with those who sought her help with English business, or to send her four hunting dogs "because mine have all died."[139] The confusion Edward and Eleanor found in Ponthieu in 1279 implies they had little contact with affairs there in the intervening years. Jeanne left sizable debts for which the king and queen assumed liability, and by providing lavishly in her testament for a son of Eleanor's brother Ferdinand, Jeanne prepared an inheritance dispute that cost Eleanor and Edward a second large sum. These challenges were met decisively and Eleanor's inheritance was prudently governed, but her status in England did not change: she never used her Ponthevin title there.[140]

Eleanor's diplomatic activity is otherwise discernible only in relations with Castile. That her efforts were of little benefit to her brother resulted from no lack of energy on her part, nor from any reluctance on her husband's: Edward recognized the ties that bound him to Alphonso (including the

Castilian king's sponsorship of Edward's son) and, after Richard of Cornwall's death, supported Alphonso's claim to the German throne until the pope pronounced against him in 1275. Only months thereafter, however, the death of Alphonso's eldest son, Ferdinand, initiated a divisive struggle that shattered the Castilian king's authority before he died nine years later. Ferdinand left two sons, heirs to the throne by primogeniture according to the law codes promulgated by Alphonso; but the king's second son, Sancho, claimed that Castilian custom made him the heir to his nephews' exclusion, and aligned himself with Castilian nobles disturbed by the threats to their privileges embodied in Alphonso's legal reforms. In 1277 Alphonso admitted Sancho as his heir.[141] The network of kinship linking the Castilian, French, and English kings ensured that the dispute would cross the Pyrenees. Ferdinand of Castile had married a sister of Philip III of France, who upheld her sons' rights; Alphonso's 1277 recognition of Sancho thus caused a Franco-Castilian rift in which Edward, at Alphonso's request, did his best to arbitrate. But efforts to arrange a meeting of the two kings at Bayonne in 1277 were hampered by that year's Welsh campaign, and by the early 1280s any likelihood of such a meeting had evaporated.[142]

As Alphonso's position deteriorated in the 1280s, Eleanor's diplomatic role is more clearly documented. In June 1282 Alphonso asked Edward to give her full credence in matters she would discuss with him; the Welsh war impeded her efforts, but that December Edward ordered the viscount of Béarn to go to Castile with one hundred Gascon knights. Late in 1282 or early in 1283, the queen was in contact with the king of Aragon about the Castilian crisis, though it is uncertain what effect the exchange might have had. The bishop of Cádiz reached England as Alphonso's envoy late in 1283, seeking help even from the queen's daughter Joan; Edward now sent Alphonso 5000 marks, but the money had not reached Seville when Alphonso died in April 1284.[143] In a 1283 testament, Alphonso complained that Edward and other princes had abandoned him, but the lack of English response was not Eleanor's fault. The moments of greatest crisis in Castile coincided with Edward's Welsh campaigns of 1277 and 1282–84, when it was impossible for him to send troops or money, and even in peacetime, distance prevented Edward from sending military aid from England.[144] While sympathetic toward the widowed Blanche of France and her sons, Edward and Eleanor had little choice but to acknowledge Sancho IV's accession in 1284. In the later 1280s they seem to have had fewer contacts with the strife-riven Castilian house, though Eleanor's links to her homeland remained strong enough for at least one Castilian chronicler to record her death in 1290, and for her son to be considered as a possible heir to that throne as late as 1304.[145]

Despite the limited role he allowed his wife, Edward cannot have objected to Eleanor's labors on behalf of her brother. Any king would expect the women of his family to do as much for him if they married foreign princes. This was an acceptable way for a royal wife, circumspectly within the family context, to maintain a visible international profile and to turn to her advantage any opportunities her connections offered (as with Alphonso X's request in 1273 that Edward increase Eleanor's dower assignment). Ultimately, however, the Anglo-Castilian link was of little benefit to Eleanor. Obsessed until 1275 with his imperial ambitions and then immersed in the struggle with Sancho, Alphonso could not have responded effectively had she needed his help. Anglo-Gascon interests were well served by the 1254 treaty sealed by her marriage, but the diplomatic history of Edward's reign was not greatly marked by the Castilian alliance. True, the interest his marriage gave him in Iberian affairs underlay his negotiation of the 1288 Treaty of Canfranc. The repute he thus acquired as an equitable arbitrator perhaps induced some Iberian nobles to offer to join him on Crusade after he took the cross a second time in 1287; but contemporaries realized that Canfranc represented no real advance for English interests.[146] Put at its simplest, the remoteness of Castile and Alphonso X's political demise narrowed Eleanor's diplomatic horizons as surely as did Edward's supervision—which was perhaps not entirely unwelcome to him. Eleanor's leverage was also impeded by a lack of ties to politically dominant Capetian circles as close as those her mother-in-law enjoyed. (Louis IX was a first cousin once removed, Philip III a second cousin, Philip IV a second cousin once removed.) Marriages projected in the 1250s and 1270s might have created such links for her, but the early deaths of the principals to these alliances emphasized the frailty of the human ties on which royal women were dependent, and perhaps help to explain Eleanor's successful 1282 objection to a daughter's premature marriage. The betrothal of Louis IX's son to Eleanor's niece Berengaria ended with his death in 1260, and her nephew Ferdinand's 1275 death left his wife, Louis' daughter, helpless and destitute; the marriages planned in 1273 for two of Eleanor's children with the heirs of Navarre and Aragon were never completed. When she died in 1290, only two of her daughters had recently married, Joan to the earl of Gloucester and Margaret to the duke of Brabant's son, and Eleanor had no time to capitalize on any advantages the marriages might have brought her.[147] Her lack of strong foreign connections meant that her vigorous development of English networks was politic, and that she deployed her maternal cousins to that end suggests that she had astutely identified the Picards as her more immediately valuable asset.[148]

It is difficult to say whether similar considerations affected Eleanor's investment in her marriage; a degree of self-interest would lead any observant queen to nourish her conjugal ties thoughtfully. But if Eleanor was not the gentling consort beloved of popular historians, her relationship with Edward was mutually constant and respectful.[149] The publicity of life at court meant that their lives could hardly be kept secret; immorality in their households was discouraged,[150] but the pair showed a healthily casual attitude toward the most intimate side of their marriage. Each year on Easter Monday, seven of the queen's women trapped Edward in his bed until he paid them a token ransom of £2 apiece, so he might rise and join her at their first opportunity to resume conjugal relations after weeks of Lenten abstinence.[151] In contrast to the austere married life of Edward's uncle Louis IX of France,[152] this half-ribald ritual witnesses a familiarity also suggested by evidence for Eleanor's understanding of Edward's moods. It seems he found formality irksome: in July 1290 he struck and injured a squire at his daughter Margaret's wedding, and when Elizabeth married the count of Holland in 1297 he threw her coronet in the fire — incidents of a piece with his failure to attend the earl marshal's wedding at Havering in June 1290, when Eleanor paid some minstrels to play for him as he sat apart during the service. As other evidence indicates that he did find comfort in music, Eleanor's gesture suggests her appreciation of his pleasures as well as a certain tolerance of his aversions.[153]

These moments lend color to such stories as the couple's escape from death in Gascony in 1287, when a bolt of lightning came through a window and passed between them as they conversed on a couch.[154] The record evidence deepens, too, Edward's most frequently quoted reference to his wife. A letter asking prayers for her soul, sent to the bishops of England on the morrow of her death, betrays a clerical hand in its scriptural allusions; but a similar letter to the abbot of Cluny in January 1291 has an entirely convincing reference to the wife "whom living we dearly cherished, and whom dead we cannot cease to love."[155] The splendid commemorations Edward endowed for Eleanor, and which he attended until his death, exalted her memory and with it his kingship. But they also imply the difficulty he had in detaching himself from her, an effort perhaps nowhere more evident than at Easter 1291, when she was five months dead: her women now had no reason to seize him in his bed, but he still gave them his token ransom as he had done in her lifetime.[156]

If it is possible to catch something of Eleanor's personality from her relationships with those around her, it is a greater task to form an idea of her preferences or aversions. That she attached some importance to her phys-

ical surroundings is implied by the speed with which refinements were supplied for her residences when she accompanied Edward during the Welsh
war of 1282–84: her chambers at Rhuddlan and Caernarvon had lead roofs,
lawns neatly turfed and fenced, even stocked fishponds.[157] The interiors of
her chambers were richly painted, windows glazed (some with colored
panes), and candles dyed in a variety of colors.[158] She preserved the
Castilian fashion for tapestries and carpets she introduced to England in
1255: four green and three red carpets were purchased for her in 1278, in
1286 a *tapiciarius* named John de Winton' was paid £5 for his wares to her
use, and "pictured cloths" from Cologne cost her 26*s*.8*d*. in 1290.[159] She
seems to have popularized the custom in England, and advertised English
work as well, sending Alphonso X hangings and vestments that he
bequeathed to the cathedral of Seville. After her death the sale of her carpets, hangings, and jewels fetched £617:11:10.[160]

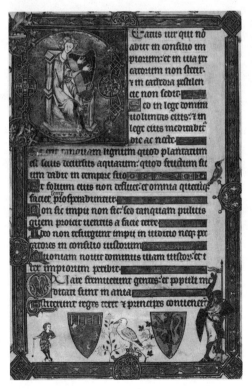

Figure 1.4. *Beatus* page of the
"Alphonso" psalter, illuminated
in 1284, for the marriage of
Eleanor's son Alphonso
(London, The British Museum,
Add. MSS 24686 fol. II).

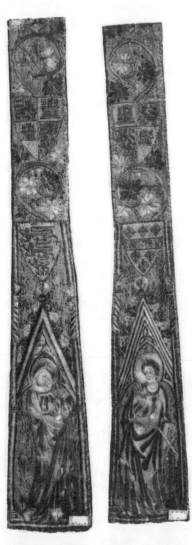

Figure 1.5. Fragments of a late thirteenth-century English maniple, embroidered with the arms of Castile and England (Lyon, Musée historique des Tissus, 1184-R6-33).

Figure 1.6. Late thirteenth-century English apparel for an alb, embroidered with the arms of England and Castile (New York, The Metropolitan Museum of Art, 17-190-186).

Precious materials also distinguished Eleanor's domestic utensils. The handles of knives she purchased in 1284 were of jasper; in 1289 a goldsmith added enamels and other ornaments to these or similar knives. Chessmen Edward gave her in 1286 were of crystal and jasper. Her mirrors were of glass and metal, with ivory mirror cases.[161] Silver and gold plate was plentiful, some given by the king, some created by Eleanor's goldsmiths. Edward's gifts to her at the Feast of the Circumcision were especially rich pieces of plate—in 1284 it was a cup made from 238 gold florins, worth £28:15:2.[162] (That many of these items, including books and chapel vestments, bore Eleanor's arms and those of many noble families supports the idea that she promoted the evolving science of heraldry.)[163]

Many of Eleanor's possessions came from abroad: Limoges caskets, vases from Venice and goods from Tripoli and Damascus, and the exotic materials for her apparel—cloth of tartarin and gold, feathers and furs from France, gilded shoes and purses. (Edward had little patience with the trappings of kingship, but it was proper that the queen concerned herself with such tokens of royal dignity.)[164] Her jewels, in the staggering quantities needed for frequent largesse, came from French, Italian, and English craftsmen and from merchants trading in the Holy Land.[165] As queen, Eleanor often secured favors for such foreign merchants, but as her taste for their luxuries did little to increase exports, the economic impact on the kingdom was negligible. Tradition credits her, however, with bringing to England the first Merino sheep—and she did import twenty-five sheep in 1280, though not certainly from Castile.[166]

Frequent references to Eleanor's gardens disclose a pronounced fondness for ornamental plantings that allowed the external appearance of her lodgings to reflect the status of their occupant. She had a quite elaborate garden at Westminster, with a pond filled by pipes from the river, which recalls the fishpond so swiftly prepared in Wales in the 1280s; replanted in 1277 with a variety of vines and roses, the Westminster garden was improved in 1279 with new cuttings and turves and an herbarium near her chapel. After the queen bought the manor of Langley in 1275, an extensive garden was planted and laid out with wells; for Langley, she obtained French apple cuttings in 1280 and in 1281 she had a *vineator* there named James Frangypany, perhaps an Italian. The decorative use of water in these gardens may represent an attempt to recreate the Islamic pleasure gardens she had known in Spain, an idea supported by her importation of Aragonese gardeners to work at Langley in 1289.[167] Her gardens were enlivened by the birds she fancied: a large aviary was put up for her at Westminster in 1279, and her accounts refer to swans, Sicilian parrots, and nightingales.[168]

A study of the foodstuffs mentioned in the wardrobe accounts would be a lengthy project, but as there is reason to think Eleanor's Castilian roots had some bearing on her dietary choices, a few references may be noted. In 1280 she sent for forty casks of olive oil and seventeen large baskets of onions from Ponthieu, and in 1289 she purchased citrus fruits and olive oil from a Castilian ship at Southampton.[169] She was well supplied with dairy products, especially cheese from Brie sent by Edward's brother Edmund, whose wife was the dowager countess of Champagne and Brie.[170] Copious purchases of fresh fruit show that Eleanor was fond of all varieties—pears, apples, cherries, quinces. The Castilian ship in 1289 provided pomegranates, figs, raisins, dates, lemons, and oranges; another, in June 1290, provided "other various kinds of fruit." Her love of fruit seems to have been well known. The earl of Lincoln sent her some when she returned to England in August 1289, and in the next months poor women twice brought her similar offerings.[171]

Figure 1.7. *Bas-de-page* from the "Alphonso" psalter showing a crowned lady hunting, here suggested as a representation of Queen Eleanor (see note 174) (London, The British Museum, Add. 24686 fol. 13v. [detail]).

While business occupied much of her time, Eleanor did indulge in leisure pastimes, especially embroidery and weaving, her fancywork kept in a coffer whose keys she carried on her person. She often rewarded the antics of fools and minstrels.[172] Edward's 1286 gift of chessmen indicates she enjoyed that game; that the book she borrowed from Cerne Abbey earlier that year could have been a chess manual suggests a focused and thoughtful approach to the game. She rarely gambled, or won more often than not, for her accounts note few losses. She favored "tables," or backgammon, and "the game of four kings," evidently a four-hand chess variation.[173] At the hunt, her tastes diverged from Edward's: he was devoted to falconry and was little interested in hunting with dogs, but Eleanor clearly preferred them.[174] She had a pack of dogs by 1270, and among the first references to her as queen is a payment to a man who took dogs to her in France in 1274. The animals were well cared for, washed in the river or run in her parks, and Eleanor used them diplomatically, as Edward secured Norwegian falcons for Alphonso X or his Sicilian cousins. As he introduced his sons to falconry, Eleanor provided her daughters with dogs; in 1285 Joan had three, cared for by one of her mother's huntsmen.[175]

Eleanor's leisure time was not entirely given over to recreation. Her childhood was passed at the most aggressively literary court in Europe, and in her adulthood the existence of her scriptorium and frequent references to "the queen's books" reveal her as a discerning patron of vernacular letters, whose literary endeavors seem, *mutatis mutandis*, to reflect interests current at the Castilian court in her youth. The range among the works she owned or that were created for her—the Vegetius translation, an ancestral romance for Ponthieu, a theological work by Pecham, saints' lives, an Arthurian romance—suggests a lively intellect and a sophistication essential to the integration of the cultural contrasts that she, like most royal brides, encountered upon arrival in a new homeland. In particular, her sponsorship of the Ponthevin romance shows the results of that process: Castilian kings never evolved an ancestral cult like those of Charlemagne, Arthur, or Edward the Confessor, but following her 1279 accession in Ponthieu, Eleanor at once ordered literary commemoration for a supposed forebear whom she can only have identified from thirteenth-century French chronicles. Her deployment through literary sponsorship of such cross-cultural perspectives proclaimed her an experienced and knowing woman; her interest in chivalric culture and secular history, nourished at the Castilian court, complemented, if it did not inaugurate, Edward's chivalric endeavors, ultimately helping him to broaden monarchy's historical focus and unify British traditions of kingship—heroic and chivalric imagery

linked to (but not wholly dependent on) the cult of Arthur now joined to the
sacralizing image of Edward the Confessor so eagerly promoted by Henry III.
By exploiting cross-cultural influences Eleanor could increase her effectiveness in other areas: Anglo-Castilian relations, mediation with the king,
and the education of their children, especially the daughters who could
profit from her example as they undertook their own marriages. In such
ways, what might have been merely a personal diversion allowed the queen
to make herself heard in more official venues, touching even the counte-
nance of kingship itself.[176]

Eleanor supported formal education as well as vernacular letters. She
and Edward patronized the universities at Oxford and Cambridge, especially
the friars there, and she left bequests to poor scholars at both schools; her
anniversary was incumbent upon all inceptors at Cambridge and all proctors
at Oxford.[177] Her interests may have been broad; her wardrobe keeper from
1277, mr Geoffrey de Aspale (d. 1287), produced commentaries on most of
Aristotle's scientific works, and in 1290 she contacted an Oxford master
about one of her books.[178] As all extant works created for her are in Anglo-
Norman or French, however, there is no reason to think she surpassed
Edward, who was exposed to Latin in youth but was uneasy with it as an
adult.[179] While Eleanor was very likely literate in the vernacular, however,
the only substantial indication of literacy among the women of Edward's family is the writing tablets purchased for their eldest daughter's use in 1286.[180]

Much evidence for Eleanor's religious observances is provided by the
wardrobes' almonry accounts.[181] As with so much else in her life, an itinerant royal pace had its impact on these practices. Travel brought the couple
on a daily basis to important churches across the realm, for example, allowing them to venerate relics and witness translations or episcopal enthronements and enabling Eleanor to display her relationships to centers of power
both secular and ecclesiastical.[182] Though royal devotion to saints' cults is
hard to document, Edward especially venerated the Confessor, St. Edmund,
and Becket, and the cult of St. George entrenched itself at court in the
1280s. Eleanor seconded his attachment to these cults; she always went with
him to Bury, and she contributed gold for the images of St. Edward and St.
George, unmistakable evocations of the spirit of Edwardian kingship, which
the couple offered at Canterbury in 1285. After her death, tile flooring evidently set below her tomb beside St. Edward's shrine showed her flanked
by St. Edmund and St. Thomas Becket, visualizing a queen's traditional
connections with dynastic cults.[183] Her support of these cults notwithstanding, Eleanor's accounts do not indicate her devotion to a particular
saint whether English, Castilian or Ponthevin.[184]

While outlines of religious practice at court are easily sketched, it is difficult to find indications of personal feeling. The most visible sign of Eleanor's religious inclinations was her support of the Dominican order, of which she has been called the "nursing mother" in England. Edward and Eleanor counted many friars among their associates, especially their confessors; her circle included prominent patrons of the Order, and the friars likely educated her children.[185] The queen founded the London and Chichester priories, was a secondary foundress of that at Rhuddlan, and enriched the houses at Salisbury and Northampton, but never realized her hopes for a nunnery at Langley.[186] The 1280 general chapter at Oxford admitted her and her children to spiritual participation in the Order's good works; her legacies to the English priories were generous, and the friars long remembered her as a devoted friend.[187]

Though Eleanor's other foundations reveal her as the most active royal foundress in England since the twelfth century,[188] her patronage is known only from Dominican writings and the records of her foundations. The monastic chroniclers' sturdy silence on Eleanor's piety is a striking failure to remark one of the qualities generally considered most important in a royal consort. It might be supposed that Augustinian and Benedictine writers looked askance at a queen who publicly put influence and wealth behind the friars—while Eleanor of Provence's sympathies lay with the Franciscans, her late profession in an aristocratic Benedictine house did much to redeem her in the eyes of monastic chroniclers. It is tempting to link Eleanor of Castile's Dominican leanings to her neglect of the old alliance between queen and hierarchy, for she seemingly preferred friars to bishops. A lack of learned bishops in late thirteenth-century England perhaps contributed to this, as it likely prompted her support of the universities where the friars had concentrated the greater intellectual energy. The sticking point was that expectations of royal piety were high and departure from customary patterns a delicate matter. Louis IX's support of the friars and his embrace of the thirteenth century's aggressive spirituality elicited direct criticism, even mockery; Eleanor's energetic patronage of the friars and her failure to advertise conventional queenly ties to the bishops and the older orders could well have led monastic chroniclers to withhold comment on her pious observances.[189]

Beyond public manifestations of wealth and power in her foundations, or in appearances at enthronements and translations, Eleanor's personal practices are witnessed by her books of hours and rosaries. As the friars' encouragement of private confession nourished such expressions of intimate personal piety, recitation of the rosary and the hours won favor as popular forms of devotion, especially among women who found in these observances some freedom from male spiritual direction.[190] Whether Eleanor obtained such fulfillment from these practices cannot be known; as a whole the evidence for her devotion does not suggest a contemplative character. Her request for Pecham's treatise on pseudo-Dionysius' *De Celesti Hierarchia*[191] witnesses a desire for informed understanding of Church doctrine, suggesting that her spiritual life was propelled by the same mental energy revealed in her literary pursuits. Her patronage of the friars and the universities likewise implies that like her descendant Margaret Beaufort, Eleanor was most concerned for the intellectual advancement of religion. As in Edward's case, moreover, her piety seemingly bred a conviction that the powers of Heaven were on her side, and this may explain one aspect of her pious practices that could profoundly and adversely affect popular opinion. While any woman's piety was most positively manifest in her charity, a queen's personal almsgiving also revealed her generosity and humility; but the language of Eleanor's accounts indicates that she left it to chaplains and almoners to make personal contact with the poor who were fed daily at her expense.[192]

While the scale of Eleanor's activities indicates a physically robust woman, her many pregnancies would have taken a toll on even the strongest constitution. (Throughout the 1270s, her children were born at an average interval of fifteen months.) Within two years after she bore her last child in April 1284, her health began to decline; in Gascony late in 1287, she was suffering from a "double quartan," probably the same "low fever" to which the Osney chronicler attributed her death in November 1290. Whether called "quartan," "tertian," "low," or "marsh" fever, malaria—endemic in the Middle Ages to the part of Europe where Eleanor was living in 1287—is rarely fatal of itself. Quite apart from the medieval regimen of alternate purging and bloodletting, the dangers lie in secondary infections to which the victim's resistance is diminished, or in injury to the spleen or liver, which invariably become enlarged and brittle; in the latter case, death results from internal bleeding or septicemia. As Eleanor's accounts imply she was gravely ill only from 20 November 1290, her death eight days later perhaps resulted from some such opportunistic infection, or injury.[193] She was in her forty-ninth year.

Queen Eleanor died in the house of Richard de Weston at Harby, still in Nottinghamshire but so near Lincoln that it seems certain the court stopped at Harby on 20 November only because she was too ill to endure the progress from Clipstone to Lincoln begun a week earlier. Her accounts record little of note until a messenger went to Lincoln on 24 November to buy urinals "because the queen was then sick."[194] In the next days urgent messages were sent to London and to Edward's friend Robert Tybotot, and on 28 November a messenger rode to Lincoln for medicines. But Eleanor died that evening, "after she devotedly received the sacrament of the dying, earnestly praying her lord the king, who was listening to her requests, that everything unjustly taken from anyone by her or her ministers should be restored, and any damages satisfied." As the king appointed in January 1291 the inquest she sought "in her last will,"[195] the dying woman must have been lucid enough to attend to matters of atonement, and her request for public inquiry suggests some sensitivity to recent events. After Edward's return to England in 1289, revelations of judicial misconduct in his absence led to a full-scale inquiry, trials, and disgrace for a number of justices; reform was in order, and in May 1290 the queen-mother —not on her deathbed—asked for an inquest into her officials' conduct. The dying queen-consort's request for reparation, moreover, forecast the extended spectacle of her funeral train and burial and the monumental commemorations Edward gave her. In death as in life, kingship in thirteenth-century Europe sought a wider stage; queens' behavior in life and provisions in death might not have the impact on the realm their husbands' had, but queens were as much a part of the image of monarchy as kings, and their public atonement as appropriate.[196]

Eleanor's private dispositions are less amply recorded. She had license in 1275 to make a will, but apart from items she left to her children,[197] her legacies are known only from her executors' accounts and petitions claiming unpaid bequests. She remembered kinsmen, friends, servants, attendants, religious houses, and poor scholars; her executors rewarded others not named in her testament, and their final account, rendered in 1294, shows they were instructed to sell whatever effects Eleanor had not bequeathed.[198]

The queen's body was eviscerated, embalmed, stuffed with barley and wrapped in linen.[199] Thoroughness was necessary, for Eleanor's final journey was to be a state progress of unprecedented splendor followed by a majestic funeral, reflecting her status as queen and mother of the king's heir—the first Plantagenet burial in England exploited to exalt the monarchy and, incidentally, to confirm Westminster Abbey's emergence as a royal pantheon, marking it as doubly significant to Plantagenet kingship.[200] The cortège left Lincoln on 3 December, after the viscera were buried in the cathedral. There were magnates in attendance, with the Chancellor and Eleanor's household; her chaplain rode near the bier, a cross propped on his saddle. Edward followed at a distance, for the focus of attention must be the dead queen, not the grieving king. Through Grantham, Stamford, and Geddington, the procession reached Northampton on 9 December and then passed by Stony Stratford, Woburn, and Dunstable, arriving at St. Albans on 13 December. The Dunstable and St. Albans' chronicles describe the honors paid the body:

> Her body passed through [Dunstable] and rested one night, and there were given to us two precious cloths called baudekyns. Of wax we had forty-eight pounds and more. And when the body of the said queen passed through Dunstable, the bier rested in the center of the marketplace until the king's chancellor and the nobles who were then present designated a fitting place, in the presence of our prior who sprinkled holy water; at which place there was later erected at the king's expense a cross of marvelous size.
>
> When the body . . . neared St. Albans all the convent, solemnly vested in albs and copes, went out to meet it at the church of St. Michael at the edge of town. Thence it was taken to the presbytery, before the high altar; that night it was honored by the entire convent with assiduous devotion, with divine office and holy vigils. In all vills and places in which the body rested, the lord king ordered to be erected a cross of wondrous height to the praise of the Crucified and the queen's memory, so that her soul should be prayed for by passersby; on which crosses the said queen's likeness was depicted.[201]

From St. Albans Edward went to Westminster as the procession continued by way of Waltham, reaching London on 14 December and stopping for the night at Holy Trinity, Aldgate. Next day, arrayed with royal insignia and followed by the king, bishops, and magnates, the body was carried to the Friars Minor for a mass and then to St. Paul's for the night. After several masses there on the morning of 16 December, the bier was taken to the Dominicans for another mass and then rested overnight in a hermitage at Charing.[202] On Sunday, 17 December the queen was buried in Westminster Abbey amid such splendor, the Barnwell annalist thought, as was not seen in England since the coming of the Christian faith; she was interred "with royal vestments, crown and scepter, dust on forehead and breast in the form of a cross, and a wax candle, with certain writings." Two days later her heart was deposited in the Dominicans' London church with those of her son Alphonso and her friend John de Vescy.[203]

SUMMARY AND SOME CONCLUSIONS

As with events in her life, the details of Eleanor's burial are, for the purposes of this work, less important in themselves than as evidence for the interaction of queen and realm. At a time when dynastic power and state power were beginning to grow apart and the secularization of society was advancing, queens' natural share in kingship's growing exploitation of ceremony allowed Eleanor in her lifetime to participate with Edward in acts that manifested the power and majesty of hereditary monarchy or fostered a sacred identity for the kingship. The association of Marian imagery with the queen's intercession and with royal childbearing rituals, for example, asserted for her, the king, and their son a sacred aura, reflecting the divine order that legitimized human order, and perhaps fortified an hereditary principle always weak in English kingship.[204] Eleanor's funeral likewise evinced the power of monarchy and the status of a royal wife, while the crosses Edward put up to her memory further obscured sacred and secular boundaries, combining chantry functions with an unprecedented forest of vertical statues of an English queen.[205] It may be said, then, that Eleanor continued in death much the same dialogue with the realm she sustained in life, and in the context of that dialogue the evidence presented here can now be evaluated insofar as it relates to the conflicting opinions about her discussed at the outset.

At first glance, these anomalies remain unresolved. Evidence for Queen Eleanor's personal life reveals an intellectually vigorous woman, a loyal wife and attentive mother, not extravagantly pious but a generous patron of her kin and (within prudent limits) those who served her. But this same woman, widely notorious for her land hunger, was capable of petty acts of vengeance against those whom she felt compromised her interests, a facet of her character known to those near her and, evidently, to many Englishmen. The chroniclers' silence on her political role is echoed by evidence that Eleanor's sway was minimal; Pecham's warnings are supported by signs that her personal influence with the king was feared. Efforts to deal with these anomalies can begin with the observation that they are rooted in the nature of the records that illustrate them. Personal matters, such as Eleanor's literary interests, are known from wardrobe accounts, a classic example of "inside" evidence, while rather less positive details come from chronicles, letters, and administrative records, which perhaps more reliably reflect what was widely believed about the queen beyond her immediate circle. To resolve such divergent testimony is exacting: contemporary perceptions of the queen were formed not from the full spectrum of evidence available to a modern investigator, but from contemporary English society's experience of the woman, and the nature of that experience must direct further discussion of Eleanor's life.

Both from Eleanor's viewpoint and that of the English people, her relations with the kingdom were focused through her queenship, which subtly informed impressions of her in many ways. Eleanor's gardens were a prodigal use of land few could afford: imported plants, foreign gardeners, and exotic birds surely made an indelible impression on those who approached her through one of her gardens. Chess, with its representation of the social order, was a conventional expression of chivalric culture, but Eleanor's chessmen in jasper and crystal reflected her preeminence. Were her literary interests known beyond her personal circle, they must have pointed up the distances between herself and most of the king's subjects, and so at the convergence of leisure and learning, a chess manual would have introduced fine overtones like those revealed at the hunt: a day in the field with her noble friends affirmed the solidarity of their aristocratic interests (echoing the coupling of royal and noble arms on vestments used in the royal chapels), but also demonstrated the queen's freedom to hunt in the king's forests with her dogs and to take as many deer as she wished. Her companions, even the greatest magnates, could never do so without license, and in most cases they would be allowed to take only the less noble, inedible prey—wolf, fox, hare, badger, or lynx.[206]

A queen could make scarcely any gift or donation, assist a petitioner, or sponsor a godchild without manifesting the resources and powers of her office. Through such encounters and exchanges she guaranteed loyalty and compliance by showing generosity and mercy.[207] Eleanor's propensity for arranging marriages among her kindred and courtiers, for example, translated wealth and power into action as she provided dowries, compelled promises of indemnity if the couple was childless, and exacted assurances that the grooms' inheritances would not be diminished. That the Burghs, Mortimers, Vescys, and Wakes married Eleanor's cousins in such circumstances acknowledged her power as well as the benefits of a marriage that linked them to the king. The marriages Eleanor promoted for her attendants are an even clearer indication of the way in which she could exercise personal inclinations while displaying her influence. Some household marriages took place at her will, and acceptance of a union she suggested won favor and reward; refusal brought serious consequences. Eleanor's choice of marriage partners in these cases is revealing: well-born husbands were found for the cousins whose marriages must not demean her, but despite the ease with which she might provide rich marriages for her attendants, they and their children were paired with spouses from similarly modest knightly families. These marriages suggest a conscious maintenance of the social order that was symbolically affirmed by a queen's way of life and death. The hierarchical ambience in which she functioned, already intimated at the hunt, was likewise figured as a queen's compliance and submission, ideally manifest in the humble posture of an intercessor, affirmed the king's superior authority and the male hierarchy he embodied. Pecham's *Jerarchie* directly evoked the social order, expounding a male hierarchy by comparing the ranks of angels to those of royal officials. As a woman, Eleanor was an outsider to such masculine arrangements; as the intimate partner of the monarch who exemplified it, however, she had to cultivate the means available to her to show herself supportive of it.

Hunting and arranged marriages were interests the queen shared with her natural associates, the magnates closest to the court. The evidence on which this chapter has focused arose within the court and the administrative circles nearest the queen, and for the most part it reveals her as being involved with those or like pursuits that were the life's warp and woof of a well-born international wife. As an aristocratic society is by nature secretive, it might seem that very little of this evidence would bear on the formation of popular opinion about Eleanor. True, as she traveled about the kingdom, most of the English people experienced the queen only amid brilliant pageantry that marked her as a figure of consequence, a woman linked in a uniquely privileged way to the centers of power. Unquestionably such episodes emphasized the image of the king's wife while obscuring her personality. But at the same time travel likely helped some scraps of knowledge about the couple to penetrate beyond their circle and give the English a sense of their rulers' individuality.[208] Thus Eleanor's personal interests were not necessarily unknown to the realm, and while the chroniclers offer few details about Eleanor, their references to her (or their silence on such matters as her piety), and others' remarks in a number of letters, can offer some clues about English perceptions of her.

An example is the Dunstable chronicle's reference to Eleanor's Castilian birth. The English were probably always aware that their kings' wives were outsiders; the more exotic the homeland—like Castile—the sharper that sense might be. That Eleanor's origins were a matter of note is clear from the 1264 rumors that her mother-in-law's hired troops included Castilians. The question here is the extent to which popular consciousness was focused or sharpened in her lifetime, and in what ways. Eleanor brought no Castilian inheritance nor diplomatic entanglements over her homeland (though the count of Bigorre's apprehension when he could not

assist Alphonso X implies that her devotion to her brother was well known).
English and French tailors, and especially the headgear from Paris and
London, indicate that she adopted northern fashions, abandoning any distinctive Castilian dress. The promotion of her kinfolk drew no adverse
comment and it was left for later centuries to assume that any cousins
imported by a Castilian-born queen must also have been Castilians.[209]

Nonetheless, certain quite visible aspects of Eleanor's behavior could
have reinforced awareness that she was an outlander. She spoke no English,
or at least chose not to converse in that tongue when she met the townspeople at St. Albans in 1275. When she came to England in 1255, the
English derided the Castilian liking for carpets; her continued use of them,
like the heraldry that visually identified her possessions, must have underscored her foreign origins. Tensions were generated at Southampton by the
Castilian merchants she protected, and though Castilians in her household
dealt mostly with Castilian business, their distinctiveness must have been
widely evident, as when Gonzalo Martini met a Castilian ship at Portsmouth
to buy for the queen earthenware jars "of strange color," and that quantity
of exotic fruit that raises the matter of Eleanor's diet. The olive oil and
onions brought via Ponthieu in 1280 are presumably the only extant
example of many such imports, but the evidence for Eleanor's love of fruit
is also pertinent, linked as it is to her love of gardens by the French apple
cuttings she imported in 1280. Aragonese gardeners and an Italian *vineator*
imply, then, that her diet offered reminders of her foreign birth, and the fruit
brought to her by poor women hints that the English were aware of the
habits that recalled their queen's origins. (The story that Edward's infant son
by his second, French, wife rejected a French nurse's milk but flourished
when an Englishwoman replaced her shows that royal diet and nationality
were indeed linked.) For all her care to avoid the impression that she was
importing foreign cousins—a matter on which the English were sensitive—
and however empowering her capacity to manipulate the cultural differences that were the integral components of a queen's life, the business of
cultural transplantation critical to her function in alliance formation
inescapably highlighted Eleanor's foreignness.[210]

It was a central conundrum of English medieval queenship that an insular kingdom had to accept an outsider as the king's wife and the mother of
his heir, the latter perhaps the more problematical—Edward was criticized
in 1263 for favoring the aliens "because his mother was of foreign birth."[211]
It bears repeating that Eleanor of Castile was the first queen of England since
1118 born a king's daughter, the importance of her descent marked in the
choice of so distinctive a name from her lineage as Alphonso for her third son.

Her pride in her lineage was strong, witnessed by the heraldry that identified her possessions, openly declared on the coffer containing the bones of
Arthur and Guinevere at the Glastonbury translation of April 1278, and
manifest in the ancestral romance commissioned upon her accession to
Ponthieu. When recording her death, a Westminster chronicler identified
Eleanor as a daughter of the illustrious King Ferdinand of Castile, linking
her alien origins to her royal birth and all it implied. Eighteen years later the
point was echoed by a St. Albans writer—with that house's ties to
Westminster—who stated that her virtues proved the glory of her ancestry:
"it is against the nature of things that bad fruit should sprout from a good
root." The provision of heirs was a queen's central function, the perpetuation
of the royal lineage inextricably linked to the realm's integrity and survival;
she alone could legitimately manifest the king's physical powers, identified
with the realm's security and prosperity. In an aristocratic society that hoped
for a glorious past to be recapitulated in each new heir, the ancestral virtues
transmitted by a queen of exalted lineage were as important as the legitimacy
of the heir's descent from his paternal forebears. For a queen and for a
noble milieu, then, her foreign origins were bound up with her royal lineage,
the guarantee of her suitability as the mother of a royal heir. But beyond the
court's immediate sway, the Dunstable annalist betrayed what was to most
Englishmen the sticking point: the king's wife, "a Spaniard by birth," was an
outsider—a marginal, not to say liminal, figure to English society.[212]

The Dunstable text speaks in one breath of Eleanor's Castilian birth and her
appetite for new lands. Though the writer surely was not attributing the one
to the other, Guisborough's "The king desires to have our gold / The queen our
manors fair to hold" shows that popular feeling did parallel her hunger for new
land with the king's demands for money. Certainly Eleanor's emphasis on her
access to Edward would not put any distance between them in the eyes of
others, and petitioners' appeals witness expectations that she could influence
him. Ptolemy of Lucca's version of Eleanor's heroics at Acre was unknown in
England until the sixteenth century, but if currency was obtained in her day
even by such details of the attempt on Edward's life as Guisborough recorded,
her devotion to him could have become a byword. Any such impressions of
their relationship must have been strengthened by their travels around the
kingdom, which displayed them as a couple on a nearly uninterrupted basis—
an image confirmed by the births of their many children. The marriage of
Edward I and Eleanor of Castile indeed may have been the model for that of
Havelok and Goldboru in the English version of that romance, written in the
1280s.[213] Eleanor's support of Edward in the 1260s also bears on such perceptions, most especially the rumors of Castilian troops in 1264 that connected

her alien origins to that support. As king, Edward needed less energetic backing from his wife than he did as heir in a time of political unrest, but there is no reason to think her support ever lagged, and a queen who showed herself helpful toward her husband could well be suspected of abetting his acts that proved unpopular. A retiring or visibly pious queen might escape censure, but Eleanor's perceived avarice and the patterns of her piety deprived her of such safeguards. These were sensitive departures from expectations of queenly behavior, points at which the queen's actions might well be seen as improperly influencing the king. An almost inevitable result surfaces in Pecham's warning that Eleanor was blamed for Edward's exacting rule: the king's foreign-born bedfellow was made to wear his unpopular face. Eleanor's leverage was more imagined than real, but anxieties for its impact on the realm would be none the less for that. It was just that kind of informal influence, commonly suspected between prominent spouses, that might escape a chronicler's notice yet move a ranking cleric to warn of hearsay and gossip.

The fraught hypostasis of queen and wife thus comes into play. Medieval women lived and functioned under male authority; even a queen's position depended on a marriage that implied her wifely subjection to the king and her isolation from his magisterial authority. When she was seen to intrude herself into the political sphere, critics dwelled on the corruption of her idealized domestic roles as wife and mother.[214] Yet a queen, whatever gendered limits governed her access to power, hardly ever occupied a purely domestic arena; ineluctable moral, diplomatic, and political factors compelled the king to take a wife, and the marriage that entailed her submission to his authority guaranteed her exaltation at his side. The Church acknowledged the importance of her office to the kingdom by urging her to counsel the king to rule justly and magnanimously, and stressed the exposed nature of her position in rituals that celebrated her even as they prescribed her chaste and submissive behavior to offer her to the realm as a model of wifely purity and compliance. If as a wife the queen was directed to a position of submission and compliance, the potential of the interstices she could seek out was heightened by her informal proximity to the center of authority. Safely in line with clerics' advice, her intercession with the king could transform into useful supporters those who sought her help. As the educator of her children, she could confirm a vital influence over the son who would one day rule; as the ideal instructor for the daughters whose marriages would replicate her own experience, she asserted a voice in that same matrimonial diplomacy to which she owed her rank. Her ability to dispense patronage could win powerful allies to her side.[215] In such ways a queen could extend her presence, and even approximate a certain autonomy; but her marginal status and interstitial tactics implied a freedom from institutional limits that could menace the order the king embodied. She might seek to bolster her position by advertising her proximity to him—by receiving petitioners before the bed she shared with him and in which she bore her children, or by publicizing their births—but in so doing she unavoidably emphasized the hazards posed by her presence near him.[216]

It is not altogether coincidental, then, that it is Eleanor's use of her influence to assist friends or petitioners that begins to reveal what people thought of her as queen and as woman. Bishop Giffard saw her as a benign protectress when he sought her intervention with the Roman Curia and with his canons; but when a prior in his diocese could not present her clerk to a church in the priory's patronage and the queen expected the bishop to use his influence in return, Giffard feared her anger. Her viewpoint can be seen in her behavior in 1290: in March she supported Giffard as a friend in the dispute with his canons, but by June, as queen, she was prosecuting him for money.[217] It was the friend whose help Giffard sought in 1282 and March 1290, but in 1283 it was the queen's wrath he feared and in June 1290 the woman's avarice—that archetypal dichotomy between perceptions of an office and the individual who occupies it. If Giffard did not make the distinction explicit, Burnell's 1290 letter to him does convey a sense that while the queen might overreach herself, the woman could be got round. Those who knew Eleanor well could distinguish queen from woman; for others not as close to her, the difference might be less obvious. The implications for her reputation are clearly profound, but they cannot be judged until more evidence is digested.

Pace Strickland, the indications are that the English always saw Eleanor of Castile as a foreigner and never entirely gave her their hearts. But such popular perceptions can have been only partly influenced by Eleanor's life as examined in this chapter. The rich display with which she surrounded herself was an instrument of queenship, the language of wealth and patronage through which the queen—in Eleanor's day largely stripped of any share in the king's authority—communicated with the realm. Such lavish panoply required immense resources, the responsibility of the queen's officials, whose acquisition and management of estates and wealth were the endeavors that brought her, albeit indirectly, into regular contact with the greater number of people. Thus her perceived appetite for land and money—and with it the harsher side of her character—may be presumed to have predominated in popular thinking about her. The financial and administrative bases of her power, and her exploitation of them, must therefore be examined before the last word can be said.

C H A P T E R

2

Prerogatives, Resources, Administration

mong the factors that influenced formation of a queen's public image, there is an obvious relationship between the money needed for royal display and patronage, and the administration that managed her wealth. Much of the history of English queenship during the thirteenth century must be understood in terms of the queens' search for revenue and materials for patronage, but these components cannot be fully grasped if they are isolated from the queens' prerogatives. In Eleanor of Castile's case the prerogatives' energizing role surfaces as early as January 1273, when the new king's lieutenants in England appointed a clerk to collect and account for her queen-gold. No orders from the new queen could have reached England so soon after Henry III's death, but the urgent need for effective management of the main source of her prerogative revenue sufficed to set her administration in motion. By March 1274 some of her officials were already claiming "royal right in all things."[1]

That these events date from the period before Eleanor returned to England in August 1274 shows that despite ritual elevation's significance to an office largely divested of authority, the queen's prerogatives were not tied to an anointed consort's status. It is well to consider briefly, then, just what the rite did confer on the queen. Unction confirmed her dignity by creating a special link with the divine, but she was anointed only on head and breast, hallowed to ensure the birth of heirs but not as a legitimate powerholder. The king's hereditary right to power was evoked by liturgical reference to Davidic patriarchs and kings; his wife's claims to dignity in her roles as an ideally submissive wife and fertile dynastic mother were anchored by allusions to Esther and to the fecundity of Sarah, Leah, Rebecca, Rachel, and the Blessed Virgin. But even as such models buttressed and exalted her office, the queen was reminded of her subordinate status. Liturgical formulae were provided only for her investiture with a ring in token of faith and a crown for glory; a scepter, symbol of the power to command, was handed to her in silence. After the rite she was directed to bow to the king, "honoring the royal majesty as is fitting," before she took her seat to his left—not to his right, the site of power. Perhaps most important, the rite did not formalize the relationship between queen and kingdom; she swore no oath, nor did she receive promises of fidelity.[2]

While she thus occupied a subordinate position that distanced her from sovereign authority, the English queen was still set above all others save her husband. A "person of dignity and excellence," she shared his public estate, the *status regis*: what touched the queen touched the king himself,[3] and the perks she enjoyed as a result of that relationship were far-ranging. Though an alien, she was dowered as a matter of course. The king's administration served his wife on virtually the same basis as himself. Fines or debts owed her were collected next after those owed the king and by the same methods; the sheriffs obeyed her orders, even on matters unrelated to the king's business. Her clerks had access to Chancery, the Exchequer, and the courts of law, and her acts were officially enrolled. The membership of her council overlapped with that of the king, and she regularly consulted with his chief ministers.[4] At law the queen, though bound by the laws of England, enjoyed capacities denied other married women in the realm. She could plead by writ in her own name, acquire land independently of her husband, and receive his grant; while lands Eleanor of Castile purchased were held to have been acquired for the king and his heirs, she granted them away with Edward's assent, and after he confirmed her grants they were construed as his.[5] Immunities paralleled capacities: the queen could be sued only by petition to the king's council, not in the courts of law. Her officials were exempt from prosecution for actions on her service; petition could be brought against them in the king's council, but he proceeded only with the queen's assent and they were summoned only before the council. Other privileges assisted the queen's administration: in lands held of the king's grant she enjoyed the return of writs, she could easily secure judicial commissions to protect her rights, and her men were exempt from tolls throughout the realm.[6]

The queen's formidable combination of privilege and resource was never formally constituted; no medieval commentator systematically described it, and its evolution is only dimly recorded. That the series of legal records begins as late as 1194 makes it impossible to ascertain whether the queen's legal capacities were acknowledged during the common law's early development, and for some of her perks there is no evidence until the thirteenth century: only from 1236, for example, does a claim survive that a new queen had the right to present one nun in every English convent.[7] But as her prerogatives informed the office through which English society experienced the queen, they cannot be ignored here, and some broad outlines may be suggested to explain how these privileges assumed the characteristics recognizable in the thirteenth century.

Seventeenth- and eighteenth-century English antiquarians supposed the queen was allowed to manage her own affairs so the king might be free to work for the kingdom, and deduced post-Conquest queens' prerogatives from Anglo-Saxon precedent. William Prynne saw the origins of queen-gold in payments to Anglo-Saxon consorts to secure their assistance or reward them for convincing their husbands to grant requests. Tenth-century consorts' active promotion of monastic reform gave them an acknowledged role as protectresses of nuns which might foreshadow post-Conquest queens' claim to present nuns throughout the realm.[8] It is unlikely, however, that an element of continuity between Anglo-Saxon and Anglo-Norman queenship is indicated by evidence that some lands held by Anglo-Saxon consorts figured in royal dower assignments down to 1254.[9] Blackstone justified later queens' freedom to control land by pointing to Anglo-Saxon consorts' capacity to do so but implied that this was unique to royal consorts, whereas later Anglo-Saxon noblewomen disposed of land with their husbands' consent if married or freely if widowed. In contrast, married women in pre-Conquest Normandy did not control land, but Matilda of Flanders as duchess of Normandy disposed of land with her husband's consent.[10] The prerogatives of queenship recognized in the thirteenth century may, then, represent an amalgam of customs both English and Norman, but their evolution is not easily traced.

In the decades after the Norman conquest, English queens were wealthy and prominent women whose inalienable dower lands, held during their marriages, were worth £1000. As the queens often acted as regents in Normandy and in England, it was necessary that they had seals and chancellors.[11] Their poorly documented administrations were presumably competent to manage their lands and revenue.[12] Matilda of Flanders and early twelfth-century queens acquired land and disposed of it with their husbands' consent, though as such transactions are known only from the charters recording disposal of property, it may be that the queens acquired the property only for purposes of patronage.[13] The queenship's high-water mark came in Stephen's reign, when Matilda of Boulogne filled the political void during the king's imprisonment; so vigorous was her presence that his party eroded after her death in 1152. Yet even at the outset of Matilda's career, the bases of the queen's power were already eroding. Early medieval queens' management of kings' households and treasure allowed them to forge valuable alliances with royal officers and gave them access to wealth; but by 1135 the English queen no longer supervised the king's household, and control of his treasure had passed to his officials.[14]

Under Henry II, there were fresh signs of contraction in the queen's role even before the rebellion of 1173 led to Eleanor of Aquitaine's eclipse. As regent (until 1165) Eleanor only implemented Henry's orders sent from abroad; she ceased to witness his acts for England within months of his accession, and issued no writs in her own name after 1163.[15] A vital factor was that, perhaps to avoid further reducing a royal demesne depleted under Stephen, Eleanor did not enter her dower lands until Henry's death.[16] Her revenue as consort came from queen-gold and from corrodies paid her stewards by the sheriffs in whose bailiwicks she resided. Since these corrodies were authorized by writs from the king or his officials, Henry apparently meant to control Eleanor's income; her efforts in the 1180s to increase revenue from queen-gold suggest the restriction was irksome. Her scheme to deprive Blyth priory of an advowson to benefit her clerk Jordan implies that limited opportunities for patronage forced her to adopt alternative methods. Only after Henry II's death did a unique combination of circumstances allow Eleanor of Aquitaine to wield authority in England, to a degree that has rightly been called anomalous.[17]

That corrodies were paid Eleanor's personnel by the sheriffs wherever she dwelled indicates that apart from the lone clerk who audited queen-gold at the Exchequer, her administration was limited to her household.[18] Since she and her immediate successors held little or no land in their husbands' lifetimes, moreover, they had little need as consorts to deploy local officials; they were not burdened with the intricacies of tenure and had little reason to use the courts of law, apart perhaps from sundry trespasses against them or their households. Unacquainted with the administration of justice in a realm she had never visited, Richard I's widow, Berengaria, did not seek her dower in English courts but turned to the Roman Curia for help in securing a settlement in 1215; John's widow, Isabella of Angoulême, did sue in the king's court for disputed portions of her dower lands, but her limited presence in

John's life and the financial dependence to which he relegated her denied her the means and opportunity to create a power base in England. She had a trifling public role during Henry III's minority and ultimately chose active command of her Poitevin inheritance over life as an English queen-dowager.[19]

If questions of personality and human relationships were complicated for eleventh- and twelfth-century English queens by the vast *regnum* that straddled the Channel, the loss of the Angevin and Norman patrimony in John's reign had an equally pervasive influence on later queens' careers. As the king no longer left England as often as in the twelfth century, there was less occasion for his anointed counterpart to act as regent. On the single occasion this did happen in the thirteenth century, administrative evolution had its impact on the queen's role: while Eleanor of Provence's rank probably decided Henry III's choice in 1253, she was appointed only in tandem with his brother, to govern in association with a council whose members Henry reserved the power to appoint.[20] Jurisprudence from the twelfth century increasingly emphasized the king as fountain of justice and sole head of orderly government; the legal writers who produced the most sophisticated thirteenth-century discussions of English government did not associate the king's wife with him, since as lawgiver he could have no equal. The impact of these developments on the queen's office was echoed in monarchy's central ritual. An eleventh-century coronation order blessed the queen as a partner in royal power, but twelfth-century revisions abandoned so potentially troublesome an association, instead incorporating exhortations and prayers to guide and limit her influence with the king—the wife's personal power would always remain a potent variable.[21] As her direct role in government declined and powerful queens were forgotten, the consort's position came to depend increasingly upon her ability to sustain impressions of power and influence by publicizing her relationship with her husband and conveying a sense of wealth and command through majestic public display, largesse, and patronage. As the thirteenth century advanced, such displays were favored as the queen claimed a share in kingship's growing use of ritual and ceremony, but the lives of Berengaria and Isabella of Angoulême show the stakes were high and the odds not necessarily favorable.

From Henry II's accession until Henry III's marriage in 1236 can thus be reckoned some eight decades in which the queens' prerogatives slowly slipped into near abeyance, their public role curtailed, revenues insufficient, and administrations strictly domestic. There was consequently great significance to Henry III's decision upon marriage to modify the manner in which his wife was provided with revenue. The financial relationship between king and queen now assumed its classic form. The king bore his wife's housekeeping expenses while she lived at court; out of court she existed on her own resources, and Henry intended funds for these periods of absence to come from wardships that were to provide £1000 yearly.[22] The role of wardships in Eleanor of Provence's finances will be judged in its place. The significant point is that the king's wife now came to hold a good deal of land that did not pertain to the royal demesne. While her control over lands held in wardship was limited, she had to assure herself the revenues while protecting the heirs' rights and rendering services owed. These obligations required that she had access to the courts of law and the Exchequer; and so the queen came into intimate contact with the powerful machinery needed for the efficient dispatch of her business.

Eleanor of Provence's actions in her early years as queen reveal a sound grasp of her situation, but reactions to her behavior show that much remained to be negotiated. She tried to present her clerks to churches connected with the wardships Henry gave her, but he reserved the advowsons to himself; like Eleanor of Aquitaine, she sought to extend the range of fines on which queen-gold was exacted, aggressively enough that complaints surfaced at the Oxford parliament of 1258.[23] While such questions of finance and patronage impressed themselves on her, however, Eleanor of Provence never showed much inclination to augment her resources by acquiring lands. As with twelfth-century queens, her independent purchases of land were for purposes of patronage and were soon granted away; only after she inherited the honor of Richmond at the death of Peter of Savoy in 1268 did she come to hold a large amount of land on a permanent basis. This situation is only partly explained by her reluctance to traffic in Christian debts to Jewish usurers, the cheapest means to acquire new estates. Henry could have granted her lands in fee but perhaps avoided doing so lest he reduce his demesne, much as he initially refused to allow her the advowsons of churches on lands granted her in wardship, lest opportunities for patronage be lost to him.[24] But wardships, the means he chose to provide for her without straining his resources, were a risky basis for any financial system: they lasted for varying lengths of time, and when heirs came of age the land had to be surrendered with no guarantee that replacements to the same value would be immediately available.[25]

A new direction was announced even before Henry III's death, as Eleanor of Castile began from 1264 to hold lands in fee both through Crown grants and her own transactions. Edward I's approach to the expansion of his demesne was more aggressive than Henry's,[26] and to augment his wife's income he gave her both opportunity and encouragement to acquire new lands on a permanent basis. The process of securing the lands honed the queen's legal capacities, while the revenues eased strain on the king's resources and provided materials for patronage that did not diminish his; as he or their son would enter the lands as her heir, she ultimately increased the royal demesne. The amount of land Eleanor acquired, however, suggested (or threatened) infinite expansion of her wealth and her ability to dispense patronage, and elicited open criticism of her activities. After eight decades during which English memories of energetic queens had faded, and at a time when noblewomen were increasingly isolated from economic activity, the efforts of the two Eleanors to augment their resources drew direct and repeated criticism. In the hands of vigorous and resolute women, the prerogatives of queenship were becoming the stuff of controversy.

REVENUE AND ITS SOURCES

The office Eleanor of Castile entered in 1272 thus represented immense potential bolstered by access to efficient means of collecting wealth; whether she was able to make use of it now has to be judged from her extant accounts. These provide more information about expenditure than revenue. Three wardrobe records cover the period between November 1287 and November 1290; only the last survives intact. An account for what are called payments (*liberaciones*) on the queen's behalf begins in January 1286 and ends at her death; the place of these records in her financial system remains to be determined. The extant accounts of her bailiffs are mere summaries of amounts rendered, uniformly and unhelpfully described as "manorial issues" and giving no details of procedure on her manors.[27] The single most important record is a summary of accounts rendered at the Exchequer by the queen's executors in March 1294, entered on the Pipe Roll for 1297–98.

The nature of the evidence requires that sources of revenue be considered before income and expenditure are discussed. As the queen's lands had a steadily increasing importance to the exercise of her prerogatives in the thirteenth century, revenue from Eleanor's estates naturally claims first attention. A distinction may be drawn between estates the queen held of her husband's grant and those she acquired otherwise; of the former, the more important were dower assignments, and though thirteenth-century queens entered their dower lands only as widows, their worth must be considered. The earliest extant charter for a queen's dower is that of John for Isabella of Angoulême, issued in May 1204, which states that Isabella's assignment was identical to Eleanor of Aquitaine's. Roger de Hoveden and John de Oxenedes report that Eleanor had held the lands assigned to the wives of

Henry I and Stephen, and some of the lands in the 1204 charter were indeed held by those queens. A 1209 papal letter threatening John with interdict on the lands Berengaria should have held in dower shows, moreover, that she, wed in 1191, was claiming virtually the same estates assigned Isabella in 1204.[28] By the late twelfth century, then, a distinct group of lands made up the queen's dower. Their worth is known from Henry III's 1235 promise that his wife would have the dower lands customarily assigned to queens of England exactly as his mother held them, or others to the same value: Eleanor of Provence's 1236 assignment was worth £1000, the sum promised Berengaria in settlements negotiated with John and Henry III.[29]

Discussion in 1253–54 over Eleanor of Castile's dower can now be put in better perspective. Henry III first offered 1000 marks, probably appropriate for the heir's wife, to be raised to £1000 when Eleanor became queen; Alphonso X demanded and got £1000 at once, to be increased by 500 marks at Edward's accession. Henry was perhaps coming to realize that £1000 was no longer an adequate sum. A widowed queen's dower replaced prerogative income that ceased with the king's death, while her expenses increased as she went permanently "out of court" with no husband to meet housekeeping costs—and the thirteenth century saw a steady increase in the size and splendor of royal households. Henry was already subsidizing Eleanor of Provence's expenses in and out of court, and in 1262 he increased her dower assignment to £4000, half in England and half in Gascony; when Edward came to the throne he could only follow suit and after some hints from Alphonso (likely engineered by Eleanor herself), the queen's dower was increased in 1275 to £4500 in English and Gascon lands.[30]

Of course, queens held their dower lands only as widows and still had to be provided for as consorts. As Edward I's solution to this problem has been explained, it remains to discuss the contributions to Eleanor of Castile's finances by her estates, both those granted her in fee and in wardship and those she secured otherwise. In the absence of detailed accounts, it is not possible to be certain what was meant by the words *exitus manerii* that recur so monotonously in her records; nor can it be discovered whether greater sums came from rents or from the sale of agricultural produce. While the records are silent on such improvements as marling, draining, or manuring, however, indications are that Eleanor's administration attached considerable importance to the agricultural yield of her manors. As the queen was an absentee landlord, her men could sell surplus grain,[31] and Eleanor's administration accordingly avoided parting with the yield of her lands in ways other than sale. A yearly rent of grain owed the abbot of St. Benet Hulme from Scottow was negotiated into a cash payment, for example, and concord was reached with the abbot of Muchelney on the amount of grain the queen enjoyed free of tithe at Somerton. Emphasis on agricultural yield explains the aggressive methods adopted to increase Eleanor's demesne: outright ejection of tenants, impeding them from cultivating land so they were ejected for nonpayment of rent, or usurping land allegedly appurtenant to the queen's manors.[32] Eleanor's mills were carefully managed,[33] and her manors developed as centers of exchange;[34] signs of husbandry are few, but the sale of horses was another source of income. When such indications are set beside a clearly marked tendency among Eleanor's officials to raise tenants' rents and withhold rents she owed others,[35] there emerges the picture of a profit-driven administration prepared to adopt any expedient to increase revenue.

Whatever the precise meaning of "manorial issues" in Eleanor's case, her lands produced income in other ways as well. Revenues were augmented, for example, when Edward granted her sums that would otherwise accrue to himself from her estates. Eleanor held pleas of vert and venison in her forests; she was granted scutage from her lands for the Welsh war of 1282–84, and in 1286, murage at Southampton to repair the castle that was in her custody.[36] Fines and amercements from eyres on her lands were allowed her, commonly from the New Forest and also from her hundreds. Those from Somerton and Horthorne were granted her in 1268 and 1281, and in 1285 those from Gartree, Barstable, and Spelhoe; she certainly had the issues from the eyre in the hundreds of Erpingham in 1286 though the grant escaped enrollment, suggesting that she had such issues more often than would otherwise appear.[37] Finally, there were the incidents that were of advantage to the queen. The churches on her manors supported her clerks; wardships granted her or falling in on her estates were the basis of patronage for attendants, friends, and local worthies.[38]

To turn to the queen's prerogative income is to enter more fully into the administrative world, for much of it was closely connected to the workings of government and the courts of law. The term as used here embraces any revenue that came to the queen by reason of her office and from any source other than her lands. Prerogative income thus includes queen-gold; the king's grants of fines, reliefs, or debts owed him at the Exchequer or through the Jewry; the chattels of condemned Jews; his gifts to the queen and payment of her expenses while she lived at court; and gifts to the queen from others.

Queen-gold (*aurum regine*) is easily defined: the queen was entitled to an additional tenth the amount of any voluntary fine made with the king above ten marks; it was also levied when the king tallaged the Jewry. The theory that queen-gold originated with Eleanor of Aquitaine's marriage settlement fails in view of doubts about its exaction before the end of Henry II's reign:[39] in the 1180s the queen was trying to exact gold on fines of ten marks, but the author of the *Dialogus de Scaccario* noted that some felt the minimum was one hundred marks. In John's reign there were doubts whether queen-gold could be exacted from anyone other than a tenant-in-chief, and at Henry III's marriage in 1236 it was still not certain that gold was due on fines below one hundred marks; some thought it was owed only on relief payments, others on voluntary fines of any amount. Eleanor of Provence tried to claim her gold on all such fines and on ecclesiastical taxation, but questions remained in 1272.[40] Detailed queen-gold receipts from Eleanor of Castile's time show that by 1285 it was exacted on relief, on fines of ten marks levied for trespass, commutation of service, for the king's confirmation or the grant of a wardship, and so forth.[41] Like her predecessors, Eleanor tried to augment her revenue from queen-gold; Edward told the Exchequer in 1276 that it must not be exacted on spontaneous gifts to him, and there was a series of reminders that the queen could not demand her gold on ecclesiastical tenths or twentieths.[42]

The king often granted his wife debts, reliefs, or fines owed him at the Exchequer. Such grants are scattered throughout the rolls of Chancery, and recognitions of debts owed the queen make up the bulk of entries regarding her business among Exchequer memoranda; but while the debtors were often prominent individuals, the rolls rarely explain how the debts originated, and it is never possible to be certain how much she received from them. Debts owed by John fitz Alan and his ancestors, for example, granted Eleanor in June 1275, were likely considerable, but the enrollment gives no sum; in contrast, a fine from Italian merchants for taking English wool to Flanders brought her £652:10:0 in 1277. Other debts range from £5 to £100.[43] On 20 April 1283 Edward granted Eleanor all issues of concealed goods and chattels of condemned Jews and from all transgressions of coin,[44] a grant that takes added significance from its relationship to the Jewry. The Crown in the thirteenth century vigorously exploited the Jews' wealth, and with the likely aim of providing money for the queen without draining his own coffers, Edward ultimately so entangled her finances with the Jewry that only the Expulsion of 1290 promised to extricate her. This was a highly controversial facet of her career since, as Pecham warned, she thus profited from usury and generated scandal.[45] Whatever the moral objections, Edward's grants were lawful. The relationship between the Crown and the Jewry made the Jew in effect a serf who acquired nothing for himself, only for his lord the king. As the Jew was liable to tallage and a third the value of a deceased Jew's goods was owed as relief, individual Jews conveyed to the king debts owed them to make up whatever sums they owed. The king thus obtained a vast number of such debts, some of which were collected to provide revenue for the Crown; others were granted or sold to third parties who could collect what was owed or, as Eleanor notoriously did, take over the lands pledged for the loans.[46]

The question here is the amount of money Eleanor realized from this source. As she used some Jewish debts to secure encumbered estates, she did not always collect the sums stated in the grants. The debts owed by John de Burgh of Lanvallay, for example, granted her in November 1275, were stated to be worth more than £1000, but in this case she secured his manor at Burgh in Norfolk. Debts granted her between 1275 and 1280 resulted in her acquisition of lands from Robert de Crevequer, William de Leyburn, John de Camoys and William de Montchensy, among others. But she is not known to have secured estates from those whose debts to Hagin f. Cress were granted her in Trinity term 1275; the total, £1207:13:4, was presumably paid her. In November 1279 she was granted debts owed Hagin f. Moses worth £5262:6:8; she secured lands from some of the debtors (Montchensy, Camoys, Adam de Neofmarche), but the others presumably paid what was owed.[47] The swiftness with which the queen's clerks prosecuted for these debts kept the sheriffs busy. After the grant of Hagin f. Moses' debts in November 1279, for example, the sheriff of Essex and Hertford reported in Hilary term 1280 that he had seized Montchensy's grain worth £120 against a debt of £250, but Philip fitz Bernard held nothing in that bailiwick whereby distraint could be levied for thirteen marks, and the bailiffs of the liberty of Westminster had not distrained Stephen de Ayswell for £48. In Bedford and Buckingham, the sheriff was to distrain Ralph Moryn for 550 marks and John fitz Alan of Wolverton for £40; the prior of Thurgarton had been distrained for £120.[48]

But realizing the stated worth of such debts was rarely quick or easy. Ayswell, for example, was later able to prove that he owed nothing, as Hagin f. Moses had previously sold his debt for £48 to the bishop of Worcester, whom Stephen had paid. After Eleanor was granted the debts owed Jacob f. Moses of Oxford in 1277, she long prosecuted Robert de Muscegros and his mother for £80 owed Jacob by a former lord of Robert's manor of Alvescot; only after Robert and the queen were dead did his mother prove before the inquest of 1291 that the debt was discharged before Henry III granted Alvescot to her husband. Adam de Neofmarche alienated a number of his encumbered manors to evade payment of his debts to the Jews; Eleanor was collecting money in 1285-87 from those who held the lands, and only shortly before her death in 1290 did she arrange to secure his manor at Carlton Scroop. St. Mary's Abbey, York, in 1282 claimed the Jews forged a charter for a debt of £500 exacted by the queen, but compromised and paid £300. (Eleanor again had the abbot before the Exchequer of the Jews in 1284.)[49] Delaying tactics and other problems in bringing debtors to book may explain the irregular references in the rolls of the Exchequer of the Jews to the sums paid by such debtors, which do not offer a regular sequence of data, nor do they add up to the known total of any individual's debts: £10 from Nicholas Tregoz in 1276, £66:13:4 from Nicholas de Menil in 1284, £13:6:8 by Urian de St. Petro in 1280, £6:13:4 from Richard de Windesore in 1284. The lack of evidence could also be attributed to the loss of most of Eleanor's wardrobe accounts, for extant records show that some Jewish debts were paid in her wardrobe rather than at the Exchequer. Over a period of time she must have collected a considerable amount of money from Jewish debts—on which, evidence suggests, she also exacted usury—but they cannot have been a regular source of funds, and their real contribution to her financial system needs further evaluation in connection with her acquisition of new lands.[50]

Prerogative income also embraced money given or lent the queen by her husband, or spent by him on her behalf. Cash gifts appear infrequently, the largest, £2000, given her through Luccan merchants in 1277. Smaller loans were common: 40 marks at Easter 1278, 200 marks in January 1281, £12:16:10 from the residue of the king's wardrobe in 1283, £17:15:0 for wine lost in a shipwreck in 1288, £66:16:3½ to acquit certain debts in 1290, £5 the same year for an ailing courtier. The queen received 2*d.* daily for alms while traveling with the king and 7*d.* for oblations at each church they visited; in 1289–90 this amounted to £19:15:0. Her confinement in January 1278 cost Edward £30. More significant were servants' wages and housekeeping expenses; in 1282–83 these were £894:12:6,[51] and by 1290 must have increased, for other similar payments rose over the years. The biggest case in point was the allowances for the robes, shoes, and oblations of the queen's *familia* and the upkeep of her chamber. Her servants received cloth for their robes until 1277, when on the advice of the king's council a money allowance was substituted; in 1290 this amounted to £1569. Edward paid 500 marks yearly for the maintenance of the queen's chamber and provided robes for her knights, ladies, and damsels; the robes cost £220 in 1284–85, £303 in 1289 and £304:6:8 in 1290.[52] In 1289–90 the total of such payments toward the queen's expenses was £2217:1:8, exclusive of wages.

Finally, there were cash gifts to the queen from persons other than the king. These were of course sporadic, the amounts variable. London gave the couple a "courtesy" of £1000 upon their return from Gascony in 1289, but the amount was probably exceptional and Eleanor's accounts do not suggest that she ever saw a penny of it. Gifts produced £674:3:10 of the £1001:10:0½ received by her wardrobe from August 1289 to November 1290; the gifts tapered off after January 1290, however, and in the next month the wardrobe began to draw on queen-gold, which suggests that these "gifts" were really "courtesies" like that from London.[53]

The above information relates exclusively to England; only limited evidence witnesses Eleanor's revenue in Ireland,[54] Gascony,[55] and Ponthieu.[56] Clearly she evolved or inherited active financial administrations in all three areas, but her income outside England cannot be accurately estimated; as these revenues cannot be shown to have had any part in her English financial system, the accounts now to be discussed deal solely with her finances in England.

THE EVIDENCE OF THE ACCOUNTS

Eleanor's finances are adequately documented only for the last five years of her life. The proper starting point for their examination is the overview provided by her executors' summary accounts, rendered at the Exchequer in March 1294. There are in fact six separate accounts:[57]

1. The account of the queen's wardrobe, Michaelmas 1288-Michaelmas 1289 (17 Edward). A balance of £188:4:4¼ was brought forward from the preceding year; receipts of £743:7:5½ were added (no details), for a total of £931:11:9¾. Expenses (no details) were £755:16:4½, leaving a balance to the good of £175:15:5¼.[58]

2. The account of queen-gold receipts from Hilary term 14 Edward (1286) to Michaelmas at the end of 17 Edward (1289), totaling £2875:0:10¼, and of issues of the queen's lands from Easter 16 Edward (1288) to Christmas 18 Edward I (1289), amounting to £4821:9:0¾. From the total £7696:9:11 were deducted £144:6:8 (a deficit from an earlier queen-gold account) and £4976:11:11 in unspecified expenses, gifts, and purchases over the same period as the receipts.[59] The balance was £2575:11:3 to the good.

3. Between Ascension 11 Edward (1283) and Michaelmas 1289, receipts from fines for transgressions of coin and concealed goods and chattels of condemned Jews totaled £3015:18:5. There were deducted undetailed expenses of £346:13:4 and three payments into the king's wardrobe totaling £2666:13:4. The favorable balance was £2:11:9.

The combined surplus of the first three accounts gave a balance to the good of £2753:18:5¼.

4. The account of the queen's wardrobe from Michaelmas 17 Edward (1289) to December 1290. Receipts were £1001:10:0½, expenses £1009:12:11¼, for a deficit of £8:2:10¾.[60]

5. Receipts from queen-gold between Michaelmas 1289 and November 1290 were £1564:17:4¼, and issues of the queen's lands from Christmas 1289 to 30 November 1290 were £2333:3:3, for a total of £3898:0:7½. Against this were expenses (some details) of £4937:8:6, leaving a deficit of £1039:7:10½.[61]

Combined deficits from the fourth and fifth accounts were deducted from the earlier surplus of £2753:18:5¼, leaving a balance of £1706:7:8. The sixth account is that of the executors' receipts and expenses:

6. In 19 Edward (1290–91) the executors took in £2654:4:5½ from the sale of ornaments and vestments from the queen's chapel, grain and other goods from her manors, and the issues of her lands that remained in the executors' hands.

In 20 Edward (1291–92) the executors collected £4389:11:2½ from the sale to the king of the queen's jewels, the issues of her lands, the sale of grain from her manors, payment of unspecified debts owed her, and the sale of jewels, tapestries, carpets, and silk cloths to persons other than the king.

In 21 Edward (1292–93) the executors received £2643:8:3¼ from the queen's lands.

In 22 Edward, from 20 November 1293 to 6 March 1294 when accounts were rendered, £1712:15:1 were taken in from the queen's lands and the payment of unspecified debts.

Between 3 January 1291 and 6 March 1294 the executors took in £11,427:19:0¼, which with the earlier surplus of £1706:7:8 made £13,534:6:8¼. From this were deducted Eleanor's bequests and legacies, damages awarded by the justices who heard complaints against her administration, the costs of her monuments at Westminster, London and Lincoln, and of the crosses Edward ordered to mark the stages of her funeral procession. These expenses amounted to £12,701:6:5¾; the executors' final balance was thus £433:0:2½ to the good.[62]

To the executors' comprehensive summary may be added some figures from other accounts.[63] The wardrobe account for 16 Edward shows total receipts of £1022:8:5; details are lacking, but other evidence does show that this sum included £833:6:8 from Eleanor's treasury. (Sources of the remaining £189:7:9 are undocumented.) Since the executors' summary shows a favorable wardrobe balance of £188:4:4¼ carried forward to 17 Edward, Eleanor's expenses paid from the wardrobe in 16 Edward were £834:4:0¾. The three surviving totals for wardrobe expenses were, then, £834 in 16 Edward, £755 in 17 Edward, and £924 in 18 Edward; the high figure for 1289–90 may indicate unusual expenses following the queen's return to England in August 1289. Comparison of these wardrobe figures with sums disbursed in *liberaciones*, for which the executors accounted separately—£4976 between 1286 and 1289, £4937 in 1289–90—confirms that some office other than the wardrobe handled the bulk of Eleanor's funds, but further analysis is needed before that office can be identified. The higher outlay in *liberaciones* in 1289–90 as compared to those for 1286–89 may, as with the wardrobe expenses in the same year, reflect heavy expenditure as Eleanor reasserted her presence through patronage after her return from an extended absence in Aquitaine.[64]

Accounts for issues of the queen's lands between 1286 and 1290 survive in useful number. In February 1286 the abbot of Westminster was appointed her treasurer and received £476:12:2¾ of her money; during his term in office, until February 1288, he collected £551:4:2¾ from certain of her manors, for a total of £1027:16:5½. His payments were £663:18:6¾, leaving £363:17:10¾.[65] The summary of issues from Eleanor's lands for 15 Edward (1286–87) shows receipts of £1204:14:8, and from 14 Edward arrears of £785:15:1¼, from which were deducted £400 the queen owed Luccan merchants, leaving £1590:9:9¼. The fragmented account of issues for 17 Edward (1288–89) starts with a balance of £1954:7:8, explicitly stated to consist of the £363:17:10¾ left from the Westminster account and the £1590:9:9¼ from 15 Edward. The executors' summary gives the issues from Eleanor's lands between Christmas 1289 and November 1290 as £2333:3:3; the total for Hilary term 1290 was £459:0:2½, and in Michaelmas term down to the queen's death, £1390:16:8.[66] (The lopsided Michaelmas figure indicates that her officials rendered their principal accounts at that time.)

Finally there are the issues of queen-gold, which Eleanor would of course cease to collect as a widow: £495:1:6½ in 14 Edward I, £941:8:2¼ in 15 Edward, £660:5:9 in 16 Edward, and £1564:17:4½ in 18 Edward. The executors' summary shows a total of £4439:18:2¾ taken in from Hilary 1286 to November 1290; if the yearly sums are deducted from this total, issues in 17 Edward were £778:5:4½. The wide fluctuation in sums produced by queen-gold echoes the varying amounts yielded by payment of debts to the queen and underlines the need for stability in her financial system; the high total for 18 Edward hints at renewed attentiveness by Eleanor's clerks after she returned to England in 1289, or may reflect the fines assessed upon those convicted in the judicial scandal of 1289.[67]

Though the variable sums produced by queen-gold and collection of debts mean that general revenue is not easily estimated, Eleanor's records can, with cautious handling, provide a reasonable picture of income and expenditure for the last few years of her life. Her lands were indeed the more stable source of income. Between Easter 1288 and Christmas 1289 her estates brought in £4821:9:0¾; as the summary of manorial issues for 17 Edward began with a balance on hand of £1954:7:8, the real issues for those twenty months were £2867:1:4¾. To this may be compared the £2333:3:3 from Christmas 1289 to November 1290 and the £2648:8:3¼ for 21 Edward. These totals suggest that the lands Eleanor held at her death were worth between £2500 and £2600 yearly—a solid increment to her income as consort, but it remains to be seen whether her resources could maintain her as a widow. Her outlay in 1289–90 included wardrobe expenses of £924:6:4¼, and *liberaciones* (less £224:6:8 sent to the wardrobe) of £4713:1:10.[68] Edward spent £2217:1:8 on her alms and oblations, the maintenance of her chamber, and the household's oblations, robes, and shoes, all of which she would pay as a widow. To the total, £7854:9:10¼, must be added the wages and household expenses the king paid, almost certainly more than the £894:12:6 he paid in 1282–83. Eleanor's full tab in 1289–90 was thus in the vicinity of £8800; but as both wardrobe expenses and *liberaciones* in that year were most likely exceptional, that figure should be revised downward for less anomalous years. Wardrobe expenses might have been £100 lower; an average yearly figure of £1660 for *liberaciones*, based on the £4976 spent in 1286–89, would probably be low as Eleanor was out of England during all that period, but a respectfully adjusted estimate might be in the neighborhood of £2000. A normal year's expenses might, then, be reckoned at around £6200; as a widow, of course, Eleanor might be induced to accept some dignified belt-tightening, but the results obviously cannot be estimated. To meet expenses, she would have the issues of her dower lands in England and Gascony extended at £4500 and of lands she acquired in England—some £2500 at first but varying as wardships she held were surrendered, as reversions she had purchased fell in, and as life tenures she granted were extinguished. Ultimately a rough total of £7000 might be estimated for her dower and other English lands,[69] in addition to which the queen could draw revenue from her lands in Ireland and Gascony, and the issues of Ponthieu. All things considered, it would appear that Eleanor's aggressive search for income was both justified and successful.

Much of the extant evidence for Eleanor's finances was created for the 1294 audit, and as her executors held her estates for five years after her death, they could indulge in "careful allocation" among accounts to reach a favorable balance.[70] These accounts thus reveal few day-to-day details, but rare notices of internal procedure suggest occasional cash shortages. The June 1290 sale of a cup and brooch for £13:6:8 might indicate a shortfall, and now and then the queen did borrow from friends, as in 1289 when Robert Tybotot and the earl of Gloucester each lent her £200 for works at Haverfordwest.[71] Debts to the Lombards are noted as early as 1275; in 1282 she transferred to the Riccardi a debt of £20 owed her, and in 1276 assigned them 300 marks from the sale of her grain. She paid them 500 marks in December 1284 and £400 in 1286–87. Her total payments to the firm between January 1286 and November 1290 were £2134:5:4; her executors repaid £686:14:6½.[72] Scattered evidence suggests these loans were a response to cash flow problems. Household expenses had her in debt before 1272; heavy outlay on the Crusade of 1270 was evidently what sent her to the Lombards by 1275.[73] Queen-gold and collection of debts always produced varying sums, and even after Eleanor accumulated a substantial group of manors, their issues were not invariably reliable. As her bailiffs rendered their principal accounts at Michaelmas, smaller amounts of income were likely in other terms, and there were at times large sums in arrears.[74] The bulk of her wardrobe receipts for 1288–89, while she was in France, are undocumented, and the *liberaciones* show no money sent to her from England; perhaps she had turned to the Riccardi for cash while abroad.[75]

In her later years, when sufficient lands had been assembled to put her finances on a stable course, Eleanor disposed of healthy lump sums with ease. The demands of patronage required ready access to large sums: in 1289–90, she made gifts of 1000 marks to Otho de Grandison, £100 each to the younger Guy Ferré and Edmund Mortimer, and £200 to Robert Tybotot, paid her cousin William de Fiennes' debts to the Rembertini amounting to £333:6:8, lent Tybotot £100 and (at the king's orders) £600 to one of the Rembertini.[76] Her treasury was a handy dip for Edward: in 1282 she gave £325 toward works at Rhuddlan, and he took £2666:13:4 out of the £3015:13:4 Eleanor realized from the chattels of condemned Jews.[77] (She still paid for new lands and met certain other obligations by means of installments.)[78] In the absence of a running series of accounts, no accurate picture can be had of the extent to which loans augmented Eleanor's finances. But to all seeming, her borrowing was prudent and never exceeded her ability

to repay comfortably: of the £13,000 that passed through their hands, her
executors repaid the Riccardi only some £686, which compares well to the
£2134—less than one year's issues from her lands—that she had repaid
between 1286 and 1290.

The weight of evidence indicates that Eleanor's revenues as consort were
adequate to her needs, provided they were vigorously collected and prudently disbursed. It is thus to those who served, gathered, and spent that
attention must now turn.

ADMINISTRATION

Evidence for English queens' administrations before the thirteenth century is meager. The wealth of the Anglo-Saxon consorts implies they had
officials to manage estates and collect revenue, though in the late tenth
century Edgar's wife Aelfthryth probably had neither a writing office nor
a system of preserving her records. Matilda of Flanders had chaplains, a
chamberlain, and presumably bailiffs on her manors. Edith-Matilda had a
seal, chancellor, and local officials; but as Adelicia's personnel are not mentioned in the *Constitutio Domus Regis*, written early in Stephen's reign, it
seems that the officials of Henry I's wives had little part in royal administration save during regencies. Extant sources rarely refer to Matilda of
Boulogne's officials.[79] Henry II controlled appointments to the retinues of
his wife and sons; when Eleanor of Aquitaine acted as regent, her chancellor attested writs issued on the king's business, but it is doubtful that the
writs were prepared by her clerks. English records ignore Berengaria's
officials, and Isabella of Angoulême's are hardly ever mentioned.[80]

The reintroduction of landed revenue for Eleanor of Provence in 1236
was thus as important for administrative developments as for the exercise
of her prerogatives, and thereafter the evolution of queens' administrations
followed lines closely related to factors discussed earlier. Though Henry III
controlled her personnel, his wife's wardrobe accounted directly with the
Exchequer;[81] as Eleanor of Provence became deeply involved in managing
lands and revenue, her administration expanded to meet new responsibilities and access to the departments of government gave her clerks valuable
experience in the conduct of business. The development of Eleanor of
Castile's administration between 1255 and 1272 parallels these changes. Her
personnel in the 1250s and early 1260s were appointed from the households
of Henry III and his wife: in 1255 the clerk John de Loundres and steward William de Cheney and in 1256 the cook John de Wodestok'. By 1262
she had a chaplain Bartholomew, who had served Henry III, and a yeoman

William de Meleford, who had long served Eleanor of Provence. Signs of growth beyond the household appear in the mid-1260s as Eleanor of Castile's interests expanded. The first grant of land to her, in April 1264, implies the presence of bailiffs (first explicitly noted in April 1265), and by September 1265 Walter de Kancia probably was her steward; a clerk with ties to Edward's household perhaps replaced Loundres by 1264, and Henry de Wodestok', a kinsman of the cook John, was Eleanor's clerk by 1271.[82]

HOUSEHOLD

Like his predecessors, Edward I kept the wardrobes and households of his family in subordination to his own; this proximity often obscures Eleanor's establishment.[83] Her ranking officials, knights, and women can be identified from wardrobe records, Chancery enrollments, and documents from their lives outside court. The king's payments for robes, shoes, and oblations identify her serjeants, yeomen, and sumpters.[84] The robe lists in fact reveal only a core group of the queen's servants whom the king supported; she presumably paid for any others deemed necessary. Thus Edward provided robes for one yeoman of her small wardrobe, but accounts in 1289–90 show there were three; in that year he clothed three messengers, but she had at least eight. Judging from the king's yearly Easter ransom, seven women were officially considered to be with Eleanor at any one time, but in 1289–90 there were nine or ten. Some servants never appear in the robe lists; her dairymaid, for example, is found only in other sources.[85] Chaplains,[86] almoners, and chapel clerks are likewise absent.[87]

At the head of a retinue that numbered some 150 souls in 1289–90[88] was the steward, a knight, who supervised operations and preserved discipline.[89] With the serjeant marshal and other officials, the steward appeared nightly before the king's officials to render the day's account for food and wine, and likely certified the king's marshal on any members of the queen's household who left or returned to court.[90] Despite the serjeant marshal's importance, the office and its sole known incumbent appear only in the king's records.[91] (He was not the individual responsible for carts, coach, and harness.)[92] Those required at the daily accounting with the steward and marshal were the master cook, pantler, and butler. Whether Eleanor's cooks had premises to themselves or fought it out for space in the king's kitchens is unclear;[93] one prepared her food, the other cooked for the household, and they shared the services of five kitchen yeomen. The serjeant butler had two or three yeomen; the serjeant pantler had a yeoman as well as the baker, and also saw to the napery.[94] The yeoman usher of the chamber preceded the queen to a new residence to prepare lodgings; in his absence, the yeoman usher of her hall assumed his duties.[95] Besides its clerks, the great wardrobe had a yeoman usher and a yeoman, the small wardrobe three yeomen.[96]

To trace serjeants, yeomen, or sumpters from year to year produces mere strings of names; more useful information is obtained when the household is examined through profiles of its personnel and patterns discernible after the sources are digested. The group most easily documented are the knights and the queen's women, both socially and officially a coherent group of uniformly modest origin. In 1289–90 Eleanor clothed twelve knights, admitted to her household by agreement with the king who paid their money fees; she almost certainly had two other knights not as explicitly identified in the accounts. Evidence is not available for earlier years, but collation of fees and robe allowances to Edward's knights in the 1280s implies some of these fourteen had been with Eleanor for some time.[97] The knights' duties are not well recorded. Probably they escorted the queen as she traveled, discharging a protective function as part of the panoply surrounding her. The younger Guy Ferré occurs among Eleanor's council in 1285–86, before he became household steward. Of the fourteen knights in 1289–90, six had witnessed acts concerning Eleanor's lands between 1268 and 1289, though the only ones to do so with any regularity were Geoffrey de Piccheford, a steward of her estates, and John Ferré, steward of her household until 1288; none of them attested in 1289–90 except the then-household steward Guy Ferré jr. (John's nephew), who witnessed once.[98] The queen's accounts indeed rarely mention her knights other than the stewards. In 1289–90 much is thus heard of Ferré, who carried oral commands from Eleanor to her clerks, gave gifts at her orders, authorized payments, and sealed some letters in her final illness; of the others, virtually nothing,[99] reflecting the fact that the queen's household had no military function. Apart from her stewards, what administrative work her knights did was on the king's business.

A queen's household of course existed not for the same administrative purposes as a king's, but to provide her an agreeable environment and way of life. Rather than those rarely glimpsed male guardians, it was Eleanor's women who were responsible for her personal needs; never drawn away on the king's errands, the intimacy of their relationships evident in the annual Easter raid on the king's bedroom, her women appear regularly in the queen's records[100] to give her retinue its unique identity. Margerie de Haustede cared for Eleanor's jewels; as other evidence shows that Margerie was considered unusually reliable, it would appear that individual qualities were taken into account as duties were assigned.[101] As with the knights, there was no obvious foreign element among the women, nor were they from prominent families. That Margerie de Haustede was married to Eleanor's knight Robert de Haustede points up the multifaceted role played by marital connections within the royal households. The queen's presence at court was unavoidable if her marriage was to provide the kingdom an example of orderly royal existence, but—a problem at courts everywhere in medieval Europe—her service required that women lived within the male enclave of the court. The queen was naturally responsible for the security of her women and in fact had a double motive for watching over them, for misbehavior by unattached females in her household could compromise her own reputation. Married women were less likely to cause gossip, especially if their husbands were nearby in the households. Hence the episcopal inquest held at Eleanor's chamber in April 1279 to examine a clandestine exchange of marriage promises between one of her damsels and the king's marshal; likewise, the girls chosen from her attendants' families to be raised with the queen's daughters married as soon as they reached a suitable age.[102]

It is, in fact, through Eleanor's women, not her knights and squires, that the matrimonial links so characteristic of her household must be traced. Of the nine or ten women with Eleanor in 1289–90, two were widows of husbands she had chosen; the other seven or eight were wives or daughters of knights and squires in her household or the king's.[103] It was the offspring of these couples who were raised with Eleanor's children, and continued to serve them as adults.[104] Fresh aspects of the queen's promotion of marriages among her attendants surface here: later medieval practice proscribed married or even related servants in noble households,[105] but in a large, itinerant court, families helped to order a potentially unruly environment, kept husbands and wives on the job, and assured a new generation of service as the attendants' children grew up with their future masters. The households thus evolved as a kind of extended surrogate family, within which the queen could claim a wider presence through her women's connections. That these links depended on women implies that Eleanor, partner in a marriage arranged to stabilize ties between kingdoms, understood women's roles in marriage and family as an effective way to assure the loyalty and dependability that were so clearly her objectives.

Members of the knightly families who attended the queen were in a sense born to service in the households, but family links also helped squires and serjeants. Ebles de Montibus, Eleanor's squire in 1289–90, was the son of a household steward to Henry III and later filled that office for Edward II's wife; many members of the Senche and Wodestok' families can be documented in one or another of the households.[106] Such ties certainly existed among lesser servants and were very probably critical in obtaining positions, but appear in the wardrobe records chiefly as a means to identify individuals: Geoffrey the kitchen ewer, "brother of mr Simon" (either Eleanor's cook or her sauser), and the chamber yeoman Richard, "brother of Hamo of the chamber."[107] Failing ties within the households, worthy service was a means to prove oneself and win promotion. Eleanor's chamber yeoman Raoulet and her tailor Gillot had served her mother.[108] John de Wodestok' cooked for Eleanor of Provence before joining Eleanor of Castile around 1256; Henry Wade, her cook in the 1280s, had served Henry III and when Wade died in 1288, his successor was Edward's former cook Simon de Goldeburgh'.[109] Eleanor's butler Geoffrey died in 1287 and was succeeded by his yeoman Wilmot de Kancia; her coachman Christian Page lost his sight in 1290, to be replaced by Michael le Charrer, her daughters' coachman. When the sauser mr Simon was paralyzed in 1289, his longtime yeoman Reginald at once took his place.[110]

Service demanded its rewards, and for knightly families this meant land. Eleanor's prudent household patronage can be observed here from a new vantage point, for the lands held by her attendants or granted to them indicate they were recruited or settled near her estates. In the New Forest, William and Iseut le Bruyn, from Candover, received lands at Rowner, Fordingbridge, and Godshill; John and Christiana de Weston were granted a manor on the Isle of Wight. Robert and Margerie de Haustede, from Kegworth near the Leicester-Derby boundary, were granted escheats in Derby hard by the Peak where Eleanor held much land.[111] (The role of female relationships in Eleanor's household surfaces again: of the couples cited here, the wives were all among her women. Stewards apart, those of the queen's knights not married to her women got no lands from her.)[112] When compared to cases in which the queen presented her clerks or obtained their presentation to churches on or near her manors, these grants suggest that with an eye to widowhood, when she would reside on her own manors and not on the great royal estates, Eleanor sought to assure that her clerks and attendants could conveniently be with her as much as possible.[113]

Favored squires, yeomen, and serjeants were granted wardships and city property. John Picard the pantler in 1280 held a wardship pertinent to the queen's lands in Somerset; she gave Philip Popiot a wardship in Berkshire, and Ebles de Montibus one in Kent. Edward gave Eleanor's squire Robert Despenser wardships in Wales and Ireland, her yeoman John de Shelvestrode a wardship in Northamptonshire, and houses in London to Martin Ferrandi.[114] Her tailors William de Somerfeld, the Ponthevin Gillot, and Richard de la Garderobe held serjeanties, lands, and houses, as did her cooks Henry Wade and Peter de Kendal, and the marshal of her coaches and horses Peter de Bardeney.[115] For servants there were gifts of money and clothing for them and their wives, 6∂. for "the boy who followed the rented carts to buy himself shoes," money for an ailing sumpter and "one with a broken leg," and new clothes for a yeoman leaving service. A Castilian woman who had served Eleanor's mother in Ponthieu was rewarded.[116] Those with legal problems might obtain a letter to Chancery requesting advice, or money, as with £13:6:8 given William de Somerfeld "to acquit his houses in London the queen gave him, against a certain woman who sought dower therein."[117] For many, the reward most anxiously awaited came at career's end, when the king might seek a corrody in a religious house to keep a servant for life. From the later 1290s, Chancery rolls contain many such requests by Edward I and Edward II on behalf of the late queen's servants; as most of them had entered other royal households, the value placed on their skills and experience cannot be doubted.[118]

As Eleanor traveled about the kingdom, her splendid entourage must have made an impressive show (as it was meant to do), but the household's role in shaping perceptions of the queen went beyond spectacle; its specialized customs and observances gave this small community a unique identity closely tied to events in the queen's life. The attendants' part in rituals to mark events in the king's family is seen on major feasts when the wardrobe remarked the presence of knights, ladies, "and others" in the chapels. Courtiers heard mass with the king's family on feast days associated with kingship, witnessed royal marriages, attended anniversary services for the king's family, friends, and administrators, and probably services in Eleanor's chapel when members of her family were commemorated.[119] The households' resemblance to an extended family was strengthened by the observance of such events in the servants' and attendants' families as well. Eleanor provided dowries and attended courtiers' weddings (which could also be celebrated away from court, still witnessed by household colleagues). Her women were sent to bear children in their own houses; a servant's wife in childbed was sent a gift, and the queen sponsored her courtiers' children at baptism.[120] Household members were knighted on the great feasts of the Church. Those who died in service were given suitable burial according to status.[121]

The ways in which Eleanor's household would have shaped popular beliefs about her can only be theorized. That the household included fewer foreigners than native English was perhaps less effective in disguising her origins than might have been hoped. But an English-speaking courtier once interpreted for her with petitioners at St. Albans, and knightly families at court undoubtedly helped spread courtly customs and usages into the shires where they had their roots. Themselves the beneficiaries of royal patronage,

Eleanor's attendants obtained favors for their neighbors, making royal munificence a reality for those who might otherwise never experience it.[122] To that extent, their modest presence in the household might have made it less an isolating buffer around Eleanor than a mediating agency between queen and kingdom.

WARDROBE, EXCHEQUER, AND TREASURY

Like the king's wardrobe, the queen's was that part of her administration most closely attached to her person. Though her travels inevitably disturbed its work, surviving records permit a close look at its responsibilities and functions. The distinction between small and great wardrobes occurs in the queen's records in 1290, the small wardrobe also designated the *garderoba robarum*; it was staffed with three yeomen including a *custos robarum*, but did not have its own clerical staff. The only reference to the *magna garderoba* suggests that it served, at least in part, to store valuables. Her chamber had no income distinct from that of the wardrobe itself.[123]

From this point, frequent reference should be made to the accompanying table of officials.[124]

Eleanor of Castile's Wardrobe and Treasury Officials, 1255–1290

Keepers or treasurers of the wardrobe (custos or thesaurarius garderobe)
John de Loundres (1255–before 1270 [?ca. 1264])
[William de Yattenden (?ca. 1264–d. November 1270)]
Henry de Wodestok' (ca. 1273 [1271?]–d. ca. 20 September 1277)
mr Geoffrey de Aspale (December 1277–d. ca. 11 June 1287)
John de Berewyk' (apptd September 1288–28 November 1290)

Controller-cofferer of the Wardrobe ("garderobarius")
Richard de Bures, fl. December 1276–d. ca. 22 March 1290

Receivers of the Wardrobe
Richard de Bures, fl. 1280–February 1287
Robert de Middelton, fl. 18 Edward I (1289–90)

Treasurers and Keepers of Queen–gold (custos or thesaurarius auri)
Walter Daubeney, apptd 22 January 1273
mr Walter de Guldeford, apptd ca. 5 August 1273–fl. ?June 1274
Walter de Kancia, apptd 25 December 1274–d. ca. July 1283
John de Berewyk', fl. Michaelmas term 1283–28 November 1290
[Walter de Wenlok, abbot of Westminster, apptd 2 February 1286;
Queen's order to audit his accounts, 16 Feb. 1288]

Keepers of queen-gold at the Exchequer of the Jews
Jacob de Oxonia, apptd 1 May 1274
Benedict de Wintonia, apptd Trinity term 1276 (hanged 1279)

The principal wardrobe officer was the keeper or treasurer whose duties paralleled those of the keeper-treasurer of the king's wardrobe: he kept the queen's private receipts and expenses, reviewed expenses on a daily basis, and at the end of his accounting year rendered accounts in the king's wardrobe.[125] There was one distinction: from Eleanor of Aquitaine's time English queens no longer had chancellors. Papal and English episcopal records, however, twice addressed Eleanor of Castile's wardrobe keepers as chancellor, implying that the queens' principal clerks had assumed the chancellor's duties if not his title.[126]

Figure 2.1. Eleanor of Castile's privy seal on an indented chirograph of May 1286, enlarged from 1¼" diameter (London, Public Record Office, Ancient Deeds LS 185; see chapter 3, appendix 1, no. 177).

For most of Eleanor's years as queen the secondary wardrobe offices were held by one clerk, a man whose obscurity complicates the history of those offices. Richard de Bures was a wardrobe clerk by December 1276; until late in 1286 he received money from the king for the queen's expenses and payments into her wardrobe from other sources. Bures prepared accounts for both the king's and the queen's wardrobes in 1282–83, and for their children in 1283–84.[127] Edward's clerks usually called him the queen's clerk, on occasion her receiver, but he prepared her accounts for 1288–89 as controller of her wardrobe, and in 1290 Edward's clerks referred to him as her cofferer.[128] In the king's wardrobe these posts involved distinct duties. The Cofferer, the Keeper's personal clerk, acted as the *locum* when the Keeper went out of court; the Controller kept a counter-roll against which the Keeper's account was checked, and held the king's privy seal. Most of Eleanor's business was moved by her privy seal, which must have been held by an officer who was with her much of the time. The queen's wardrobe keeper was often out of court, however, and since as quasi-chancellor he would have held her great seal, it is unlikely he held the privy seal as well.[129] As red wax for the privy seal was twice purchased by Bures' subordinates, he was presumably responsible for the privy seal. This would suggest that his office was comparable to that of the king's Controller; but Bures accounted as Eleanor's receiver in 1282–83 and as her controller only in 1288–89. A likely explanation is that as the queen's wardrobe did not require, and most probably had not evolved, the degree of specialization needed in the king's wardrobe, one clerk could discharge a variety of secondary functions. Given Bures' jumbled titles and duties, it is well to follow the clerk who in 1293 called him the queen's *garderobarius*, a usefully imprecise term that still conveys a strong sense of the important day-to-day work Bures obviously shouldered.[130]

The part of Eleanor's financial administration that did not travel with her consisted of an exchequer and treasury. The issues of her lands were kept in her treasury, as were her muniments; its security can be judged from a 1286 incident in which one of the stewards carried off the keys so that a messenger had to go retrieve them. Its location is uncertain. A depository existed at Westminster, but a good deal of the queen's money was kept at the hospital at Clerkenwell and some of her business was transacted there. Eleanor's treasury clerks in the late 1280s also used, for unspecified purposes, some houses in London that were connected with Otho de Grandison.[131] Documented from 1286, the queen's exchequer may have evolved from an office known under Eleanor of Provence as the queen's receipt (*recepta*); in 1289 its checkered table was recovered in green, and new counters and other accounting paraphernalia were purchased. The two clerks in residence received £10 yearly for expenses, the ushers 2*s.* Eleanor's bailiffs were summoned to account at the exchequer, but none of its records survives and there are no indications that a system of enrollments existed by 1290. Nor is there any reason to think the queen's exchequer had any judicial competence; as Eleanor used the king's Exchequer to enforce her rights and prosecute tardy bailiffs, her exchequer probably was no more than a well-developed accounting office similar to those of many lay and ecclesiastical magnates whose estates generated enough business to require such machinery.[132]

The relationship between exchequer and treasury is clarified by examining the duties of the *custos auri* or *thesaurarius auri Regine* (the keeper or treasurer of queen-gold), the only one among the queen's officials whose appointment was recorded at the Exchequer. The office is likely traceable to the twelfth-century clerk who audited for queen-gold, which was then the queen's chief contact with the Exchequer; as the volume of her business expanded in the thirteenth century, it would have been convenient for that clerk, accustomed to attend the Exchequer in her name, to take charge of all her affairs there. By Eleanor of Castile's time the *custos auri* was in effect the queen's official representative at the Exchequer, where in addition to collecting queen-gold he secured distraint upon those who owed her money for any reason, testified that she had agreed to pay debts owed by others, and acted as her attorney at the Exchequer of Pleas or the Exchequer of the Jews.[133] He was also responsible for sums the queen collected from debts granted her by the king, especially fines and amercements from eyres on her lands.[134] Eleanor's records in fact reveal that her goldkeeper and treasurer were one man under different titles, depending on whether he was at a given moment representing her at the king's Exchequer or was presiding at her exchequer or treasury: Walter de Guldeford was appointed goldkeeper in August 1273 but in December 1274 was her "former treasurer"; Walter de Kancia in 1282 was "treasurer of the gold of the king's consort," and John de Berewyk', named goldkeeper in 1283, was called treasurer in Michaelmas term 1284. (He became wardrobe keeper, or treasurer, only in September 1288).[135]

The realization that the goldkeeper and treasurer were the same person facilitates reconstruction of the relationships among exchequer, treasury, and wardrobe. The original account for Berewyk's *liberaciones* in 1289–90 agrees in every case with the few details in the fifth section of the executors' summary: among other entries, both documents record the payments to John de Hardington for the manor of Whitfield and to Piers de Montfort for his son's marriage, the money fee to Eleanor's daughter Mary, and issues to the queen's wardrobe. The executors' summary identifies the sources of revenue for these *liberaciones* as the receipts of queen-gold, issues of the queen's lands, and the chattels of condemned Jews, all explicitly stated to have been paid into the treasury. Further proof of the funds' provenance is obtained by collating the *liberaciones*' payments to the wardrobe with the 1290 wardrobe receipts: eight issues match receipts on 20 February, 6–7 May, 6 June, 25–26 June, 13–14 July, 18–19 July, 23–24 July, and 28 August 1290, and in three of these cases the wardrobe specified the source as the issues of queen-gold.[136]

The same relationship surfaces in the *liberaciones* for 1286–89. The second section of the executors' summary again gives the source of funds as receipts of queen-gold and issues of the queen's lands, while the original account for those issues for 1286–87 explicitly states that those issues were deposited in the treasury. The path followed by the money is also made clear by the first "expense" in the original account for *liberaciones* between 1286 and 1289, in fact a deficit (also noted in the executors' summary) from the lost preceding account for queen-gold. While wardrobe accounts for 1287–88 and 1288–89 preserve no details of receipt, issues to the wardrobe can be traced in the *liberaciones* for those years and in the abbot of Westminster's account as treasurer. Queen-gold, fines, amercements from eyres on her lands, and other debts owed the queen were, then, collected at the king's Exchequer by her goldkeeper, and the issues of her lands were paid at her exchequer to the same clerk as treasurer; all the money went to her treasury, which issued cash to the wardrobe and made the *liberaciones* as directed by the queen or her ranking officials.[137] (The *liberaciones* are therefore treasury accounts, not wardrobe records, and it now becomes clear that it was the treasury that dealt with the bulk of the queen's funds.)

While the outlines of Eleanor's financial system are reasonably clear, routine is less easily described. The mechanics of accounting are witnessed only by purchases of counters, parchment, ink, scales for the wardrobe in 1286, and wax tablets in 1289. Her wardrobe perhaps accounted by the Exchequer year—from Michaelmas—not by regnal years. Eleanor's clerks took a conservative course; by 1286–87 the king's wardrobe accounted in book form, with expenses divided into categories, but her accounts exist only in roll form, with the exception of a book for 1289–90. This is clearly a journal of expenses identical in content to earlier rolls of account produced by her wardrobe, but copied in book form, an anomaly explained by the circumstances of its compilation: it was not really "kept" in 1289–90, but was written up as late as 1294 for her executors' audit at the Exchequer.[138]

The organization and methods of the queen's central administration reveal the framework within which her clerks worked. The labors of these men were critical to the queen's position, for it was they who oversaw Eleanor's robust finances, collecting and managing the treasure that was the vital force of a queenship shorn of official authority. Descriptions of clerks' duties and responsibilities alone, however, cannot create a comprehensive picture of the queen's administration; recruitment, tenure, rewards, and promotion are also pertinent matters, best studied in the details of her clerks' careers.

The first keeper of her wardrobe, appointed before September 1255, was John de Loundres, formerly Eleanor of Provence's clerk. Loundres was still in Eleanor of Castile's service in September 1265 but had returned to Eleanor of Provence by 1268–69; during Eleanor of Castile's absence on Crusade, he was in the household of her children in England. Just after the new queen reached England in 1274, she attorned John touching her interest as executrix in the testament of Alina de Bathe, but a petition from the queen-mother for various favors from Edward shows Loundres in her service in the autumn of 1275.[139] He may have left Eleanor of Castile's service by the mid–1260s, when sums granted her by Henry III were being received by one William de Yattenden. Possibly a brother of Bartholomew and Nicholas de Yattenden, respectively in the service of the Lord Edward and Eleanor of Provence, and a brother-in-law of Alina de Bathe, William went on Crusade with Eleanor and died in Sicily in November 1270; she was involved with the execution of his testament in August 1275.[140]

Yattenden's immediate successor was probably Henry de Wodestok', whose family were longtime royal servants. He was certainly Eleanor's clerk by February 1271 and her chief clerk by April 1273, when Gregory X dispensed him to hold multiple benefices—a privilege he repeatedly exploited. Active both in and outside Eleanor's service, at his death in September 1277 Henry was found to be deeply in debt to the king and queen, and his accounts were in arrears. She prosecuted for what Henry's heirs owed her, seized his goods, and sued for debts owed him; her executors made restitution to his family.[141] Wodestok's successor, probably by December 1277, was mr Geoffrey de Aspale. Son of a Suffolk man and a London heiress, Aspale had Henry III's favor by 1264 and evidently joined the Crusade of 1270. A pluralist like Wodestok', he was rebuked by Pecham but died a rich man.[142] Aspale was the first keeper to witness Eleanor's surviving acts, but he left very few traces on her financial records; Richard de Bures' labor on accounts in the 1280s was perhaps needed as Aspale, a university man who commented at length on Aristotle's scientific works, may have had little interest in the financial side of his duties. His death in June 1287 revealed Eleanor's accounts again in confusion; the deficit in the lost queen-gold account for that year might suggest a raid on treasury funds to meet wardrobe debts, some of which from his time in office were still being paid in 1290.[143]

Aspale was succeeded in the wardrobe by John de Berewyk', formerly clerk of King's Bench who had acted as Robert Burnell's attorney. King's clerk from 1279, Berewyk' had acquired considerable administrative experience before he became Eleanor's goldkeeper in 1283; he was involved in her land transactions from 1284 and attested her acts as often as Aspale. He was named wardrobe keeper in September 1288, combining the two most important financial offices in her administration while still handling a good deal of business for the king. The care with which John managed Eleanor's finances is evident in her executors' accounts. She must have had some regard for him; he was the only keeper who received property from her, and he was among her executors. The more significant years of his career in Edward's service came after 1290; in 1312 he left his niece a wealthy woman.[144]

The keepers of Eleanor's wardrobe present a heterogeneous profile unlike that for the keepers of fourteenth-century queens. The circumstances of John de Loundres' 1255 appointment and the later stages of his career suggest that Henry III and Eleanor of Provence confided their daughter-in-law's finances to him as part and parcel of their appointments to the households of Edward and his wife; after Eleanor of Castile began to direct her own affairs in the 1260s, Loundres rarely worked for her. Yattenden and Wodestok' were probably helped by relatives. Aspale's learning perhaps appealed to Eleanor's literary side, but his apparent inattention to duty is a good argument against letting academics handle money. A mixed lot, and worthy of remark considering the experienced royal clerks among whom Eleanor might have chosen.[145]

The importance of the queen's goldkeeper is reflected in the earliest appointment to that office while Eleanor was queen. On 22 January 1273 the archbishop of York, a guardian of the realm in Edward's absence, presented Walter de Albini at the Exchequer "to keep the gold of Eleanor, consort of the said king." No orders from her could have reached England by that date, and that Walter had long served Eleanor of Provence implies that the guardians appointed him only until the king's wife announced her own choice—though an August 1273 order that Walter de Guldeford receive queen-gold came not from Eleanor but from Edward. The quick turnover in this office seems to have resulted from Eleanor's absence from England until August 1274 and the readjustments that followed her return: Walter's successor, Walter de Kancia, was carrying out his duties by 13 December 1274, though her letters appointing him are dated 25 December of that year. As this is the only case in which her letters exist in near completeness, it is useful to quote the text in full:

> To the barons on behalf of the Queen, the King's consort, in this form. Whereas we have committed to our dear and faithful clerk Walter de Kancia the custody of our lands and tenements in England and of our gold of England, and the receiving of the issues therefrom

and the ordering of the same as he shall see best for us, and as there are certain matters touching the said custody that by your care may be well concluded, we therefore ask you affectionately that without any delay you shall receive the said Walter to the custody of our said gold, and that at our prayers and for love of us you shall advise and assist him in the said office and in all other our business to be carried out before you, as the need shall arise. Given at Woodstock the twenty-fifth day of December, in the third year of the reign of our lord [the king].[146]

Walter's abilities had recommended him to Eleanor by September 1265, and she nominated him her attorney at her departure on Crusade in 1270. His tenure as goldkeeper lasted from 1274 until he died in 1283. No accounts for queen-gold survive from these years, but as goldkeeper Kancia received money owed Eleanor at the Exchequer. The Exchequer of the Jews acted as her attorney at both Exchequers and audited accounts of the receiver in Ponthieu. Like Wodestok', Aspale, and Berewyk', Walter sought advancement and wealth for his relatives, including a brother John and a nephew Richard, who also became the queen's clerk. Walter left goods worth over £102:13:4; Eleanor took them, and his executors were compensated only after she died.[147]

While there is no enrollment of Berewyk's appointment as *custos auri*, he was in office within a few months after Kancia's death. His activities as goldkeeper do little to distinguish his duties from Kancia's, though the same prudence he showed in the wardrobe is apparent in his treasury records. He testified to payment of debts to the queen at the Exchequer and the Exchequer of the Jews, audited accounts in Ponthieu and, in February 1288, audited the abbot of Westminster's account as the queen's treasurer.[148]

Though little is heard of the office or its incumbents, the queen seems to have had a distinct goldkeeper at the Exchequer of the Jews. On 1 March 1274 Eleanor nominated as goldkeeper Jacob de Oxonia, a Jew with whom she had business since 1268, and in 1276 Edward told the barons to admit Benedict de Wintonia to keep queen-gold "as other Jews have been accustomed to do." Neither appeared as goldkeeper at the Exchequer, and unless Edward's choice of words is taken to mean that Eleanor had employed Jews as keepers of her Irish gold before 1272 (of which there is no record), it is likely that these men represented her at the Exchequer of the Jews, though there is no reference to their activities there. After Benedict was hanged in 1279 for clipping the coin, the history of this office is obscure.[149]

The wardrobe handled personal expenses, and since the treasury supplied a good deal of its revenue, the wardrobe treasurer did not collect the funds he disbursed; the goldkeeper, in contrast, was burdened with the collection of revenue. The importance of this office can be seen as appointments to it are reviewed in terms of alignment between treasury and wardrobe. Kancia was goldkeeper and steward of Eleanor's lands during the years when she was most rapidly increasing her estates (1274–83). The reason for confiding these two offices to one man was the role played by debts owed the Jewry by Christian landlords from whom the queen secured many of her new estates—the process Kancia's offices would allow him to control most conveniently. This linkage between local and central administrations was not preserved after his death; later stewards had no hand in Eleanor's finances. From 1288 Berewyk' combined treasury and wardrobe, the first time the chief offices in Eleanor's financial administration were entrusted to one man;[150] after the motley succession of earlier keepers, it was perhaps thought well to appoint to the wardrobe a man who had already proved himself. Berewyk's prudence made this arrangement as much a success for the queen's finances as the union of goldkeepership and stewardship had been under Kancia for the increase of her lands. There is, of course, no assurance that the two keeperships would have remained united had Berewyk' left service before the queen died: fresh realignments might well have been essayed as old hands disappeared and new candidates emerged.

The chief officers of Eleanor's administration were frequently out of court, and it was the work of subordinates such as Richard de Bures that remained critical to daily operations. Many of them vanish from the records after one or two notices,[151] but more information exists about others. Kancia's nephew Richard[152] benefited from a family connection, though as with the servants such links are rarely specified for the clerks. William Burnell, rector at the queen's manor of Westerham in 1289, was Robert Burnell's nephew, his presentation likely her thanks for the Chancellor's counsel.[153] Robert de Middelton, the wardrobe receiver in 1290, may have been related to Eleanor's damsel Grace de Middelton, daughter of Edward's wetnurse Alice de Luton.[154]

The closeness and informality of relations between the administrations of king and queen are shown by Eleanor's letters addressing as "her dear clerks" Edward's men who were not associated with her service.[155] Access to his clerks was vital to the queen's ability to project the image of an influential wife; as intercessor, she forwarded to them petitions with requests to expedite the supplicants' affairs, and manipulated the process to her profit by promising favors to them—provided the petitioners were told that her intervention had carried the day.[156] There are no indications that Eleanor tried to intrude into Edward's service clerks who could further her interests; rather, a sedate reciprocity prevailed. John Bacun left Edward's service for Eleanor's in the mid–1280s;[157] some, like Aspale and Berewyk', served both at once. Clearly this was to the queen's advantage but the king profited too: a number of her clerks, John de Caen among them, entered his service after she died.[158] Some of Eleanor's clerks were entrusted with the king's business for which their backgrounds—and hers—made them especially suited, reinforcing the role in Edward's diplomacy implied by Eleanor's family connections. John de Montibus was a "Burgundian" or Savoyard, so it was natural that Edward sent him to Savoy and Montferrat in 1282.[159] In 1268 Eleanor secured license for her merchant Gil Martini to trade in England and later obtained protection and safe-conducts for him and his brethren, including Gonzalo, a clerk who entered the queen's service and was assigned to embassies to and from Castile, or to purchase Castilian goods for her.[160]

To attract able men to her service, the queen had to show that she could reward their proficiency. To accomplish this she relied on the benefices to which she could present her clerks or could induce others to present them. Patterns in her patronage are typified by the case of Walter de Kancia, who held a stall at Lichfield and at least six churches, one on the queen's manor at Great Bowden and others near her manor of Macclesfield at Stockport and Prestbury, to which her neighbors presented him. Henry III in 1270 promised Kancia a benefice in the patronage of St. Andrew's priory at Northampton; Walter probably thus obtained the church of Little Billing, near Kingsthorpe (which Eleanor held from 1267). In 1274 Edward presented Kancia to Taxal, near Macclesfield and Eleanor's lands in the Peak.[161]

The churches on or near her manors, whether held in wardship or in fee, were clearly crucial to Eleanor's provision for her clerks. Her acquisition of a new manor included the advowson whenever possible, and other advowsons were purchased separately; her clerks soon appear as rectors of many of these churches, and Edward continued to use them to provide for her clerks after her death.[162] Despite Eleanor's initiatives, however, the number of churches at her disposal was limited, and other means of supporting her clerks had to be pursued: papal mandates, for example, provided prebendal stalls, allowed for multiple benefices, and permitted nonresidence.[163] Alternative methods were also explored. Eleanor failed to usurp the church at Hardwick, claimed as appurtenant to the wardship of James Russell's lands, but did wrest that at Bockingfold from Leeds Priory, and in two cases her purchases of advowsons—or claims to have purchased them—seem to have been of a questionable nature and may have resulted in conflict and at best temporary possession.[164] The lengths to which Eleanor could go to induce others to present her clerks to churches in their gift is evident in the protracted litigation over the presentations of her nephew and her physician to the church of Crondall; her swiftness to punish those who failed to comply is amply illustrated by the sad ordeal of Richard de Stokepord', who was unable to present Eleanor's clerk John de Caen at Stockport as she required him to do upon Kancia's death, and was consequently tormented by her men at her orders for seven years. Bishop Giffard's 1283 warning to the prior of Deerhurst, who found himself in a situation identical to Stokepord's, shows that this aspect of her behavior was no secret. His admonition is echoed by Archbishop Pecham's concern for royal indignation in the Crondall affair and by Nicholas de Moels' politic offer, after he recovered the church at Hardwick against the queen, to present her clerk Edmund de Loundres, whom she evidently sought to intrude there.[165] However ungraceful it may appear, Eleanor's aggressive pursuit of advowsons served an important double purpose: effective exertion of her powers provided for her clerks without depleting her coffers and convincingly manifested her capacity to influence the actions of others. Her exertions were necessary as well since Edward was not entirely helpful to her in this area. He presented some of his wife's clerks to Irish stalls, but generally remembered them only when vacant sees or wardships put new benefices temporarily at his disposal; she, on the other hand, presented two of his clerks to churches she held in wardship by his grant—the advowson to one of which she had recovered at her own expense.[166]

LOCAL ADMINISTRATION

For the most part, household, wardrobe, exchequer, and treasury were rarely entered by those who had no business there. The queen was represented to the majority of the English people by those of her officials who labored among them—stewards, auditor, bailiffs, and reeves. Eleanor of Castile's local administration was significantly different from those of other magnates, not only because of its privileges and exemptions but because it was freshly installed on estates newly assembled over little more than a quarter century with the sole purpose of producing revenue. For her lands to be properly managed, the issues collected and delivered to her, called for knowledgeable and energetic officials willing to do whatever was expected of them.

As the most valuable single source for her local administration is the inquest that followed Eleanor's death, a few details on its records will not be out of place here. Three justices, assisted by three Dominican and three Franciscan friars, were commissioned on 6 January 1291 to hear and determine complaints touching unjust exactions, transgressions, and injuries committed by the queen or her ministers. The querents' convenience and a desire to expedite matters were clearly Edward's objectives; the justices sat at locations near Eleanor's lands (Westminster, Salisbury, Chester, Bury St. Edmunds), and the procedure adopted was by bill, not the more cumbersome and expensive writ. Four rolls of proceedings survive; another is lost if not two, while collation of the rolls with payments for damages in the queen's executors' accounts, with Chancery enrollments and other sources, proves that the extant rolls are incomplete. The justices did not determine all cases. Many end with a note that discussion with the king was needed; some querents withdrew or failed to prosecute.[167] By their nature these rolls give a negative impression for which due allowance must be made. In the summer of 1290, moreover, Eleanor of Provence requested a similar inquest into the conduct of her officials; none of its records survives, but there is other evidence that at various times her ministers were accused of actions similar to those revealed by the 1291 inquest, and like offenses were perpetrated by officials of both Isabella of France and Philippa of Hainaut.[168] The sheer bulk of the material from the 1291 rolls must not, then, unduly influence the conclusions drawn from it: many who served a queen might abuse the powers and immunities of her office.

At the hub of Eleanor's local administration were the stewards of her lands. Walter de Kancia likely held that office by September 1265, though he appears with the title only from 1273.[169] In the years after Eleanor's return to England, the rapid expansion of her lands required an associate; Geoffrey de Piccheford was co-steward by September 1276 and held office until the queen's death.[170] Kancia was probably succeeded in 1283 by William de St. Claro,[171] in turn replaced before the end of 1286 by Hugh de Cressingham, who served until Eleanor died.[172] There is no reason to think the stewards' duties were divided along geographic lines, as was the case in Queen Philippa's administration in the next century.[173] There was, however, a separate steward for the New Forest, an office Eleanor acquired in 1270. Kancia probably took office at that time and made John de Budesthorn' his deputy.[174] Hugh de Digneveton' was steward in October 1276,[175] but was soon replaced by John fitz Thomas, who served until 1291. That fitz Thomas accounted for the forest on the same footing as bailiffs from Eleanor's other manors shows that the forest steward was not the equal of the other stewards, who did not account.[176]

Allowing for the greater dignity of her administration, the activities of Eleanor's stewards reflect contemporary practice.[177] Cressingham is named as a member of her council in 1290, and other stewards probably advised her there. That it was desirable for them to work closely with the queen is shown by the complaint of Richard Maylle, who took the manor of Weeting at farm from St. Claro in Eleanor's absence; unaware of this, she gave custody of the manor to Petronilla de Toeny, who ejected the lessee. When the queen secured new lands, the stewards took extents to determine their value. They did not dispose of wardships, marriages, escheats, or dowers without her warrant; Albreda de Ewelle sought her dower "from the queen and her stewards," and Eleanor herself assigned Joan de Lyndon's dower at Lyndon. Piccheford in 1280 ordered the queen's tenants at Upton to be intendent to Adam de Stratton, to whom she had granted a wardship there; in 1286, he was to extend lands in Essex she would exchange with the earl of Essex for his moiety of the barony of Haverfordwest, and in 1289 he received John de Hardington's conveyance of a manor at Whitfield. Exceptionally, Cressingham appeared for the queen at the Exchequer; in 1288–89 he leased Tatlington to Kenilworth priory, and in 1289–90 he saw to Eleanor's new interests at Haverfordwest, holding courts, taking tenants' fealty, and acting as her attorney in parliament against William de Valence who held part of that barony in right of his wife. All four stewards were named to commissions touching Eleanor's estates. Trained in the law or with access to counsel, they easily had complaints against them dismissed during the inquest. Piccheford noted that the prior of St. Albans' bill did not mention his abbot and that he had no letters of attorney, that John de Grymstede had not put in his claim on a fine, and that John de Lisle had an identical action pending in another court; Cressingham forced others to admit actions were pending elsewhere.[178]

The circle of local administrators closest to the queen was completed by the auditor of her accounts, the importance of whose office increased during the thirteenth century as the procedure of account became a practical means to assure honesty and efficiency. The 1291 inquest shows Eleanor's auditor John de Lovetot indeed occupied a highly authoritative position. John was in her service by 1273–74, became a justice of Common Pleas in 1275, and presided on occasions when the queen's business was before the court. He was one of her council in the 1280s, witnessed her acts as often as the stewards, was named to commissions on her lands, and audited accounts in Ponthieu.[179] His authority is shown by the complaint of Robert de Mauteby, whom the queen's bailiffs in Norfolk distrained and twice hauled before parliaments for eighty-five marks allegedly owed her; the sub-bailiff and bailiff absolved themselves by claiming they were under orders from Lovetot, "whom they dared not refuse." To a significant degree, however, Lovetot's role in Eleanor's administration differed from the description of the auditor found in contemporary sources. These indicate that auditors were often eminent men chosen from outside the lord's entourage, men whose station commanded respect and whose lack of affinity to the lord's stewards and bailiffs postulated a capacity to do impartial justice to those, free and villein alike, who might complain of the lord's officials during the audit.[180] However eminent and experienced in the law, Lovetot was no outsider to the queen's administration. By all signs he was a permanent fixture whose service she well rewarded, even extending her favor to his children. So far from acting as a check on the actions of her other officials, John is commonly found acting hand in glove with them, entering as customary in his extents of the queen's lands, for example, the inflated amounts the stewards claimed as rents and services. He did well for himself but in 1290 was disgraced as a justice for taking a false verdict.[181]

The daily tasks of administering the queen's manors were the province of bailiffs and reeves. There is little information about the latter; except for Maurice at Ditton Camoys, none was impleaded in 1291, and otherwise they are mere names in the manorial issues. These confirm, however, that reeves accounted with bailiffs. Reeves at Burgh paid the lesser tithe to the bailiff, but it was denied the parson since the auditor disallowed it in the bailiff's accounts; past and present reeves gave evidence, their number showing that, as was common practice, Eleanor's reeves changed office frequently. She secured Burgh in 1278 and by 1290 there had been nine reeves there.[182]

The bailiff's most important role was as the chief financial officer for lands in his charge, supervising trade with the lord's goods and produce, and preparing yearly accounts testifying to his competence. Otherwise the bailiff functioned as a general superintendent of the manor, occupied especially with the manor court, where he served as a prosecutor before the steward; he took pledges, made attachments, levied distraint, and collected amercements.[183] Most of Eleanor's bailiffs are known only by name, but some details survive about a few of them. Three were clerks (probably all *laici*): John de Ponte, Thomas de Macclesfeld', and Humphrey de Waleden.[184] Adam de Cretyng and Robert de Bures were knighted, apparently after they left office.[185] As three bailiffs in 1291 easily had complaints dismissed in the same fashion as the stewards, they must have had access to legal counsel.[186] It is not clear that Bures was a relative of Eleanor's *garderobarius*, but some bailiffs did benefit from the influence of relatives and patrons—Ponte, for example, was beyond question a creature of Walter de Kancia.[187]

Only one bailiff's appointment is recorded, that of John de Shelvestrode at Feckenham in May 1290. An experienced royal falconer and huntsman, he was briefly preceded to Feckenham by John fitz Thomas, steward of the New Forest, so it would seem his particular expertise decided his appointment to a manor that included a forest among its appurtenances. Other bailiffs were recruited from Eleanor's manors or from places nearby and thus had intimate knowledge of the neighborhood.[188] Robert de Petra, at Cawston, came from Aylsham, and Alexander de Horshegh, subbailiff in North Erpingham, was presumably from Horsey; John de la Woderowe at Didmarton most probably came from Eleanor's manor nearby at Woodrow. Eleanor of Provence deprived the Strecche family of the hereditary office of forester while she held Feckenham (1273–88), but Robert Streche, Eleanor of Castile's bailiff at Hope (1283–84), was perhaps of the same family. Walter de Chidecroft had kept the warren at Bockingfold before Robert de Crevequer's lands came to Eleanor in 1278; he then became her bailiff in Washlingstone and at Brenchley. Roger de Walcote, bailiff in Lincolnshire, was probably from one of the Walcotts near Eleanor's lands at Nocton. Thomas de Macclesfeld' came of a locally prominent family at Macclesfield. John de Cretingham, at Bentley Dodnash, clearly came from Cretingham, not immediately near Bentley but close to Aspall and to Creeting St. Mary, home of the queen's knight and sometime bailiff Adam de Cretyng; both men perhaps owed their posts to Geoffrey de Aspale. Minor officers at Soham were from that vill and nearby Fordham; those at Hope Castle and in the Maelor Saesneg were clearly of local origin.[189] John le Botiller, bailiff at Woodrow in Wiltshire in the early 1280s, appears to have been from that county; he was of great help to Eleanor when she acquired land near Woodrow at Didmarton in Gloucestershire and may have assisted with her acquisition of lands in Essex and Hampshire.[190] Some bailiffs were shifted from one area to another: Ponte worked in Lincoln, Somerset, Norfolk, Hampshire, and Kent; Waleden in Somerset, Norfolk, Wiltshire, and Worcester; and John le Forester in Norfolk and later in Essex.[191]

The form of the account of manorial issues for 1286–87 reveals the seven bailiwicks (ballive) in which Eleanor's lands were then arranged, each identified by the name of its principal bailiff. The "bailiwick of John de Horstede" lay in Somerset, Dorset, Gloucester, and Wiltshire.[192] That of John fitz Thomas, centered on the New Forest, was entirely in Hampshire. Richard de Hoo's manors sprawled across Buckingham, Hertford, and Essex. Moses de Wautham had charge of estates in Warwick, Hugh de Lyminstr' had those in Snowdon and Anglesey, and Thomas de Macclesfeld' that manor with Ashford in the Peak. The manors in Northampton, Lincoln, Rutland, and Leicester were assigned to Roger de Walcote. None of the later summaries of manorial issues were written up in the same form as that for 1286–87, but with the complaints of 1291–92 they can amplify the organization sketched here. The Maelor Saesneg and lands at Hope made up a well-defined unit with a bailiff subordinate to the man at Macclesfield. In Pembroke, Haverfordwest was a bailiwick to itself. Issues for 1290 show that lands at Washingley in Huntingdon, granted to the queen in 1289, were attached to the Northampton-Lincoln-Rutland-Leicester group. A bailiwick in Norfolk, Suffolk, and Cambridge is attested by the roll of complaints arising only from those shires; none of the summaries of issues refers to Eleanor's estates in Kent, but the 1291 inquest shows they were a distinct unit.[193] There are no details for the queen's lands in York, Sussex, or Surrey.

The degree to which the queen's administration valued the geographical coherence within each bailiwick can be judged from the fact that it was most common for her to grant away or to confer in wardship those manors that lay at some distance from her other estates. Gayton and Tothill in Lincoln, for example, she surrendered to Edward in 1274 to be granted in fee to her knight John Ferré. Aust in Gloucester, which came to her with the wardship of James Russell's lands in 1280, was nowhere near the other Gloucestershire estates she then held, and she quickly granted it in wardship to her friend Bishop Giffard of Worcester. She would have held the town of Bristol in dower had she survived Edward, but that she did not yet hold it may explain her 1278 grant of tenements acquired there in 1277 to her marshal Thomas de Bardeney. She held Weeting in Norfolk by reason of the wardship of Ralph de Playz' lands from 1284; isolated from her estates around Burgh and Aylsham, it was granted to Petronilla de Toeny, mother-in-law of the king's household steward Walter de Beauchamp. The hamlet of Tatlington in Worcester, which pertained to the wardship of Robert Walerand's lands, was leased in 1288 or 1289 to Kenilworth Priory. In Somerset, Eleanor leased lands she acquired at Uphill and Christon, at some distance from her other lands in that county. The lands she held of the king's grant in Anglesey and certain parts of North Wales, administered by a bailiff in 1286–87, were later leased to the tenants and the rents collected by the king's chamberlain in North Wales.[194]

The principal bailiff of each bailiwick collected from reeves, farmers, or lessees the issues of the manors in his charge and carried them to the queen's exchequer. (Subbailiffs did not account; they are known only from complaints brought against them in 1291 of ejections, disseisins, or seizures of goods at the bailiffs' orders. The steward of the New Forest had the foresters in fee to assist with the forest itself; reeves accounted for manors in the Hampshire bailiwick outside the forest.[195]) The chief bailiff accounted personally for one manor, presumably the administrative center for his bailiwick.[196] In the New Forest this was at Lyndhurst, where tenants from outlying areas were compelled to transport rents in grain though they had previously taken them to more convenient locations. Somerton was the center for the Somerset-Dorset group. The lands in Chester, Stafford, and Derby were administered from Macclesfield; those in Flint attached to Macclesfield were under a bailiff at Hope, with subbailiffs at Overton. Bailiffs of the Northampton-Lincoln-Leicester-Rutland group accounted for Gartree hundred; the center was probably at Market Harborough. Langley was the seat for the Essex-Hertford-Oxford group, and in Kent it was at Leeds Castle.[197]

The tangled story of the additions to Eleanor's estates is discussed in Chapter Three; for the moment, the focus must be the assimilation of these additions as members of her financial system. Eleanor lost no time in setting administrative wheels in motion when new estates were at hand; told of an advantageous wardship in Gloucestershire in late August 1280, she secured it within three weeks. The stewards worked with equal dispatch. Piccheford's mandate to the queen's tenants at Upton after she granted land there to Adam de Stratton is dated 25 November 1280; her letters telling Piccheford of the grant are dated 24 November.[198] After the queen was in seisin, the first need was to determine how much income the new manor might produce, and this meant taking an extent by sworn testimony. Complaints in 1291 revealed only the preparation of fraudulent extents but prove they were taken as a first step. The stewards inflated the rents and services entered in Lovetot's extents, for which the bailiffs were made responsible; Lovetot refused to allow the bailiffs part or all of certain sums — for example, 3d. daily Eleanor granted Alice widow of Robert Follet of Exbury to support her daughters. Inquest at Thorness in 1286 showed Wilton Abbey had 2s. yearly rent from the manor until Hugh de Cressingham refused to enter it in the extent. At Hope, tenants were burdened with 12s.5d. above the customary rent; nine acres materialized at Overton where there had been seven, and the rent shot from 6d. to 7d. the acre. Cressingham's methods caught up with him when a fresh inquest at Kynarton identified the false extent he had proffered in evidence. (False inquisitions benefited tenants too: the men of Lavington in 1288 swore they owed suit at the bishop of Winchester's hundred only twice yearly, though they should have offered it every three weeks.)[199]

Once Eleanor's men were installed the pace hardly slackened, as is clear from her three-week tenure at Barwick in 1265, when her officials seized the Michaelmas rent as well as the relief due from a tenant. A quick sequence of events can be documented after she acquired the custom of the port of Sandwich from Christ Church priory in the spring of 1290. She was put in seisin on 28 or 29 June; on 13 July she was granted three yearly fairs there, and on 18 July she reminded her bailiff to allow the priory's men to enjoy their houses and quays. On 20 July she told the mayor and town bailiffs to do right to a Breton merchant whose wines had been seized by the priory's men.[200] That her bailiff knowingly or otherwise infringed on the priory's rights after he arrived at Sandwich parallels other encroachments by her officials when new lands came to her. Within three months of taking office in the Maelor Saesneg, Adam de Cretyng seized lands of the barony of Wem, initiating a dispute settled only in Edward II's reign. Six weeks after Eleanor was granted Hope Castle in 1283, her officials seized a moor from John Beydele, who recovered it in 1291. The best-known case was Eleanor's dispute with William de Valence and his wife, after Eleanor in 1288 acquired a share of Haverfordwest in Pembroke.[201]

The bailiffs' most important function was to collect and transmit to the queen's coffers the money drawn from the lands in their care and to account reasonably therefor. Those who failed were given short shrift: Adam Basset probably lost his post around 1280 because he was £30 in arrears, and Gartree hundred was seized in 1279 because William de Boyville had not paid his farm.[202] All that remain to show the results of the bailiffs' labors are the summaries of manorial issues; in only a few instances can the estimated value of her lands be compared to what was rendered.[203] Langley was valued at £40; issues in 1286–87 were £35 and at Michaelmas 1290, £35:4:0. The lands in Somerset and Dorset secured from Henry de Newburgh were valued at £25 and in 1289–90 produced £23. Scottow, extended at £40, was farmed for and produced that amount in 1289–90; Somerton and its hundred were farmed to that vill for £60, the amount rendered in 1289–90. Worth £12:15:9, Gartree hundred yielded £16 in 1285–86, the same in the next year, and £10:12:10 in Michaelmas term 1290. Uphill and Christon, worth £6:4:6¼, were farmed for £8 in 1286–87 and 1289–90. Lands at Nocton were worth £60; issues in 1286 were £54. In 1291 the New Forest was extended at £168:2:2¼; in 1285–86 the issues were £180:18:6¾, in 1286–87 £149:0:0, and at Michaelmas 1290 £120:0:0.[204]

As these bare figures cannot reveal the bailiffs' methods, it is the inquest of 1291–92, supplemented by other relevant material, that paints the clearest picture of the local officials' behavior. Even bearing in mind the limitations of these records, it is difficult to avoid the conclusion that under pressure to maximize revenue and secure in their freedom from prosecution while on the queen's service, stewards and bailiffs adopted whatever expedients suggested themselves. Their most common method was to exact increased rents and services from tenants, often as demanded by the stewards' inflated extents, though the bailiffs did arbitrarily raise rents and services: Bures exacted from English tenants in his bailiwick the rent from their lands before the end of the ten years during which they should have been held rent-free, and 1d. for pasture though tenants previously paid nothing. Payments for herbage and cheminage were raised by Kancia in the New Forest, and in Anglesey full rents were exacted though Eleanor had reduced them because of the tenants' poverty.[205]

The search for income was conducted with remarkable thoroughness. Under Henry III, Nigel de Bokland took at farm in the New Forest a croft of the king's waste at a rent of 2s., but Bokland's enemies showed the king that this arrangement damaged the forest and the steward took back the croft. Nigel and his son Roger, the querent in 1291, should have been quit of the 2s. but when Eleanor held the forest, Kancia "determined from the rolls that the same rent was subtracted and thereafter caused [it] to be taken" for eighteen years; Roger recovered 36s. and the croft. Kancia found as well that 30s. rent for a cow pasture in the forest was not paid by Richard de Burele, who also owed twelve marks' rent for the bailiwick of Burley; both were levied anew though the cows were lost in the Barons' Wars and Burele's father ejected from the bailiwick. In a like case the abbot of Beaulieu had to pay the full farm for the vill of Exbury after a widow recovered 22s. dower there. The abbot of St. Benet Hulme paid £22:10:0 on an amercement, but Ponte failed to give quittance and the abbey was repeatedly distrained for that sum. Not even the queen's favorites escaped the net: John fitz Thomas exacted from William and Iseut le Bruyn 30s. rent from lands Eleanor gave them in the New Forest, so in 1288 she had to certify that she remitted the rent when she made the grant in 1286.[206]

Rents or services were also withheld from those of whom the queen held her manors: from Clive Abbey at Camel, from John de Mandeville at Lyme Regis, and from Southwark priory at Westerham. St. Albans lost a rent from Langley after the queen purchased the manor in 1275, the earl of Cornwall £30 yearly from Whitchurch after 1286, Peterborough Abbey £54:8:9 for rents and services from Torpel and Upton, and St. Benet Hulme £25 from Scottow. Amesbury priory—where the queen-dowager and Eleanor's daughter Mary lived—lost a rent from Woodrow, and the priory's men were distrained by the steward of the New Forest to pay cheminage and to offer suit of court.[207] On a less impressive scale, Simon Pypard lost 2s.2d. yearly from Jordan le Forester's lands, and bailiffs detained a "small rent of villeins" assigned by Henry de Bathe to his chantry at Uplambourne. The bailiffs impeded suit owed by Eleanor's tenants in the courts of the abbot of Peterborough, the bishop of St. Asaph, and the bishop of Winchester. Views of frankpledge were usurped from the earl of Norfolk and the abbot of St. Benet Hulme, and in 1280 it was found that tenants of the see of Canterbury were compelled to offer suit in the queen's court at Leeds.[208]

While no records survive from any of the queen's manorial courts, it is clear from the inquest of 1291–92 that these courts afforded the bailiffs many opportunities for abuse. In Norfolk, Waleden distrained John de Antingham for 8*s.* without accepting John's pledges though he was willing to let himself be attached; William de Wileby distrained William Gryndel for 8*s.* after accepting a false indictment and refusing pledges. Richard Cole compelled Robert Baldwin to offer suit at Lyndhurst though Robert held nothing of the queen whereby he should have done so; he was twice amerced for £13:6:8, for which Cole seized six of his oxen and sold them for 6*s.*8*d.* apiece though they were worth 10*s.* each. Cole also took Baldwin's grain worth £20. In this and other wrongdoing, Cole was upheld by John de Budesthorn' and Walter de Kancia, the latter well known for using his office to enrich himself and to torment those who crossed him. At Overton, Henyt wife of Gylyn ap Ievan was maliciously amerced for one mark after following up a judgment for detention of chattels against the subbailiff by the justices of Chester. David ap Ythel, subbailiff at Hope, falsely accused Thomas del Pek of putting alien beasts into the king's pasture and distrained him for 3*s.*6*d.*, and by a like false accusation tried to conceal exaction from Thomas of the farm of lands that should have been held free of farm. At Overton, Bures alleged that Philip de Crumbes was surety for debts of Hywel ap Iorwerth and distrained him until he fined for half a mark. He also claimed that Baldrus de Worthingebury plotted to kill him, refused contrary testimony, and jailed Baldrus until he fined for half a mark; when Baldrus' brother dared criticize Bures, he too was amerced for one mark.[209]

More blatant cases included the exaction of £666:13:4 from executors of Bishop Nicholas of Winchester, indicted for trespass of venison in the New Forest in 1280; he died before he was convicted or amerced, but the queen's bailiffs levied the money from his goods "although by the laws and customs of England none may be amerced after he is dead." At Cawston, Robert de Petra withheld the king's writ of right touching two messuages and nine acres of arable, so Cecily and Beatrice Cleynknayl were kept out of their inheritance. John fitz Thomas entered into collusion with Joan Senche to eject Geoffrey de Immere from a messuage and two carucates at Imber; Immere brought a writ of mort d'ancestor, but Joan and fitz Thomas swore that Eleanor granted the land to Joan. Kancia falsely asserted that a New Forest tenant had died intestate, seized goods worth £35:10:8, and kept them himself, though he claimed to act in the queen's name.[210]

As no rolls from her manorial courts exist and her officials were exempt from prosecution, the number and severity of the cases reported in 1291–92 are the only signs that conflict was generated as the queen's men asserted her presence on her new estates. That most victims had to wait for redress until 1291 reveals how the prestige and power of a queen's administration allowed her officials to assure her tenants' deference and submission, and guarantee the increase and collection of revenue. Their behavior makes unattractive reading, but as shown earlier, it was not uncommon for queens' officials to engage in dubious activities. The question here is not whether Eleanor's ministers were any worse than those of other queens, but the extent to which their behavior shaped her reputation. From this standpoint the remarkable cases from the 1291 inquest are those in which querents sought remedy for personal grievances by falsely claiming that the culprits were the queen's men. All these complaints were soon disproved, but they suggest that the real bailiffs' notoriety was such as to give the querents reason to think their strategies might succeed. Official references to the bailiffs' conduct in Eleanor's lifetime are few, but support the idea that their behavior was well known; such knowledge could have bolstered impressions of the queen as a harsh and grasping woman.[211]

The phenomenon of a woman presiding over an extensive administration was not so anomalous as to elicit a gendered criticism of Eleanor's administrative actions: medieval England was accustomed to heiresses and widows controlling broad estates, most prominent among them in Eleanor's day the countesses of Aumâle and Devon. When he remonstrated with her about the exactions on her tenants, Pecham did not isolate the queen's sex as the factor that made this side of her behavior unseemly. It was in an altogether different context that he urged her, as a woman, to manifest her pity and alleviate impressions that she made the king rule severely; but as some aspect of her conduct was clearly creating exactly that impression, it is not out of place to consider how her managerial activity might have been read into her relationship with Edward to color opinions of his lordship.[212] The social, legal, and administrative contexts here are complex. On one hand, her auditor's failure to control her stewards and bailiffs left Eleanor's tenants with no immediate remedy against their exactions, a situation that ran counter to that strain in Edward's legislation concerned with such officials' accountability to the community as well as to the lord. Indeed, the high-handedness of the queen's men contrasts markedly with Edward's efforts in the 1270s to restrain his officials and to provide for review of their conduct. From another viewpoint, the picture is subtly different: the ease with which the queen could secure commissions and inquisitions, and her ready exploitation of those advantages, presumably would associate her, not by contrast but directly, with the more exacting aspects of Edward's lordship.[213] Such perceptions typify the varied ways in which a queen's relationship to the king might be understood by observers. In neither case would they have worked to Eleanor's advantage, and they might well have heightened suspicions that she favored the energy of Edward's rule. If the queen's alien origin is factored in as well, might not her administrative behavior, as supported by legal immunities and advantages, have recalled for some the extent to which Henry III turned the course of his justice to the benefit of foreign favorites? Just such a combination of factors—including the presence of the Castilian merchants Eleanor protected—kept her dealings with Southampton at the simmer, and any similar cases would have offered so many opportunities for resentment to build up against her.[214]

That Eleanor felt herself responsible for her officials' behavior is shown by her dying request that administrative wrongs be set right, but her sense of liability must not be pushed too far. It should not be supposed, for example, that she told the reeve at Ditton Camoys to eject Richard fitz Adam and his wife from a tenement in Newmarket and jail them on charges of breaking into the house. Probably she did not tell Thomas le Taverner to compel tenants at Overton to give half their catch of fish to his wife, who sold it to her own profit. Nor is it likely that Ponte consulted with her before ejecting John Bolytoute from his house in Norwich, jailing him, and using the house to entertain a prostitute.[215] On the other hand, few cases of misconduct reported in Eleanor's lifetime led to discharge. The only cause for which she dismissed or prosecuted her officials was failure to produce revenue, her only move to impose general reforms a July 1285 commission to the steward St. Claro touching exactions on her poor tenants[216] —which clearly achieved very little by 1290. Stokepord's case, moreover, proves that Eleanor was indeed capable of ruthless tactics, and the letters cited here from Burnell, Pecham, and Giffard confirm fairly widespread misgivings about her on these grounds.

SUMMARY AND SOME FURTHER CONCLUSIONS

Examining Eleanor's personal role in the direction of her administration is thus an integral part of an investigation aimed at uncovering the image her contemporaries had of her. That she was indeed aware of events on her manors is indicated by official records and by extant reports informing her of such developments. In 1279–80 the bailiff at Woodrow told her a neighboring knight had ejected her men from newly purchased land at Didmarton; another agent soon notified her that the knight had died leaving a young son and urged her to seek the wardship from the king. In 1283 the bailiff at Hope informed Eleanor that her tenants there had been attacked by John Boydel, "so they pray you that as their liege lady you shall command Sir John to retire from these outrages and allow them to remain in peace and have their profit from their lands. . . . Know, my lady, that I would have come myself to tell you this but for my illness, which troubles me grievously. . . ."[217] The last sentence implies that she expected full reports from her officials, and certainly some problems did result from a lack of communication. Obvious examples are the Weeting lease, granted by the stewards in Eleanor's absence but then defeated by her grant of custody to another, and the rent exacted from lands she had granted quit of rent to the Bruyns. On occasion she was deliberately misled, and reversed decisions when she learned the truth. In 1289–90 the Treasurer of Ireland told Richard de Morlee that John de Folebourne was indebted to the queen and John's Irish lands were taken into her hand; she restored them when he proved he owed nothing. When John de Budesthorn' died, fitz Thomas told the queen John had been her bailiff; she seized his lands and goods, but the widow disproved the allegation and recovered everything.[218]

As bailiffs would hardly report their own wrongdoing, tenants' appeals were an important way for the queen to keep abreast of affairs on her lands. After she assigned Joan de Lyndon's dower, the buildings at Lyndon were found in ruins and Eleanor personally ordered them rebuilt; John de Cauz' court near Lyndhurst was damaged by her men, and she told the steward of the forest to undertake repairs. Kinsmen of a Welsh boy in the queen's ward apparently came to her in 1290 after a bailiff refused to provide for the boy's maintenance. Margaret de Bromfeld', unjustly ejected from ten acres at Overton, got them back by the queen's own mandate. In 1290 John de Upton, the rector of Hanmer, came to Eleanor at Macclesfield seeking hunting and fishing rights denied by her bailiff in the Maelor, and tenants from Overton sought relief from Bures' exactions. Her response to these pleas, and her reaction to the poverty of the tenants in Anglesey whose rent she reduced, suggest that Pecham's letter on behalf of tenants at Westcliffe, reduced to near indigence by her bailiffs' exactions, would not have gone unheeded.[219] Such individual cases were dealt with favorably as they came to the queen's attention, but it must be kept in mind that while Eleanor of Provence evidently did aim for a general reform of her administration in 1290, Eleanor of Castile made no effective moves toward corrections until she was on her deathbed.

Upton's statement that he met with Eleanor and her advisors neatly leads to consideration of the makeup and role of her council and her part in its workings. This body existed by 1270 when Richard de Seez met with Eleanor and her council to arrange the ransom of his lands granted her after Evesham. Her bailiff John le Botiller advised in 1280 that she consult her council on the wardship of Robert Burdon's lands; in the same year the council assisted in an agreement with Romilley priory on advowsons and rents the queen would help the priory recover and on the purchase of John de Montfort's marriage. The council's makeup is witnessed by two of the 1291 complaints. John de Wauton the elder stated that he came into Eleanor's council through John de Kirkby, and there met with Berewyk', Lovetot, and Guy Ferré. Those at Upton's 1290 meeting were Cressingham, Ferré, and Edward's confessor Walter de Winterbourne OP, to whom Upton likely presented himself to reach the queen.[220]

The queen's council was thus drawn from her household as well as her central and local administrations, and its operations confirm her officials' role in shaping strategies to develop and exploit the bases of her power, both financial and (as with the Montfort marriage) social. She also sought advice outside her immediate entourage. Her 1283 letter to the Roman Curia on Bishop Giffard's behalf praises his counsel, and John le Botiller's 1280 letter on the Burdon wardship shows that she consulted as well with Edward's council.[221] Here her most valuable contacts were Burnell and Kirkby. Burnell's name is seldom missing from witness lists to the queen's acts after 1274, and she sought him out in a variety of situations; a letter from Lucy de Grey of Codnor, seeking help with debts exacted at the Exchequer, reminds Eleanor of a meeting she arranged with Burnell, who had advised Lucy to gather the summons and tallies she now had ready.[222] Eleanor was accustomed to work with Kirkby by 1265; a 1279 letter to her on the seizure of Gartree hundred implies they met often. Most of her extant letters to Chancery are to Kirkby; one, dated at Aberconway on 15 April 1283, recalls "that business we discussed with you at your departure," reminds him that she had sent fresh particulars, and asks what can now be done to further the matter.[223]

That Eleanor's personal role in decision making was an active one is thus beyond question, though evidence to pinpoint it is rare. Her wardrobe seldom detailed the contents of letters sent on local business, but two pairs of her original letters bear on the question. The first pair is dated at Winchester on 5 May 1278: one orders the steward of the New Forest to permit enclosure of four acres she had granted Breamore priory, and the other orders allocation, in the accounts for the king's prise wines at Southampton, of three tuns Eleanor took to her use at Lyndhurst. The second pair survives among those already noted in regard to Eleanor's tenure at Sandwich in 1290: her order from Westminster on 18 July that her bailiff allow men of Christ Church priory to enjoy their quays and houses, and from Watford on 20 July, an order that the mayor concern himself with a Breton merchant's goods seized by the priory. Two letters on the Valence dispute, from Quenington in March 1290 and from Westminster that June, can be seen in the same light, as can her May 1286 confirmation at Dover of a con- veyance among tenants at Overton.[224] With tenants' petitions, bailiffs' reports, and meetings of her council, these prove that business followed the queen and that she was the final authority within her administration.

Given the assurance with which she exerted her prerogatives to inform its operations, the care with which she deployed marriages among her ret- inue, the energy with which she obtained churches for her clerks, and the patterns in her patronage that show much forethought, Eleanor begins to emerge rather more visibly as a personality. The other side of the coin is that, directly or indirectly, she must bear responsibility for her officials' actions— a tacit understanding that she asked no questions, provided her expectations were met, would have allowed her officials to take up the rich variety of methods they adopted. But that a distinction could be observed between Eleanor's actions and her officials' behavior appears from the proceedings of 1291, when many complaints ended with prayers for remedy "for the good of the late queen's soul." Such words echo her admission of responsi- bility for her officials, but do not impute their actions to her. Indeed the majority of complaints, from her tenants and townspeople, do not directly implicate Eleanor: if such people did mention her, it was as a remote figure to whom querents had appealed over the heads of abusive officials—the benign queen whom the townspeople of St. Albans in 1275 asked for help against the abbot's exactions.[225] It is in complaints from those whose estates she obtained, whose lands her bailiffs seized, or from whom her officials withheld services that she appears as an immediate presence, treacherous and vengeful, who breaks her promises and robs them of lands and rights: the grasping harpy suggested by the Dunstable and Guisborough texts and the letters of Pecham, Burnell, and Giffard.[226]

This distinction relates to conclusions in Chapter One that opinions of a queen might vary among different social groups. Despite the obvious cul- tural links she shared with the aristocracy, for example, it was not unlikely that a queen would come into conflict with those with whom she shared a common idiom of lordship and patronage. The Stokepord' case, Pecham's letter to the nuns of Hedingham Castle, and Giffard's to the prior of Deerhurst, all concern patronage, a matter critical to magnate and queen alike, while the disseisins, exactions, and detentions of rents or services revealed in 1291 show that her administration seized any chance to add to her income — just as did many of the lords whom she despoiled. The pattern implied earlier thus comes into sharper focus: those who knew the queen or who shared her sphere of interests had reason to be wary of her, but those at a distance could shape their image of the king's wife in keeping with their hopes of her mercy and pity. That so many complaints from members of the landed classes were connected in one way or another with Eleanor's lands indicates that the next key to the puzzle of her reputation indeed lies in the intricate tangle of her estates.

CHAPTER

3

Outcry and Gossip, Rumor and Scandal

Chapter Two demonstrated that, from the 1230s, a major factor in the evolution of English queens' prerogatives and administrative machinery was their need for adequate revenue and the means to assure its collection. The king had to find some way to provide that revenue without compromising his income—or his ability to dispense patronage, for the queen also had to be able to reward her followers with money, property, or ecclesiastical benefices. The present chapter will consider Edward I's response to that dilemma: the rapid accumulation of a substantial and stable landed endowment for the queen, an endeavor that occupied much of Eleanor's attention and energy over a quarter century. Examination of this aspect of her life is central to an understanding of the evolution of the resources of queenship and Eleanor's exploitation of them, but it is a facet of her career previously examined only from a variety of ancillary viewpoints, not from the perspective of the royal establishment within which it was conceived and directed, nor as a process in itself, with its own aims, rhythms, and patterns.

The reasons for investigating Eleanor's land gathering are not, of course, limited to her financial resources; as often remarked here, this side of her career was plainly controversial. Four contemporary sources, two from the same hand, witness the effect Eleanor's activities had on popular opinion. It might be questioned whether anyone not fortified by youth's immortality would have dared speak to Edward I as derisively as in Guisborough's doggerel, allegedly recited to the king by his courtiers' sons ("The king would like to get our gold / The queen, our manors fair to hold"), but the Dunstable epitaph with its reference to the queen's land hunger ("A Spaniard by birth, who obtained many fine manors") corroborates the doggerel as a reflection of popular opinion on her behavior. More direct testimony is offered by two letters from Archbishop Pecham, the first of them sent to the queen probably in the autumn of 1283:

> . . . for God's sake, my lady, when you receive land or manor acquired by usury of Jews, take heed that usury is a mortal sin to those who take the usury and those who support it, and those who have a share in it, if they do not return it. And therefore I say to you, my very dear lady, before God and before the court of Heaven, that you cannot retain things thus acquired, if you do not make amends to those who have lost them, in another way, as much as they are worth more than the principal debt. You must therefore return the things thus acquired to the Christians who have lost them, saving to yourself as much as the principal debt amounts to, for more the usurer cannot give you. My lady, know that I am telling you the lawful truth, and if any one gives you to understand anything else he is a heretic. I do not believe that you retain in any other manner things thus acquired, but I would wish to know it by your letter, so that I can make it known to those who think otherwise. . . .

Pecham's second letter was sent in December 1286 to Geoffrey de Aspale, then keeper of Eleanor's wardrobe:

> A rumor is waxing strong throughout the kingdom of England, and much scandal is thereby generated, because it is said that the illustrious lady queen of England, whom you serve, is occupying many manors, lands and other possessions of nobles, and has made them her own property, lands which the Jews extorted with usury from Christians under the protection of the royal court. It is said that day by day the said lady continues to acquire plunder and the possessions of others by this means, with the assistance (though we ourselves do not believe it) of certain clerks who are of the tribe of the

devil and not of Christ. There is public outcry and gossip about this in every part of England. Wherefore, as gain of this sort is illicit and damnable, we beg you, and firmly command and enjoin you as our clerk, that when you see an opportunity you will be pleased humbly to beseech the said lady on our behalf, that she bid her people entirely to abstain from the aforesaid practices, and restore what has been seized in this way, or at any rate make satisfaction to those Christians who have been wickedly robbed by usury.[1]

These records and letters affirm opinions of the queen's behavior current outside the royal establishment. The detailed sources for her land gathering that are the basis for this chapter, however, reflect an "inside" perspective not accessible to most of Eleanor's contemporaries. As with the divergent pictures that emerge from her wardrobe accounts and from sources such as legal records, information from "inside" sources may be difficult to reconcile with that from "outside" sources; alternatively, each may extend the other's meaning. Commentators often turn, for example, to a schedule appended to the Close roll for 9 Edward I, listing manors, rents, and advowsons the queen had acquired by 1281. The list is not comprehensive; a number of purchases were omitted, and as can be seen from Appendix I to this chapter, the schedule barely hints at the full extent of Eleanor's acquisitions.[2] The accessibility of so concentrated a résumé of her activities has naturally brought it much attention, however, and its repeated references to vendors' debts to the Jewry echo Pecham's letters as well as a much-quoted clause in the Barons' Petition of 1258, complaining that magnates were acquiring the property of knights indebted to the Jews. Chronicles, letters, schedule, and petition together have shaped recent descriptions of Eleanor as "the greatest acquirer of them all," "particularly notorious" in securing lands pledged to the Jews, and "a dynamic and important landowner" who "seems to have been everywhere in the property dealings of her day." These remarks are drawn from studies involving either a limited district of England in which Eleanor happened to acquire a number of manors, some aspect of the history of the English Jewry, or the episcopate of John Pecham—all contexts in which his letters, the Guisborough and Dunstable texts, the Close roll schedule, and the 1258 petition, jointly or singly, could easily be given disproportionate weight. Nonetheless, this combination of evidence has led some to posit an almost paradigmatic relationship among knightly indebtedness to the Jews, magnates' greed, and Eleanor's accumulation of property.[3]

It remains to be seen whether this seductive alliance of "inside" and "outside" evidence is secure. As most of the transactions omitted from the 1281

schedule did not involve the Jews, for example, the schedule may give misleading prominence to Eleanor's dealings with them. The silence of the
Guisborough and Dunstable texts on the Jews is thus potentially significant.
Until it becomes clear why the 1281 schedule was written up when it was
and in the form it was given, its bearing on her transactions and, more
important, its relationship to Pecham's letters and the petition may not be
fully grasped. There is no doubt as to the extent of the queen's property dealings, but the questions they pose cannot be answered until they are examined less as a regional phenomenon, or one linked to a particular social
stratum or group, than as what "inside" sources imply was a process controlled from within the royal establishment, in fact a direct outgrowth of
Edward I's policies.

This approach, however, at once suggests that Eleanor's property dealings
were so atypical that they should be related neither to the economic crises
of one group, the strengths of another, or to the moneylenders. A sense of the
anomalous is indeed inescapable if discussion begins, as it must, with review
of the factors underlying Eleanor's acquisition of land. By Edward I's reign,
the traditional sources of an English queen-consort's income were manifestly
inadequate. Sums drawn from queen-gold and from debts granted by the
king were erratic and, even at their highest, failed to meet her needs. Wardships proved an evanescent source of funds for Henry III's wife, and his
retention of advowsons on the manors granted Eleanor of Provence in wardship highlights the fact that the queen's need for materials for patronage com-
peted with the king's needs. The history of the royal demesne in the
thirteenth century offers further reason to link Eleanor's activities to
Edward's interests. After the loss of the Angevin patrimony, the Plantagenets
were compelled to increase their lands in England to support themselves and
their families. By reacting to chance opportunities, Henry III acquired the
earldoms of Cornwall, Chester, Derby, and Leicester, all granted to members
of his family. Edward I aggressively initiated transactions and acquired,
with much other property, the Isle of Wight, the honor of Aumâle, and the
earldom of Norfolk (the last later given to one of his younger sons), but his
domanial revenues were still estimated in the 1280s at less than £19,000.[4] He
could not follow twelfth-century practice and allow his wife to hold her
dower lands in his lifetime: his widowed mother already held dower lands
from the royal demesne in England worth £2000, and to have handed
another £2000's worth to his wife would have reduced his revenues by an
unmanageable amount, quite apart from his mother's £2000 dower in
Aquitaine and the queen-consort's promised £2500 there (much of which was
supposed to be supplied by the reversion of the dowager's lands).

There was, then, every argument that Edward should allow and encourage Eleanor to secure lands to support herself and to afford the needed resources for patronage, in effect strengthening both their positions: the process would hone her legal prerogatives, and as Edward or their son would be her heir, her lands would ultimately increase the royal demesne. Eleanor's activities are further linked to the Crown by the Jewish debts through which she acquired certain estates. Between 1269 and 1275 legislation proscribed the practice of usury in England, ended the pledging of land held in fee to secure loans from the Jewry, and forbade the transfer of such debts between individuals. While means were soon found to circumvent the prohibition of usury, the Crown succeeded in closing down the traffic in Jewish debts to all save those who obtained them through royal grant or by royal license. This effectively made Jewish debts a medium of patronage that Edward used to the advantage of his adherents and his family, especially his wife. Thus the bulk of the debts Eleanor used to acquire land came to her either by Edward's grant or as the result of his tallages on the Jewry, when queen-gold was exacted and the Jews conveyed debts to her to make up the sums demanded. Original documents and official enrollments for Eleanor's purchases such as the Close roll schedule of 1281, moreover, often state that while she entered the lands, they were in fact conveyed to both the king and queen, and that Edward paid the vendor. If any of the £2000 he gave Eleanor in 1277 was for the purchase of English land, like the £1000 he provided in 1281 to buy land in Ponthieu, his direct contribution to her acquisitions was imposing indeed.[5] Whether or not his intent was to acquire a group of estates as the basis for later queens' dower lands, successors to the lands assigned in the twelfth century, there is no question that this was the result. After 1290 Eleanor's estates kept their identity as *terre Regine* and were separately administered as such until Edward married Margaret of France in 1299; the lands then became the English half of Margaret's dower—leaving the royal demesne untouched—and they formed the nucleus of later queens' dower assignments into the next century.[6] The signs of Edward's promotion of Eleanor's land gathering, then, imply that to examine her acquisitions will contribute less to an understanding of the thirteenth-century land market, or of the knights' status in this period, than it will add to what is known of Edward's expansion of his demesne lands.

This chapter, therefore, is neither a detailed study of the knights, of the Anglo-Jewish community, nor of the thirteenth-century English land market. The ways in which these factors converged to expedite one arm of Edward I's policy will be dealt with, but the focus here remains the effect that policy had upon the queen's reputation, as witnessed by the sources cited earlier. Pecham's echo of the 1258 complaint that knights were losing lands through the Jewry may be taken as indicating an initial line of approach. It is clear that despite a generally buoyant English economy in the thirteenth century, the lower ranks of the landed classes were facing a crisis in the struggle for resources. The complex background to this situation has been well described elsewhere and only a broad outline is needed here.[7] The consequences of the English inflation of 1180–1220 included a movement away from twelfth-century lords' reliance on rental incomes and toward increasing the profitability of the estate through intensive demesne farming, increasing rents when possible, and closer definition of villein obligations. This transition was difficult for the many thirteenth-century knights who inherited smaller estates. The fragmentation of knightly holdings began at about the same time as the great inflation, helped along by a land law that partitioned estates among female coheirs and by evolution of the final concord as a convenient means to convey land. The result was the creation of many small holdings that were worked by wage labor, as sufficient villeins owing labor service were lacking; even if one man inherited several such holdings, they were often so widely scattered as to impede efficient administration, and produced little or no surplus with which the lord might share in the market. Fragmentation also divided rights to manorial courts among coheirs, limiting profits from the courts' operation and weakening them as a means to control the manor. At the same time, the common law protected free tenants, whom lords could not eject to reclaim their holdings for the demesne; attempts to encroach on others' lands, clear forest land, or reclaim waste could be foiled by tenacious tenants or neighbors. Increasingly, the only means of adding to the estate or of reforming it was by the purchase of land or buying out others' rights, but many knights found this impossible.

The lack of profits left smaller lords with scant resources to meet the increasing costs of assuming knighthood, of providing themselves with military equipment, and of maintaining a chivalric way of life as knighthood came to imply membership in a social elite. For some knights there were crusading expenses; for the many whose declining interests led them to support Simon de Montfort against Henry III in the hope of gaining relief from their plight, there were heavy fines and ransoms after Montfort's defeat. There were the additional burdens of the administrative role assigned the knights by Angevin government and of providing for family members. Daughters' dowries and the landed endowment for which sons hoped were burdensome for small estates; many thirteenth-century knights were unable to provide even ecclesiastical livings for younger sons, as their twelfth-century predecessors had often granted away the advowsons that would have provided such opportunities.

The crisis facing English knights in the thirteenth century appears to be similar to that facing lesser lords in northwestern France at the same period. The financial crises of Ponthevin knights allowed Edward and Eleanor after her accession there in 1279 to purchase much land to repair earlier losses from the comital demesne, but there was one significant difference to the English knights' situation. None of the Ponthevin knights who sold lands to the royal couple is stated to have been indebted to Jewish money-lenders,[8] but into the 1260s many English knights did pledge their estates to secure Jewish loans. The lands were lost when the creditors, often under the pressure of royal taxation on the Jewry, which increased throughout the century, conveyed the debts to the Crown, or, until the practice was halted by legislation, sold them to third parties who exacted payment. Additional debts came to the Crown as one-third of a Jew's goods descended at his death to the king, and the Crown's role in collecting or selling these debts had attracted controversy since John's reign. According to the 1258 petition, it was the magnates who bought up the Jews' obligations and acquired the knights' encumbered lands; but it has been shown that the higher aristocracy were in fact not inclined to acquire estates in this way. Knightly debts to the Jews were more commonly purchased by wealthy religious houses or rising *curiales* such as Simon de Wauton, Walter de Merton, Geoffrey de Langley and Adam de Stratton, who could rely on official connections to ensure rapid collection of the debts or swift acquisition of lands pledged for the loan. Some knights, locally well connected, ambitious, or far-sighted, were able to reform their estates and made the changeover to profitable administration; many others were less able or less lucky. That some rose while others fell is a reminder that for many the situation remained open either to progress or retreat. But those who did lose lands might well complain, like those in 1258 or Geoffrey de Southorpe in the 1280s.[9]

As the Jews' role as middlemen whose capital facilitated the movement of estates from one hand to another comes into focus, and most especially as the magnates' supposed share in the acquisition of knights' land is clarified, the relationships among sources just cited with regard to Eleanor's activities begin to weaken. Her activities are perhaps not quite so readily paralleled with the magnates'; the restriction of traffic in Jewish debts and the queen's emergence as a beneficiary of this area of Edward's patronage again emphasize the anomalous nature of her purchases and highlight her accumulation of land as an outgrowth of Edward's policy. The role played by that policy becomes clearer as certain patterns, established in the early stages of the additions to the queen's lands, are followed throughout the course of her acquisitions.

That Eleanor's accumulation of property was carefully thought out at a high level from its initiation in the mid–1260s is discernible in the patterns of Henry III's grants to her. As noted earlier, these reveal a proclivity for arranging her lands in neat groups. Ashford, granted her in April 1264, lay within her dower expectations in the Peak, as did most of the rebels' lands granted her after Evesham, at Haddon, Bakewell, and Codnor. In March 1265 Henry granted her in wardship the manors of the purparty of a daughter of William de Vivonne, including Dundon in Somerset; when he granted her the nearby manor of Somerton a month later, Henry expressly noted that her men already in the vicinity (at Dundon) would find it easy to attend to Somerton, and early the next year he gave her neighboring manors at Pitney and Wearne. In Leicestershire her first manors were Great Bowden and Market Harborough, granted her in November 1267; Henry in March 1268 added Gartree hundred, which included both manors. There was an identical profile in Northamptonshire: Kingsthorpe came to her in November 1267 in the same grant with Bowden and Harborough, and in May 1270 Henry added Spelhoe hundred as appurtenant to Kingsthorpe. Eleanor's 1270 acquisition of the New Forest stewardship embodied the same approach. Edward granted her in 1266 the manor of Ringwood and the issues of the forest; in August 1270 she surrendered to the king Pitney and Wearne, to be granted to Alan Plogenet in exchange for the stewardship and the manor of Lyndhurst. The outlines of Eleanor's evolving estates were completed by Henry's October 1269 grant of Aylsham with North Erpingham hundred and Edward's 1270 grant of Macclesfield near the Peak. In May 1270, probably in anticipation of her absence on Crusade, a single grant put all the manors and hundreds granted by Henry III in Eleanor's hands in fee for life, with the provision that they not be separated from the Crown.[10]

By 1270, the accumulation of Eleanor's estates was well in hand and was following reasoned guidelines. Up to that time, the expansion had been accomplished almost entirely by grants from Henry and Edward: there is no reason to think she purchased land in the years before Edward's accession, nor that she dealt widely with the Jews before 1272. Her earliest recorded contact with the moneylenders came in April 1268, when Henry III gave her all debts owed by William fitz William of Hartwell to Jacob f. Moses of Oxford and to any other Jews in England, and before Henry's death she was granted the debts owed by Richard de Ernham of Froyle and Thomas Basset of Welham. Benedict de Wintonia attracted Eleanor's favor by December 1269, when she got Henry III to promise that Benedict's debts would not be interfered with for ten years. The signs are few, but they do show that before Eleanor left England on Crusade in 1270, she had encountered some of the Jews who were later involved in her business, that she had intervened with the king on behalf of one of them, and that she was most probably aware of the mechanics through which land could be acquired through debts to the Jewry. That knowledge may explain Henry III's February 1270 payment, at her request, of £66 owed Aaron f. Abraham by William Fyliol, father-in-law of Eleanor's cousin Giles de Fiennes.[11]

By the time of Edward's accession, then, Eleanor's administration had had opportunity to develop a deliberate approach to the expansion of her estates and had a grasp of the potential offered by the Jewry for increasing her lands and her wealth. That her clerks were prepared to put their knowledge and experience to early use is shown by an order of March 1274, before the queen returned to England from the Crusade, that a remedy be taken concerning her officials who were usurping royal right pertaining to the Jews. Apart from three wardships granted her by the king, however, there was little movement toward increasing her estates between her return in August 1274 and October 1275, when Edward, following his father's example and after some hints from Alphonso X, augmented Eleanor's dower assignment to provide £4500 in English and Gascon lands, the former in twenty-two shires. The 1254 dower, worth £1000—the Peak, Stamford, Grantham, and Tickhill—was abandoned save for the Peak, which was retained probably because it lay near Macclesfield, which was granted her in 1270; Eleanor had secured no new lands near Stamford, Grantham, or Tickhill.[12]

That no new permanent acquisitions are recorded between August 1274 and October 1275—the period during which the new dower assignment was presumably mapped out—suggests that purchases were postponed pending the assignment. But a large number of Jewish debts was granted Eleanor during these same months. In December 1274 Edward granted her the debts Richard de Redlee of Essex owed Benedict f. Jacob of Lincoln; before February 1275 he gave her the debts owed Jacob de Oxonia by Norman Darcy of Lincolnshire. In the spring of 1275 some debts owed Hagin f. Moses by Stephen de Cheyndut of Hertford came to her by the king's order, in May those owed by Bartholomew de Redham, and by June all debts and chattels of Sadekin f. Vives, in the king's hands as Sadekin was excommunicate. In Trinity term 1275 she was given all chattels and debts of Hagin f. Cress, also excommunicate, and by Michaelmas term that year, probably through payment of queen-gold, she acquired some interest in the debts owed Manser f. Aaron of London by Robert de Crevequer of Kent.

And on 13 November 1275, a month after the new dower assignment, Edward granted her all debts owed the Jewry by Cheyndut, John de Burgh of Lanvallay, and William de Leyburn of Kent.[13]

The acquisition of these debts is significant in that it accelerated so swiftly after Edward and Eleanor returned to England, during a quiescent time in the growth of her estates that coincided with the preparation of the new dower assignment and with the Statute of the Jewry of 1275, which completed the process whereby the traffic in Jewish debts was shut down save with royal license or the king's grant. It is likely that these debts were meant to provide cash, either for Eleanor's expenses or to finance the purchase of new lands, but a closer look suggests that the selection of these debts was not determined solely by the amounts to be collected. Estates the queen acquired from some of the debtors (especially Crevequer, Leyburn, Burgh, and Redham) were critical components in the next stages of the growth of her estates, and their examples point to an emerging relationship between her dower assignment and the opportunities offered by knightly debts to the Jews. The bulk of John de Burgh's estates came from his mother, the heiress to the Lanvallay barony, and it has been plausibly suggested that he alienated his patrimony willingly, to clear an inherited burden of debt to the Crown: in 1273 he surrendered most of those estates to Edward, who then made them part of the queen's new dower assignment. That she was given Burgh's debts to the Jewry barely a month after the assignment was published suggests that a royal eye was trained on the vestiges of his patrimony; by June 1278 Eleanor had taken advantage of his debts to secure his manor at Burgh in Norfolk, next Aylsham, which she had held from 1269. Edward at almost exactly the same moment added adjacent Cawston with South Erpingham hundred—which Burgh also surrendered in 1273, but which the queen would otherwise enter only in dower. The compact unit thus established was augmented before January 1281 by lands at Scottow and Hautbois secured from Bartholomew de Redham by reason of his debts to the Jewry, granted the queen in May 1275 while the new dower assignment was being planned. Another example comes from Kent, where the queen had no dower lands: the debts given her in 1275 resulted in her 1278 acquisition of the Crevequer barony of Chatham, the nucleus of the lands she built up in Kent. This was no coincidence. The barony had been fragmented as Robert de Crevequer alienated his estates to meet his debts; the queen secured one member of the barony from him and another from William de Leyburn, both of whose debts to the Jewry came to her hands in 1275 while her dower assignment was in the planning stages. A third member was purchased from Roger Loveday, who was not indebted to the Jews. All three Kentish conveyances took place between June and November 1278, just as the Burgh-Cawston-Aylsham group in Norfolk was assembled.[14]

These cases make it evident that the accumulation of Eleanor's lands was a complex process in which Crown grants, lands purchased or acquired in other ways, and her dower expectations were jigsawed together. While Eleanor would not enter her dower in Edward's lifetime, the assignment provided a backdrop against which purchases could be planned in anticipation of her dower tenure, repeating on a wider scale the pattern remarked in Henry III's grants to her in the 1260s. To assign a central role in this process to any one method of securing lands — Christian debts to the Jewry, for example — is to obscure the scope of the endeavor and the planning that underlay it. To discuss Eleanor's transactions on an individual basis would likewise sacrifice comprehensiveness to detail; Appendix I to this chapter provides an account of each acquisition. Here it will be of greater value to consider the ways in which the larger patterns already observed were repeated or elaborated as the queen's lands were aggressively expanded in the 1270s and at a rather more leisurely pace in the 1280s.

A convenient starting point will be the growth of Eleanor's estates in the counties of Gloucester and Wiltshire. Her dower assignment included the castle and town of Bristol, and in Wiltshire the farms of Bedwyn and Wexcombe. In Gloucestershire Eleanor first acquired tenements in Bristol, surrendered to her in 1277 by William de Montrevel; with the exception of a certain garden, she soon granted these to her marshal Thomas de Bardeney. A regular series of acquisitions began in 1279–80, when Eleanor purchased from John Besilles the Wiltshire manors of Great Sherston within twenty miles northeast of Bristol, and Woodrow next Melksham, about the same distance southwest of Bristol and some thirty miles west of Bedwyn and Wexcombe. These manors were administered from Woodrow, and within what must have been a few months after the purchase Eleanor's bailiff there sent her the following letter:

> To the high and very noble lady, my lady Eleanor by the grace of God queen of England, lady of Ireland and Duchess of Aquitaine, her valet John le Butiller, if it please her, sends greeting and as much as he can of reverence, service and honor. Know, my lady, that I had spoken on your behalf with a woman of Didmarton named Cecily Tosard, concerning a carucate of land which she wished to leave, the which is adjacent and very convenient to your manor of Sherston. It was agreed in this form, that she would enfeoff you of the remainder to the extent of that carucate and would

retain it for her life. And on your behalf I so manoeuvred, by the good will of this woman, to have seisin of the land for four days. And then there came a knight, Sir Robert Burdon, who has ejected you from this land and is entered in seisin of the land. Therefore, my lady, if the council of our lord the king and your own so advise you, procure if you please writs of our lord the king to the sheriff of Gloucester that this land be taken into the hand of our lord the king so that right may be done you. My lady, may God keep you.[15]

This letter may have been followed by an urgent warning that the land be taken into the king's hand lest it be irretrievably lost to the queen, but apparently before anything was done another letter reached her, sent by the same John Besilles who conveyed Sherston and Woodrow to her:

To his dear lady the queen of England, if it please her, her own John Besilles sends greeting and as much as he can of reverence, service and honor. Know, my lady, that the knight Sir Robert Burdon, who ejected your men from the vill of Didmarton, is commanded to God and left this life on the Saturday next after the decollation of Saint John. And know, my lady, that he held of our lord the king in chief a manor in Devonshire called Kingsteignton, which was formerly a manor of the king and is worth £20 yearly. And of other lordships he held easily £60 worth of land, of which he held a manor near Sherston in the county of Gloucester that is called Oldbury, and another near Devizes that is called Poulshot, and other manors in different counties whose names I know not. The heir of the said Sir Robert is a son of twelve years, and he will be the heir of Sir William de Kaune of Wiltshire whose daughter the said Sir Robert had married, the which [de Kaune] is dead, and the father [Burdon] had everything, and the boy will be heir to the one and the other for all their lands, of which our lord the king will have the wardship as well as the marriage of the heir since Teignton in Devonshire is held of the king in chief. And pray the king, my dear lady, that he grant you this wardship and marriage, for it will be of great profit to you. Sir Hildebrant de Londres, sheriff of Wiltshire, has the child in his guard, and if it please you, my dear lady, that I have the custody of him, order that he be delivered to me and I will keep him safely until you order your will to be done. To God, my lady, and may He keep you always.[16]

Eleanor apparently had no interest in the Devonshire manor since she held no lands there, but on 20 September 1280 she was granted wardship of Oldbury, very near Sherston and Didmarton; Poulshot, hard by Woodrow in the southerly group of her Wiltshire estates, was granted her in wardship the next December. She obtained custody of Burdon's son Nicholas, who grew up in her children's household. It appears she took advantage of his minority to regain seisin at Didmarton: just come of age, he brought a complaint before the 1291 inquest and proved that Cecily Tosard's conveyance was invalid. She held the land by the enfeoffment of Nicholas' father; Botiller, maliciously or otherwise, had misled Eleanor as to the facts.[17]

The explicit documentation on the Didmarton transaction is tacitly echoed in further additions to Eleanor's estates in Gloucestershire and Wiltshire. Toward the end of 1280 she was granted the wardship of the lands of James Russell, which with estates in Dorset and Somerset included lands at Aust on the Severn; Aust was not in immediate proximity to Eleanor's other lands in Gloucestershire, and she quickly granted custody of it to Bishop Giffard of Worcester. When she was granted wardship of some Fitzalan lands in 1284, however, she retained the manor at Acton Turville, near Sherston, until the heir came of age in 1287. The promise of manors near both the Wiltshire groups came in 1287, when the king and queen purchased from Matthew fitz John the reversion to his estates in Gloucester, Wiltshire, Devon, and elsewhere. To the northern group of Eleanor's manors along the Gloucester-Wiltshire border, this would add Uley, seven miles north of Oldbury; and to the southerly group, Erlestoke and Rowde, the former just south of Poulshot and the latter roughly a mile to the north, with a manor at Yatesbury nine miles to the northeast. Three manors were added to the southern group in 1288, when the queen received the wardship of lands formerly held in dower by Maud Walerand: another manor at Yatesbury, one at Market Lavington four miles east of Erlestoke, and one at Keevil three miles southwest of Poulshot.[18]

The deliberate arrangement of Eleanor's estates could not be more clearly illustrated, explicitly mentioned as it is in the letters just quoted and in Edward's grants remarking Oldbury and Poulshot's proximity to Woodrow and Sherston.[19] A glance back at the Aylsham-Burgh-Cawston group created in Norfolk in 1278 and the Chatham barony in Kent reunited in the same year shows that this was not a unique case; similar progression can be traced in Appendix I for other shires (Essex, for example), and it can be recalled that Eleanor preferred to grant away only those of her manors that were at some distance from the major groups that were so neatly constructed.[20] The value attached to a coherent arrangement of the queen's manors in fact lies behind an incident mentioned earlier, involving the Northamptonshire knight Geoffrey de Southorpe. Eleanor in 1280 secured the manors of Torpel and Upton through John de Camoys' debts to the

Jewry, and in 1281 farmed them to Southorpe. Geoffrey already owed her £56:6:4, and by Easter term 1285 owed her a further £84:13:4 for three years' arrears in the farm of the manors. Later that year he went to prison. He had clearly had opportunity, however, to familiarize himself with the conduct of the queen's administration, and he now tried to escape from his dilemma by drawing her attention to what he could be reasonably certain she would regard as a choice property. He told her (presumably by letter) that he had sold his manor at Southorpe to Stephen de Cornhill who, in collusion with the abbot of Peterborough, enfeoffed the king's clerk Elias de Bekyngham of the manor; Elias then conveyed it to the abbey against the statute of mortmain. To emphasize the manor's desirability, Geoffrey pointed out that it lay just between Torpel and Upton. Then in Gascony, Eleanor accordingly went to the king and demanded that he take the manor into his hand, with the likely intent that he should grant her custody of it. Edward, however, deferred action until his return to England, and Geoffrey's account, though based on at least a grain of truth, won him nothing. He was freed in 1289 upon conveying to Eleanor seven librates at Lolham, near Torpel and Upton.[21]

Consolidation on the large scale as observed here for Eleanor's lands in Norfolk, Gloucester, Wiltshire, and Kent was followed up on a smaller scale within a manor once the estate was secured—the sort of large- and small-scale consolidations, common among thirteenth-century lords both ecclesiastical and lay, that increased administrative efficiency, added to the lord's demesne, and got into the lord's hands such valuable incidents as the advowsons the queen so industriously pursued.[22] An example is her April 1282 exchange with Geoffrey de Piccheford, whereby she granted him her manor at Drayton in Sussex in return for his right in Sheldon, a member of Ashford in the Peak. In Kent, the lands of the Crevequer barony reassembled in 1278 were augmented by purchase, ejection, and usurpation; the manor at Langley in Hertfordshire acquired from Stephen de Cheyndut was similarly improved. Subsidiary interests were purchased at Macclesfield, at Burgh, and in anticipation of the queen's dower tenure at Banstead in Surrey (another of John de Burgh's manors).[23]

It is in connection with such additions to the queen's estates that an element of disorder surfaces. Bartholomew de Redham claimed that her bailiffs disseised him of ten librates at Hautbois allegedly appurtenant to Scottow, and John de Antingham was ejected from land at nearby Witchingham and Alderford. William Payforer was ejected from 380 acres in Kent claimed as appurtenant to Bockingfold (a member of Leeds), and at Bockingfold itself the advowson was usurped from Leeds Priory. By 1278 the queen's men seized a wardship at Marple in Chester, allegedly appurtenant to Macclesfield, and after Hugh Despenser in 1287 surrendered to her his right at Denton in Macclesfield, her men ejected Hugh de Dutton from his holding. After Eleanor in 1276 purchased from Henry de Newburgh the manor of Hurcott in Somerset, she occupied a further ten and one-sixth fees in Dorset and Somerset, claimed as appurtenant to the lands originally purchased. After Edward's 1283 grant of the Maelor Saesneg, her bailiffs disputed its boundaries with Shropshire and Chester, so that the Botiller barony of Wem was shorn of one hundred acres, recovered only in Edward II's reign. At Hope Castle the bailiffs ejected John de Beydele from a moor at Duddleston claimed as a member of Hope, and Roger Mortimer of Chirk was disseized of a vill and a wood that were claimed as part of other lands whereof Roger had lawfully enfeoffed the queen.[24]

If in the drive to consolidate Eleanor could be a disagreeable neighbor, she was an equally unpleasant lord. A particularly unfortunate case involved Agnes de Garkevylle, widow of a tenant at Langley; the bailiffs so tormented her for six years after her husband died that she could not cultivate her land and was finally obliged to leave it. In the New Forest, William de Minstead' and Margaret de Budesthorn' were disseised of some sixty acres in Blackfield; the forest steward ejected the widow and sisters of Eustace Fucher from a messuage and three carucates, and Henry Toluse was disseised of some forty acres claimed as appurtenant to the forest. In other cases, Eleanor's officials refused to honor arrangements made by former lords of manors she acquired: after Robert de Crevequer surrendered Wood Ditton to her, Henry de Wotton was ejected from a messuage and forty acres there that Robert had granted him, and the abbot of Thorney was detained from a wood at Torpel sold to the abbey by John de Camoys before he conveyed the manor to the queen.[25]

That these usurpations were not redressed until the inquest of 1291–92 confirms that the queen's prerogatives, powers, and judicial immunities gave Eleanor a distinct advantage in adding to her lands as well as in managing them. Not only was she able to purchase and control land by herself (which she did do in a number of cases independently of the king), as those whom she disseised, ejected, or detained from land or rights had no remedy against her, she surmounted the contention and conflict that other lords could not sustain against tenants or neighbors upon whose rights they tried to encroach. This sense of high-handedness is congruent with evidence that Eleanor was greatly assisted in adding to her estates by her access to the king's clerks and the vital information they could supply. This aspect of her endeavors is most clearly glimpsed in cases suggesting that once the queen caught the scent of a potential windfall, she kept after it until the prize was won. An obvious example is the Didmarton affair discussed earlier; parallels also could be drawn with the Crevequer lands in Kent. A like case is that of Norman Darcy, whose debts were granted Eleanor by February 1275. After an agreement in that month that she would pay Jacob de Oxonia 200 marks in return for a ten-year lease of Darcy's lands at Nocton worth £40, there seems to have been a scurry to uncover the full extent of Norman's debts to the Jews (said in 1281 to be £950); in November 1275 their agreement was modified to give Eleanor lands at Nocton worth £60 for fourteen years. In other cases she did not stop with the grant of an individual's debts to the Jewry, but later obtained further grants of debts owed the king at the Exchequer. In cases like that of John de Camoys it was probably the later grant that enabled her acquisition of land from the debtor. The grant to her in Hilary term 1280 of all debts owed Hagin f. Moses brought her Camoys' obligations; to meet these, John in March 1280 demised to her for a term of years his manors at Torpel and Upton, but four months later she secured all his debts to the king at the Exchequer, and the manors were conveyed to her outright the next November. Stephen de Cheyndut came to Eleanor's notice in the spring of 1275, when one of his debts to the Jewry was granted her after it was established that another debtor was no longer liable; in November 1275 she received more of his debts, and in that month he conveyed to her his manor at Langley. The manors of Tothill and Gayton in Lincoln were secured around 1270 because Richard de Seez failed to ransom them after the Barons' Wars; when the manors were in her hands, Eleanor was granted Richard's debts to the Jewry and acquired further interests at Tothill. In 1280 Aaron f. Vives gave her all debts owed by Gilbert Pecche; she then obtained Pecche's debts to the king at the Exchequer, and Gilbert in consequence conveyed to her in June 1280 his manor at Westcliffe in Kent, followed early in 1284 by most of his lands in Essex, Cambridge, and Suffolk.[26]

It was this kind of thoroughness that won Eleanor Robert de Camville's manors in three counties. A tallage on the Jewry brought Eleanor Camville's debts by the fall of 1279, when he conveyed to the king and queen manors at Fobbing and Shenfield in Essex and Godington in Oxford; he retained for life manors at Westerham and Edenbridge in Kent. At just the same moment — October 1279 — Eleanor agreed to assist the prior and convent of Romilley in recovering a £20 rent and various advowsons detained from the convent by Camville; the priory would then enfeoff her of the whole for 250 marks, or a smaller sum if less were recovered. Everything was duly conveyed to the king and queen in Easter term 1280: the rent and two advowsons were at Fobbing and Shenfield, and the others were at Little Laver, High Ongar, and Stanford-le-Hope nearby. Though there were clearly two phases here, it is significant that the clerks who wrote up the 1281 schedule regarded the Camville acquisitions as a single transaction; it can only be surmised, however, that the same view was taken in other cases in which the queen acquired one man's lands piecemeal.[27]

Eleanor's resorting to collusion in the Camville case was not unique. She entered into other such agreements that were unsuccessful, and three querents at the 1291–92 inquest alleged that their estates came to her hands after she connived with third parties who unjustly obtained seisin and then conveyed the lands to her; in two of these cases there is reason to regard the complaints as well founded. In two other cases a role approximating that of the third parties mentioned in those 1291 complaints was taken by one John le Botiller, who is likely the same bailiff who arranged the unlawful Didmarton purchase. The number of cases in which members of the households were parties to the queen's transactions may, then, extend a network of collusive practices. Even less engaging is the queen's circumvention of such agreements after entering into them, as in the case of Hugh Venables' lands at Hope and Estun in Flint, which she obtained by Edward's grant after promising to assist Venables to recover them in consideration of twenty librates there. A comparable case is that of William de Montchensy of Edwardstone. Eleanor in 1280 or 1281 acquired his Essex manor at Quendon by reason of his debts to the Jewry, but only after she reached an agreement with St. Osyth's Abbey very much like those with Romilley priory and Hugh Venables. This was not the end of her interest in William's estates, which she continued to acquire bit by bit right down to the month of her death.[28]

The broad patterns discussed here may suggest calculated if not necessarily ruthless exploitation of the vendors' troubles, but the evidence also indicates some humane consideration for their dignity. The compensation the queen offered, for example, argues that she was not out to ruin them. Available evidence implies that monetary payments were generous; Crevequer and Camoys were granted life tenure in other lands, Pecche was scrupulously provided with rents worth as much as the lands he conveyed, and Camville demised only some of his estates, retaining others for life.[29] These men were not reduced to indigence, and Eleanor seems to have been well inclined toward some of them. Crevequer became a knight of her household. Robert de Camville's son Thomas was taken into her daughters' household; she paid for candles at Robert's 1286 funeral, left dowries for his daughters, and provided for his widow and even a widowed daughter-in-law. There can be

no doubt that her 1278 purchase from William de Leyburn was of great benefit to him. His father, Roger, was a good friend of both Edward and Eleanor
and had assisted her as she began to obtain lands in 1265; as it was Roger
who bought Leeds Castle from Crevequer, the manor was not anciently
part of the Leyburn inheritance, and after William agreed to part with it,
Eleanor obtained for him pardons of his and Roger's debts to the Jewry and
at the Exchequer.[30] Such courtesies do not suggest contentious conveyances.
Sedate transactions appear to be reflected as well in a lack of reference to
these purchases among the complaints at the 1291 inquest by those seeking
to recover lands Eleanor had held. Many complaints were brought by those
whose lands were not encumbered by Jewish debts but who now disputed
their conveyances to the queen, or those who were disseised or ejected from
lands. But of the fourteen who conveyed lands to her by reason of Jewish
debts, only one is known to have come before the justices—and as John de
Wauton's complaint implies that he did not leave his land willingly, he may
not have been as well treated by her as were other vendors.[31]

The patterns of discovery and pursuit, collusion and evasion nonetheless
pose intriguing questions. It would be satisfying, for example, to know just
how Eleanor (or her clerks) found that Camville was detaining advowsons
and rents from Romilley priory when she was already engaged in securing his
lands, but it is difficult to do more than hint at possibilities. The letters quoted
earlier on the Didmarton transaction show that Eleanor's local officials were
probably expected to pass along helpful information; some sleuthing by alert
clerks must be assumed. However these opportunities were identified, certain
factors must be kept in mind regarding the consequences: the degree to
which the king and queen consulted each other, her access to necessary information, and her powerfully enabling prerogatives. All these elements—thorough planning, the value of her relationship to the king, the emphasis on the
coherence of her estates—come together in an intriguing if obscure case, the
wardship of the dower lands of Robert Walerand's widow Maud. A prominent supporter of Henry III in the Barons' Wars, Robert was indirectly
involved in Eleanor's acquisition of the New Forest stewardship in 1270; the
office was hereditary in his family, but the childless Robert had given it to his
nephew Alan Plogenet, from whom Eleanor secured it. Robert died in 1273
leaving Maud and, as his chief heirs, a late brother's teenage sons, both half-
witted. Perhaps in anticipation of this situation, Walerand had himself and his
wife jointly seized of many of his manors, and conveyed others to Plogenet.[32]
But it was inevitable that most of Robert's lands would remain in the king's
hands long after the heirs actually came of age, and this made the Walerand
wardship an unusually secure, long-term prospect.

That Edward confided it to Eleanor has passed almost unnoticed by local historians, some of whom, unaware of the heirs' incapacity, could not explain why neither of them ever held the lands. There is no doubt that Eleanor held them; the manors are named in the summary accounts for her manorial issues in 1290 and in the enrolled accounts kept separately for the issues of her lands as late as 1300–1. A 1291 complaint against her officials states that the Wiltshire manor of Market Lavington came to Eleanor's hands at Maud Walerand's death, and in a letter to Burnell Eleanor herself stated in so many words that the manor of Hurst in that county was granted to her by the king with others of Maud's lands. The confusion may be explained by the lack of an enrolled grant to the queen, but the reasons for the omission are unclear. At Maud Walerand's death in 1288, the king and queen were in Gascony, but other grants to Eleanor during her residence abroad were duly enrolled. Possibly, however, Eleanor's tenure of the Walerand lands had been decided some time earlier. She became acquainted with the Walerand lands at the time of the New Forest transaction in 1270; one of the nephews was living with her children in 1274, so she must have known of his incapacity, and it seems she did keep an eye on Maud's affairs over the years.[33] However patchy the evidence, from 1270 Eleanor was surely aware that the estates would be in the king's hand for some time, and the location of Maud's dower manors as compared to some of the queen's estates suggests that the expectation of this wardship influenced some of the queen's acquisitions in the years before Maud's death.

Eleanor's accounts show that the Walerand wardship brought her manors or interests in Somerset, Dorset, Gloucester, Wiltshire, and Hampshire, five shires in which she had accumulated significant estates before 1288. It has been seen that Walerand manors contributed to the development of two well-defined groups of manors, one along the Wiltshire-Gloucester border and the other around Woodrow. Walerand lands at Steeple Langford and Winterbourne Isherton, together with lands at Compton Chamberlayne held in respect of the Haversham wardship granted the queen in 1274, helped link the Woodrow group to Eleanor's manors in the vicinity of Salisbury. East and south of Salisbury, Walerand manors at Broughton, West Tytherley, Sparsholt, and Meonstoke Walerand linked Salisbury and Southampton, where Eleanor held custody of the castle. Walerand manors at Broughton, West Tytherley, and Sparsholt, moreover, fitted neatly with lands Eleanor held of the Chaworth wardship from 1283 at Somborne, Weston Patrick, Longstock, and Stockbridge, the interests at Redbridge she held by Edward's grant, and a manor at Lockerley purchased from John de Cobham. And Walerand lands stretched southward from Bristol into

Somerset, expanding the queen's dower expectations at Axbridge, Cheddar, and Congresbury and her lands in the vicinity of Somerton. In Dorset, a Walerand manor at Moreton was near the Newburgh lands the queen purchased or seized at Poorstock, Winterbourne Belet, Winterbourne Came, and Woodsford.[34] The rate of coincidence between wardship and purchases seems rather high to reject out of hand the hypothesis that the 1270 New Forest exchange was the moment at which Eleanor first took notice of the Walerand estates and, presumably with Edward's concurrence, included them in her planning when she made later acquisitions.

Eleanor's criteria and methods in choosing and pursuing the estates she found desirable will now be evident, as will the fact that their accumulation was in its essentials an arm of Edward's policies. To restate the main points that have been established: the expansion of Eleanor's lands was effected in consistent consultation and cooperation with Edward's administration, with the object of providing her revenue and materials for patronage. The accumulation of estates was dovetailed with her dower assignment: initial acquisitions, many of them near manors Eleanor could expect to hold in dower, were followed up by additions nearby—the former held by Crown grant or secured through the lord's debts to the Jewry, the latter by purchase or a variety of methods that echo the exotic range of expedients adopted by Eleanor's bailiffs to increase her revenue. The planning that informed the process is evident in the choice of Jewish debts granted Eleanor in 1274–75, apparently selected to bring her specific estates that would fill out her dower expectations in certain areas. It would seem, indeed, that Eleanor could rely on Edward to grant her exactly those debts that would allow her to acquire particular estates—as with his 13 November 1275 grant of the Burgh, Leyburn, and Cheyndut debts and his order of 26 July 1280 to levy debts owed by Camoys, Montchensy, and Pecche, which led almost immediately to Eleanor's acquisition of lands from each man.[35] In the Venables case and in that of a 1290 grant of William de Montchensy's lands, Edward granted her the estates outright.

The preceding discussion is, of course, built up largely from evidence not available to those outside the administrative circle around the king and queen, but what her contemporaries could see of Eleanor's land gathering makes it hardly surprising that, as the Guisborough and Dunstable texts indicate, she was regarded as one who craved fine manors and obtained many of them. As the chroniclers' reports are thus well founded, Eleanor's relations with the Jewry should be examined too, as the background to Pecham's letters, the remaining sources for opinions about the queen's acquisitions.

As a child in Castile, Eleanor must have become accustomed to meeting with Jews on a regular, even familiar, basis. More numerous than the English

Jews and less culturally distinct from their Christian neighbors, Castilian Jews offered that monarchy a learned and cosmopolitan labor pool whose members had important positions in royal financial administration and diplomacy, and whose numbers were helpful in resettling uninhabited areas following the thirteenth-century reconquest. Castilian kings took special advantage of Jewish learning: Jewish physicians had attended Eleanor's ancestors from the eleventh century—including both her parents—while Jewish astronomers and translators were prominent among Alphonso X's scholarly collaborators. When Eleanor arrived in England in the mid–1250s, however, anti-Jewish sentiment there was growing. Very shortly before her arrival, the death of "little" St Hugh of Lincoln had newly inflamed Christian feeling against the Jews; the December 1255 pardon for that murder granted to a Jew by Henry III at the instance of Eleanor's *ayo* García Martínez suggests a Castilian sympathy for the Jews that contemporaries might have suspected Eleanor of retaining throughout her life in England. Her relations with them require reexamination to see if she was as openly familiar and cordial with them as her background suggests she might have been.[36]

Certainly Eleanor's property dealings involving the Jewry contrast with the attitude of the queen-dowager, who was not averse to taking a profit from the Jews but generally held aloof from the possibility of obtaining land by trafficking in Jewish debts. In 1275 the dowager induced Edward to expel all Jews from towns she held in dower, and she was said to have urged him to order the Expulsion of 1290. It has been suggested that Eleanor of Provence's attitude toward the Jews was shaped by her Franciscan spiritual advisors, and it may be noted here that John Pecham, who rebuked Eleanor of Castile for her traffic with the Jews, was of that Order.[37] The question naturally arises whether Eleanor of Castile's favored Dominican friars influenced her relations with the Jews. The special responsibility for conversions entrusted to both Orders meant that the friars were in frequent contact with Jews, and many were intimately acquainted with Jewish scholarship. Their familiarity with Jewish society made the friars one of the groups most vulnerable to Jewish influence; some few embraced Judaism, but others reacted by expressing violent antagonism against the Jews. Such men were unlikely to regard complacently the novelty of a prominent Christian laywoman, educated and cosmopolitan, mingling with Jews on a regular basis. Indeed, as the cultural background the queen shared with the Jews was a factor not likely to be lost on experienced and well-traveled churchmen, her literary activity and sophistication could well have heightened the friars' anxieties. If the

Dominicans did anything to shape Eleanor's attitude toward the Jews, probably it was not to encourage her to consort with them. On the other hand, the fact that they did not convince her to abandon transactions with the Jewry calls for attention to the spiritual advice the friars were offering her. The subtle evolution of thirteenth-century Church teachings on usury to admit the distinction between usury and interest (understood as compensation for risk assumed in extending a loan) could not apply to Eleanor, who was not an original party to the Jewish debts she exploited. But she might appeal to the distinction evolved in the wake of the Fourth Lateran Council (1215) between "excessive" usury, which was condemned, and "moderate" usury, held by some to be permissible. As in some cases the sums Eleanor exacted were noticeably reduced from the amounts owed, perhaps the Preachers whom she evidently favored over the bishops drew a line here to her advantage. (Was this the Franciscan Pecham's meaning when he condemned anyone who told her usury was not mortal sin? Or was he referring to some such individual as Walter de Kancia?)[38]

The foregoing implies that while Eleanor was willing to profit from Jewish debts, she did not openly associate with Jews. What is known of her behavior toward them seems, indeed, less in keeping with the appreciative attitude toward the Jews attributed to Alphonso X than with that of Edward I, inspired by what has been called "sincere bigotry," or with that of Louis IX, informed by a crusader's religious zeal and reforming spirit. A second look, moreover, indicates that Alphonso X was less benevolent toward the Jews than has been thought. Like Christians everywhere in medieval Europe, he esteemed the talents of individual Jews and rewarded those who served him; but it was easy for a Jewish official to lose his favor, and toward Jewish society as a whole he maintained a less welcoming stance.[39] Eleanor, too, favored certain Jews, as when in May 1281 she induced Edward to confirm as archpresbyter the former excommunicate Hagin f. Cress, later known to royal clerks as "the queen's Jew"; but scrutiny reveals that her acts of patronage profited only those individuals who were of some service to her. There were also acts of pillage, including the reduction to indigence of the family of Jacob f. Moses, whom Eleanor had named her goldkeeper at the Exchequer of the Jews in 1274.[40] It is noteworthy too that the circle of Jews most regularly involved in Eleanor's land transactions was a small one. Hagin f. Cress was not the only member of his distinguished family involved in Eleanor's business; his uncle was mr Elias of London, with whom the queen had financial contacts as early as 1275, and some of whose debts were granted her after his death in 1284.[41] Aaron f. Vives was not a member of the same family, but he was "the Jew of the king's brother," and from 1280 was connected with Eleanor's acquisition of the estates of Gilbert Pecche and later those of John de Wauton in Surrey.[42] Her relations with Benedict de Wintonia dated from 1269, and in 1276 she named him her goldkeeper at the Exchequer of the Jews; he was among those hanged for clipping the coin in 1278.[43] (These five account for the majority of Eleanor's transactions involving debts to the Jewry, but of course they were not the only Jews with whom she had business; Edward's comprehensive grants of individual Christians' debts to the Jewry, and the payment of queen-gold when the Jewry was tallaged, brought her into contact with many other lenders, who appear only briefly in her records.)[44] So far, from revealing Eleanor as well disposed to the Jews, the profile sketched here implies opportunistic exploitation,[45] reflecting the fact that the sole reason for her relations with them was that they offered a convenient means to secure land or cash.

As anticipated by consideration of the Dominicans' influence on Eleanor's ties to the Jews, there exists no proof that she actively fraternized with the Anglo-Jewish community. Wardrobe and treasury accounts offer no evidence for her personal contacts with Jews, no sign that the intellectual vitality of the Anglo-Jewish community attracted her interest, no hint that Jewish merchants conveyed her exotic purchases. Her records identify neither Jewish servants nor physicians; they refer to a Jew but once, obliquely and not by name. Only one of her extant letters addresses a Jew.[46] Evidence for Eleanor's contacts with the Jewish community is confined to the rolls of the Exchequer of the Jews, the rolls of Chancery, and queen-gold accounts, all of which associate her with the Jews in name only and with exclusive reference to estates and revenue, or to the few for whom she obtained favors from the king. While it is possible now and again to read between the lines and suppose that Eleanor might have met personally with a moneylender in connection with the debts of a particular lord or a certain estate in which she was interested, the records leave the impression that her business with the Jews was usually negotiated by her shrewd and experienced clerks, Walter de Kancia as always the craftiest among them.[47] The queen's relations with the Jewry were, then, remote, and almost certainly they involved little more than her exploitation of Jewish debts to secure lands or cash. These distant and businesslike dealings recall the signs that her land gathering followed well-defined guidelines, and further indications of a reasoned approach are discernible in patterns in the land transactions she effected through Jewish debts. These imply that a precisely calculated use of the debts was integral to the process as Eleanor's lands were accumulated.

It will be evident from Appendix I that the expansion of the queen's lands was most rapid in the late 1270s, down to 1280–81. None of her accounts survives for that period, but clearly at the outset of the additions to her estates, her income could not have reached the impressive totals of the later 1280s. The copious grants of Jewish debts between 1274 and 1279 would appear to have provided cash for Eleanor's expenses and for her initial purchases of land (assisted by Edward as necessary). By the late 1280s her lands were ample enough for their issues to finance new purchases, as recorded in her wardrobe and treasury accounts from those years.[48] Eleanor's acquisition of lands by means of Jewish debts in fact tapered off markedly after 1281, and it may be no coincidence that the much-cited Close roll schedule was drawn up in that year. Jewish debts were exploited early in the expansion of her estates to secure well-located or sizable amounts of land from such men as Crevequer, Leyburn, Burgh, Pecche, or Camville, as a means to establish the foundations of growth in the major groups of her lands. The schedule would appear to mark the point in the process at which the debts had achieved that initial purpose. With the obvious exceptions of lands Eleanor was granted or acquired in Wales after 1283, most of her acquisitions in the 1280s expanded or consolidated the interests she established in the 1270s and are not stated to have involved vendors' debts to the Jewry. Of the four who conveyed lands to her by reason of Jewish debts after 1281, moreover, two had done so before 1281 and the later purchases most probably represent the second phase of acquiring their estates, as already discussed.[49]

The lessening of Eleanor's reliance on Jewish debts to secure land in the 1280s may relate as well to the 1269 prohibition of the pledging of land held in fee to secure loans from the Jews; the amount of property thus encumbered must have declined thereafter. The Jews' worsening financial position in the 1280s also has to be taken into account. The last comprehensive grant of an individual Jew's debts came to her in 1279; nor did she thereafter obtain any Christian's total debts to the Jewry. She continued in the 1280s to acquire debts through queen-gold and the operations of the Exchequer of the Jews—from Jews' amercements for default, for example —and certainly exacted them from the debtors; the difficulties in securing payment of such debts, noted in Chapter Two, may mean that some granted her in the 1270s were still being collected in the 1280s. But there is no reason to think debts were granted her after 1280 on the scale seen in the 1270s. In 1283, rather, she was granted the profits of concealed goods and chattels of condemned Jews, perhaps thought more likely than fresh grants of debts to provide worthwhile income as the desperate moneylenders were driven to commit transgressions of coin and to conceal the goods of deceased family members.[50]

In any event, as can be seen in Appendix I, the majority of the queen's acquisitions did not involve Jewish debts. The impression given by Pecham's letters and the Close roll schedule notwithstanding, Eleanor did not exploit Jewish debts to sweep away poor knights on a scattergun basis across the realm;[51] indeed, as she apparently could rely on Edward to grant her precisely those debts that would enable particular purchases, Jewish debts might have functioned rather as effective guarantees that lords would compliantly part with certain estates identified as suitable and convenient to Eleanor's purposes; like John de Burgh and William de Leyburn, they might even have been glad of the chance to clear their debts. These points raise obvious questions about the activity Pecham lamented as late as 1286, but it will be better to defer discussion of this point until more material is digested.

The planning and organization that imply a calculated exploitation of Jewish debts can be seen as well in the bursts of activity evident among the records for Eleanor's purchases. Edward's orders of July 1280 and the acquisitions that soon followed can be recalled in this regard, as can his grants in November 1275 of the Burgh, Leyburn, and Cheyndut debts made at almost the same moment Eleanor finalized the arrangements for Stephen Darcy's manor at Nocton. There was a similar sequence between June and November 1278, when she secured manors in Kent and Norfolk. Comparable arrays can be seen in November 1280, July 1281, February 1284, June and July 1285, and February 1286. Such concentrations of activity have been found significant in other areas of Eleanor's administration, and they merit examination here too.[52] Terminal dates for thirteenth-century parliaments are not readily available, for example, but the dates of a number of documents for the queen's purchases show they were enacted around the times parliaments were convened.[53] This coincidence may explain the availability of the prominent witnesses to the queen's acts. Unlike Eleanor of Provence's acts—usually attested only by her family, householders, and those party to the acts—Eleanor of Castile's acts were witnessed by royal officials, earls, members of the king's council, justices, and prominent royal clerks, but rarely by members of her household other than the stewards or her chief clerks.[54] The queen-dowager's acts thus appear almost as those of a private individual; Eleanor of Castile's, in contrast, as those of a queen whose transactions were of some consequence to the king. The association of these transactions with parliaments and their dignified attestations were an obvious expression of Edward's approval of his wife's purchases and could have helped to legitimize her activities by casting over them the figurative mantle of his authority and protection. But

reports of the queen's purchases must have spread through the crowds in
attendance at parliaments, to be publicized as participants made their way
home, full of gossip about goings-on in high places. (The queen's own incessant travels could be remarked again in this connection, for her visits, with
the king, associated them visibly and physically with her new properties. In
the last fifteen months of her life, there were visits to Leeds, Burgh,
Lyndhurst, Feckenham, Thurrock, Langley, Torpel, and Macclesfield.)[55]

Impressive witness lists may confirm the significance of the queen's acquisitions, but they relegate Eleanor herself to the background and plainly raise
questions about her personal role in these acquisitions. It was seen in
Chapter Two that she was the final authority regarding the administration
of her manors, but—given the fact that Edward had a strong interest in
many of her purchases—it has to be asked whether it was she, her clerks,
or even the king's officials who really arranged and effected her purchases.
As might be anticipated, however, the sources here are rarely as commu-
nicative as could be wished. It is significant that while Eleanor's council is
only fitfully documented, it often appears in connection with acquisitions of
one kind or another, helping to assess the ransom for Richard de Seez'
lands before 1270, in 1279 advising on the rents and advowsons to be
secured from Robert de Camville through Romilley Priory, and in 1280 on
the acquisition of John de Montfort's marriage.[56] A unique account of the
council's role regarding Eleanor's estates is found in John de Wauton's
1291 complaint, which states that he was brought into Eleanor's council by
John de Kirkby, and that those present included John de Berewyk', John
de Lovetot, and Guy Ferré. The evidence implies a date around 1286 for this
meeting, at which Wauton showed Eleanor that Aaron f. Vives had
"seduced" him into a number of heavy loans, and asked for help in paying
them without risking the loss of his lands. This was not so suicidal a move
as might appear; Eleanor had helped others in this way, and she now
promised Wauton her assistance. The rolls of the Exchequer of the Jews
confirm that Wauton was deeply indebted to Aaron—and they also show
that in July 1286 he contracted a number of new debts to Hagin f. Cress,
"the queen's Jew," to whom he was not previously bound. Soon thereafter
Hagin gave these new debts to Eleanor, so that Wauton lost to her his
manor at West Betchworth.[57] The council's advisory role is clearly implied,
though it is not stated whether they connived as a body at what was almost
certainly collusion between Eleanor and Hagin. (The council's membership
at Wauton's interview is not without its own interest. Lovetot will be remembered as the accommodating auditor of Eleanor's accounts and as a lively
accumulator of manors in Essex. In 1286 Berewyk' was her goldkeeper, a

position that kept him in contact with the Exchequer of the Jews, and it may not be coincidental that Edward granted him the manor at Betchworth after Eleanor's death.)

While Wauton's complaint indicates that Eleanor worked directly with her advisors, it does not verify her personal role. Evidence for the queen's real involvement in the accumulation of her estates is provided by letters that passed between her and her advisors, most revealing among them a series from the summer of 1279 that prepared the king's seizure of Gartree hundred from William de Boyville, to whom Eleanor leased it at farm but who failed (like Geoffrey de Southorpe) to pay her the farm. The first of these letters is anonymous, but another, from the justice Geoffrey de Leukenore, makes it clear that the unknown informant was Eleanor's steward, Walter de Kancia, whose brisk address shows that Eleanor and her steward were accustomed to deal with each other in the closest confidence:

> My Lady, know that I have spoken with Sir Geoffrey de Leukenore of the matters concerning William de Boyville, and I have so done that he will send you by his son in a letter the things he has found about him [Boyville] in his rolls, the which it is good you shall show to Sir John de Kirkby and so do, if it please you, that the hundred of Gartree shall be seized into the king's hand so the truth may be better determined. And I pray that you will speak fairly to the bearer of this letter, and if his father has anything to do with Sir John de Kirkby, ask of him [Kirkby] what seems good to you. And order his father that he send you the other things he has about William [de Boyville]. To God, my Lady; may He keep you.

> To his very dear lady, Lady Eleanor by the grace of God queen of England . . . her liege knight, if it please her, Geoffrey de Lewkenore sends greetings and all his duty. Dear lady, I lately received letters of our lord the king that I should send him the inquests that were taken by Sir Gilbert de Preston and me in the time of his father our lord King Henry, concerning Sir William Morteyn and Sir William Bagot and William de Boyville and others in the county of Leicester. And, my lady, because the said Sir Gilbert de Preston was with me and I with him, I do not have those rolls with me. I cannot certify you as fully as if I had them in my keeping, but what I can find in my rolls I send you by my son, the bearer of this letter, according to the form agreed between Sir Walter de Kancia your clerk, and myself. And I send you, as my lady, by the same valet whatever I found in my rolls or may yet find about anyone of whom the said Sir Walter spoke to me. And when

I may enquire further, I will send it to you loyally and fully, as my
dear lady whose I am and wish ever to be. God in His mercy
grant that you do His will on earth, and to reign in Heaven without end.[58]

Eleanor's letter on a purchase in Ireland is also helpful, as demonstrating her
participation in the exchange of information:

Eleanor by the grace of God queen of England . . . to her dear clerk
Sir John de Kirkeby greeting. Since we have spoken with Sir
Roger de Clifford concerning certain lands and tenements that he
has in Ireland which we will buy from him, for the ordering of
which in proper form we send to you on this matter our dear clerk
R. de Geyton, bearer of the presents, and ask you strictly that you
give full attention to this matter, which our said clerk will explain
fully to you, so that by your discreet industry, in whatever way
seems best to you, this affair will be concluded to our profit.
Farewell. Given at Rhuddlan, the fifteenth day of February, under
our privy seal.[59]

Clifford's conveyance of this manor was dated 15 February 1283, most
probably the same day as Eleanor's letter. This letter recalls her April 1283
letter, also to Kirkby, reminding him "of that business we discussed with you
at your departure" and asking what should be done to further the matter.[60]
Like the letters on the wardship of Robert Burdon's lands, moreover, the
Leukenor and Clifford letters confirm that planning and deliberations for
the acquisition of her lands followed the queen, which must raise the
assumption that her role was an active one.

The speedy response in the case of the Burdon estates was repeated for
Gartree hundred and the Clifford manor, reactions that could have been
those of clerks or advisors acting in the queen's name. One letter, however,
does reveal Eleanor herself formulating plans and instructions on the
basis of information reported to her in much the same way Leukenore
must have done. On 18 September 1265 she was granted wardship of a
manor at Barwick in Somerset in the minority of William de Cantilupe's
heir, but by some oversight it was shortly thereafter regranted to another.
Before 30 September the following letter was dispatched to Eleanor's
clerk John de Loundres:

Eleanor, consort of the Lord Edward, to her loyal and faithful Sir
John de Loundres, health and good love. Know that our lord the
king gave us the other day the manor of Barwick with its appurtenances, at the solicitation of Sir Roger de Leyburn; and because it

is appurtenant to the guardianship of Cantilupe, my lord has given it to another, so that nothing of it is remitted to us. But there is another manor close by, in the county of Somerset, which is at the town of Haselbury, which belonged to Sir William le Marshal, who is dead, and held it of the king in chief; wherefore we would desire that you should ask of Sir John de Kirkby if the guardianship of that manor is granted, and if it is not, then that you should pray Sir Roger de Leyburn and the bishop of Bath on our behalf, that they should procure from our lord the king that he should grant us the manor until the coming of age of the heir of Sir William. And if it is given, there is another manor in the county of Dorset, which is called Tarrant, which belonged to Sir William de Keenes, who is dead, and he held it in chief of the king. Wherefore we would that if we cannot have the other, you should pray them on our behalf that they should apply to the king to allow us this one. The manor of Haselbury is worth less. And if neither, pray Sir Roger in this way. Tell him that the manor of Barwick that the king gave us at his suggestion has been taken from us, for this will tend to make us seem less covetous; and say the same to the bishop of Bath. And if the letters which you have concerning it can profit nothing for this affair, give them to the bearer of this letter, for he will carry them to Walter de Kancia, our clerk. Be careful to dispatch this affair, for it will be to our profit; and so suitably procure the affair that they shall not set it down to covetousness. Farewell.[61]

The letter has no dating clause and there is neither reference to, nor trace of, the seal needed to authenticate an order sent in Eleanor's name. Her direct involvement with the letter is also implied by its emphasis on avoiding suspicion that the new manor was sought out of greed; a clerk who merely put an order into written form would not necessarily include such a sentiment, and likely would not repeat it so emphatically, unless he was writing at Eleanor's direction. Whoever shaped the letter's precise directions was well acquainted with the king's circle and with Edward's advisors. Roger de Leyburn had been Edward's steward until Eleanor of Provence in 1263 accused him of leading her son astray; after he was sacked, it was suspected that he had misappropriated much of Edward's money. Subsequently Leyburn's allegiance to Henry III won him readmission to favor, and by 1265 he was once more among Edward's closest associates. It is noteworthy that Henry's initial grant had been made at Leyburn's request; Eleanor of Castile's hopes for his continued support—surprising given Roger's labors to restore peace to the kingdom just at this time—suggest that Edward was already interested in adding to her lands.[62] The bishop of Bath in 1265 was an equally strong choice as advocate with the king. Walter

Giffard was a brother of Bishop Godfrey Giffard of Worcester, whose family was close to the court and with whom Eleanor was friendly; a staunch royalist in the troubles, Walter was made Chancellor after Evesham.[63] The reference to John de Kirkby, then a clerk in Chancery, shows that Eleanor already had access to the records of Chancery, knew what was to be found there and whom to ask for it. Everything about this letter—its informality, personal language, knowledge of the king's circle—marks it as a confidential communication Eleanor sent to someone intimately familiar with her business; and John de Loundres fits that description exactly.[64]

As early as 1265, then, Eleanor was personally involved in the additions to her lands, and the location of her manors near each other was already a fixture of the process. It remains unclear whether she herself formulated this reasoned approach or whether it was suggested to her, and hence the importance of her reference to Walter de Kancia, some account of whose career has already been given. The 1265 letter is the first evidence Walter had entered her service, just as the outlines of her land gathering were being laid down. Her instructions that he should be given letters on the Barwick affair if all else failed suggests that she was already confident in his ability to see matters through to a satisfactory finish, and his actions on her service in the 1270s suggest that her reliance was not misplaced. As both steward of her lands and goldkeeper in the years after her return to England in 1274, he had at his fingertips just the kind of information needed to increase her estates most efficiently, and in both roles he was closely involved with her transactions, especially those through the Jewry. It was he who received the charters in May 1275 for Bartholomew de Redham's debts to the Jews and that November those for debts owed by Roger de Leyburn and John de Burgh. Kancia was also given the charters for debts owed Hagin f. Cress in 1275 and in 1280 those for debts owed Hagin's uncle Hagin f. Moses that had just been granted the queen. All these debts enabled Eleanor's acquisition of manors important to the early growth of her estates, especially in Norfolk and Kent, where the location of manors near each other was strictly pursued, in both shires by the piecemeal accumulation of the lands of one man: John de Burgh in Norfolk and Robert de Crevequer in Kent. Walter was prosecuting for Eleanor in 1280 for debts owed the Jewry by Gilbert Pecche, John Camoys, and Adam de Neofmarche; from Pecche and Camoys, Eleanor in that year acquired lands by reason of those debts and later arranged to secure Adam's manor at Carlton Scroop. That Kancia's uniquely devious abilities justified the combination of offices with which he was entrusted is implied by their separation after he died in 1283. It cannot, of course, be proved that it was Kancia who showed Eleanor the advantages of arranging her estates conveniently, though he is as strong a candidate as is likely to emerge. Like his sleuthing to increase Eleanor's revenues, Walter's labors behind the scenes were critical to the growth of her estates. It is tempting to link his death in 1283 to the slower rate of her acquisitions thereafter, though the slackening is more convincingly explained in other ways.[65]

Finally, the 1265 letter's reference to Kirkby points again to Edward's interest in Eleanor's land gathering. His stake in the expansion of her lands casts fresh light on her relations with his advisors, especially Kirkby and Robert Burnell: Kirkby evidently assisted with the arrangements preceding the king's 1283 grant to Eleanor of the Maelor Saesneg, and Burnell may have given her information of value in her pursuit of Jewish wealth.[66] Kirkby's name has surfaced repeatedly as the queen sought and received information from him—further proof that research was constantly carried out—conferred with him, and interceded with him as in Leukenore's case, presumably to assure the latter's future cooperation. (Leukenore's reference to "anyone of whom the said Sir Walter spoke to me" implies that inquiry was indeed ongoing.) Kirkby's function, evidently as a "fixer" of the first order, offers perhaps the most consistent evidence for the supporting role of the king's establishment in Eleanor's land gathering and the very careful planning that underlay it.

SUMMARY AND YET MORE CONCLUSIONS

Now that the record evidence has revealed the official side of Eleanor's land gathering and her personal role in it, the essential facts remain almost as they were at the outset: she acquired a great amount of land by means that were often questionable, and popular reaction was negative. The quantity of detail here added to these facts, however, suggests many ramifications to be pondered, and the effects the resulting tensions had on opinions of Edward and Eleanor are best approached by considering the strains her activity was likely to place on her relations with those segments of English society upon which her activities had the most immediate impact. The potential consequences advance an evolving theme in these pages—the chords a queen's behavior could strike across the social scale.

The relationship between Eleanor's purchases and the knights' problems, for example, requires reconsideration. The combination of Pecham's letters, the Close roll schedule and the 1258 petition implied that criticism of her activities centered on her use of Jewish debts to secure lands from indebted knights. This in turn would suggest that she was criticized chiefly by those who lost estates to her through the Jewry, or those at risk of doing so. But her generosity to the few whose lands came to her through the Jewry, and their apparent lack of ill will toward her, makes them (except perhaps for John de Wauton) unlikely critics. The relationships between Pecham's letters and the Close roll schedule have weakened, moreover, as the schedule's purpose and the chronology of the queen's purchases through the Jewry have been examined; and as magnates obtained lands through the Jewry less often than was believed to be implied by the 1258 petition, the petition appears to bear less directly on the queen's activities than was thought. Dismantling the connections among these sources suggests that just as Eleanor's methods in acquiring estates were more varied than allowed for by emphasis on her transactions through the Jewry, so reactions were likely to vary and hence may have been more broadly based than has been supposed. All those who had lost lands to other lords by reason of Jewish debts, or those at risk of doing so, might well feel menaced by Eleanor's few though highly visible acquisitions through the Jewry, and could react angrily against the usurers or, as in 1258, any who were thought to be profiting from them.[67] That a minority of Eleanor's purchases involved the Jewry, and that neither the Guisborough nor the Dunstable text refers to the moneylenders, suggest further that opinions of her land gathering did not rest solely upon her acquisition of lands encumbered by Jewish debts. Those who were financially troubled but not bound to the Jews could well have been agitated by her purchases from those in like case, and even those not burdened with debts but whose lands lay near Eleanor's new estates had the disturbing prospect of the many disseisins and ejections her men perpetrated.

Segregated from the 1258 petition and the Close roll schedule, Pecham's repeated insistence on the outcry caused by Eleanor's relations with the Jews has to be reexamined. At the time of Pecham's first letter in 1283, current gossip could well have centered on lands she acquired through the Jewry. That stage of the expansion of her lands had only recently peaked. But as in the later 1280s she used Jewish debts less often to secure land, Pecham's 1286 letter implies that the ongoing outcry he described was caused by her exaction of the debts—including usury, as indicated by her 1282 demand of St. Mary's Abbey, York, for a debt of £500 "and usury incurred."[68] As exaction of these debts must have affected many more people—most of them far from illustrious—than the relatively small number from whom Eleanor acquired land through their debts to the Jewry, Pecham implies a basis for gossip and outcry much broader and, for her soul, more perilous than the mere acquisition of land. There are echoes here too of the anxieties of those who feared in 1258 that the example of Jewish usury might lead Christians to engage in such lending, fears that underlay the Montfortians' ferocious savaging of the Jews.[69] On one level, then, Pecham was legitimately and genuinely concerned for Eleanor's soul, as was proper for the Primate, *ex officio* a spiritual advisor to the king and queen. On another level, Pecham took up an old strain in clerics' advice to Christian queens when he reminded Eleanor in his second 1283 letter that she must be a model of virtue to the realm.[70] He did not associate her traffic with the Jewry to her implied failure to offer such an example, but it can hardly be doubted that the notoriety of those associations was a detriment to her ability to do so. And as the scandal she thus caused might lead others astray, her traffic with the Jewry likely did dismay the bishops, contributing to Eleanor's remote relations with them—perhaps manifest in the fact that save for Burnell, few bishops are named among those stately witness lists to her acts.[71]

As English magnates acquired land through Jewish debts less frequently than was formerly thought, the connections inferred from the petition of 1258 between the queen's activities and aristocratic land purchases have become attenuated as well. But as the many ways in which queen and aristocracy could come into conflict involved land, wealth, and patronage, it is likely that her land gathering did compound the elements of tension in her relations with the higher nobility. Quite apart from the question of purchases involving the Jews, thirteenth-century English magnates showed little interest in securing land on the entrepreneurial scale implied by Eleanor's purchases. Differences in outlook are significant: for the aristocracy, land represented prestige, not money, but what the queen needed, and urgently, was revenue. The scale of Eleanor's activities implied extraordinary expense, but no English earl turned so much of his revenue to the purchase of land; even so energetic an improver as Prior Henry of Eastry at Canterbury applied only a small percentage of the priory's income to such purchases. Comment would have been excited by any lord who, exclusive of inheritance, acquired in a quarter-century lands worth some £2500. A queen who did so could well have seemed *arriviste* to her well-born subjects. The disputes over rents or advowsons that often followed Eleanor's acquisitions were conflicts common among knights desperate for resources, but which for the magnates might put her in an undignified light. (William and Joan de Valence found that even royal relatives were not safe from the queen's expansionist tendencies.) There is a contrast, moreover, between the swiftness with which Eleanor's clerks exacted Jewish debts or secured lands pledged for the debts, and the relaxed pace at which the Crown collected such debts; such briskness recalled the odious *parvenus* Merton, Langley, Stratton, and Simon de Wauton, who exploited their privileged access to the Exchequer to secure quick payment of Jewish debts.[72] The elder Hugh Despenser, stepgrandson of an earl of Warwick, stepson of an earl of Norfolk, and married to an earl of Warwick's sister, perhaps betrayed such a patrician wariness of Eleanor in 1287 when he pledged a manor at Soham for 1000 marks he owed her for his marriage without license. She might be expected to show some interest in adding Hugh's manor to her dower expectations there; after he acknowledged the debt he asked the Exchequer to promise that his manor — and the charter for the debt — would be restored once his fine was paid.[73] Despite the cultural interests a queen naturally shared with the aristocracy, Eleanor's resolute pursuit of property may have done little to endear her to the higher nobility.

It is harder to assess reactions among the rest of the population, those not immediately affected or threatened by the queen's activities. It was noted in Chapter Two that reactions to Eleanor's administrative behavior were not necessarily based on gendered assumptions; women often controlled substantial estates. That women rarely engaged in economic activity on the scale implied by Eleanor's acquisition of property, however, suggests that the same may not obtain for her land gathering and her financial operations. True, neither the Guisborough nor the Dunstable text deals with Eleanor's land acquisitions in gendered terms, echoing the lack of explicitly gendered language in which English chroniclers from the twelfth century discussed getting and spending; avarice was a sin in male or female. But queenly avarice was often suspected in earlier centuries if a consort applied herself too eagerly to management of the king's household and treasure, and Pecham's 1283 letter warning Eleanor of suspicions that she caused Edward to rule harshly does point toward a gendered criticism of her economic activity. As a woman, Pecham told her, she should show more mercy and pity than a man, and as queen she should provide the realm with an example of virtue; therefore she should behave better than anyone else in the kingdom. A corollary was that since as woman she was the more likely to fall into sin, she must as queen show that she strove the harder to avoid it. Yet her behavior openly showed her to be avaricious.

Eleanor's relations with the Jewry also implied her failure to adopt the gently persuading posture of the wife depicted in sermon *exempla*, confessional manuals, and canon law as the agent who might dissuade a usurious husband from such behavior to assure his salvation. The queen's exaction of usury cannot have advertised her as so meek a figure; as noted earlier, this most probably entered into Pecham's thinking on her inability to offer a properly virtuous image to the realm, and the actions that revealed her as the opposite number to the humbly dissuading wife might sharpen fears of her baneful influence on her husband. A queen's influence was acceptable so long as she exercised it on behalf of others and in a way that acknowledged the king's authority (by assuming an intercessor's idealized submissive role, for example). But the belief that Eleanor caused Edward to rule harshly would mean that she was thought to have rejected such modest demeanor, implying her failure to conform to Scriptural directives that women should exert influence only from postures of humility and weakness (Mark 9:34; 1 Corinthians 1:27; 2 Corinthians 8:9). With this in mind, it is appropriate here to raise the matter of Eleanor of Castile's known acts of intercession with Edward, which are rather fewer than those recorded for her mother-in-law or for Edward's second wife, Margaret of France. Other factors of course played a part here, among them an individual queen's reasons for exploiting the intercessory role; Margaret, brought to England by an unpopular peace treaty as the second wife of a king four decades her senior, and not the mother of his heir, would have had every reason to exert herself as an intercessor to win popular favor and support. Eleanor's sporadic appearances as an intercessor will be analyzed in their place. For the moment, the possibility cannot be discounted that her behavior made her appear an unlikely target for those seeking the king's favor.[74] In this respect it seems significant that the St. Albans encounter took place in April 1275, just before Eleanor's land gathering was undertaken in earnest.

The uncommonness of noblewomen's economic activity and the possibility of a gendered criticism of Eleanor's behavior suggests attention to the degree to which her unique legal status might be supposed to have allowed her to act autonomously. Certainly those of her consolidating acquisitions effected by ejection or disseisin, not to mention the fact that most of her victims had to wait until 1291 for restitution and compensation, testify to the advantages her prerogatives gave her. But the evidence for Edward's involvement with Eleanor's acquisitions argues that she enjoyed limited autonomy. Admittedly, the labors behind the scenes that supported her acquisitions—the search for information, the planning, the securing of grants—were probably not widely evident outside an administrative inner circle, but signs were not lacking that Edward extended his approval and protection to Eleanor's land gathering, and his control over her lands confirms her activities as an aspect of his policy as plainly as does his initial encouragement of the endeavor. Her capacity to exploit for purposes of patronage the lands she held of Edward's grant was restrained by the explicit provision that the lands not be separated from the Crown;[75] his control of the patronage she dispensed from the lands she acquired is evident from his confirmations of grants she made from that property.[76] The queen's prerogatives were put to good use for the benefit of the king and his house:

what she acquired was acquired for him and his heirs, and the resulting wealth must not be used to confound him. It is possible, too, that by encouraging Eleanor to acquire new estates—not forgetting the consequent preoccupation of managing them—the king channeled the energies of a vigorous and intelligent woman away from matters of state. The possibility also exists that in seizing upon the Jews to supply his wife with land and money, Edward in effect assigned her that means of adding to his demesne most likely to attract the sharper criticism and thus avoided it himself. (The idea that he thus exploited Eleanor may jar at first, given his efforts and those of his Chancellor, remarked earlier, to control her behavior; but he could restrain her moves against such individuals as Hugh Despenser or Bishop Giffard while still deploying her to implement policy in a manner likely to attract unfavorable attention.)[77]

It is understandable, then, that Eleanor's transactions shared the same "devious and grasping" nature of Edward's acquisitions, which were likewise criticized in his time.[78] The unpopularity of the pair's shared endeavors in this area could have done much to reinforce the idea that the queen was to blame, sharpening the very troubling possibility that the king was susceptible to her goading. The impact of Eleanor's economic activity on perceptions of the couple's relationship was probably heightened by that particular English touchiness about its alien queens, which gave charged overtones to Edward's decisions regarding Eleanor's lands and finances. By associating his wife with the Jews, aliens like herself, and with a financial role peculiar to them, Edward unavoidably intensified that alien aura that always clung to her. That she imported Castilian customs to England would already have emphasized the Mediterranean cultural origins she shared with northern European Jewry, likely eliciting something of the same distrust inspired among the insular English by Jewish wealth and sophistication. Given the notoriety of her dealings with the moneylenders, such misgivings could have fostered a belief among the English that Eleanor favored the Jews almost as fellow countrymen; though her personal relations with them were in fact distant, impressions of privileged links between queen and Jewry could have been unsettling to many.

A liminal figure as alien and woman alike, a queen was routinely linked to such marginal characters as the desperate, powerless petitioners who hoped for her assistance. A classic example is Eleanor's 1275 encounter with the townspeople at St. Albans; the abbot was discomfited at the prospect and turned her coach in another direction, but the mob pursued her with loud cries and she upbraided the abbot for trying to keep them away from her. Such moments could associate a queen with a liminal leveling inimical to the male hierarchy represented by both abbot and king. Though Eleanor was apparently less often approached by such people than were other consorts, she was associated with other marginals, such as the Jews and the alien Castilians and Picards she kept about her. Such links to the marginal or the institutionally disempowered could threaten the center of authority to which a queen was visibly if informally linked. It will be recalled that Eleanor openly advertised her proximity to Edward; that he showed his approval of her land gathering by associating her transactions with parliaments and with his officials further narrowed that sensitive distance between himself and her disruptive behavior. If Marian allusions could legitimize a queen's intercessory association with the disempowered, however, no such imagery existed to legitimize Eleanor's links to the Jews or the scale of her land gathering.[79]

Eleanor could not have been ignorant of reactions to her activities. She surely knew the contents of Pecham's letters; whether or not Guisborough's doggerel was repeated to Edward, it probably reflects gossip that must have been known to her circle.[80] To what extent she heeded such criticism can never be known. She dealt graciously with complaints of excessive demands on her tenants when she learned of them; but though also aware of the responses to her land gathering and her exaction of usury, she reacted less cordially, continuing (if less often after 1281) to secure lands from those indebted to the Jews, exacting usury from others, and retaining lands, advowsons, dowers, or wardships that had been usurped or detained.[81] A like contrast can be indicated between her anxiety as wife of the heir to the throne to avoid any impression of covetousness at a politically sensitive time, and her actions as queen, which created exactly that perception of herself. If the evidence presented in this chapter suggests a woman rigorously applying plans devised with care and attention to detail, there are hints as well of a keen eye for the main chance and a grasp of the occasional advisability of dissimulation.

Further questions are raised by the 1291–92 inquest. If Eleanor requested it in response to Church teachings that reparation was necessary to atone for usury, her real intent seems either to have been misconstrued or ignored. The justices' commission did not mention the exaction of usury; no complaints were heard concerning her collection of debts contracted to the Jewry, and as noted earlier, only one complaint was brought by a knight whose debts to the Jewry had cost him a manor. That estate remained with the queen's grantee, and the justices settled very few of the other complaints over her lands that did not involve debts to the Jewry. Except for blatant cases of disseisin or ejection, none of these actions ended in recovery of the lands; some were dismissed on technicalities or delayed so the king might be consulted, in which cases the lands remained in his hands.[82] One case, indeed, suggests that there was in some quarters a sense that proceedings should be controlled. The justices evidently grasped the implications of Richard de Stokepord's complaint—the only case on the extant rolls that accuses Eleanor of willful administrative vindictiveness—and heard the evidence in secret. After the bailiff at Macclesfield admitted that it was by her orders that he mistreated Stokepord', Richard tried to force the matter back into the open by asserting that Burnell knew the truth. The justices then relieved themselves of responsibility by telling Richard to take up his complaint with Eleanor's executors, including Burnell, who could handle it with his usual discretion.[83] The letter of the queen's request was honored, but public atonement apparently had its limits.

The attempt to conceal the Stokepord' claim suggests a conscious effort to manipulate Eleanor's reputation—not improbable, really, at a time when her funeral procession and burial were still fresh in the kingdom's memory, when Edward was commissioning the memorial crosses, religious services were being endowed, prayers for her soul encouraged, and indulgences offered to those who responded. In a real sense this discussion has now come full circle, and it remains to consider the ways in which these elaborate provisions have resounded as Eleanor's reputation has evolved over the centuries since her death.

Appendix I

Queen Eleanor's Lands†

The following catalogue is arranged by pre-1974 shires. Within each shire, lands held by Eleanor of Castile appear under three headings: her dower assignment, lands held by crown grant, and lands acquired. The queen did not enter her dower lands upon marriage or the king's accession, though some estates included in her dower were especially granted her by the king to hold during his lifetime; these last appear as both dower and crown grants, with appropriate cross-references. For the dower assignment made to Eleanor in July 1254, see *CPR 1247–1258*, 351; *RG*, i, no. 4277; Cuttino, *Gascon Reg. A*, no. 177(5); and *Foedera*, i, p. 304. This was superseded in October 1275 (*CChR*, ii, 192–93; lands described therein as "quit-claimed to the king by John de Burgh," identified from *CPR 1272–1281*, 41, and *EFF*, ii, 5 [no. 18], are marked in the catalogue with an asterisk [*]). Final adjustments made in 1280 are, in the catalogue below, nos. 24, 29, 221–22.

For Eleanor's Gascon dower assignment see *CChR*, ii, 143 (November 1275), and *CPR 1272–1281*, 380 (June 1280). She was not dowered in Ireland, but held lands there of the king's grant and by purchase. In December 1274 she was granted the ward of lands late of John le Poer of Dunoyl (*CPR 1272–1281*, 74; *CDI*, i, no. 1535, and ii, no. 169). In 1280 she and the king acquired lands in Wexford, Connaught, Kildare, and Galway of the inheritance of Christiana de Mareis; valued in 1282 at £181:11:8½, these were granted her by Edward, December 1284 (*CDI*, i, nos. 1771, 1798–1800, and ii, no. 279; *CPR 1281–1292*, 146).[84] The manor of Ratoathe (Meath) was conveyed to Eleanor by Roger de Clifford, February 1283 (*CCIR 1279–1288*, 230 bis; *CDI*, i, nos. 2055–56); she granted it that July to the earl and countess of Ulster (*CDI*, i, no. 2012; *CChR*, ii, 267). Eleanor had some interest in the wardship or marriage of Theobald le Botiller, who came of age in 1290 (*CHEC*, 84; *GEC*, ii, 449; *CCIR 1288–1296*, 320), and in the marriage of Juliana, widow of John de Cogan (*CCIR 1288–1296*, 147).

A contemporary list of rebels' lands granted Eleanor after Evesham requires comment. According to this source she received "all the lands of William son of Hugh Paynel, Richard de Sees, Robert son of Andrew le Blund except his land in Ginge, the manor of Bakewell that was Ralph Gernon's, [and] all the lands of Hugh Wake."[85] The lands of Richard de Sees or Seez, the manor of Bankwell and at least one of Hugh Wake's manors were indeed granted Eleanor between October and December 1265 (see nos. 38, 39, 134), but the list omits manors at Haddon and Codnor (Derbs.) formerly of Richard de Vernon and Richard de Grey, and John Despenser's manor of Martley (Worcs.), granted her about the same time (nos. 38, 237). There appears to be no further documentation for Eleanor's interest in the Paynel or Blund lands, but as there was clearly some confusion over grants made her in the months following Evesham (see nos. 188–89), grants of the Paynel and Blund lands were perhaps ineffective.[86] A confused case is that of Gilbert le Fraunceys, whose October 1268 acknowledgment that he owed Eleanor £250 at the next feast of St. John Baptist, to be levied in default on lands in Yorks., Bucks., and Cumbs., is identical (including the amount) to an acknowledgment at the same time by Richard de Vernon, which was unquestionably for the ransom of Vernon's lands (compare no. 38 and *CIR 1268–1272*, 95–96). No grant of Frauncey's lands to Eleanor is known. In January 1266 Henry III confirmed Edward's promise to Gilbert (who delivered the castle of the Peak to Edward in the troubles) that none of Gilbert's lands would be granted to anyone (*CIR 1264–1268*, 233). In Cumbs., Fraunceys held Rockliff of the Vernons (*CIPM*, i, no. 738) and in Derbs. held with other lands Nether Haddon (*CIPM*, ii, nos. 246, 455);

---

†Abbreviations used in the appendices are identical to those used in the footnotes (see Abbreviations, pp. xiii-xix).

Vernon's manor at Haddon was ransomed from Eleanor (no. 38). Fraunceys' October 1268 agreement almost certainly related to a ransom, but unless he agreed to pay half Vernon's ransom, further evidence for Eleanor's interest in Fraunceys' lands is lacking.

Eleanor's May 1280 agreement with Piers de Montfort of Beaudesert on the marriage of his son John (*CCIR 1279–1288*, 52) provided that she would acquit Piers' manor of Elmdon from Nicholas Sifrewast, and then hold the manor until she recovered any sums expended; when she had arranged John's marriage, Peter would enfeoff John and his wife of that manor, saving the queen's term therein. This is exactly similar to the terms on which she held Martock and Carshalton after providing the dowry for her cousin Maud de Fiennes' marriage to the earl of Hereford's son, and perhaps Marcle after Margaret de Fiennes married Edmund Mortimer (see nos. 196b, 214, and note 206). The financial aspect of her agreement with Montfort seems to have been observed (see Chapter Two, note 78), but it is unclear whether the terms concerning Piers' lands were implemented. He d. 1286 or early 1287; his son, of age by 1285, m. bef. March 1287. In April 1287, Eleanor wrote from Gascony to the earl of Cornwall, king's lieutenant in England, stating that before he died Piers enfeoffed John of all his estates (not only Elmdon), but that on Piers' death the lands were taken into her hands by her bailiffs. As the earl of Warwick now claimed that the lands were held of him, Eleanor ordered Cornwall to make inquiry into the matter and report to her (S.C. 1/20/45). Her accounts for 1286–90 do not, however, reveal any Montfort manors in her hands during that time, nor is any of them found in the records for the 1291–92 inquest.

Note may be made here of the many cases in which contemporary scribes or modern editors confuse the two Queens Eleanor, Provence and Castile. Cuttino, *Gascon Reg. A*, no. 177.vi, for example reads that Edward I in September 1273 granted his wife the isle of Oléron, but the editor notes that other texts of the enrollment read "matri" instead of "consorti." That Eleanor of Castile in November 1275 was granted the reversion to Oléron and other Gascon dower lands of the king's mother (*CChR*, ii, 193) proves the correct reading is "matri." Any such anomalies affecting this catalogue are noted in the apparatus, and wherever possible, evidence is cited to resolve confusion. Throughout the appendices, dates in square brackets are conjectural.

ANGLESEY AND SNOWDON[87]

Dower: None

Crown Grants:
1. 1284 (21 Oct.). In Anglesey, the manor of Rhosfair with the commote of Menai and a carucate of land at Llynfaes; in co. Arvon, the manors of Dolbenmaen and Penhethen, to be held for life and not separated from the Crown (*CChyV*, 290, 291–92; E. B. Fryde, *Welsh Entries*, no. 144; W. Rees, ed., *Anct Petitions*, no. 268; *CPR 1307–1313*, 101).

2. 1289 (6 Nov.). Wardship of the land of Glyndyfrdwy, half the land of Cynllaith Owain with the manor of Sycharth, and the manor of Rhuddalt in Bromfield, in minority of the h. of Gruffydd Vychan (*CChyV*, 321; *CFR*, i, 286; W. Rees, ed., *Anct. Petitions*, nos. 23–25; N. M. Fryde, "Royal Enquiry," 369–70; J. E. Lloyd, *Owen Glendower*, 8–13; *CHEC*, 62).

Acquisitions:
3. [1289 Nov. X 1290 Nov.]. lands at Bromfield (no. 2) of the inh. of William de Bromfeld'.[88] The Q perhaps only leased them; Bromfeld' released them to the K bef. 8 Jan. 1291 when in compensation he was gtd the Q's manor at Frant (no. 221; *CPR 1281–1292*, 414; *CCIR 1288–1296*, 335).

BEDFORD

Dower:
> 1254: None
> 1275:
4. Town of Bedford

Crown grants:
5. 1290 (3 and 12 Nov.). Custody of manors at Bromham, Renhold, "Dylewick" (?Wick End, in Stagsden), and Cardington, late of William de Montchensy of Edwardstone (*CCIR 1288–1296*, 108; *CPR 1281–1292*, 394; *CHEC*, 128; *CIPM*, ii, no. 610). As these were gtd the Q in the month of her death they do not appear in accts from her lifetime, but were later held by her exors (S.C. 6/1090/4); other lands in this gt are nos. 19, 59, 104, 209. On Montchensy, GEC, ix, 411–17; Moor, *Knights*, iii, 179–80; H. G. Fowler, "Montchensy of Edwardstone," 1–10; *Manners*, 113, 117, 126, 136. He also appears in connection with nos. 58, 60, 63.

Acquisitions: None

BERKSHIRE

Dower: None

Crown Grants:
6. 1280 (25 May). Wardship of a manor at Waltham in minority of Joan, dau. h. of John Jordan *als* le Forester, hereditary forester of Windsor (*CPR 1272–1281*, 371; *VCH Berks.*, iii, 172; for other lands appurt. to the wardship, no. 168). CPR states the gtee was Eleanor of Provence, perhaps a scribal error or editorial slip, though possibly the Q acq. this ward from the queen-mother. The Q in Apr. 1281 secured from John Jordan's br. Richard a release of all right in the inh., and ca. 1294 the h. Joan m. the Q's cousin John de Fiennes (*CCIR 1279–1288*, 119; *Kalendars*, i, 59; *CHEC*, 53). Before she d. the Q gtd Robert le Forester (?error for Richard abovenamed) wardship of the lands at Ascott in minority of John le Forester's h. (*CCIR 1288–1292*, 159; see no. 168).

7. [1280?]. Wardship of a manor at Upton, in minority of the hs of Ralph and James Russell. The date of the enrolled gt, 13 Feb. 1281 (*CPR 1272–1281*, 424), cannot be correct. Russell d. by Feb. 1280 (*CFR*, i, 122) and the Q gtd land at Upton to Adam de Stratton, 24 Nov. 1280 (E 40/87; *DC*, i, 8); her gt to Philip Popiot of £10 yrly from the issues of Upton predated that to Stratton, as in M1282 Adam was held to pay Philip the £10 (E 159/56 *m.* 4; *Manners*, 108). See also *CCIR 1279–1288*, 108; *CCIR 1288–1296*, 24. On the Russell family, Sanders, *Baronies*, 68; other lands connected with this wardship are nos. 12, 45, 77, 192.

Acquisitions: None

BUCKINGHAM

Dower:
> 1254: None
> 1275:
8. Farm of Aylesbury

9.   Manor and Forest of Brill

10.   Farm of Wycombe

Crown Grants.[89]

11.   1274 (8 Nov.). Wardship of a manor at Haversham in minority of Maud, dau. h. of
      Nicholas de Haversham (*CPR 1272–1281,* 64; *CCIR 1272–1279,* 109; *CIPM,* ii, no. 738,
      and iv, no. 371; *Feudal Aids,* i, 73; *RO,* i, 38; *RH,* i, 37). Maud m. Eleanor's cousin James
      de la Plaunche, 1289 (*CHEC,* 50 and note 182). Other lands appurt. are nos. 126, 167,
      229.

12.   [1280?]. Wardship of a manor at Hardwick in minority of the hs of Ralph and James
      Russell (documentation ident. to no. 7; see also *CCIR 1279–1288,* 108; Hill, ed., *Rolls
      and Reg. Sutton,* viii, 137–38). Other lands appurt. are nos. 45, 77, 192.

Acquisitions:[90]

13a. 1286 (Feb.). Two parts of a manor at Isenhamstede (now Chenies), purchased from
      Stephen de Cheyndut who had gtd it to Hugh fitz Otes "against the Jews" (on 29 Mar.
      1279, the K for Hugh's service gtd that he and his hs not be distr. in Isenhamstede
      for Cheyndut's debts to the Jewry [E 9/31 m. 4d]). *CPR 1281–1292,* 416, states that
      the Q held custody of Isenhamstede at a rent of £20, by gt of Stephen de Cheyndut
      of whom fitz Otes held by knt service; but see *DC,* i, 7 *bis; Kalendars,* i, 58 (no. 181);
      VCH Bucks., iii, 207–8; and no. 13b. Held for 1 fee of the honor of Wallingford (*BF,*
      466, 467, 470; *RH,* i, 46). In 1275 the Q acq. Cheyndut's manor at Langley (no. 105a)
      by reason of his debts to the Jewry; in Nov. 1279 a debt for his for £50 came to her
      when she was gtd all debts owed Hagin f. Moses (*CCIR 1272–1279,* 547; E 9/33 m.
      6), but it is unclear if the Isenhamstede conveyance resulted from the 1279 gt. The
      date is known from the Q's payment of £20 to Joan wife of Stephen de Cheyndut,
      for a quitcl. of all her right in Isenhamstede (Westm. Abbey, muniments 23627).
      Other transactions involving Cheyndut are nos. 105a, 137, 141, 246b.

13b. [1286 X 1290]. A third part of the manor at Isenhamstede, purchased from Sir John
      de Suleye to whom the Q's exors paid £10, M1291 (*Manners,* 99, 100).

14.   1286 (Feb.). A manor at Turweston with the adv., purchased for 200 marks from
      Simon de Ellesworth, rector of Thrapston. *VCH Bucks.,* iv, 252, states the manor
      escheated to the Crown and was gtd to the Q, but Westm. Abbey, muniments 23627
      has the above payment; *Kalendars,* i, 62 adds the adv. *VCH Bucks.,* ibid., shows the
      tenure acq. by the Q was ident. to the ½ fee held in 1242–43 by Humphrey de Scovill
      of Alan de la Zouch (*BF,* 870; in 1253–54 Scovill was said to hold one fee of Zouch
      here [*RH,* i, 33]); Scovill enfeoffed Ellesworth bef. 1284–86 (*Feudal Aids,* i, 79).
      Ellesworth owed the Q £25 in E1275, but the reason is not stated (E 159/49 m. 25),
      nor is it clear why he conveyed to her. The Q beq. the manor for life to Otho de
      Grandison (*CPR 1281–1292,* 417), who restored it to the K 1292 to be gtd to
      Westm. Abbey for her anniversary service (*CChR,* ii, 424–26; Harvey, *Westm. Abbey
      and Its Estates,* 31). Her exors in 1293–94 bought out tenants' rights at Turweston,
      presumably so Westm. might hold it unencumbered (*Manners,* 136, 138–39).

15a. 1287 (June). A manor at Denham, surr. to the K and Q by mr Robert de Fyleby, br.
      of Adam de Filby, rector of Denham from 1271.[91] In M1276 John de Bohun of
      Midhurst conveyed a life interest in Denham to Adam, who acq. the manor from
      Bohun and Joan his wife by fine, July 1281. Adam made over the manor to Robert,
      who attorned Adam de Hamwell to put the K and Q in seisin, 16 June 1287

(*Kalendars,* i, 38 [no. 34], 47–48 [nos. 107–9]; C 146/9953 [Robert's letters attorning Hamwell]; *VCH Bucks.,* iii, 257; Lathbury, *History of Denham,* 63–71; Harvey, *Westm. Abbey and Its Estates,* 32). Edward in Jan. 1292 gtd Denham for the Q's anniversary service at Westm. Abbey, which already had interests at Denham. Joan de Bohun sought to recover Denham 1300, 1314, and 1337 X 1339 (*CChR,* ii, 411; *CCIR 1337–1339,* 510; *RH,* i, 43; Lathbury, *Denham,* 74–76).

15b.   15 Edward I (1286–87). *Kalendars,* i, 48 (nos. 110–11) show a messuage at Denham acq. from Robert "ad molendinum," *als* "son of William the Miller of Woxebrigg'."

CAMBRIDGE

Dower:
           1254: None
           1275:
16.   *Soham (see nos. 23b, 24, 29a)

Crown Grants:
17.   1265 (20 Mar.). Wardship of a manor at Dullingham in minority of Cecily, dau. coh. of William le Fort *als* de Fortibus (*CPR 1258–1266,* 415). Cecily was b. 1257, her father d. 1259; the date of her marr. to John de Beauchamp of Hatch is not known, but their son was b. 22 July 1274 (GEC, ii, 48, and iv, 198). Other manors appurt. are nos. 186, 213; for John de Beauchamp, see no. 193.

18.   1284 (11 Feb.). Wardship of a manor at Foulmire or Fowlmere in minority of the h. of Ralph de Playz (*CPR 1281–1292,* 113; *CIPM,* iv, no. 121; *RH,* ii, 546; Sanders, *Baronies,* 83; GEC, x, 535–39). Other lands apuurt. are nos. 57, 149, 217.

19.   1290 (3 and 12 Nov.). Custody of a manor at Haslingfield late of William de Montchensy of Edwardstone (documentation identical to no. 5; see also nos. 58, 59, 60, 63, 104, 209).

Acquisitions:
20.   1281 (May). A manor at Wood Ditton *als* Ditton Camoys, demised to the K and Q by John de Camoys for 15 years from 6 May 1281 (*CCIR 1279–1288,* 120; further transactions, nos. 23a, 159a. Held of the hs of Ralph de Stivichale for £10 yearly (*CIPM,* ii, no. 212).

21.   [1284 (Feb.)]. 9¾ knights' fees at Haslingfield (no. 19), Kingston, Wimpole, Eversden, Guilden Morden, Bourn, Madingley, Rampton, Lolworth, and Long Stanton, acq. from Gilbert Pecche by reason of his debts to the Jewry (*CCIR 1288–1296,* 285; *RO* i, 47; Miller, *Abbey and Bishopric of Ely,* 177). The date is inferred from no. 22 and the Q's gt to Gilbert, 14 Feb. 1284, of certain of her lands elsewhere, to be held for life (*CPR 1281–1292,* 114). In M1284 Pecche ackn. the Q had gtd him £54 at Westcliffe (no. 118) and £8 in cash for her half of £124 yrly for life in cons. of lands lately surr. to the K and Q (E 159/58 *m.* 13d); the K on 27 Dec. 1284 assigned Pecche the farms of Ipswich and Chesterton and 78s. cash (C 62/61 *m.* 9; E 159/58 *m.* 5; compare *CChR,* ii, 281). This arrangement superseded the Q's Feb. 1284 gt to Pecche; her accts show the lands in that gt (nos. 128, 152, 159) were not in Gilbert's hands 1286–90. On Gilbert, GEC, x, 334–35; for other of his manors that came to the Q, nos. 22, 64, 118, 211.

22.   1284 (Feb.). Gilbert Pecche conveys to the K and Q the adv. of Barnwell Priory
        (*Barnwell*, 51–52; *CIM*, ii, no. 1847; *CPR 1281–1292*, 162–63).

23a.   1285 (5 July). A manor at Wood Ditton *als* Ditton Camoys, surr. to the K and Q by
        John de Camoys (*CCIR 1279–1288*, 360; *CIPM*, i, no. 443, and ii, no. 212; see also nos.
        20, 159a; GEC, ii, 506; Sanders, *Baronies*, 19–20). The Q beq. Ditton for life to Otho
        de Grandison (*CPR 1281–1292*, 417; *CChR*, ii, 424–26; *CPR 1313–1317*, 656).

23b.   1285 (5 July). Robert de Crevequer surr. to the K and Q his right at Wood Ditton
        (*CCIR 1279–1288*, 360). In 1278 the Q acq. Robert's manor of Chatham and mem-
        bers of that barony in Kent (nos. 114–116). In compensation Crevequer was gtd for
        life the Maelor Saesneg, but this he surr. to the Crown 1283 (no. 69), when he was
        gtd for life manors at Soham (nos. 16, 24) and Ditton (*CChR*, ii, 266; *CCIR 1288–1296*,
        225–26).

23c.   [July 1285 X Nov. 1290]. In 1291 Henry de Wotton' complained that he held for life
        of Robert de Crevequer's enfeoffment a messuage and 40 acres arable with appurts
        in Ditton Camoys, but after Crevequer surr. his right at Ditton to the Q, her men
        ejected Wotton. Inq. pr. Wotton's cl. but his action was not determined (JUST 1/836
        m. 6d).

24.   1289 (30 Sept.). A moiety of the manor at Soham, surr. to the K and Q by Robert
        de Crevequer who held it for life in compensation for his 1283 surr. of the Maelor
        Saesneg (*CCIR 1288–1296*, 56, 225–26; *CHEC*, 74 note 77). In M1289 Robert recd
        from the Q's treas. £14:5:4 for this quitcl. and 20s. for expns while in London
        (*Records 1286–1289*, no. 3194 = S.C. 6/1094/25 m. 4; *CHEC*, 74–75). See also nos.
        16, 23b, 29a, 69, 114, 115, 116.

CHESHIRE

Dower: None

Crown Grants:
25.   [1270? (bef. 8 Sept.)]. The manor of Macclesfield with its hundred and forest, gtd
        Eleanor by the Lord Edward (*CPR 1266–1272*, 459 is Henry III's conf. on the above
        date). Members incl. Adlington and Bollington, noted in the Q's accts in 1290 (S.C.
        6/1089/25 m. 2); appurts in Staffs. (no. 200) are mentioned, May 1281 (*CPR
        1272–1281*, 471–72).

Acquisitions:
26.   [1270 X 1278]. The wardship of lands at Marple and Wibberleigh, usurped from John
        de Mohaut (*als* Montalt). In parlt in 6 Edw. I, Mohaut cl. the Q seized the wardship
        though it pertained to the manor of Poynton whereof his wife was dowered; he
        sought it according to the law and custom of Chester and was advised to prosecute
        before the K's justices (*RP*, i, 10). ?Seized at the death of Gilbert le Frounceys, whose
        lands were perhaps gtd Eleanor after Evesham (see intr. to appx); Gilbert d. ca. 7 Mar.
        1278 holding Marple and leaving s. h. Richard, 15 (*CIPM*, ii, nos. 246, 455).

27.   283 [ca. 1 Apr.?]. A moor at Duddleston, usurped from Sir John Beydele as appurt.
        to Hope Castle (no. 67), though held in chief of the K as of the earldom of Chester.
        Beydele recovered the moor and £20 damages, 1291; his complaint, at the quinz. of
        St. John Baptist, dated the ejection eight yrs earlier, or to spring 1283 (JUST 1/1149

m. 2d). Hope was gtd the Q 24 Feb. 1283 (no. 67); a letter from her bf there informed her that on Thursday after mid-Lent Sir John "de Boydel" inflicted damages on her Welsh tenants (S.C. 1/11/46, s.d.). It cannot be doubted that "Boydel" and "Beydele" are the same man who, according to the letter, would have attacked the tenants on 1 Apr. 1283, eight yrs before the 1291 complaint. It is not clear whether the seizure of his moor was consequence or cause of his (alleged) trespass. Boydel held land in Duddleston at his death, 1307 (*CIPM*, v, no. 74; Ormerod, *Chester*, ii, 848).

28.   1283 (5 June X 2 Aug.). One hundred acres of land appurt. to a manor at Dodington, with the land called Hadley and "Hadley's Cnoll'," usurped from William le Botiller of Wem as appurt. to the Maelor Saesneg after 5 June (no. 69) and bef. 2 Aug., 1283 (*CChyV*, 11; *RP*, i, 279; *CIM*, ii, no. 195; *CPR 1313–1317*, 686–87). The lands lay in Chester and Salop. (see no. 181). Another usurpation from the Botiller family is no. 234.

29a.   15 Edw. I (Nov. 1286 X Nov. 1287). Hugh Despenser releases to the K and Q his right in Bollington in Macclesfield (*Kalendars*, i, 62 [no. 210]). In Aug. 1283 the Q was gtd the wardship of lands late of Payn de Chaworth (no. 89), and Despenser by 1286 m. Chaworth's widow without license (GEC, iv, 265–66). A letter from William de Valence to John de Kirkby states the Q exacted 1000 marks from Hugh because of the marr. (S.C. 1/10/109, s.d.). Bollington was taken into the K's hands Jan. 1285, as Hugh took emends of ale without warrant (Stewart-Brown, ed., *Rolls of Chester*, 214, 225). Hugh on 27 Jan. 1287 ackn. he owed the Q 1000 marks to be paid by 29 Nov. follg, and pledged his right at Soham, Cambs. (no. 16; E 159/60 *m.* 15d); on 15 Feb. 1287, Hugh came bef. the Exch. and asked assurance that on payment of the 1000 marks, Soham would be restored to him with the charter for the debt (E 159/60 *m.* 4d). At the K's order the Q pardoned the 1000 marks, 25 June 1287 (E 159/61 *m.* 1d); Edward on 8 Nov. 1287 pardoned 2000 marks for the marr. (*CCIR 1279–1288*, 462), probably in cons. of Hugh's surr. of Bollington. See also nos. 29b, 175.

29b.   [June 1287? X Oct. 1288]. A third part of the manor at Bollington, incl. a third of the chief messuage and a third of a mill with appurts, from which the Q's bfs ejected Hugh de Dutton after Hugh Despenser surr. Bollington. Dutton brought an action to recover his right in the eyre at Macclesfield, Oct. 1288; the bfs answered that the K was fully enfeoffed by Hugh Despenser and was in peaceable possession, but Dutton might sue against the K (Stewart-Brown, ed., *Rolls of Chester*, 239–40). In 1291 Dutton sought to recover the land; his complaint was dismissed as he had a like action pending in another court (JUST 1/1149 *m.* 10). See *CIPM*, iii, nos. 219, 220.

CORNWALL

Dower: None

Crown Grants: None

Acquisitions: None[92]

CUMBERLAND

Dower: None

Crown Grants: None[93]

Acquisitions: None

DERBY

Dower:
>   1254:
> 30. Castle and town of the Peak (= no. 35)
>   1275:
> 31. The hundred of Ashbourne (exch. 1280 for Burstwick and Hedon, Yorks. [= nos. 243, 244]: *CPR 1272–1281,* 380).
>
> 32. Castle and town of Bolsover
>
> 33. Town of Derby
>
> 34. Castle and town of Horston
>
> 35. Castle and town of the Peak (= no. 30)
>
> 36. The hundred of Wirkesworth (exch. as above, no. 31)

Crown Grants:[94]
> 37. 1264 (18 Apr.). A manor at Ashford in the Peak, gtd Eleanor by Henry III at the Lord Edward's instance (*ClR 1264–1268,* 28, says Edward gtd it; E 159/60 *m.* 4 has the inf. given here. Wrongly in Kent, E. B. Fryde, *Welsh Entries,* no. 25.) Members in Great Longstone and Sheldon (*RH,* ii, 287; see no. 40).
>
> 38. 1265 (17 Oct.). Manors at Bakewell, Haddon and Codnor, late of the K's enemies Ralph Gernoun, Richard de Vernon and Richard de Grey, to be held for life (*CPR 1258–1266,* 466). Bakewell was then to be held for 14 yrs from Feb. 1268 to pay the ransom (*ClR 1264–1268,* 518–19; *CPR 1266–1272,* 213; *RH,* i, 58). None of these manors is in the Q's accts, 1286–1290; all were presumably ransomed under the Dictum of Kenilworth.
>
> 39. 1265 (19 Dec.) A manor at Chesterfield, late of Baldwin Wake the K's enemy, to be held for life (*CPR 1258–1266,* 522). Prob. ransomed as were the rebels' manors in no. 38.

Acquisitions:
> 40. 1282 (8 Apr.). Twenty librates at Sheldon (no. 37), surr. to the Q by Geoffrey de Piccheford in exch. for her manor at Drayton, Sx (no. 219; *CChR,* ii, 261; *RH,* ii, 288). This land was gtd to Piccheford by Gruffydd Gwenwynwyn, whose widow sought dower in Sheldon and showed his charter to Geoffrey, 1291 (JUST 1/1149 *m.* 2d; E. B. Fryde, *Welsh Entries,* no. 25).

DEVON

Dower: None

Crown Grants: None[95]

Acquisitions:
41. 1285 (26 Nov.). The marr. of Amice, dau. h. of James de Boulay of Blackborough, sold to the Q for £20 by Henry de la Pomeray of whom de Boulay held by knt service (E 159/59 m. 19; *BF*, 791). The Q's exors sold the marr. to Guy Ferré for £40 (*CFR*, i, 288, 333). No. 251 involves others of the Pomeray family.

42. 1287 (17 May). Reversion to manors at Start Point, Yealmpton, Stokenham, Pyworthy, and Hockford Waters, conveyed to the K and Q by Matthew fitz John, who retains them for life (*CCIR 1279–1288*, 480; *CPR 1281–1292*, 270). This conveyance was made follg an agreement between the K and Matthew at Bordeaux, Feb. 1286, according to which Matthew would surr. lands worth £500 (*CChR*, vi, 294–95 = *Kalendars*, i, 49 [no. 122]). In 14 Edw. (1285–86) Matthew was paid £120 (*Records 1285–86*, no. 2338), and on 12 July 1287 another £120 (*Records 1286–89*, no. 4415). See also *CFR*, i, 242, 529; *CCIR 1307–1313*, 87, 510; Pugh, ed., *Feet of Fines relating to Wilts.*, nos. 184, 186; Beardwood, ed., *Trial of Walter Langeton*, 161–62. The final concord, 6 Oct. 1287, is E 159/61 m. 5. On fitz John, GEC, v, 442–45; Sanders, *Baronies*, 42, and *VCH Wilts.*, vii, 82–83; as he d. 1309, the Q never entered these lands. For other manors appurt., see nos. 82, 98, 235.

DORSET

Dower:
    1254: None
    1275:
43. *Winfrith Newbury (see no. 48c)

Crown Grants:
44. 1269 (26 June). A manor at Trente, late of Humphrey de Bolesden the K's enemy (*CPR 1266–1272*, 360). This manor is not among the Q's later accts, and was presumably ransomed like the lands of other rebels gtd her (nos. 38, 39, 134, 237).

45. [1280]. Wardship of manors at Mappowder, Haselbury Bryan, Sturminster and Kingston Russel in minority of the hs of Ralph and James Russell (documentation identical to no. 7; see *CFR*, i, 99). Other lands appurt. are nos. 7, 12, 77, 192.

46. 1285 (28 July). The Q is apptd at pleasure to custody of cos. Dors. and Soms., John de St. Laud to exercise the office of sheriff (*CPR 1281–1292*, 186).

47. [1288]. Wardship of the manor at Moreton lately held in dower by Maud, widow of Robert Walerand whose nephew and h. is an idiot in the K's ward (*CIPM*, ii, no. 6; Moor, *Knights*, v, 147–48). The background to this gt is discussed above, pp.136–38; other lands involved are nos. 79, 91, 102, 195, 232, 238.

Acquisitions:[96]
48a. 1276 (Octave of Mich.). Lands at Melbury Bubb, Swanage and Wraxall, amounting with other lands in Somerset (no. 197, below) to 6¾ fees, purchased from Henry de Newburgh for £200. E. Green, ed., *Pedes Finium for Somerset*, 318 (no. 48); E. A. Fry, ed., *Dorset Fines*, i, 243.

48b. [1276 X 1281]. In 1281, no. 48a was described as involving "an estate and fourteen knight's fees" (*CCIR 1279–1288*, 81). In fact the Q occupied as allegedly appurt. to the lands purchased further Newburgh lands in Dorset and Soms. extended at 7¾ fees. Those in Dorset were at Lyme Regis,[97] Gillingham, Powerstock, Woodsford, Winterborne Belet and Winterborne Came (*Cal. Memoranda Rolls*, no. 815). On Lyme, see also no. 51.

48c. [1276 X 1281?]. The Q also entered, as appurt. to no. 48a, one-third a manor at Winfrith Newbury (no. 43), which Newburgh's s. John apparently recovered, 1290 (*RP*, i, 21–22; *Manners*, 113–14, 118). His efforts to recover the other lands in 1291 failed (JUST 1/1014 *mm.* 4–6); he recovered lands at Powerstock and Gillingham in 1305, but those at Winterborne Belet, Winterborne Came, Woodsford, and Lyme remained with the K (*AP*, 256; Maitland, ed., *Memoranda de parliamento*, 158).

49. [M1276 X 11 Mar. 1279]. A manor at Chilfrome, conveyed to the Q by Henry de Newburgh (*CIPM*, ii, no. 298). Details are lacking; records cited for no. 48a–c do not mention Chilfrome.

50. 1280 (ca. 4 Mar.). The vill and port of Melcombe Regis (Weymouth), conveyed to the K and Q by the abbot and convent of Cerne (*CPR 1272–1281*, 365, 367). In 1291 the convent sought to recover their right, cl. the Q never paid them. They proffered a letter (Exeter, 1 Jan.; undoubtedly 1286 [*Records 1285–86*, nos. 1326, 1344–53, 1977, 1992–96]), in which she promised to promote the convent's interests, but as it did not address the Melcombe transaction the justices dismissed the complaint (JUST 1/1014 *m.* 7d).

51. 1281 (12 July). Land in Lyme Regis, with the hamlet of "la Burste" and the Cobb, conveyed to the K and Q by Elie de Rabayn and Maud his wife (*CCIR 1279–1288*, 130–31; *Kalendars*, i, 35 [no. 11]). This was Maud's inh., held as of her barony of Thoresway for ¼ fee (*CIPM*, i, no. 159; Sanders, *Baronies*, 88–89). Other transactions with this couple are nos. 138, 233; on Lyme Regis, see no. 48b.

ESSEX

Dower:
    1254: None
    1275:
52. *Eastwood

53. *Rayleigh

54. *The hundred of Rochford

55. *Nayland (with members in Suffolk, no. 207)

Crown Grants:[98]
56. 1280 (26 July). The Essex lands of Richard de Ewelle are committed to the Q at pleasure (*CCIR 1279–1288*, 29; see also no. 62).

57. 1284 (11 Feb.). Wardship of manors at East Ham and West Ham, in minority of the h. of Ralph de Playz (documentation identical to no. 18; see also nos. 149, 217).

58. 1286 (11 Jan.). Custody of manors at Pilton in Dansey (Delemeres in Bradwell), Willinghale Spain in Dunmow, and Finchingfield in Hengford, formerly of John de Ispannia, an idiot who had been induced to sell them to William de Montchensy (CIPM, ii, nos. 591, 610; CCIR 1279–1288, 381). In 1291 Ispannia's br. h. Richard cl. the Q continued to hold the manors after John d. two years earlier; the justices could do nothing since she held the lands of the K's gt and even if living could not be held to answer without him (JUST 1/542 m. 1d; Sayles, ed., Select Cases, ii, 120–22). On Montchensy, nos. 5, 19, 59, 60, 63, 104, 209.

59. 1289 (3 and 12 Nov.). Custody of manors at Sibil Hedingham[99] (with the hamlet of "Rokehaye"), Brendhall in Bollington (Ugley), Stanstead and Weston in Hengford, Belchamp Walter, "Manhale" (with hamlets of "Brenyng" and "Bolesgrave"), and Layer de la Haye, late of William de Montchensy of Edwardstone (documentation identical to no. 19; see nos. 5, 58, 60, 63, 104, 209).

Acquisitions:[100,101,102]
60. 1279 (4 Mar.). The two hundreds of Barstable, quitcl. to the Q by Robert Giffard with the assent of his parents William and Gundred (Kalendars, i, 61 [no. 204]; E 159/53 m. 5; EFF, i, 43, 50, 83, 106, 122).[103] In M1280 William Giffard, perhaps Robert's father, was indebted for £71:6:4 to John le Botiller, who gave the debt to the Q (E 159/54 m. 3d). This John le Botiller is perhaps the Q's bf of that name in Wilts. and Glos. (above, pp.129–30); on him see also no. 88.

61a. M1279. Manors at Fobbing and Shenfield with appurts, secured from Robert de Camville by reason of his debts to the Jewry, which came to the Q when the K tallaged the Jews, for the arrears in a certain rent owed the prior of Romilly, and in cons. of 200 marks paid by the K (CCIR 1279–1288, 80; held for three fees of the honor of Boulogne [BF, 667, 678]). In M1278 Camville paid Isaac le Eveske £9 (E 9/29 m. 9), but the debts stated in CCIR to have come to the Q must have amounted to much more than that. Camville conveyed the manors M1279 (EFF, ii, 28–29, incl. lands in Oxon. and Kent [nos. 117, 171]). Fobbing and Shenfield were among the lands the Q exch. with the e. of Essex for his moiety of Haverfordwest, ca. 1288 (see no. 177).

61b. 1280 (Easter and Mich. terms). A further £20 rent in Fobbing and Shenfield, with advs there and at Stanford, Little Laver, and High Ongar, conveyed to the K and Q by the prior of Romilley who recovered them agst Robert de Camville with the Q's help (CChR, i, 85; CCIR 1272–1279, 577–78; EFF, i, 152, and ii, 25–26; Kalendars, i, 61 [no. 202]); see also nos. 61a, 106, 117, 171.

62. 1280 (Mich. term). (?ca. 7 November). Reversion to a manor at Farnham with appurts, conveyed to the K and Q by Richard de Ewelle who holds it for life at the rent of a red rose at the feast of St John Baptist (EFF, ii, 28). Wardrobe buyer to Henry III (Tout, Chapters, vi, 34), Ewelle was gtd Farnham Aug. 1262 (CPR 1266–72, 729). From 1278 he was impleaded by Italian merchants for debts from his time in office (E 13/6 m. 17); it was likely for this that his lands in Essex were taken into the K's hand and custody gtd the Q, July 1280 (no. 56). The fine between Ewelle and the K and Q was levied M1280; his pardon for debts owed Henry III or Edward I, 7 Nov. 1280 (CPR 1272–81, 402), almost certainly issued in cons. of the fine. The Q gtd Farnham for life to her knt John Ferré, 2 Nov. 1281 (CChR, ii, 256). In 1291, Richard de Ewelle jr cl. that the Q, angered at his sister Eleanor's refusal to m. Philip s. of the K's physician Simon de Beauvais, caused the elder Ewelle to be jailed until he conveyed Farnham; he d. bef. his cl. was settled (JUST 1/542 m.1).[104] Albreda, widow of Richard sr, pr. 1291 that £50 of his goods were seized at Farnham by the

Q's bfs, but withdrew from a complaint that she was denied dower there (JUST 1/542, *mm.* 4, 1d).

63. [1280 July X 1281 Nov.]. A manor at Quendon, conveyed to the K and Q by William de Montchensy by reason of his debts to the Jewry and to the K, and in consideration of £200 paid him by the K (*CCIR 1279–1288,* 80; *CChR,* ii, 254; *CIPM,* i, no. 301; Hall, ed., *Red Book,* i, cxxix). In E1280 the Q was assisting St. Osyth's Abbey to recover Quendon; Montchensy had unlawfully regained seisin after pledging it to the abbey for payment of his debts (E 13/8 *m.* 19). On 26 July 1280 the Treas. was ordered to levy all debts Montchensy owed at the Exch., as the K had gtd them to the Q (*CCIR 1279–1288,* 28–29 [= E 159/54 *m.* 1]). On 15 Nov. 1280 she was gtd £250 he owed Hagin f. Moses (E 9/33 *m.* 6); by H1281 the sher. of Essex had seized to her use grain worth 180 marks from William's lands (E 9/34 *m.* 6). In Nov. 1281 the Q gtd Quendon for life to her knt John Ferré (*CChR,* ii, 256); after his death ca. 1289, Quendon was among lands she exch. with the e. of Essex for his moiety of Haverfordwest (no. 177). On Montchensy see also nos. 5, 19, 58–60, 104, 209.

64. [1284, ?Feb.]. Reversion to the manor of Netherhall in Gestingthorpe and one-sixth part of a knt's fee in Middleton, secured from Gilbert Pecche prob. by reason of his debts to the Jewry. Prob. incl. in the same transaction that brought her Pecche's lands in Cambs. (no. 21). In 1289 the Q gtd the reversion to Guy Ferré jr, who held it after Pecche's death until he d. 1323 (*CCIR 1288–1296,* 285; *CPR 1281–1292,* 325; *CIM,* ii, no. 603; *CIPM,* iii, no. 459, and vi, no. 422; *Feudal Aids,* ii, 143). On Pecche see also nos. 21–2, 118, 211.

65. E1286 (bef. 25 April). A manor at Aythorp Roding, incl. a messuage, 300 acres land and 12 acres wood, quitcl. to the K and Q by Robert de Rothynges (*EFF,* ii, 53). The Q on 25 Apr. 1286 gtd the manor to Guy Ferré jr. and his wife Margerie, dau. h. of Peter fitz Osbert (*CChR,* ii, 330). At his death in 1323 Guy held it of the e. of Oxford for two fees (*CIPM,* vi, 422).

66. [1286 Nov. X 1290 Nov.]. Wardship of a manor at West Thurrock in minority of the h. of Bartholomew de Brianzun, acq. from John of Brittany, e. of Richmond. Held of the honor of Richmond for ½ fee; the h. was aged three and more in Nov. 1286 (*CPR 1281–1292,* 414; *CIPM,* ii, no. 624).

FLINT

Dower: None

Crown Grants:

67. 1283 (24 Feb.). The castle and land of Hope, late of David ab Gruffydd (JUST 1/1149 *m.* 6; *CChyV,* 265, 273; N. M. Fryde, "Royal Enquiry," 375).

68. 1283 (10 May). A manor at Bangor Iscoed (Bangor-on-Dee, Bankerbury), late of Owain ab Gruffydd Madog (*CChyV,* 271; *CChR,* ii, 266).

69. 1283 (5 June X 2 Aug.). the Maelor Saesneg (Flints. detached, with *caput* at Overton). The Maelor was gtd for life to Robert de Crevequer in cons. of lands in Kent conveyed to the K and Q, 16 Nov. 1278 (*CPR 1272–1281,* 283). Crevequer surr. it to the K 5 June 1283, in exch. for Soham and Ditton, Cambs. (nos. 23b, 24; *CChR,* ii, 266). The Q held the Maelor by 2 Aug. 1283 (*CChyW,* 11).

Acquisitions:[105, 106]

70.   [ca. 1283]. The vill of "Lankemyn" and the wood of "Wennahald", usurped from Roger Mortimer of Chirk as appurt. to lands of which he enfeoffed the Q; detained for eight years. Roger pr. his cl. 1291 (JUSt. 1/1149 *m*. 3d; N. M. Fryde, "Royal Enquiry," 374).

71.   [ca. 1283]. Two hamlets in the vale of Mold, incl. 400 acres land and pasture, usurped from Roger de Mohaut and detained for eight years; recovered in 1291 (JUST 1/1149 *m*. 1).

72.   [1283 X 1284]. Adv. of the ch. of Hanmer in the Maelor, bought to the Q's use by Adam de Cretyng and Robert de Bures (JUST 1/1149 *m*. 10, where it is cl. the agreed price was never fully paid). Cretyng and Bures were the Q's bfs in the Maelor; the purchase perhaps took place around the time Bures succeeded Cretyng (about a year after the Maelor came to the Q, according to another 1291 complaint [JUST 1/1149 *m*. 9]).

73.   15 Edw. 1 (1286–87). Right in mills around Hope castle, conveyed to the Q by coparceners (*Kalendars*, i, 120–21 [nos. 44–52]).[107]

74.   [1283 X 1290]. Two acres land, a messuage, and a mill at Bangor-on-Dee, acq. by fine from Iorwerth ab Neuner who in 1291 cl. ejection. Robert de Bures pr. conveyance by proffering the fine (JUST 1/1149 *m*. 7).

GLOUCESTER

Dower:
      1254: None
      1275:
75.   Castle and town of Bristol

Crown Grants:
76.   1280 (20 Sept.). Wardship of a manor at Oldbury in minority of the h. of Robert Burdon (*CCIR 1279–1288*, 34; *CIPM*, ii, nos. 29, 380). For the background, above, pp.129–30, and no. 81; on the family, *VCH Bucks.*, iii, 392, and Moor, *Knights*, i, 158. The h. Nicholas was aged 11 in 1280 (*CIPM*, iii, no. 430).

77a. [1280]. Wardship of a moiety of the town of Aust, in minority of the h. of Ralph and James Russell (documentation identical to no. 7; for other lands appurt., nos. 12, 45, 192). The Q gtd the ward of Aust, 5 Nov. 1280, to Bp Giffard of Worcester (*CCIR 1288–1296*, 24, reads that the gtee was G. bp of Winchester, impossible in Nov. 1280 when the bp was John de Pontissara; compare Bund, ed., *Reg. Godfrey Giffard*, 311).

77b. [1288?] Russell also held a manor at Dirham, Glos. (*CIPM*, iii, no. 400); this was gtd by Ralph Russell in free marriage with his dau. Maud to Robert Walerand. Maud d. s.p. 1288 (*Cal. Genealogicum*, i, 194; see also nos. 47, 79, 91, 102, 195, 232, 238).

78.   1284 (11 Feb.). Wardship of a manor at Acton Turville, lately held in dower by Maud wife of Richard de Amundeville, of the inh. of Richard fitz Alan, a minor (*CPR 1281–1292*, 113; *CIPM*, ii, no. 563; Bund, ed., *Reg. Godfrey Giffard*, 342; see no. 178). Maud (de Vernon) m. first John fitz Alan, *de jure* 9th e. of Arundel (d. 1267) and then Richard de Amundeville; she d. 27 Nov. 1283. Her grs. h. Richard fitz Alan (b. Feb. 1267) was to

have seisin 8 Dec. 1287 (GEC, i, 239–40); the Q held Acton Turville in 15 Edw., i.e., to Nov. 1287 (S.C. 6/1089/22 m. 1). See also nos. 180, 216, 218, 231.

79.   [1288]. Wardship of manors at Siston next Bristol, Coberley next Gloucester, and Frampton Cotterell, lately held in dower by Maud, widow of Robert Walerand whose nephews are idiots in the K's ward (CIPM, ii, no. 6; Moor, Knights, v, 147–48). Further documentation identical to no. 47; see also nos. 91, 102, 195, 232, 238.

Acquisitions:
80.   1277 (6 Feb.). Land and tens in the town and suburbs of Bristol late of Christiana wife of Peter le Clerc, quitcl. to the Q by William de Montrevel[108] who held them of the K's gift (CCIR 1272–1279, 412). Christiana, fl. 29 Dec. 1277 (CPR 1272–1281, 249), d. by 29 Mar. 1278 when the K ordered inq. to determine what right in her lands pertained to Roger Kantok, Jordan la Warre, and George de Lydyerd (CPR 1272–1281, 288–89). Save for a garden "under Brandon hill," the Q gtd these, 27 Sept. 1278, to her marshal Thomas de Bardeney who held them at his death, 1296 (CPR 1272–1281, 278; CIPM, iii, no. 351).[109]

81.   8 Edw. I (1279 Nov. X 1280 July). A messuage and 1½, or 2, virgates at Didmarton, purchased of Cecily Tosard (Kalendars, i, 58 [no. 183]). As a result of the Oldbury wardship (no. 76), the Q must have regained seisin of this land from which Robert Burdon ejected her, for when his s. Nicholas Burdon came of age in 1291 he sought to recover the land; he pr. Cecily Tosard held it of Robert Burdon's gt and had no right to alienate (JUST 1/542 m. 2d). In 29 Edw. a messuage and 2 virgates at Didmarton were still adm. with lands of the late Q (E 372/146 m. 43).

82.   1287 (17 May). Reversion to a manor at Uley, conveyed to the K and Q by Matthew fitz John, who retains it for life (documentation identical to no. 42; see also nos. 98, 235).

HAMPSHIRE and ISLE OF WIGHT

Dower:
       1254: None
       1275:
83.   Castle and town of Odiham

Crown Grants:[110]
84.   1266 (15 Sept.). Henry III conf. the Lord Edward's gt to Eleanor of the manor of Ringwood, with the adv. and the issues and profits of the New Forest (CPR 1258–1266, 63; see also no. 86).

85.   1270 (2 Aug.). Henry III conf. to Eleanor the stewardship of the New Forest, secured from Alan Plogenet the former steward, and gts her the manor and bailiwick of Lyndhurst in the New Forest (CChR, ii, 149–50; CPR 1266–1272, 460, 484). Manors exch. with Plogenet for the stewardship are no. 187b–c.[111]

86.   1276 (26 May). Custody of the K's houses in Southampton, incl. the castle (CPR 1272–1281, 144).[112]

87.   1279 (3 Nov.). The hundred of Redbridge within the New Forest, to be held at pleasure (CFR, I, 118, 190; CCIR 1272–1279, 543; CPR 1281–1292, 76; RO, i, 34, 46).

88.   1280 (15 Feb.). Custody of a manor at Ringwood at pleasure, during voidance of the
       see of Winchester. The manor was taken into the K's hand 1272 X 1275 after John
       fitz John sold it without lic. to the bp of Winchester and his hs, but in 1275 was conf.
       to the see. In Dec. 1280 a John le Botiller gave up all right in the manor in return for
       £60 in lands elsewhere, though it is unclear what right Botiller had. He is possibly the
       Q's bf in Glos. and Wilts. (above, no. 60). The Q held the manor until her death (CPR
       1272–1281, 362, 426, 445; VCH Hants., iv, 607–8; CCIR 1272–1279, 80; Martin, ed.,
       Reg. Peckham, i, 313–14).[113]

89.   1283 (11 Aug.). Wardship of a manor at King's Somborne with the hundred, and lands
       at Longstock, Weston Patrick, and Stockbridge in minority of the h. of Patrick de
       Chaworth (CCIR 1279–1288, 214; CIPM, ii, no. 477, showing the h. was b. 2 Feb.
       1282). Somborne manor was assigned in dower to the widow, who held it with her
       second husband Hugh Despenser (CCIR 1279–1288, 217, 220; VCH Hants., iv, 471);
       the Q retained the hundred (S.C. 6/1089/25 m. 1). See also no. 29.

90.   [1284 5 Apr. X 1287 Nov.]. A manor at Swainstone, with member at Brixton
       (Brighstone), surr. to the K by the bp of Winchester (Hall, ed., Red Book, i,
       cxxix–cxxx; Deedes, ed., Reg. Pontissara, i, xv–xvi, 282, and ii, 719; VCH Hants.,
       v, 218–19). No gt to the Q is known, but her accts show she held Swainstone 15–18
       Edward (S.C. 6/1089/22 m. 1; S.C. 6/1089/25 m. 1).

91.   [1288]. Wardship of manors at West Tytherley, Sparsholt, Broughton and Meonstoke
       Walerand, lately held in dower by Maud widow of Robert Walerand whose nephew
       and h. is an idiot in the K's ward (CIPM, ii, no. 6; Moor, Knights, v, 147–48). Further
       documentation identical to no. 47; see also nos. 79, 102, 195, 232, 238).

Acquisitions:[114, 115, 116]
92.   [1275 X 1276?]. A piece of land called Blackfield, containing 60 acres and more, from
       which William de Minsted' jr and Margaret de Budesthorn' were ejected by Hugh de
       Digneveton, then Q's steward in the New Forest, fifteen yrs bef. William and
       Margaret recovered it, H1291 (JUST 1/1014 m. 8; Manners, 105, shows William had
       £10 damages from the Q's exors). For Digneveton as forest steward, see above,
       Chapter Two.

93.   [1276 X 1277?]. A messuage and three carucates of land in the New Forest, usurped
       from Eustace Fucher whose widow and sisters recovered it in 1291. Apparently the
       ten. in Battramsley in which Fucher's widow recovered 50s.8d. dower (Stagg, CNFD,
       i, nos. 367, 369); prob. in the Q's hands by Oct. 1277 (CCIR 1272–1279, 405).
       Fucher, forester in fee of the New Forest, placed himself in the Q's grace for tres-
       passes charged agst him Nov. 1276 (Stagg, CNFD, i, no. 149; see no. 96). In 1291 her
       men cl. Eustace held the land as her bf, but his widow and cohs proved this untrue;
       the widow won 20 marks and 14d. in damages (JUST 1/1014 m. 6d; Manners, 134).

94.   [before 1280 20 Mar.]. A manor at Middleton, I.o.W., which the Q gtd on this date
       to John de Weston and Christiana his wife (CChR, ii, 234; VCH Hants., v, 161–62). Held
       of John de Lisle for one fee (BF, 1301).

95.   [1279 X 1280]. Roncesvaux house in Southampton, recovered by Roncesvaux pri-
       ory, 1291. The priory had leased the house to Claremunde de Suhant' (d. by Sept.
       1260; CPR 1258–1266, 104–5; Hockey, Quarr Abbey, 94–95; Kaye, ed., Cartulary of
       God's House, index p. 421 s.v. "Claramunda, dna"). At her death, her nepotes William
       and Richard de Gloucestr' entered it and pledged it to Benedict de Winton', hanged

for clipping in 1279–80 (Roth, *History of the Jews in England*, 75–76); as the Q recd by the K's gt the property of condemned Jews, the house came to her hands. The priory sought to recover it; two inqs were held and the K's steward was to restore the house to the priory, 1280–81 (*Cal. Genealogicum*, i, no. 76b; *CCIR 1279–1288*, 87). But the steward of the New Forest objected that the Q was not summ. to those inqs and she retained the house (JUST 1/1014 m. 7d). "For their houses in Southampton" the priory had £14:2:0 damages, H1292 (*Manners*, 105).

96. [bef. 1281 15 July]. Forty acres of land in Battramsley in the New Forest, from which Henry Toluse was ejected by Walter de Kancia with the collusion of Eustace Fucher; Toluse recovered this in 1291 (JUST 1/1014 m. 8). Fucher's role dates the disseisin bef. his death, in 9 Edw. bef. St. Swithin's transl. (i.e., 20 Nov. 1280 X 15 July 1281; JUST 1/1014 m. 6d). Possibly the Toluse ejection was ca. 1276, when Fucher was disgraced (no. 93).

97. 1286 (Feb.). A messuage and three carucates of land with appurts at Thorness in Northwood, I.o.W., purchased from John Morice *als* Morize. At the octave of St. Martin 14 Edw. (Nov. 1285) by fine *coram rege* at Fordingbridge, Alice dau. of John "Illeybon" ackn. this property to be the right of John de Grymstede, who conceded it in fee to John Morice (*Kalendars*, i, 52 [no. 140]). In Feb. 1286 the abbot of Westm. as Q's treas. paid John Morice £66:13:4 "pro quadam terra ab eo empta" (Westm. Abbey, muniments 23627). In 1291 Andrew, s. h. of John de Grymstede (on whom see no. 229) cl. ejection from Thorness by collusion between Alice de Lillebon and John Morize, who were advised and supported by the Q. At the death of her br. Richard Alice brought a writ of mort d'ancestor against Andrew, who had John de Lillebon's charter of enfeoffment and Richard's quitcl. John de Grymstede cl. Andrew was threatened by life, limb, and lands until he conveyed the manor to Morize who sold it to the Q. Grymstede's action was dismissed as he had not put in his cl. on the Nov. 1285 fine (JUST 1/1014 m. 9d).

98. 1287 (17 May). Reversion to the manors of Warblington and Hinton Waldrist, conveyed to the K and Q by Matthew fitz John who retains them for life (documentation identical to no. 42; see also nos. 82, 235).

99. 1287 (E 15 Edw.). Reversion to the manor of Whitfield in Brading, I.o.W., purchased from John de Hardington. The Q's treas. accts show payment of £20 to Hardington for "Wytlesfeld," E1287 (*Records 1286–1289*, no. 3138), and £40 in H1290 (S.C. 6/1089/25 m. 4). Berewyk' ackn. 1291 that £40 of the £100 agreed on for the manor were still owing (JUST 1/1014 m. 4d); paid, H1292 (*Manners*, 105). Held for one fee of the lady of Gatcombe (*BF*, 1302). Hardington cl. 1291 that he was compelled to convey Whitefield to the Q under threat of imprisonment from the K's Treas. and Geoffrey de Piccheford; the justices found no proof of coercion (JUST 1/1014 m. 4).[117] Hardington held the manor at his death, Aug. 1293 (*CIPM*, iii, no. 196). *VCH Hants.*, v, 159–60 is unaware of these documents.

100. 1288 (ca. June). Manors at Lockerley and Avon, acq. by fine from John de Cobham. In 1291, John de Lisle cl. ejection from these manors on 23 June 1288 by the steward of the New Forest in the Q's name; Lisle brought a writ of novel disseisin but the steward won judgment by proffering a fine between the Q and John de Cobham. Lisle asserted that the "origo" of that fine was Maud de Columbars who held the manors only in dower; Lisle cl. them as Michael de Columbars' right h. Cobham answered that he was enfeoffed by Michael de Columbars by fine, which he proffered; Lisle cl. Columbars was not lawfully seized of the lands when that fine was levied.

Lisle's action was dismissed as his writ of novel disseisin was pending (JUST 1/1014 m. 7). According to *VCH Hants.*, iv, 501, 515, these were Columbars manors. Maud's husband Matthew d. 4 Nov. 1281 X 25 May 1282, leaving br. h. Michael, who had liv. 13 July 1282 and *d.* by 27 Sept. 1284 (Moor, *Knights,* i, 228, and iii, 44). Michael's undated gt of the lands to Cobham (*CCIR 1307–1313,* 327) was made while Philip de Heyville *als* Hoville was sher. of Hants., thus bef. 15 Oct. 1282 (PRO, *List of Sheriffs,* 54);[118] if bef. Michael de Columbars had liv. in July 1282, Lisle rightly asserted its invalidity. Lisle m. ca. 1281 Nichola, dau. h. of Michael de Columbars, and d. 1304 (GEC, viii, 39–41; *CCIR 1279–1288,* 104); his s. John sought to recover the manors in 1310 (*CCIR 1307–1313,* 327 bis).

101.   [1276 X 1290, ?ca. 1276]. In parlt. 8 Edw. II (1315) Richard de Burle *als* Burely cl. that his great–grandfather Richard was gtd the bailiwick of Burley in the New Forest in fee farm at a rent of 12 marks. After the forest came to the Q's hands, William the querent's father was ejected but the rent was still exacted from Richard. Inq. was ordered on the rent, and Richard might sue *coram rege* as to the ejection; he held Burley in 1316 (*RP,* i, 313; *Feudal Aids,* ii, 317). William de Burely, forester in fee Oct. 1276, was convicted of trespass of vert Nov. 1276 (Stagg, *CNFD,* i, nos. 94, 118, 143, 146, 148, 150–51) and was perhaps ejected then. In 1291 Richard de Burely cl. ejection in the New Forest, but the membrane is damaged and it is unclear if he was then cl. Burley (JUST 1/1014 m. 6d). Richard also cl. 1291 that 30 cows held by his ancestors in the forest at a rent of 30s. were stolen in the troubles under Henry III; but the rent was exacted after the forest came to Eleanor (JUST 1/1014 m. 6d bis)—the rent for which he had £20 from the Q's exors, 1292 (*Manners,* 106)? He owed 30s. rent for 30 cows in the forest, ca. 1300 (Stagg, *CNFD,* i, no. 388). He *d.* by 1330 (Stagg, no. 541; *VCH Hants.,* iv, 611).[119]

HEREFORD

Dower: None

Crown Grants:
102.   [1288]. Wardship of a manor at Lugwardine, lately held in dower by Maud, the widow of Robert Walerand whose hs are idiots in the K's ward (Moor, *Knights,* v, 147–48, and *CIPM,* ii, no. 6). Further documentation identical to no. 47; see also nos. 79, 91, 195, 232, 238.

Acquisitions: None[120]

HERTFORD

Dower: None

Crown Grants:
103.   [1289 X 1290]. The Q's accts show that in 1289–90 she held the year and waste of Adam de Stratton's lands at Little Stanmore and Shenley (S.C. 6/1089/25 *mm.* 1, 2). No gt from the K is known; *VCH Herts.,* ii, 265 does not connect the Q with Adam's lands. But in 1291 four complaints alleged ejection or disseisin by her bfs at Shenley: in two cases it was shown that querents alienated to Stratton bef. his downfall (JUST 1/542 *mm.* 1–1d); for the others, no. 107a–b.

104.   1290 (3 and 12 Nov.). Custody of a manor at Patmere, late of William de Montchensy of Edwardstone (documentation identical to no. 5; see also nos. 19, 58, 59, 60, 63, 209).

Acquisitions:
105a.   1275 [Nov]. A manor at Langley secured from Stephen de Cheyndut by reason of his debts to the Jewry, which came to the Q partly by the K's gift and partly for her gold when the Jewry was tallaged. She pardoned 300 marks of the debt, and for the other 700 marks "and for other great bounty that the Q has done to [Stephen]," the K retained the manor (*CCIR 1279–1288,* 80 [worth £40]; held of the e. of Cornwall as of the honor of Berkhamstead for 5 fees and two parts of one fee [*VCH Herts.,* ii, 235]). On Cheyndut, Moor, *Knights,* i, 204. He had lost four manors to Walter de Merton in 1268 by reason of his debts to the Jewry (Coss, "Geoffrey de Langley," 33). He owed the Q 100 marks in 1275, not certainly a Jewish debt (*CCIR 1272–1279,* 238). His involvement with the Q through the Jewry appears from June 1275, when his debt to Hagin f. Moses for £200 was to be levied, £140 for the Q and £60 for the K. Hagin had agreed with Amicia de Say and John her s. to quit them towards all Jews in England for 200 marks, but did not quit them towards Benedict f. Cok whom they owed £140; Benedict gave that debt to the Q for her gold but when she exacted payment Amicia and John pr. their agreement with Hagin quit them of the debt. The £200 Cheyndut owed Hagin was substituted (*CCIR 1272–1279,* 198; *CPEJ,* ii, 308; S.C. 1/17/19, s.d., is the Treas. Joseph de Cauncy's order that Walter de Kancia be given the charter for £200). On 13 Nov. 1275 the Q was gtd all debts Cheyndut owed Manser f. Aaron, dated 23 July 1275 (*CPEJ,* iv, 82–83; as the Q was evidently first aware of Cheyndut's indebtedness from June 1275 and his debts to Manser were dated the follg month, there was perhaps collusion with Manser along lines suggested by the case of John de Wauton [no. 205]). Cheyndut's conveyance of Langley to the Q is E 326/4326, s.d.; *Kalendars,* i, 58 (nos. 177, 179) are dated 3 Edw., or bef. 19 Nov. 1275; the e. of Cornwall's conf. (11 Dec. 1275) is E 329/191. Other transactions touching Cheyndut are nos. 13a, 137, 141, 246b.

105b.   1280 (unknown date). The prior and convent of Langley convey to the K and Q the adv. of the ch. of Langley (*Kalendars,* i, 58 [no. 178, dated A.D. 1280]).

105c.   [1275 Nov. X 1283 Feb.?]. Land in the manor of Langley, gtd to the K and Q by John s. of Alexander de Reda, who bought it from Alan le Huirer *als* le Hemrer (*DC,* i, 2 [s.d.]; *Kalendars,* i, 58 [no. 180, s.d.]).[121]

105d.   [1275 Nov. X 1290 Nov.]. Lands held of the manor of Langley by Geoffrey Garkevylle, whose widow Alice cl. 1291 that after her husband's death the Q's bfs troubled her so that she could not cultivate nor take profit from the lands and so surr. them to the Q (JUST 1/542 *m.* 3, too damaged to allow any determination to be read). William "Jarkevylle" and three others held one fee of the Q appurt. to Langley, 1284–86 (*Feudal Aids,* i, 77).

106.   [1284 Nov. X 1287 Easter (13–15 Edw.)]. The adv. of the ch. of Tring, conveyed to the Q by the prior and convent of Romilley. This was among advs she agreed to assist the prior to recover agst Robert de Camville, Oct. 1279 (*CCIR 1272–1279,* 577–78), but not among those conveyed to her, E1280 (*EFF,* ii, 25). *RP,* ii, 48, and Phillimore, ed., *Coram Rege Roll,* 88, show the prior conveyed his cl. on the Tring adv. to the Q betw. the quinz. of St. Martin 13 Edw. and E1287, while he prosecuted agst the abbot and convent of Faversham a writ of right touching the same; the abbot of Faversham released his right to the K in 30 Edw. (1301–2). The Q bef. 1290 pres. Gilbert de

Ivinghoe to Tring (*Coram Rege Roll*, 88); in 1295 this pres. was conf. by the bp of Lincoln as by the abbot and convent of Faversham (Hill, ed., *Rolls and Reg. Sutton*, v, 90, and viii, 85). See *CPR 1291–1301*, 136; *RP*, ii, 48; *VCH Herts.*, ii, 292; nos. 61a–b, 117, 171.

107a.   [1289 X 1290]. A croft of 5 acres at Shenley, cl. 1291 by Matilda Moriz, widow of Hugh Faber who alienated it to Adam de Stratton though it was Matilda's inh. bef. she m. Hugh. Matilda pr. her cl. but the justices did not determine the case *rege inconsulto* (JUST 1/542 *m.* 1).

107b.   [1289 X 1290]. Five acres of land and 2s. rent in Shenley, of which Adam de Stratton was enfeoffed by Robert s. of John de Tytelhurst to hold of the same Robert, who cl. 1291 that the Q's bfs detained it after Shenley came to her hands. A charter pr. his cl. but he did not prosecute (JUST 1/542 *m.* 1d); see no. 103.

HUNTINGDON

Dower:
        1254: None
        1275:
108.   Farm of Brampton

109.   Rent of the fair of St. Ives

Crown Grants:
110.   1289 (7 Feb.). Wardship of two parts of a manor at Washingley in minority of the h. of Ralph de Wassingele (*CClR 1288–1292*, 373; *Records 1286–1289*, no. 3229; *BF*, 923, 928, 1173, 1217; *RH*, ii, 634). The chief manor at Washingley and half the vill were held of the barony of Lovetot (for which Sanders, *Baronies*, 80–81). This explains why the wardship was first gtd, 27 Nov. 1288, to John de Lovetot, the Q's auditor and a cadet of the baronial family, as stated in the *CClR* reference. In M1286 and M1287 Ralph "de Wassinglee" of Cambs. paid the Q 10 marks of the debts owed Meyr f. David (E 101/505/19 *m.* 1; E 101/505/20 *m.* 1); this is likely the Ralph whose lands were gtd the Q in 1289 but no proof is available. On Ralph, Dewindt, *English Royal Justice*, 668.

111.   1290 (28 June). Custody during pleasure, at a rent of 100s. yrly, of the hundred of Normancross, which the K lately recovered agst the abbot of Thorney (*CPR 1281–1292*, 396; *RP*, ii, 42).

Acquisitions: None

KENT

Dower: None

Crown Grants:[122, 123]
112.   1285 (27 June). The hundreds of Washlingstone and Littlefield, to be held for life (*CPR 1281–1292*, 180; worth £60, *RH*, i, 218).

113.   1289 (1 Apr.). Wardship of lands and tens at Brenchley, with appurts and marr. of the h., in minority of the h. of Roger Loveday (*RG*, ii, no. 1279; see no. 114.) See also Beardwood, ed., *Trial of Walter de Langeton*, 106–7: *CIPM*, iv, no. 456.

Acquisitions:[124]

114. 1278 (May X June). A manor at West Farleigh with member (or another manor) at Teston, which the Q purchased for £200 from Roger de Loveday who held it of the inh. of Robert de Crevequer (nos. 115, 116a; *CCIR 1272–1279*, 498; *CCIR 1279–1288*, 80 [Farleigh worth £24]; *CChR*, ii, 357; *CIPM*, i, no. 563; *RH*, i, 224 [the manors worth £30 together]). There is no indication that Loveday was indebted to the Jewry; on him, Moor, *Knights*, iii, 66; and see no. 113. The Q gtd West Farleigh and Teston for life to John Ferré, July 1285 (*CPR 1281–1292*, 180); after his d. ca. 1289 they were among lands she exch. with Christ Church Priory, Canterbury, for right in Sandwich, 1290 (no. 120). A ward at Farleigh, sold by the Q's exors 1293–94, must have fallen in before that exch. (*RO*, i, 80).

115. 1278 (ca. 22 June). The castle and manor of Leeds *als* "la Mote," with the park of Ashleigh and other appurts, secured by reason of 1020 marks owed the Jewry by William de Leyburn whose father held Leeds of the enfeoffment of Robert de Crevequer, and in cons. of 500 marks the Q paid William (*CCIR 1272–1279*, 221, 481, 499 *ter*; *CCIR 1279–1288*, 80 [worth £40]; *CPEJ*, iii, 78–79; *Kalendars*, i, 57 [no. 174]). The Q ackn. she owed Leyburn 400 marks, 22 June 1278 (*CCIR 1272–1279*, 499); at her inst. Leyburn was pardoned all debts owed by him and his ancestors to the Exch. or to any Jews, 15 Nov. 1279 (*CPR 1272–1281*, 335; see also *CCIR 1272–1279*, 334). On Crevequer, see no. 116a.

116a. 1278 [May X Nov.]. The manor of Chatham and the adv. of Leeds priory, secured by reason of debts owed the Jewry by Robert de Crevequer. This transaction was not incl. in the summary of lands the Q acq. by 1281 (*CCIR 1279–1288*, 80–81); Sanders, *Baronies*, 31–32, seems unaware she obtained Chatham. By M1275, prob. for her gold on a tallage, the Q acq. Crevequer's debt to Hagin f. Moses for £333:6:8 (*CPEJ*, iii, 110–11); the later stages of this transaction are obscure but see *Kalendars*, i, 61 (no. 201, 6 Edw. I); *CPR 1272–1281*, 283 (where in compensation for the conveyance Crevequer is gtd for life the Maelor Saesneg [no. 69], 16 Nov. 1278). Crevequer was in seisin of Chatham ca. 19 May 1278 (see no. 116d); on 15 Nov. 1279, like William de Leyburn (no. 115), he was pardoned all debts to the Jewry (*CPR 1272–1281*, 334–35). Members of the Crevequer barony incl. 2⅚ fees at Tilmanstone, Southden, Chevening and Foots Cray, which the Q gtd the see of Canterbury in 1281 (Lambeth Palace MS 1212, f. 37v; *CPR 1272–1281*, 436; *RH*, i, 207).[125] On Crevequer see also nos. 23b–c, 24, 69, 114–15, 116d, 116g.

116b. [1278 Nov. X 1290 Nov.]. The fair of Chatham with all rights and liberties, conveyed to the K and Q by the prior and convent of Leeds (*Kalendars*, i, 61 (no. 200, s.d.).

116c. [1278 Nov. X 1290 Nov.]. A rent of 9 measures of winter barley in Chatham, conveyed to the K and Q by John "de Aula" de Maydenstan'[126] (*Kalendars*, i, 61 (no. 203, s.d.).

116d. [1278 Nov. X 1290 Nov.]. A ten. of 380 acres called "Beggebrok," appurt. to Bockingfold in Yalding (member of Chatham) usurped from William Payforer, who had been put in seisin by Robert de Crevequer 19 May 1278, upon payment of 100 marks. The Q's steward cl. she was put in seisin by Stephen de Penecestr' who was vouched to warranty. Inq. was summoned but Payforer failed to prosecute and was in mercy (JUST 1/542 m. 1d; *CIPM*, i, no. 563; *RH*, i, 221). On Bockingfold see further, note 195.[127]

116e. [1278 Nov. X 1290 Nov.]. The adv. of the ch. of Bockingfold, usurped from Leeds priory as allegedly appurt. to Chatham (Hasted, *Kent*, v, 163–64; see no. 114d).

116f. [1278 Nov. X 1290 Nov.]. Pasture for one cow at Bockingfold, usurped from John Morel who won 8s. damages, paid him by the Q's exors 1292; known only from that payment (*Manners*, 106).

116g. [1278 Nov. X 1290 Nov.]. In Brenchley, 5 acres sometime held in dower by Cecilia widow of Robert Ayllard. These she demised for term of years to Robert de Crevequer, who within that term conveyed his lands to the Q, whose bfs would not allow Cecilia to re–enter the land. She recovered seisin and 20s. damages in 1291 (JUST 1/542 *m*. 9d).[128]

116h. [1278 Nov. X 1290 Nov.]. At Brenchley, 5 acres lately held by Thomas de Crevequer, a bastard, who was enfeoffed thereof by Robert Ayllard; when Thomas d., the Q's bfs seized the land. Recovered in 1291 by Hamo Wodcok' and Dulcia his wife, dau. of Robert Ayllard (JUST 1/542 *m*. 9d).

116j. [1278 Nov. X 1290 Nov.]. At Brenchley, a garden and 16 acres lately held by the bastard Thomas de Crevequer of Robert s. h. of Robert Ayllard and other sons of the elder Robert, deceased. Since Thomas' death, Robert jr was detained from his share of the land though his brothers recovered their right (JUST 1/542 *m*. 11d, where Robert pr. his right and wins arrears of 6s., paid him by the Q's exors. 1292 [*Manners*, 106]).

117. M1279 Reversion to manors at Westerham and Edenbridge with appurts (the adv. at Westerham conveyed to the K and Q at once) secured by reason of debts owed the Jewry by Robert de Camville, who retains the manors for life at the rent of a chaplet of roses at the feast of St. John Baptist (payment recorded in 1283–4 and 1284–5 [E 159/57 *m*. 9; E 159/58 *m*. 10]). Further documentation identical to no. 61a–b; see also nos. 106, 171. Camville d. 1286 (*Records 1286–1289*, no. 3114; for the family, *VCH Oxon*, vi, 147–48). In 1290 the Q gtd the Westerham adv. to Canterbury Priory for the custom of the port at Sandwich (no. 120). Camville's s. h. Roger tried to recover the manors in 1291, cl. that the Q had not kept a promise to promote Robert's children; he failed to pr. his cl. but was shown mercy "quia pauper" (JUST 1/542 *m*. 3).[129] Though no record of such action appears, Roger recovered a ten. in Westerham called "Brokelond" by Apr. 1292 (*CPR 1281–1292*, 484); he had some money from the Q's exors, perhaps to clear Westerham of rent-charges bef. the K gtd it to Westm. Abbey for the Q's anniversary service (*Manners*, 105, 126, 133; *CChR*, ii, 424–26; Harvey, *Westm. Abbey and Its Estates*, 32). Robert's widow Joan had £42 for damages and exactions at Westerham (*Manners*, 126, 135).[130]

118. 1280 (June). A manor at Westcliffe with the adv., acq. from Gilbert Pecche of whose debts to the Jewry the Q had one debt of 500 marks; in cons. of £30 owed the K at the Exch., and 200 marks paid by the K (*CCIR 1279–1288*, 25, 28–29, 80 [worth £60, though *RH*, i, 206, says £40]; one fee, held in chief of the honor of Perche [*BF*, 655, 676]). On Gilbert Pecche see also nos. 21, 22, 64, 211. On 26 Feb. 1280 the K informed the Treas. and barons that Aaron f. Vives had lately given and conceded the Q all debts in which Gilbert Pecche was bound to him (E 9/35 *m*. 6; E 159/53 *m*. 4), possibly the debt of 1000 marks Aaron gave the Q shortly bef. 20 Jan. 1280 (*CCIR 1279–1288*, 5). Walter de Kancia was prosecuting for Gilbert's debts, amounting to 640 marks, H1280 (E 9/34 *m*. 6); on 6 June 1280 the Q by letters patent told Aaron to quit Pecche for the debts as he had satisfied her therefor (E 9/36 *m*. 7), and on

26 July 1280 the K ordered the Treas. to levy all debts Gilbert owed at the Exch., as the K had gtd them to the Q (*CCIR 1279–1288*, 28–29 [= E 159/54 m. 1]). Gilbert's undated charter of conveyance for the manor, adv. and other appurts, in cons. of 1000 marks paid him by the K and Q, is Hall, *Red Book*, i, cxxviii; see also *Kalendars*, i, 57 (no. 175), and Miller, *Abbey and Bishopric of Ely*, 177. The Westcliffe adv. and one acre of land there were among lands the Q exch. in 1290 with Canterbury Priory for right in the port of Sandwich (no. 120).

119. [ca. 1280?]. Rents at Woolwich and Mottingham, gtd by the Q to John de Vescy and Isabella his wife (*CPR 1281–1292*, 474; *CIPM*, ii, no. 723). These appear to have been considered as appurt. to the manor of Eltham and were perhaps worth £33:6:0¾ (*RO*, i, 36; *Kalendars*, i, 62 [no. 208]). Isabella de Beaumont, the Q's cousin, m. John de Vescy ca. 1280 (*CHEC*, 46–47). Later tradition had it that Vescy enfeoffed Antony Bek of Eltham so it might be conferred on John's bastard s. William (whose existence is doubtful), and that Bek instead gave it to the Q (Camden, *Britannia*, ed. Gibson [1695], col. 189).

120. 1290 (June). The custom and rent of the port of Sandwich, acq. from the prior and convent of Canterbury, in exch. for the advs of Westerham and Westcliffe and one acre of land in each manor (nos. 117, 118), and manors at West Farleigh and Teston (no. 114). The K's commrs, incl. John de Berewyk', were apptd 18 May 1290 to treat with the convent about this exch.; the Q was not mentioned and lands in Kent to be given in exch. were said to be the K's, not his wife's (*CPR 1281–1292*, 358), but soon thereafter her squire was in Kent to extend lands apparently connected with this transaction (see note 152). The Q's gts are Canterbury, dean and chapter library, Reg. I, f. 136 (20 June 18 Edw.); *CChR*, ii, 357 *bis*; *MA*, i, 98 (s.d.). Cont. Gervase of Canterbury, 296, says the Q was put in seisin at Sandwich 29 June, the day she gave the priory land and adv. at Westcliffe; the priory had seisin at West Farleigh and Teston on 30 June. On 28 June the prior notified the mayor and bfs of Sandwich that the exch. had taken place and required them to be intendent and respondent to the Q, reserving the priory's quays and houses (Canterbury, dean and chapter library, Cartae Antiquae S. 274).

121. 1290 (autumn?). E 101/249/20, a small roll listing ten. formerly of the Jews in Canterbury, includes (m. 2d) one held jointly by Hagin "the Q's Jew" and Aaron f. Vives, Jew of the K's br. Edmund; worth £1:18:5, this was held of Canterbury priory at a rent of 11s. At the Expulsion, Aaron's moiety came to Edmund; the Q's ordered her bfs to take into her hands Hagin's moiety, with a vacant place worth 30s. from which Richard le Ioeuene was owed 19d. *MA*, i, 98, notes at least 13 ten. in the Jewry at Canterbury were gtd the Q or taken into her hand at the Expulsion, and were later gtd to the priory; but it is unclear if Eleanor so gtd them or if the K did so after her death.

LEICESTER

Dower:
    1254: None
    1275:
122. Farm of Goscote hundred

123. Ouston

Crown Grants:

124a. 1267 (22 Nov.). The manors of Great Bowden and Market Harborough, committed to the Lady Eleanor at pleasure (*CPR 1266–1272*, 168).

124b. 1268 (6 Jan.). Great Bowden and Market Harborough are committed to Eleanor for ten years from last Michaelmas (*CPR 1266–1272*, 179).

124c. 1270 (26 May). Great Bowden and Market Harborough are gtd Eleanor for life, not to be separated from the Crown (*CChR*, ii, 133).

125. 1268 (28 Mar.). The hundred of Gartree, to be held at pleasure notwithstanding that it was lately committed to William de Boyville (*CPR 1266–1272*, 213–14). In 1291 Boyville cl. he held Gartree from 50 Henry III (1265–66) until 7 Edw. (1278–79), when the Q's steward ejected him; it was answered that he surr. the hundred after admin. difficulties. His action was to be continued (JUST 1/542 *m.* 5), perhaps at the Northampton sitting for which the roll is lost. Eleanor in fact farmed the hundred to Boyville, who failed to pay her the farm and in Aug. 1279 the hundred was taken into the K's hand (*CFR*, 116; *RO*, i, 34; Sayles, ed., *Select Cases*, i, clxviii–clxix). The unpaid farm may explain Boyville's indebtedness to the Q, 1271–73 (*CIR 1268–1272*, 431; *CCIR 1272–1279*, 46). On him, Moor, *Knights*, i, 27.[131]

126. 1274 (8 Nov.). Wardship of ¼ knight's fee at Claybrooke in minority of the h. of Nicholas de Haversham (documentation identical to no. 11; see also nos. 167, 229).

Acquisitions:

127. M1276. Sixteen virgates with appurts at Welham, to be held by the Q for six years from M1276, each virgate extended at 18 acres arable and 7 rods of park, worth 20s. For this and for 11 marks of silver paid her by Thomas Basset of Welham, the Q agreed to quit him of 140 marks owed Benedict f. Moses of London, and £10 owed Solomon of Stanford (E 159/50 *m.* 9). Debts owed the Jewry by Thomas Basset of Welham were said in June 1275 to have been gtd Eleanor by Henry III, "so that she may make her profit out of them as shall seem fit to her" (*CCIR 1272–1279*, 184).

128. 1281 (May). A manor at Newton Harcourt, demised to the K and Q by Walter de Kancia, who is gtd it for life with reversion to the Crown (*CCIR 1279–1288*, 61; *CPR 1272–1281*, 430; held of the e. of Warwick for one fee, *CIPM*, i, no. 411; *VCH Leics.*, v, 432, where it appears Kancia unlawfully gained seisin of the manor before demising it. Saer de Harcourt, predecessor of the Richard from whom Kancia obtained the manor, was indebted to the Jewry and had lost his manor at Kibworth to Walter de Merton, 1270 (Coss, "Geoffrey de Langley," 33). Saer owed the Q 50 marks, 1275 (*CCIR 1272–1279*, 238), but it is not clear if this debt bears on the conveyance to Kancia. In T1275, £300 of Richard's debts to the Jewry came to the Q when she was gtd all debts owed Hagin f. Cress (*CPEJ*, ii, 310); it is not known if these debts played any part in Kancia's acq. of the manor or his conveyance to the K and Q. Kancia held the manor until he d. 1283; on 14 Feb. 1284 the Q gtd Newton for life to Gilbert Pecche in return for lands lately surr. to her (*CPR 1281–1292*, 114; see no. 21). In Sept. 1284, 30 librates at Newton were gtd for life to John le Lou and Amice his wife, in cons. of Amice's release to the Q of her inh. in Warks. and Yorks. (nos. 226, 247; *DC*, iv, 132–33).

LINCOLN

Dower:
    1254:
129.   Grantham (omitted from 1275 assignment)

130.   Stamford (omitted from 1275 assignment)
        1275:
131.   Soke of Caistor

132.   Town of Grimsby

133.   City of Lincoln

Crown Grants:
134.   [1265, autumn]. Manors at Gayton le Marsh and Tothill in Lindsay, late of the K's
        enemy Richard de Seez *als* Seos or Sayes (Hunter, ed., *Rotuli selecti*, 249 [mention-
        ing in the same gt Bakewell, Derbs., no. 38]). See no. 135a.

Acquisitions:
135a.   [1265 X 1274]. Manors at Gayton le Marsh and Tothill (no. 134), secured after
        Richard de Seez failed to pay the ransom for his lands. Held in chief as of the honor
        of Chester for one fee (*BF*, 1059, 1077; *CIPM*, vi, no. 422). Seez ackn. his debt to
        Eleanor 2 Jan. 1268, and on 2 Feb. follg accepted a ransom of 590 marks for his
        manors (*ClR 1264–1268*, 505, 514; *CPR 1268–1272*, 434). Gayton and Tothill were
        in the Q's hands Oct. 1274 (*CClR 1272–1279*, 224); the next month she surr. them
        to the K to be gtd to John Ferré (*CChR*, ii, 188; *Kalendars*, i, 69 [no. 7]). In 1291 Seez
        cl. that after he agreed (in Jan. 1268?) with Eleanor's council on terms for payment
        of his ransom, Walter de Kancia refused to accept an installment in June 1270 and
        cl. it was not offered, so that Richard lost the lands. Seez could not pr. this and took
        nothing for his claim; the K of his grace gave him a knt's robe (JUST 1/542 *m.* 5).

135b.   E1275 Further lands at Gayton, secured from Richard de Seez by reason of his debts
        to the Jewry. Bef. 12 Dec. 1274 Hagin f. Moses gave the Q debts Seez owed him (*CPEJ*,
        iv, 42–43; *CClR 1272–1279*, 140; *ClR 1268–1272*, 296). On 1 June 1275 Seez ackn.
        he owed her £40 for a trespass (*CClR 1272–1279*, 237), and her suit against him for
        that trespass, E1275, shows the debts Seez then owed her through the Jewry totaled
        260 marks; she was to hold the land at Gayton until this sum was paid her (K.B. 27/16
        m. 16d). The K later gave her debts of £80 Seez owed Aaron Crispin (*CClR
        1272–1279*, 391).

136.   1275 (18 Nov.). Lands in the manors of Nocton and Dunston to the value of £60,
        to be held by the Q for 14 years in cons. of her acquitting Norman Darcy of debts
        to the Jews. This transaction seems to be more complex than implied by Roth, *Jews
        of Medieval Oxford*, 71–73. Late in 1274 or early 1275, Darcy ackn. he owed the Q
        200 marks, to be paid in installments of 40 marks yrly from Easter 1275; thus his debt
        of 200 marks to Jacob of Oxford would be quit and cancelled (*CPEJ*, ii, 178). *CPR
        1272–1281*, 80, is a Feb. 1275 agreement between the Q and Darcy that the Q would
        hold lands worth £40 for 10 years, in return for which she would acquit him of £280
        owed Hagin of London and £133:6:8 owed Jacob of Oxford, which debts the K had
        gtd her. There is ref. in June 1275 to debts Darcy owed Moses de Clare and Aaron
        of Rye, which the K had gtd the Q; Jacob of Oxford is said to have conveyed to her
        a debt of 200 marks (*CClR 1272–1279*, 182; *CPEJ*, ii, 309, and iv, 87). The 18 Nov.

1275 agreement is *CPR 1272–1281*, 113, where the debts are £280 to Hagin, £133:6:8 to Jacob, and £50 to Elias f. Moses of London (*CCIR 1279–1288*, 81, however, has £950 owed mr Elias and Manser f. Aaron, which the Q had "partly of the gift of the Jews and partly for her gold," of which at the prayer of Antony Bek she pardoned £250). On the same day, 18 Nov. 1275, the K ordered the Q given debts in which Darcy was bound to the Jews, as he had gtd them to her; she received charters for 200 marks owed Jacob f. Moses (of Oxford) and for £280 owed Hagin f. Moses (*CPEJ*, iv, 83). She did acquit Darcy towards Jacob f. Moses and Elias f. Moses (*CPEJ*, iii, 74–75), but ca. 25 Nov. 1275 Darcy ackn. he owed her £35:13:4 by Christmas, and that in the next fortnight he must add 60s. of land to that she already held (*CPEJ*, iii, 59). The K in M1280 gtd the Q Darcy's £100 relief (E 159/54 m. 3d), but in Jan. 1284, for Darcy's service in the Welsh war, pardoned his debts to the Jewry and his relief (E 159/57 m. 3; E9/44 m. 5). On Darcy, Moor, *Knights*, i, 265–66.

137.   [T1277 X E1280?]. Houses in Lincoln taken into the Q's hands apparently by reason of Stephen de Cheyndut's debts to the Jewry, though Adam de Neofmarche cl. prior right (Rigg, ed., *Select Pleas, Starrs*, 109–10). Presumably the houses noted in a list of debts owed Hagin f. Moses by Cheyndut and others, gtd the Q T1277 (E 13/5 m. 22). On Cheyndut see also nos. 13a, 105a, 141, 246b; on Neofmarche, no. 139.

138.   [1288 X 1290]. A manor at Welbourn, acq. by fine from Peter Mallore and his wife Maud, widow of Elias de Rabayn. *CIM*, i, no. 1964 shows the Q gtd the manor to her cousin Isabella de Beaumont, widow of John de Vescy who d. Feb. 1289 (no. 117 is another gt to this couple; for land acq. from Elias and Maud, nos. 51, 233). Maud was h. of John de Bayeux (d. 1249) who held Welbourn in chief as of his barony of Thoresway, worth £20:15:11 (*CIPM*, i, no. 159; Sanders, *Baronies*, 88–89). Rabayn d. 1285; in May 1286 the Q was gtd the marr. of his widow, still unm. May 1288 (*CIPM*, ii, no. 689; *CPR 1281–1292*, 248; Moor, *Knights*, iv, 108–9; Sanders, 88–89, says Maud and Mallore m. 1288 or 1289). As the Q obtained Welbourn from Maud and Peter, the conveyance must have followed their marr.; she may have exacted it for her lic. to marry or as penalty for marr. without lic. Mallore owed the Q's exors. £100 in Sept. 1291 (*CCIR 1288–1296*, 203), but this seems unrelated to further arrangements in Feb. 1293 (*CFR*, i, 305).

139.   1290 (13 Oct.). The Q sealed at Clipston a chirograph with Peter de Cestre, guaranteeing his life tenancy of a manor at Carlton Scroop in Kesteven, which she was to purchase from Adam de Neofmarche; Peter promised not to impede her entry and would retain his term therein (D.L. 25/2909). Held of the e. of Surrey for one fee (*RH*, i, 330; *BF*, 1040, 1094). There were two Adams de Neofmarche, father and son, and until the father d. 1282–83 it is hard to distinguish them; one or both were in financial troubles from 1278 (GEC, ix, 547–48; Moor, *Knights*, iii, 263; Wrottesley, *Pedigrees*, 538, 541; see also no. 137). After 1282–83, rolls of the Exch. of the Jews show the yr Adam indebted to several moneylenders; he owed Hagin f. Moses £900, M1280 (E9/33 m. 6d). Some of these debts came to the Q when she was gtd debts owing Hagin f. Moses, 1279 (E 9/33 m. 6–6d). Queen-gold accts for 14–15 Edw. show payments to Eleanor by some who held lands late of Adam de Neofmarche, who had apparently alienated them to evade payment of his debts (*Records 1286–1289*, no. 3088; E 101/505/19 m. 2). The Q's death in the month after this agreement seems to have ended royal interest in the manor.

MIDDLESEX

Dower:
>   1254: None
>   1275:
140.   Kempton

Crown Grants: None[132]

Acquisitions:
141.   [bef. Jan. 1276]. A messuage in Milkstrete, London, acq. from mr Moses and gtd by the Q, 21 Jan. 1276, to Stephen de Cheyndut (*CPR 1271–1281*, 129, 131, 137). Other transactions involving Cheyndut are nos. 13a, 105a, 137, 246b.

142.   [bef. Feb. 1290]. Houses in London acq. from persons unknown, gtd by the Q bef. 19 Feb. 1290 to her tailor William de Somerfeld, who on that date had £13:6:8 "to acquit his houses in London that the Q gave him, against a certain woman who sought dower therein" (*CHEC*, 89).

143a.   [bef. July 1290]. The Q perhaps acq. from Otho de Grandison houses in London used by her wardrobe; ?ident. to 143b (*CHEC*, 110). Apparently still used by clks of the Q's exors, M1291 (*Manners*, 96).

143b.   [bef. Nov. 1290]. The Q gtd Otho de Grandison houses in London formerly of Hagin f. Moses. These Otho afterwards surr. to the K, who restored them to Otho on 12 July 1296, to be held by him and hs by services due. ?Ident. to 143a (*CChR*, ii, 465).

144.   [bef. Nov. 1290]. Houses in Seving Lane, London, gtd by the Q to her wardrobe keeper John de Berewyk', who held them at his death, 1312 (*CPR 1307–1313*, 481).

NORFOLK

Dower:
>   1254: None
>   1275:
145.   Farm of Ormsby

146.   *Cawston with the hundred of South Erpingham (= no. 148)

Crown Grants:
147a.   1269 (24 Oct.). The manor of Aylsham, committed to the Lady Eleanor at pleasure (*CPR 1266–1272*, 372).

147b.   1270 (26 May). Aylsham is gtd Eleanor in fee for life, with remainder to her hs by Edward (*CChR*, ii, 133). Though neither 147a–b so states, Aylsham was held with N. Erpingham hundred and members incl. lands in Scottow (no. 152): *RH*, i, 505, 513.

148.   1278 (28 May). The manor of Cawston (no. 146), gtd the Q for life (*CPR 1272–1281*, 265). Held with S. Erpingham hundred, both formerly of John de Burgh (*CIPM*, ii, no. 82; *RP*, i, 299; *CFR*, i, 452–53; *RH*, i, 513).

149. 1284 (11 Feb.). Wardship of manors at Weeting and Toftrees in minority of the h.
of Ralph de Playz (documentation identical to no. 18; see also nos. 57, 217). The Q
gtd wardship of Weeting to Petronilla de Toeny (JUST 1/836 m. 5).

150. 1285 (11 Sept.). Wardship of a manor at Wood Dalling in minority of the h. of
William Cummyn (CPR 1281–1292, 193; CCIR 1279–1288, 337; for Cummyn fees in
Norfolk, BF, 911). In 1289–90 one "Comyn'," perhaps the Dalling h., was in Edward
of Caernarvon's household (C 47/3/22).

Acquisitions:
151a. [1278 May/June]. A manor at Burgh next Aylsham, secured from John de Burgh
through his debts to the Jewry reckoned at 400 marks, for £140 owed the K at the
Exch., and in consideration of £66:13:4 paid by the Q (Kalendars, i, 60 [no. 193]; CCIR
1279–1288, 80 [worth £30 yrly]). On Burgh's debts, CPEJ, iii, 82; CCIR 1272–1279,
221; CPEJ, iv, 64–65. These, amounting to £1000 or more, were gtd the Q 13 Nov.
1275; when she was gtd in 1280 all debts owing Hagin f. Moses, John de Burgh was
found to be indebted to him for 250 marks (E 9/33 m. 6), and in cons. of her decision not to distr. the abbot of Hyde for £71 owed through the Jewry, she was given
a debt of 100 marks Burgh owed Manser f. Aaron (S.C. 1/19/3, s.d.). The date of this
transaction is inferred from nos. 148 (another of John's manors near Burgh) and 151b.

151b. 1278 (June). All the lands Ralph de Hauville held in the manor of Burgh, released with
all appurts to the K and Q, lords of the manor of Burgh (CCIR 1272–1279, 497). John
de Burgh's former manor of Cawston was gtd the Q in the preceding month (no.
146), suggesting that Burgh was conveyed to her about the same time to create a
compact group of estates in Norf. Compare nos. 114–16 in Kent, also in 1278.

152a. [1275 26 May X 1281 5 Jan.]. A manor at Scottow (see no. 147b), with the adv. and
member at Great Hautbois, secured from Bartholomew de Redham whose debt to
Hagin for £200 was gtd the Q by the K, and other of whose debts to the Jewry came
to her for her gold (CCIR 1279–1288, 80 [worth £40]; RP, i, 312). It is not clear which
"Hagin" is meant here; neither the gt of Hagin f. Cress' debts to the Q, T1275 (CPEJ,
ii, 310), nor that of his uncle Hagin f. Moses' debts, 15 Nov. 1279 (CCIR 1272–1279,
547; E 9/33 m. 6–6d), mentions Redham, but new debts could have been contracted
with either Hagin after those gts. Other of Redham's debts were gtd the Q 26 May
1275, "that [she] may deal with them as it may seem to her most expedient," and
his creditors were allowed appropriate amounts in the tallage (CPEJ, ii, 310; CCIR
1272–1279, 184; CPEJ, iv, 86–87 [= CCIR 1272–1279, 205], 123–24). In Feb. 1284 the
Q gtd Scottow for life to Gilbert Pecche in return for lands lately surr. to her (CPR
1281–1292, 114).

152b. 1281 (5 Jan.). At Hautbois, nine messuages, six acres land, 20 acres meadow and pasture, a free fishery, and 5s. yearly rent, from which the Q's bfs at Scottow ejected
Bartholomew de Redham, as allegedly appurt. to Scottow. See no. 152c.

152c. [1281 Jan. X 1290 Nov.]. At Hautbois, four acres of alder-wood, one and one-half
acres called "Duffusyerd," one acre called "Gerardesacre" and a free fishery; and at
Scottow, 12 acres, from all of which Bartholomew de Redham unjustly disseized
Robert and William Baynard before conveying Scottow to the K and Q, whose men
refused to restore the lands to the Baynards. Redham in 1291 sought to recover 10
librates in Hautbois; inq. was summoned but the action was not determined (JUST
1/542 m. 11d). In 1301 Redham and the Baynards recovered the lands in nos. 152b–c
(CPR 1281–1292, 207; CCIR 1296–1302, 415–16; CCIR 1302–1307, 39–40).

153.   1282 (29 Mar.). The adv. of the ch. of Stow Bedon, with an acre of land at Wyveton, acq. by fine from Geoffrey de Southorpe. The Q in May 1290 obtained papal license for appropriation of the adv. to Marham Abbey; the K effected the gt Feb. 1292 (Nichols, ed., *History and Cartulary of Marham*, 242; Bliss, i, 513, 530; *CChR*, ii, 416). On Southorpe, see no. 160.

154.   [1288 Jan. X 1290 Nov.]. At Witchingham and Alderford, nine messuages, 80 acres land, seven acres meadow, two parts of one acre of wood, two acres pasture, 17s. yearly rent and appurts usurped from John de Antingham after the death of his br. Bartholomew, who had enfeoffed him thereof. Known only from Antingham's 1291 complaint, dismissed when the Q's officials pr. he had a writ of novel disseisin pending in another court (JUST 1/836 m. 1). Bartholomew de Antingham d. Jan. 1288, when his lands were taken into the K's hand on the assumption they were held in chief (later found to be untrue). As some of his lands were at Scottow (no. 152), the disseisin might have been perpetrated on grounds that they pertained to the Q's tenure (*CIPM*, ii, no. 687; *CFR*, i, 253).

NORTHAMPTON

Dower:

        1254: None
        1275:
155.   Apethorpe

156.   Castle and forest of Rockingham

Crown Grants:[133]
157a.   1267 (22 Nov.). The manor of Kingsthorpe, committed to Eleanor at pleasure (*CPR 1266–1272*, 168).

157b.   1268 (6 Jan.). Kingsthorpe is to be held for ten years from last Michaelmas (*CPR 1266–1272*, 179).

157c.   1270 (26 May). Kingsthorpe with the hundred of Spelhoe, gtd in fee to Eleanor for life, with remainder to legitimate hs by Edward (*CChR*, ii, 133).

Acquisitions:[134]
158.   [bef. 1279 July]. A well outside Northampton, gtd by the Q in this month to the Dominican friars of the town (*CPR 1272–1281*, 322).

159a.   1280 (25 Mar. and 4 Nov.). Manors at Torpel and Upton, secured from John de Camoys, who owed to the Jewry 500 marks which the Q had of the K's gift, and in consideration of 600 marks paid by the K (*Kalendars*, i, 61–62 [no. 205]; *CCIR 1272–1279*, 81 [worth £80]). Held of the abbot of Peterborough in chief with other lands for 6 fees (*CIPM*, ii, no. 212; *Feudal Aids*, iv, 443; E. King, *Peterborough Abbey*, 38–40; GEC, ii, 506; Sanders, *Baronies*, 19; Coss, "Geoffrey de Langley," 31–33). Camoys was bound to merchants as well as the Jewry (E 13/7 m. 3; *CCIR 1279–1288*, 28, 48, 52, 54). Debts his father Ralph (d. ca. Mar. 1277) owed Hagin f. Moses were gtd the Q, T1277 (E 13/5 m. 22d), and John's debts, amounting to 1000 marks, were among those owed Hagin f. Moses gtd the Q 15 Nov. 1279 (*CCIR 1272–1279*, 547; E 9/33 m. 6). In H1280 the sher. of Surrey was to distr. Camoys (E 9/34 m. 6); Walter de Kancia was suing for the debts T1280 (E 9/36 m. 5d). Camoys demised Torpel and

Upton to the K and Q for term of years, 25 Mar. 1280, but on 26 July 1280 the Q was gtd all debts Camoys owed at the Exch., and conveyance of the manors came on 4 Nov. (*CCIR 1279–1288*, 28–29, 46, 66; *CPR 1272–1279*, 366–67). See also nos. 20, 23a.

159b. [1280 Mar. X 1290 Nov.]. At Torpel, the Q's bfs refused to allow the abbot of Thorney to enter a wood purchased for 50 marks from John de Camoys before the manor came to the Q. The abbot pr. his right 1291, but the justices refused to proceed *rege inconsulto* (JUST 1/542 *m.* 9).

160. M1289. At Lolham, seven librates conveyed to the K and Q by Geoffrey de Southorpe (*PA*, 220; E. King, "Large and Small Landowners," 36). For Southorpe, above, no. 153. He acq. the land in Lolham in 1276–77; this was held of John de Camoys as of the manor of Torpel for ½ fee (*CIPM*, iv, no. 47; see no. 159a).

161. See no. 179a (Easton, member of Lyndon, Ruts. q.v.)

NORTHUMBERLAND

Dower:
    1254: None
    1275:
162. Farm of Corbridge

Crown Grants: None

Acquisitions: None

NOTTINGHAM

Dower:
    1254: None
    1275:
163. Clipston

164. Mansfield with the soke

165. *Wheatley

Crown Grants: None

Acquisitions: None

OXFORD

Dower:
    1254: None
    1275:
166. Wootton, with the hundred

Crown Grants:[135]

167.   1274 (8 Nov.). Wardship of ⅛ fee at Thrup in minority of the h. of Nicholas de
        Haversham (documentation identical to no. 11; see also nos. 126, 229).

168.   1280 (25 May). Wardship of 12 virgates with appurts at Ascott in Great Milton, in
        minority of the h. of John Jordan *alias* le Forester (documentation identical to no. 6;
        see also *CCIR 1288–1292,* 159).

169.   [uncertain]. The Q is said to have been gtd, or cl. to have been gtd, all issues and prof-
        its of the city of Oxford (Roth, *Jews of Medieval Oxford,* 76, 89–90, 157).

Acquisitions:[136]

170.   [bef. 1279 12 Nov.]. A messuage with solar and a garden with well, in the parish of
        St. Martin within Oxford, formerly of Jacob f. Moses; and a solar opposite the church
        of St. Martin, gtd by the Q, 12 Nov. 1279, to Henry Oweyn of Oxford (*CPR
        1272–1281,* 332–33; Roth, *Jews of Medieval Oxford,* 76–78, 89–90).

171.   M1279. A manor at Godington with appurts including some land in Bucks., secured
        from Robert de Camville by reason of his debts to the Jewry (documentation iden-
        tical to no. 61a–b; see also nos. 104, 117). Held of the earl of Lincoln for ¼ fee (*CIPM,*
        vi, no. 422). Stated in M1279 to be held for life by Stephen de Pencestre (*d.* 1299;
        EFF, ii, 28–29; Moor, *Knights,* iv, 32–35), but gtd by the Q to Guy Ferré jr, Feb. 1281
        (*CChR,* ii, 248, 249; Salter, *Feet of Fines for Oxon.,* 212 (no. 60).

172.   1281 (July). The manor of Headington with its members, gtd to the K and Q by Hugh
        de Plessis (*CCIR 1272–1279,* 128; *Kalendars,* i, 140 [no. 114]; Hall, ed., *Red Book,*
        i, cxxviii [where the Q is not named]; held in chief for 1 fee [*RH,* ii, 710]). Details are
        lacking. On de Plessis see GEC, x, 548–49; he owed the Q £53:10:0 in 2 Edw., per-
        haps because she paid the farm due from him for Headington in that year (E 159/48
        m. 28).

173.   [1275 X 1285]. A messuage called "la Oriole" in Sideyard street, Oxford, conveyed
        to the Q by mr Bevis de Clare bef. 1285, when she gtd it for life to her nephew James
        de Ispannia. James was allowed in 1329 to convey his interest to the college now
        known as Oriel (Shadwell and Salter, ed., *Oriel College Records,* nos. 98–102, 105;
        Rannie, *Oriel College,* 17–18 [where "the wife of Edward I" is wrongly Eleanor of
        Provence]; Highfield, "The Early Colleges," 238). For James de Ispannia, Emden,
        Oxford, iii, 1737–38; on Bevis de Clare, Emden, i, 423–24, and Parsons, "Piety,
        Power," 112–13.

174.   1286 (Feb.). A manor at Whitchurch, purchased by the Q from Roger la Ware (or
        de la Ware) for 200 marks (Westm. Abbey, muniments 23627; *Kalendars,* i, 57 [no.
        173]; *CIPM,* iii, no. 145). Details are lacking.

175.   15 Edw. (1286 Nov. X 1287 Nov., "at Bordeaux"). A manor at Kirtlington, released
        by Hugh Despenser the elder whose grandmother Ela held it in dower of his inh.
        (*Kalendars,* i, 43 [nos. 65–66] has Hugh's release of the manor and his letters *de inten-
        dendo* to Ela in favor of the K; *VCH Oxon.,* vi, 222, is unaware of this). Edward I
        annulled the release 1 Oct. 1296 (*DC,* ii, 160); his letters *de intendendo* to Ela in favor
        of Hugh (3 Oct. 1296) are *CPR 1292–1301,* 206. The 1286–87 release is almost cer-
        tainly related to no. 29a, which took place at about the same time.

PEMBROKE

Dower: None

Crown Grants:
176. [ca. 1265?]. Eleanor of Castile appears to have held the wardship of some lands of the Bohun inheritance (*CIR 1268–1272*, 206, with which compare GEC, vi, 463 note "h"). Further details are lacking; ?related to no. 177.

Acquisitions:
177. [1286 7 May X 1288 3 June]. The two parts of the barony of Haverfordwest (including the castle) that were of the inh. of Humphrey de Bohun, earl of Hereford and Essex, acq. through an exch. of manors. D.L. 27/185 is an indented chirograph between the Q and the e. (Leeds castle, 7 May 1286) agreeing he would enfeoff her of his moiety of Haverfordwest in exch. for lands in Essex to the same value; officials were chosen to extend the lands and arbiters nom. in case of dispute. The Q was in seisin at Haverfordwest by 3 June 1288 (Edwards, *Anct Correspondence*, 170, giving S.C. 1/31/36 [3 June s.a.] with a suggested date in 1288 or 1289 "with a probable preference for 1288"). *CPR 1281–1292*, 330–31, shows the exch. was effected well bef. 15 May 1289 and by Feb. 1290 the Q had been in seisin two full years (*RP*, i, 30). *CIPM*, iii, no. 552, identifies the manors given Bohun by the Q as Quendon, Fobbing, and Shenfield (nos. 61a, 63). See Edwards, *Littere Wallie*, no. 306, and *Kalendars*, i, 43 (no. 69).

178. 18 Edward I [1290 May X 1290 19 Nov.]. The homage and service of Robert de Valle, of Hill, Bickton and Molhock, surr. to the K and Q by Walter de Monte, lord of Molhock, and Thomas de Roche (*Kalendars*, i, 63 [nos. 211–12], 119–20 [no. 42]). Disputed in 1290 by William de Valence and Joan his wife, h. to the third part of Haverford. *CPR 1281–1292*, 330–31, states that de Valle was forced to do homage to the Q's officials bef. 15 May 1289; John de Wogan who responded for William and Joan in Feb. 1290 said he entered Haverford castle just in time to prevent de Valle doing homage to Cressingham (*RP*, i, 33). As the homage was still disputed in May 1290 the conveyance may have come later, perhaps in or after June 1290 when the Q won judgment against the Valences through Joan's default (*RP*, i, 31; *CHEC*, 108). See also *CCIR 1296–1302*, 226; *CPR 1292–1301*, 258.

RUTLAND

Dower: None

Crown Grants: None

Acquisitions:
179a. 1285 [July]. A manor at Lyndon, with member at Easton-on-Hill, Northants. (no. 161), acquired from Simon de Lyndon and mr Henry Sampson the elder.[137] (*CCIR 1279–1288*, 375; *CIPM*, iii, no. 446; ref. to lands in Casterton held by service of 1/6 fee as of the manor of Easton acq. by the Q, *CFR*, i, 405–6). Lyndon and Easton were held together for one fee (*BF*, 931). In 1291 Joan widow of Simon de Lyndon pr. that after the Q assigned her dower at Lyndon, the buildings there were found in ruins; the Q promised repairs but nothing was done (JUST 1/542 *m*. 9; *CIM*, ii, no. 258).

179b. [1285 July X 1290 Nov.]. In 1291 Joan de Lyndon further pr. that the Q's bfs seized the wardship of lands of Peter de Relegh', tenant of Simon de Lyndon in Easton, though Relegh' died bef. Simon and the wardship should have remained with Joan as her husband's executrix. She was to recover the wardship (JUST 1/542 *m.* 9).

SHROPSHIRE

Dower: None

Crown Grants:
180. 1284 (11 Feb.). Wardship of manors at Acton Round, Upton Magna, Wroxeter and Cound, lately held in dower by Matilda, wife of Richard de Amundeville, of the inh. of John fitz Alan, a minor in the K's ward (documentation identical to no. 78; see also nos. 216, 218, 231).

Acquisitions:
181. See nos. 3, 28, 234.

SOMERSET

Dower:
  1254: None
  1275:
182. Farm of Axbridge

183. Farm of Cheddar

184. Farm of Congresbury

185. *Camel (Queen's Camel) and Kingsbury (or Camel Kingsbury); see no. 191.

Crown Grants:
186. 1265 (20 Mar.). Wardship of a manor at Dundon, with member at Long Sutton, in minority of Cecily, dau. coh. of William le Fort *als* de Fortibus (documentation identical to no. 17; see also no. 213, and *VCH Soms.*, iii, 157–58).

187a. 1265 (30 Apr.). The manor and hundred of Somerton, to be held at farm (*CPR 1258–1266*, 420).

187b. 1266 (17 Feb.). The manor and hundred of Somerton, to be held free of farm with the manors of Pitney and Wearne, until Eleanor be better provided for by the K (*CPR 1258–1266*, 555).

187c. 1266 (7 Apr.). Somerton with the hundred, and the manors of Pitney and Wearne, to be held for life (*CPR 1258–1266*, 578).[138] Pitney and Wearne were surr. to the Crown Aug. 1270, to be transferred to Alan Plogenet in exch. for the stewardship of the New Forest (no. 85).

188. 1265 (18 Sept.). Wardship of manors at Barwick and Stokewood in minority of the h. of William de Cantilupe (*CPR 1258–1266*, 453; *CIM*, i, no. 575). Ineffective (Shirley, ed., *Royal Letters*, no. 647). See also nos. 190, 208, 224.

189. 1265 (30 Sept.). The manor of Haselbury Plucknett, to be held at pleasure for the Lady Eleanor's maintenance. The manor was, however, gtd in fee to Alan Plogenet, 19 Oct. 1265 (*CPR 1258–1266*, 458, 476).

190. 1274 (11 Nov.). Wardship of a manor at Barwick in minority of John Hastings, nephew coh. of George de Cantilupe (*CPR 1272–1281*, 64; *CCIR 1272–1279*, 148). This George was the h. in whose minority the wardship of Barwick was briefly gtd Eleanor, 1265 (no. 188). He d. in the autumn of 1274 just after reaching his majority, leaving as cohs a sister and John Hastings aged 14–15, son of a deceased sister (*CIPM*, ii, no. 17; Moor, *Knights*, i, 179). John was in the Q's ward in 1276 when she recovered the adv. on one of his manors in Warks. (see no. 224).[139]

191a. 1276 (8 Apr.). The manor of Camel, to be held at pleasure (*CFR*, i, 68).

191b. 1276 (1 May). The manor of Camel, to be held at will (*CPR 1272–1281*, 139).

191c. 1278 (28 May). The manor of Camel, to be held for life and not separated from the Crown (*CPR 1272–1281*, 265; *Feudal Aids*, iv, 285; *RO*, i, 70). Though enrollments do not so state, Camel was held with the hundred of Horethorne and the rent of assize at Milborne (S.C. 6/1089/22 m. 1; *CFR*, i, 305; *RO*, i, 70).[140]

192. [1280]. Wardship of a manor at Horsington in minority of the hs of Ralph and James Russell (documentation identical to no. 7; see also nos. 12, 45, 77, and *CFR*, i, 290).

193. 1284 (Feb.). Wardship of a manor at Stoke sub Hamden, in minority of the h. of John de Beauchamp of Hatch (*CCIR 1272–1279*, 251). John de Beauchamp (d. Oct. 1283) m. Cecily le Fort, Eleanor's ward in 1265 (nos. 17, 186, 213). The Beauchamp h. was b. 25 July 1274 (GEC, ii, 186).

194. 1285 (28 July). The Q is apptd to custody of cos. Soms. and Dors., John de St. Laud to exercise the office of sheriff (*CPR 1281–1292*, 186).

195. [ca. 1285]. Manors at Stogursey and Rodway with the vill and hundred of Cannington, held in dower by Maud widow of Robert Walerand whose hs are idiots in the K's ward. Documentation identical to no. 47; see also *Feudal Aids*, iv, 218, and *CIPM*, iv, no. 457. The Q's connection with the Soms. lands of the Walerand inh. appears to have begun in 13 Edw. I, when she held Cannington (*Feudal Aids*, iv, 282). Indications (*CCIR 1288–1296*, 22) that she held Stogursey in 13 Edw. and half of 14 Edw. are borne out by accts for arrears in her manorial issues for 14 Edw. (S.C. 6/1089/22 m. 2) and by payment from mr Thomas de Button, dean of Wells, of £73:6:8 for the farm of Stogursey in 14 Edw. (E 159/59 m. 28). But Maud Walerand survived until 1288, and it was only then that other lands of that inh. came to the Q (nos. 47, 79, 91, 102, 232, 238). Further details are lacking.[141] Stogursey and Rodway were still admin. with the Q's lands in 29 Edw. (E 372/146 m. 43d). See also nos. 79, 91, 102, 232, 238.

Acquisitions:[142]

196a. 1270 (3 May). A manor at Martock next Somerton, leased by Eleanor from William de Fiennes for six yrs from the Invention of Holy Cross 54 Henry III (*CPR 1266–1272*, 459; *CCIR 1279–1288*, 88, reads "Walter," but the lord of Martock in 1270 was William de Fiennes [*CHEC*, 44–46]).

196b. 1275 (15 June). Martock is leased for three years from Midsummer 3 Edw. so the Q may recover a portion of the £1000 she agreed to pay as dowry for William de Fiennes' dau., who is to m. the e. of Essex' h. (*CChR*, ii, 190–91; see also no. 214).

197a. 1276 (Octave of Mich.). A manor at Hurcott with lands at Ash Herbert and
       Atherstone, amounting (with lands in Dorset, no. 48) to 6¼ fees, purchased from
       Henry de Newburgh for £200.

197b. [M1276 X 1290 Nov.]. The Q occupied as appurt. to Hurcott lands in Frome Belet,
       Raddington, Upcott, Tuxwell, Charlton Mackrell and Huish Champflower (docu-
       mentation for no. 197a–b identical to nos. 48–9; see also VCH Soms., iii, 83, 97–98,
       138; CIPM, iii, no. 152). Newburgh's s. John tried to recover some of these lands, 1290
       (RP, i, 21–22); he failed again in 1291, as did Henry's widow Alice who sought dower
       in Hurcott and elsewhere (JUST 1/1014 mm. 4, 5; Manners, 110). John recovered
       some lands, 1305, but most remained with the K (see nos. 48–49).

198.   1279 (20 Oct.). and 1281 (Quinz. of Easter). A manor at Dulverton with the hundred,
       demised to the K and Q by Thomas du Pyn and his wife Hawise. On 20 Oct. 1279
       the couple demised manor and hundred to the Q who would provide them with
       lands to the same value elsewhere (CCIR 1272–1279, 578). By fine in E1281 the
       couple ackn. the manor to be the right of the K and Q, and were to hold it for their
       lives at a rent of 1d. at Easter (E. Green, ed., Pedes finium for Soms., 254 [no. 58]; CCIR
       1279–1288, 80). Held in chief for 1/3 fee (CIPM, iii, no. 263). Nothing is known of
       the "great bounty" the Q is said to have done du Pyn (CCIR 1279–1288, 80); on him,
       Moor, Knights, iv, 68–69.

199.   [ca. 1280]. A manor at Uphill with land at Christon, making in all 2 carucates held of
       William Martin for ¼ fee, whereof the Q was enfeoffed by Agnes de Sparkeford in
       cons. of 10 marks yrly for life, after the Q helped Agnes recover the lands agst
       William de Pateneye sr, whom Agnes enfeoffed when he promised to marry her
       (Sayles, ed., Select Cases, i, 65–66; ii, 20–23; iii, xcix n. 4). William de Pateneye jr. tried
       to recover the lands in 1290 (RP, i, 53), and again in 1291 when inq. supported Agnes;
       his bill stated that the manor at Uphill was worth £4:6:3 3/4 and the land at Christon
       38s.2¾d., a total of £6:4:6¼, roughly the 10 marks Agnes had yrly for the conveyance
       (JUST 1/542 m. 8). In 15 Edw. the lands were farmed for £8 (S.C. 6/1089/22 m. 1).

STAFFORD

Dower: None

Crown Grants:
200.   1270 (before 8 Sept.). Lands at Leek and Densington, appurt. to Macclesfield, Ches.
       (no. 25) (Ormerod, Chester, iii, 63; CPR 1272–1281, 471–72; CPR 1281–1292, 76;
       Stewart-Brown, ed., Rolls of Chester, 232–33, 237).

201.   1279 (Feb.) The year, day and waste of the manor of Handsworth, late of William
       de Parles who was hanged for felony (CCIR 1272–1279, 521; Moor, Knights, iv, 6).
       Parles was hanged 1 July 1277 X 10 Feb. 1279; his felony seems to be unrelated to
       the problems noted in RH, ii, 116. His sons long troubled the Q and others over his
       lands (CCIR 1279–1288, 179; RP, i, 51, 95; Sayles, ed., Select Cases, i, 103; Coss,
       Lordship, Knighthood and Locality, 277–80).

Acquisitions:
202.   1290 (2 May). A manor at Rowley (Rowley Regis), acq. by fine from William de Etling
       als Detling, saving to Roger de Somery life tenancy (Wrottesley, "Final Concords,"
       44); held in socage of the K in chief, rendering 16s.4d. yearly (Feudal Aids, v, 9; CIPM,

ii, no. 813 [at 494, 497]). Detling was paid £10 "pro manerio de Rulegh'" from the Q's wardrobe on 14 Feb. 1290 and gave her letters of quittance; on 20 May follg he had another £10 for the manor from her treas. (CHEC, 88; S.C. 6/1089/25 m. 4). In 1291 Detling cl. that while he might have had £90 and a horse worth 10 marks for the manor, he conveyed it to the Q after she promised to promote himself or his children, and that he was never paid more than 30 marks. His complaint was not determined (JUST 1/542 m. 3). Compare no. 117, a like cl. by Roger, s. h. of Robert de Camville. In that case the Q kept her promise; perhaps her death soon after the Rowley purchase prevented her advancement of Detling or his family.

SUFFOLK

Dower:
> 1254: None
> 1275:
203. Farm of Dunwich
204. Farm of Combe

205. Farm of Ipswich

206. Castle and town of Orford

207. *Lands in Suffolk appurtenant to Nayland, Essex (no. 55).

Crown Grants:
208. 1274 (11 Nov.). Wardship of a manor at Badmondisfield in minority of the hs of George de Cantilupe (documentation identical to no. 190; compare nos. 188, 224).

209. 1290 (3 and 12 Nov.). Custody of a manor at Edwardstone with five manors and other tens, making in all 12 fees late of William de Montchensy of Edwardstone (documentation identical to no. 5; compare nos. 19, 58–60, 63, 104).

Acquisitions:[143]
210a. [ca. 1274?]. A manor at Bentley Dodnash and lands at Tattingstone, demised to the Q by John Carbonel. Most information on this obscure transaction comes from a 1291 complaint by Sybil and Theobald de Bellus (JUST 1/836 m. 6). John Carbonel m. Agnes, dau. h. of Hugh de Doddeneys (dead in 3 Edw. [RH, ii, 190]) and his wife Sybil, whose second husband was Theobald de Bellus. In 1291 Sybil and Theobald recovered her dower in lands at Dodnash and Tattingstone demised to the Q by John Carbonel sixteen years earlier; they recd £2:13:7 of the grace of the Q's exors and 8 marks to remit all demands (Manners, 106, 127). The widow of John Carbonel released to the Q all lands settled on her by her father Hugh de Dodenesse (Kalendars, i, 57 [no. 172, s.d.]). Two debts owed Elias Bagard, a Jew, by one John Carbonel came to the Q in 1284; these amounted to £13:13:8 (E 9/44 m. 6), but it is not certain this John was the vendor at Tattingstone and Dodnash; there were perhaps three of the name active in Suffolk in Eleanor's time (Moor, Knights, i, 182).

210b. [ca. 1275 X 1290 Nov.]. The Q held lands in Dodnash formerly of Charles son of Charles, of the inh. of Edward Charles his nephew; these were to be restored to Edward Charles 3 Feb. 1291 (CCIR 1288–1296, 161). On the family, Moor, Knights, i, 193–94. Edward Charles was s. h. of William Charles (d. ca. 1271), knt in Eleanor's household who m. ca. 1262 her damsel Joan "de Valle Viridi." Born ca. 1269, Edward

Charles would have come of age around the time the Q d. in 1290, suggesting she had obtained, or cl., an interest in his wardship and thus may have held the uncle's lands after he d., evidently during Edward Charles' minority. Further details are lacking.

211.   1284 (ca. Feb.). Three fees at Sogenhoe (in Ufford), Blaxhall and Culford, secured from Gilbert Pecche by reason of his debts to the Jewry (documentation identical to no. 21; see nos. 22, 64, 118). This transaction may also have incl. the adv. of the ch. of Dalham (*CCIR 1288–1296*, 284), though apparently not the manor itself.

SURREY

Dower:
        1254: None
        1275:
212.   *Banstead[144]

Crown Grants:
213.   1265 (29 Mar.). Wardship of a manor at Woodmansterne in minority, of Cecily, dau. coh. of William le Fort *als* de Fortibus (documentation identical to no. 17; see no. 186).

Acquisitions:
214.   1277 (24 June). A manor at Carshalton, leased from William de Fiennes for 9 years from Midsummer 1278 so that from the issues (reckoned at 100 marks yearly) the Q may recover part of the £1000 she agreed to provide for the dower of William's dau., who is to marry the e. of Essex' h. (identical to no. 196b).

215.   [ca. 1286?]. A manor at West Betchworth secured from John de Wauton sr by reason of his debts to the Jewry. From T1280, Wauton ackn. many debts owed Aaron f. Vives, "Jew of the K's brother"; a partial list of these totals £950, secured on stated amounts of grain (E 9/36 *m.* 7d; E 9/39 *m.* 3; E 9/40 *m.* 5; E 9/44 *m.* 5d). All John's debts were owed Aaron f. Vives until T1286 when he contr. a debt to Hagin f. Cress, "the Q's Jew," and with the K's lic. enfeoffed Hagin of Betchworth, 8 July 1286, to hold until the 500 marks was repaid (E 9/47 *mm.* 3d, 5d, 9, 9d). In 1291 Wauton cl. he was intr. into the Q's council by John de Kirkby, then Treas., and there reached agreement that with the help of Hagin f. Cress he would be relieved of his debts to the Jewry without losing his lands. As his complaint mentions only debts owed Aaron f. Vives, this meeting prob. predated the July 1286 loan from Hagin. At some point after 8 July 1286, Hagin at the Exch. of the Jews ackn. transferral to the Q of debts owed by John de Wauton of Surrey (E 9/47 *m.* 9); it is impossible to doubt that the Q thereby acq. Betchworth. Wauton's complaint was not determined as many of those needed to give evidence were with the K in Scotland (JUST 1/542 *m.* 4d). The K in 1291 gtd the manor to John de Berewyk' who held it of the e. of Glos. at his death, 1312 (*CIPM*, v, no. 397); it was found that Wauton had enfeoffed the e. of the manor bef. it came to the Q (*CChR*, ii, 403; *CCIR 1307–1313*, 483).[145] See also Moor, *Knights*, v, 149–50; *VCH Surrey*, iii, 173, 316, and no. 221.

SUSSEX

Dower: None
Crown Grants:[146]
216.   1283 (5 June). Wardship of manors at Stanstead (in Stoughton) and Burne with its
       hundred, lately held in dower by Isabella de Albini sometime ctss of Arundel, of the
       inh. of Richard fitz Alan, a minor in the K's ward (*CPR 1281–1292*, 65, possibly inef-
       fective; see the identical gt in aid of works at Vale Royal Abbey, 11 June 1283 [*CPR
       1281–1292*, 66]). See also nos. 78, 180, 218, 231.

217.   1284 (11 Feb.). Wardship of a manor at Wanningore and its member Wapsbourn,
       with advs of the chs of Worth and Chailey, in minority of the h. of Ralph de Playz
       (documentation identical to no. 18; see nos. 57, 149).

218.   1284 (11 Feb.). Wardship of the hundreds of Easewrithe, Bury, Easebourne and
       Rotherbridge, and manors at North Stoke, Donhurst and Eastdean, lately held in
       dower by Matilda wife of Richard de Amundeville of the inh. of Richard fitz Alan,
       minor in the K's ward (*CPR 1281–1292*, 113; *CIPM*, ii, no. 536; further documenta-
       tion identical to no. 78, and see nos. 180, 216, 231).

Acquisitions:
219.   [before 1282 Apr., ?after 1281 ca. July]. The manor of Drayton in Oving, acq. from
       John Tregoz, quitcl. to the Q by Roger de Clifford who held it for life of Tregoz' enfe-
       offment (*CChr*, ii, 261 shows that on 8 Apr. 1282 the Q exch. Drayton with Geoffrey
       de Piccheford in return for all his right in Sheldon, Db [no. 40]). As this transaction
       is not included on the Close Roll schedule of 1281 (*CCIR 1279–1288*, 80–81), it per-
       haps took place after the schedule was drawn up ca. July 1281. Held of the honor of
       Arundel for one fee (*BF*, 688). Piccheford acq. interest in Drayton bef. 1282 (*CIPM*,
       ii, no. 144), but details of his exch. with the Q are obscure (see *VCH Sussex*, iv, 166–67).
       Salzman, "Tregoz," 34–58, suggests Clifford's debts explain the Q's acq. of the
       manor. Thomas Tregoz sought to recover Drayton, 1321 (Wrottesley, *Pedigrees*,
       553–54).

220.   [bef. 30 Apr. 1286]. A plot of land in the town of Chichester, purchased of John s.
       of Nicholas the Goldsmith, which the Q gtd 30 Apr. 1286 to the OP of Chichester
       (recited in the K's conf. of June 1290, *CPR 1281–1292*, 376, the two witn. lists con-
       flated). Her treas. accts for E 14 Edw. (1286) show payment "pro quadam placia
       empta ad opus fratrum predicatorum Cicestr'" (*Records 1286–1289*, no. 3121).
       Perhaps two transactions were involved as the Q had lic. 28 July 1285 to alienate in
       mortmain to the OP of Chichester, to enlarge their site, a plot of land purchased from
       John le Blel (*CPR 1281–1292*, 186).

221.   [1274? X 1290 Nov.]. A manor at Frant, gtd the Q by the K's brother Edmund. The
       earliest ref. to the Q's tenure at Frant is the K's gt of it, 8 Jan. 1291, to her squire
       William de Bromfeld (see no. 3 above; *CPR 1281–1292*, 414). In 1293 it was ordered
       that Bromfeld not be troubled in Frant for debts of John de Wauton who formerly
       held the manor (*CCIR 1288–1296*, 335); Joan, widow of John de Wauton, sought
       dower in Frant in 8 Edw. II (*RP*, i, 304). On Wauton, see no. 215.

WARWICK

Dower:

      1254: None

      1275:

222.   *Cumpton

223.   Farm of Kineton

Crown Grants:

224.   1274 (11 Nov.). Wardship of the manor of Aston Cantlow in minority of the h. of George de Cantilupe (documentation identical to no. 190; see also no. 208). The Q recovered the adv. of Aston Cantlow against the prior of Stodley, 1276 (*PA*, 266).

225.   1280 (20 Jan.). Wardship of the manors of Hampton Arden, Knowle, Ardens Grafton *als* Grafton Minor, Over Whitacre, Elmdon and Longdon, with lands at Wootton and Solihull, of the inh. of Richard de Ardern, an idiot (*CPR 1272–1281*, 361; *CIPM*, ii, no. 198; see also nos. 226a–b, 245, 247).

Acquisitions:

226a.   1284 (27 Sept.). John le Lou and Amice his wife release to the K and Q all right in Amice's inh. in the manors of Hampton Arden, Grafton, Knowle, Wootton and Solihull (no. 225), for which the Q assigns them 30 librates in Newton Harcourt, Leics. (no. 128; *CCIR 1279–1288*, 304–5; *DC*, iv, 132–33); bef. 8 June 1285 a like release was given by Philip le Lou and Margery his wife (*CPR 1281–1292*, 175 *bis*). Hampton Arden was held for ½ fee of the honor of Mowbray (*CIPM*, ii, no. 198). At Grafton there were three hides held for ½ fee (ibid.; *VCH Warks.*, iii, 198). At Wootton there was perhaps one virgate (*VCH Warks.*, iii, 200, but one fee there is noted in a fine by Thomas de Ardern, 1195–96 [E. Stokes, ed., *Warks. Feet of Fines*, I, 2]). Knowle was held by unspecified service 1276 (*CIPM*, ii, no. 98; *VCH Warks.*, iv, 91–99). For Solihull and Longdon in Solihull (*als* Longdon la Launde), *VCH Warks.*, iv, 221–22; *CIPM*, i, 198; *CFR*, i, 74; *CIM*, i, no. 1673.[147] Amice and Margery le Lou were sisters, cousins coh. of Richard de Ardern at whose death the sisters were prob. underage. They m. a widowed father Philip le Lou, and his s. John (*VCH Warks.*, iv, 82–83, and v, 202; see also nos. 128, 245, 247, and Coss, *Lordship, Knighthood and Locality*, 192 note 156). In 1291 Philip and Margery le Lou tried to recover her right in the inh., cl. their agreement with the Q was made in Philip's nonage (unlikely if he had a son old enough to m. his wife's sister 1280 X 1284). Hugh de Cressingham answered that at the time of the release the couple were content with the £100 and 12 librates (presumably at Humberton, nos. 245, 247) the Q gave them. No determination seems to have been reached (JUST 1/542 m. 6d); the Ardern lands were among those gtd to Westm. Abbey for the Q's anniversary service, Oct. 1292 (*CChR*, ii, 424–26; Harvey, *Westm. Abbey and Its Estates*, 31). Philip and Margery tried again to recover in 1297 (*CCIR 1296–1302*, 72–73; *CIM*, i, no. 1762), and in 1332 (*VCH Warks.*, iii, 98).

226b.   [1284 X 1290]. As a result of no. 226a, the Q occupied all Hampton Arden and the other lands agst John Pecche of Wormleighton, a third coh. to the Ardern estate who did not convey his interest to the Q. He came from a different family from the Gilbert Pecche who conveyed to her lands in Cambs. and Essex (nos. 21, 22, 64, 118, 211; GEC, x, 339). Though there is no record in the existing rolls of the 1291 inq. that John Pecche brought a complaint, in 1292 he was to recover his moiety of lands in Warks. late of Richard de Ardern his kinsman (*CPR 1281–1292*, 519; *CIPM*, iii, no. 360; *CCIR 1323–1327*, 143).

WILTSHIRE

Dower:

      1254: None

      1275:

227.   Farm of Bedwyn

228.   Farm of Wexcombe

Crown Grants:[148]

229.   1274 (8 Nov.). Wardship of lands at Compton Chamberlain in minority of the h. of Nicholas de Haversham (documentation identical to no. 11; see also nos. 126, 167).[149]

230.   1280 (3 Dec.). Wardship of a manor at Poulshot in minority of the h. of Robert Burdon (documentation identical to no. 76; see also no. 81).

231.   1284 (11 Feb.). Wardship of a manor at Keevil lately held in dower by Matilda the wife of Richard de Amundeville of the inh. of Richard fitz Alan, a minor in the K's ward (*CPR 1281–1292*, 113; *CIPM*, ii, no. 536; other documentation identical to no. 78, and see nos. 180, 216, 218).

232.   [1288]. Wardship of manors at Yatesbury, Market Lavington, Hurst (in Westbury), Steeple Langford and Winterbourne Isherton (in Berwick St. James), lately held in dower by Maud widow of Robert Walerand. Documentation identical to no 47; see also nos. 79, 91, 102, 195, 238.

Acquisitions:

233.   1280 (Octave of T 8 Edw. I). Manors at Great Sherston and Woodrow purchased from John Besilles (Pugh, *Feet of Fines relating to Wilts.*, no. 50; *Kalendars*, i, 62 [no. 206]). Great Sherston, held in chief, worth £36 (Meekings, ed., *Crown Pleas of the Wilts. Eyre*, no. 217). Woodrow was formerly held by Elias Rabayn, who conveyed to John Besilles in 1272 (*VCH Wilts.*, vii, 102); Elias conveyed other lands to the Q, 1281 (no. 51), and his widow conveyed a third manor (no. 138). In 1275, Besilles had added to the manor a messuage, 36 acres of land and four acres meadow (Pugh, no. 16).

234.   [1283 ca. Dec.]. At Bramshaw, the Q's steward of the New Forest disseized Thomas de St. Omer of the wardship of lands late of William le Botiller of Wem, although William held nothing there of the K or the Q in chief, only of others in socage (*CIPM*, ii, no. 529; no. 28 is a disseisin against Botiller in Chester).

235.   1287 (17 May). Reversion to manors at Erlestoke (incl. ½ fee in Yatesbury), Haxton in Fittleton, and Rowde, secured from Matthew fitz John who retains the lands for life (most documentation identical to no. 42; see nos. 82, 98, *CCIR 1279–1288*, 480, and Pugh, *Feet of Fines relating to Wilts.*, nos. 184, 186). Held in chief for one fee (*BF*, 716, 728–29).

236.   1289 (30 Sept. X 8 Dec.). A yearly rent of 16s. in Fisherton next Salisbury, purchased from Henry fitz Aucher.[150] Eleanor's treas. accts for M 17–18 Edw. show payment to fitz Aucher of 16 marks for the rent (S.C. 6/1089/25 m. 4 = *Records 1286–1289*, no. 3201). The Q gtd this to the Dominicans of Salisbury; the K's conf. is dated 8 Dec. 1289 (*CChR*, ii, 345).

WORCESTER

Dower: None

Crown Grants:
237.   [1265, ca. Sept.?]. A manor at Martley, late of John Despenser the K's enemy, who afterwards ransomed it for £220. It must be assumed that this manor was granted Eleanor at the same time as the lands of other rebels (nos. 38, 39, 44, 134). On John's ransom, for which he had final quittance Apr. 1274, *CIR 1268–1272*, 559; *CCIR 1272–1279*, 46, 56, 119.

238.   [1288]. Wardship of a manor at Tatlington, lately held in dower by Maud widow of Robert Walerand (documentation identical to no. 47; see also *CIPM*, ii, no. 6; *CIPM*, v, no. 148). The Q's steward Cressingham demised the manor at farm to Kenilworth priory for nine years, but the priory was ejected after one year; in 1291 the prior won damages of 40s. but did not seek to recover his term (JUST 1/542 *m.* 12d). See also nos. 79, 91, 102, 195, 232, 238.

239.   1289 (22 Aug.). Custody during pleasure of the manor and forest of Feckenham (*CPR 1281–1292*, 320, 361). Assigned in dower to the K's mother, Eleanor of Provence, who entered it 1273 (*CCIR 1272–1279*, 31; *CPR 1272–1281*, 27, 71). After she took the veil in 1286, she surr. most of her lands, incl. Feckenham and its forest (*CPR 1281–1292*, 218; *Worcester*, 496).[151]

Acquisitions: None

YORK

Dower:
       1254:
240.   Castle and town of Tickhill (omitted from 1275 assignment)
       1275:
241.   Farm of Bardsey

242.   Farm of Collingham

243.   Farm of Burstwick (see nos. 31, 36)

244.   Town of Hedon (see nos. 31, 36)

Crown Grants:[152]
245.   1280 (20 Jan.). Wardship of a manor at Humberton (in Kirby-on-the-Moor), lately of Richard de Ardern, an idiot (*CPR 1271–1281*, 361; further documentation identical to nos. 225–26, and see no. 247).

Acquisitions:
246a. [before 15 Nov. 1279]. Land and houses in the city of York, with buildings thereon, gtd by the Q on this date to John Sampson and Roger Basy of York (*CPR 1272–1281*, 334, where they are concurrently pardoned debts owed the Jewry by reason of this ten.). Details are lacking. Possibly identical to no. 246b.

246b.   [T1277 X E1280]. Houses in York acq. from Stephen de Cheyndut by reason of his
         debts to the Jewry (Rigg, ed., *Select Pleas, Starrs,* 109–10). Qy if the houses noted in
         a list of debts owed Hagin f. Moses by Cheyndut and others, gtd the Q T1277 (E 13/5
         m. 22). On Cheyndut see also nos. 13a, 105a, 137, 141.

247.   1284 (27 Sept.) X 1285 (8 June). The manor at Humberton (no. 245) released by
         Philip and Margery le Lou to the Q, who gts it to them as ¼ fee in cons. of their
         release to her of Margery's right in the inh. of her kinsman Richard de Ardern (*CPR
         1281–1292,* 175; see also nos. 128, 225–6, 245). Hugh de Ardern held three caru-
         cates at Humberton, 1224 X 1230 (*BF,* 1461); William de Ardern *d.* 1276 holding ten
         bovates here of the hon. of Mowbray and 30 acres of the earl of Cornwall (*CIPM,* ii,
         no. 198).

248.   [before Nov. 1290]. The houses of certain Jews in York. After the Q's death, these
         were to be sold for the K by the escheator beyond Trent in the presence of some
         "discreet subject," and the K was to be certified of the buyer (*CPR 1281–1292,* 417).

249.   [before Nov. 1290]. Houses in York sometime the property of Isaac le Veil, that the
         Q leased or gtd to the Jew Bonamy who held them of her. These the K gtd, 1291–92,
         to Hugh de Cressingham (*RO,* i, 76; on Bonamy, Roth, *History of the Jews in England,*
         87–88, 274).

LOCATION NOT ESTABLISHED

Acquisitions:
250.   [before 1275 Feb.]. Lands of Richard de Ernham, acq. by reason of his debts to the
         Jewry; now gtd to William de Somerfeld the Q's tailor. ?At Froyle, North Froyle,
         Ernham or Halyburn, Hants. (*CPR 1266–1272,* 360, 402; *CPEJ,* i, 308, 309, and ii,
         169–70; *CCIR 1272–1279,* 151 [= E 159/49 m. 9]).

251.   1290 (Feb.). Land bought from Matilda de la Pomeray for £18:13:4 (*CHEC,* 86–87).
         In 1290 the head of the Pomeray family was the Henry who conveyed to the Q the
         marr. of Amice de Boulay, 1285 (no. 41). Matilda was widow of another Henry, cadet
         of the same family, who *d.* 1275 holding at Clistwick, Up Ottery, Ovington, Ruddon,
         Buckerell, and perhaps Stoke Rivers (Devon). Matilda held only dower in those
         manors and could not alienate, but her husband had acq. land at Ibsley and Gorley,
         Hants., nr Lyndhurst (no. 85), and this was perhaps what she sold the Q (Powley,
         House of de la Pomeray, 30–31; *VCH Hants.,* v, 572, 579–80, knows of no such sale).
         Neither the Q's accts nor the 1291 inq. refer to other land connected with the
         Pomeray family (*Records 1286–1289,* no. 3079, has a payment of queen-gold on a fine
         by Geoffrey de Kaunvill' to have the wardship of the lands and h. of Henry de la
         Pomeray, but this does not imply the Q held the ward).

Appendix II

Witnesses to Queen Eleanor's Surviving Acts†

Names of members of the Q's household or administration are preceded by an asterisk (*); the same in square brackets [*] indicates an individual who was in her household at some date but was not certainly at the time of the act.

1. 1268 (2 January). Richard de Seez' agreement for the ransom of his lands (*ClR 1264–1268*, 505; Appendix I, no. 135a). Witn.: [*]William Charles, Hugh de Dyve, Peter de Chauvent, Nicholas de Cugeho, [*]John de Weston.

2a. 1275 (15 June). Agreements for the marr. of Maud de Fiennes and Humphrey de Bohun (*CChR*, ii, 190–92; Appendix I, no. 196b). Witn.: Robert Burnell bp of Bath and Wells, Walter de Merton bp of Rochester, John fitz John, Walter Helyun, *John de Lovetot, Hugh fitz Otes, John de Geynton.

2b. 1275 (20 June). Further agreements on the same (ibid.). Witn.: Robert Burnell bp of Bath and Wells, Robert Tybotot, Henry de Bohun, John de Bohun, [*]John Ferré, Roger le Rus, Antony Bek, Robert de Hales, [*]Richard de Bures.

3. 1275 (ca. 11 November). Stephen de Cheyndut surr. to the Q his manor at Langley (E 326/4326; Appendix I, no. 105a). Witn.: Robert Burnell bp of Bath and Wells, Thomas de Cantilupe bp of Hereford, Walter de Merton bp of Rochester, William de Valence, Roger Mortimer, John de Vescy, William de Fiennes, Payn de Chaworth, Hugh fitz Otes.

4. 1278 (May/June). Ralph de Hauville surr. to the K and Q right in the manor of Burgh (*CCIR 1272–1279*, 497; Appendix I, no. 151b). Witn.: Robert Tybotot, Payn de Chaworth, Richard de Bruys, Bartholomew de Sulleye, Hugh fitz Otes, Walter Helyun, Antony Bek, John de Kirkby, *Geoffrey de Aspale, [*]Walter de [Kancia?].[153]

5. 1278 (ca. June). Roger de Loveday surr. to the K and Q the manor of West Farleigh (*CCIR 1272–1279*, 496; Appendix I, no. 114). Witn.: Thomas de Cantilupe bp of Hereford, William de Middelton bp of Norwich, Robert Tybotot, Bartholomew de Sulleye, Stephen de Pencestr', John de Cobeham, Walter Helyun, *John de Lovetot, *Geoffrey de Piccheford, Antony Bek, John de Kirkby, *Geoffrey de Aspale.

6a. 1278 (June). William de Leyburn surr. to the K and Q the manor of Leeds (*CCIR 1272–1279*, 499; Appendix I, no. 115). Witn.: Thomas de Cantilupe bp of Hereford, William de Middelton bp of Norwich, Robert Tybotot, Bartholomew de Sulleye, Stephen de Pencestr', John de Cobham, Walter Helyun, *John de Lovetot, *Geoffrey de Piccheford, Antony Bek, John de Kirkby, *Geoffrey de Aspale.

6b. 1278 (June). Further document touching the same (ibid.). Witn.: Thomas de Cantilupe bp of Hereford, William de Middelton bp of Norwich, Gilbert de Clare e. of Gloucester, Roger Mortimer, Roger de Clifford, Robert Tybotot, Antony Bek,

†Abbreviations used in the appendices are identical to those used in the footnotes (see Abbreviations, pp. xiii-xx).

Stephen de Pencestr', Richard de Tany, *John de Lovetot, Walter Helyun, John de Kirkby, *Walter de Kancia.

7. 1279 (4 November). The K and Q, as ct and ctss of Ponthieu, gt privileges to the market at Crécy in Ponthieu (Paris BN, lat. 10112 fol. 134b, of which a French draft without witnesses is S.C. 1/12/165). Witn.: Robert Burnell bp of Bath and Wells, William de Middelton bp of Norwich, Henry de Lacy e. of Lincs,, Otho de Grandison, John de Vescy, Robert Tybotot, Stephen de Pencestr', Hugh fitz Otes, *Geoffrey de Piccheford.

8. 1279 (12 November). The K conf. Q's gt of tens in Oxford to Henry Oweyn (CPR 1272–1281, 332–33; see Appendix I, no. 170). Witn.: John de Vescy, *John de Lovetot, *Geoffrey de Piccheford, Bartholomew de Brianzun, *Geoffrey de Aspale, *Walter de Kancia.

9. 1280 (20 March). The K conf. Q's gt of the manor of Middleton, I.o.W., to [*]John and Christiana de Weston (CChR, ii, 234; Appendix I, no. 94).[154] Witn.: Geoffrey de Piccheford, [*]Giles de Fiennes, [*]Andrew de Sakeville,[155] John de Lisle, Thomas de Evercy, Thomas de la Halle, Robert de Glamorgan, William Spileman, Robert Folyet.

10. 1280 (16 November). Agreement for the marr. of John de Vescy and the Q's cousin Isabella de Beaumont (CCIR 1279–1288, 67–68). Witn.: Robert Burnell bp of Bath and Wells, Robert Tybotot, Hugh fitz Otes, *John de Lovetot, Robert fitz John, Antony Bek, John de Kirkby.

11. s.d. (1275 Nov. X 1283 Feb.).[156] John de Reda gives to the K and Q lands at Langley, Herts. (E 40/18, s.d.; Appendix I, no. 105c). Witn.: John de Vescy, Otho de Grandison, Hugh fitz Otes, Robert fitz John, Richard de Bosco, *Geoffrey de Piccheford, [*]John de Weston.

12. 1281 (22 February). The K conf. Q's gt of the manor of Godington to Guy Ferré jr. (CChR, ii, 248–29; Appendix I, no. 171). Witn.: Robert Burnell bp of Bath and Wells, Antony Bek, John de Kirkby, Hugh fitz Otes, Robert fitz John, William de Montrevel, *Geoffrey de Piccheford, Richard de Bosco, [*]Eustace de Hacche,[157] Peter de Huntingfeld, Alan fitz Roald, Fulk de Reykote, John le Waleis, John fitz Nigel.

13. 1281 (ca. 8 March). Christiana de Mareis surr. to the Q lands in Ireland (CDI, i, no. 1800; intr. to Appendix I). Witn.: Robert Burnell bp of Bath and Wells, William de Middelton bp of Norwich, Antony Bek, William de Valence, Gilbert de Clare e. of Glos., Henry de Lacy e. of Lincs., Humphrey de Bohun e. of Herefs., John de Kirkby, Robert fitz John.

14. 1281 (ca. 6 May). John Camoys surr. to the K and Q for 15 yrs the manor of Wood Ditton (Ditton Camoys) (CCIR 1279–1288, 120; Appendix I, no. 20). Witn.: Robert Burnell bp of Bath and Wells, John de Vescy, Robert Tybotot, Hugh fitz Otes, John de Kirkby, *John de Lovetot.

15. 1281 (July). Hugh du Plessis releases to the K and Q the manor of Headington (CCIR 1279–1288, 128; Appendix I, no. 172). Witn.: John de Vescy, Otho de Grandison, Robert Tybotot, Stephen de Pencestr', Hugh fitz Otes, *John de Lovetot.

16. 1281 (12 July). Elie Rabayn and Maud his wife release right in Lyme to the K and Q (CCLR 1279–1288, 61; Appendix I, no. 51). Witn.: John de Vescy, Robert Tybotot, Hugh fitz Otes, *John de Lovetot.

17. 1281 (July/August). Walter de Kancia releases to the K and Q the manor of Newton
     Harcourt (*CCIR 1279–1288*, 61; Appendix I, no. 128). Witn.: Robert Burnell bp of
     Bath and Wells, Thomas Bek, *Geoffrey de Aspale, Richard de Bruys, Patrick de
     Chaworth, Peter de Chauvent, Hugh fitz Otes, Robert fitz John, Richard de Bosco,
     [*]Eustace de Hacche.

18. 1281 (2 November). K conf. the Q's gt of the manors of Farnham and Quendon to
     John Ferré (*CChR*, ii, 256; Appendix I, nos. 62–63). Witn.: *Geoffrey de Piccheford,
     [*]Giles de Fiennes, [*]Andrew de Sakeville, [*]John de Weston, William Arnaud.

19. 1282 (8 April). K conf. the Q's exch. of the manor of Drayton with Geoffrey de
     Piccheford for right in Sheldon in the Peak (*CChr*, ii, 261; Appendix I, nos. 40, 219).
     Witn.: Robert Burnell bp of Bath and Wells, Godfrey Giffard bp of Worcester, John
     de Kirkby archdcn of Coventry, Henry de Brandeston' archdcn of Dorset, Hugh fitz
     Otes, Robert fitz John, Richard de Bosco, Peter de Huntingfield, [*]Eustace de
     Hacche.

20. 1283 (15 February). Roger de Clifford and Comitissa his wife release to the Q the
     manor of Ratoath in Ireland (*CCIR 1279–1288*, 230). Witn.: Robert Burnell bp of Bath
     and Wells, Hugh de Turbeville, *Geoffrey de Piccheford, Robert fitz John, John de
     Kirkby, William de Luda, [*]Adam de Cretyng.[158]

21. 1283 (24 February). K gts Hope Castle to the Q (*CChyV*, 265 (Appendix I, no. 67).
     Witn.: Edmund e. of Lancs., Gilbert de Clare e. of Glos., John de Warrenne e. of
     Surrey, William de Beauchamp e. of Warks., Roger Lestraunge, Griffin Gwenwynwyn,
     Fulk fitz Warin.

22. 1283 (10 May). K gts the Q the manor of Bangor-on-Dee (*CChyV*, 271; Appendix I,
     no. 68). Witn.: Edmund e. of Lancs., Gilbert de Clare e. of Glos., William de
     Beauchamp e. of Warks., John de Vescy, Otho de Grandison, Robert de Ros, Reginald
     de Grey, Robert fitz John, Hugh de Turbeville, [*]Eustace de Hacche, Richard de
     Bosco.

23. 1283 (25 June). K gts the Q a market at Hope Castle (*CChyV*, 273; Appendix I, no.
     67). Witn.: Robert Burnell bp of Bath and Wells, Henry de Lacy e. of Lincs., Roger
     le Bigod e. of Norfs., Robert de Brus sr lord of Annandale, Robert de Brus jr. e. of
     Carrick, Robert fitz John, Peter de Chauvent, *Geoffrey de Piccheford, [*]Eustace de
     Hacche.

24a. 1283 (2 July). Q gts the manor of Ratoath to the e. and ctss of Ulster (*CDI*, i, no. 2102
     = *CChR*, ii, 267; intr. to Appendix I). Witn.: Robert Burnell bp of Bath and Wells,
     Thomas de Normanville, *Geoffrey de Piccheford, *Giles de Fiennes, [*]John de
     Weston, *Geoffrey de Aspale, William Arnaud.

24b. 1283 (2 July). K conf. no. 24a (*CDI*, i, nos. 2100–1). Witn.: Robert Burnell bp of Bath
     and Wells, Henry de Lacy e. of Lincs., Robert de Brus jr. e. of Carrick, Richard de
     Bruys, Peter de Chauvent, [*]Eustace de Hacche.

25. 1284 (27 September). Q's agreement with John le Lou and Amice his wife on Amice's
     right in the inh. of her cousin Richard de Ardern (*DC*, iv, 132–33; *CCIR 1279–1288*,
     304–5; Appendix I, no. 226a). Witn.: Robert Burnell bp of Bath and Wells, John de
     Vescy, Otho de Grandison, Robert Tybotot.

26. 1285 (Easter term). Geoffrey de Southorpe ackn. he owes the Q £80:13:4 in arrears for the farm of Torpel and Upton (E 159/58 m. 6; Appendix I, no. 159a). Witn.: John de Kirkby, Thomas de Weylaund, Roger de Norwode, John de Cobeham, [*]John Ferré, *John de Lovetot, *William de St. Claro.

27. 1285 (8 June). Q agrees with Philip le Lou and Margery his wife on Margery's right in the inh. of her cousin Richard de Ardern (CPR 1281–1292, 175; Appendix I, nos. 226a, 247). Witn.: John de Vescy, [*]John Ferré, *John de Lovetot, Thomas de Normanville, *Geoffrey de Piccheford, John de Lithegreyn sheriff of York.

28. 1285 (15 June). K conf. the Q's agreement of 8 June with Philip le Lou and his wife (CPR 1281–1292, 175; Appendix I, nos. 226a, 247). Witn.: John de Vescy, [*]John Ferré, *John de Lovetot, Thomas de Normanville, *Geoffrey de Piccheford, John de Lithegreyn sheriff of York.

29. 1285 (5 July). mr Henry Sampson releases to the K and Q right in the manor of Lyndon (CCIR 1279–1288, 375; Appendix I, no. 179a). Witn.: Thomas Weylaund, *John de Lovetot, William de Brumpton, Roger de Leycestr', [*]John Ferré, *Geoffrey de Piccheford, *John de Berewyk'.

30a. 1285 (5 July). John de Camoys surr. right in the manor of Ditton to the K and Q (CCIR 1279–1288, 360; Appendix I, no. 23a). Witn.: Thomas Weylaund, *John de Lovetot, William de Brumpton, Roger de Leycestr', [*]John Ferré, *Geoffrey de Piccheford, *John de Berewyk'.

30b. 1285 (5 July). Robert de Crevequer surr. to the K and Q right in the manor of Ditton (CCIR 1279–1288, 360; Appendix I, no. 23b). Witn.: Thomas Weylaund, *John de Lovetot, William de Brumpton, Roger de Leycestr', [*]John Ferré, *Geoffrey de Piccheford, *John de Berewyk'.

31. s.d. (1275 X 1285). Bevis de Clare surr. to the Q his ten in Oxford called "la Oriole" (Shadwell and Salter, ed., Oriel College Records, no. 99; Appendix I, no. 173). Witn.: Robert Burnell bp of Bath and Wells, Gilbert de Clare e. of Glos., John de Vescy, Otho de Grandison, Richard de Bruys, Hugh de Turbeville, William de Leyburn, *Geoffrey de Piccheford, Nicholas de Kingeston' mayor of Oxford, William ypotecario, Henry Oweyn.[159]

32. 1286 (30 April). Q gts land in Chichester to the OP friars of that city; K's conf. 16 July 1290 (CPR 1281–1292, 376, where the witn. lists to the two documents appear to be conflated;[160] Appendix I, no. 220). Witn.: bp of Chichester, Robert Burnell bp of Bath and Wells, Gilbert de Clare e. of Glos., Henry de Lacy e. of Lincs., Richard de Pevenese, Luke de Vian', John Pecche, John le Fauconer, *Geoffrey de Aspale, Giles de la Garderobe, *John de Berewyk', William de Hertham mayor of Chichester, Henry de Merlawe, Roger Germeyn, Roger Ploket, William Bewlf.

33. 1286 (13 June). Q gts land at Godshill to William and Iseut le Bruyn (RG, ii, no. 1569; Appendix I, note 179). Witn.: Antony Bek bp of Durham, Robert Burnell bp of Bath and Wells, Edmund e. of Cornwall, John de Vescy, Richard de Bruys, *John de Lovetot, [*]John Ferré, *John fitz Thomas.

34. 1287 (Ascension term). Matthew fitz John surr. to the K and Q the reversion to his lands (CCIR 1279–1288, 480; Appendix I, no. 42). Witn.: John de Kirkby bp of Ely,

Philip de Wilughby, Peter de Cestre, John de Cobeham, William de Middelton, William de Carleton, *John de Lovetot.

35.   1287 (19 October). Q arbitrates a dispute over burial rights between the OSB monks and OP friars at St-Sever in Gascony (Mont-de-Marsan, arch. dépt. des Landes, H.2[18]). Witn.: Robert Burnell bp of Bath and Wells, John de Kirkby bp of Ely, William de Middelton bp of Norwich then seneschal of Gascony, John de Vescy, Otho de Grandison.

36a.   1287 (6 October). Fine levied in the K's court between the K and Matthew fitz John touching lands Matthew will convey to the K and Q (E 159/61 m. 5; Appendix I, no. 42). Justices: Thomas de Weylaund, *John de Lovetot, William de Brumpton, Roger de Leycestr', Elias de Bekingham.

36b.   1287 (October). A second fine levied in the K's court touching the same (E 159/61 m. 5; Appendix I, no. 31). Justices: Thomas de Weylaund, William de Brumpton, Roger de Leycestr', Elias de Bekingham.

37.   1289 (30 September). Robert de Crevequer surr. to the K and Q right in the manor of Soham (CCIR 1288–1296, 56; Appendix I, no. 24). Witn.: Robert Burnell bp of Bath and Wells, Henry de Lacy e. of Lincs., John de St. Johanne, *Guy Ferré, Ralph de Sandwico, *John de Lovetot.

38a.   1290 (20 June). Q gts land and advs in Kent to Canterbury Cathedral Priory in exch. for the custom of the port of Sandwich (Canterbury, Dean and chapter library, Reg. I fol. 136; Appendix I no. 120). Witn.: Robert Burnell bp of Bath and Wells, Antony Bek bp of Durham, Gilbert de Clare e. of Glos., Henry de Lacy e. of Lincs., Otho de Grandison, John de St. Johanne, Stephen de Pencestr', *John de Berewyk'.

38b.   1290 (20 June). The K confirms no. 38a (CChR, ii, 357). Witn.: as for no. 38a, with the addition of John de Warrenne e. of Surrey.

Legend and Reality

This examination of Eleanor of Castile's life has been neither an attack nor a rehabilitation, but an attempt to identify the factors that underlay the contradictions in her reputation that were described earlier. Chapter One accordingly examined, first, the evidence for her personal life, the extent to which her activities and preferences might have been known to the kingdom at large, and the ways in which such knowledge might shape opinions about her. Chapter Two turned to Eleanor's administrative activity, an aspect of her career that made her rather more widely known to the realm; Chapter Three dealt with her land gathering, the facet of her activities for which she was most generally notorious. The outlines of Eleanor's life that have thus taken shape do much to confirm indications that contemporaries did not regard her as the paragon of queenly excellence praised by many later writers. The present chapter concerns itself with the posthumous evolution of a gracious Eleanor and with the reasons why that image has for so long eclipsed the reality.

Eleanor's legend originated soon after her death, as the splendor of her funeral procession was echoed by the twelve monumental crosses Edward ordered to mark its stages, and as her burial was commemorated by elaborate tombs in Westminster Abbey, the London Dominican church, and Lincoln Cathedral. These multiple monuments call for remark. Many English kings' bodies had been divided after death, but a tripartite royal burial was unknown in England. Henry I's viscera were buried in Rouen Cathedral, his body in Reading Abbey; Richard I's body rested at Fontevraut, his heart at Rouen, and his viscera at Châluz, where he died. John's body lay at Worcester and his viscera at Croxton, whose abbot performed the embalming. Richard of Cornwall's heart rested in the Franciscan church at Oxford, his body at Hayles Abbey; Henry III's heart was buried at Fontevraut. Eleanor of Castile evidently planned only for the separate burial of her heart in the London Dominican church; in 1284 she had her son Alphonso's heart kept for burial there, and before her death she paid £100 for construction of the chapel where the hearts would be buried. The separate interment of her viscera at Lincoln was, like that of Richard I at Châluz, probably the expedient result of her embalming at Harby or Lincoln.[1] The three burials thus did not represent Eleanor's real intentions, but they combined with her funeral procession to give Edward the opportunity for an unprecedented program of visual tributes to his queen.

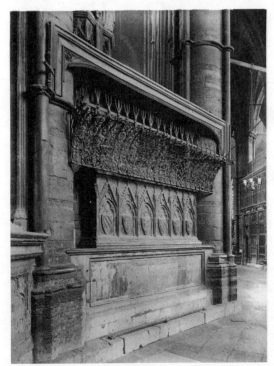

Figure 4.1.
Queen Eleanor's tomb in Westminster Abbey, from the North Aisle (National Monuments Record).

Of the monuments that marked Eleanor's interments, only her Westminster tomb survives. Long regarded as one of the finest of medieval tombs, its graceful effigy the largest cast-metal work executed in England down to 1291, the tomb still conveys an incomparable aura of majesty despite the loss of its scepter, of paste jewels from sockets in crown and mantle, and the painting of the tomb chest.[2] The tomb inextricably mingles the sacred and the secular; the effigy could be interchangeable with a statue of the Virgin Mary (and around 1296 the goddess Diana was represented almost identically). A painting on the ambulatory wall beneath the tomb is thought to depict Otho de Grandison praying for Eleanor in the Holy Land, perhaps as a visual invitation to others to pray for her; the floor of the ambulatory beneath the tomb was apparently set with tiles depicting the queen between St. Edmund and St. Thomas Becket.[3] The tomb chest's heraldic shields, so different to the Cosmatesque tomb of Henry III next to it, proclaim Eleanor's exalted ancestry; the shields include her maternal Ponthevin arms as well as those of Castile to suggest again that invisible network among medieval royal women.[4]

The shields are, like the crown and scepter, reminders of who the woman was in life. Apart from its wall painting and its inscription's conventional request that passersby should pray for the queen's soul, the tomb does not in fact look to the hereafter. The recumbent effigy is not that of a recognizably dead person but of a crowned woman standing erect, simply robed, and with hair unbound as prescribed for a queen's coronation. The hands are not folded in prayer but are deployed in gestures of power, the right positioned to carry a lost scepter, the left toying with the mantle's cord in a gesture identifiable among the early thirteenth-century sculpture of the façade of Wells Cathedral and that at Reims.[5] The derivation of the effigy's costume from the Wells façade is disputed, but the costume's extreme simplicity, like the effigy's unbound hair, does recall the provision that the queen wear unadorned robes for her coronation. The effigy's echoes of the moment of coronation suggest that the tomb is a visualization of monarchy's continuity—not inappropriate for the monument of a queen, whose chief function was the perpetuation of the royal lineage. As it was in fact Eleanor's interment that marked Westminster as both a coronation and a burial church that juxtaposed royal beginnings and endings to visualize monarchy's endless renewal, her tomb, which itself compresses the moments of coronation and burial, cannot be viewed separately from its share in the abbey's emergence as an arena for royal ritual. Her tomb was the end point of the cortège that bore her body from Lincoln to Westminster; the very act of returning her body to the South, followed by a lavish funeral, marked Westminster as a royal "center" whose aura Edward exported to the kingdom through the other monuments erected to her.[6]

Figure 4.2.
Queen Eleanor's tomb effigy *in situ*, from above (National Monuments Record).

As the tombs in Lincoln Cathedral and the London Dominican church are no longer extant, they may be dealt with briefly. The Lincoln tomb was wrecked by Cromwell's troops, but a seventeenth-century drawing by William Dugdale shows it was a double of that at Westminster. (A copy of the Westminster effigy was installed in the cathedral at private expense in 1891, but on the south side of the retro-choir, not on the original site at the east end of the "angel" choir's north aisle.)[7] The London heart tomb disappeared in 1550 when the Dominican priory became a parish church and its monuments were sold, but details of its construction exist in the accounts of Eleanor's executors. Its distinctive use of materials — including as many as three small metal images and an evidently larger metal angel that held the heart or a portrayal of it — aligns the London monument more closely with a goldsmith's reliquary or shrine than with sculpted heart tombs like that of Henry III's half brother Bishop Aymer de Valence of Winchester (d. 1250).[8] (The use of varied media on the London tomb, including wall paintings by the same artist who worked on the Westminster tomb, recalls the marble chests and gilt latten effigies of the Westminster and Lincoln monuments.)[9]

Figure 4.3.
Bishop Aymer de Valence's heart tomb in Winchester Cathedral (Dr. Phillip Lindley).

However sumptuous, the three tombs pale beside the twelve crosses Edward erected to mark the stages of Eleanor's funeral procession between Lincoln and Westminster. No English precedent existed for such a forest of crosses, for though commemorative crosses were not unknown in England, earlier specimens were isolated: Henry III put up a cross at Merton for his kinsman the earl of Surrey (d. 1240), one was erected at Reading by 1279 for King Edward's sister Beatrice (d. 1275), and by 1294 one stood near Windsor in memory of Eleanor of Provence (d. 1291).[10] The inspiration for Edward's project is commonly said to have been the series of crosses in France, known as the *montjoies*, which marked the stages of Louis IX's 1271 burial cortège. Henry III was an enthusiastic imitator of Louis' use of visual statements to impress his subjects with the legitimacy and sanctity of Capetian kingship; and as Edward proved even more competent than Henry as an assimilator of Capetian models, it is likely that the *montjoies* did provide the impetus for the Eleanor crosses. The monuments must, then, be taken primarily as a statement of the dignity and prestige of kingship, and only secondarily as a king's tribute to his wife.[11]

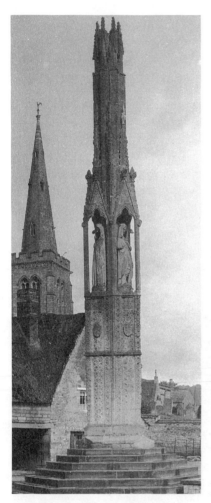

Figure 4.4.
The Eleanor cross at Geddington,
co. Northants (National Monuments
Record, © B. T. Batsford Ltd.).

Figure 4.5.
The Eleanor cross at Hardingstone near
Northampton (National Monuments
Record, © B. T. Batsford Ltd.).

Figure 4.6. Sketch of the Eleanor cross at Waltham (Essex) in 1812–13 (National Monuments Record, © B. T. Batsford Ltd.).

Figure 4.7. The Eleanor cross at Waltham after restoration (National Monuments Record, © B. T. Batsford Ltd.).

Three Eleanor crosses survive—at Hardingstone near Northampton, at Geddington, and at Waltham. These share a three-tiered design, polygonal at Hardingstone and Waltham, triangular at Geddington, and probably derived from the *montjoies*: a solid lower story and a second stage opened with niches for statues, surmounted by a spire that, if the chroniclers are right, probably terminated in a cross.[12] The identity of the woman commemorated by the crosses was left in no doubt; Eleanor's arms appear repeatedly on them, as on her Westminster tomb and the lost Lincoln monument. The multiple statues of the queen on each cross offer in their frontality a uniformly restrained and idealized image of aristocratic calm, as if to distance her image from the unattractive aspects of her reputation. Heads gently inclined, a quiet smile on the lips, bodies gracefully curved, the left hand playing with the cord of the mantle, which is itself in some cases gathered under the arm to emphasize both the richness of the apparel and the woman's modesty—these images plainly suggest power tempered by amiable benevolence. The statues thus encapsulate medieval English queenship's ritual construction, which exalted the queen even as it inscribed her seclusion from the king's authority and her subordination as an instrument of lordship and order. All the statues are crowned, the hair loose as on the Westminster tomb; each held in the right hand a scepter, which enhanced the majestic aura created by the crosses while reinforcing the image of a compliant and submissive consort, for in a queen's hand the scepter developed Marian, and hence intercessory, resonances.[13]

Described as representing "a key moment in the history of English art, one of those sudden evolutionary shifts after which nothing is quite the same again," the crosses are as remarkable in their artistic impact as for any statements they made about English kingship or about Queen Eleanor. Their original appearance is hard to imagine today; their painting and gilding are lost. But their lavish deployment of architectural forms on a small scale—arches, gables, pinnacles, buttresses, battlements, and parapets—their early suggestions of ogival arches, and their surfaces, diapered with rosettes where they are not elaborately carved with foliage or blind tracery, were something new in stonework, as though a goldsmith's intricate miniatures were translated into monumental stone. The effusive surface treatment is traceable to the Sainte-Chapelle in Paris, a centerpiece of Louis IX's deployment of visual statements on behalf of French kingship, and to the interior ornamentation of Westminster Abbey. The crosses in fact mark a decided step forward in that fusion in English style of the monumental and miniature, the sculptural and architectural, which irretrievably blurred such distinctions for the rest of the Middle Ages. The artisans who created the crosses appear to have been localized in London and Westminster; they perhaps worked on St. Stephen's Chapel in Westminster Palace, and probably on other royal monuments in the abbey: the tombs of Edward's brother Edmund (d. 1296), Edmund's first wife Aveline de Forz (d. 1274), the king's uncle William de Valence (d. 1296) and his son Earl Aymer of Pembroke (d. 1324), all of which, like Eleanor's tomb, furthered the abbey's emergence as a Plantagenet ceremonial center. The crosses perpetuated the role of her funeral cortège in designating that center even as they disseminated the stylistic developments that embellished it.[14]

The outlines of the program enunciated by the tombs and crosses are now clear. The monuments advertised the glory and might of monarchy, affirmed and complemented by feminine benevolence. With specific reference to Eleanor, the gracious and majestic images scattered about the kingdom might help to dispel unpleasant memories associated with her. And like Eleanor's monument near St. Edward's shrine in Westminster Abbey, her Lincoln tomb near St. Hugh's shrine showed that a consort as well as a king could associate monarchy with sacred authority both at the center and on the periphery.[15] It has been thought that Edward's monuments for his father and his wife imply that he hoped for the canonization of one or both. But the skepticism with which he is said to have greeted the report of a miracle at Henry III's tomb rather defeats the notion that he expected his father's canonization, and there is no reason to believe that he thought of his wife in such terms. To suggest that Edward's program enhanced his family's reputation for sanctity is misleading; rather, it evoked and supported the special relationship between kingship and the divine.[16]

The blurring of sacred and secular boundaries, motifs, and functions in Eleanor's tombs and the crosses alike is a reminder that the monuments had the additional purpose of soliciting prayers for her soul—which was in fact done in a variety of ways even before the monuments were completed. In April 1291 Archbishop le Romeyn of York ordered his official to cause prayers to be offered for the queen's soul in all collegiate and parish churches and chapels within that diocese; the dean and chapter of York were to pray for her soul every Wednesday for the next year. On 7 June 1291, le Romeyn informed Edward that 47,528 masses had already been celebrated for the queen in his diocese, exclusive of those celebrated for the health of the king and his family, and an indulgence of forty days from enjoined penance had been proclaimed for all who devoutly said a Pater Noster and Ave Maria for the souls of the queen and all faithful. On the first anniversary of Eleanor's death Bishop Sutton of Lincoln granted a like indulgence in his diocese and in May 1293 granted forty days' indulgence to those who went to a cross at Easingwold and the Virgin's chapel there, and devoutly prayed for the souls of the two Queens Eleanor, John de Vescy, and William Grivel of Easingwold. Schedules of the prelates' indulgences "for the good of the queen's soul" were drawn up for her executors early in 1294.[17]

The services Edward caused to be celebrated for the first anniversary of Eleanor's death were as splendid as the funeral itself, if not more so. There were masses in Westminster Abbey and the London Dominican priory, with an elaborate hearse in either church and 3000 pounds of wax for candles; the clergy were exhausted by the ritual. The nature of the occasion can be judged from the description of a service for Eleanor the king caused to be celebrated in his presence some years later:

> He caused to be burned around the tomb of the queen forty-eight square candles each weighing sixteen pounds, twenty-four of the same shape around the tomb of King Henry, and twelve small candles each weighing one pound around the shrine of St. Edward. He caused a framework [i.e., hearse?] to be placed reaching from the marble columns on either side of the shrine to the end of the choir, and candles of the same size were fixed there and burned; the space between each candle was one foot and a half. Each monk, all the religious friars of the city of London, and all the clerics and layfolk who were present at the mass held in their hands candles of an identical size. Candles were also given to the poor and the beggars in the church, and the glow from the burning lights, like the starry heavens, exhilarated the souls of the beholders with pervasive joy.[18]

To the encouragement of prayers for the late queen's soul succeeded the proliferation of endowed religious services in her memory. For a year after Eleanor's death, Edward made a special distribution of alms each Tuesday to as many as might approach him. In January 1292 he began to endow a yearly observance at Westminster for the queen's soul, initially granting the abbey Eleanor's manor at Denham (Bucks.) and later adding to it those at Westerham and Edenbridge (Kent), Turweston (Leics.), and Knowle and Grafton (Warks.); another manor at Birdbrook (Essex), which Eleanor had not held, was added to make up the sum Edward meant to endow the service. The 1292 grant specified almost every detail of the observances. Thirty large candles were to be kept about Eleanor's tomb at all times, two to be lighted daily and all of them on great feasts. Each week on Monday, the eve of her obit, the entire convent was to gather in the abbey choir to sing Placebo and Dirige, with nine lessons and a tolling of bells. On the Tuesday, the convent would celebrate mass with the tolling of bells, and a silver penny each was to be distributed to 140 paupers or as many as might come; before and after receiving the coin, each was devoutly to recite the Pater Noster, Credo, and Ave Maria for Eleanor's soul. The yearly anniversary was to begin on the vigil of St. Andrew, with one hundred candles each weighing twelve pounds to burn from the start of the vigil (at six in the evening of 28 November) until after high mass next day. Bells were to be rung without ceasing and divine office chanted hourly, with Placebo, Dirige, and nine lessons. At the commemoration's end, alms were to be given to the poor, the mendicant friars, and the London hospitals. The letters patent were to be read out in chapter yearly on the anniversary to ensure proper observance.[19]

The Westminster service was only the most elaborate of the many endowed around the realm in Eleanor's memory in the decades after her death. Edward founded chantries at Maidenheath and in the Dominicans' London church, and it was probably he who established the chantry that was at first in the church of North Clifton (the parish including Harby), but was moved in 1310 to Lincoln Cathedral.[20] Others soon followed his lead. In January 1291 Edward granted license for alienation to Peterborough Abbey by his clerk Elias de Bekyngham, on condition that the abbot and convent find two chaplains to celebrate mass daily forever for the queen's soul, and three to celebrate at Southorpe on the anniversary of her death, with 200 paupers to be fed. Mr Henry Sampson, who had sold Eleanor a manor at Easton in Rutland, endowed a chaplain in September 1291 to celebrate there for her soul, his parents', and all faithful departed. In 1294 a yearly service was founded at St. Albans, and the archbishop of York provided for a chaplain celebrating for the queen's soul in the chapel at Harby.[21] By 1294 William and Juliana de Copstone of Coventry provided a rent of 100*s.* for a chaplain to celebrate at the altar of St. Edward the Confessor in Coventry Cathedral for their souls and the soul of the late queen. The friars of the Sack in London had license in March 1305 to assign Robert f. Walter in fee simple a chapel in Colmanstreet, formerly a synagogue, so that he and his heirs should find two chaplains to celebrate daily for the soul of the queen, Robert's ancestors, and all faithful departed. Bishop Heselshawe of Bath in December 1306 provided for chaplains to celebrate two masses daily in that cathedral for King Edward and his second wife, Queen Margaret, while they lived, for the king's children, and for the soul of the late queen. The dean and chapter of Lincoln in 1315 established a chaplain there to pray for Edward II, his wife and children, and for the souls of the late King Edward and Queen Eleanor. While certain proof is lacking, licenses for alienations to religious houses Edward I and Edward II granted for the good of Eleanor's soul as late as 1323 may also have been intended to support chantries for her.[22]

It has been suggested that the Westminster anniversary service made a great impression on the realm and that many imitated it by founding chantries for themselves and their families. True, aspects of Eleanor's commemorations were emulated: when Bishop Nicholas Longespee of Salisbury died in 1297, his body was buried in his cathedral, his heart at Lacock Abbey, and his viscera at his manor of Ramsbury. But the idea that Eleanor's service had a lasting impact on later foundations is an illusion; her inclusion in several of the chantries just noted was likely no more than the founders' way to obtain license for the alienations to endow their chantries. The greater likelihood is that new royal commemorations periodically stimulated such foundations, as with Edward III's observances for his mother after 1358 and for his wife after 1369.[23]

Edward's program nonetheless would ultimately have the impact on Eleanor's reputation that he probably intended. This evolving authorized version of her image obtained written form during the year or so after his death in 1307, when an anonymous monk at St. Albans undertook the first continuation since Matthew Paris' death in 1259 of the tradition of historical writing that had existed at St. Albans since the twelfth century. Known as the *Opus chronicorum*, the 1308 work was meant to continue Matthew's chronicle from 1259 until 1307, but breaks off in 1297. In contrast to the silence of the monastic chronicles written in Eleanor's lifetime, the *Opus* never misses an opportunity to praise her extravagantly, as in connection with the Crusade of 1270:

> [Edward] took with him his wife, Eleanor by name, born of noble stock, who surpassed all women of that time in wisdom, prudence and beauty; indeed, except that it would appear to be flattery, I would say that she was not unequal to a Sybil in wisdom.

When he discussed Eleanor's children, the chronicler repeated that she "went before all women in that time in wisdom and prudence," but it was when he came to record her death that he outdid himself:

> In the year of our lord's incarnation 1290, which is the nineteenth year of King Edward's reign, the Lady Eleanor the younger, queen of England, left this world at the vill of Harby, near Lincoln; whose soul God keep. Seeing that I have said a little of her excellent qualities, on account of grief at her death and the sorrow of my heart, I have thought it fitting to add her genealogy briefly and truthfully, so that when a diligent investigator shall examine the uprightness of her forefathers, how virtue shone forth and how piety was resplendent in them, he may recognize how natural it

may be to abound in riches, to blossom with virtues, to be made famous by victories, and what is more than all these, to shine in the Christian faith and the prerogative of justice. For to know oneself to come from the best of those whose nobility of blood accords with merit, is the greatest incentive to preserve the best qualities. It ever shames a noble spirit to be found degenerate in its posterity, and it is against the nature of things that bad fruit should sprout from a good root. Howbeit she did not lose a kingdom but changed it, abandoning the temporal and attaining the eternal, her passing was tearfully mourned by not a few. For she was as a pillar of all England, by sex a woman but in spirit and virtue more like a man. In her days, foreigners troubled England but little. As the dawn scatters the shadows of the waning night with its rays of light, so by the promotion of this most holy woman and queen, throughout England the night of faithlessness was expelled, . . . of anger and discord cast out.[24]

Dead kings and their wives were always susceptible to greater praise or condemnation than living ones but even so, such fulsome extravagance is quite startling, coming as it does only two decades after the death of a woman who was barely noticed by earlier chroniclers. Of course, this was an "inside" view: St. Albans was the premier abbey in England, the shrine of the English protomartyr, and it might be expected that so privileged a house, with its ties to historical writing at Westminster under the court's influence, would shape and transmit a positive image of Eleanor.[25] But the really significant factor seems to have been the *Opus'* composition in the year of the accession of her son, Edward II. He was five and a half when she died, and had been entirely separated from her for more than three of those years, while she was in Aquitaine between May 1286 and August 1289; by the time she returned to England, she was sickening to her death and in the months before she died, she was not much in her son's company. It must be presumed that Edward II had few clear memories of his mother, save as an aging, ailing woman. After she died, the boy spent much of his childhood at her manor at Langley, very near St. Albans, and he retained a lifelong affection for the monastery.[26] Young Edward's awareness of his mother could, moreover, have been especially related to St. Albans. One of those crosses "of wondrous height" stood in the town market place and must have been known to him; it is not unlikely that he and his household attended at least on occasion the yearly service for the queen at the monastery. And while it cannot be proved that local lore told him of her meeting with the townspeople there in 1275, when she listened to their complaints against the abbot and scolded him for trying to keep the crowd from her, the possibility cannot be discounted that her son knew of the incident.

With strong reminders of her thus localized near his residence, young Edward could have been led to ask his attendants about his mother and perhaps he even queried the monks, who at any rate could easily have known of his curiosity; there would have been many opportunities for an exchange of such information between manor and monastery. One of these can be documented and is especially suggestive: in 1305 young Edward asked the abbot to receive John le Parker of Langley, who had long served the late queen, and to find him a place where he might end his days in prayer for her soul.[27] It is idle to speculate as to whether the monks told Edward anything about his mother before 1307. But the *Opus'* astonishingly positive depiction of her does suggest an exercise in public relations, not duplicitous but diplomatic. The work was intended to be a history of Edward I's reign, plausibly though not certainly meant for presentation to Edward II by the monks of whose house he was so fond, and the writer (or his abbot, identified by the chronicle's incipit as its instigator) likely thought it well to flatter the new king by praising the mother he could barely remember. At the same time, there is every possibility that the writer fashioned his account of Eleanor, and the equally fulsome encomium of Eleanor of Provence that immediately precedes it, to send Edward II a hint at the outset of his reign that he must show himself worthy of his glorious ancestry, so resplendent with noble virtues on all sides—or to offer discreet suggestions on proper queenly behavior to the new king's young wife.

The *Opus chronicorum* was as much a dehistoricization of the queen's image as were the Eleanor crosses. The chronicle was never finished, however; it would be widely known only to a later age and in a different form, and for the moment, Eleanor's reputation remained equivocal. At the time the *Opus* was composed and for some decades thereafter, a contrasting "outside" view is provided by a stream of legal actions, as the heirs of those who had conveyed property to the queen in the 1270s and 1280s attempted to recover the lands. Joan de Bohun of Midhurst repeatedly tried to recover Denham between 1300 and 1339, John de Antingham and the brothers Robert and William Baynard recovered lands at Hautbois and Scottow in 1301, John de Newburgh recovered some of his father's lands in Somerset and Dorset in 1305, John de Lisle tried to recover Lockerley in 1310, Thomas Tregoz failed at Drayton in 1321, Margerie le Lou tried in 1323 and 1332 to recover Grafton, Quarr Abbey sought the manor of Whitfield from 1333 to 1341, and Faversham Abbey claimed the advowson at Tring in 1337. Gilbert Pecche's son tried to recover Birdbrook in the 1330s.[28] A claim to the manor of Westerham in Kent was brought in 1341 by two granddaughters of Robert de Camville, ironically daughters of that Thomas de Camville who became

a squire in the household of Eleanor's daughters. The sisters alleged that the
queen was angered when Robert declined to convey Westerham to her, on
the grounds that he had already settled it on a son and daughter-in-law.
When summons were later issued for the king's war in Wales, the queen plotted with the marshal of the army to make it appear that Camville had not performed the military service he owed. At the war's end she sent two knights
to arrest him; he was imprisoned until he conveyed Westerham to her, and
within nine months he died. The facts surrounding Eleanor's acquisition of
Westerham and other Camville manors in Oxfordshire and Essex (none
named in the 1341 claim) do not support this claim. Camville lost his lands
to Eleanor through his debts to the Jewry; he conveyed the manors in 1279,
retaining Westerham for life, and so far from dying within nine months, he
lived until 1286.[29] Its falseness notwithstanding, the 1341 claim serves along
with the others to suggest that in the decades after Eleanor's death, and outside the court milieu, virtue and generosity were not necessarily qualities that
sprang to mind when her name came up in conversation.

If, indeed, it came up at all. By the mid-fourteenth century the lawsuits
tapered off as heirs tired or died, and those who had personal memories of
the queen were becoming thin on the ground. Of her family, only Margaret,
Mary, Elizabeth, and Edward II outlived the king; Margaret, the last sur-
vivor, was alive in 1333 but had not lived in England since 1297. The last
of the many cousins Eleanor brought to England, Clemence d'Avaugour,
widow of the younger John de Vescy, died in 1343.[30] The queen's attendant
Margerie de Haustede died in 1338 at a great age; her husband Robert had
died in 1321 and of their sons, William died in 1322, Robert junior around
1330, and John in 1336.[31] Eleanor de Ewelle, who around 1280 had refused
a husband urged on her by the queen and lost her dowry in consequence,
died unmarried in 1349. Among the last of those who could have spoken
knowingly of the queen was Maurice, the son of Iseut and William le Bruyn,
who died in 1355.[32]

It was during this period, as living memory of Eleanor was receding, that
two St. Albans chroniclers fashioned and repeated an estimate of her character derived from the *Opus chronicorum*. The anonymous earlier writer,
whose work was long believed to be by William Rishanger, wrote some time
after the death of Edward II in 1327. In likening Eleanor to a pillar of the
realm and noting that foreigners troubled England but little in her day, the
chronicler clearly drew on the *Opus chronicorum*, which was expanded with
a statement that Edward mourned Eleanor all the days of his life and with
a remark about oppression by royal officials that suggests some wishful
thinking about conditions in the writer's own time. Eleanor was also praised

as a mediator, an image possibly inspired by her 1275 encounter with the townspeople at St. Albans, an account of which was preserved at the monastery. The pseudo-Rishanger's passage on Eleanor's character was repeated verbatim in Thomas Walsingham's *Historia Anglicana* (after 1392):

> She was a most pious, modest, and merciful woman, a lover of all the English, and like a pillar of the entire realm. In her time foreigners did not trouble England. The inhabitants were not oppressed by royal officials, if the slightest claim of oppression came to her ears in any way. Everywhere, as her dignity permitted, she consoled the afflicted, and to the utmost of her power, she reconciled those in discord.[33]

In 1338, at roughly the same time the pseudo-Rishanger paraphrased the 1308 text, Robert Mannyng of Brunne prepared an English version of Piers Langtoft's Anglo-Norman verse chronicle, originally written soon after Edward I's death. Mannyng did not translate strictly; he freely interpolated, and one of his additions adds color to Langtoft's few notices of the queen. Piers gave her death two lines, and later referred to the king's reaction merely to say that as she left but one son, Edward in 1293 began to think of remarrying to father more sons. Mannyng's version is significantly more nuanced:

> On fell things he thought, and waxed heavy as lead,
> How chances on him sought, and that the queen was dead.
> His solace was all bereft, that she from him was gone,
> And no son left to him, but young Edward alone.[34]

Just how widely any of these chronicles was circulated in the century or so after their composition is impossible to determine. But compared with the pseudo-Rishanger's remark that Edward mourned Eleanor all his life, Mannyng's refashioning of Langtoft implies that by the mid-fourteenth century, tradition indeed held that Edward had long grieved for her. By the century's end, as living memory of the queen was lost, and as any gossip surrounding actions to recover her manors dissipated as heirs abandoned their claims or died, her reputation would have been preserved chiefly by such traditions as pseudo-Rishanger and Mannyng witness—beliefs likely inspired if not enhanced by the dignified aura of the Eleanor crosses. When Walsingham chose to repeat pseudo-Rishanger's tribute in the 1390s, he probably had good reason to regard it as genuine and appropriate. By the early fifteenth century, this courtly image appears to have triumphed: in

1425 Eleanor was called Edward I's "rayr wife" in a dispute over precedence among the earls, who trotted out royal descents to buttress or attack each other's claims.[35] That their recitations wrongly made her Alphonso X's daughter anticipates the fact that during the fifteenth century Eleanor surfaces only as a name in royal pedigrees that proliferated in an era of uncertain succession and civil war.[36] The decline in any real interest in her that might have modified the parroted St. Albans eulogy is not surprising; she had now been dead for a century, and was of interest only in the sense in which the earls mentioned her in 1425 or the pedigree writers included her—as an ancestor whose virtues might glorify her descendants. In this context her father's identity was, as implied by the 1308 eulogy, less important than the general truth of her royal ancestry.

Though the inevitable deterioration over time of the fabric of the great crosses can have had little to do with this diminished interest in Eleanor, an echo exists between the two. William Worcestre's *Itineraries* never mention them; other sources show that by the mid-fifteenth century several had lost their tops, or were said to be decayed through age. The St. Albans monument alone was still "very stately" in 1596; that at Stony Stratford was "not very splendid" in 1586 and by 1590 Charing cross was "defaced by antiquity".[37] In the 1530s John Leland mentioned them as crosses like many others he remarked; he did associate the Hardingstone cross with a queen— "a right goodly crosse, caullid, as I remembre, the Quene's Crosse"—but did not identify the woman whom it celebrated. (He did indicate that memories of Eleanor's three burials had persisted, perhaps proliferated: Leland identifies a monument in the Franciscan church at Bedford as that of an otherwise-unknown Queen Eleanor.)[38] The decay of the Cheapside and Charing crosses in London was deemed an affront to civic pride, and efforts were made to repair them. These inflicted further damage, physical and stylistic: the Cheapside cross was entirely gilded for state occasions in the sixteenth century, and new statues ill suited to its original purpose were added—the Resurrection, St. Edward the Confessor, the Virgin and Child, and the goddess Diana, spouting water through appropriate if indecorous orifices.[39]

Tudor chroniclers merely codify Queen Eleanor's appearance as a name in royal pedigrees, and perhaps predictably after the Reformation, they make very little of the crosses. The English *Brut*, first printed in 1480, mentions her twice, noting that she bore her daughter Joan in Palestine and that she was with Edward in Gascony in the 1280s. Raphael Holinshed's compilation of chronicles adds nothing to the little that writers contemporary with Eleanor had said about her; he included neither the Guisborough nor the Dunstable text, and his chief contribution to the evolution of Eleanor's reputation was to provide an English text of the later version of the St. Albans eulogy. Richard Grafton mentions Eleanor's marriage, her journey to the holy land with Edward, her coronation, her death, and her children — very similar to his treatment of other past queens of England save for the prominently disruptive Isabella of France and Margaret of Anjou. The rhyming John Hardyng notes her only in connection with Edward's Crusade, incredibly making her a daughter of the king of Aragon. Robert Fabyan refers to Eleanor only to identify Edward's wife, and mistakenly puts her death in the twentieth year of the reign (1291–92); Polydore Vergil has it that she brought Edward Ponthieu as her dowry in 1254 (implying that it was a Castilian honor, not French), and his failure to remark her death leaves unsettling questions hovering over his account of the king's second marriage in 1299. The confusion over Ponthieu may have been caused by the anonymous verses that formerly hung over the royal tombs in Westminster Abbey (perhaps as early as the fourteenth century), which in Eleanor's case stated that Ponthieu was her dowry:

> Queen Eleanor is here interred, a worthy noble dame,
> Sister unto the Spanish king, of royal blood and fame.
> King Edward's wife, first of that name and Prince of Wales by right.
> Whose father Henry just the third was sure an English wight.
> Who crav'd her wife unto his Son; the Prince himself did go
> On that Embassage luckily as chief, with many moe.
> This knot of linkèd marriage her brother *Alphonse* lik'd,
> And so 'tween Sister and this Prince the marriage up was strik'd.
> The dowry rich and royal was, for such a Prince most meet,
> For *Pontive* was the marriage gift, a dowry rich and great.
> A woman both in counsel wise, religious, fruitful, meek,
> Who did encrease her husband's friends, and larg'd his honour eke.
>   *Learn to die.*[40]

Meager attention to medieval queens in Tudor historical writings implies that the theory of increased interest in the lives of royal women when England has a reigning queen cannot apply to the reign of Elizabeth I. It is not too difficult to understand why this should have been so. The medieval consorts upon whom John Foxe dwells longest in *Acts and Monuments* (1563) were Matilda the Empress, Eleanor of Aquitaine, and Margaret of Anjou, women whose careers cannot have broadcast queenship as a conciliatory or benevolent office. Such emphasis on earlier queens as the origin of disorder may have served to emphasize Elizabeth I as a force for tranquillity and order.[41] Elizabeth's presence on the throne, moreover, meant that there was no market for works that offered former queens as models for a living con-

sort. It is likely too that discussions of past English queens and their monuments would inevitably have roused memories of the Roman faith at a time
when Reformation England had not yet had a successful Protestant queen-
consort. Neither Anne Boleyn, Anne of Cleves, nor Katherine Howard
was particularly well suited as a role model. Conventionally represented as
a properly meek and self-effacing Christian wife and queen, Jane Seymour
had borne the Protestant Edward VI but as she barely survived the event
there was no question of representing him as learning his catechism at her
knee. Learned and eloquent, Katherine Parr was a good friend to the
Reformers but when her views threatened to become too extreme for Henry
VIII, she saved her life only by reconfiguring herself as a weak and ignorant wife. If any of Edward VI's stepmothers shaped his beliefs it was
Katherine, who might have had an important role in his reign but for her
remarriage and death in childbirth shortly after his accession; her reputation for prudence and sagacity was stained by her widower's execution for
treason for allegedly plotting (perhaps in Katherine's lifetime) to marry
Elizabeth Tudor.[42]

Late in Elizabeth's reign, however, the dawning age of the antiquary
contributed significantly to the development of Queen Eleanor's reputation.
Archbishop Parker's 1574 edition of Walsingham's *Historia Anglicana* first
made accessible the late version of the St. Albans eulogy, which attained
even wider currency three years later when an English translation appeared
in Holinshed's *Chronicles*.[43] William Camden, who published another Latin
text of Walsingham in 1603, introduced the Acre legend to England in
Britannia (1586). The story of Eleanor's selflessness allowed him to avoid the
Eleanor crosses' religious context: he interpreted them as a richly deserved
tribute by a grieving king to the devotion of a much-loved and widely
respected queen, giving them a new identity that profoundly marked
Eleanor of Castile's reputation. Camden's reasons for emphasizing this
meaning in the crosses become clear when it is recalled that he took the Acre
story not from Bartolomeo Fiadoni's *Historia Ecclesiastica*, where it is
acknowledged to be a popular tradition, but from the fifteenth-century
Spanish chronicler Rodrigo Sánchez de Arévalo, whose work, printed by
Robert Bel in 1579, gave the story as fact and tricked it out with praise of
the queen as a devoted wife:

> What then can be more rare than this woman's expression of love?
> or what can be more admirable? The tongue of a wife, anointed (if
> I may so say) with duty and love to her husband, draws from her
> beloved those poysons which could not be drawn by the most
> approv'd Physician; and what many and most exquisite medicines
> could not do, is effected purely by the love of a wife.[44]

Camden elaborated on this view of Eleanor in *Remains of a larger work concerning Britain* (1605) where, after inventing her admirable reasons for accompanying Edward to Palestine, he extolled her wifely devotion at some length:

> When king *Edward* the first was in the holy land, hee was stabbed with a poysoned dagger, by a Sarazen, and through the rancor of the poyson, the wound was judged incurable by his Physitions. This good Queene *Eleanor* his wife, who had accompanied him in that journey, endangering her owne life, in loving affection saved his life, and eternized her owne honour. For she daily and nightly sucked out the ranke poyson, which love made sweete to her, and thereby effected that which no Arte durst attempt; to his safety, her joy, and the comfort of all England; So that well woorthy was shee to be remembered by those Crosses as monuments, which in steade of Statues were erected by her husband to hir honour. . . .[45]

With both Walsingham's and Camden's very positive portraits of Eleanor in circulation, it is shocking to encounter within ten years of *Britannia*'s publication the appalling queen who lurks in the pages of George Peele's historical play *Edward the First*, probably written between 1590 and 1592. This Eleanor insists that her coronation be delayed so she may send to Spain for tailors to prepare her robes; when her daughter Joan urges her not to disdain the English in such manner, Eleanor swears to keep them in "a Spanish yoke" and teach them who their lord and master really is. In Wales she declares the soil too base to receive her foot, and longingly recalls the rich carpets on which she trod the streets of Jerusalem. Most disturbingly, she demands that Edward order all Englishmen to shave their beards and every Englishwoman to lose her right breast, a demand that Edward adroitly evades, to her irate frustration. Out of jealousy, the queen subsequently does away with the lady mayoress of London by applying a serpent to her breast. She denies any role in the murder, invites the earth to swallow her if she has lied, accordingly vanishes into Charing green, and surfaces on Potter's hithe. Duly chastened, she takes to her bed and summons two friars to hear her confession. Edward declares that he and his brother Edmund of Lancaster will don friars' robes and shrive her themselves, but much to his dismay, Eleanor reveals that she surrendered her maidenhead to Edmund the night before her wedding, and later fornicated with a French friar who fathered Joan. She expires, Edmund is sentenced to death, and Joan dies of shame when Edward reveals her true paternity. The play ends as Edward commands that Eleanor and Joan be interred with due solemnity, with a cross erected to Eleanor's memory at Charing.[46]

The questions raised by this troubling representation of Eleanor are most helpfully approached by the theory that the extant text of *Edward the First*, which is profoundly corrupt, represents the revision of an original in which Edward and Eleanor figured as a loving couple; when this was reworked (whether by Peele or another is unclear), chiefly to create the proud and savage persona for Eleanor, new passages were jammed in so that two Eleanors exist chaotically alongside each other. The Eleanor of Peele's original is a loving and human queen who speaks lyrically of her affection and adoration for the king, familiarly addressed as Ned. She comfortably mentions her advancing age, works up a good sweat through the heat and dust of travel, and lustily encourages the earl of Gloucester to woo her daughter Joan:

> Give me my pantables[47]
> Fie this hot wether how it makes me sweate,
> Hey ho my heart, Ah I am passing faint.
> Give me my fanne that I may coole my face,
> Hold, take my maske but see you romple not,
> This wind and dust see how it smolders me,
> Some drinke good Gloster or I die for drinke,
> Ah Ned thou hast forgot thy Nell I see,
> That shee is thus inforst to follow thee.
>
>   ❁   ❁   ❁
>
> Faith Jone I thinke thou must be Glosters bride,
> Good Earle how neare he steps unto her side,
> So soone this eie these younglings had espide,
> Ile tel thee girle when I was faire and young,
> I found such honny in sweete Edwards tongue,
> As I could never spend one idle walke,
> But Ned and I would peece it out with talke.
> So you my Lord when you have got your Jone,
> No matter let Queene mother be alone.
> Old Nell is mother now and grandmother may,
> The greenest grasse doth droupe and turn to hay,
> Woo on kinde Clarke,[48] good Gloster love thy Jone,
> Her heart is thine, her eies is not her owne.
>   (*Edward the First*, sc. 6, ll. 1016–24, 1061–73)

She develops a pregnant woman's cravings, in this case a desire to box the king's ear; she summons Ned and administers a solid clout, which he takes in good stead. After bearing a son, she scolds the maid who lets the baby cry in the king's presence.[49] This is a thoroughly regal but companionable

Eleanor, a queen out of Merrie Olde Englande whom Peele possibly based on and developed from the Edward and Eleanor of Robert Greene's *Friar Bacon and Friar Bungay* (ca. 1589); as the sources used by both playwrights most probably included Holinshed's *Chronicles,* the Walsingham text of the St. Albans eulogy perhaps influenced Peele's original version. But neither Greene nor Peele (at least in the extant version of *Edward the First*) refers to the Acre incident, though Camden had published it probably well before either play was written.[50]

The sources for the revised portrayal of Eleanor perhaps included the 1571 edition of Matthew Paris' *Chronica Majora* by Archbishop Parker, the only source that records the Londoners' caustic reactions in 1255 to the Castilian fashion for carpets—possibly the point of departure for the speech in which Eleanor recalls the "costly Arras points, Faire Iland tapestrie and Azured silke" on which she rode through Jerusalem.[51] Very certainly the revision rests upon two ballads about earlier English queens named Eleanor, the more important of them "The Lamentable Fall of Queene Elnor, who for her pride and wickednesse, by Gods Judgment, sunke into the ground at Charing crosse, and rose up againe at Queene hive." There is no conclusive evidence for the date at which "The Lamentable Fall" originated, but there is much to be said for the theory, advanced by an eighteenth-century printer, that it dates from the reign of Mary Tudor. The Eleanor of this ballad is obsessed with all things Spanish, as Mary might have been thought to be, and the ballad's queen is murderously jealous of the mayoress who has borne a son while the queen has none, as Mary's hopes of a child were humiliatingly disappointed. The ballad's queen demands the shaving of Englishmen's heads and beards and the mutilation of Englishwomen, which may refer to the restoration of the monasteries and the sufferings of the Protestants in Mary's reign. "The Lamentable Fall" also introduces Eleanor's admission of adultery with a friar, though not all texts of the ballad identify the child born of that coupling. The relationship of the "Lamentable Fall" to the revision of *Edward the First* is immediately obvious:

> When Edward was in England king
> The first of all that name,
> Proud Ellinor he made his queen,
> A stately Spanish dame:
> Whose wicked life, and sinful pride,
> Thro' England did excel;
> To dainty dames and gallant maids,
> This queen was known full well.

She was the first that did invent
In coaches brave to ride;
She was the first that brought this land
To deadly sin of pride.
No English taylors here could serve
To make her riche attire:
But sent for taylors into Spain,
To feede her vain desire.

             ✿   ✿   ✿

She crav'd the king, that ev'ry man
That wore long lockes of hair,
Might then be cut and polled all,
Or shaved very near.
Whereat the king did seem content,
And soon thereto agreed;
And first commaunded that his own
Should then be cut with speed;

And after that to please his queen,
Proclaimed thro' the land
That ev'ry man that wore long hair,
Should poll him out of hand.
But yet this Spaniard, not content,
To Women bore a spite,
And then requested of the king,
Against all law and right,

That ev'ry womankind should have
Their right breast cut away;
And then with burning irons sear'd,
The Blood to staunch and stay!
King Edward then perceiving well
Her spite to womankind,
Devised soon by policy
To turn her bloody mind;

He sent for burning irons strait,
All sparkling hot to see;
And said, "O queen, come on thy way;
"I will begin with thee."
Which words did much displease the queen,
That penance to begin;
But ask'd him pardon on her knees,
Who gave her grace therein.

But afterwards she chanc'd to pass
Along brave London streets,
Whereas the mayor of London's wife
In stately sort she meets;
With music, mirth, and melody,
Unto the Church they went,
To give God thanks that to th'lord mayor
A noble son had sent.

It grieved much this spitefull queen,
To see that any one
Should so exceed in mirth and joy,
except herself alone:
For which she after did devise,
Within her bloody mind,
And practis'd still most secretly
To kill this lady kind.

Unto the mayor of London then
She sent her letters straight,
To send his lady to the court,
Upon her grace to wait.
But when the London lady came
Before proud El'nor's face;
She stript her from her rich array,
And kept her vile and base.

      ✿   ✿   ✿

But this contented not the queen,
But shew'd her most despite;
She bound this lady to a post
At twelve a clock at night.
And as poor lady she stood bound
The queen (in angry mood)
Did set two snakes unto her breast,
That suck'd away her blood.

      ✿   ✿   ✿

But coming then to London back,
Within her coach of gold,
A tempest strange within the skies
This queen did there behold:
Out of which storm she could not go,
But there remained a space;

Four horses could not stir the coach
A foot out of the place.

A judgment surely sent from heav'n,
For shedding guiltless blood,
Upon this sinful queen that slew
The London lady good!
King Edward then, as wisdome will'd
Accus'd her of that deed;
But she deny'd and wish'd that God
Would send his wrath with speed:

If that upon so vile a thing
Her heart did ever think,
She wish'd the ground might open wide,
And she therein might sink!
With that at Charing-cross she sunk
Into the ground alive;
And after rose with life again,
In London, at Queenhithe.

When, after that, she languish'd sore
Full twenty days in paine,
At last confess'd the lady's blood
Her guilty hand had slain:[52]
And likewise how that by a fryar
She had a base-born child;
Whose sinful lusts, and wickedness,
Her marriage-bed defil'd.

Thus have you heard the fall of pride;
A just reward of sin;
For, those that will forswear themselves
God's vengeance daily win.
Beware of pride, ye courtly dames,
Both wives and maidens all,
Bear this imprinted on your mind,
That pride will have a fall.[53]

The second ballad used to revise *Edward the First*, "Queen Eleanor's Confession," contributed the motifs of the king and a henchman disguised as friars to hear the queen's confession and her admission of adultery with the henchman. The ballad does not identify its Eleanor beyond her marriage to a King Henry. That name, that there were no friars in the twelfth century, and

that the title of earl marshal did not then exist, suggest Eleanor of Provence
as the queen of the ballad's title; but among the sins this Eleanor admits is the
poisoning of Fair Rosamund at Woodstock, which identifies her as Eleanor
of Aquitaine. This ballad's origins are even more obscure than those of "The
Lamentable Fall," though perhaps the "Confession" relates to Foxe's emphasis on the "turbulent" queens who included Eleanor of Aquitaine; certainly in
the sixteenth century her reputation was none too good.

> Queene Elianor was a sicke womàn
> And afraid that she should dye:
> Then she sent for two fryars of France
> To speke with her speedilye.
>
> The king calld downe his nobles all,
> By one, by two, by three;
> 'Earl marshall, Ile goe shrive the queene,
> And thou shalt wend with mee.'
>
> 'A boone, a boone;' quoth earl marshàll,
> And fell on his bended knee;
> 'That whatsoever queene Elianor saye,
> No harme therof may bee.'
>
> 'Ile pawne my landes,' the king then cryd,
> 'My sceptre, crowne, and all,
> That whatsoever queen Elianor sayes
> No harme thereof shall fall.'
>
> ❁   ❁   ❁
>
> When that they came before the queene
> They fell on their bended knee;
> 'A boone, a boone, our gracious queene
> That you sent so hastilee.'
>
> 'Are you two fryars of France,' she sayd,
> 'As I suppose you bee?
> But if you are two English fryars,
> You shall hang on the gallowes tree.'
>
> 'We are two fryars of France,' they sayd,
> 'As you suppose we bee,
> We have not been at any masse
> Sith we came from the sea.'

'The first vile thing that ever I did
I will to you unfolde;
Earl marshall had my maidenhed
Beneath this cloth of golde.'

      ✿   ✿   ✿

'The next vile thing that ever I did,
To you Ile not denye,
I made a boxe of poyson strong,
To poison king Henrè.'

      ✿   ✿   ✿

'The next vile thing that ever I did,
To you I will discover;
I poysonèd fair Rosamonde,
All in fair Woodstocke bower.'

'That's a vile sinne,' then sayd the king,
'May God forgive it thee!'
'Amen, amen,' quoth earl marshàll;
'And I wish it so may bee.'

'Do you see yonders little boye,
A tossing of the balle?
That is earl marshalls eldest sonne,
And I love him the best of all.

Do you see yonders little boye,
A catching of the balle?
That is king Henrye's youngest sonne,
And I love him the worst of all.'

      ✿   ✿   ✿

The king pulled off his fryars coate,
And appeared all in redde;
She shrieked, and cryd, and wrung her hands,
And sayd she was betrayde.

The king lookt over his left shoulder,
And a grimme look lookèd he;
'Earl marshall,' he sayd, 'but for my oathe,
Or hangèd thou shouldst bee.'[54]

By appropriating both ballads, the revised *Edward the First* makes Eleanor
of Castile doubly adulterous as well as murderous, a foreigner whose behavior is inimical to English society. It may well be asked why a depiction
vouched for (and perhaps based on) Walsingham's eulogy was so drastically
transformed at a time when Camden's positive representation of Eleanor was
also available. One explanation has been found in the debates on the succession to the throne during the reign of Elizabeth I. There were suggestions
from the 1570s into the 1590s that her heir should be Philip II of Spain's
daughter Isabella—not as strange an assertion as it may seem, for Isabella
was twice descended from John of Gaunt: through his eldest daughter
Queen Philippa of Portugal, and a younger daughter Queen Catherine of
Castile. A basic point in these arguments turned on a foreigner's capacity to
inherit the English Crown and whether the Crown could transform an alien
heir into an Englishman (or woman). An unpublished but influential 1567
treatise by Edmund Plowden supporting Mary Stuart's claim to the throne
took the position that as in law the Crown made a king's foreign wife an
English subject, it could make an alien heir English as well. This argument
clearly favored Isabella of Spain as well as Mary Stuart, and it has been theorized that both Greene's *Friar Bacon and Friar Bungay* and the revised *Edward
the First* address the point by asking if the Crown could indeed "English" an
alien queen—the only context in which medieval queens seem to have been
of much interest to Tudor England.[55] But as will be seen, the succession theory
applies more neatly to Greene's work than to Peele's.

Greene's *Friar Bacon and Friar Bungay* is little concerned with Eleanor herself, who appears in only four scenes and has little to say. The work obviously
plays on her foreign origins, but the threat to England by foreign domination
is evoked rather through her kinsmen the king of Castile and the emperor, who
accompany her when, after receiving Edward's portrait, she enters England
on her own initiative to offer herself to him in marriage. Greene emphasizes
Eleanor's precipitate behavior by having her admit that Castilian ladies are
"not very coy" and stresses her foreignness by bringing her onstage only with
the Castilian king and emperor. (Unless Greene's reference was to Alphonso
X's attempt to win the German throne, the historical Eleanor was not closely
related to an emperor; the sixteenth-century Habsburg infanta was.) Edward's
marriage to this impulsive alien is thus potentially perilous for the kingdom;
but Friar Bacon's magic protects the tree of royal succession whose golden
boughs are threatened by Hercules, identified as Jove's bastard—a very likely
hint that bastard lines cannot claim the throne. In the end, the alien rulers are
reduced to attendants who bear swords of state before Henry III in a wedding
procession signifying Eleanor's subjection to her English husband.[56]

Peele's *Edward the First* of course emphasizes Eleanor's persistent Spanishness and her disdain for all things English,[57] her sexual misconduct, and her manifestly destructive enmity for the English people. The succession argument would explain *Edward the First*'s transformation of the adulterous earl marshal of "The Queen's Confession" into the play's adulterous Edmund, for by making Edmund a traitor the play bastardizes the descent through which Isabella of Spain's claim to the throne was reckoned: John of Gaunt's first wife Blanche of Lancaster, heiress of Edmund's line, was the mother of Queen Philippa of Portugal. But the idea that the play deals with the succession debate clearly applies only to the revised *Edward the First*, which vilifies Eleanor, and in any event, the Eleanor material makes up only one of the play's three plots. It might be supposed, however, that the political implications of Peele's original Eleanor were only belatedly grasped and that the ballads were then seized upon to refashion his queen.[58]

The succession theory is attractive, but it should not blind the modern reader to other contexts in which late-Elizabethan audiences experienced the hideous Eleanor of *Edward the First*, an image derived from ballads that had existed independently of the play and had other audiences and contexts before they were appropriated to it. Indeed, assuming that "The Lamentable Fall" dated from Mary I's reign, its original political overtones would likely have dissipated after her death, before the ballad was adapted for Peele's play, so that the "Fall" could have had a second, intermediate existence before it was used in *Edward the First*. In the same vein, the succession theory applies to *Edward the First* for only a brief period after its revision: James VI of Scotland's 1594 affirmation of the Protestant faith eclipsed the infanta's claims and made him, for the majority of Elizabeth's subjects, her most likely heir. (The strongest defense of the infanta's claim, Robert Doleman's *A conference about the next succession to the Crowne of Ingland*, was published in the year of James' affirmation and may represent a last attempt to justify Isabella's rights.)[59] As *Edward the First*'s audiences after 1594 might have become less aware of Eleanor of Castile as the political symbol proposed by the succession theory, they would have been free to interpret her image in other ways. A look for alternative readings is thus in order.

Both "The Queen's Confession" and "The Lamentable Fall," especially the latter, have strong undercurrents of misogyny linking them to that debate on the value of women, successor of the late-medieval *querelle des femmes*, around which considerable literary ferment revolved in the sixteenth and seventeenth centuries. The evils with which "The Lamentable Fall" credits Eleanor amount to a conjugation of the charges most commonly leveled against women in that debate: a love of finery and garish apparel — and the extravagance it implied—pointed to an excess of pride (made explicit in the concluding stanza of "The Lamentable Fall"), while through their seductiveness and malice women incited men to discord and cruelty.[60] That the debate dwelled especially on a wife's subordination to her husband's authority suggests fresh nuances to Peele's characterization of Eleanor, shades of meaning imbedded in the ballads before they were adapted to Peele's play, and which could have been plain to *Edward the First*'s audiences both before and after the question of Elizabeth's heir became a less anxious matter for her subjects.

By having Eleanor demand the shaving of Englishmen and the mutilation of Englishwomen just after the birth of her son, for example, the play utterly inverts the benign image of medieval English queens, who following childbirth requested the king's pardons or grants on behalf of petitioners. The queen's implied rejection of her nurturing maternal role at the moment of her own maternity (". . . thy Nell had skil to choose her time") is echoed by the lady mayoress' death, bitten on the breast by a serpent after the queen tauntingly appoints her nurse to the new prince (". . . draw forth her brest/ And let the Serpent sucke his fil, why so/ Now shee is a Nurse, sucke on sweet Babe").[61] The mayoress' death irresistibly recalls the fate of Cleopatra, who in the debate on women was both praised for constancy and vilified for seductiveness; as the mayoress dies with a tender farewell to her husband, she is aligned with Cleopatra's constancy, by opposition implying that Eleanor is not so constant a wife and thereby preparing her later confession of adultery.[62]

The double demand for shaving and mutilation also implies an eradication of sex characteristics, which takes added meaning from its juxtaposition with the queen's reproductive activity. The play renders this unmistakable by emphasizing only the shaving of beards, not heads as in the ballad, and by compressing both requests into a single quatrain rather than presenting them sequentially as in the ballad. The unity of the requests is also underscored by Eleanor's withdrawal of both when Edward declares that he will be the first to shed his beard and that she must lose her breast first of all: the ballad's Eleanor withdraws only her demand for mutilation—she does not object to the king's shearing, and his order for shaving goes out to the realm. (A problem surfaces here in fitting *Edward the First* into the succession theory; if the queen must lose her breast like other Englishwomen it surely follows that she had somehow been "Englished.") The context here hints at an independent spirit among English wives during the reign of a female sovereign; the play's Eleanor might lead her newly-minted Amazons to lord it over their emasculated former masters. Amazons were praised in the debate on women as adventurous, hardy beings whose able government showed that a society could exist without men, but they were also symbols of sexual ambiguity. Eleanor's vexed renunciation of her project to create a realm of such beings thus reaffirms the sexual distinctions that were threatened by an aggressive and vindictive woman. As it is only Edward's masculine good sense that restrains Eleanor and shows her the folly of her requests, *Edward the First*'s adaptation of "The Lamentable Fall" implies that the play, like the ballad before it, can be read regardless of political context as part of the debate on the worth of women—a manifesto against the turbulent wife who must be subjected to her husband's authority. The revised *Edward the First* thus manipulates its dehistoricized Eleanor to approve the image of an ideally submissive wife, ironically the same thing Camden had suggested by stressing her wifely devotion; the play dramatizes the argument by inverting Camden's image to depict a more violently disruptive royal shrew, tamed by a reasonable master. It can only be wondered what the reviser might have done with Pecham's warning about Eleanor's influence on Edward, or the Dunstable or Guisborough texts.[63]

Peele's *Arraignment of Paris*, written for performance in Elizabeth I's presence probably in the winter of 1581–82, some years before the creation of *Edward the First*, set Elizabeth firmly in an harmonious female community, reduced the erotic differentiation between the sexes, and considered the power of women in political contexts as an active, benevolent force for peace and cooperation—creating a new world in which Elizabeth could act politically as only men had previously acted. But *Edward the First*, probably not intended for performance in the sovereign's presence, emphasizes differences between the sexes through the queen's attempt to annihilate them, treats women's power not as political but as highly emotional, devious, and inimical, and obviously distances her from a community of women as well as from the community of England as a whole.[64] Not only does the Eleanor of "The Lamentable Fall" and *Edward the First* in her malice threaten the physical well-being of the English people and the natural order of relationships among them; by corrupting her function as perpetuator of the royal lineage, the promiscuous queen of both ballads and *Edward the First* threatens the succession, that vital token of the realm's identity and integrity so intimately associated with her office, and she contaminates relations between the king and those who are most held to show him loyalty—his ranking earl or his brother.[65] Another context is thus suggested for *Edward the First*, one that could have evolved after James VI became the front runner as Elizabeth I's heir. Fear of the influence of alien queens is clear throughout the play, bringing to the fore Elizabeth's 1563 remark to the Commons that while England might in future have many alien stepmothers, she alone was their natural mother.[66] *Edward the First* thus hints at English anxieties as the childless Elizabeth aged — not for the identity of her heir, but for the foreign women who would again inevitably figure on the English stage as Elizabeth's successors married. (The most recent foreign-born English queens — Anne of Cleves, Katherine of Aragon, and Margaret of Anjou — were not particularly reassuring examples.) James VI's 1594 affirmation thus sharpened some anxieties even as it relaxed others; there is, for example, a probable link here to the gradual disappearance around 1594 of the Marian imagery associated with Elizabeth from the mid-1570s, as James' emergence as her probable successor eased the fears that had elicited such imagery to mask Elizabeth's childlessness and to camouflage her decaying physical body with the Virgin's agelessness.[67] As Peele's *Edward the First* was experienced in these changed circumstances after 1594, the audience's focus could well have shifted from fears for the succession to apprehension over the influence of future alien queens.

Indeed, the seventeenth century was no more propitious for English queens than it was for the status of Englishwomen in general: all the Stuart consorts in fact aroused controversy and suspicion. Anne of Denmark lived apart from James I for most of his English reign and disagreed endlessly with him over the education of their children; around 1600 she had secretly embraced the Roman faith. Henrietta Maria was a Roman Catholic, and her openly partisan role in the struggles between Charles I and Parliament was profoundly damaging to the notion of the king's wife as an impartial mediator. The queens of Charles II and James II were Catholic and both complicated the succession — Catherine of Braganza by failing to produce an heir, Mary Beatrice of Modena ironically by succeeding where Catherine had not. After James II's flight, the anomalous position of Mary II, though she was indisputably Protestant, posed problems for her apologists. She was crowned simultaneously with William III as queen in her own right, but thereafter William's control of English administration and Mary's admission to a limited regency only in his absence made it unclear whether she was a queen-regnant or a consort — and whether she should be praised as a dutiful spouse or vilified as an unnatural daughter who connived at her father's deposition.[68] The lives of such women, like those of the Empress Matilda, Eleanor of Aquitaine, Isabella of France, or Margaret of Anjou at the hands of Tudor writers, were not likely to kindle interest in the queens of the distant past. Little was written about them in this period — though significantly, "The Lamentable Fall" and the "Confession" continued to circulate, the former well into the eighteenth century. The destruction of most of the monuments to Eleanor of Castile in the Stuart era was nonetheless not a result of her image in the ballads or *Edward the First* but of religious fanaticism during the Civil War, when her Lincoln tomb was wrecked and the crosses pulled down at Grantham, Stony Stratford (1646?), Woburn (1643), St. Albans (1643), Cheapside (1646), Charing (1643), and perhaps Stamford.[69]

In 1643, however, Sir Richard Baker published *A History of the Kings of England*, which included a brief account of the Acre incident in which Eleanor "suckt out the poison of his wounds with her mouth, thereby effecting a cure, which otherwise had been incurable," and reflected that "It is no wonder, that love should do wonders, which is it self a wonder." A lack of scholarly merit did not prevent Baker's work from becoming a popular manual of English history that disseminated the Acre legend afresh, and Edmund Gibson's 1695 English edition of *Britannia* gave new currency to Camden's portrayal of Eleanor. The resulting drift in a new direction may be glimpsed in the latest extant copy of "The Lamentable Fall," dating from around 1720, which carries a printer's note excusing the publication of something so much at variance with what was known to be Eleanor's true history.[70] About this time, too, there were signs of interest in preserving the remaining Eleanor crosses, probably helped along by the Gothic revival. The first attempt to restore the Hardingstone cross came in 1713 and was followed by their repeated publication by antiquaries, most notably in the second volume of the Society of Antiquaries' *Vetusta Monumenta* (1780). By the end of the century they were well enough known to the public to furnish the material for a satirical Cruikshank engraving of antiquaries marveling at the Hardingstone monument.[71]

Perhaps the popularity of George II's wife Caroline of Ansbach, the first influential Protestant queen of England, had some effect on the development of interest in earlier queens, but if so it is ironic that the century's best-known and most positive view of Eleanor of Castile came about as an expression of opposition to Caroline's husband. James Thomson's 1739 play *Edward and Eleanora: A Tragedy*, based on the Acre legend (for which Thomson credited Baker's *History*), presented the Plantagenet couple as heroically devoted to each other and the welfare of England. While Edward and Eleanor may have been so devoted a couple, Thomson exploited their dehistoricized images for openly political purposes. Thomson was a client of George II's heir Frederick Louis, who was on notoriously bad terms with his father. Frederick openly espoused the opposition to Horace Walpole, the minister in whom King George and Queen Caroline placed their confidence; when *Edward and Eleanora* was written, the prince was forbidden the king's presence, and in 1737 had been kept away from his mother's deathbed.[72]

Figure 4.8.
A Cruickshank
engraving of
1796, showing
antiquaries at
the Harding-
stone cross
(London,
The British
Museum).

Edward and Eleanora implies from start to finish that Edward—heir to the
throne at the time of the Acre incident—was more devoted to the interests
of England than was his father. He is repeatedly urged to return to England
to correct abuses there, and is reminded of his privilege and duty as the king's
first counsellor. Eleanora's selfless sacrifice is clearly intended to imply that
Edward (read Frederick Louis) had in Eleanora (read Augusta of Saxe-
Gotha) a wife fit to support his noble struggles for England's welfare. As
Edward and Eleanora is dedicated to Augusta, the address is worth quoting:

> In the Character of *Eleanora* I have endeavoured to represent,
> however faintly, a PRINCESS distinguish'd for all the Virtues that
> render Greatness amiable. I have aimed, particularly, to do justice
> to her inviolable Affection and generous Tenderness for a
> PRINCE, who was the Darling of a great and free People.
> Their Descendants, even now, will own with Pleasure, how
> properly this Address is made to your Royal Highness.

Thomson's Eleanora is indeed an heroic if wordy creature, who upon learning from Daraxa, an Arab princess captive in the English camp, that Edward's life can be saved only if a willing victim sucks the poison from his wound in the certain knowledge that he or she will then suffer the venom's fatal pangs, at once accepts that the sacrifice must be hers:

> Then hear me, Heaven!
> Prime source of Love! Ye Saints and Angels, hear me!
> I here devote me for the best of Men,
> Of Princes and of Husband [*sic*]. On this Cross
> I seal the cordial Vow: confirm it to Heaven!
> And grant me Courage in the Hour of Trial!
> (*Edward and Eleanora* I.vi)

Despite his desperate illness, Edward also manages to deliver some thoughts on his wife:

> Ah, my GLOSTER,
> You have not touch'd on something that here pleads
> For longer Life, beyond the Force of Reason,
> Perhaps too powerful pleads—my ELEANORA!
> To Thee, my friend, I will not be asham'd
> Even to avow my Love in all its Fondness.
> For Oh there shines in this my dearer Self!
> This Partner of my Soul! such a mild Light
> Of careless Charms, of unaffected Beauty,
> Such more than Beauty, such endearing Goodness,
> That when I meet her Eye, where cordial Faith,
> And every gentle Virtue mix their Lustre,
> I feel a Transport that partakes of Anguish!
> (*Edward and Eleanora* II.iii)

As Eleanora in turn lays dying from the poison the sultan, impressed by her devotion, disguises himself and enters the English camp to administer an antidote. The drama ends as news of Henry III's death arrives and Edward declares his intention to return to England and restore it to its former glory among nations. It lies not within the scope of this book to determine whether Frederick Louis was the darling of a great and free people or whether Augusta of Saxe-Gotha was distinguished for any of the virtues that render greatness amiable. But it was certainly the play's political overtones that led the censor to forbid its performance. Aware that the ban would only increase public interest, Thomson quickly published the work, and whether because of its politics or in spite of it, *Edward and Eleanora* sold well. John Wesley praised the nobility of its sentiments and called it "quite [Thomson's] masterpiece"; in an adapted form it was frequently mounted from the 1770s into the 1790s, its political undercurrents by then doubtless forgotten.[73]

The passages just quoted make it clear that Thomson's play, despite its titular claim to tragedy, was among the first stage works to move away from the conventions of neoclassical tragedy and toward a romanticized, even sentimentalized, drama. Insofar as it relates to the play's subject matter, this approach may have been suggested to Thomson by Baker's reflections on Eleanor's love for Edward — "that love should do wonders, which is it self a wonder." And in this sense the portrayal of Eleanora and Edward as devoted spouses and (especially in Eleanora's case) parents, seems likely to have contributed to that gradual reshaping of cultural expectations of love that underlay far-reaching changes in marriage and domestic life in the eighteenth century.[74] With the authority of Camden and Baker behind it, the cult of the romantic in full bloom, and interest in the Gothic growing apace, this very positive image of Eleanor swiftly overcame any lingering traces of the vile queen of the Tudor ballads and Peele's *Edward the First*; it was in the Camden-Baker-Thomson transfiguration that Eleanor's reputation soared into the nineteenth century. The effect is evident in the earliest systematic effort to examine her career, Joseph Hunter's 1842 article on Edward's commemorations of her. A careful worker, Hunter was evidently the first to dismiss the Acre legend; he dealt competently with the narrative sources available to him, but used few unedited records, and for his estimate of Eleanor's character relied on Walsingham, Holinshed, and Camden. Hunter's reputation as an antiquarian and historian served to legitimize those earlier accounts for the Victorian era, and his work strengthened regard for Eleanor of Castile as an exemplary consort.[75]

By far the more significant nineteenth-century development for Eleanor's reputation, indeed for all the English medieval queens, was the publication of Agnes Strickland's *Lives of the Queens of England* (1840–48). No work has had more influence on beliefs about the medieval queens of England, and as its impact continues to be felt despite its age, a good deal of attention must be given it here. Agnes Strickland (1796–1874) and her sister Elizabeth 1795–1875, a silent collaborator who wrote the lives of most of the medieval queens including Eleanor of Castile, were daughters of a prosperous merchant who gave them a thorough classical education. When Agnes was fourteen, her father bought a Suffolk estate near Southwold called Reydon Hall, but later suffered reverses; after he died in 1818 his unmarried daughters turned to their pens to support themselves. The reception accorded Agnes' poems convinced her by the 1830s to pursue the writing of history.

Thereafter she and Elizabeth, who had written for a women's magazine, turned to study in the British Museum; they learned paleography from staff members and became the first women allowed to consult in the State Paper Office. Agnes entered into correspondence with Englishmen familiar with records of history, such as Sir Harris Nicolas and Sir Thomas Phillipps, who provided the sisters with moral support and much information from manuscripts; the French historian Guizot helped them consult records in that country. It was no coincidence that the *Queens* was dedicated to the new sovereign. The work was inspired by renewed affection for the monarchy upon Victoria's accession, and Strickland (or her canny publisher Henry Colburn) believed that the presence of a queen on the throne would renew interest in the histories of other royal women, which proved to be as true for Victoria's reign as it had not been for Elizabeth I's.[76]

A biographical context is helpful to understand Strickland's work, for the *Queens* reflect many early influences in their lives. Agnes in particular labored to improve what was for her a painfully ambiguous family situation, neither gentry nor merchant elite. She obsessively claimed gentle birth, repeating her father's belief in an unverifiable descent from the Stricklands of Sizergh. The *Queens* advertised and legitimized these claims: Agnes dated her prefaces from Reydon Hall, later editions featured engraved vignettes of the house, and alleged ancestors were identified in footnotes. That Agnes saw her work as initially directed to a gentle readership is clear in her preface to an 1872 printing, in which she announced her pleasure that this edition was priced to make it accessible to "all classes."[77] Strickland also sought to legitimize herself as a woman writer not of verse or novels but of serious history, and so offered the *Queens* as "a national undertaking, honourable to the female character, and generally useful to society."[78] The work was less explicitly but nonetheless firmly attached to the fashionably renewed literary interest in the medieval past inspired by the works of Sir Walter Scott and derived additional legitimacy from association with the burgeoning Record Movement: Strickland repeatedly insisted that the *Queens* rested upon original evidence—"incorruptible witnesses" that yielded "facts not opinions." And she spoke—(in surprisingly modern accents) as one historian to another when she told her readers that "documentary historians alone can appreciate the difficulties, the expense, the injury to health [and] the sacrifice of more profitable literary pursuits, that have been involved in this undertaking."[79]

The spectrum of tastes to which Strickland's work appealed was broad, its success consequently enormous. Press reviews appended to later editions of the *Queens* hailed the work as "a remarkable and truly great historical work," ". . . which has conferred upon its authoress an enviable and lasting

celebrity." Strickland was praised as "a lady of considerable learning, inde-
fatigable industry, and careful judgment," "to our mind the first literary lady
of the age," "beyond all comparison the most entertaining historian in the
English language." Agnes' insistence that her work was of national utility
struck a resonant chord: "no one can be said to possess an accurate knowledge of the history of the country who has not studied this truly national
work." She exploited the immense prestige she wrested from the *Queens* to
make her way in from the margins of gentility, haunting the royal drawing
rooms and enjoying the attentions of titled readers. On an 1865 visit to
Oxford she heard her work cheered (by the undergraduates) and in 1870
was granted a Civil List pension of £100 "for her services to literature."
Elizabeth Strickland's vital collaboration was never revealed to the *Queens'*
vast readership.[80]

Social ambition was not the only factor that shaped Strickland's *Queens*.
The work's medieval lives were limited by the sisters' Anglicanism and
their staunch Tory politics. Agnes conscientiously faced the need to deal
with the Roman Catholic faith, a religion obviously distasteful to her; she
made an extended visit in a convent near London and attended many services in French churches while researching there. But these encounters with
nineteenth-century Catholicism in no way modified her perception of an
oppressive Roman Church or what she called "the old superstitions." Like
most of her audience, she was profoundly ignorant of the vital force the
Christian faith exerted in medieval life, and could suggest that certain of her
queens "would have been better women if their actions had been more con-
formable to the principles inculcated by the pure and apostolic doctrines of
the church of England."[81] And even allowing for early Victorian ignorance
of the medieval constitution, few nowadays will fail to react with surprise
to the information that England at Edward I's accession was "happy in the
permanent settlement of her ancient representative government, now, for the
first time, firmly established since the reign of St. Edward," as manifest
when Edward entered London in 1274 to find "both houses of Parliament
assembled to welcome and do honour to their constitutional sovereign and
his virtuous consort."[82]

Strickland makes it clear, too, that she is ready to stake out and defend
the queens as her own, explicitly female, territory. Blackstone's *Commentaries*,
for example, glossed the ancient custom of allowing the queen the tail portion of any whale that washed up on shore as a means to provide whalebone
for the royal corset. Strickland abruptly dismisses such nonsense with the
remark that the learned Blackstone, J., would have been well advised to ask
a lady about this: whalebone for corsets comes not from the tail but from the

head (which went to the king). And she was roused to scathing disdain by
the male writers who had presumed to question whether Matilda of Flanders
had really embroidered the Bayeux tapestry:

> ... with due deference to the lords of creation on all subjects con-
> nected with policy and science, we venture to think that our
> learned friends the archaeologists and antiquaries, would do well
> to direct their intellectual powers to more masculine objects of
> inquiry, and leave the question of the Bayeux tapestry ... to the
> decision of the ladies, to whose provinces it peculiarly belongs. It
> is a matter of doubt to us whether one out of the many gentlemen
> who have disputed Matilda's claims to that work ... would know
> how to put in the first stitch.[83]

The distinction Strickland so sharply drew between the male and female
spheres reveals the vacuum at the heart of her work. Dependent upon
records created by men that reflected male concerns, Strickland could find
her queens only by turning to such matters as embroidery and corsets. She
was otherwise unable to isolate them from the political history of their husbands' reigns, and for long stretches loses sight of them as political and military matters are discussed, as the ruins of monasteries and castles are
minutely described, or as tomb effigies and manuscript illuminations are
expounded as portraits from the life. As noted earlier, political affairs must
at times claim precedence in considering a medieval queen's life, but it is by
no means impossible to consider her career afresh within that context, and
certainly it can be viewed from vantage points other than the political. But
Strickland's *Queens* reinforces a gentility that implied feminine virtues embed-
ded in the domestic; the result is at best a primitive feminization of history
whose household rootedness, insofar as it related to royal women, was likely
also modeled by Victoria's aggressive domesticization of her court. In the last
analysis, while the *Queens* suggest the novelty of women's history or at least
of history ostensibly approached through women's lives, the authors only
solidify distinctions between male and female spheres. Strickland's efforts to
legitimize herself as a writer of history notwithstanding, she bowed to "the
lords of creation" in other conventional male spheres—most explicitly when
Agnes later refused to exploit in the cause of married women's property
rights the celebrity the *Queens* had brought her.[84]

With her disdain for anything that smacked of ideology in the writing of
history, Strickland would never have acknowledged that her work might
prove a point or serve a purpose. But hers was not an age that looked for
unbiased history. This was especially true for writers like Strickland, whose

earnest readership expected instructive moral lessons from the individuals and events of whom they read. Strickland obliged handsomely: the contrast to be drawn between "good" queens like Eleanor of Castile and "bad" ones like Eleanor of Aquitaine or Isabella of France was too inviting to be passed over in silence, and so, by comparison, "good" queens were further glorified. As Strickland never could establish her queens in a context independent of their husbands' political careers, moreover, she tended to transform queens into kings' moral pendants, which made it the easier for historians to pair "good" and "bad" kings with appropriately "virtuous" or "wicked" consorts. But for all its limitations, given the medieval materials the sisters could use and current standards of historical writing, the *Queens* was not without value: Strickland deserves credit for bringing the queens to public notice, and the work's popular success did open doors for women as writers of history.[85]

If much has been said here about the composition of Strickland's *Queens*, it is because the factors just noted all had their impact on her influential accounts of the medieval consorts. Strickland's queens are, ideally, refined and genteel, pious, and generous; they are devoted, chaste, and modest wives, and devoted mothers. They are supplied with forks, soap, tubs, and combs, so they neither eat with their fingers nor are offensive in their persons. And they own books, one item without which the Stricklands, with their literary leanings, clearly felt no woman could be considered a lady. (Despite the benefits the sisters reaped from their excellent private training, the social implications for female education were not developed: the royal books are mere tokens of gentility, not means to knowledge or power.) When a queen like Eleanor of Aquitaine meddles in politics or behaves immodestly, forcing Strickland to consider her in relation to matters outside this domestic arena, she is sharply criticized.

A more serious complication in Strickland's work is that her claims of original evidence for her medieval lives are suspect. Much original material is cited for the Tudor and Stuart queens, but this was exactly the period in which the sisters were most passionately interested, and, of course, much more material survives from that period than from earlier centuries. In comparison with her Tudor and Stuart lives, Strickland's appeals to original material for many medieval queens are conspicuously few. Her life of Eleanor of Castile is supported by citations to medieval chronicles, but only those available in print or from which extracts were provided by collectors or archivists. These are cited with a fine disregard for contemporaneity, and a preference for long quotes from rhyming chroniclers and ballads betrays Agnes' early hopes for a poet's career. What record evidence is cited was likewise either accessible in print or was provided by others. A good deal of what was already in print was, however, ignored by the Stricklands, evidently because much of it, like the Hundred Rolls and most of the entries concerning Eleanor in the Parliament Rolls, suggested her less attractive side. Strickland was not unaware of these sources; two entries from the parliament rolls are cited in the *Queens'* life of Eleanor, but both date from after her death and concern her only in that they seek Edward's consideration in certain matters "for the good of the late queen's soul"—from which Strickland infers that Eleanor was well remembered by her subjects.[86] The wardrobe accounts and related sources that might have spurred Strickland to explore new paths in her queens' lives were likewise not unknown to her, and that they could be used in a lengthy survey, despite the primitive arrangement and cataloguing of the public records at that time, is proved by Mary Anne Everett Green's *Lives of the Princesses of England* (1849–55). Inspired by the *Queens* and for the medieval period far more closely documented from such sources than Strickland, Green's *Princesses* is a work of its time and offers its masses of detail in a purely narrative framework. But the details themselves suggest attention to fresh aspects of medieval queens' lives, and Strickland's failure to use these sources (or the *Princesses*) when revising the *Queens* remains a baffling anomaly.[87]

The single most important record source for Eleanor's life then in print, Beriah Botfield and Thomas Turner's edition of her executors' accounts (1841), was cited in Strickland's later editions with manifest wariness. Entries in those accounts for the payment of damages awarded from the 1291 inquest are clearly identified by marginalia; their purpose is unmistakable but Strickland never mentions them. Her failure to do so is thrown into conspicuous relief by her use of the chronicle known to her as "Matthew of Westminster," otherwise the *Flores historiarum*—the one source that records Eleanor's deathbed prayer for the 1291–92 inquest. Strickland's claims to thorough research would thus presume that she knew of that request and could have deduced its relationship to the damages paid by the queen's executors; but nothing is said to indicate that the damages entries exist, even when such payments occur in the accounts side by side with the entries Strickland ostensibly (and approvingly) cites to illustrate Eleanor's literary interests or to identify her ladies-in-waiting and physicians. In fact, an obvious lack of explicit citations to the accounts themselves strongly implies that Strickland never looked at them, but relied exclusively on Botfield's lengthy introduction—the only part of the work she specifically cites.[88]

For the most part, Strickland's account of Eleanor relies on the Tudor writers who had so little to say about her, and on the antiquarians—Carte, Pennant, Speed, Stow, Strype—who provided lore about ruined castles

Eleanor might have occupied but who, like Strickland, turned to Camden for what they said of Eleanor herself. In essence, Strickland reported whatever she found consistent with Camden or Walsingham, and there must be strong suspicions that she deliberately bypassed, or at best remained ignorant of, available material that pointed in a different direction. Eleanor thus emerges in Strickland's pages as a creature of refinement, not medieval barbarism; here, for the first time, appears the gentle wife who tamed the Plantagenet lion; Strickland emphasizes Eleanor's literary interests and praises her taste in dress (as witnessed by her tomb effigy) as more befitting her rank than the excessive display of the modern age. Eleanor's avoidance of the "superfluous devotion of the middle ages"[89] is lauded, and so much attention is paid to items of personal refinement that she emerges almost as a housewife with all the modern conveniences, a domesticization furthered by Strickland's portrayal of Eleanor as a model of conjugal purity and maternal solicitude. This Eleanor is the epitome of noble womanhood, supplied with every token of gentility and rank—all of which Strickland intimated that she herself was equipped to appreciate, both by birth and by breeding.

The impact of the *Queens* was immediate and lasting; in its wake there came a seemingly endless stream of parroted, sentimentalized biographical sketches of English queens that, not coincidentally, reached a nadir with Victoria's 1897 Diamond Jubilee.[90] Quite apart from Strickland's legacy, it was not unlikely that interest in medieval royalty would increase in a century that saw a rebirth in Great Britain of popular affection for the monarchy, renewed attention to royal ritual with all its medieval evocations, and a gradual enhancement of (and renewed antiquarian interest in) Westminster Abbey's role in the nation's public life. And in Eleanor of Castile's case, the Eleanor crosses' hold on popular imagination was strengthened by events within the contemporary royal family. The crosses were Gilbert Scott's model for the Martyrs' Memorial in Oxford (1841), and in the 1860s he avowedly returned to the "most touching monuments ever erected in this country to a Royal Consort" as his inspiration for the Albert Memorial in London; his linking of the Eleanor crosses and the Memorial gave Queen Victoria's extravagant grief the historical precedent of Edward's elaborate mourning for Eleanor, and made Strickland's sentimentalized portrayal of Eleanor more believable by affording Edward's bereavement a modern parallel. Either the Memorial, or a collection of photographs of the original crosses John Abel published in 1864, may have inspired the imitation Eleanor cross erected in that year near Charing Cross station in London as an advertisement for a local hotel.[91]

Strickland's work was sustained beyond its viability largely through the impression that further research on the queens was now unnecessary, if not downright presumptuous. But despite Strickland's influence, the evolution of Queen Eleanor's reputation was not complete; indeed, Strickland in a sense had anticipated later developments when she dismissed the sinister queen of "The Lamentable Fall" as a tradition of the common people.[92] Thus anointed by implication as a "learned" commodity, the Walsingham-Camden-Strickland Eleanor was in turn vulgarized as Strickland disseminated her to "all classes." But Strickland's audience had to deal too with the long-term effects of the Record Movement, which steadily brought to light signs that Camden and his heirs were wide of the mark; those conditioned by Strickland found this evidence painful, and the process of assimilation has been long and difficult. Francis Child may have been unaware of the Pecham letters, Guisborough, or Dunstable, when he fumed in 1889 that the excesses of "The Lamentable Fall" were better suited to Henry II's queen than "that model of women and wives, Eleanor of Castile." In preparing a short life of Eleanor for the *Dictionary of National Biography,* published in the same year, the antiquary W. H. Stevenson found himself unable to ignore the contemporary sources, and tried to reconcile the contradictions with a carefully-worded but awkward estimate that Eleanor was pious and gentle but "rather grasping." Unfettered by scholarly objectivity, popular feeling resented the encroachment of erudition: K. A. Patmore in 1910 regretted that "cold research" had tainted Eleanor's image as "the amiable and selfless being of our dreams." At midcentury, Thomas Costain ignored edited sources just as doggedly as had Strickland, and even coaxed new mileage out of the Acre legend by assuring his readers that Eleanor would not have hesitated to suck Edward's wounds had she taken it into her head to do so.[93] Costain's publications in the 1940s coincided with Vivian Galbraith's challenge to traditional views of "good" and "bad" kings; postwar interest in social and economic history brought evidence for Eleanor's land hunger to wider notice, hinting at a less affable queen than Strickland or Patmore dreamed of, and feminist studies have prepared her disentanglement from the gendered portrayals of past ages. The image of a harsh queen Strickland so genteelly dismissed thus slowly acquired its own "learned" legitimacy, but cherished traditions die hard: much of the renewed interest in Eleanor at the seventh centenary of her death in 1990 was plainly inspired by the romance of the crosses.[94]

For centuries, then, the Eleanor crosses and the St. Albans eulogy together have made Eleanor of Castile's reputation susceptible to manipulation that has approved an idealized image of wife and queen, defined according to gendered roles. Indeed, the first steps in this evolution can be discerned in her own lifetime. John Pecham cautioned that since as woman she was naturally

more merciful than man, she must as the most exalted of women be more
clement than anyone else in the realm; he rebuked her for the bad example
her avarice gave the kingdom and warned that she was thought to urge the
king to rule harshly. Eleanor's contemporaries in effect affirmed their expectations of merciful and generous queenly deportment not by praising
Eleanor's compassion and virtue but by criticizing her perceived lack of
them, or by remaining altogether silent. Her image was distanced from an
unhelpful reality by monuments that advertised a submissive and gracious
queen, mourned by king and realm alike. As living memory faded, such ide-
alization favored new identities for a long-dead queen. Amid fifteenth-century dynastic crises, she was the consort who assured the realm's integrity
by perpetuating a line of worthy rulers: a royal brood mare who passively
transmitted ancestral virtues. When a woman ruled in England and many
wives chafed at the marital yoke, both the Fiadoni-Arévalo Eleanor
expounded by William Camden, and the viperous queen of "The Lamentable
Fall," endorsed a wife's subjection to her husband. The sentimentalization
prepared by Camden was cultivated by Geoffrey Baker and brought to full
bloom by James Thomson, whose Eleanora embodied a wife's romantic
and heroically selfless devotion to her husband, a royal couple ideally
pledged to England's welfare. Strickland and Costain both witness a post-
industrial separation of the public and private spheres, from which Eleanor's
domestic virtues emerged as the perfect complement to Edward's military
skill and executive mastery—a sovereign pair decorously happy in the taste-
fully appointed home life provided by an industrious and unobtrusive queen.

IN CONCLUSION

So much, then, for legend. Can a woman be recovered from that mingling
of deference and inventiveness characteristic of the lives of most medieval
women but nowhere so clearly observed as in the lives of queens, witnessed
in Eleanor's case by limited male-centered sources that only fitfully indicate
female contexts in which to consider her life or her queenship and that ultimately appear always to return her (and queenship itself) to a masculine
frame of reference? Pecham's *Jerarchie*, written to answer an intellectually
vigorous queen's questions about angels, expounds the Heavenly hierarchy
to her by likening its ranks to those of an implicitly male royal officialdom.
Her embrace of the Dominicans, suggestive of an individual refashioning of
traditional queenly postures, tested her relationship to the Church's male
hierarchy and the older monastic orders, who took an evidently dim view
of her actions. That Eleanor appears infrequently in the archetypically gen-

dered role of intercessor suggests that his subjects did not have uniform expectations of all queens but took notice of personal qualities—or even that individual queens had differing approaches to their office; it also inexorably recalls Pecham's admonition that she was not giving the realm a proper example of the compliant wifely virtues. Uncommunicative though they are in detail, her letters are those of a woman accustomed to the exercise of power, but clearly her access thereto was subject to the pleasure of a watchful husband.

As the wife of an energetic and competent king, Eleanor of Castile was not among that endlessly-discussed handful of medieval queens whose atypical importance is almost invariably attributable to the absence or incapacity of a male ruler: a sonless father or brother whose death without sons left a daughter or sister to inherit, a husband who died leaving a widow as regent, or whose illness or incompetence allowed or compelled his wife to occupy an ominous political vacuum (another sign that medieval queenship always had a male referent, physically present, proficient, or not). No such anomalies characterized Eleanor's life; so commanding was Edward's presence that it is virtually impossible to fit her into the official history of his reign. But if Eleanor's engagement with her society's conventions was politically less eventful than that of an Eleanor of Provence or a Margaret of Anjou, it will be clear by now that Edward's proximity itself gave his wife's negotiation of those narratives its own intricacies, demanding her acquiescence and inviting her creativity. Her life is thus a reminder that the full range of experience within a group—here the queens of medieval England—is fully discerned only when the less conspicuous are scrutinized alongside the anomalously prominent. With this in mind, consideration of medieval queenship's gendered settings may help isolate Eleanor of Castile from the male contexts that shadow her.

The ruling houses of medieval Europe handled gender in a variety of ways, but royal consorts in general were directed during their husbands' lifetimes to informal, unofficial spheres of activity. Their claims to power rested on the bearing and rearing of children, the family connections to which they were born or which they created by marriage, and various forms of patronage; their freedom of action was paradoxically dependent upon their compliance and collaboration with male authority. This was territory accessible and familiar to many wives, but its importance to a queen was magnified by the wealth she might command, by the international stage upon which her family connections and marriage established her, and most especially by her access to the king. Eleanor's life reveals some of the ways in which these informal, relational arenas allowed queens to traverse the cloudy limits between unofficial and official, margin and center, "private" and "public": her literary interests, the marriages she arranged, the cultivation of her relatives, the training of her daughters, all extended her reach within the diplomatic and curial milieux in which she functioned. Louis IX's restriction of his wife's role in their children's education, and of her ability to form close relationships with his officials through patronage, implies that kings understood well the advantages their wives might develop in such ways.[95] Given Edward's control over her actions, Eleanor's effective performance in these unofficial arenas and her invaluable relationships with such men as Burnell and Kirkby suggest that he saw no danger in the benefits she might derive from methods likely to be seen as uncontroversially appropriate to his wife—or else that he trusted her more than Louis IX trusted Margaret of Provence. In Eleanor's deference to Edward, then, a hint may be caught that she was both prudent and resourceful.

It may be questioned whether the English at large were cognizant of a queen's curial and diplomatic manoeuvres. But as other areas of Eleanor's activities were certainly well known to the kingdom, her life can be used to study some of the ways in which even a politically inconsequential queen became the focus of distrust and contention despite her prudence and resourcefulness and regardless of rituals that deployed her as an instrument of conciliation and order. The cultural boundaries Eleanor traversed, made widely apparent to a kingdom acutely sensitive to any foreign presence around its king, were not gendered save in that she was, like most queens, an in-marrying female; but her engagement with other, gendered, limits was controversial enough to touch the magisterial face of the king whose life she shared. Edward's inability to supply her with sufficient income and materials for patronage thrust her into an economic sphere no previous queen had entered and brought her into contact with English society in ways earlier queens had not experienced. Her rapid accumulation of land and wealth with Edward's approval, the evolution of a highly aggressive administration for her estates and revenue, and the vigorous exploitation of her prerogatives, led some to link the unwelcome assertiveness of an alien queen to the energetic rule of the king to whom her intimacy was so industriously touted. Given the significance of a gracious female figure to representations and perceptions of sovereignty in the medieval West, Eleanor's intermittent appearances as a wifely intercessor propose fresh nuances to impressions of Edward as a severe king that accent the complexities of gender in the construction of medieval kingship and queenship. Suspicions that she incited him to rule harshly implied the troubling prospect of a king under his wife's sway; that she only sporadically appeared as the benevolent queen who led him to show his subjects justice and magnanimity could have reinforced anxieties for her malign domination—or may have suggested that Edward, like the brutal king in the fourteenth-century English romance *Athelston,* was arrogantly refusing to allow a woman's salubrious counsel to modify his magisterial behavior.[96]

Eleanor's life serves as well, then, as a reminder that what was thought about queens influenced what was thought of kings, and that queens constructed kingship in their mundane behavior as well as through their share in ceremony and ritual. The reverse was also true, to the extent that a king's perceived faults might be projected on his wife, or blamed on her. This posits that a queen was judged on her conformity to conventional behavior that complemented the king's male office. In this, Eleanor was like other consorts, but she stands apart in her failure, real or perceived, to comply with such customs, as intimated by the patterns of her piety (especially her charity) and again implied in the preceding paragraph. The matter of a queen's individual agency as she negotiated her society's conventions is thereby raised. It was suggested in Chapter Three that Eleanor was not seen as a likely target for petitioners seeking her help with the king; that she seemingly did not bother herself to better that impression by adopting the postures of a "good" queen—by dispensing her alms in person, for example, or cultivating opportunities to mediate with the king—poses questions the sources cannot quite answer. The letter she sent John de Loundres at a time of crisis in 1265 shows her anxious to avoid criticism of her avarice, and in the years following Evesham she benefited both Henry III and herself by exploiting numerous opportunities to reconcile the king with supporters of Simon de Montfort. But it appears that she jettisoned concerns about her reputation for covetousness once crisis was past and she was the wife of a victorious and confident king, with the result that those who sought a mediator with Edward ceased to approach her. Any hints that Eleanor adopted or rejected certain lines of conduct on her own initiative, especially those that implied a departure from approved standards, would suppose that her deference to Edward was also an individual decision—one perhaps periodically renegotiated?—and that her resourcefulness was also unique. Here, however, a caveat must be entered against pushing such reasoning too far: the extant sources cannot reveal whether her actions reflect an arrogant calculation, whether Edward's self-assurance had persuaded Eleanor to forget early worries, or even if she justified her land gathering on the grounds that she was following paths her husband indicated for her.

For similar reasons only cautious efforts can be made to define Eleanor as an individual woman against the common experiences she shared with her sister queens. Reactions to Eleanor's behavior were recorded in chronicles and documents, all created by males, that were never meant to convey personal revelations about men, let alone a woman. Even the sources of a more intimate nature contain little information about her; her *ipsissima verba* are nowhere preserved (save perhaps in the 1265 instructions to John de Loundres), nor do her letters reveal anything like the attractive personality evident in Eleanor of Provence's correspondence.[97] Any attempt to reconstruct a character seven centuries after the fact will be tentative, and much of what can be surmised about Eleanor of Castile as an individual must be couched in general terms. Intelligent and spirited, she was well prepared to deal with the situations she encountered as queen of England, a consort whose acquiescence merited the esteem, and whose energies warranted the attentive supervision, of a strong and capable king. Though she could react swiftly if circumstances required, the watchful planning that prepared Eleanor's actions implies an organized mentality, consistent with the sophisticated literary tastes that reveal an intellectual vitality also apparent in her spiritual life. Ideas that the resolve and tenacity Eleanor showed were genetically available to the women of certain royal lineages are defeated by the self-evident reality that any queen had to cultivate such qualities to safeguard her position. These are by no means offensive attributes, but they can manifest themselves in unpleasant ways and there is no denying that in Eleanor's case they did exactly that. The same may well prove to be true when the lives of other medieval queens revered in recent centuries are at last subjected to thorough investigation.

It is paradoxically out of that intersection of common experience and individual initiative, of deference and creativity—the dove's innocuousness and the serpent's sagacity—that Eleanor of Castile speaks most clearly, even touchingly, in the concern for her daughters that reveals her awareness of the patterns of medieval royal women's lives, perceptions that suggest a queen's understanding of herself as a daughter, wife, and mother. Her protection of her daughters, the heraldic displays that included her mother's arms, the many marriages she arranged for her female cousins and attendants—surely these mean that Eleanor understood herself in terms of her membership in a female network that effectively, if silently, paralleled the political alliances among princes. That membership propelled her across boundaries that were cultural as well as geographical, eliciting choices and decisions that could be a powerful impetus to self-realization, and placing at her command the cross-cultural currents she manipulated to advantage through literary patronage. It may be argued that these were her responses to an arranged marriage that itself exemplified her subjection in a male society, and that emphasizing them only embeds her again in a male context. To an extent this is true. But here at least it can be answered that these were exactly the responses that would be shaped by a woman aware of herself through her experiences within that system; and this woman, her husband's surveillance notwithstanding, identified and occupied with a certain effectiveness the interstices that were open to her. The fortunes of such women can and should be as accurately assessed in their recognition and exploitation of such opportunities as in the extent to which they were or were not able to claim official political power.[98]

I. Eleanor's Ancestry

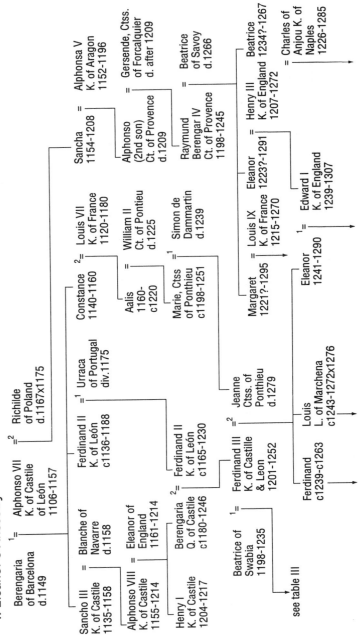

see table III

see table III

II. Eleanor's Potential Husbands in 1250

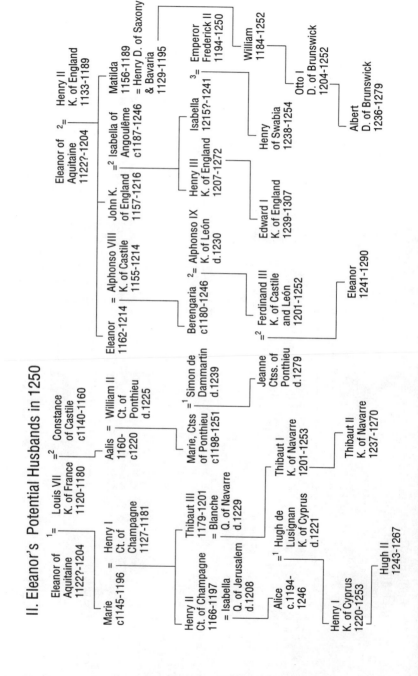

III. England, Castile and France in the Thirteenth Century

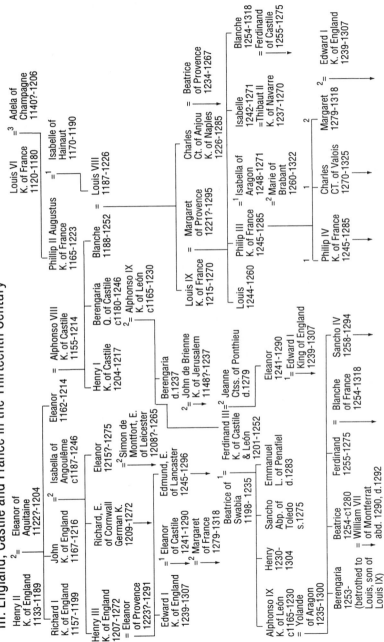

Notes*

CHAPTER ONE

1. Galbraith, "Good Kings and Bad Kings," 119–32; J. W. Alexander, "Historiographical Survey," 94–109; Hanawalt, "Golden Ages for the History of English Medieval Women," 9. On queens, Johnstone, "Queen's Household" in Tout, *Chapters*, v, 231–89, and idem, "Queen's Household," *English Government*, i, 250–99; Myers, "Household of Queen Margaret of Anjou," 1–75, and "Jewels of Queen Margaret of Anjou," 113–31; Richardson, "Letters and Charters," 193–213; Myers, "Household of Queen Elizabeth Woodville," 207–35, 443–81; Blackley and Hermansen, eds., *Household Book of Queen Isabella*; Doherty, "Date of the Birth of Isabella," 246–48; Kibler, ed., *Eleanor of Aquitaine*; *CHEC*; Given-Wilson, "Merger of Edward III's and Queen Philippa's Households," 183–87; Leyser, *Rule and Conflict*, 49–73; Blackley, "Isabella of France," 23–47; Menache, "Isabelle of France," 107–24; J. C. Parsons, "Year of Eleanor of Castile's Birth," 245–65; Stafford, *QCD*; Lee, "Reflections of Power," 183–217; Howell, "Resources of Eleanor of Provence," 372–93; Erler and Kowaleski, eds., *Women and Power in the Middle Ages*; Fradenburg, ed., *Women and Sovereignty*; J. C. Parsons, ed., *Medieval Queenship*.

2. Strickland, *Queens*, i, 447, 448 note 1; Costain, *Magnificent Century*, and *Three Edwards*; Powicke, *Thirteenth Century*, 268; Salzman, *Edward I*, 18–19, 98; Stuard, "Fashion's Captives," 62–63.

3. *RP*, i, 10, 21–22, 30–31, 50, 299, 310, 312–13, ii, 4–5; *RH*, ii, 288; *Manners*, 95–139; *Dunstable*, 362; Martin, ed., *Reg. Peckham*, ii, 555, 619–20, 767–68, iii, 937–38. From the rolls, e.g., *CIM*, i, no. 875; *CCIR 1272–1279*, 70, 405; *CCIR 1279–1288*, 16; *CChyW*, 11 (compare *RP*, i, 279, and *CPR 1313–1317*, 686–87); *CIPM*, ii, nos. 529, 629, v, no. 137; *CPR 1281–1292*, 207, 210; *RG*, ii, no. 1570. *Guisborough*, 216 (author's trans.; compare Johnstone, *A Hundred Years of History*, 153, and Cam, *The Hundred*, 237). As noted by *Guisborough*'s editor (216 note), the doggerel appears in a late, isolated MS tradition; Johnstone, *A Hundred Years of History*, 153, thinks it genuine and suggests a date for the incident ca. 1278.

4. Riley, ed., *Gesta Abbatum Sancti Albani*, 411–12; for Barnwell see Chapter Three, Appendix I no. 22; *Worcester*, 500; Trevet, *Annales*, 310; Rutherford, ed., *Anglo-Norman Chronicle of Nicholas Trivet*, 346 (a reference I owe Prof. Frank Mantello); *Foedera*, i, 651.

5. Stafford, "Portrayal of Royal Women"; Huneycutt, "Female Succession." On Eleanor of Provence, Paris, *CM*, iii, 338, 477, 497, iv, 510, and v, 298, 510, 549, 597, 678, 741; *Waverley*, 355; *Tewkesbury*, 175, 177, 179; *Wykes*, 133, 136, 154–55; *Cotton*, 139; *Bury*, 26–27, 29; *Flores*, ii, 481–82, 500; *Dunstable*, 223, 227, 233–34; *London*, 59–60; cont. Gervase of Canterbury, 224–25; *Worcester*, 448, 452–53; Halliwell, ed., *Chron. of William de Rishanger*, 36; Treharne, *Baronial Plan of Reform*, 308. On Eleanor of Aquitaine, Facinger, "A Study in Queenship," 1–47; Warren, *Henry II*, 118–21; E. A. R. Brown, "Eleanor of Aquitaine," 9–34.

6. Martin, ed., *Reg. Pecham*, ii, 555 (Anglo-Norman), 765-66 (English trans., used here with some modifications).

7. Gillingham, "Richard I and Berengaria," 157–73; E. A. R. Brown, "Political Repercussions of Family Ties," 573–95; Lane, *Royal Daughters*, i, 83–84; Gonzalez, *El reino de Castilla en la época de Alfonso VIII*, i, 190–91, 864–75.

8. Lourie, "Society Organized for War," 54–76; Powers, "Two Warrior-Kings," 95–129; Ruíz, "Unsacred Monarchy," 109–44; Gonzalo, *Conquistas*; O'Callaghan, *Medieval Spain*, 338–40, 344–46, 351–54.

9. Ximenez de Rada, *De rebus Hispaniae*, bk. 9, Chapter One; Menendez Pidal, *Primera crónica*, c. 1048. (Ferdinand's reputation for sanctity notwithstanding —he was canonized

---

*Abbreviations used in the appendices are identical to those used in the footnotes (see Abbreviations, pp. xiii-xx).

in 1671—Berengaria may have felt she had reason to worry: her husband had scattered the royal seed widely [Florez, *Reinas*, i, 368–81; Fernandez de Retana, *Albores del imperio*, 24]). On the 1235 betrothal, Paris, *CM*, iii, 327–28; *CPR 1232–1247*, 25, 74, 175; Bliss, i, 153; *Foedera*, i, 216–19, 231, 277, 284; Cuttino, *English Medieval Diplomacy*, 56; J. C. Parsons, "English Administration in Ponthieu," 389.

10. Ferdinand was b. 1201; all Jeanne's parents' children living 1225 were b. after 1214 (Prarond, *Cartulaire*, no. 87). On the 1237 marr., J. C. Parsons, "Year of Eleanor of Castile's Birth," 245–46; Menendez Pidal, *Primera crónica*, chaps 1048, 1063; de Manuel Rodríguez, *Memorias*, 497–98. On Jeanne's children, "Year of Eleanor of Castile's Birth," 245–49, and J. C. Parsons, "English Administration in Ponthieu," 387–88; Ximenez de Rada, *De Rebus Hispaniae*, bk. 9, Chapter One, is explicit on the choice of Eleanor's name. See genealogical table 1.

11. Ballesteros Beretta, *Sevilla en el siglo XIII*, 51–52, and *Alfonso X*, 52–53, 102, 108; Menendez Pidal, *Primera crónica*, Chapter One. Ferdinand III was based in Valladolid in the winter of 1241–42, the period during which Eleanor was probably b. (Gonzalo, *Conquistas*, 86–87), but this does not pr. Eleanor was b. there as Jeanne might have been living elsewhere.

12. Eleanor's literary interests are remarked below and discussed further in J. C. Parsons, "Of Queens, Courts and Books." The *Partidas*' ideas on the education of royal children (Real Academia, *Siete Partidas*, II.vii.11–12) have their closest affinity to Guillaume Peyraut's *De Eruditione Principum* (ca. 1264); in that work Peyraut drew from his own *Summa de vitiis et virtitibus* (finished by 1249 and known to Castilian Dominicans by 1250) and from Vincent of Beauvais' *De Eruditione Filiorum Nobilium*, finished by 1249 and perhaps sent to Ferdinand III with other of Vincent's works by Louis IX (Dondaine, "Guillaume Peyraut," 162–236; Steiner, "Guillaume Perrault and Vincent of Beauvais," 51–58; Vincent of Beauvais, *De Eruditione*, ed. Steiner, xv–xvi; Steiner, "New Light on Guillaume Perrault," 519–48; Hinnebusch, *Dominican Order*, ii, 243). For Dominican influence on the *Partidas* in general, Giménez y Martínez Carvajal, "San Raimundo de Peñafort." Eleanor's Dominican patronage and her children's education are remarked below. Ferdinand III's yr son Frederick in 1253–54 sponsored a Castilian translation of the Arabic *El Libro de los Engaños e Asayamientos de las Mugeres* (ed. Keller, trans. idem as *The Book of the Wiles and Tricks of Women*); see Keller, *Alfonso X*, 47.

13. Goodman, "Alphonso X and the English Crown," 39–41; while trade was likely discussed, Childs, *Anglo-Castilian Trade*, and Ruíz, "Castilian Merchants in England," do not deal with the period under review here. On the 1249 inquest, *Foedera*, i, 270, 277; for the dispensation, Berger, *Registres d'Innocent IV*, no. 4782. The background to the inquest is obscure; I am grateful to Margaret Howell for correspondence. Ignorant of critically important Spanish sources and not in command of edited English and French documents, Mugnier, *Les Savoyards en Angleterre*, 76–77, 104–7 (229, 256–59 in the serial version) does not support Ridgeway's implication that Anglo-Castilian marriage talks dated from 1249 ("Lord Edward and the Provisions of Oxford," 92, citing Mugnier in the serial version). See also below, note 16.

14. Eleanor was related to Edward and Henry of Swabia in the third degree touching the fourth; a fourth-degree dispensation could apply, but if meant for either of them it likely would have stated the exact relationship. She was related to Albert of Brunswick in the fourth degree, and to Hugh of Cyprus in the fourth touching the fifth. See genealogical table 2. On Berengaria of León and John de Brienne, Wolff, "Morgage and Redemption of an Emperor's Son," 46–47. On the 1247 Brabantine embassy, Paris, *CM*, iv, 623, 645; English chroniclers' mystification on Castilian brides in 1253 is noted below.

15. Paris, *CM*, v, 277–78; Marsh, *English Rule in Gascony*, 5, 7–9; Lodge, *Gascony under English Rule*, 25–26; Bémont, *Simon de Montfort*, 73–128; Powicke, *Thirteenth Century*, 110–13; Trabut-Cussac, *L'administration anglaise*, xxxix-xxx, xxxiv; Prestwich, *Edward I*, 8–9.

16. Older works have Alphonso moving first (Paris, *CM*, v, 365, 370; Marsh, *English Rule in Gascony*, 135, 143, 151; Lodge, *Gascony Under English Rule*, 42–43, 48). Recent works take the opposite tack: Ballesteros Beretta, *Alfonso X*, 92–96; Trabut-Cussac, *L'administration anglaise*, xxix-xxx; O'Callaghan, *Medieval Spain*, 361–62; Hillgarth, *Spanish Kingdoms 1250–1516, I*, 318; Socarras, *Alphonso X*, 93–5, 126 note 31; Childs, *Anglo-Castilian Trade*, 12–13; Cuttino, *English Medieval Diplomacy*, 56–57; Goodman, "Alphonso X and the English Crown," 41. Powicke, *King Henry III*, 232, sees the marriage as Alphonso's goal, contradicting however Powicke's later implication (*Thirteenth Century*, 116) that Ferdinand III and Henry III favored it bef. 1252. (If that were so, Alphonso would have had little reason to intervene in Gascony, were the marriage his only object).

17. Henry perhaps reported this in good faith, but it was untrue (*Foedera*, i, 295; Paris, *CM*, v, 365, 424, 440; Cuttino, *English Medieval Diplomacy*, 56; Powicke, *Thirteenth Century*, 116). Alphonso was a grandnephew of Blanche of Castile, whose husband Louis of France was offered the English crown in her right (as Henry II's granddau.) and invaded England in 1215, very nearly supplanting John and Henry III.

18. Paris, *CM*, v, 381–83, 396–97; *CPR 1247–1258*, 230; *Foedera*, i, 290. Trabut-Cussac, *L'administration anglaise*, xxxv note 67, shows that the original writ of 15 May does not name the principals to the marriage; the *Foedera* text adds the names. See also *Dunstable*, 188; *Glastonbury*, 222. Baylen, "John Maunsel," 482–91, thinks Maunsel suggested the marriage, but compare Stacey, *Politics, Policy and Finance*, 181.

19. *Foedera*, i, 290 *bis*; *CIR 1251–1253*, 355, 475–76; Paris, *CM*, v, 396–97. On 5 July Henry added to Edward's household Eleanor's cousin William de Fiennes (*CIR 1251–1253*, 486; *CHEC*, 44–46), also Eleanor of Provence's cousin (Berger, *Registres d'Innocent IV*, no. 7693). Baylen, "John Maunsel," 487, thinks agreement was reached quickly but misconstrues Powicke, *King Henry III*, 232.

20. On the knting, Paris, *CM*, v, 397–98; Socarras, *Alphonso X*, 117–19, Ruíz, "Unsacred Monarchy," 124, and below, note 29. Henry III meant to knt Edward himself (*CIR 1251–1253*, 37–38, 191, 442–43, 465, 508). The dower offer is *CPR 1247–1258*, 219, perhaps carried by a second embassy noted only in *Dunstable*, 188; for Alphonso on royal dower see Real Academia, *Siete Partidas*, II.vii.12. See also *CPR 1272–1281*, 380, *CChR 1257–1300*, 192–93. On Eleanor's dower see Chapters Two and Three.

21. Huici Miranda and Cabanes Pecourt, eds., *Documentos de Jaime I*, iii, no. 624; Gonzalez, *Reinado y diplomas de Fernando III*, i, 266–69; O'Callaghan, *Medieval Spain*, 223, 346, 361; Ballesteros Beretta, *Alfonso X*, 89, 96–99. See genealogical table 2.

22. Trabut-Cussac, *L'administration anglaise*, xxx-xxxv; Gonzalez, *Reinado y diplomas de Fernando III*, i, 107–10; Ballesteros Beretta, *Alfonso X*, 104–20; Socarras, *Alfonso X*, 114–15; Gonzalo, *Conquistas*, 122.

23. Paris, *CM*, vi, 284–86. García Martínez perhaps became Eleanor's *ayo* (governor) in regard to renewed talks (below, note 27). See *CPR 1247–1258*, 321 (= *RG*, i, no. 3948); *Foedera*, i, 309; Studd, "Henry III and the Lord Edward," 4–19. Given Paris' criticism (*CM*, v, 450), it may be asked if Henry would have been so liberal were Alphonso less exacting on dower; but Eleanor of Provence's family also pressed Henry to provide for his son (Prestwich, *Edward I*, 11; Ridgeway, "Lord Edward and the Provisions of Oxford," 91). Henry III m. Eleanor of Provence without dowry (*Foedera*, i, 220 *ter*); Paris, *CM*, iv, 505–6, wrongly says four Provençal castles made up her dowry (compare *CLR*, ii, 213; *CPR 1232–1247*, 416, 418). It is untrue that Ponthieu was Eleanor's dowry (see Chapter Four); she inherited the county in 1279 only because both her full brothers predeceased their mother—Louis perhaps as late as 1276 (J. C. Parsons, "English Administration in Ponthieu," 387–89).

24. *Foedera*, i, 290, 297–301; Chaplais, ed., *Diplomatic Documents*, i, nos. 270, 217–74.

25. Cuttino, *English Medieval Diplomacy*, 56–59; Goodman, "Alphonso X and the English Crown," 54. On Louis IX, Paris, *CM*, v, 509–10. Thibaut II did homage to Alphonso Dec. 1255, without ackn. his supremacy (Ballesteros Beretta, *Alfonso X*, 128; O'Callaghan,

Medieval Spain, 361); Henry never was absolved from his crusading vow (Cuttino, ed., *Gascon Reg. A*, i, no. 177.vii; *Foedera*, i, 372).

26. Cuttino, ed., *Gascon Reg. A*, nos. 177.i, iii, v; *RG* i, nos. 3854, 4277; *Foedera*, i, 304–5; *CPR 1247–1258*, 312, 351; d'Achéry, ed., *Spicilegium*, iii, 633; on the feast of St. Edward, Ballesteros Beretta, *Alfonso X*, 99, and Prestwich, *Edward I*, 10.

27. *CPR 1247–1258*, 324 bis; *RG*, i, no. 3845. Martínez' presence is anomalous; Alphonso X felt royal ladies should have female attendants (Real Academia, *Siete Partidas*, II.vii.10). The *ayos* of Eleanor's brothers so identified themselves in private acts, but Martínez did not do so in May, only in Nov. and Dec. 1253 (Ballesteros Beretta, *Sevilla en el siglo XIII*, 51–52 and his appx. nos. 14, 56, 118; *Alfonso X*, 83–84, 323, 346, 349). Was he apptd only to represent Alphonso in renewed talks? See also Cuttino, ed., *Gascon Reg. A*, nos. 177.ii, vi; *RG*, i, nos. 3947, 3950; *Foedera*, i, 305–6; *CPR 1247–1258*, 321; Teulet, ed., *Layettes*, iv, nos. 5416, 5559 (where Castilian bps certify Louis IX on the age of Alphonso's son, about to m. Louis' dau.). On Edward and Eleanor's consanguinity, see genealogical tables 1 and 2.

28. On royal women's attention to the marriages of their daughters and kinswomen, J. C. Parsons, "Mothers, Daughters"; Adair, "Countess Clemence," 67; Vann, "Medieval Castilian Queenship," 136–37; *Foedera*, i, 553, 556. Did Jeanne's bad relations with Alphonso date from his failure to m. her sister Philippa, as anticipated in 1237 (J. C. Parsons, "Eleanor of Castile and the Viscountess Jeanne," 284)? On Henry of Castile, Ballesteros Beretta, *Sevilla en el siglo XIII*, 55–56, and *Alfonso X*, 112–16; Gonzalez, *Reinado y diplomas de Fernando III*, i, 109–10; Gonzalo, *Conquistas*, 122–24; Segura Graiño, "Semblanza humana de Alfonso el Sabio," 16. See also *CPR 1247–1258*, 311, 330, 347, 351; *RG*, i, nos. 3841–42; de Lhomel, ed., *Cartulaire de la ville de Montreuil*, 122–23; du Fresne du Cange, *Histoire des comtes de Ponthieu*, 168.

29. Bury, 19; *Crónica de Cardena*, in Florez, *España Sagrada*, xxiii, 374. For the date, Trabut–Cussac, *L'administration anglaise*, 7; Ballesteros Beretta, *Alfonso X*, 100. On the knting, *RG*, i, no. 3436; for a year Alphonso used it to date his privileges (Procter, "Materials," 39, where "more than a year" rests on the erroneous date of Edward's arrival in Burgos). The latest privilege so dated that has come to hand is to the Premonstratensian canons at Retuerta, 26 Oct. 1255 (Madrid, AHN, Clero, carpeta 3436, no. 12). See also *Foedera*, i, 310; *RG*, i, no. 3714; Chaplais, ed., *Diplomatic Documents*, i, no. 275; Ballesteros Beretta, *Alfonso X*, 101–2.

30. Trabut–Cussac, *L'administration anglaise*, 7; J. C. Parsons, "Year of Eleanor of Castile's Birth," 257 (see below, note 46); *RG*, i suppl., no 4555 (the wardrobe or principal accting office is discussed in Chapter Two); *CLR*, iv, 243. John de Wodestok', her cook by Nov. 1256, was from Eleanor of Provence's household (*CPR 1258–1266*, 55–56; *CIR 1256–1259*, 5; *CLR*, vi, no. 1180). For her arrival, *CIR 1254–1256*, 128, 136, 144–45, 225; *CLR*, iv, 234, 241, 244, 247, 271; Paris, *CM*, v, 513. Cont. Gervase of Canterbury, 204, inexplicably says she reached Dover 9 Jan. 1255.

31. Douie and Farmer, eds., *Magna Vita Sancti Hugonis*, ii, 142, 156; *Records 1286–1289*, no. 3217; Binski, "Reflections on *La estoire de Seint Aedward le rei*," 339–40; Brieger and Verdier, *Art and the Courts*, i, 90–91, and ii, pl. 27–28; Alexander and Binski, *Age of Chivalry*, no. 39 and p. 143; N. Morgan, *Early Gothic Manuscripts, II*, no. 123. See also Ruíz, "Unsacred Monarchy," 114, 128; J. C. Parsons, "Family, Sex, and Power," 4, and idem, "Of Queens, Courts and Books." On touching for scrofula, see Barlow, "King's Evil."

32. Paris, *CM*, v, 653–54; *Tewkesbury*, 166; was she with Edward when he went to Chester, July 1256 (*Chester*, 128–29)? For the rings, E 101/349/26 m. 3 (the knt is unnamed). On Albreda (de Caumpeden), *CIR 1264–1268*, 342, *CPR 1272–1281*, 134, *CCIR 1272–1279*, 270; in 1290 the Q gave her a ten marks' *maritagium* (S.C. 6/1089/25 m. 3), perhaps for her dau. Eleanor, to whom the Q's exors gave £5 (*Manners*, 104). Imagination has filled the gaps in the Q's life in the 1250s: Strickland, *Queens*, i, 420, 422; Galloway, *Eleanor of Castile*, 5–6 (but compare *CLR*, vi, no. 91, and Powicke, *Thirteenth Century*, 249 note 2).

33. Shirley, ed., *Royal Letters*, ii, no. 802. On 24 Mar. 1260 at St-Omer, Eleanor of Provence gave Ferdinand a ruby ring (E 101/349/26 m. 1); for the merchants, *CIR 1259–1261*, 117, 259. On the stags, *CIR 1259–1261*, 134, 301. Unlike Edward's sisters, Eleanor had no gifts from Eleanor of Provence at Christmas 1260 (E 101/349/26); the next thing heard of her is *CPR 1258–1262*, 220. Henry III paid some of her expenses, Oct. 1260 X Oct. 1265 (E 372/113 m. 2.)

34. Paris, *CM*, v, 509–10, 513–14; *Foedera*, i, 325 ter, 328; *CLR*, iv, 234; Ridgeway, "Foreign Favorites," 590–616, and idem, "King Henry III and the 'Aliens'," 81–92. On Henry's promises and Eleanor's kinsmen, *CPR 1247–1258*, 324 bis, 385 bis; *RG*, i, no. 3845; *CHEC*, 42, 51; Paris, *CM*, v, 509–10; Trabut-Cussac, "Enrique de Castille," 51–58. One cousin entered Edward's household in July 1253 (above, note 19). See also *CLR*, iv, 254 bis.

35. Trabut-Cussac, *L'administration anglaise*, 9–10, 20, 25; Shirley, ed., *Royal Letters*, ii, no. 506; *Foedera*, i, 372; Goodman, "Alfonso X and the English Crown," 47–49. On the 1257 election, Paris, *CM*, v, 649; Powicke, *King Henry III*, 214–15, 250 note 2, and *Thirteenth Century*, 119; Hilpert, "Richard of Cornwall's candidature," 185–98.

36. *CIR 1254–1256*, 389–90 (= Shirley, ed., *Royal Letters*, no. 506); *Foedera*, i, 372; Goodman, "Alphonso X and the English Crown," 45–46, 48. It may be that Alphonso was less interested in seeing Beatrice m. his brother than in stopping her marr. to the Aragonese heir, Henry III's original plan. By May 1259 Henry was pursuing another husband for Beatrice (*Foedera*, i, 382).

37. Ballesteros Beretta, *Alfonso X*, 117–18, 171–72.

38. Paris, *CM*, v, 575–76; Goodman, "Alphonso X and the English Crown," 47; Trabut-Cussac, "Enrique de Castille," 55–58; the consequences of his visit are noted below.

39. She was informally called ctss though Edward used no title (*Oxenden*, 203; Hockey, ed., *Account-Book of Beaulieu*, 10–11, 301; Prestwich, *Edward I*, 11–12); in 1265 she styled herself only "companion of the Lord Edward" (Shirley, ed., *Royal Letters*, ii, no. 647). *Tewkesbury*, 166, in 1258 isolates her at the end of the K's family, not with Edward but after his br. Edmund (still allowed precedence as K of Sicily?), and just before other ctsses.

40. Paris, *CM*, v, 509; R. H. C. Davis, *King Stephen*, index, p. 153 s.v. "Constance of France"; Appleby, *Reign of King Stephen*, index, p. 213 s.v. "Constance, daughter of Louis VI"; *RRAN*, iv, nos. 139, 229a; Eyton, *Court, Household and Itinerary of King Henry II*, index, p. 321 s.v. "Henry II, Henry, son of, Margaret of France, wife of"; Barlow, *Thomas Becket*, 206.

41. Paris, *CM*, iii, 334–35, 581 (see Isenburg-Büdingen and Freytag von Loringhoven, *Stammtafeln*, 1.ii, tables 45, 110; E. L. Cox, *Eagles of Savoy*, 9, 21; Sivéry, *Marguerite de Provence*, 11). For 1282, *RG*, ii, no. 597; J. C. Parsons, "Year of Eleanor of Castile's Birth," 260, and idem, "Mothers, Daughters," 61–76.

42. Born in 1230 (Gonzalez, *Reinado y diplomas*, i, 109–10), he was remembered as "powerful in war and exceedingly crafty, but most wicked and not a diligent follower of the practice of the catholic faith" (*Gesta Sancti Ludovici, RHF*, xx, 428).

43. Snellgrove, *Lusignans in England*; Ridgeway, "Foreign Favourites," idem, "King Henry III and the 'Aliens'," and idem, "Lord Edward and the Provisions of Oxford," 91–97; Carpenter, "What Happened in 1258?," 106–19; *CHEC*, 42; above, note 30. On Henry of Castile, *CPR 1247–1258*, 561, 567; Trabut-Cussac, "Enrique de Castille," 54 and note 2.

44. Carpenter, "What Happened in 1258?," 112–17; Ridgeway, "Lord Edward and the Provisions of Oxford," 97; Prestwich, *Edward I*, 24–27; J. C. Parsons, "Eleanor of Castile and the Viscountess Jeanne," 141–44. The wedding was perhaps late in 1260, when Edward met his uncles at Paris; as noted below, Eleanor was likely with him (Prestwich, *Edward I*, 26, 34–35).

45. Prestwich, *Edward I*, 22, 28–29, 31; Trabut-Cussac, "Enrique de Castille," 55–58; the next stage of Henry's career is noted below. S.C. 1/11/3 (Paris, Thurs. after the decollation of St. John, s.a. bef. 1272) is from Gaston of Béarn asking Eleanor to intercede

with Edward for the vct's knt Fortulle Amanevi (who cannot be identified as Gaston's unnamed Jan. 1259 envoy).

46. Prestwich, *Edward I*, 27–38; Denholm-Young, "Tournament in the Thirteenth Century," 252–63; Barker, *Tournament in England*, 56–59, 190–92. On 1262–63, *CPR 1258–1266*, 220, 226; cont. Gervase of Canterbury, 215, 218; *Dunstable*, 219; *Foedera*, i, 423 (= *CIR 1261–1264*, 272–73). The dau. bur. in Bordeaux was perhaps b. during the "exile," but in 1261 and 1262 it is impossible to verify Eleanor's presence in Bordeaux in the month of May, when the child d.

47. *Burton*, 499; cont. Gervase of Canterbury, 219; Stapleton, ed., *Antiquis Legibus*, 54–55; *Flores*, ii, 481; J. C. Parsons, "Towards a Social History," 57. A 1258 demand that Edward's household be reformed did not mention his wife's (Richardson and Sayles, "Provisions of Oxford," 299–300, 317–21); were the two seen as one, and were the couple thought to be acting in concert?

48. *CIR 1261–1264*, 308–9; Stapleton, ed., *Antiquis Legibus*, 58; *CIR 1261–1264*, 313, *CPR 1258–1266*, 292; *CLR*, v, 131; *CIR 1261–1264*, 334. The story that she fled to France in 1263 evidently originated in Strickland, *Queens*, i, 422, citing *Wykes*, 179, which notes Eleanor of Provence's return to England 29 Oct. 1265 but does not mention Eleanor of Castile (see also *Winchester*, ii, 103, and *Bury*, 32, where Eleanor of Provence is accompanied by her s. Edmund, not Edward's wife). Blaauw, *Barons' Wars*, 229, realizes Eleanor of Castile was at Windsor June 1264 (as below) but supposes she fled to France thereafter.

49. That she used the lack of a safe-conduct as her excuse for not leaving Windsor for more than a week implies her departure was not voluntary (*CPR 1258–1266*, 324–25, 329); on the Castilians, Halliwell, ed., *Chron. of William de Rishanger*, 35–36. Katherine is the first child known to have been b. since the dau. bur. in Bordeaux but the date of her birth is unknown (J. C. Parsons, "Year of Eleanor of Castile's Birth," 258). Compare Henry's order of 17 June to his pregnant sister-in-law Joan de Valence, also at Windsor, to await her delivery in some religious house nearby (*CPR 1258–1266*, 325).

50. An attempt to free Edward from prison put his life in danger (Prestwich, *Edward I*, 47). On Joan, J. C. Parsons, "Year of Eleanor of Castile's Birth," 258. Henry sent Eleanor a messenger in Mar. 1265 (E 101/308/2 *m.* 1). For the loan, *CLR*, v, 145, 170. See also *CIR 1264–1268*, 8, 28, 41–42, 365–66; Prestwich, *Edward I*, 48. This Despenser fell at Evesham in 1265; his s., the "elder" Hugh Despenser—notorious in Edward II's reign—conveyed lands to the Q in the 1280s, but it is unlikely those conveyances involved any enmity she harbored from the events of 1265 (see Chapter Three, Appenix I nos. 29a, 175).

51. J. C. Parsons, "Year of Eleanor of Castile's Birth," 258–59; *CPR 1258–1266*, 617; *CLR*, v, 229, vi, no. 555; Stapleton, ed., *Antiquis Legibus*, 87; W. Brown, ed., *Reg. Walter Giffard*, 101.

52. The marr. Edward promoted ca. 1262 between Eleanor's damsel Joan "de Valle Viridi" and William Charles, her knt in 1264, was perhaps meant to anchor supporters in their households (*CPR 1258–1266*, 212–13, 324–25, 376–77). See also above, note 47.

53. Loengard, "Of the Gift of her Husband," 215–55; Howell, "Resources of Eleanor of Provence," 380–81. For Eleanor of Castile's dower, see Chapters Two and Three. On Edward's revenue, Prestwich, *Edward I*, 20, 22, 36, 37–38; lands gtd Eleanor in 1264–65 were perhaps as much to relieve his resources as to improve hers. For his gts before 1270, below, chap. 3, Appx I nos. 25, 84; the capacity of the wives of the K and his heir to take their husbands' gts is discussed in Chapter Two.

54. See Chapter Three, Appendix I nos. 17, 38, 134, 186, 187, 213; see also *CIR 1264–1268*, 347, 449; (compare *CPEJ*, i, 289; *CChR*, ii, 117, suggests Eleanor conveyed these debts to Alice de Luton, for whom *CIR 1256–1259*, 203; *CPR 1258–1266*, 220; *CChR*, ii, 84); *CIR 1268–1272*, 347–48; *CCIR 1279–1288*, 386. She held Barwick for three weeks, Sept. 1265 (as below), but took the Mich. rent and relief for fees held there (*CIM*, i, no. 575; E

13/6 m. 9). Cash gifts are *CLR*, v, 131, 145, 170, 267; vi, nos. 308, 352, 761; *CIR 1268–1272*, 5–6. E 101/350/7 m. 3 has payments to Edward's creditors "antequam esset Rex et consortis sui" in London, Oxford, Northampton, "et pluribus aliis locis" for necessities "ad hospicia eorundem."

55. S.C. 1/11/25 (= Shirley, ed., *Royal Letters*, no. 647); *CPR 1258–1266*, 453, 458. For lands, see Chapter Three, Appendix I nos. 25, 84–85, 124–25, 157; on admin., *CIR 1268–1272*, 96, 431; *CIR 1264–1268*, 520. Kancia's career is discussed below, chs 2–3. Loundres *fl*. Dec. 1264 (*CIR 1264–1268*, 5); on Yattenden, *CLR*, v, 131, 145, and below, Chapter Two.

56. Cont. Gervase of Canterbury, 249; *CHEC*, 32–35, 36, and J. C. Parsons, "Towards a Social History," 51–71.

57. Such links among the households in the 1250s are noted above. On the Senches, J. C. Parsons, "Towards a Social History," and for the Ferrés, *CHEC*, 32–35. The latter surname is not often rendered with the accented final "é," but frequent occurrence in contemporary records of such forms as "Ferry," "Ferree," and (confusingly) "Ferrer'," inarguably with reference to members of this family, amply justify the spelling used here.

58. *CPR 1266–1272*, 434. On Hawise, *CPR 1258–1266*, 678. For the Haustedes, *CHEC*, 35–38; their sons, ordained 1295–96, were prob. b. in the early 1270s (Graham, ed., *Reg. Winchelsey*, ii, 909, 913; Hill, ed., *Rolls and Reg. Sutton*, ii, 136, and vii, 82, 88, 98). Eleanor's household is discussed in greater detail in Chapter Two.

59. On John le Picard, *CPR 1258–1266*, 324; one of this name had Henry III's wages, 1264–65 (E 372/115 m. 1), was Eleanor's squire, Mar. 1278 (C 47/4/1 fol. 13), and later her pantler (chap. 2). On merchants, *CChR*, ii, 133; *CPR 1266–1272*, pp. 169, 317; Childs, *Anglo-Castilian Trade*, 13–14. For pardons, *CPR 1258–1266*, pp. 400, 567–68; *CIR 1264–1268*, pp. 330, 335, 466–67; *CPR 1266–1272*, 262, 305, 346, 391. On her alleged intercession for Adam Gurdon in 1266, Powicke, "King Edward I in fact and fiction," 129–32; the version of a ballad in which she obtains Henry III's pardon for Adam (Strickland, *Queens*, i, 290–91), differs from that in T. Evans, *Old Ballads*, iv, 122–29, where Eleanor of Provence is the pivotal figure (as Powicke demonstrates was the case in fact). Eleanor of Castile did pardon Gurdon for offenses in the New Forest in 1280 (Stagg, *CNFD*, no. 223).

60. J. C. Parsons, "Year of Eleanor of Castile's Birth," 259–60; *CLR*, vi, nos. 57, 91; *CIR 1268–1272*, 4, 6–7, 45–46, 210; Hockey, ed., *Account-Book of Beaulieu*, 10–11, 301; *CHEC*, 53. Henry III paid for "una roba breudanda ad opus domine Alienore vxoris domini Edwardi" 1265 X 1268 (E 372/115 m. 1d). A sword-belt found in Ferdinand of Castile's tomb, worked with the arms of families related to Henry III, was perhaps Edward's gift at the wedding (Ballesteros Beretta, *Alfonso X*, 483–85, 487, though identifying the English Edward at the wedding as Edward II).

61. The extant late thirteenth-century English MS (Oxford, Bodleian, Laud Misc. 537) is ed. in Cerulli, *Il libro della scala*, and in Muñoz Sendino, *La Escala de Mahoma*. See Procter, *Alfonso X*, 16–19; Keller, *Alfonso X*, 150–52; Lasater, *Spain to England*, 32. Eleanor's literary interests are remarked later in this chapter and in J. C. Parsons, "Of Queens, Courts and Books." A MS of the first portion of the *Siete Partidas*, a product of Alphonso X's scriptorium in the 1260s, may have reached England at this time but its provenance is unknown (London, BL, Add. 20787; see Herriott, "A Thirteenth-Century Manuscript of the Primera Partida," and Procter, *Alfonso X*, 113).

62. Trabut-Cussac, "Le financement de la croisade anglaise de 1270," 113–40; Beebe, "English Baronage and the Crusade of 1270," 127–47; Strayer, "Crusades of Louis IX," 514–18; S. D. Lloyd, "Lord Edward's Crusade," 120–33; Prestwich, *Edward I*, 75–78; S. D. Lloyd, *English Society and the Crusade*, 113–53; Tyerman, *England and the Crusades*, 124–32.

63. It is unclear if Eleanor formally took the Cross with Edward in 1268. On preparations, *Wykes*, 236; *CLR*, vi, nos. 1133, 1162. *Dunstable* does not confirm Strickland, *Queens*,

i, 424, on a pilgrimage bef. leaving England. On young Henry, *CPR 1266–1272*, 412, and cont. Gervase of Canterbury, 249 (*Flores*, iii, 18, and *Bury*, 46, are muddled here). See also Camden, *Remains*, ed. Dunn, 236–37, 444; Eleanor's patronage of merchants is discussed later in this chapter.

64. Henry III's permission for Edward to make disposition of his children is E 40/15187 (Westm., 20 July 1270); see also *Foedera*, i, 484, and *CPR 1266–1272*, 479–80. On the Spanish visit compare Stapleton, ed., *Antiquis Legibus*, 125, and *Wykes*, 236. See also J. C. Parsons, "Year of Eleanor of Castile's Birth," 259–61; Thorpe, "Mastre Richard, a Thirteenth Century Translator of the `De Re Militari'," 39–50, and "Mastre Richard at the Skirmish of Kenilworth," 120–21; Legge, "Lord Edward's Vegetius," 262–65; Prestwich, *Edward I*, 50; Keen, *Chivalry*, 111–12. N. Morgan, *Early Gothic MSS II*, no. 150, dates the work 1265 X 1270, but compare Folda, *Crusader Manuscript Illumination*, 16–17, 129–30, 199; see also Giles and Wormald, *Descriptive Catalogue*, i, 82–84. The extant MS was perhaps made ca. 1306 for the knting of Edward of Caernarvon, who owned the work in the 1320s (Vale, *Edward III and Chivalry*, 49–50).

65. *Guisborough*, 208–10; Beebe, "English Baronage and the Crusade," 132 note 2; *Foedera*, i, 512; *Wykes*, 248–50; *Bury*, 53; Stapleton, ed., *Antiquis Legibus*, 156; *L'Estoire de Eracles*, 462; T. Wright, ed., *Political Songs*, 132; Ormrod, "Personal Religion of Edward III," 871–72.

66. Fiadoni, *Historia Ecclesiastica*, XXIII.vi, in Muratori, ed., *Rerum Italicarum Scriptores*, xi, col. 1168; *Brevis Annales*, ed. Schmeidler, 169–71.

67. Camden took the story not from Fiadoni, but from Rodrigo Sánchez de Arévalo's chronicle, printed in 1579 in Robert Bel's *Rerum hispaniarum scriptores* (Camden, *Remains*, ed. Dunn, 237 and note); Arévalo, a papal diplomat, presumably saw Fiadoni's work in Italy. See Camden, *Britannia*, i, cols. 390–91, and Camden, *Remains*, ed. Dunn, 237; Holinshed, *Chronicles of England*, ii, 474–75; Prestwich, *Edward I*, 78–79.

68. Holder-Egger, ed., *Chronica Monasterii Sancti Bertini*, 856–57; Clifford, *Knight of Great Renown*, 10, 30. For the illness, Bliss, i, 446, *Wykes*, 263, *CCIR 1272–1279*, 197–98; for their Italian itinerary see note 71; Eleanor's Dominican patronage is discussed in J. C. Parsons, "Piety, Power," 116–22. Dr. Faye Getz advises that sucking was not prescribed for snake bites at this period. Later medieval female mystics are represented as sucking the wounds of Christ, but Dr. Aviad Kleinberg finds no parallel for the Acre story in twelfth- or thirteenth-century hagiography; in any case, removing poison from a human wound is hardly comparable to sucking Christ's wounds.

69. *L'estoire de Eracles*, 462; E 372/121 m. 22; Bruce, *Evolution of Arthurian Romance*, i, 26–28; E. G. Gardner, *Arthurian Legend*, 44–63, 154; de Malkiel, "Arthurian Literature in Spain and Portugal," 406–7; Pickford, "Miscellaneous French Prose Romances," 350–52. *Meliadus* was perhaps sent to Castile (Entwhistle, *Arthurian Legend*, 109, 113–14). On Charles of Anjou and Charlemagne, Spiegel, "*Reditus Regni*," 145–71. Edward's interest in Arthuriana must not be exaggerated (Prestwich, *Edward I*, 120–22).

70. Imperiale, ed., *Ann. Ianuensis*, xiv, 157–58 and note 1. For a 1274 attempt by Jaime I of Aragon to obtain Henry's release, Forster, ed., *Chronicle of James I*, ii, 653–54.

71. *Foedera*, i, 497 ter; Stapleton, ed., *Antiquis Legibus*, 158; S.C. 7/16/4 = *Foedera*, i, 499. On their journey, *Wykes*, 254–55; Bliss, i, 445; Frati and Sorbelli, ed., *Memoriale Matthaei de Griffonibus*, 20; Torrace, ed., *Chron. Petri Cantinelli*, 11, 15–16; *Foedera*, i, 504, 512, 523; Holder-Egger, ed., *Cronica Salimbene de'Adam*, 488; Bonazzi, ed., *Chron. Parmense*, 30; Muratori, *Annali d'Italia*, vii, 402; *Wykes*, 255; *Flores*, iii, 30–31; Cuttino, ed., *Gascon Reg. A*, no. 115; *Guisborough*, 210–12; Prestwich, *Edward I*, 83–85.

72. *Wykes*, 255; Stapleton, ed., *Antiquis Legibus*, 159; Powicke, *King Henry III*, 614 note 1; Trabut-Cussac, *L'administration anglaise*, 41 note 2. S.C. 1/16/10 reads "Dat' Sibill' xviij. Junii. Anno Domini .M.CC.Lxxxij. Johannes Andree de mandato domini Regis litteram istam scripsit." In *Foedera*, i, 503, "xviij" was perhaps read "xxiij," and "Lxxxij" as "Lxxiij." Ballesteros Beretta, *Alfonso X*, 980, correctly discusses the letter under the year 1282.

73. *Majus chron. Lemovicense, RHF* xxi, 780–81; Ballesteros Beretta, *Alfonso X,* 666; *Wykes,* 255; Stapleton, ed., *Antiquis Legibus,* 159; Trabut-Cussac, *L'administration anglaise,* 41 note 3; *Waverley,* 385; *Foedera,* i, 541; *CPR 1272–1281,* 380; *CChR,* ii, 192–93. The name Alphonso likely would not have been chosen were the newborn heir to the throne; a year later the death of the elder surviving s. Henry left young Alphonso the heir. (King Stephen's sons Baldwin and Eustace and Henry IV's son Humphrey, named for maternal lineages that had contributed rich inheritances, were b. bef. either man had any immediate prospect of the throne; the son b. after Stephen took the throne was named William.) It is unclear what part the Q had in the choice of name, the likely result of Alphonso X's adventitious presence at the baptism (compare Dunbabin, "What's in a name?" 949–50).
74. Walter de Guldeford was made kpr of queen-gold ca. 5 Aug. 1273; she apptd Jacob de Oxonia to that office at the Exch. of the Jews 1 Mar. 1274 (E 159/48, *mm.* 7, 5). On the children, cont. Gervase of Canterbury, 282; Johnstone, "Wardrobe and Household of Henry," 14 and note 4, 15, 17; Prestwich, *Edward I,* 315, 320–21, 324–26.
75. *Bliss,* i, 446; *Foedera,* i, 513; *CClR 1272–1279,* 70–71; Stapleton, ed., *Antiquis Legibus,* 167, 171; Langlois, *Règne de Philippe III,* 73–74; Prestwich, *Edward I,* 303. An acct for Alphonso's expns "et pro Johanne sorore eiusdem commorante secum . . . antequam traderetur per Regem comitisse de Pontif' matri Regine consortis Regis educanda" is E 372/121 *m.* 22; they were still together 4 June 1274 (C 62/50 *m.* 6), and Alphonso reached London 14 June (Stapleton, ed., *Antiquis Legibus,* 170). The Q was at St-Riquier ca. 25 July (E 101/350/5 *m.* 3). See also *Foedera,* i, 514; cont. Gervase of Canterbury, 282; *Flores,* iii, 43; Johnstone, "Wardrobe and Household of Henry," 36 and note 2.
76. Stapleton, ed., *Antiquis legibus,* 172–73; *Wykes,* 259–60; *Flores,* iii, 44; *Rishanger,* 84; Aungier, ed., *French Chronicle,* 13; Richardson, "English Coronation," 190–202; Ruíz, "Unsacred Monarchy," 109; Brühl, "Les auto-couronnements," 452–57. The English distinguished anointed from unanointed kings (Luard, ed., *Roberti Grosseteste Epistolae,* 350; *Ann. Regni Scotiae,* in *Rishanger,* 341; Stones and Simpson, eds., *Edward I and the Throne of Scotland,* ii, 259). In Castile, Alphonso XI's wife was not crowned (1332) as she was pregnant (Ruíz, "Unsacred Monarchy," 109 note 1); Eleanor was pregnant in Aug. 1274 (J. C. Parsons, "Year of Eleanor of Castile's Birth," 262), as was Philippa of Hainaut in Feb. 1330 (*Ann. Paulini,* 349).
77. *Records 1285–1286,* nos. 170, 175; *CHEC,* 30–31, 71 *bis,* 74, 78, 94, 95, 102, 117; *Chester,* 112; Trevet, *Annales,* 395.
78. Riley, ed., *Gesta Abbatum Sancti Albani,* 411–12 (Apr. 1275); *Bury,* 57, 66, 83, 92; *Winchester,* 120; *Glastonbury,* 243, 245; *Dunstable,* 266, 355; *Osney,* 268, 278–79, 325; *Rishanger,* 92; *Waverley,* 391, 402; *Chester,* 108; cont. Gervase of Canterbury, 292; J. C. Parsons, "Ritual and Symbol," 68. Compare Geertz, "Centers, Kings and Charisma," 13–20.
79. J. C. Parsons, "Year of Eleanor of Castile's Birth," 262–65. The Q arrived at Westminster from Pershore 24 Dec. 1277 and had a child there ca. 3 Jan. 1278 (BL, Add. 36762 *m.* 1; J. C. Parsons, "Year of Eleanor of Castile's Birth," 263–64). Margaret was b. Windsor 15 Mar. 1275 (compare *CPR 1272–1281,* 113); if Riley, ed., *Gesta Abbatum Sancti Albani,* 411–12 is right, she was at St. Albans 11 Apr., and at Bury 17 Apr. (*Bury,* 57). Apart from a 1264 purchase for "the third day before her confinement" (*CLR,* v, 150), there is no evidence that Eleanor observed the formal "taking the chamber" of later centuries (Staniland, "Welcome, Royal Babe!" 1–13, and "Royal Entry into the World," 297–313).
80. J. C. Parsons, "Year of Eleanor of Castile's Birth," 264; *CPR 1272–1281,* 306 *ter,* and Johnstone, "County of Ponthieu," 435–52; *CFR 1272–1307,* 109 (compare *CPR 1272–1281,* 139, and Parsons, "Year of Eleanor of Castile's Birth," 263); on the Q's gts from the K, see Chapters Two and Three); Bund, ed., *Reg. Godfrey Giffard,* 110.

81. *CHEC,* 35–40, 154–56. On Eleanor of Provence's women, *CIR 1242–1247,* 272, *CCIR 1272–1279,* 445 (Juliana de Albini fl. 1250–78); *CPR 1258–1266,* 220, *CPR 1266–1272,* 52 (Claricia de Albini, 1262–67); *CLR,* ii, 137, *CLR,* iv, 113 (Ada de Boeles, 1242–53); *CPR 1232–1247,* 103, 282 *CIR 1237–1242,* 424, Paris, *CM,* iv, 200 (Margerie Biset d. 1242); *CLR,* i, 295, 315, *CPR 1232–1247,* 211, *CLR,* iii, 85 (Emma Biset d. 1242); *CLR,* iv, 320, 412, *CIR 1256–1259,* 456 (Joan Gorges, 1256–59); *CIR 1242–1247,* 163, *CLR,* iii, 75–6 (Roberga, 1244–46, occ. as a Gorges 1252 [E 101/349/13 m. 1]); *CLR,* ii, 278 (Anastasia, 1244); *CPR 1258–1266,* 678 (Hawise de Weston, 1266); *CPR 1272–1281,* 79–80 (Amabilia de Mortuo Mari, 1275). Willelme de Attelis accompanied Eleanor to England 1236 and d. 1260 (*CIR 1237–1242,* 132, 285, *CPR 1232–1247,* 423, *CPR 1247–1258,* 613–14, *CLR,* iv, 502).

82. Two Ferrés were household stewards (see Chapter Two), but cousins incl. only Giles de Fiennes and one Rotheric (*CHEC,* 53, 76; on Rotheric, below, note 91). Three Castilians were among her 150 householders 1289–90, with others elsewhere (*CHEC,* 70, 75, 154–59). Physicians incl. mr Nicholas de Menona (Deedes, ed., *Reg. Pontissara,* i, 249, 264; Douie, *Pecham,* 108–9), mr Peter de Portingale (*CHEC,* 19, 24, 78, 106, 122, 134), an Aragonese (*Manners,* 102), and mr Leopardus or Jordan de Leopardo (*CHEC,* 80); see Talbot and Hammond, *Medical Practitioners in Medieval England,* 202–3, 228, 252.

83. For Isabella of France's women, 1311–12, Blackley and Hermansen, eds., *Household Book,* 156–205; for Philippa's, who incl. a ctss, 1330, *Cal. Memoranda Rolls 1326–27,* 373–76.

84. The Charles-Valle Viridi marr. is above, note 52; on Blakenham, *Manners,* 104, *CIPM,* ii, no. 266, and *CPR 1266–1272,* 358, 573, 604. Compare the Sakevilles (*CHEC,* 14–15), Westons (above, note 58), and Eleanor de Cretyng (Beardwood, ed., *Trial of Walter Langeton,* 106–7); on Hemmegrave and Ewelle, see Chapter Three, Appendix I no. 62.

85. Prestwich, "Royal Patronage under Edward I," 43, 52, and *Edward I,* 154–56; *CHEC,* 32–40; see MacFarlane, "Had Edward I a 'Policy'?," 266–67. On the Bruyns, GEC, ii, 355; Moor, *Knights,* i, 154–55; *RG,* ii, nos. 1569–71; on the Haustedes, GEC, vi, 402–4; Moor, *Knights,* ii, 203–4; Farrer, *Honours and Knights' Fees,* ii, 79–80; *CChR,* ii, 346; *CCIR 1279–1288,* 8, 147; *CFR,* v, 20–21; *CIPM,* ii, no. 752). Both couples were gtd marriages in England and Ireland (*CPR 1292–1301,* 197, 198; *RG,* ii, no. 1099; *CPR 1281–1292,* 415–16).

86. For the Vescies, *CHEC,* 46–48, Moor, v, 118–19, GEC xii part 2, 278–80, and below, note 185; he witn. thirteen acts for the Q, 1275 X 1287 (see below, chap. 3, Appx Ii). Lincoln, who witn. for her seven times 1279 X 1290, was her exor (*CHEC,* index, p. 174 s.v. "Lacy, Alisa de", and "Lacy, Henry de"; GEC, vii, 680–87; Moor, iii, 24–25; below, chap. 3, Appx Ii). On Otho, who witn. eight times for the Q, 1279 X 1285, Clifford, *Knight of Great Renown,* 125–26; Moor, *Knights,* ii, 136–37; GEC, vi, 69–73; below, Chapter Three, Appendix I nos. 14, 23, 143, and Appendix II. Otho's nephew John de Strattlingen, Q's knt by 1286 and in 1289–90, m. by 1286 a kinswoman of Bp Giffard of Worcester, for whom see immediately below (*CHEC,* 74 note 73; Bund, ed., *Reg. Godfrey Giffard,* 136–37; *CCIR 1279–1288,* 432; *Records 1286–89,* nos. 3130, 3167; Moor, *Knights,* iv, 301).

87. GEC, 12.i, 368–72; Moor, *Knights,* i, 74–75; *Br. chronology,* 74; Bliss, i, 503; Bund, ed., *Reg. Godfrey Giffard,* 367–68. On Eleanor de Beauchamp, *CHEC,* 103; on Petronilla de Toeny, Parsons, *CHEC,* 64–65, GEC, 12.i, 770–71, and Chapter Three, Appendix I no. 149. Other goddaus appear to be Eleanor de Sakeville (*CHEC,* 14–15); Eleanor de Cretyng (Beardwood, ed., *Trial of Walter Langeton,* 106–8; GEC, iii, 532; *CHEC,* 154]); Eleanor Ferré (*CHEC,* 33–34); Eleanor de Hacche (*CHEC,* 63, 154; GEC, vi, 387–90); Eleanor de Burgh (J. C. Parsons, "Eleanor of Castile and the Countess Margaret," 336–37); Eleanor de Caumpeden (above, note 32). The Q's interest in Eleanor de Ewelle (above, note 84) hints she was a goddau., and the arms in the Tiptoft Missal imply Eve Tybotot was another (B. Watson, "Artists of the Tiptoft Missal," 25–39).

88. *CHEC,* 155 note 7; *CPR 1232–1247,* 247; *CIR 1247–1251,* 247; W. Brown, ed., *Reg. Walter Giffard,* 101; *CCIR 1288–1296,* 24; *Worcester,* 500. In Dec. 1283 the Q wrote the Roman Curia to ask favors for Godfrey, "quem fidum protectoris nostri consilium, et nostram manum dexteram reputamus" (Worcs. and Herefs. Record Office MS 713 fol. 198).

89. GEC, 12.ii, 89–93; Moor, *Knights,* v, 20–23; *CHEC,* 100 note, 132; Rigg, ed., *Select Pleas, Starrs,* 109–10; S. D. Lloyd, "Lord Edward's Crusade," 128; *Foedera,* i, 495. Tybotot witn. ten acts for the Q, 1275 X 1284 (below, chap. 3, Appx li). John de Vescy's death in 1289, and Grandison's departure for the Holy Land in summer 1290, could mean Tybotot was the K's closest friend in England at the Q's death. For the Q's chaplains, below, chap. 2; on Robert and Eve's dau. Eve, perhaps the Q's goddau., see note 87.

90. Compare the cousins apparently sent from by Ponthieu by Eleanor's mother in the 1250s, the marr. of Eleanor's cousin to Edward's uncle ca. 1260, and the mercenaries provided by Ponthieu and (perhaps) Castile in 1263–65, discussed above; and Eleanor's pride in her lineage, noted later in this chapter.

91. Emden, *Oxford,* iii, 1736–38 (the "nephews" were called sons of Alphonso X, but their paternity is unclear). Rotheric *Ispannus,* Edward of Caernarvon's kinsman 1300–1, was K's squire 1282 (Lysons, ed., "Roll of Expenses," 49; *CHEC,* 76; Johnstone, *Edward of Carnarvon,* 6, and idem, ed., *Letters,* 70–71; *CPR 1281–1292,* 339); Eleanor left him £20 (*Manners,* 96).

92. Henry of Castile has already been mentioned in this chapter; see also *CHEC,* 119, 123, 126. S.C. 6/1089/25 *m.* 4 shows £5 given, 17 Feb. 1290, to his knt Peter Gunsalves, who was in England with him in Jan. 1257 (*CLR,* iv, 353). Ferdinand's widow is noted later in this chapter; literary exchanges with Castile in the late 1260s were noted earlier.

93. *CHEC,* 41–55, "Eleanor of Castile and the Countess Margaret," 335–40, and "Eleanor of Castile and the Viscountess Jeanne," 281–88. Only Edmund Mortimer's marr. was remarked (the Wigmore *Fundationis et Fundatorum Historia* [*MA,* vi, 351]; Hayles Abbey chron., BL, Harley 3725 fol. 16–16v; neither is critical, though both note royal influence, and the *Historia* makes the Picard bride Castilian, probably reflecting the Q's role). See also Holt, "Feudal Society and the Family, iv," 26–28; Waugh, "Marriage, Class and Royal Lordship," 199–203; Ward, "Caesar's Wife," 214–16. On the exceptions, *CHEC,* 53. Some male cousins had eccl preferment (e.g., the "nephews" discussed above: see Deedes, ed., *Reg. le Romeyn,* i, 390–91; *Fasti 1066–1300,* iii, 121, and iv, 23, 54; Bliss, i, 544, 601, 606).

94. *CHEC,* 48 note 174, 151 note 20; *CCIR 1279–1288,* 52, 67–68 (compare *CCIR 1272–1279,* 551); *CPR 1281–1292,* 340; *CCIR 1288–1296,* 144; *CCIR 1302–1307,* 417.

95. The exception was Richard of Cornwall's son, who d. *s.p.* 1300. See R. A. Griffiths, "Crown and Royal Family," 15–26; Wagner, *English Genealogy,* 39–41; *CHEC,* 42, 44–46; L. D. Lloyd and D. M. Stenton, eds., *Book of Seals,* 29 (with *VCH Oxon.,* vi, 147–48).

96. *Records 1286–1289,* nos. 3215, 3217, 3225 bis, 3234, 3235 bis, 3240, 3241, 3244, 3245; *CHEC,* 10–11, 70, 113–14; J. C. Parsons, "English Administration in Ponthieu," 382–83.

97. *Bury,* 86; *CHEC,* 45, 68–69, and "English Administration in Ponthieu," 393, 399; *Records 1286–1289,* nos. 2684, 2722, 2820, 2829–30, 3046, 3224, 4428; Prestwich, *Edward I,* 263, 307–8, 539; G. W. Watson, "Families of Lacy, Geneva, Joinville and la Marche," 241–42. On Brienne's marriage, *CPR 1247–1258,* 499, 561, and *CHEC,* 41, 45.

98. Nelson, "Queens as Jezebels," 39–45, 55–60; Stafford, "Sons and Mothers," 79–100.

99. GEC, vii, 378–87; Powicke, *King Henry III,* 733, and idem, *Thirteenth Century,* 235–36, 236–41, 518; Rhodes, "Edmund, Earl of Lancaster," 19–40, 209–37; *Records 1286–1289,* nos. 3208, 3242; *CHEC,* 70, 96, 108, 111; below, Chapter Three, Appendix I no. 221. He witn. two of the K's gts to Eleanor, 1283 (*CChyV,* 265, 271), and gtd her his manor at Frant, Sussex, 1274 X 1290 (below, Chapter Three, Appendix I no. 221).

100. GEC, iii, 433; Prestwich, *Edward I,* 218, 348, 363, 410, 522. He owed 700 marks' queen–gold 1284 (E 159/57 *m.* 9; C62/61 *m.* 8 [K pays 160 of 200 marks owing, Dec. 1284]; still owing, Apr. 1288 [E 159/61 *mm.* 7, 7d]). In 1286 the Q bought a manor at

Whitchurch held of him; a rent owed him was £135 in arrears, 1290 (see Chapter Three, Appendix I no. 174; JUST 1/542 m. 11). See CCIR 1279–1288, 59–60; Deedes, ed., Reg. Pontissara, ii, 462–63. He witn. the Q's act, 1286 (RG, iii, no. 1569).

101. Prestwich, Edward I, 122–23; Richard, Saint Louis, 126–27; Records 1286–1289, nos. 3214, 3221, 3229, 3230, 3231; CHEC, 75, 116, 124, 126.

102. Paris, CM, iii, 392, 479; VCH Dorset, ii, 88; CIR 1242–1247, 13; CChR, ii, 160, 227; CCIR 1272–1279, 290; Palmer, "Friar-Preachers of Guildford," 7–20.

103. Johnstone, Edward of Carnarvon, 24; RG, ii, no. 597.

104. Below, Chapter Three, Appendix I no. 86; CPR 1281–1292, 229. Eleanor of Provence's letter, S.C. 1/23/21 (Marlborough, 22 Apr.), uses the royal title she dropped upon her profession in July 1286; Eleanor of Castile's, S.C. 1/30/44 (Blanquefort, 17 Jan.), mentions the dowager's letter.

105. Stafford, "Sons and Mothers," 79–100, idem, QCD, 143–68, and idem, "King's Wife in Wessex," 24–27; Nelson, "Queens as Jezebels," 35, 38, 43–4, 48–52. Louis IX's wife made her son swear to remain in her tutelage until thirty (Teulet, Layettes, iv, no. 4859); compare Turner, "Eleanor of Aquitaine," 321–35. The K's 1290 provisions affirm his daus' rights, but imply some anxiety for female succession (Foedera, i, 742; Powicke, King Henry III, 732–33, 788–90).

106. CHEC, 9–10; compare Turner, "Eleanor of Aquitaine," 324, 332. Young Eleanor (b. 1269) was at court at times 1277–78, the first year for which records exist (BL, Add. 36762). Two daus went to Nottingham with the Q, 7 Edw. (C 47/3/11 m. 4); at least two children were at the trans. of St. Hugh at Lincoln, Oct. 1280 (Peterborough, 40). Alphonso (b. 1273) was at court, Pentecost 1278 (Add. 36762 m. 3), and a tournament that July (Lysons, ed., "Roll of Purchases," 307–8; C 47/3/11 m. 3). On Elizabeth (b. 1282) and Edward (b. 1284) in 1290, Johnstone, Edward of Carnarvon, 24–25; for the older daus, M. A. E. Green, Princesses, as cited below. In 1289–90 Mary, eleven, was living with the queen-dowager in their convent at Amesbury. Leeds Castle was never a regular residence for the children; Edward's works at Leeds (KW, 695–702) do not prove any particular affection for the place, there is no evidence that the couple visited Leeds any more frequently than other royal manors, nor did they reside there for unusually long periods of time. The Q's partiality for Leeds appears to be the invention of a later age.

107. Records 1285–1286, no. 66, and Records 1286–1289, nos. 1060, 3229). Messengers often went to the Q from the children's household; these in 1290 carried news of the health of her cousin John de Fiennes (C 47/3/22 m. 1), and "medicinal waters" from young Edward to his mother (CHEC, 24).

108. Records 1286–1285, nos. 1992–2002, and Records 1286–89, no. 2574; CPR 1281–1292, 222–23 (= Westm. Abbey muniments, 1577); Trabut-Cussac, "Itinéraire d'Édouard Ier en France," 160–203 notes. Eleanor's letter to Leeds Priory announcing provision for a Leeds Castle chantry asks prayers for herself and children (JUST 1/542 m. 10d [Libourne, 24 Oct. 1286]). In May 1290 Edward gave £15 for five windows in the London Dominicans' church for five of his children ("pro .v. liberis," C 47/4/5 fol. 22v), prob. his five daughters then surviving.

109. Riley, ed., Opus chronicorum, 33; Rishanger, 76–77 (but see Powicke, "Edward I in fact and fiction," 122–24). A. J. Taylor, "Royal Alms," 107–8, notes Edward's accts show no masses said after his son Alphonso d. 1284, but he prob. asked bps to celebrate (compare M. A. E. Green, Princesses, ii, 355, and his similar request at the time of the Q's death, as noted below). The K gave 12s.9d. when the boy's obit was kept on 18 Aug. 1285 (C 47/4/2 fol. 28v; it was kept in young Edward's household in 1290 [C 47/3/22 m. 2]).

110. Johnstone, Edward of Carnarvon, 23; Riley, ed., Opus chronicorum, 48; Chaplais, "Private Letters of Edward I," 86.

111. J. C. Parsons, "Year of Eleanor of Castile's birth," 257 (no. 1), 258–59 (nos. 4, 5).

112. For Alphonso's armor (1278), Lysons, ed., "Roll of Purchases," 307–8; he had a toy castle, 1279 (E 372/123 m. 21), and a falcon and saddle, 1283 (RG, iii, no. 5060; E 101/351/12 m. 1). See Martin, Reg. Peckham, iii, 992–93; Douie, Pecham, 51; Flores, iv, 72; London, p. 99. The uncertainty with which his death faced his parents perhaps intensified their reactions. The new heir, Edward, was five months old; it would be many years before the K, already forty-five, could look to him for support, and the boy might succeed as a minor. The Q was in her forty-third year; hopes for another son were slight, and as remarked earlier the K had to face the possibility that a dau. might succeed him.

113. BL, Add. 36762; M. A. E. Green, Princesses, ii, 275–317; Prestwich, Edward I, 315, 320–21, 324–26; Johnstone, "Wardrobe and Household of Henry"; E 101/350/12.

114. Johnstone evolved differing views of the Q's absence from her son's side ("Archbishop Pecham," 171, and "Wardrobe and Household of Henry," 395–96). Henry d. Guildford ca. 16 Oct. 1274. S.C. 1/22/29 (Guildford, 14 Oct. s.a.), in which Eleanor, Q of England, tells the Chancellor of wrongs done to Henry of Almain's widow, is ascr. to Eleanor of Castile by Wood, ed., Letters of Royal and Illustrious Ladies, i, 46–47; but in the autumn of 1274 it was Eleanor of Provence who was watching over the interests of the widow (CPR 1272–1281, 58, 63–64), a dau. of her uncle the vct of Béarn.

115. M. A. E. Green, Princesses, ii, 318–62; GEC, v, 702–12, and x, 140–43. For the two yeomen in 1290, C 47/4/5 fol. 8r as written makes no sense: "pro duobus vallettis conductis ad opus domine Johanne predictos .ix. dies quia quelibet aliarum filiarum habuit viij. vallettos et ipsa .x. . . . ix.s." A clk must have reversed "viij" and "x." On Clipstone, C 47/4/5 fol. 52v; Joan's s. was b. May 1291 (Osney, 328). For 1305, Johnstone, ed., Letters, 60–61.

116. M. A. E. Green, Princesses, iii, 1–59; CHEC, 24. Edward II's favors to his former nurse suggest a strong bond (Johnstone, Edward of Carnarvon, 9; Parsons, CHEC, 107; Blackley and Hermansen, eds., Household Book, index p. 247 s.v. "Legrave"; CIPM, iv, no. 53; Moor, Knights, iv, 228; CPR 1324–1327, 87; CCLR 1318–1320, 174, 611; CCIR 1307–1313, 581). See also Turner, "Eleanor of Aquitaine," 325–26; CIR 1256–1259, 2–3; CPR 1258–1266, 220; CChR, ii, 84; CPR 1266–1272, 530; CCIR 1288–1296, 27–28; CFR, i, 347; CIPM, iii, no. 171. For Margaret, M. A. E. Green, Princesses, ii, 363–401, esp. 383, 387.

117. M. A. E. Green, Princesses, ii, 404–42; MA, ii, 337–40; Guilloreau, "Marie de Woodstock," 341–59. The Q's gifts to Mary incl. silver plate in 1285 (BL, Add. roll 6711). On her pension, Records 1286–1289, nos. 3111, 3124, 3128, 3141, 3149, 3165, 3177, 3192; Edward raised it to £100 at the Q's death (C 62/67 m. 2). Surrey's bride was underage (1304); he was living with another woman by 1311 (GEC, xii.1, 511; Bliss, iii, 116, 168, 173; R. A. Wilson, ed., Reg. Reynolds, 28–29). By 1344 all Mary's siblings were dead; as a celibate, she left no children to be offended by Surrey's allegation.

118. Prestwich, Edward I, 127–29; compare E. A. R. Brown, "Prince is Father of the King," 300–1, 303–7. On Elizabeth, Johnstone, ed., Letters, 70, 75; Mary's letter is S.C. 1/19/111 (Woodstock, Sunday after St. Bartholomew, 1292 or later as she styles herself "humble nun . . . of Amesbury").

119. As noted earlier, Eleanor of Provence had supervised Edward's education; compare J. C. Parsons, "Mothers, Daughters," esp. 72–75. One example of female networking, not altogether positive, would be the efforts remarked earlier, seemingly made by Eleanor's mother in the 1250s to exploit her daughter's presence in England.

120. CHEC, 10, 95–6; Louis IX's wife was forbidden to hire her children's svts (W. C. Jordan, Louis IX, 6). For the friars, C 47/4/5 ff. 13r, 29r (compare Johnstone, Edward of Carnarvon, 18–22); the writing tablets are cited below. On Trevet, Legge, Anglo-Norman in the Cloisters, 77, and Anglo-Norman Literature, 300; Dean, "Nicholas Trevet, Historian," 339–49. Reasons for ascr. Trevet's vernacular chron. to Mary's patronage are discussed in J. C. Parsons, "Of Queens, Courts, and Books." See also Bell, "Medieval Women Book Owners," 136–37, 148–51, 159–60.

272   Notes to Chapter One

121. Johnstone, *Edward of Carnarvon*, 8; *CHEC*, 15, 139; *Records 1286–1289*, nos. 3224 *bis*, 3225, 3227–30. During the 1277 campaign, Eleanor lived at Shotwick (Ches.), 13 July–15 Sept. (E 101/350/26 *mm.* 4, 5; C 47/4/1 fol. 13v). They were apart for eight days, 20 Nov. 1288 X 25 Sept. 1289 (compare *Records 1286–1289*, no. 2552, and Trabut-Cussac, "Itinéraire d'Édouard Ier en France," 196). See also below, Chapter Two, note 90.
122. Martin, ed., *Reg. Peckham*, i, 56–57.
123. Herefs. and Worcs. Record Office, MS 713, ff. 155v–156r: "Litteras domine nostre, Domine Alianore dei gracie Regine Anglie, necnon Reverendi patris Domini . . . Bathonensis et Wellensis Episcopi, pro Domino Nicholao de Cler' ipsius Regine Capellano nobis directas, vobis inspiciendas mittimus . . . pro quo quidem Domino Nicholao vobis consulendo salubrius vestram dilectionem requirimus cum affectu, quatinus eundem .N. ad ecclesiam de Welreford . . . inspectis periculis que ex ipsius domini Regis indignacione si eam forsan incureretis, quod absit . . . in agendis possent multipliciter iminere, presentare velitis." "Ipsius domini Regis" is anomalous, as the K is named nowhere else in the letter; did a clerk merely muddle the abbreviations for "ipsius domine Regine," or did Giffard really mean to imply that the Q might turn the K against him? On the Crondall dispute, *CPR 1281–1292*, 32; Deedes, ed., *Reg. Pontissara*, i, xiv–xv, 249, 264; Douie, *Pecham*, 108–9. In a similar case involving a br. of her steward Walter de Kancia, Pecham noted that the Q had interested herself in the matter (Douie, ed., *Reg. Pecham*, ii, 115 [compare Hill, ed., *Rolls and Reg. Sutton*, i, 9, and viii, 93]). See also below, note 129.
124. S.C. 1/15/66: "Item domine Reverende cum reverenda domina nostra illustrissima . . Regina nos si placet excusetis nam nobis datum est intelligi quod ipsa nos habet odio eo quod minus in Navarram quod vitare nequimus cum fuissimus moniti . . . sub amissione tocius terre nostre . . . ferre." For the 1277 Navarrese crisis, Ballesteros Beretta, *Alfonso X*, 793–97.
125. S.C. 1/30/44: "Kar sachet ke nous auons dit au Rey . . . <ke> nous garnierons vous. . . de totes les choses auandites [for know that we have said to the King . . . [that] we would inform you . . . of all the aforesaid things]".
126. E 159/61 *m.* 1d (Barp, 25 June 15 Edw.): "nus a la requeste de lui et de ses amis et par le comaundement nostre seigneur le Rey ke sur ce nus fu fet a la priere del devantdit sire huge ceus memes mil mars lui avoms relesse e pardonne." Valence's letter is S.C. 1/10/109 (to John de Kirkby, s.d.). See below, Chapter Three, Appendix I nos. 29a, 175.
127. Mellows, *Pytchley's Book of Fees*, 64, 71–72.
128. Herefs. and Worcs. Record Office MS 713 fol. 329v: "Credimus tamen quod cum colloquium habueritis cum dicta domina nostra Regina, dictum negocium feliciarem optinebit effectum, nobis presentibus."
129. In 1291 Richard de Stokepord' complained that at the Q's orders her bf at Macclesfield unjustly impleaded and distrained him, as he could not present her clk to the ch of Stockport. The bf ackn. this, "Et quia predictus Ricardus dicit quod Episcopus Bathon' [Burnell] bene nouit istam veritatem, Ideo fiat supplicacio et demonstracio Executoribus domine Regine predicte" (JUST 1/1149 *m.* 2). If charges agst Stokepord' there, 1285–88, were part of this abuse, he suffered indeed (Stewart-Brown, ed., *Rolls of Chester*, 214, 215, 230, 239). On the K and Burnell, Powicke, *Thirteenth Century*, 338–39; Prestwich, *Edward I*, 233–34.
130. *Dunstable*, 223; *Flores*, ii, 482; Prestwich, *Edward I*, 45.
131. *Foedera*, i, 484, 495. Henry III's will of 1242 made his wife regent and guardian for Edward (the late Rev. Michael M. Sheehan C.S.B. kindly allowed me to consult his typescript of this text); when Henry left England in 1253, his wife was made custodian of his lands in England should he die before Edward was of age (*Foedera*, i, 290–92). See also J. C. Parsons, "Family, Sex, and Power," 7.
132. On the earls, *CCIR 1272–1279*, 504, S.C. 1/8/55, s.d. (Hereford to John de Kirkby, asking at the Q's orders transcripts on the dispute for a meeting at Abergavenny), and

Prestwich, *Edward I*, 348–52. See also *CCIR 1279–1288*, 59–60; *RG*, ii, nos. 916, 918, 1142; *RG*, iii, no. 1064; Trabut-Cussac, *L'administration anglaise*, 266; *RG*, ii, no. 1069; a request from the vct of Béarn that she intercede with Edward for the vct's follower, 1265 X 1272, is cited above, note 45; see also J. C. Parsons, "Piety, Power," 116 and note 30. A full list of petitions cannot be included, but see *CPR 1272–1281*, 184, 202, 301; *CCIR 1272–1279*, 483; *CPR 1281–1292*, 29, 38, 194, 218; *CCIR 1279–1288*, 205, 263; *RG*, iii, no. 5074; Bliss, i, 514; Sayles, ed., *Select Cases*, ii, 20–23. S.C. 1/9/34 (Wells, 25 March 1283) is from Burnell to Kirkby forwarding the Q's letter with a certain petition enclosed, which Kirkby was instructed to expedite.

133. Huneycutt, "Intercession and the High Medieval Queen"; J. C. Parsons, "Queen's Intercession," and idem, "Ritual and Symbol," 60–77. Further consideration of Eleanor of Castile's particular behavior as an intercessor will be found below in Chapters Three and Four.

134. Waugh, *Lordship of England*, esp. 191–92, 214–15 (the marr. at 192 note 172 was in fact arr. by the Q); *CHEC*, 50 note 183. On godchildren, see above, note 87.

135. E 101/351/14 (12 Edw.) shows cups for two French knts, the wife of Piers de Geneville and her damsel; BL, Add. roll 6711 (1284–85) has cups for the legate, the dowager's minstrel, a prioress, and the bp of Verdun's seneschal and steward; see also *Records 1285–1286*, nos. 1983, 1988, 1989, 1991, 2006. Compare Enright, "Lady with a Mead-Cup," 170–203.

136. *Records 1286–1289*, nos. 1649, 1730, 3225, 3229, 3238 (with the last compare *CHEC*, 112). A later source says Eleanor de Montfort was in the Q's household bef. her 1278 marriage to Llywelyn of Wales (*Rishanger*, 87 [but compare *Wykes*, 266–67]).

137. Edward apptd Montibus and Hugh de Negres 19 Mar. 1282 (C 47/29/1/12); S.C. 1/20/126 (s.d.), from Amadeus of Savoy, informs Edward of their return from Montferrat: "e sachez sire ie ay entendu por les messages avandiz quil se puet mult emender en cete besoigne por le mandement ma dame la Royne od le vostre." As Savoy-Montferrat relations were chronically troubled (E. L. Cox, *Eagles of Savoy*, 423–34), perhaps the K and Q favored Beatrice's marr. to improve their mutual capacity to deal with the situation; that an Anglo-Montferrat connection was deemed desirable is suggested by the marquis' first marriage (1257) to a dau. of Earl Richard de Clare of Gloucester. In June 1290, 100s. were paid the Q's messenger to "Le markys de mounferraunt" (S.C. 6/1089/25 m. 4), probably at the time her grandnephew John I succeeded his abdicating father. (In 1284 Eleanor's grandniece Yolande of Montferrat m. Emperor Andronicus II Palaeologus, but nothing has surfaced to suggest the Q cultivated that connection.) For the Montferrat marriages, Isenburg–Büdingen and Freytag von Loringhoven, *Stammtafeln*, ii, tables 47, 136. Montibus' career is discussed further, below, Chapter Two, note 154; for queens' manipulation of marriages, J. C. Parsons, "Mothers, Daughters," 64.

138. *Foedera*, i, 643, 658; *Records 1285–1286*, no. 280. Lovetot's career is considered further, see Chapter Two; for Gueldres, *CHEC*, 113.

139. S.C. 1/16/1 (s.d., 1274 X 1279: "vous pri sire ke vous menvoies .iiij. bons kiens convenables ad chers, car li mien sont avan tout mort."); S.C. 1/16/2 (s.d., 1278 [compare *Foedera*, i, 561], on the Abp of Rouen's homage); S.C. 1/16/4 (see J. C. Parsons, "Eleanor of Castile and the Viscountess Jeanne," 141–42).

140. Johnstone, "County of Ponthieu," 435–52; J. C. Parsons, "English Administration in Ponthieu," 371–96. The title and arms do appear on the Q's tomb and the Eleanor crosses (discussed in Chapter Four).

141. *Foedera*, i, 522–23, 540–41 (see Chaplais, ed., *Treaty Rolls, I*, nos. 179–181). Ballesteros Beretta, *Alfonso X*, esp. chaps 15–16; MacDonald, "Law and Politics," 192–97, and "Alfonso the Learned and Succession," 647–53.

142. In general, Daumet, *Mémoire sur les relations de la France et de la Castille*; Chaplais, *Treaty Rolls I*, nos. 155–62, 164–65, 170–72, 175, 177.

143. For the 1282 letter, above, note 72. S.C. 1/12/112 (Edward to Alphonso, s.d.), notes a recent Castilian embassy but says the Welsh uprising detains the K. See *Foedera*, i, 620–21, 625, 629, 634, 638; Ballesteros Beretta, *Alfonso X*, 1047. E 101/308/11 is an acct for Bp Suero's expns, some paid by Edward on 4 Dec. 1283 (E 101/351/12 *m.* 1); Suero's letter to Joan is S.C. 1/30/3 (s.d.). For the 5000 marks, *CPR 1281–1292*, 113, 122.

144. Anon., ed., "Testamento del Rey Don Alonso [*sic*] X," 116–17. Gascon knts and ships were sent to help Alphonso (*RG*, ii, nos. 174, 380).

145. *Records 1286–1289*, nos. 2333, 2592, 3224, 4390; *CHEC*, 82, 88, 111; Lehmann-Brockhaus, nos. 6263, 6266. See also *Foedera*, i, 649, 662; *Records 1285–1286*, index p. 287 s.v. "Sancho IV, king of Castile," and *Records 1286–1289*, index p. 634 s.v. "Sancho IV, king of Castile." With *Records 1286–1289*, no. 3232, and *CHEC*, 129, compare Hillgarth, *Spanish Kingdoms 1250–1516 I*, 311–120. The Q's death is noted in *Ann. Toletanes III*, in Florez, *España Sagrada*, xxiii, 414; see further, Tolley, "Eleanor of Castile and the 'Spanish' Style," 172–73.

146. Prestwich, *Edward I*, 323–26; for the nobles, *Foedera*, i, 787, 793 (compare Powicke, *Thirteenth Century*, 268–69 and note).

147. Prestwich, *Edward I*, 323–26; Teulet, ed., *Layettes*, iii, no. 4192, and iv, nos. 5416, 5559. I owe to Dr. Prestwich the observation on the Q's lack of close Capetian ties, illustrated in genealogical table 3.

148. It is tempting to take the chronology of these Anglo-Picard unions as an indication that the Q turned to the Picards only after Alphonso X died. Giles de Fiennes m. Sybil Fillol by 1270; his sister Maud m. Humphrey de Bohun 1275. Margaret de Fiennes m. Edmund Mortimer 1285; her sister Joan m. John Wake 1286. Alice de la Plaunche m. John de Montfort bef. Mar. 1287. In 1289 James de la Plaunche m. Maud de Haversham, and Marie de Picquigny m. Almeric de St. Amand. Clemence d'Avaugour m. the yr John de Vescy 1290; later that year the Q arr. Eleanor de Fiennes' marr. to Richard de Vernon (*CHEC*, 41–54). But this chronology is misleading: the Q obtained John de Montfort's marr. as early as 1280 (*CCIR 1279–1288*, 52), and while proof is lacking, the others too could have been arr. long bef. they took place. The St. Amand marr., however, prob. was not arr. bef. ca. Oct. 1287, when Almeric's married elder br. Guy d. *s.p.* at eighteen (*GEC*, xi, 295).

149. The 1269 rumors of Edward's familiarity with the ctss of Gloucester were unfounded, and it is unlikely he fathered John Botetourt (*Bury*, 45; Denholm-Young, *History and Heraldry*, 38–39; Given-Wilson and Curteis, *Royal Bastards*, 135–36; Prestwich, *Edward I*, 60–61, 131–32). Young Edward in 1305 addressed the offspring of Richard of Cornwall's bastards as cousins, but did not call Botetourt his brother (Johnstone, ed., *Letters*, 65 *bis*, 67 *bis*, 115).

150. Tout, *Chapters*, i, 162.

151. In 1278 (C 47/4/1 fol. 27v), 1287 (*Records 1286–89*, no. 980), 1290 (C 47/4/5 fol. 45v); as noted below, the K gave the women his ransom the Easter after the Q died. A different interpretation is given these incidents by Chaplais, *Piers Gaveston*, 8–9 (though allowing it does bear on sexual behavior). See also *Records 1286–1289*, nos. 947–49. On conjugal abstinence in penitential periods, Vauchez, *Les laïcs au moyen âge*, 203–9, and Weinstein and Bell, *Saints and Society*, 75–81; Elliott, *Spiritual Wedlock*, deals with married couples who observed perpetual chastity or converted to it later in their marriages.

152. Delaborde, "Une oeuvre nouvelle," 285. Louis rarely spoke of his family (Joinville, *History of St. Louis*, 176); Edward often did so (Riley, ed., *Opus chronicorum*, 48).

153. C 47/4/5 fol. 47v; M. A. E. Green, *Princesses*, iii, 15; for Havering, E 101/352/12 fol. 17, and for Edward and music, Prestwich, *Edward I*, 118.

154. Two servants were killed (*Rishanger*, 114; Hayles Abbey chron., BL, Harley 3725 fols. 16v–17). Local tradition says Edward in 1287 f. a Franciscan house at Libourne after

escaping death by lightning there (Dedieu, "Quelques traces de religion populaire," 241; Wadding, *Annales Minorum*, v, 185–86, dates the foundation 1287, without noting the lightning incident).

155. Raine, ed., *Letters from Northern Registers*, 91; Ramsey, 369; Deedes, ed., *Reg. le Romeyn*, i, 33; *CHEC*, 133; *Foedera*, i, 743.

156. Riley, ed., *Opus chronicorum*, 50; *Liber Quotidianus*, 29, 38; *Ann. Paulini*, 255; M. A. E. Green, *Princesses*, ii, 382, 420, and iii, 19, 33; the anniversary service is discussed in Chapter Four. For Easter 1291, J. C. Parsons, "Eleanor of Castile: Legend and Reality," 44, note 88.

157. *KW*, 324, 372; compare preparations for Q Margaret, 1306 (ibid., 862–63).

158. At Clarendon the wainscoting of her chamber was green starred with gold, the walls painted as green curtains (C 47/3/48/2); on windows at Westminster in 1288–89, E 101/467/20 *m.* 4, and at Langley 7–9 Edw., E 372/125 *m.* 2d. See also *KW*, 896–97, 904, 915, 919; for candles, *CHEC*, 80.

159. Lysons, ed., "Roll of Purchases," 308; Westm. Abbey, muniments 23627A; *CHEC*, 83, 86, 90, 92.

160. E 372/143 *m.* 36; *CCIR 1288–1296*, 20 (compare *CHEC*, 96); Daumet, "Les testaments d'Alphonse X," 90.

161. For knives, E 101/351/12 *m.* 7; *CHEC*, 81; *Records 1286–1289*, no. 3227. On the chessmen, *Records 1286–1289*, no. 2009 (see Prestwich, *Edward I*, 114–15). For mirrors, J. C. Parsons, "English Administration in Ponthieu," 397, 398; *Records 1286–1289*, no. 3219; in 1284 a mirror case cost 20s. (E 101/351/12 *m.* 7). See also *Records 1286–1289*, no. 3225.

162. For 1284, E 101/351/14 *m.* 1. See *CCIR 1279–1288*, 388; Byerly, *Records 1285–1286*, nos. 424, 1977, 1989, 2011, 2015, 2017; *Records 1286–1289*, nos. 106, 3190, 3196; *CHEC*, 59, 134–35; *Manners*, 95. E 101/684/56/3–4 are an indenture (London, 4 Jan. 1296), for plate delivered to the K by the Q's exors, incl. twelve pitchers, one hundred plates, four spice plates, twenty-six cups, eight fruit plates and many liturgical vessels.

163. *Kalendars*, i, 57; *Records 1285–1286*, no. 432; Johnstone, "Wardrobe and Household of Henry", 28; James, *Apocalypse in Latin and French*; Sandler, *Gothic Manuscripts 1285–1385*, ii, nos. 1, 10. On vestments, Kendrick, *English Embroidery*, 29–32; Brieger and Verdier, *Art and the Courts*, i, no. 91, and ii, pl. 120; Lehmann-Brockhaus, nos. 239, 919, 930, 934, 2911, 2913, 2916, 2930. See Denholm-Young, *History and Heraldry*, 45–47; E. Salter, *English and International*, 96–97; Brault, "Arthurian Heraldry," 81–88; Wagner, *Heralds*, 2–3, 17; Lachaud, "Embroidery for the Court of Edward I," 33–35; Cherry, "Heraldry as Decoration," 123–34.

164. Stafford, *QCD*, 106–7; Prestwich, *Edward I*, 108; Lysons, ed., "Roll of Purchases," 305–6, 308; *RG*, iii, no. 5090; J. C. Parsons, "English Administration in Ponthieu," 397; *CHEC*, 11, 65–66, 85–86, 94, 108–9, 122; *Records 1286–1289*, nos. 2004, 2143, 3188, 3221, 3233, 3236, 3237, 3239, 3242, 3244; *Manners*, 97, 137.

165. *CPR 1272–1281*, 212, 215; *Manners*, 97; Turner, "Will of Humphrey de Bohun," 348; Lehmann-Brockhaus, no. 6262; *CHEC*, 80–81, 84–85, 102, 106 *bis*, 130 *bis*, 134–35, and "English Administration in Ponthieu," 397; *Records 1286–1289*, nos. 2143, 2385, 3181, 3188, 3241, 3242. Jewels from Paris incl. two diamonds for £6:12:4 and a cut emerald for 40s. (E 101/684/56/13, s.d.). An acct of Eleanor of Provence's jewels shows most items given away as gifts (E 101/349/26). For Syrian goods, *CHEC*, 11, 85; *Records 1286–1289*, nos. 3188, 3222, 3244; *Manners*, 97.

166. Eleanor's intervention on behalf of Castilian merchants bef. 1272 were noted earlier. For the period after 1272, *CPR 1272–1281*, 184, 196; Childs, *Anglo-Castilian Trade*, 71–72, 77–78, 84, 96; Ruíz, "Castilian Merchants in England," 182. At the Q's instance writs of aid issued, Jan. 1288, to Gascon merchants suing for debts in England (E 159/61 *mm.* 6–6d); on 20 July 1290 she told the mayor and bfs of Sandwich to restore to a Breton merchant wines seized by the men of Canterbury priory (Canterbury, Dean and Chapter Library, Reg. I fol. 197v). For the sheep, J. C. Parsons, "English Administration in Ponthieu," 400.

167. E 372/121 *m.* 22, E 372/123 *m.* 21 (7–9 Edw. I); J. C. Parsons, "English Administration in Ponthieu," 398; for Frangypany, E 372/125 *m.* 2. For the Aragonese gardeners, *CHEC*, 104; there was a vineyard at Leeds Castle where Ferdinand *Ispannus* worked (*Manners*, 102; *CHEC*, 70). Islamic models for the Q's gardens are suggested by Tolley, "Eleanor of Castile and the `Spanish' Style," 175–76. No proof has surfaced that the Q first imported the hollyhock to England.

168. E 372/123 *m.* 21; E 101/352/13 *m.* 2; *CHEC*, 63, 111, 112. On illumination of a psalter for her son (1284), Yapp, "Birds of English Medieval Manuscripts," 343, sees an interest in natural history among thirteenth-century patrons and doubts that "artists would make the lavish use that they did of birds in [the] Alphonso [psalter] . . . unless the patron who commissioned the book requested it." See also Hutchinson, "Attitudes Toward Nature," 5–37.

169. J. C. Parsons, "English Administration in Ponthieu," 399; C 47/4/5 fol. 2.

170. Her *daia* and *custos vaccarum* occ. Nov. 1277 (E 101/350/26, *mm.* 4, 5). A bldg was put up at Caernarvon for the *daia* May 1284; that Aug. payment was made for taking her milk, butter and cheese from Caernarvon to "Baladeruelyn'" (E 101/351/9 *mm.* 6, 12). See *Records 1285–1286*, nos. 417, 666; *Records 1286–1289*, nos. 517, 3231. For cheese, *Records 1286–1289*, nos. 740, 1679; Lysons, ed., "Roll of Purchases," 308; J. C. Parsons, "English Administration in Ponthieu," 397; *RG*, iii, no. 5090; Robo, *Mediaeval Farnham*, 167; *CHEC*, 133. Edmund sent Brie, Aug. 1289 (E 101/352/14 *m.* 7); cheese also came from Ponthieu (J. C. Parsons, "English Administration," 402).

171. J. C. Parsons, "English Administration in Ponthieu," 398, 402; *Records 1285–1286*, nos. 585, 666; C 47/4/5 fol. 10v; *CHEC*, 119. For gifts, *Records 1286–1289*, nos. 3243, 3224, 3245; *CHEC*, 100, 124, 150 note.

172. *Records 1286–1289*, nos. 3231, 3232, 3234; *CHEC*, 66, 76, 85, 111, 112, 117; Lachaud, "Embroidery for the Court of Edward I," 36–37.

173. *CHEC*, 12; Murray, "Medieval Games of Tables," 61, 67; Prestwich, *Edward I*, 114–15, 123–24. A book she borrowed at Cerne Abbey, Dec. 1285 (her letter including thanks for the volume is JUST 1/542 *m.* 7d) was perhaps the Anglo-Norman chess treatise written there in her day (Eales, "Game of Chess," 28).

174. Tanqueray, "Lettres du Roi Edward I," 487–503; Prestwich, *Edward I*, 115–17; *Foedera*, i, 568. The Q had a *parturcarius, bernarii, veutrarii,* and *venatores*; her birdcatcher did little but "take birds," "for the king's amusement" (*Records 1286–1289*, no. 3229; *CHEC*, 12, 72, 76, 78, 79, 82, 84, 86). Her dogs and the K's falcons suggest the illuminations of a crowned lady hunting with dogs and a knight with falcons in the "Alphonso" psalter, begun for their son (1284), represent the couple (see above, note 168 on the birds in the psalter—perhaps reflecting the Q's interest in birds remarked earlier).

175. Hockey, ed., *Account-Book of Beaulieu*, 301; E 101/305/5 *m.* 3; *Foedera*, i, 569, 579, 621; *CPR 1272–1281*, 137, 263; *Records 1285–1286*, no. 42; *Records 1286–1289*, nos. 705, 723, 3245; *CHEC*, 114. In 1278 Llywelyn sent her dogs (C 47/4/1 fol. 38); E 101/371/8/15 [for Edward's second wife?] shows £11:7:4 spent to take 34 of the Q's dogs to the French K). For the Q's dogs in 15 Edw., *Records 1286–1289*, nos. 2773–2901. On parks, *CCIR 1272–1279*, 210, 263, 481; *CCIR 1279–1288*, 142, 148; *CPR 1272–1281*, 182, 471–72, 475; *CPR 1281–1292*, 48, 351, 406; Stagg, *CNFD 1244–1334*, nos. 92–141, 142–46, 150, 152–60, 162–65, 167–71, 173–74, 176. For the children, Johnstone, "Wardrobe and Household of Henry," 25; *RG*, iii, no. 5060; E 101/351/20 *m.* 4.

176. J. C. Parsons, "Of Queens, Courts and Books," and idem, "Mothers, Daughters," 71–73; works perhaps sent her from Castile in the 1260s were noted earlier, and a religious work written for her by Abp Pecham is remarked below. On Edward's interest in Arthuriana, Prestwich, *Edward I*, 120–22. Eleanor's role in Anglo-Castilian diplomacy is discussed above.

177. Pensions to friars at both universities are, e.g., E1290 (C 47/4/4 fol. 41 *bis*). See *Manners*, 96, 103, 107, 108, 135–36; Gibson, ed., *Statuta Antiqua*, 13, 16; Hackett, ed., *Original*

Statutes, 233; Aston and Faith, "University and College Endowments," 276, 278, 283. She sent one Edmund de la Hyde to study at Salisbury (JUST 1/1014 m. 11; see also *Manners*, 126).

178. Emden, *Oxford*, i, 60–61; Macrae, "Geoffrey of Aspall's Commentaries," 94–134; *CHEC*, 14.

179. Galbraith, "Literacy of the Medieval English Kings," 215; Denholm-Young, *History and Heraldry*, 54. That a courtier spoke with a petitioner at St. Albans in 1275 implies Eleanor could not (or did not) converse in English (Riley, ed., *Gesta Abbatum Sancti Albani*, 411–12).

180. *Records 1285–1286*, no. 403; Galbraith, "Literacy of the Medieval English Kings," 215. See *Records 1285–1286*, no. 3226, and parchment "to the queen's use for writing books" (*CHEC*, 107–8). Ivory "tables" bought in 1288 were perhaps gaming pieces (*Records 1286–1289*, no. 3225; compare Murray, "Mediaeval Games of Tables," 58). Eleanor's goldsmith Adam paid 2s. "pro tablettis ad libros . . . liberatis Regine" (E 101/684/56/13, fragm.); tablets bought by Richard du Marche were prob. to bind a psalter he had illuminated (*Manners*, 103 bis). Adam bought "tabliaus a liure" for young Eleanor, 1291 (E 101/684/56/2 m. 1).

181. *Records 1285–86*, index 297, s.v. "Almonry" and "Alms and Oblations," 298 s.v. "Clergy and Religious," and 308 s.v. "Religious Articles, Houses and Shrines"; *Records 1286–89*, nos. 2477–2578 (272–305), and index pp. 652, s.v. "Almonry" and "Alms and Oblations," 657 s.v. "Clergy and Religious," 676 s.v. "Religious Articles, Houses and Shrines"; *CHEC*, 98–100, 113, 117, 124, 132; Johnstone, "Poor-Relief in the Royal Households," 149–67; A. J. Taylor, "Royal Alms," 93–125; Prestwich, "Piety of Edward I," 120–28. See also Armstrong, "Piety of Cicely," 135–56; A. Crawford, "Piety of Late Medieval English Queens," 48–57; Ormrod, "Personal Religion of Edward III," 849–877; J. C. Parsons, "Piety, Power," 107–23.

182. She was dispensed for a portable altar, 1278 (Bliss, i, 456; see also Ullmann, ed., *Liber regie capelle*, 66). On shrines, Phillips, "Edward II and the Prophets," 190 (compare *Bury*, 83); *Dunstable*, 355. Eleanor sent her clks to offer at distant shrines (*Records 1286–1289*, nos. 1639, 3215; *CHEC*, 95); her daus went on pilgrimages to shrines linked to Plantagenet kingship (M. A. E. Green, *Princesses*, ii, 293–95, 303, 364, 426–27). The liturgical vestments she gave Lichfield cathedral were prob. solicited by her steward Walter de Kancia or her wardrobe kpr Henry de Wodestok', prebendaries there, like the vestments with her arms "procured" from her chapel for Bath cathedral by Bp Burnell (Swanson, "Medieval Liturgy as Theatre," 248 [on Kancia and Wodestok', see Chapter Two]; Lehmann-Brockhaus, no. 239); see also Lachaud, "Embroidery for the Court of Edward I," 35.

183. A. Taylor, "Royal Alms"; Prestwich, "Piety of Edward I," 121–22, 123–24, 128; *Commendatio Lamentabilis in Transitu Magni Regis Edwardi*, in Stubbs, ed., *Chronicles of Edward I and Edward II*, ii, 3–21, esp. 19. The 1285 images cost £347:14:1½ (BL Add. 6711 m. 1; A. J. Taylor, "Edward I and the shrine of St. Thomas," 22–28). The Canterbury chron. and necrology both note the images (cont. Gervase of Canterbury, 292; BL, MS Arundel 68, fol. 33–33v). On the tiles, Alexander and Binski, *Age of Chivalry*, no. 367; compare Stafford, *QCD*, 120–22.

184. Accts in *CHEC*, *Records 1286–1289*, and A. Taylor, "Royal Alms," show fewer English saints commemorated in the Q's chapel than the K's. She made a vow to St. Thomas, 1289 (*CHEC*, 99), and gave St. Nicholas' finger to Westm. Abbey (Lehmann–Brockhaus, nos. 2517, 6262).

185. Palmer, "Friar-Preachers of Guildford," 8; *Records 1285–86*, nos. 400, 544; *CHEC*, 16–17, 127 note 197; compare Hinnebusch, *Early English Friars Preachers*, 471–72; the friars dwelling with her children in 1289–90 were noted earlier. Patrons at court incl. the Ferrés and the Q's cousin Isabella de Vescy (Hinnebusch, 97; Clapham, "On the Topography of the Dominican Priory," 82; Palmer, "Friar Preachers of Guildford," 12).

186. Hinnebusch, *Early English Friars Preachers*, 78–79, 34–37, 44–45; Clapham, "On the Topography of the Dominican Priory," 58; *Records 1286–1289*, no. 3121; *CPR 1272–1281*, 322; see Chapter Three, Appendix I nos. 158, 236. On Langley, Bliss, ii, 207, 217; v, 501–2; *KW*, 257–63. Tradition says she gave a site for the OP at St-Sever; she only mediated a dispute on burial rights there with the local OSB, patrons of the parish burial ground (Arch. dépt. Landes, H 2, pièce 18, notarial copy [5 July 1685] of a lost original [St-Sever, 19 Oct. 1287]); Bernardus Guidonis, *De fundatione*, 207; *GC*, i, col. 1178.

187. Hinnebusch, *Early English Friars Preachers*, 73; *Manners*, 95, 96, 99, 101, 102, 103; Bernardus Guidonis, *De fundatione*, 207.

188. For her other foundations, J. C. Parsons, "Piety, Power," 114 and note 24. Her letters patent allowing Breamore Priory to enclose five acres she gtd them in the New Forest are E 327/551 (Winchester, 5 May 6 Edw., unknown to *MA*, vi, 328–29, or *VCH Hants.*, ii, 168–72). See also *CPR 1272–1281*, 436 (= Lambeth Palace MS 1212, fol. 37v [16 May 9 Edw., with the K's *inspeximus* and conf. 20 May]); *CHEC*, 61 and note 23, 65; *RP*, i, 53; *CChR*, ii, 416; below, Chapter Three, Appendix I no. 153, and Appx I, note 134.

189. J. C. Parsons, "Piety, Power," 116–23; W. C. Jordan, *Louis IX*, 184–85, and "*Persona et Gesta*, 2," 214–15. Compare Musto, "Queen Sancia of Naples and the Spiritual Fanciscans," 185–86.

190. A point perhaps related to the Q's distance from the bps. J. C. Parsons, "Piety, Power," 119–20; *CHEC*, 63–64; *Manners*, 136. Lachaud, "Embroidery for the Court of Edward I," 37 note 16, 46, thinks coral and jet beads purchased for the Q were for embroidery and has one later example of that use of such beads. But these beads were purchased from a jeweller, not a mercer, at the same time as paternosters that Lachaud apparently overlooked (*CHEC*, 80, 106). The well known popularity of jet and coral rosary beads in the medieval period argues that Eleanor's beads were indeed for that purpose.

191. J. C. Parsons, "Of Queens, Courts and Books."

192. Prestwich, *Edward I*, 128; J. C. Parsons, "Piety, Power," 118–19; Vauchez, "Lay Peoples' Sanctity," 30–32; Stafford, "Portrayal of Royal Women," 145. On Margaret Beaufort, Armstrong, "Piety of Cicely," 152, and A. Crawford, "Piety of Late Medieval English queens," 54–57.

193. Cartwright, *Disease and History*, 142–43; *CHEC*, 23–26; *Osney*, 326. *Barnwell*, 226, implies a sudden death, but in other cases records correct the chroniclers in such matters (Bond, "Notices of the Last Days of Isabella," 462–63).

194. *CPR 1292–1301*, 19; *CHEC*, 132; Crook, "Last Days of Eleanor of Castile," 17–28. C 47/34/18/10 *m*. 4 are memoranda prob. written at Harby, incl. a gt of warren to Weston, 23 Nov. (*CChR*, ii, 382). For the Q's iter in Nov. 1290, *CHEC*, 151–52; she dated a letter at Marnham on 19 Nov. on the adv. of Westerham she had gtd Canterbury priory in June 1290 (Canterbury, Dean and chapter library, Register I, fol. 137; compare *CChR*, ii, 357).

195. *CHEC*, 132–33; *Flores*, iii, 71; Fenwick, "Inquiry into Complaints against the Ministers of Eleanor of Castile," xxxi–xxxiii.

196. Tout and Johnstone, *State Trials*; Brand, "Edward I and the Justices," 31–40; *CPR 1281–1292*, 405; E. A. R. Brown, "Royal Salvation," 1–8.

197. *CPR 1272–1281*, 79; Eleanor of Provence had such lic. Aug. 1271, Eleanor of Aquitaine July 1202 (*CPR 1266–1272*, 567; *Foedera*, i, 86). On the daus, *CHEC*, 134; Turner, "Will of Humphrey de Bohun," 348; M. A. E. Green, *Princesses*, iii, 37; Chaplais, *Piers Gaveston*, 126, 129 (but was "reigne Alianore" Eleanor of Provence?)." Eleanor's dau. Elizabeth later owned the "Alphonso" psalter, but it is not certain the Q left it to her (Alexander and Binski, *Age of Chivalry*, no. 357; Hutchinson, "Attitudes Toward Nature," 29–33). The K reclaimed or bought the chessmen he gave her in 1286 (above, note 161); Edward II owned two literary works associated with his mother (above, note 64; J. C. Parsons, "Of Queens, Courts, and Books"), but not certainly by her legacy.

198. *Manners,* 95–139; *CCIR 1288–1296,* 187; *CCIR 1288–1296,* 203; *CPR 1281–1292,* 478; *CPR 1281–1292,* 420; Johnstone, ed., *Letters,* 40 (compare *RP,* i, 477); *CCIR 1307–1313,* 481 (compare *CChyV,* 384, *CPR 1307–1313,* 508, and *KW,* 252–53); Cole, ed., *Documents Illustrative of English History,* 33. The 1294 acct is analyzed in Chapter Two.

199. *CHEC,* 132; Riley, ed., *Opus chronicorum,* 50; E. A. R. Brown, "Death and the Human Body," 221–70, and idem, "Authority, the Family, and the Dead," 803–32. Compare preparation of the body of Anne of Hohenburg (d. 1281), wife of Rudolf I of Habsburg (Pertz, ed., *Chronicon Colmariense,* 253–54).

200. Beaune, "Mourir noblement," 126, 138–39; Finucane, "Sacred Corpse, Profane Carrion," 40–60; Cannadine, "Context, Performance and Meaning of Ritual," 150–51; Hope, "Funeral Effigies," 520–29; Mason, "'Pro Statu et Incolumitate regni mei'," 99–117; Hallam, "Royal Burial," 359–80; E. A. R. Brown, "Burying and Unburying," 241–45, 242 note 1; Giesey, "Models of Rulership," 46–48.

201. *CHEC,* 133; Powicke, *King Henry III,* 734 note 2; *Dunstable,* 362–63; Riley, ed., *Opus chronicorum,* 50; *Flores,* iii, 171–72; Galloway, *Eleanor of Castile,* 12–19. Anne of Hohenburg's body, drawn by 40 horses, was escorted by friars, ladies in 3 coaches and 400 men, with copious distribution of alms (Pertz, ed., *Chron. Colmariense,* 253).

202. Shorter stages near London imply greater crowds, or that progress was coordinated to allow for preparations in London and Westminster. Edward's 1307 funeral took the same route in London (*Flores,* iii, 71–72; *Guisborough,* 379). It seems the Q's embalmed body was exposed (Anne of Hohenburg's face was treated with balsam but her coffin was closed [Pertz, ed., *Chron. Colmariense,* 253]). On Holy Trinity, *CPR 1281–1292,* 420. Charing was not named for Edward's "chère reine"; in 1257–58 Henry III paid a hermit at "Cherringe" 50s. for masses for his dau. Katherine (E 403/15A m. 3).

203. *Barnwell,* 226; *Flores,* iii, 171–72; *Osney,* 326; *Lanercost,* 137; Douie, *Pecham,* 323; *London,* 99; *Manners,* 103; *CHEC,* 88; *KW,* 482–83; Galloway, *Eleanor of Castile,* 30–31; Hinnebusch, *Early English Friars Preachers,* 44–45; Pertz, ed., *Chron. Colmariense,* 253–54. The writing was prob. an indulgence (J. C. Parsons, "Piety, Power," 120). On royal vestments, see Johnstone, "Queen's Household," Tout, *Chapters,* v, 249; Hope, "Funeral Effigies," 544; Blackley, "Isabella of France," 26. *Dunstable,* 363, says the Q was bur. "in sepulcro Henrici regis," prob. the grave near the high altar in which Henry III's body lay until May 1290 (Binski, "Cosmati at Westminster," 19–21).

204. J. C. Parsons, "Ritual and Symbol," and idem, "Queen's Intercession."

205. Lindley, "Romanticizing Reality," 82–83. The Eleanor crosses are discussed in Chapter Four.

206. Eales, "Game of Chess," 12–34; Cummins, *Hound and the Hawk,* chaps 2, 6–10. The liturgical vestments embroidered with the arms of the K and Q and those of various noble families, remarked earlier, also evoke a community of interests linking the couple and the aristocracy.

207. On "royal exchanges," Hayden, *Symbol and Privilege,* 130–46.

208. Staines, "Havelok the Dane," 621–22, 622 notes 41, 42.

209. *CHEC,* 44; compare above, note 93. On the sociopolitical significance of Qs' clothing, Hughes, "Regulating Women's Fashion," 138–40; Zanger, "Fashioning the Body Politic," 101–20; Zweig, *Marie Antoinette,* 13.

210. On the Crondall case, see above, note 123; the Q's relations with Southampton are discussed below, Chapter Two. See also Fradenburg, "Rethinking Queenship," 4–5; for Eleanor's Dominican patronage in this context, J. C. Parsons, "Piety, Power," 122–23. Tolley, "Eleanor of Castile and the 'Spanish' Style," suggests other Castilian customs the Q may have imported, though admitting (at 191) that his suggestions "may be too speculative for some." On Thomas of Brotherton's nurse, *Rishanger,* 438–39, and Prestwich, *Edward I,* 131 (it is not verifiable that the first nurse was French and her replacement English, but it is significant that nationality became part of the story).

211. *London,* 57, 59; *Rishanger,* 438–39.

212. *Glastonbury*, 245; J. C. Parsons, "Year of Eleanor of Castile's Birth," nos. 9, 11, and idem, "Of Queens, Courts, and Books"; *Flores*, iii, 44, 71; Riley, ed., *Opus Chronicorum*, 49–50. For kingdom, lineage, and reproduction, Kertzer, *Ritual, Politics and Power*, 46–47; Alcuin, *Epistolae*, no. xviii, remarked by Klaniczay, "Sacral Kingship to Self-Representation," (1986), 64–65; J. Nelson, "Inauguration Rituals," 63, 71; Spiegel, "Pseudo-Turpin," 214–17.
213. Staines, "Havelok the Dane," 621–22.
214. Collier, "Women in Politics," 89–96; J. M. Taylor, *Eva Perón*, 10–13, 145–46; Hanawalt, "Lady Honor Lisle's Networks," 188. On the terms authority, power, and influence, Rosaldo, "Woman, Culture and Society," 21, and Lamphere, "Strategies, Cooperation and Conflict," 99–100.
215. Ks' marriages are broadly treated by A. Crawford, "The King's Burden?" 33–56. See also J. C. Parsons, "Ritual and Symbol," 60–77, idem, "Mothers, Daughters," 63–78, idem, "Family, Sex, and Power," 3–4, and idem, "Queen's Intercession." To writings cited in Casagrande, "The Protected Woman," 78–79, compare Peter of Blois' letter to Eleanor of Aquitaine ca. 1173 (*PL* 207, cols. 448–49), and Pecham's 1283 letter to Eleanor of Castile (Martin, ed., *Reg. Peckham*, ii, 555).
216. On Eleanor of Castile's bed, J. C. Parsons, "Ritual and Symbol," 67–68. English Qs evidently formally announced royal births (W. Brown, ed., *Reg. Walter Giffard*, 101 [1266]; J. C. Parsons, "Year of Eleanor of Castile's Birth," 265 [1282]; Costain, *Three Edwards*, 134 [1312]; DeMolen, "The Birth of Edward VI," 362 [1537], 364 [1533]).
217. Compare her relations with Bogo de Clare (J. C. Parsons, "Piety, Power," 112–13).

CHAPTER TWO

1. *CPR 1272–1281*, 70; the 1273 appt is discussed further below.
2. Never crowned, Edward's second Q enjoyed all the perquisites of her office (Johnstone, "Queen's Household," Tout, *Chapters*, v, 239–41, 272–73; Prestwich, *Edward I*, 129–30). On coronations, J. C. Parsons, "Ritual and Symbol," 60–77; Dupront, "Sacre, autorité, pouvoir," 321; Richardson, "Coronation in Medieval England," 121–23 (the 1274 directory edited by Richardson at 197–202 barely notices the Q's presence); Stafford, *QCD*, 87, 127–34; L. G. W. Legg, ed., *English Coronation Records*, lvii–lix, 21–22, 37–39; Schramm, *English Coronation*, 29–30, 39–40, 60, 84–85; Nelson, "Inauguration Rituals," 283–307 (generous advice from Drs. Nelson and Stafford is gratefully acknowledged).
3. Ehrlich, *Proceedings*, 207; Cam, "Cases of Novel Disseisin," 104; "cum . . . domina Regina habuisset statum domini Regis" (JUST 1/1014 m. 11) was argued in 1291 to justify the Q's entry to a manor during another's term. See also Post, "*Status, id est, magistratus,*" 55–61, 74–75.
4. Prynne, *Aurum Reginae*, 23. The Q in 1283 ordered the sher. of Hants. to collect and pay her the issues of Redbridge hundred, as she testified at the 1285 *visus* (E 159/58 m. 21d). On 30 Dec. 1289 she told the sher. of Northumbs. to survey a Scottish manor assigned in dower to her cousin Isabella de Vescy (S.C. 1/30/50; *RP*, i, 48). For Chancery, Shirley, ed., *Letters*, no. 647, and *CPR 1268–1266*, 453, 458; her council is discussed further below. Compare Louis IX of France's restrictions on his wife (W. C. Jordan, *Louis IX*, 5–6).
5. Ehrlich, *Proceedings*, 206–11; Blackstone, *Commentaries*, i, 212–17. On the Q's lands, *CCIR 1279–1288*, 80–81; for gts and confs, below, Chapter Three, Appendix I, e.g., nos. 116a, 117, 120, 135a; see also *CChR*, ii, 353, 422, 423.
6. Johnstone, "Queen's Household," *English Government*, i, 289–90; Clanchy, "Return of Writs," 59–82; McIntosh, *Autonomy and Community*, 25. As dowager, Eleanor of Provence reminded the Chancellor that writs touching her dower should come to her (S.C. 1/23/13 [Aug. 1275]). Commissions will be cited in context; of unedited cases, e.g., E 159/50 m. 14d (E4 Edw.) orders the sher. of Soms. to inquire by oath what rents and issues come yearly from Somerton "per se, preter redditus et exitus pervenientes de

manerio de Somerton et quantum dicti redditus et exitus predicti hundredi per se valeant et pro quanto Karissima Consors Regis A. Regina Anglie . . . tradere possit idem hundredum ad firmam." Burnell on 16 Apr. 1283 ordered Kirkby to cause to be relaxed distr. upon the Q's men at Southampton as they were free of toll "per totum regnum" (S.C. 1/9/86).

7. *CPR 1232–1247*, 155; S.C. 1/30/49 (s.d., *temp.* Hen. III) orders the sher. of Beds. to distr. Chicksands priory who refuse to admit a nun pres. by the Q "ex antiqua et approbata consuetudine . . . racione sue noue creacionis." Abp Pecham's letter to Hedingham Priory about a woman sponsored by the Q possibly relates to a similar situation (discussed in Chapter One).

8. Prynne, *Aurum Reginae*; Blackstone, *Commentaries*, i, 213–16 (compare Hincmar, *De Ordine Palatii*, 74); Meyer, "Women and the Tenth-Century English Monastic Reform," 337–45, 354–61. It is tempting to connect that custom to Edgar's association of his wife Aelfthryth with English nunneries (Symons, ed. and trans., *Regularis concordia*, 2), but no evidence exists to support such conjecture.

9. For Anglo-Saxon royal dower in general, M. Meyer, "The Queen's 'Demesne'," noting at 82–84 almost complete discontinuity between the lands held by the Confessor's wife and those held by Matilda of Flanders; see also note 28 below. Lands of the Confessor's wife are badly indexed in Ellis, *General Introduction to Domesday*, ii, 81–83; see *Domesday*, i, 65.a2, 100.b2, 337.b2, and *VCH Soms.*, iv, 84. On ninth-century dowers, Keynes and Lapidge, *Alfred the Great*, 323 notes 86–89; Stafford, "King's Wife," 22–23. Twelfth-and thirteenth-century dowers are discussed further below.

10. Blackstone, *Commentaries*, i, 212–13; Klinck, "Anglo-Saxon Women and the Law," 114–18; M. Meyer, "Land Charters and the Legal Position of Anglo-Saxon Women," 60–1, 67–8, links such freedoms to the individual woman's social class. On Matilda of Flanders, Pollock and Maitland, *History of English Law*, ii, 407–8; Fauroux, ed., *Recueil des actes des ducs de Normandie*, nos. 197, 231; Musset, ed., *Les actes de Guillaume le Conquérant et de la reine*, no. 2.

11. Dower assignments' value is discussed further, below. Early French Qs sealed only as widows (Bedos-Rezak, "Women, Seals and Power," 63–64). English Qs' authority as regents is debated (Richardson and Sayles, *Governance*, 152–53, 162; Sayles, *Medieval Foundations*, 379; Hollister, "Viceregal Court of Henry I," 131–44). It should be emphasized that these regencies were effective only during the K's temporary absence; no widowed Q of England was ever formally constituted regent for her minor son.

12. For Matilda of Flanders, *RRAN*, i, no. 193; *Domesday*, i, 163.b2, 170a. For Edith-Matilda, *RRAN*, ii, xi, nos. 544, 571, 613, 624, 675, 971, 1108–9, 1190. For Adelicia, Brett, *English Church under Henry I*, 107. For Matilda of Boulogne, *RRAN*, iii, x, xiii, and nos. 117, 162, 195, 554, 830, 843.

13. On Matilda of Flanders, *RRAN*, i, nos. 26, 114, 135 (compare *Domesday*, i, 67.a2), 149–50, 183; *Domesday*, i, 36.b1 (compare Maitland, *Domesday Book and Beyond*, 69; R. A. Brown, *Origins of English Feudalism*, 44 note 63), 38.a1, 68.b1, 75.b1, 75.b2, 78.b1, 83.a2, 83.b1, 84.b2, 113.a1, 118.a2, 163.b2; Edith-Matilda, *RRAN*, ii, nos. 674, 676, 742), 743 (compare *Domesday*, i, 291.a2), 908–9 (compare no. 525); Adelicia of Louvain, *RRAN*, iii, nos. 140, 220, 679, 697, 793; Matilda of Boulogne, *RRAN*, iii, nos. 24–26, 149, 194–95, 221–22, 243, 511–12, 843.

14. R. H. C. Davis, *King Stephen*, 37, 48–50, 62–64; Stafford, *QCD*, 49–50, 99–114, 161; Enright, "Lady with a Mead-cup," 194–97; *Constitutio Domus Regis*, in Johnson, *Dialogus*, 129–35.

15. Delisle and Berger, eds., *Recueil*, intr. 171–74; Eyton, *Court, Household and Itinerary*, 6–7; Richardson and Sayles, *Governance*, 153–54; Richardson, "Letters and Charters," 195–99; Gibbs, ed., *Early Charters of St. Paul's*, no. 48; Davies and Landon, eds., *Cartae Antiquae Rolls*; M. G. Cheney, "Geoffrey de Lucy," 750–63. Few of her acts for England date from Henry's reign, but see Delisle and Berger, *Recueil*, i, no. 45; most of her acts

in Teulet, ed., *Layettes*, i–iv, date from after 1189 and involve only her Aquitanian lands.

16. Richardson, "Letters and Charters," 195, 198 note 6, is unreliable on dower. That in 1183 she visited manors she later held in dower implies neither that she held them bef. 1173 nor that Henry had restored them; nor does her 1184 visit to Berkhampstead prove it was then in her hands. Exeter and its fair, Lifton, Kenton and Wyke were "in manu regis" four years after Richardson thinks they were restored (Round, ed., *Pipe 33 Henry II*, 143, 147–48), but see Stenton, ed., *Pipe 9 Richard I*, 4, and idem, ed., *Pipe 10 Richard I*, 177). See also Warren, *Henry II*, 217–18, 272–74.

17. Eyton, *Court, Household and Itinerary*, e.g., 50–51, and index p. 321 s.v. "England, Eleanor queen of;" Richardson, "Letters and Charters," 200; Johnson, ed., *Dialogus*, 123; Timson, ed., *Cartulary of Blyth Priory*, lxxxiii, 349 (on Jordan, see "Letters and Charters," 198); Richardson and Sayles, *Governance*, 153–54.

18. The Qs prob. apptd that clk (Johnson, ed., *Dialogus*, 122–23; Richardson, "Letters and Charters," 208–9, 210–11); the office is discussed further below. Most of Eleanor of Aquitaine's personnel are known only from her charters for Aquitaine ("Letters and Charters," 193–213; Delisle and Berger, eds., *Recueil*, i, nos. 23–24, 74, 278, 495, 508).

19. On Berengaria, C. R. Cheney and M. G. Cheney, eds., *Letters of Innocent III*, nos. 210, 217–19, 355, 531, 580–81, 765–66, 789, 836, 868, 1022, 1050–52; Bliss, i, 15, 18, 29, 33, 35, 42, 43, 48, 54, 77, 78, 82; *Foedera*, i, 84, 94, 97, 126, 137–38, 140, 161; *Waverley*, 278; Howden, iv, 164, 172–73. On Isabella, *CRR*, viii, 184, ix, 172 (Eleanor of Aquitaine and Berengaria do not appear in *CRR*); on her dower see further below, and *Foedera*, i, 88, 166, 183. John in 1207 made collection of queen-gold incumbent on the Exch. but perhaps kept it himself (Richardson, intr. to Stenton, ed., *Mem. Roll I John*, xxxix, xcvj; Howell, "Resources of Eleanor of Provence," 373 note 3, 376). See also Carpenter, *Minority of Henry III*, 44, 47, 155, 167; *Foedera*, i, 148.

20. Facinger, "A study of Medieval Queenship," 32–33, 36, 45–47, sees similar developments in France at the same time, for the same reasons. Henry III's 1242 testament named his wife regent should he die in Edward's minority (the late Rev. Michael M. Sheehan, C.S.B., generously shared his typescript text of this will); compare *CPR 1232–1247*, 244, 280, 294, and *CIR 1251–1253*, 480, 497.

21. Bracton, *De Legibus*, fol. 5 (ed. Woodbine and Thorne, ii, 33); Kantorowicz, "Kingship," 89–109; Strayer, "Laicisation," 103–15. On ritual, Brückmann, "English Coronations"; J. Legg, ed., *Three Coronation Orders*, 63; L. G. W. Legg, ed., *English Coronation Records*, 38–39; J. C. Parsons, "Ritual and Symbol," 60–77, and idem, "The Queen's Intercession." A directory for the 1274 coronation barely notices the Q (Richardson, "Coronation in Medieval England," 190–202).

22. *CPR 1266–1272*, 682; Howell, "Resources of Eleanor of Provence," 387–88. Miss Howell informs me that an enrolled account of Eleanor of Provence's wardrobe suggests this system was adopted by 1239–40 (E 372/83 m. 7). Queen-gold revenues contributed to expenses both in and out of court.

23. Paris, *CM*, v, 299; Treharne and Sanders, eds., *Documents of the Baronial Movement*, 78–79; Howell, "Resources of Eleanor of Provence," 378–79, 385–86. Henry also denied her advs on her dower lands (*CChR*, i, 218), implying concern lest occasions for patronage be lost to his hs; compare his tardiness in gting her lands in fee, below. From 1266 she was, in some cases, allowed to present to chs on lands held in wardship (*CPR 1258–1266*, 574; *CPR 1266–1272*, 372, 682).

24. Howell, "Resources of Eleanor of Provence," 389–90; Wolffe, *Royal Demesne*, 52–53. For correspondence on Eleanor of Provence's lands I am grateful to Miss Howell, who suggests that Eleanor's Franciscan sympathies shaped her attitude to the Jews, expelled in 1275 from her dower towns (*CPR 1281–1292*, 76; *Bury*, 61; the Expulsion of 1290 was also imputed to her influence [*Waverley*, 409]); Richardson, *English Jewry*, 131, regards her attitude toward the Jews as a financial sacrifice on her part. Whether

Eleanor of Castile's Dominican sympathies shaped her relations with the Jewry is considered further in Chapter Three.

25. In 1256–57 Eleanor surr. lands of Roger de Toeny and the e. of Devon (GEC, iv, 318–20, xii.1, 771–73; CPR 1232–1247, 283; CPR 1247–1258, 151); new wardships soon replaced them (CPR 1247–1258, 536, 540, 574, 614), but the losses may relate to an increase in the K's subsidies to her wardrobe (Ramsay, Dawn of the Constitution, 295, and critique of these figures by Howell, "Resources of Eleanor of Provence," 373, 387, 390–91). There was the further disadvantage that her bfs were repeatedly uprooted and resettled on new lands.

26. MacFarlane, "Had Edward I a 'Policy'?" 145–59; Prestwich, Edward I, 103–4; Wolffe, Royal Demesne, 53–54.

27. Detailed accts exist only for 1296–97, after the Q's exors returned her lands to the K (S.C. 6/1090/4). Dr. James Masschaele has prepared a transcript of these; it is hoped they will be published in the near future.

28. Foedera, i, 88 (compare Eleanor's death [Apr.], Isabella's charter [May], and C. R. Cheney and M. G. Cheney, eds., Letters of Innocent III, no. 580); Howden, iii, 27; Oxenden, 73. Norman lands are not considered here. Edith-Matilda, Adelicia, and Matilda of Boulogne held Waltham (RRAN, ii, nos. 525, 1986, and iii, nos. 915, 917); Adelicia and Eleanor of Aquitaine held Wilton (RRAN, iii, no. 793; Stenton, ed., Pipe 4 John, 122); Eleanor held Ilchester, Exeter with its fair and Lifton (Pipe 4 John, 84, 244). Anglo-Saxon dowers were noted earlier; Edith (d. 1075) held Grantham and Lifton (Domesday, i, 100.b2, 337.b2), the former assigned to Eleanor of Castile in 1254 (below, Chapter Three, Appendix I nos. 129–30). Berengaria's claim is Bliss, i, 33, seemingly based on a lost earlier assignment; note that Arundel had remained with Adelicia's issue by her second husband (GEC, i, 233–35), Eleanor of Aquitaine had gtd Lifton to John's nurse (M. G. Cheney, "Geoffrey de Lucy," 759–60), and Eustace of Boulogne held Martock by 1125 (VCH Soms., iv, 84–85), perhaps by gt of Edith-Matilda whose sister he m. As the Domesday lands held by Matilda of Flanders incl. virtually none of those in the later charters, and as Adelicia was the last dowager to hold Arundel, the basis of Eleanor of Aquitaine's assignment (and Berengaria's claim) was almost certainly Edith-Matilda's assignment; given Henry II's emphasis on his right to the throne as Henry I's grandson, he would naturally adopt the assignment made to the latter's wives.

29. Isabella of Angoulême's dower was confiscate in 1236; Henry III allowed for the possibility she might recover it (Foedera, i, 219; CChR, ii, 218; CPR 1266–1272, 736–37, where the first "£10,000" is an error). The amount is identical to that Henry meant his wife to have in wardships to support herself out of court. Lands in Gascony, not dealt with here, replaced the lost Norman lands. On Berengaria, Foedera, i, 84, 161; Howden, iv, 172–73; CLR, i, 2, 33–34, 79, 104, 133, 153. Compare the £900 estimated for Edith's lands (Barlow, Edward the Confessor, 74).

30. When Edward I betr. a son to the h. of Navarre in 1273, she was promised 1000 marks' dower (Foedera, i, 508). On royal households, Treharne and Sanders, eds., Documents of the Baronial Movement, 110; Bury, 31; cont. Gervase of Canterbury, 249. For the 1262 and 1275 dower assignments, CPR 1266–1272, 736–37 (though Isabella of Angoulême was dead, the 1262 dower was unrelated to twelfth-century lands); CChR, ii, 192–93. English Qs were dowered with £4500 into the fourteenth century (Johnstone, "Queen's Household," Tout, Chapters, v, 281).

31. Grain from three manors in 1283 fetched 300 marks (E 159/56 m. 5d); that from Acton Turville £9:1:4 in 15 Edw., and from Ringwood, £20:4:4¾ (S.C. 6/1089/22 mm. 1, 2). Grain from Upton was sold "in grosso" in 1290 for £9, and from Stanmore for £12:5:4 (S.C. 6/1089/25 m. 1). The accts distinguish these sums from "exitus manerii" entries. Dr. James Masschaele notes that the 1296–97 accounts (S.C. 6/1090/4) show seeding rates almost double normal rates at the time; compare Stacey, "Agricultural Investment and the Management of the Royal Demesne Manors," 928–32.

32. JUST 1/836 *m*. 4d (Scottow owed 50 measures of barley and 50*s*., changed to £10 yearly, £25 in arrears by 1290); Bates, ed., *Cartularies of Muchelney and Athelney*, 91–92, 99–100. Neighbors in the New Forest were burdened with rents of grain formerly offered as gifts to the foresters (JUST 1/1014 *mm*. 8d *bis*, 12). For ejections and usurpations, below, Chapter Three, Appendix I nos. 27, 28, 48b–c, 92, 93, 96, 101, 105d, 107a–b, 116d, f–j, 197b.

33. Below, Chapter Three, Appendix I nos. 73–74; JUST 1/1149 *mm*. 9, 8. At Hope and Overton, coparceners were ejected, one from an eighteenth share (JUST 1/1149 *m*. 8 *bis*, 6). At Bockingfold the water to Michael de Elhurst's mill was diverted to the Q's; a weir was put up at Horstead so the abbess of Caen was left high and dry (JUST 1/542 *m*. 13d; JUST 1/836 *m*. 3d). Dr. Masschaele notes careful attention to the mills on the Q's manors in 1296–97 (S.C. 6/1090/4).

34. *CChyV*, 273; *CChR*, ii, 368. A 1291 complaint stated that a bf impeded tenants at Overton from going to market (JUST 1/1149 *m*. 6d); compare Stewart-Brown, ed., *Rolls of Chester*, 214, 215, 230, 239. Eleanor acq. interests in the ports of Lyme Regis, Melcombe Regis, Swanage, Sandwich, Southampton and Milford Haven (below, Chapter Three, Appendix I nos. 48a–b, 50–51, 86, 120, 177). On her interest in trade at Milford Haven, *RP*, i, 84, 138–42; W. Rees, *South Wales and the March*, 40–41; John, *Pembrokeshire*, 60–63; Soulsby, *Towns of Medieval Wales*, 139–42.

35. On horses, *CHEC*, 76, 95; compare *CCIR 1279–1288*, 516. In 1282 she was gtd Baldwin Wake's stud (*CCIR 1279–1288*, 166–68, 322; S.C. 1/29/205 [s.d.] informs her on those animals, one seized by the abp of York). S.C. 6/1089/25 *m*. 1 shows horses sold for £15:16:6 in 1290, noted like the sale of grain separately from "exitus manerii." For sheep, J. C. Parsons, "English Administration in Ponthieu," 400. The raising of rents is discussed further below.

36. Stagg, *CNFD*, i, nos. 92–141; *CPR 1281–1292*, 229, 398; *CChyV*, 368.

37. On the forest, *CPR 1266–1272*, 367 (arrears paid, M1273 [E 159/48 *m*. 2]; quittance of one such debt, June 1274 [C 62/50 *m*. 5]); *CCIR 1279–1288*, 19, 24 (order for quittance for payment, M1281 [E 159/55 *m*. 2]). For hundreds, *CIR 1264–1268*, 472; *CIR 1268–1272*, 12–13; *CCIR 1279–1288*, 93 (= E 159/54 *m*. 7d "hac vice"); *CCIR 1279–1288*, 341–42 (= E 159/59 *m*. 16d). E 101/505/19 *m*. 2 shows £40 "pro exitibus Hundredi de Sutherpyngham' de Itinere S. de Roff' anno . . . xiiij"; in 14 Edw. she received £19:11:9 from the eyre at Somerton (S.C. 6/1089/22 *m*. 2; no gt is known). For 13–14 Edw., *Records 1286–1289*, nos. 3061, 3069–70, 3075.

38. Advs are discussed further below; for wards, below, Chapter Three, Appendix I nos. 116a note 125, 149, 190 note 139, 191c note 140.

39. Prynne, *Aurum Reginae*; Howell, "Resources of Eleanor of Provence," 373–74. Stacey, *Politics, Policy and Finance*, 145 note 62, says gold was exacted on a Jewish tallage only once under Henry III, but see *CIR 1254–1256*, 24; for temp. Edward I, e.g., *CPEJ*, iii, 57, and iv, 42; *CCIR 1272–1279*, 198; *CCIR 1279–1281*, 80–81; E 9/29 *m*. 8d (M1278), where Benedict de Wintonia pays gold on a tallage from 2 Edw. (= *CPEJ*, v, no. 823). Richardson, "Letters and Charters," 209–11, gives undue weight to the fact that the earliest undoubted reference to queen-gold is from *temp*. Henry II (Barnes, ed., "The Anstey Case," 22; Richardson, intr. to Stenton, ed., *Mem. Roll 1 John*, xxxix and note 2). Compare Howell, "Resources of Eleanor of Provence," 373 note 3.

40. Johnson, ed., *Dialogus*, 122–23; Madox, *History and Antiquities*, 240–41; Hall, ed., *Red Book*, iii, 759–60; Howell, "Resources of Eleanor of Provence," 378–79.

41. *Records 1286–1289*, nos. 3056–3100 (14 Edw.), E 101/505/19 (15 Edw.), E101/505/20 (16 Edw.); S.C. 6/1089/25 *mm*. 6–7 are fragm. for 18 Edw. In addition to payments identified here, Eleanor's queen-gold accts carried sums from the Exch. of the Jews and payment of debts to the Jewry (e.g., *Records 1286–1289*, nos. 3086, 3087, 3095, 3102). The relationship between the Q's clk responsible for queen-gold and the Exch. of the Jews is analyzed below.

42. E 159/50 *m.* 8d: "*Baronibus pro Auro Regine.* Rex mandat eisdem quandam cedulam coram se et consilio suo super auro Regine prouiso ordinatam presentibus interclusam mandat et [sic] eisdem quod ea que super hoc prouisa sunt et ordinata decetero firmiter obseruari faciant etcetera"; the text is in Madox, *History and Antiquities,* 241 note "m" (9 July 1276). Orders touching tenths and twentieths issued in 8, 9, 10 and 13 Edw. (E 159/53 *m.* 6d; E 159/54 *m.* 5d; E 159/55 *m.* 3d *bis*; E 159/58 *m.* 5d).

43. The first such gt appears to be of 30 marks from Dartmouth and Totness, amerced for contempt in 55 Henry III (E 368/44 *m.* 8d). A brief sample shows Robert Lucas of Guildford ackn. £16:16:3, H1275 (E 159/59 *m.* 24d); Thomas de Sandwiz' 60 marks, T1275 (E 159/59 *m.* 26d, with a later note of payment); Robert de Mucegros 20 marks, Sept. 1279 (*CCIR 1272–1279,* 574); Elias de Hauville 10 marks, M1283 (E 159/57 *m.* 11). For fitz Alan (of Wolverton), *CPR 1272–1281,* 96. See also *CCIR 1272–1279,* 394, 448, 543.

44. *CPR 1281–1292,* 62; in H1284 the K reminded the Exch. that he also gtd the Q all silver plate pertaining to such concealment, and ordered a search for information on such goods, to be given to her goldkpr (E 159/57 *m.* 4). A 1280 gt from the issues of transgressions of coin brought her 300 marks (*CCIR 1279–1288,* 19). See also *CFR,* i, 216; *CPR 1281–1292,* 184; *CPR 1281–1292,* 173, 193, 213; *CCLR 1288–1296,* 91, 224–25. In M1284 Simon de Stanbrigg', chaplain, ackn. he owed the Q £10 for concealing such chattels (E 159/58 *m.* 13d). S.C. 1/30/53 (Blanquefort, 10 Jan. [1287]), is the Q's letter to Solomon de Rocestre, K's justice for the Jews, thanking him for pains on her affairs over such chattels and ordering him to take as his assoc. the K's justice William de Carleton in place of Henry le Galeys; S.C. 1/30/53A (anon. to William de Hamelton, s.d.), clearly related to the last, orders that "Hagin" (i.e., Hagin f. Cress, "the Q's Jew") be told of these provisions and that Carleton have his warrant to act as the Q directs.

45. Martin, ed., *Reg. Peckham,* ii, 767–68, and iii, 937–38; Johnstone, "Queen's Household," Tout, *Chapters,* v, 270; Roth, *History of the Jews in England,* chaps 3–4; Richardson, *English Jewry,* 107; Postan, *Medieval Economy and Society,* 183–84. Whether the Q exacted usury on such debts is considered in Chapter Three.

46. Picciotto, "Legal Position of the Jews," 69–70, 73; Painter, *Studies in the History of the English Feudal Barony,* 186–88. Eleanor, of course, obtained additional debts since queen-gold was exacted when the Jewry was tallaged (as noted earlier).

47. On Burgh, *CCIR 1272–1279,* 221, 497; *CPEJ,* iii, 64–65; below, Chapter Three, Appendix I no. 151a; on the others, Chapter Three, Appendix I nos. 63, 115, 116, 159. The likelihood is discussed below in chap. 3 that the Q was gtd these debts precisely in order that she might obtain specific manors. For the 1279 gts, *CPEJ,* ii, 310; E 9/33 *m.* 6–6d; Chapter Three, Appendix I nos. 63, 139, 159a.

48. E 9/34 *m.* 6 (sher. of Beds. said the writ was late and was ordered for the quinz. of Easter); on Thurgarton, E 9/35 *m.* 4d (the prior held land lately of one indebted to Elias, but pr. Elias promised to pay the Q and was quit).

4 9. For Ayswell, E 9/36 *m.* 3d, and for Neofmarche, Chapter Three, Appendix I no. 139. On Muscegros, below, Chapter Three, Appendix I no. 191c note 140; *RP,* i, 2 (where "un Grey" is prob. misread for "un Gieu" or the like); the Q was prosecuting for these debts, totalling £80, T1280 (E 13/8 *m.* 25; Robert's petn in *RP* says £90). His mother's 1291 complaint is JUST 1/542 *m.* 12. See also Craster and Thornton, eds., *Chronicle of St. Mary's,* 21; E 9/45 *m.* 2. *Dunstable,* 290, notes that house's payments for queen-gold in 1282, but it is unclear if further payments there "pro defaltis de Judaismo" were owed the Q or the Exch. Other houses owing the Q Jewish debts incl. Carrow Priory, E1281 (E 9/66 *m.* 5) and Spalding Priory, Bardeney Abbey, and Halsey Park Priory, M1284 (E 9/45 *m.* 2 ter).

50. For the payments mentioned, *CPEJ,* iii, 123; E 9/44 *m.* 7d, E 9/36 *m.* 8d, E 9/45 *m.* 3d. For one debt paid at the wardrobe and another the Q pardoned, *CHEC,* 63, 123; for other pardons, *CCIR 1279–1288,* 271, and E 9/44 *m.* 7d, where Nicholas de Menil is

pardoned 50 marks of his debt. The Jews too were slow to pay (e.g., *Records 1286–1289*, no. 3058). The Nicholas Tregoz mentioned here was among those whose debts to Hagin f. Cress came to the Q in T1275 (*CPEJ*, ii, 310); he was a kinsman of the John Tregoz who conveyed a Sussex manor to the Q in 1282, a transaction unrelated to Nicholas' debts (below, Chapter Three, Appendix I no. 219). Evidence that the Q exacted usury on the Jewish debts she collected is considered in chap. 3, below.

51. The various prests are respectively C 47/4/1 fol. 16; E 101/352/12 fols. 2, 16v; E 101/352/21 *m.* 4; *CPR 1272–1281*, 193, 422; Lysons, ed., "Roll of Expenses," 50. For alms, C 47/4/4 fol. 42v (her personal alms in 1289–90 totaled £74:2:0: *CHEC*, 63–135). On the confinement, BL, Add. 36762 *m.* 6. The 1282–83 figure is from Lysons, ed., "Roll of Expenses," 50 (not a wardrobe sum, but for the *hospicium*). The only other sources are enrolled accts of the K's wardrobe which give global figures, e.g., in 3 Edw.: "in expensis Regis et Regine quando fuit in Curia per totum predictum tempus . . . . viij. mill'.xlvj.li.vj.s.xvj.d. [sic] sicut continetur in rotulo de particulis" (E 372/119 *m.* 22).

52. For chamber maintenance and attendants' robes, E 372/124 *mm.* 24, 30; E 372/138 *m.* 26. A writ of *liberate* in 9 Edw. for allocations to a retiring kpr of the K's wardrobe notes the decision to give money not cloth for servants' robes (C 62/57 *m.* 4). For robes, E 372/124 *m.* 30 (7–8 Edw.); E 101/351/17 *m.* 3 (13 Edw.); *Records 1285–1286*, no. 1717 (14 Edw.); E 101/351/25 *m.* 3 (15 Edw., damaged); BL, Add. roll 6710 *m.* 2 (16 Edw., £290:13:4); *Records 1286–1289*, no. 2941 (17 Edw.); E 101/352/24 *m.* 3 (18 Edw.). The robe, shoe and oblation accts indicate payment from the K's wardrobe to individual svts; funds for her chamber and attendants' robes were paid to the Q. Her extant wardrobe accts contain only one pertinent entry showing that a knt's summer robe in 1290 cost her £2:13:4 (*CHEC*, 110).

53. Sharpe, ed., *Letter-Books of the City of London: A*, 224; *CHEC*, 59–63 (incl. sale of a brooch, cup, and sturgeon given by King's Lynn). Louis IX forbade his wife to accept gifts of importance (W. C. Jordan, *Louis IX*, 6).

54. *CDI*, i, nos. 1490, 1634, 1801, 2056, 2088, and ii, no. 807; *CPR 1281–1292*, 67, 419; Lawlor, *Fasti of St. Patrick's*, 124; *Records 1286–1289*, nos. 3153, 3243, 3255; Cole, ed., *Documents Illustrative of English History*, xix); *CHEC*, 123. For her Irish lands, below, intr. to Chapter Three, Appendix I; *CPR 1272–1281*, 74; *CDI*, i, no. 1535, and ii, nos. 169, 608, 693, 796; *CHEC*, 84, 155; Sayles, ed., *Select Cases, ii*, 128.

55. *CPR 1272–1281*, 106, 156; *RG*, ii, nos. 189–90, 487, 1130–31, and iii, nos. 2009, 2019, 2023–26, 2028; Trabut-Cussac, *L'administration anglaise*, 61–64.

56. J. C. Parsons, "English Administration in Ponthieu," 371–403.

57. E 372/143 *m.* 36. Refs are given to surviving subordinate accounts.

58. The original acct for 17 Edw. is E 101/352/13 (*Records 1286–1289*, nos. 3229–3246); that for 16 Edw., E 101/352/11 (*Records 1286–1289*, nos. 3206–3228). Both are damaged and are missing details of receipt; the first membrane of E 101/352/13 is altogether lost.

59. The original queen-gold acct for 14 Edw. is E 101/505/18 (*Records 1286–1289*, nos. 3056–3104); the two follg gold accts, E 101/505/19 and 20, are unedited. The original acct of expns is E 101/352/7 (*Records 1286–1289*, nos. 3105–3205), also beginning with the deficit of £144:6:8 (total expns were £5120:18:7, not £5120:18:8 as in no. 3205).

60. The original is BL, Add. 35294 (*CHEC*, 59–135).

61. The original, S.C. 6/1089/25 *mm.* 3–4, is filed with accts for issues of the Q's lands in 18 Edw. and two fragm. of queen-gold receipts in that year. Continuity between E 101/352/7 (*Records 1286–1289*, nos. 3105–3205) and S.C. 6/1089/25 *mm.* 3–4 is beyond doubt; the first paragraph of the latter is virtually identical to the last paragraph of the former (duplicate entries, in the order in which they appear in S.C. 6/1089/25 *m.* 4, are *Records 1286–1289*, nos. 3205, 3191, 3194, 3203, 3194, 3195, 3204, 3192, 3201, 3196, 3197, 3198. 3199, 3200).

62. The exors' accts are *Manners*, 95–139. Some legacies may have remained unpaid: *CClR 1307–1313*, 481; Johnstone, ed., *Letters*, 40 (compare *RP*, i, 477), 69–70; Cole, ed., *Documents Illustrative of English History*, 33.

63. A roll of daily expns of the Q's household at Rhuddlan in late summer 1282 (E 101/684/62/1) is too dilapidated to offer any pertinent information.

64. *Records 1286–1289*, nos. 3146, 3156, 3163. Bef. 16 Edw. the only relevant sources show that between 26 Apr. and 8 May 1286, the abbot of Westm. acting as Q's treas. sent to her wardrobe £175:1:10¾; her permanent treas. sent £66:13:4 (Westm. Abbey, muniments 23627 dorse; *Records 1286–1289*, no. 3112). The relationship between the wardrobe and the *liberaciones* is discussed further below; see also Howell, "Resources of Eleanor of Provence," 373–74, 391–92.

65. Westm. Abbey, muniments 23627; see Harvey, *Westminster Abbey*, 31–32.

66. S.C. 6/1089/22; S. C. 6/1089/23; S.C. 6/1089/25 *mm*. 1–2.

67. I am grateful to Dr. Brand for the latter suggestion; unfortunately, the fragmented queen-gold acct for 18 Edw. cannot confirm it.

68. Wardrobe expns for the twelve months Mich. 1289–Mich. 1290 were £924:16:6¼ (*CHEC*, 63–122); to these were added expns for the last weeks of the Q's life and her funeral procession (30 Sept.–30 Dec. 1290), totaling £224:6:8 (*CHEC*, 123–35).

69. Extent and yield seldom agreed even for royal widows (Johnstone, "Queen's Household," Tout, *Chapters*, v, 282). After the K's death, moreover, the Q would have to supply her household's food; consuming the yield of her manors might meet that need, but would reduce amounts available for sale and thus lessen revenue. Among reversions outstanding in 1290 was that to Matthew fitz John's lands, extended at £500 (below, Chapter Three, Appendix I no. 42).

70. *CPR 1272–1281*, 79; Johnstone, "Queen's Household," Tout, *Chapters*, v, 272.

71. *CHEC*, 62; the loans were repaid in 1290 (S.C. 6/1089/25 *mm*. 3, 4).

72. *CPR 1272–1281*, 79; E 159/55 *m*. 17d (for which the Riccardi's letters of receipt are S.C. 1/24/1, s.d.); E 159/60 *m*. 3. The barons of the Exch. in M1286 were to view her accts with the Riccardi who cl. an error of 50 marks in their last reckoning with her; on 21 May 1287 a bag sealed by the Treas., containing accts viewed on this matter, was returned to her auditor and steward (E 159/60 *mm*. 3, 7). For payments 1286–89, *Records 1286–1289*, nos. 3131, 3143, 3157, 3175, 3180, and two payments of 500 marks in S.C. 6/1089/25 *m*. 3; E 372/143 *m*. 36 (the total is £2820:19:10½). The Riccardi seem to have been the Q's "official" bankers (*CPR 1272–1281*, 422 does not pr. she borrowed from a Venetian). With the exception of one notice of 350 marks Eleanor owed Elias f. Moses of London in H1275, canceled as Elias owed the K that sum on a tallage (E159/49 *m*. 7d), there is no hint that the Q borrowed from the Jewry. The reason for her debt to Elias is not stated; it might have arisen as a loan from him but could, for example, have resulted from the Q's agreement to pay a third party's debts to Elias.

73. Above, Chapter One note 54; *CPR 1272–1281*, 79.

74. A tallage on Kingsthorpe gtd her by Henry III was fully paid only in 1287 (*CClR 1279–1288*, 386; E 159/60 *m*. 3d); the queen-gold acct for 18 Edw. has arrears from 10 Edw. (S.C. 6/1089/25 *mm*. 6–7). In the absence of a longer series of accts it must be assumed that as the Q's clks used the "Westminster" form, "arrears" are prob. sums owing from earlier accts (Denholm-Young, *Seignorial Administration*, 151–54; Oschinsky, ed., *Walter of Henley*, 218–19).

75. Or the Templars. S.C. 1/11/108 (anon, s.d, *temp*. Edw. I) begins: "ma dame le tresorier du temple de pariz nous tient mult court pour cink cenz et quarante neuf livres de paris keus nous li devons" and urges she obtain the K's letters asking the treas. of the Temple that "de la terre [?Ponthieu] les peussons convenablement lever." *Records 1286–1289*, no. 3125, shows 100 marks paid the Temple via the Luccans M1286; did she borrow at Paris in the spring of 1286? *Records 1286–1289*, no. 3099 is an E1286 loan of 200 marks from the Hospital of St. John in England.

76. E 372/143 m. 36, in the exors' summary of queen-gold, 18 Edw. (below, Chapter Three, Appendix I no. 172.) Edward's order to repay her the £100 lent Tybotot is C 62/65 m. 7, her loan to Huberto Douchy of the Rembertini, S.C. 6/1089/25 m. 4. Gifts among the *liberaciones* for 1286–89 totaled £1422:6:3½ of the total £4976 (*Records 1286–1289*, nos. 3105–3205). Gifts from the wardrobe 1289–90 were £300:8:10½ of total expns of £924:16:6¼ (*CHEC*, 63–122). But a partial total of *dona*, loans, and *maritagia* in the damaged *liberaciones* acct for 1289–90 is £3385:7:7 of the total £4937 given in the exors' summary (S.C. 6.1089/25 mm. 3–4). The lesser amount in 1286–89 may reflect the Q's absence from England, the higher total in 1289–90 the need to reassert her presence through patronage after her return.

77. The £2666:13:4 prob. incl. the 1000 marks she gave him in 1289 (*Records 1286–1289*, nos. 3189, 3245 bis). S.C. 1/32/51 is indexed as payments to the Q's wardrobe in 10 Edw., but deliveries in her wardrobe of £225 to Thomas de Gonneys and £100 to another clk do not connect the document to her. It is in fact a list of receipts of the K's wardrobe (compare Lysons, ed., "Roll of Expenses," 32–33, where the payments from lady de Baliol, the lord of Greystoke and the abbot of Glastonbury are identical to S.C. 1/32/51).

78. The 500 marks paid for the manor of Leeds (*CCIR 1279–1288*, 80) were by installments, 1278 (*CCIR 1272–1279*, 499 bis); for a 1287 case, below, Chapter Three, Appendix I no. 99. Compare provision for Maud de Fiennes' dowry, 1275, and perhaps for Margaret de Fiennes' dowry, 1286 (below, Chapter Three, Appendix I nos. 196b, 214, and note 120). The financial side of the Q's 1280 agreement with Piers de Montfort for his son's marr. and her payment of Piers' debts (*CCIR 1279–1288*, 52) implies a long-term arrangement: Piers ackn. he owed her 50 marks, E1281 (E 159/54 m. 21, the reason unstated); in H1286 she owed £108:13:4 to four of Piers' creditors incl. Walter de Langeton and Baroncino Gualteri (E 159/59 m. 6d).

79. On Aelfthryth, Whitelock, ed., *English Historical Documents*, i, no. 120. For Matilda, *Domesday*, i, 86.b1; *RRAN*, i, xxv and no. 193. On Edith-Matilda, *RRAN*, ii, xi and nos. 632, 675, 1090, 1108–9; Johnson, *Dialogus*, 129–35. For Matilda of Boulogne, *RRAN*, iii, x, xiii, and nos. 117, 162, 195, 554, 830, 843.

80. Stubbs, ed., *Gesta Regis Henrici*, i, 43; Richardson, intr. to Stenton, ed., *Mem. Roll I John*, lxxxiii. On Eleanor's regencies, ibid., lxviii and note 4; Richardson, "Letters and Charters," 208–9; Gibbs, ed., *Early Charters of St. Paul's*, no. 48. For Isabella's steward, Stenton, ed., *Mem. Roll I John*, 47.

81. *CLR*, i, 303; *CIR 1237–1242*, 342; *CPR 1242–1247*, 152, 237; *CIR 1247–1251*, 305; *CIR 1251–1253*, 344–45; Johnstone, "Queen's Household," Tout, *Chapters*, v, 233–36.

82. For Bartholomew, *CPR 1258–1266*, 244, *CPR 1266–1272*, 243, and *CCIR 1272–1279*, 385. On Meleford, *CIR 1259–1261*, 137, *CPR 1258–1266*, 220, and *CPR 1266–1272*, 617. For later developments, below, Chapter Three, Appendix I no. 37 (compare *CIM*, i, no. 1184); *CPR 1258–1266*, 420; Shirley, ed., *Royal Letters*, no. 547. Her clks are discussed further below, as regards her central administration.

83. Tout, *Chapters*, i, 162, and ii, 42; Johnstone, "Queen's Household," Tout, *Chapters*, v, 236, and *English Government*, i, 294–95; *CHEC*, 154 note; Prestwich, *Edward I*, 134–69. What follows is indebted to Mertes, *English Noble Household*; Given-Wilson, *Royal Household*, 1–28, sketches the K's household but not the Q's.

84. BL, Add 36762 m. 3; E 101/372/5 m. 1; E 101/351/17 m. 3; *Records 1285–1286*, nos. 978, 1708–18; *Records 1286–1289*, no. 1451, nos. 2937–39, 2941; BL, Add. roll 6710; E 101/352/24 m. 3 and C 47/4/5 fol. 38–38v. On "squire," "serjeant" and "yeoman," *CHEC*, 156–57; Mertes, *English Noble Household*, 26–31. Here "squire" is used for *scutifer*, "serjeant" for *serviens*, "yeoman" for *vallettus*, "attendant" or "courtier" for those of knightly rank, "servant" for lesser workers.

85. For the wardrobe, E 101/352/24 m. 3, but see *CHEC*, 157–58. The Easter ransom was noted in Chapter One; on the Q's women in 1289–90, *CHEC*, 155–56 (the last four

domicille were not attendants). Compare Andrivète's seven women in *Escanor*, written for Eleanor in the 1280s (Michelant, ed., *Der Roman von Escanor*, II. 9771–73, at 258). The dairymaid was noted earlier, in Chapter One.

86. Roger fl. 1264, d. 1272 (Bliss, i, 412–13; Davis, ed., *Rot. Gravesend*, 224). Bartholomew de Haye fl. 1268–77 (*CPR 1258–1266*, 224; *CPR 1266–1272*, 243; E 101/350/5 m. 4 [1273–74]; E 101/350/23 m. 1 [Nov. 1276]; *CCIR 1272–1279*, 385). Payn de Exonia *als* de Chaworth fl. 1275–1284 (*CPR 1272–1281*, 78; E 101/350/23 m. 1; C 47/4/1 fol. 36v ["de Chaworth"]; *CPR 1272–1281*, 364; E 101/351/15). Nicholas de Clere occ. May 1283 (Herefs. and Worcs. Record Office, MS 713 ff. 155v–156r). William de Windesore fl. Dec. 1283–1290 (E 101/351/12 m. 1; C 47/4/2; *Records 1285–1286*, no. 527; *CPR 1281–1292*, 415). Robert Achard fl. 1283–90 (E101/351/9 mm. 8–9; E 372/ 130 m. 5; *Records 1285–1286*, no. 437; *Records 1286–1289*, index 559 s.v. "Achard [Acard], Robert"; E. B. Fryde, ed., *Book of Prests*, 35, 187). Roger de Clare fl. 1285–1290 (C 47/4/2 fol. 27; le Neve, *Fasti*, iii, 201; *Records 1286–1289*, nos. 82, 122; *CHEC*, 122).

87. William de Windesore occ. 19 Mar. 1283 (C 47/4/2 fol. 14). Ralph de Staunford fl. 1286–90 (Deedes, ed., *Reg. Pontissara*, i, 48, 85, 184–86, 263, 288, and ii, 456–57, 733; *Records 1286–1289*, index p. 628 s.v. "Ralph, Q's almoner"; *CHEC*, index p. 176 s.v. "Ralph, Q's almoner"; *CCIR 1279–1288*, 152; *CCIR 1288–1296*, 152, 404; *CPR 1281–1292*, 238). Robert de St. Albano fl. 1289–90 (*CHEC*, 64, 133; Harvey, ed., *Docts. of Walter de Wenlok*, 32, 175; *CPR 1281–1292*, 413; Bliss, i, 550; Hill, ed., *Rolls and Reg. Sutton*, iii, 198–200). Roger de Assherugg' fl. 1288–90 (*Records 1286–1289*, index p. 562 s.v. "Ashridge, Roger de"; C 47/4/4 fol. 16; *CHEC*, 154; *Manners*, 137; E. B. Fryde, ed., *Book of Prests*, index p. 238 s.v. "Assherugg'").

88. *CHEC*, 153–60

89. William de Cheney occ. Oct. 1255 (*CLR*, iv, 243–44; *CIR 1254–1256*, 144–45; *CDI*, i, no. 1976; *CPR 1258–1266*, 324; *CPR 1281–1292*, 8), John de Weston sr in June and Dec. 1264 (*CPR 1258–1266*, 324–25; *CIR 1264–1268*, 8). After 1272 no steward occ. until Exch. records so describe John Ferré, 1287 (E 159/60 m. 16); the many cases 1275 X 1286 in which he witn. her acts (Chapter Three, Appendix II) imply he was then steward (though Tout, *Chapters*, i, 162, implies there was no steward with that title in Nov. 1279). Ferré fl. Mar. 1289, d. by June 1290 (*Records 1286–1289*, nos. 3214–15, 3217–18, 3221, 3230, 3231; *CHEC*, 34; below, Chapter Three, Appendix I nos. 114, 120). John de Weston jr. occ. June 1288 (*Records 1286–1289*, nos. 3219, 3220). The steward in 1289–90 was prob. Guy Ferré jr, John Ferré's nephew (*CHEC*, 154, and index p. 172, s.v. "Ferré, Guy [younger]").

90. Tout, *Chapters*, i, 162; Johnstone, "Queen's Household," *English Government*, i, 266–67. C 47/3/50 m. 2 records the Q's departure "cum familia sua" 15 May 1279, her return next day, and her absence 19–26 May. Acct was kept of time out of court (*Records 1285–1286*, nos. 1177, 1297; *Records 1286–1289*, no. 1302, 2942–3009, 2970; *CHEC*, 81, 87); compare Mertes, *English Noble Household*, 69.

91. John le Blount (*Records 1285–1286*, nos. 201, 405, 528, 735, 869; *Records 1286–1289*, nos. 71, 1650, 1833, 1946); occ. May 1290 (C 47/4/5 fol. 9v); served the K until 1296 (*CCIR 1288–1296*, 510). ?Sub-usher of the Q's chamber, 12 Edw. (E 101/372/5 m. 1), usher 15 Edw. (E 101/351/25 m. 3). Not to be confused with John le Blond, yeoman of John de Weston (*Records 1286–1289*, index p. 568 s.v. "Blount, John le"; *CHEC*, 70).

92. Thomas de Bardeney occ. Mar. 1277, d. 1296 (E 101/350/26 m. 2; *CPR 1272–1281*, 278; Lysons, ed., "Roll of Expenses," 47; *DC*, iv, 405; C 47/4/3 fol. 2; *Records 1285–1286*, index p. 290 s.v. "Thomas, marshal of the queen"; *Records 1286–1289*, index p. 613 s.v. "Marshal, Thomas le"; *CHEC*, index p. 169 s.v. "Bardeney, Thomas"; *CCIR 1279–1288*, 425; *Manners*, 97; *CIPM*, iii, no. 351; below, Chapter Three, Appendix I no. 80).

93. A potentially serious problem as the Q's growing children acq. their own households and cooks (in 1289–90, C 47/4/5 fol. 37v for the two elder daus; C 47/3/22 mm. 1–2 for young Edward).

94. *Records 1286–1289*, nos. 1451, 1618; *CHEC*, 29–30, 157–58.

95. The chamber usher Hamo occ. 6 Edw. (BL, Add. 36762 *m.* 3; E 101/351/17 *m.* 3; *Records 1285–1286,* nos. 7, 47, 1708; *Records 1286–1289,* nos. 304, 403, 865, 1483, 1724, 1755, 1835, 3208, 3210–12; *CHEC,* 81, 94, 122); also porter and viewer of works at Windsor (*CCIR 1279–1288,* 447). The hall usher Walter le Blunt occ. from 14 Edw. (sub-usher of the chamber 13 Edw. [E 101/351/17 *m.* 3]; *Records 1285–1286,* nos. 355, 474, 981, 1710; *Records 1286–1289,* nos. 1755, 1844).

96. John fl. 6–13 Edw. (BL, Add. 36762 *m.* 3; E 101/372/5 *m.* 1; E 101/351/17 *m.* 3); occ. 14 Edw. (*Records 1285–1286,* no. 1710) but Hugh de la Penne replaced him that year (*Records 1285–1286,* no. 981, *Records 1286–1289,* nos. 1451, 2937; E 101/352/24 *m.* 3; BL, Add. roll 6710 *m.* 2; *CHEC,* 89; *Manners,* 111, 128, 130, 132, 134). Penne and one yeoman slept in the wardrobe (*Records 1285–1286,* nos. 812, 814; Tout, *Chapters,* i, 163).

97. For 1289–90, *CHEC,* 154–55 (John Besilles was admitted for two years "per pactum initum inter Regem Reginam et ipsum" [C 47/4/5 fol. 34]). The other two were the yr Guy Ferré, Q's knt 1288–89 and prob. the household steward 1289–90 (*Records 1286–1289,* no. 2959), and John de Weston jr, steward 1288 (*Records 1285–1286,* nos. 1678, 1722; *CHEC,* 70, 88); as stewards they had lands from the Q (as noted below) and prob. were not held to need robes (see Prestwich, *Edward I,* 147 note 38). In 14 Edw. (1285–86) Ferré, Besilles, Adam de Cretyng, Robert de Crevequer, Simon de Creye, and Peter d'Estavayer (all Q's knts 1289–90) had fees but not robes from the K (*Records 1285–1286,* nos. 1677–80, 1720–23); in 17 Edw. (1288–89), Ferré, d'Estavayer and Weston had K's fees but not robes (*Records 1286–1289,* nos. 2905, 2959, 2994).

98. As counsellors, Blackley and Hermansen, eds., *Household Book,* xv; *Records 1286–1289,* no. 1859; Eleanor's council is discussed further below. Seventy-two surviving *acta* or references to lost acts were identified (incl. Edward's gts to Eleanor); for those with witness lists, see below, Chapter Three, Appendix II. Piccheford witn. fifteen times, 1278 X 1285, years in which is it is certain he was the steward of the Q's lands and a household knt. John Ferré, Q's household steward, witn. eight times (1275 X 1286); the sr John de Weston, her steward in 1264, once (1268). Problems with the witn. lists to the Q's acts are compounded by difficulties in ascertaining the time at which an individual became the Q's knt (see note 97). Adam de Cretyng, certainly the Q's knt in 1289–90, witn. once (1283) at a time when his household status is unclear; Giles de Fiennes, her cousin and prob. her knt throughout her years as Q, witn. three times (1280 X 1283). Eustace de Hacche witn. six times (1280 X 1283) though not certainly her knt until the later 1280s, and John de Weston jr, briefly her steward in the late 1280s, witn. twice (1281 X 1283) when not certainly her knt. William Charles, certainly her knt in 1264, witn. once (1268). Andrew de Sakeville, husband of the Q's woman Ermentrude de Sakeville and most prob. (though not certainly) a household knt, witn. twice (1280 X 1281).

99. *CHEC,* 83, 101, 103, 111, 116, 117, 122, 123, 124, 126, 128, 129, 131, 132 (see also 63, 65, 71, 110, 127–28). The same profile appears in earlier years when only the then-steward John Ferré occ. regularly (*Records 1286–1289,* nos. 3121, 3214, 3215, 3217, 3218, 3221, 3230); John de Weston jr. occ. while steward (nos. 3219, 3220) but not later.

100. *CHEC,* 155–56. Bef. the Q's extant accts begin in 1286, Joan "de Valle Viridi" occ. 1262 (see Chapter One, note 52); Margaret Wake 1277 (E 101/350/26 *m.* 4); Maud de Columbars 1278 (below, Chapter Three, Appendix I no. 100); Grace de Middelton 1279 (below, note 154); and a "domina de Hacche," perhaps Eustace de Hacche's wife Amice, 1282 (Lysons, ed., "Roll of Expenses," 46; GEC, vi, 389; Harvey, ed., *Docts. of Walter de Wenlok,* 167). Columbars, Wake and Hacche were traveling in the Q's train, as apparently was Amice de Weston, 1279 (Bund, ed., *Reg. Godfrey Giffard,* 110).

101. On Margerie, *CHEC,* index p. 173 s.v. "Haustede, Margerie de"; Chaplais, "Private Letters of Edward I," 86; Turner, "Will of Humphrey de Bohun," 346. S.C. 1/30/52

(Westm., 7 June) is the Q's letter to the warden of Dover asking him to assure "Crestyen' de Weston' nostre chere Dameysele ke passe la mer pur noz bosoygnes . . . hastif passage e sauf"; on her see below, Chapter Three, Appendix I no. 94; *CHEC*, 70, 110. For Iseult le Bruyn, *Records 1286–1289*, nos. 1858–59.

102. Morality clearly underlay the 1279 inquest (Bund, ed., *Reg. Godfrey Giffard*, 110; Moor, *Knights*, ii, 205–6, and v, 183); for the Castilian Q's women, Vann, "Medieval Castilian Queenship," 132 note 31. See also Hincmar, *De Ordine Palatii*, 72–74; S. Agobardi *Liber apologeticus*, PL 140, cols. 313–14; *Lamberti Ardensis Historia*, 625; Tout, *Chapters*, i, 162; Mertes, *English Noble Household*, 179. Maud de Haversham (b. 1274), with the Q's daus 1287, m. 1289 (*CHEC*, 50 note); Beatrice, dau. of Iseult le Bruyn, with the Q's daus 1290 (C 47/4/5 fol. 3), m. by 1293 (*CCIR 1288–1296*, 277; *CPR 1292–1301*, 82; *VCH Hants.*, iii, 263, 363, and iv, 172, 202, 539). Joan de Haustede, with the daus 1289–90 (C 47/4/5 fol. 3), m. soon thereafter (*CPR 1281–1292*, 415–16; Councer, "Heraldic Painted Glass in the Church of St. Lawrence," 61–62; Hasted, *Kent*, v, 73–74; anon., "Kent Fines, 8 Edward II," 301; the suggested identification of Joan de Mereworth as Q's laundress [*CHEC*, 83 note] must be withdrawn).

103. Ermentrude de Sakeville was widow of Andrew, prob. Q's knt in the 1280s (*CHEC*, 14–15; *Records 1285–1286*, nos. 1678, 1722; *CChR*, ii, 234, 256). Sybil le Poer's husband d. ca. 1284 (Moor, *Knights*, iv, 276; she m. Henry de Bodrugan after Dec. 1288 (*Records 1286–1289*, no. 1989) and had a son in Jan. 1290, when the K sent her £9:6:8 (GEC, ii, 199; Moor, i, 103–4; *Records 1286–1289*, no. 2416). For the others, *CHEC*, 32–40, 155–56. Alice le Breton (*CHEC*, 130; *Records 1285–1286*, no. 175) was prob. dau. of Iseult le Bruyn (*CIPM*, iv, no. 83; *VCH Hants.*, iii, 88, 225–26, 228). A like profile has been noted for Isabella of France's women, 1311–12 (Blackley and Hermansen, eds., *Household Book*, xiii–xv); the same may be true for those of Q Philippa in 1330 (*Cal. of Memoranda Rolls*, no. 2270 [i, ii, iii, v]).

104. Maurice le Bruyn and Robert de Haustede jr. were with young Edward 1289–90 (*CHEC*, 37–38). Margerie wife of John de Ingham, with the Q Oct. 1284 (E 101/351/12 m. 4), was with Joan of Acre 1289–90, her son Oliver with young Edward (C 47/4/5 fol. 37v; *CHEC*, 155). Sybil le Poer's sons were with the Q's children 1289–90 (C 47/3/22). Ermentrude de Sakeville's dau. Eleanor was at court 1290 (*CHEC*, 92), her nephew John Chandos with young Edward (C 47/3/22; *CIPM*, ii, no. 98; Wrottesley, *Pedigrees*, 260; Banks, *Baronage*, i, 261–62; Johnstone, ed., *Letters*, xv, 117–18, and idem, *Edward of Carnarvon*, 116–17). A s. of the Q's goldsmith Adam and his wife (the Q's woman from 1285) worked for the K, 1299 (Lehmann-Brockhaus, no. 6256; *CHEC*, 155).

105. Mertes, *English Noble Household*, 57–58, 64, 74, 167–68, 179–80.

106. J. C. Parsons, "Towards a Social History"; the Wodestoks are considered in greater detail below. On Montibus, Moor, *Knights*, iii, 194–96; Johnstone, "Queen's Household," Tout, *Chapters*, v, 242; perhaps "Ebles de la Reine," 1279 (Tout, *Chapters*, i, 163; *Records 1285–1286*, nos. 1685, 1689). His mother was perhaps Joan de Somery (d. 1282), who m. the sr Ebles as her third husband 1246 X 1253 (*VCH Cambs.*, v, 229–30; *CPR 1247–1258*, 220, 239). Joan took the Q's son Henry to France, 1270 (*CPR 1266–1272*, 412); a chamber was built for her at Westm., 1279 (E 372/123 m. 21).

107. Possibly related were Simon and Thomas Lowys; William and Reginald Heyne; the sjt marshal John le Blount and Walter le Blount, usher of the hall; mr Robert de Picheford, Edward's physician bef. 1272, and the Q's knt Geoffrey de Piccheford (*CHEC*, 71, 77, 156, 158; on the Blunts, above, notes 91, 95; for Picheford, Adams and Donohue, eds., *Select Cases*, 265 and note 5). For Geoffrey, Simon, Richard, and Hamo, *CHEC*, 94, 158. Richard occ. from 6 Edw. (BL, Add. 36762 m. 3; *Records 1286–1289*, nos. 3222–23, 3233; *CHEC*, 81, 110).

108. J. C. Parsons, "English Administration in Ponthieu," 398; Brunel, *Recueil*, no. 466; *CIR 1264–1268*, 520; *CPR 1272–1281*, 109; *Records 1286–1289*, no. 1649; *CHEC*, 76.

109. On Wade, *CIR 1259–1261*, 107, 453–54; *CPR 1258–1266*, 134, 142, 215, 382, 523, 549; *CPR 1266–1272*, 54, 80, 116, 164, 190, 225, 363, 651; *CPR 1272–1281*, 315; *CCIR 1272–1279*, 397; *CCIR 1279–1288*, 64, 135, 254, 299, 360, 540; *CPR 1281–1292*, 29, 52, 70, 179, 239; *Records 1285–1286*, no. 1708; *Records 1286–1289*, nos. 243, 1052, 1536; GEC, ii, 9–10; Roth, *Jews of Medieval Oxford*, 79, 90–91, 159; *VCH Berks.*, iii, 101–2; *VCH Hants.*, iii, 159, 158, 168; *CIPM*, ii, no. 620. The "mr Simon" of the wardrobe records (Parsons, *CHEC*, 72, 156), occ. as "de Goldeburgh'" in his private acts (White et al., eds., *Chertsey Cartularies*, ii, nos. 667–75); he had a money gift from the Q, autumn 1290 (S.C. 6/1089/25 m. 3).

110. *CHEC*, 32, 156, 158; *Records 1286–1289*, nos. 1451, 1618, 1947; Reginald was admitted to K's wages as Q's sauser 1 Aug. 1289 (C 47/4/4 fol. 13).

111. For the Bruyns, *RG*, ii, nos. 1569–71; Stagg, *CNFD*, i, no. 548; Moor, *Knights*, i, 154–55; GEC, ii, 355; on the Westons, below, Chapter Three, Appendix I no. 94. For the Haustedes, *CChR*, ii, 346; *CIPM*, vi, no. 316; *CCIR 1279–1288*, 8, 147; *CIPM*, vi, no. 316. In 1290 they bought a manor at Harpole, near the Q's manor at Kingsthorpe (*CPR 1281–1292*, 371; *CIPM*, ii, no. 752; *CPR 1313–1317*, 365; *CPR 1327–1330*, 232). The alien Ferrés initially had no lands in England, but the Q gave manors in Kent and Lincs. to her steward John Ferré; Guy jr, prob. the steward in 1289–90, got manors in Essex and Oxon. (Chapter Three, Appendix I nos. 62, 63, 65, 114, 135a, 171). For John see also *CPR 1272–1281*, 359; *RG*, ii, nos. 189–90; for Guy, *CIPM*, vi, no. 422. Alice de Luton, a knt's wife, Edward's former wetnurse and governess of Eleanor's children, obtained William de Hertewelle's lands through his debts to the Jewry, seemingly gtd her by Eleanor (above, Chapter One note 54).

112. The steward John Ferré's wife Joan was the Q's woman (*CHEC*, 33–34). The yr Guy Ferré's first wife Margerie was perhaps not, though Guy was later steward (*CHEC*, 34–35; for her, whom he m. 1286 and who d. *s.p.* bef. 1289, Moor, *Knights*, ii, 13–14; GEC, v, 445–48; *Cal. Genealogicum*, i, lix, 199; *CIPM*, iv, no. 392). For lands the Q gtd John Ferré and Guy Ferré jr, see above, note 111. Philip Popiot, the Q's Ponthevin knt, was gtd a wardship in Berks. (E 159/56 m. 4); his wife Edeline was not the Q's woman, but she was governess of her dau. Joan (*CHEC*, 38–39).

113. The Q's clks are discussed below; compare her pres. of Burnell's nephew to the ch. of Westerham, and Nicholas son of her auditor John de Lovetot to Great Bowden, as below.

114. For Picard, E 159/55 m. 7 (E 159/56 m. 4 shows Popiot sold his right to Adam de Stratton for £10); for Montibus, *CPR 1281–1292*, 411, and below, Chapter Three, Appendix I no. 116a note 125. On Despenser, *CPR 1272–1281*, 59; *CChyV*, 325; *CCIR 1296–1302*, 535–46; he occ. 5 Edw. (E 101/350/24 m. 2), in 1282 (Lysons, ed., "Roll of Expenses," 49), and 1290 (*CHEC*, 70, 78, 157). On Shelvestrode, below, Chapter Three, Appendix I note 133. For Martin, *RO*, i, 75; *Records 1285–1286*, nos. 809, 845–46; *Records 1286–1289*, nos. 112, 188, 744, 1652, 1767, 3217–18, 3224, 3238, 3242; *CHEC*, 69, 76, 77; *Escanor*, ed. Michelant, mentions at ll. 24434–35 Guinevere's squire "Martin d'Espaigne," whom Michelant, at 644, thought might be modeled on one of Eleanor's svts. One svt had land from the K after the Q died (*CChR*, ii, 382).

115. For Somerfeld *als* de Horton, *CPR 1258–1266*, 496; *CPR 1266–1272*, 360, 402 (see below, Chapter Three, Appendix I no. 250); *CPR 1272–1281*, 379; *CCIR 1272–1279*, 151; *CPR 1281–1292*, 55; *Kalendars*, i, 35 (no. 8); *CHEC*, 89; *Manners*, 122; Lehmann-Brockhaus, nos. 2913, 2916. On Gillot, *CIR 1264–1268*, 520; *CPR 1272–1281*, 109; *CHEC*, 76, 156. On Richard, *CPR 1272–1281*, 101; *CCIR 1279–1288*, 6; *Records 1285–1286*, index p. 285 s.v. "Richard, tailor of the queen," and *Records 1286–1289*, nos. 135, 1488; *CHEC*, 132, 156. On Wade, above, note 109. For Kendal, *CPR 1281–1292*, 119–20, 187; *CCIR 1279–1288*, 342; *Records 1285–1286*, no. 1708; *RO*, i, 51; *CFR*, i, 227. On Wade's death Kendal took his place (*Records 1286–1289*, no. 1536), but d. bef. the Q (*Manners*, 109). On Bardeney, Chapter Three, Appendix I no.

80. Other royal cooks had lands near Windsor (*VCH Berks.*, iii, 101); on tenants of Windsor in the royal households, Parsons, "Towards a Social History," 55–56.

116. *Records 1286–1289*, nos. 3240 *bis*, 3244 *bis*; *CHEC*, 76 *bis*. A gift from the e. of Lincoln to her messenger Simon (*CCIR 1288–1296*, 87) could have been sought by the Q. Compare E 101/352/21 *m.* 1 [27 Feb. 1290]: "Thome de Boueneye qui fuit aquarius filiarum Regis . . . totaliter licenciato de Curia ad unam Robam sibi emendam de dono Regis Regina precipiente ex parte Regis xiij.s.iij.*d.*" A gift to the widow of a "cook" (*Manners*, 104) in fact concerns a kitchen yeoman who *fl.* 1278–1286/87 (BL, Add. 36762 *m.* 3; *Records 1285–1286*, nos. 981, *Records 1286–1289*, nos. 747, 794, 1451). On Constance le Espanoyl, J. C. Parsons, "English Administration in Ponthieu," 400.

117. E.g., S.C. 1/23/46 (Long Bennington, 17 Feb. 1284): the Q asks Burnell to expedite affairs of Jakke her chandler. Jakke or Jakemin *candelarius* (le Chaundeler), de Arraz (de Attrabato), or Jakemin Usurer, occ. from 1284–85 (E 101/351/17 *m.* 3 has "Jacobus Bochard de Candelaria;" *Records 1285–1286*, nos. 194, 216, 763; *Records 1286–1289*, nos. 25, 66, 100, 138, 180, 537; *CHEC*, 80 and note); *Records 1285–86*, nos. 904, 961, and *Records 1286–1289*, nos. 1438, 1691, 2038, 2070, 2933, imply that John Buchard "de candelaria" and Jakke the Chandeler are the same. See also Tout, *Chapters*, i, 160 (Nov. 1279). For Somerfeld's house, *CHEC*, 89.

118. Prestwich, *Edward I*, 155–56; *CPR 1272–1281*, 137; *CPR 1281–1292*, 470, 505; *CPR 1292–1301*, 52; *CCIR 1288–1296*, 506 (see *CHEC*, 32); *CCIR 1296–1302*, 296; *CPR 1292–1301*, 503; *CChyW*, 175, 219, 242, 467; *CCIR 1307–1313*, 220; Johnstone, ed., *Letters*, 115–16 (see *Manners*, 108, 135). On the Q's scribe Hugh de Hibernia, J. C. Parsons, "Of Queens, Courts and Books."

119. *Records 1286–1289*, nos. 2478, 2484, 2487, 2491, 2496, 2498, 2504, 2506, 2533 *bis*, 2542, 2549, 2556, 2559, 2565, 2570; in 1289–90, C 47/4/4 ff. 38r (Christmas 1289), 39v (mass for the K's aunt, 19 Mar.; burial of Richard de Bures at Feckenham, 23 Mar.), 40r (mass for the K's sister, 29 Mar.), 43r (Ascension, St. John Baptist), 45r (Assumption), 47r (All Saints), 48v (mass for Henry III). On the Q's family, *CHEC*, 95, 100. Svts' oblations show they were expected to attend mass, though prob. not with the K's family (*KW*, 137–45; Alexander and Binski, *Age of Chivalry*, 324–25).

120. On marriages, Mertes, *English Noble Household*, 152–57. Treas. accts 1289–90 show *maritagia* to ". . . La Panetere," Agnes dau. of Eined, Albreda de Caumpeden', Malyna de Wyndesor', and "Maroye" (S.C. 6/1089/25 *m.* 3; on Albreda see Chapter One, note 32, and on Malyna, *Manners*, 111). Compare below, Chapter Three, Appendix I nos. 62 note 104, 113; for weddings, *Records 1286–1289*, nos. 3235, 3243; *CHEC*, 48, 64, 103; *CCIR 1279–1288*, 54; *CIPM*, ii, no. 566). Compare gts to Joan and William Charles, 1262 (above, Chapter One note 52) and Ermentrude and Andrew de Sakeville, 1275 (*CHEC*, 14–15), and Eleanor's encouragement of marriages remarked in Chapter One. On childbirth, *CIPM*, ii, no. 98; *Records 1286–1289*, no. 3239; for Sybilla le Poer, above, note 103. Christiana de Weston was with the Q in Gascony until Dec. 1288 when she went to England to bear a child (*Records 1286–1289*, no. 1989, misreads "ad peregrinandum" for the correct "ad pregnandum" [E 101/352/14 *m.* 10]). On godchildren see above, Chapter One note 87 (see also *CIPM*, ii, no. 436).

121. For knthoods, *Records 1286–1289*, no. 1302; *CHEC*, 37–38, 155 note. For burials, see discussion of Henry de Wodestok' and Richard de Bures below; *Records 1286–1289*, nos. 371, 1618–19, 1625, 1633–34, 1637, 1719, 1722, 2503, 3233, 3361–62; *CHEC*, 129). Clks and svts were bur. where they d. but kntly bones were sent from Gascony to England in 1287 (*Records 1286–1289*, nos. 483, 1628, 1632).

122. Riley, ed., *Gesta Abbatum Sancti Albani*, 412; for gts obtained by courtiers, e.g., *CPR 1292–1301*, 82; *CChR*, ii, 182, 184 *bis*, 349, 455, 467.

123. For disruptions, *CHEC*, 65, 74–75, 88–89, 112, 114 (with which compare gaps in the Q's itinerary, 20–24 June and 20–24 July 1290, at 146–47), 115. On chamber and wardrobe, *CHEC*, 122, 125, 127, 135, 156–59; Johnstone, "Queen's Household," Tout, *Chapters*,

v, 234, 242–43, and *English Government,* i, 275–77; B. P. Wolffe, *Royal Demesne,* 69–70. The lack of wardrobe receipts bef. 1289 isolates payment at her wardrobe in 1290 of the issues of some of the Q's Welsh lands in 1290, when those lands were being admin. for her by the K's chamberlain in N. Wales (*CHEC,* 62–63; Edwards, ed., *Anct. Correspondence,* 118; *CHEC,* 62 [C 62/65 m. 4, has the K's order of 1 June 1290 that the £79:12:10½ be allowed the chamberlain's accts]). This payment was anomalous; in earlier years these lands were admin. by a bf who paid the issues to the Q's treas. (S.C. 6/1089/22 m. 2 [14 Edw.]; Westm. Abbey, muniments 23627 [1286]).

124. Sources will be cited in the course of discussion. "Fl." indicates the individual was in office at the time indicated, "d." that he died in office. On Walter de Wenlok's anomalous appt as treas. (Westm. Abbey, muniments 23627, 9492), see Harvey, *Westminster Abbey,* 31–32.

125. Tout, *Chapters,* ii, 34–35; Johnstone, "Queen's Household," *English Government,* i, 273–74. The acct of the Qs exors was audited at the Exch. in 1294, as discussed earlier, but the statement (*Records 1286–1289,* xiv) that Eleanor of Castile's wardrobe regularly acctd there perhaps arises from some confusion with that of Eleanor of Provence, which did acct at the Exch. (Johnstone, "Queen's Household," Tout, *Chapters,* v, 233).

126. Bliss, i, 454–55, 456; R. G. Griffiths, ed., *Reg. Cantilupo,* 18–19, 203–4; Johnstone, "Queen's Household," *English Government,* i, 268.

127. Prob. in Q's service June 1275 (*CChR,* ii, 190–92); recd money from the K for her, Dec. 1276 (E 101/350/26 m. 1), in 6 Edw. (C 47/4/1; BL, Add. 36762), 12 Edw. (E 101/351/12; E 101/351/14), 13 Edw. (BL, Add. Rot. 6711), 14 Edw. (C 47/4/3); and from the abbot of Westm., 1286–88 (Westm. Abbey, muniments 23626 dorse). See *Records 1285–1286,* index p. 260, s.v. "Bures, Richard de," and *Records 1286–1289,* index p. 574 s.v. "Bures, Richard de." For his accts 1282–84, Lysons, ed., "Roll of Expenses," 32, 50; E 372/130 m. 5.

128. Q's clk, E 101/351/14 (12 Edw.); BL, Add. rot. 6711 (13 Edw.); receiver, *CCIR 1279–1288,* 61, 386. He had £3:0:3 from the K for plate for the Q, Feb. 1286 (C 47/4/3 fol. 8). In H1287 a payment to him as receiver was ackn. at the Exch. by the wardrobe kpr (E 159/60 m. 3d); see *Records 1285–1286,* nos. 923, 981. In 1289–90 Robert de Middelton recd payments at her wardrobe (S.C. 6/1089/25 m. 4 [from her treas.]; C 47/4/5 fol. 5v [from K]). E 101/352/13 is ident. as Bures' work as controller by the exors' summary (E 372/143 m. 36); see *Records 1286–1289,* no. 3204. As cofferer, C 47/4/5 fol. 38. He was bur. at Feckenham Mar. 1290 (C 47/4/4 fol. 39v). There can be no doubt Bures acctd for the wardrobe from Geoffrey de Aspale's death (June 1287) until John de Berewyk's appt as kpr in Sept. 1288.

129. A photograph obtained of Eleanor's great seal (British Museum Add. Charter 8129) was unsuitable for reproduction. A pointed oval 3½" in height, the seal shows (obverse) a queen standing, crowned and holding a scepter in her right hand, surrounded by the castles of Castile and lions of León; reverse, a shield of England hanging from a tree.

130. For the K's officers, Tout, *Chapters,* ii, 37–39; by Edward III's reign, controller and cofferer in the Qs' wardrobe were clearly distinguished (Johnstone, "Queen's Household," *English Government,* i, 268). For the Q's seal, *CHEC,* 94, 116, 122. Of Eleanor's 47 extant letters identified for this study (distinct from charters and other acts), thirteen preserve a seal or contain a sealing clause; eleven issued under the privy seal, also used for a May 1286 chirograph (D.L. 27/185 [below, Chapter Three, Appendix I no. 177]). Berewyk' as kpr was out of court at least four times, 1289–90 (*CHEC,* 78, 95, 109, 116). On purchases by Bures' clks, *Records 1286–1289,* nos. 2269, 3237; *CHEC,* 64, 94. The term *garderobarius* is applied to Bures in *Manners,* 135.

131. S.C. 6/1089/22 m. 1 ("Rotulus de denariis . . . depositis in Thesauro domine Regine . . . apud Westmonasterium de Exitibus quarundam terrarum suarum . . ."); *CPEJ,* iii, 302–3;

CPR 1279–1288, 61; *CCIR 1288–1296*, 56 (for her muniments, catalogued temp. Edw. II, *Kalendars*, i, 36–37, 38, 47–48, 53, 57–63, 69). On money sent to Clerkenwell, *Records 1286–1289*, nos. 3132, 3171, 3172, 3203; also £1100 at the morrow of All Souls 1289, and in M1290 an unstated sum from "from the houses of Sir Otho de Grandison" (S.C. 6/1089/25 *mm.* 4, 3; on these houses see below, Chapter Three, Appendix I no. 143a). The 1290 ref. to those who "ate at the treasurer's house" (*CHEC*, 112), refers to the treas.-kpr of the wardrobe, not the goldkpr-treas. Richard de Seez was to proffer the ransom for his lands at Clerkenwell June 1270 (JUST 1/542 *m.* 5; compare *Records 1286–1289*, no. 3127).

132. "Receipt" and "exchequer" were interchangeable (*Manners*, 133; Johnstone, "Queen's Household," Tout, *Chapters*, v, 232–35, and *English Government*, i, 279; idem, "Queen's Exchequer," 143–53). The older queen's receipt was repaired, Feb. 1274 (E 101/467/6/1 *m.* 2). On equipment, *Records 1286–1289*, nos. 3116, 3119, 3133, 3137, 3158, 3162, 3183, 3187, 3204 (S.C. 6/1089/25 *m.* 3 gives the clks in 1289–90 as Richard de Kancia and John Bacun). For comparison with other exchs, Johnstone, "Queen's Household," Tout, *Chapters*, v, 247, 250–51; Denholm-Young, *Seignorial Administration*, 145–46.

133. Letters of appt are quoted below; see Howell, "Resources of Eleanor of Provence," 379–80. For distr., e.g., E 159/53 *m.* 19d (H1280): Kancia, goldkpr, has two in Wilts. distr. for debts of Philip le Blund which the K gtd the Q. On debts, e.g., E 159/59 *m.* 6d (H1286): Berewyk', goldkpr, ackn. the Q will pay £42 Piers de Montfort owes John le Graunt and Hugh de Bolonia, £40 to Walter de Langeton, 40 marks to the Luccans. Kancia, goldkpr, was Q's atty for debts owed her by Henry de Wodestok' (E 13/6 *m.* 21 [6 Edw. I]); in E1284 Berewyk', goldkpr, ackn. payment of one such debt (E 13/11 *m.* 13). For the Exch. of the Jews, *CPEJ*, ii, 308, 311; Rigg, ed., *Select Pleas, Starrs*, 87–88. Kancia, goldkpr, ackn. receipt of £10 owed Hagin f. Moses by Nicholas Tregoz E1276 (E 9/52 *m.* 4). Berewyk', goldkpr, was to be told of concealed goods of condemned Jews H1284 (E 159/57 *m.* 4; *CPR 1281–1292*, 173, 283); he ackn. payment at the Exch. of the Jews T1283 (E 9/44 *m.* 7d), and of debts from the Jewry M1283 (E 9/45 *m.* 3d). This aspect of the goldkpr's duties explains why queen-gold accts carry payment of debts to the Jewry and the Q's profits from the operations of the Exch. of the Jews (e.g., *Records 1286–1289*, nos. 3080–90, 3095, 3102).

134. In 1280–81, Kancia as goldkpr was to have issues from the eyre in Hants. (*CCIR 1279–1288*, 24; E 159/55 *m.* 2 perhaps concerns that gt); in 1285 those from Gartree, Barstable and Spelhoe hundreds were to be paid the goldkpr Berewyk' (E 159/59 *m.* 16d). His accts for queen-gold include such issues, 1286–90 (*Records 1286–1289*, nos. 3061, 3069–71, 3075, 3100); those from the eyre in S. Erpingham appear in 15 Edw. (E 101/505/19 *m.* 2).

135. For Guldeford, *CPEJ*, iv, no. 140; E 13/10 *m.* 4 (oct. of St. Martin 1282) refers to a "serviens Walteri de Kancia Thesaurarii auri Consortis Regis." On Berewyk', Madox, *History and Antiquities*, i, 361; *Records 1286–1289*, no. 3226. The goldkpr-treas. must not be confused with the wardrobe treas. (Johnstone, "Queen's Household," *English Government*, i, 278, muddles them.) Wodestok' was called treas. and wardrobe kpr Sept. 1277, and Aspale occ. as treas. Feb. 1286 (*CPR 1272–1281*, 229; Westm. abbey, muniments 23627); neither was ever goldkpr. Berewyk' occ. as wardrobe treas. 1289–90 (*CHEC*, 59; Deedes, ed., *Reg. Pontissara*, ii, 30–31, 184–86).

136. S.C. 6/1089/25 *m.* 4; *CHEC*, 61–63 (the receipts "de exitibus auri Regine" are those for 20 Feb., 6 May and 28 Aug.).

137. For issues from lands 1286–87 and issues to the wardrobe 1286–90 are discussed above. See *Records 1286–1289*, nos. 3105, 3146, 3148, 3156, 3163; Westm. Abbey, muniments 23627 (above, note 123). S.C. 6/1089/25 *mm.* 3–4 have payments authorized by Berewyk' and John de Lovetot the auditor.

138. C 47/4/3 fol. 17 (scales, July 1286); *Records 1286–1289*, no. 3204; *CHEC*, 64; *Manners*, 96. The wardrobe accts for 17–18 Edw., prepared for the 1294 audit, run from Mich.

but could have been written up differently to earlier years; that for 16 Edw., however, not created for the audit, does run from Mich. (*Records 1286–1289*, no. 3206 and note). On accting in the K's wardrobe, Johnson, "System of Account," 51–52. For innovation in Isabella of France's wardrobe, Tout, *Chapters*, v, 118–20, and Johnstone, "Queen's Household," *English Government*, i, 295.

139. *RG*, i, suppl., no. 4555; *CLR*, iv, 244, 247. Loundres' identification with the poet John de Hoveden (Stone, "Jean de Howden," 496–519) is unlikely. For 1265, Shirley, *Royal Letters*, no. 647. Cash for the children's expns was paid him Jan. 1273 and July 1274 (C 62/49 *m.* 1; C 62/50 *m.* 5); a letter on the children's safety amid rumors of armed conspiracy was sent the Chancellor by Loundres and the constable of Windsor (S.C. 1/7/179, s.d.). The Q's letters of attorney are S.C. 1/7/100 (3 Sept. 1274, from Eleanor, Q of England [not K's mother]); on Alina, widow of Henry, d. 1260, see *CFR*, i, 26; *CIPM*, ii, no. 45; Paris, *CM*, v, 213–14; *VCH Berks.*, iv, 255. That her exor was Eleanor of Castile is shown by John de Bathe's 1291 complaint touching a rent of villeins usurped by that Q's bfs, noted below. The petition, S.C. 1/16/208 (s.d.), seeks the ward of Barking Abbey (see *VCH Essex*, ii, 121), and dower in Rye (see *CPR 1271–1281*, 104, 106). Loundres occ. on Eleanor of Castile's service June 1277 (*CPR 1272–1281*, 212), and fl. 1280–81; one of this name occ. 1289 but is not certainly the same man (Tout, *Chapters*, vi, 119; *CHEC*, 60).

140. On William, *CLR*, v, 131, 145; W. Brown, ed., *Reg. Walter Giffard*, 101; *CPR 1266–1272*, 480; Adams and Donohoe, eds., *Select Cases*, 236–64; *VCH Berks.*, iv, 126. Herefs. and Worcs. Record Office MS 713 fols 61v–62 has Bp Giffard's letter (1 Aug. 1275) that he will inform the Q on William's goods at the next parlt (Bund, ed., *Reg. Godfrey Giffard*, 83, clumsily calendars the letter; *Select Cases*, 245, mistakenly assigns it to Eleanor of Provence). Nicholas, kntd with Edward 1254 (*CLR*, iv, 69; *RG*, i, no. 3436), was const. of Windsor Jan. 1269 and d. ca. Oct. 1272 (*CPR 1266–1272*, 315–16, 684; *CIPM*, ii,·no. 5); Bartholomew d. ca. 1288 (*CIR 1259–1261*, 305; *CPR 1266–1272*, 358; *CChR*, ii, 160).

141. Missed by Johnstone, "Queen's Household," Tout, *Chapters*, v. His family incl. the cook John, the K's clk Andrew, and Robert the K's marshal (*CPR 1272–1281*, 168; *CPR 1272–1281*, 229 bis; *CCIR 1272–1279*, 292; *Manners*, 100; *CLR*, vi, no. 1180; *CPR 1258–1266*, 55–6; *CIR 1264–1268*, 339). A Henry de Wodestok', K's kitchen sumpter 1261, had land at Hordley in Woodstock (*CIR 1259–1261*, 392; *CPR 1258–1266*, 603), as did the Q's clk Henry (*CPR 1272–1281*, 168). He had 20 marks for expns going to the Q Feb. 1273, £20 that Dec., and went to her in Gascony 1273–74 (E 101/350/5 *mm.* 3, 6 *ter*). Papal chaplain, disp. Mar. 1277 for addl benefices which later incl. stalls at Dublin, Hereford, and Lichfield (Bliss, i, 445, 453–54; *CPR 1272–1281*, 54, 83, 229 [see Lawlor, *Fasti*, 167–68]; *CPR 1272–1281*, 89, 110; *CCIR 1272–1279*, 280; Bund, ed., *Reg. Godfrey Giffard*, 64; le Neve, *Fasti*, i, 520; J. C. Cox, "Catalogue of the Muniments," 203, 210 note 55). See also *CCIR 1272–1279*, 269, 309, 349, 389; *CPR 1272–1281*, 153, 161, 168; Stagg, *CNFD*, i, nos. 99, 102, 128; for his accting duties see Kemp, ed., *Reading Abbey Cartularies*, i, 257–58. Fl. 15 Sept. 1277, when recd money from the K for the Q's expns out of court (E 101/350/26 *m.* 5); a gt of his Dublin stall on 20 Sept. was made "immediately" after he d. (*CPR 1272–1281*, 229, 262), and the K heard mass for his soul 21 Sept. (E 101/350/23 *m.* 2). On his debts, *CPR 1272–1281*, 229 bis.; E 13/6 *m.* 21 (6 Edw.: Kancia agst Andrew de Wodestok' and Robert le Marechal, who respectively owed the Q £5:7:0 and £2:9:4 [E 159/52 *m.* 11d]); E 13/9 *m.* 22d (E1281) shows three indebted to Henry answering to the Q for 55 marks; his tailor complained the Q jailed him for concealing Henry's jewels (JUST 1/542 *m.* 1d); Berewyk' recd 20 marks from his exors, E1284 (E 13/11 *m.* 13). See also *Records 1286–1289*, no. 3091 bis; *Manners*, 100, 120.

142. Bliss, i, 456, and R. G. Griffiths, ed., *Reg. Cantilupo*, 302, are the same doct, the former dated Dec. 1278, the latter (prob. correctly) 1277: he was in the Q's wardrobe Mar. 1278 (C 47/4/1 fol. 12), and witn. her acts from June 1278 (*CCIR 1272–1279*, 497). On his family, BL, Add. 19115, ff. 214v–215r; Rye, ed., *Feet of Fines for Suffolk*, 65, 80; G. A. Williams, *Medieval London*, 50–53, 324–25; Churchill, ed., *Kent Fines*, 308; *CIPM*, ii, no.

635. See also Emden, *Oxford,* i, 60–61. On his wealth, *CIPM,* ii, no. 635; *CPR 1272–1281,* 268, 326; *CIPM,* v, no. 348; *CPR 1281–1292,* 276; Graham, ed., *Reg. Winchelsey,* ii, 1147; Gapes, ed., *Reg. Swinfield,* 33–34 (= Douie, ed., *Reg. Pecham,* ii, 245), 170–71. A nephew Robert, steward to Edward II's wife, m. the h. of the Q's steward Cressingham (Johnstone, "Queen's Household," *English Government,* i, 282; GEC, 12.ii, 95).

143. Russell, *Dictionary of Writers,* 28–31; Macrae, "Geoffrey de Aspall's Commentaries," 94–134. For his attestations, below, Chapter Three, Appendix II nos. 4–6a, 8, 16, 24a, 32. See also *CPR 1272–1281,* 408, 469; *CCIR 1279–1288,* 386; *Records 1285–1286,* nos. 1252, 2277. He ackn. at the Exch. Jan. 1287, that men of Kingsthorpe had paid a tallage gtd Eleanor by Henry III (E 159/60 m. 3d). For his accts in 1287, *CPR 1281–1292,* 229; Harvey, *Westminster Abbey,* 374; for 1290, *CHEC,* 75.

144. I owe to Dr. Brand information on Berewyk's early career. The John de Berewyk' in E. Green, ed., *Pedes finium for Somerset,* 242, is another man. See also *DNB,* s.v. "Berewyk, John de (d. 1312)"; *EFF,* ii, 18–19. For his attestations, below, Chapter Three, Appendix II nos. 29, 30a–b, 32, 38a–b. He did not go to France with the Q, 1286, but remained in England until May or June 1288 (*Records 1286–1289,* nos. 3056–3104, 3105–3163, 3226; *CCIR 1279–1288,* 490, 506; *CPR 1281–1291,* 294–95); *Records 1286–1289* emends no. 3212 to read that "mr John de B[erewyk']" was with the Q in France Feb. 1288, but John was not a university man and is not otherwise designated "mr" in wardrobe docts. For the Q's gts to him, Chapter Three, Appendix I nos. 144, 215. See also *CCIR 1288–1296,* 203; Maitland, ed., *Memoranda de Parliamento,* xliii–xliv; *Fasti 1300–1541,* iii, 36; v, 31; vi, 48; viii, 48; ix, 23–24; x, 55; Deedes, ed., *Reg. Pontissara,* i, 30–31, 184–86; *CIPM,* v, no. 397; GEC, vii, 12.

145. Johnstone, "Queen's Household," *English Government,* i, 272. The appts of her wardrobe kprs are undocumented, but relations between the Q's admin. and the K's, that her clks were regarded as his and carried out his business as well as hers (as remarked below) mean that she can have made no appts without his approval. Compare W. C. Jordan, *Louis IX,* 6.

146. For Jan. 1273, E 159/47 m. 4; Bliss, i, 350. On Guldeford, E 159/48 m. 5: "*Baronibus pro magistro Waltero de Guldeford'.* Rex vult et mandat eisdem Baronibus quod magistrum Walterum de Guldeford ad recipiendum aurum Alienore Regine Consortis Regis ad scaccarium admittant. Et hoc nullatenus omittant. Dat' Paris .v. die Augusti. anno regni regis E. primo." E 101/350/5 m. 3 has an undated entry for Guldeford's expns in London "pro negociis domine Regine," in sequence with expns for her son's arrival in England, June 1274 (for which see Stapleton, ed., *Antiquis Legibus,* 170). On Kancia's appt, *CPEJ,* iv, 42 shows Kancia functioning bef. the date of the letter quoted, which is E 159/49 m. 5d (where the copyist omitted the salutation and "the king").

147. Shirley, ed., *Royal Letters,* no. 647; *CIR 1268–1272,* 252. Edward's attys gave him custody of the Peak, Eleanor's dower (*CPR 1266–1272,* 461, 642; *CCIR 1272–1279,* 45, 46, 119). Her atty 54 Henry III (JUST 1/542 m. 5), in 1271 (JUST 1/1014 m. 7d), and I Edw. (JUST 1/1014 m. 1d); her atty at the Exch. H1273 (E 159/47 m. 16d). For his accting duties, *CCIR 1272–1279,* 198, 499; *CPR 1272–1281,* 332–33; *CPEJ,* ii, 308; E 9/36 m. 6 (T1280). He was to receive from Richard de Seez an installment of his ransom, 1270 (JUST 1/542 m. 5), and in 3 Edw., £200 from Edmund de Hemmegrave who refused to m. Eleanor de Ewelle (JUST 1/836 m. 3); on Ponthieu, *RG,* iii, no. 5050. His benefices are noted below. He witn. acts touching the Q's lands in 1278–79 (below, Chapter Three, Appendix II nos. 4, 8, ?6b). His will was pr. 26 July 1283 (Sharpe, ed., *Wills in the Court of Husting,* i, 65); Hill, ed., *Rolls and Reg. Sutton,* ii, 28, 30; see also *Manners,* 111, 112–13, 120, 127–28, 130, and Chapter Three, Appendix I no. 128. He unjustly amerced a canon of Salisbury who ejected John from his house, as Walter did not pay rent or board as agreed while John studied there (*CCIR 1279–1288,* 398; JUST 1/1014 m. 6); on John (d. 1286), Douie, ed., *Reg. Pecham,* ii, 115; *Rolls and Reg. Sutton,* i, 9, and viii, 93, 103; *CPR 1272–1281,* 462. Richard's career is discussed below.

148. In T1283 three ackn. a debt to the Q; as goldkpr Berewyk' ackn. payment "after Michaelmas in the follg year" (E 159/56 m. 5d). As he occ. as goldkpr H1284 (E 159/57 m. 4) "the follg year" prob. refers to the change of regnal year on 20 Nov. 1283, meaning he was goldkpr by autumn 1283. Ackn. payment by Nicholas de Menil of a debt owed the Q through Cok Hagin, T1284 (E 9/44 m. 7d); for 1288, Westm. Abbey, muniments 9492. See CPR 1281–1292, 173; CCIR 1279–1288, 341–42; RG, iii, no. 5073.

149. CIR 1251–1253, 271, suggests the existence of such an official temp. Henry III (a reference I owe Dr. Brand). For Jewish acctants and svts in contemporary Castilian royal admin., Mayer, História de las instituciones, ii, 54; Fernandez de Retana, Albores del Imperio, 405; Sánchez de la Cuesta y Gutierrez, Dos Reyes enfermos, 46. Jacob's appt is E 159/48 m. 7: "Baronibus pro A. Regina Anglie consorte Regis Edwardi. Eadem A. mandat eisdem quod assignauit Jacobum de Oxon' Judeum ad recipiendum ad dictum scaccarium nomine suo aurum suum et illud custodiendum quamdiu etcetera. Et ideo mandat eisdem Baronibus quatinus dictum Judeum ad hoc admittant et faciant admiti eundem in hiis que pro utilitate dicte Regine per ipsum factis fuerint. Dat' Lactor' primo die marcii etcetera." See CIR 1264–1268, 449. Benedict's is E 159/59 m. 8d (T 4 Edw.): "Baronibus pro Alienora consorte Regis. Cum karissima consors Regis Alienora Regina Anglie assignauit Benettum de Wynton' Judeum ad aurum ipsius Consortis custodiendum et ad alia negocia ipsam contingentia exequendum prout alii Judei super hoc facere consueuerunt Rex mandat eisdem quod prefatum Benettum ad hoc admittant in forma predicta. Teste etcetera." He was likely apptd ca. 6 June 1276 (CCIR 1272–1279, 296); see also Corcos, "Extracts," 203. Queen-gold accts in the late 1280s incl. fines on Jews for default, false claims, contempt, etc., which must have arisen from the Exch. of the Jews (Records 1286–1289, nos. 3056–3104), perhaps indicating that after Benedict's fall, the goldkpr-treas. assumed the duties of goldkpr at the Exch. of the Jews.

150. Note, however, that after 1288 clks long subord. in the Q's exch., like John Bacun and Richard de Kancia (whose careers are noted below), remained there and did not cross over into the wardrobe.

151. CHEC, 154. Robert le Clerk fl. 1270 (CPR 1266–1272, 480). Of Kancia's clks, Roger de Wylton' was beaten in his house, 1279 (E 13/7 m. 6), and Henry de Norwic' owed the Q £15:5:4 in 1282; a purse he said held £6:0:1 had £5:0:1, 1284 (E 9/36 m. 8d; E 159/55 m. 17d; E 159/57 m. 5d). Of Berewyk's subords, Elyas ackn. receipt of 20 marks from Wodestok's exors E1284 (E 13/11 m. 13); Walter de Meudon was owed a debt 1284 (E 159/57 m. 15). For Bures' subords, see Records 1286–1289, nos. 1328, 3246. William de Eure was Q's atty 1278 and 1281 (JUST 1/542 m. 1d; E. Salter, ed., Feet of Fines for Oxon., 212); Walter de Castello was Berewyk's atty 1284 (E 159/47 m. 5d).

152. Walter's clk 10 Edw. (E 159/55 m. 17d); Berewyk's clk 12 Edw. (E 159/57 m. 17); atty for the Q's exors. (CPR 1281–1292, 246, 420; CCIR 1288–1296, 3, 113, 172, 248). Walter's exor and h. for houses in London (Sharpe, ed., Wills in the Court of Husting, i, 65; JUST 1/1014 m. 8d). Had his fee for E1293, but Robert de Middelton was in his place T1293 (Manners, 127 bis); dead Mar. 1294 when the Q's exors acctd (E 372/143 m. 36, stating Middelton was his replacement).

153. One of this name was bf in Gartree 1287 (S.C. 6/1089/22 m. 1); accused of usurping the sher.'s tourn, 1288 (E 13/13 m. 37). As Q's officer exempt from prosecution, but may already have left office as the Gartree bf 1289–90 was Roger de Walecote (S.C. 6/1089/25 m. 1). The rector at Westerham, b. ca. 1268 (Emden, Oxford, i, 316), res. when the Q gave that adv. to Canterbury Priory, 1290 (Canterbury, Dean and chapter library, Reg. I, ff. 136r–v; below, Chapter Three, Appendix I no. 117).

154. Berewyk's subord. Aug. 1288 (C 47/4/5 ff. 5v, 24v); recd issues to the wardrobe 1290 (S.C. 6/1089/25 mm. 4, 3). See CHEC, 88, 112, 133, 135; Manners, 95–139; CPR 1281–1292, 519, and above, note 152. On Alice, CIR 1256–1259, 2–3; CPR 1258–1266, 220; CChR, ii, 84; CPR 1266–1272, 530; CIR 1268–1272, 119–20; CCIR 1288–1296,

27–28; *CFR,* i, 347; *CIPM,* iii, no. 171. On Grace, *CPR 1272–1281,* 310; *CIPM,* ii, no. 505; *CCIR 1288–1296,* 382, and *CPR 1292–1301,* 28, 342.

155. S.C. 1/30/51 (Caernarvon, 13 Aug., s.a.) to Walter de Odiham and Hugh de Kendale, for whom *CDI,* i, no. 2100 and *CPR 1281–1292,* 126. She told Kirkby Edward had pres. Thomas de Gonneys to the ch. of Fordingbridge, June 1279 (S.C. 1/10/54); Gonneys had £200 from her wardrobe, Aug. 1282 (S.C. 1/32/51) but was controller of Edward's wardrobe (*Oxenden,* 326–36). For Robert de Hulmo, *CHEC,* 63, and Bliss, i, 546.

156. J. C. Parsons, "Queen's Intercession."

157. Dr. Brand thinks Bacun may have been Berewyk's assoc. 1280–81 (citing JUST 1/788 *m.* 30d); see *CPR 1281–1292,* 91. Clk in the Exch. of the Jews T1284 (E 9/44 *m.* 2); Berewyk's clk Feb. 1288, when named with others to audit abbot of Westm.'s accts as Q's treas. (Westm. Abbey muniments 9492). See also *CCIR 1279–1288,* 506–7; *CCIR 1288–1296,* 3, 56; *CPR 1281–1292,* 420; *Records 1286–1289,* no. 2407; *Manners,* 95–139.

158. On Caen, C. R. Cheney, *Notaries Public,* 143–51; Stones and Simpson, eds., *Edward I and the Throne of Scotland,* i, 79–80; *Records 1285–1286,* no. 79; *Records 1286–1289,* nos. 2112, 2169, 2172, 2253, 3216, 3221, 3223; *Manners,* 96. Edmund de Loundres d. 1333 (Tout, *Chapters,* ii, 24, 129; *CPR 1281–1292,* 147; *CPR 1313–1317,* 166; *Records 1286–1289,* 909, 2307, 3242, 3244, 3246; *CHEC,* index p. 174 s.v. "London, Edmund de"; Hill, ed., *Rolls and Reg. Sutton,* viii, 137–38; *Fasti 1300–1541,* i, 16). Hugh de Lyminstr', bf in Anglesey 1286–90 (Westm. Abbey, muniments 23627; *Records 1285–1286,* no. 2364; *CHEC,* 63), was later controller of Edw. II's wife (Blackley and Hermansen, eds., *Household Book,* xii). Berewyk' and Aspale are discussed above.

159. This appt is remarked above, Chapter One, note 137. Montibus was the bp of Verdun's clk, on Q's errand to France Dec. 1277; K's envoy to the German K Jan. 1278 (BL, Add. 36762 *mm.* 1, 2); K's clk, canon of Verdun May 1290 (*CPR 1281–1292,* 354). See also Deedes, ed., *Reg. Pontissara,* i, 184–86; *CPR 1281–1292,* 321, 409, 410, 476; *CCIR 1288–1296,* 8, 107; *Records 1285–1286,* nos. 268, 274, 1681, 2370, and idem, *Records 1286–1289,* nos. 3176, 3179; *CPR 1281–1292,* 30; Bund, ed., *Reg. Godfrey Giffard,* 93, 140.

160. *CPR 1266–1272,* 265; Childs, *Anglo-Castilian Trade,* 14. On Gonzalo, *CPR 1272–1281,* 196; *CChyW,* 4; J. C. Parsons, "English Administration in Ponthieu," 401; *Records 1285–86,* nos. 109, 650, 845–46, 2078; *Records 1286–89,* nos. 166, 258, 318, 566, 3215; *CHEC,* 154. In 1289 he met a Spanish ship at Portsmouth and bought goods for the Q (C 47/4/5 fol. 2).

161. It was upon Kancia's death in 1283 that the Q told Richard de Stockpord' to present John de Caen to that ch. (above, Chapter One, note 129); for Gt Bowden, Stocks and Braggs, eds., *Market Harborough Records,* 19–20. On Little Billing, *CIR 1268–1272,* 252; Hill, ed., *Rolls and Reg. Sutton,* ii, 30; *VCH Northants.,* ii, 102, and iv, 76. For Taxal, *CPR 1272–1281,* 44; on Prestbury, Tait, ed., *Chartulary of St. Werburg,* ii, 329 and note. On Helmdon, *Rolls and Reg. Sutton,* ii, 28; for Lichfield, Martin, ed., *Reg. Peckham,* iii, 1064, and Douie, ed., *Reg. Pecham,* ii, 106.

162. Below, Chapter Three, Appendix I nos. 14, 22, 61b, 72, 105b, 116a, 116e, 117, 118, 152a, 153, 190, 211. With *CCIR 1279–1288,* 80–81, compare pres. of Edmund de Loundres to Shenfield bef. 1284 (*CPR 1281–1292,* 147), William Burnell to Westerham by 1289 (Bliss, i, 506, 517–18), John de Caen to Little Laver (*CPR 1281–1292,* 488), and John de Berewyk' to Scottow by H1291, though perhaps by St. Benet Hulme (E 13/15 *m.* 11; *MA,* iii, 76–77; note 164 below). (Note that Robert de Camville conveyed to the Q the reversion to the manor of Westerham, but she took the adv. at once [Chapter Three, Appendix I no. 117].) Her nephew James was pres. to Cawston by 1282 and to Ringwood ca. 1283 (Emden, *Oxford,* iii, 1737; Chapter Three, Appendix I nos. 84, 88, 148, and *CCIR 1279–1288,* 81). She pres. Gilbert de Ivinghoe to Tring; the K pres. her clk Robert de St. Albano to Great Bowden 1291, her chaplain William de Windesore

to St. Peter's, Northampton, with chapels at Torpel and Upton (Bliss, i, 550; *CPR 1281–1292*, 415; Chapter Three, Appendix I nos. 106, 124, 159). On Aston Cantlow, Chapter Three, Appendix I nos. 78, 224; *PA*, 266; Bund, ed., *Reg. Godfrey Giffard*, 93; Bliss, i, 507.

163. *CPR 1272–1281*, 256; *CPR 1281–1292*, 67; Bliss, i, 445, 453–54, 456, 507, and ii, 11–12. A damaged letter from Edward to the papal chamberlain refers to John de Caen's prebend, "Regine Anglie dudum ab apostolica sede concessa" (S.C. 1/14/83, Dec. 1284).

164. On Hardwick, Hill, ed., *Rolls and Reg. Sutton*, viii, 137–38; on Bockingfold, below, Chapter Three, Appendix I no. 116e. It was cl. 1281 that she bought the adv. of Curry Rivel, but if so it was restored to Henry de Urtiaco by 1322 (Chapter Three, Appendix I note 142). It was also cl. 1281 that she bought the adv. of Scottow from Bartholomew de Redham (Chapter Three, Appendix I no. 152a), but that adv. is also said to have been held by St. Benet Hulme (*MA*, iii, 76–77); her clk John de Berewyk' occ. 1291 as rector at Scottow (above, note 162), perhaps pres. by Hulme to resolve conflict, as Nicholas de Moels offered to pres. Edmund de Loundres to Hardwick when Moels recovered that adv. agst the Q (see text). On the frequency with which religious houses appear in connection with the Q's efforts to obtain advs, compare Coss, *Lordship, Knighthood, and Locality*, 204, 268–69.

165. On Stockport and Giffard, above, Chapter One notes 123, 129. Other cases in which the Q asked or attempted to compel pres. of her clerks by others are Douie, *Pecham*, 108–9; Deedes, ed., *Reg. Pontissara*, i, xiv–xv, 249, 264; Martin, ed., *Reg. Peckham*, i, 359, and ii, 115; Hill, ed., *Rolls and Reg. Sutton*, viii, 137–38. Giffard consulted her steward in 1289 when assigning custody of the ch. at Acton Turville to the archdcn of Glos., as the Q held the manor in wardship (Bund, ed., *Reg. Godfrey Giffard*, 342).

166. Lawlor, *Fasti of St. Patrick's*, 76–77, 95, 124, 167, 177; *CPR 1272–1281*, 44, 425; *CPR 1281–1292*, 30; an exception was Wodestok's stall at Wolverhampton (*CCIR 1272–1279*, 280). As noted above, the Q pres. Ralph le Alemaunt to Aston Cantlow 1278 after recovering that adv. (Bliss, i, 507; *CPR 1281–1292*, 353; *Records 1285–1286*, nos. 612, 618; *Records 1286–1289*, index p. 560 s.v. "Alemand"); and Walter de Bathe to Oldbury 1283 (below, Chapter Three, Appendix I no. 76; Emden, *Oxford*, iii, 2150; Harvey, ed., *Docts of Walter de Wenlok*, 30–31; Bliss, i, 468, 482; *Records 1285–1286*, nos. 69, 224, 2382).

167. *Manners*, 100–1, 120; a text of the commn (BL, Harl. 645 fol. 208v) is in Fenwick, "Inquiry into Complaints," xxxi–iii. In two cases juries were to be at Northampton in June 1291 (JUST 1/542 m. 2d; JUST 1/836 m. 6) but no roll of proceedings there is known to exist. Judgment in a case from Salisbury was to be entered on a "new London roll" (JUST 1/1014 m. 6) but JUST 1/542 does not preserve it. No complaints refer to *Manners*, 99 (Fysseburn'), 105 (Beaulieu, Crevequer, Chidcroft, Faversham, Barshale, Norhamtona), 107 (Baliol, Chilham), 111 (St. Claro), 126 (Mandeville, Enefeud), 135 (Tynten), 129 (Southwark); nor to cases in *CPR 1281–1292*, 484, 519 or *CPR 1292–1301*, 49. The roll of complaints heard at Salisbury (JUST 1/1014) has no complaint relating to Reading Abbey's rights to pannage and herbage in the New Forest, stated to have been determined by the justices assigned to the inquest at Salisbury at the oct. of the Purification 1291 (Kemp, ed., *Reading Abbey Cartularies*, i, 321).

168. *CPR 1281–1292*, 405; *RH*, i, 49, 180, 331, 405; Prynne, *Aurum Reginae*, 108; Johnstone, "Queen's Household," *English Government*, i, 298–99.

169. Shirley, ed., *Royal Letters*, no. 647; *CPR 1272–1281*, 8; occ. 3 Edw. (JUST 1/836 m. 3), 1275 (JUST 1/542 m. 1), 5 Edw. (JUST 1/1014 m. 10d), 7 Edw. (JUST 1/542 m. 5).

170. ?S. of Ralph de P. and Margerie le Strange (JUST 1/1149 m. 1d; *VCH Salop.*, viii, 118; Strange, ed., *Le Strange Records*, 98; Moor, *Knights*, iv, 63–65; Stagg, *CNFD*, i, no. 111). Oversaw Q's works at Langley 1275 X 1279 (KW, 971); her steward Nov. 1280 (*DC*, i, 8). ?Burnell's protégé (Johnstone, "Wardrobe and Household of Henry," 386; *CCIR*

1279–1288, 347). For his attestations to the Q's acts, below, Chapter Three, Appendix II.

171. As steward, after Feb. 1284 farmed a manor at Weeting to William Maylle (noted below). Commr for Q's lands May and (as steward) July !285 (*CPR 1281–1292*, 207, 210); witn. Geoffrey de Southorpe's ackn. of arrears from Upton and Torpel, E1285 (E 159/58 *m.* 6); handed Q's money to abbot of Westm. Feb. 1286 (Westm. Abbey, muniments 23627). Dead Nov. 1287 (Moor, *Knights*, iv, 171–72).

172. At the Exch. for the Q, M1286 (as below); had £50 for expns 1289–90 (E 372/143 *m.* 36); *DNB*, s.v. "Cressingham, Hugh (d. 1297)"; *CIPM*, iii, no. 405.

173. Johnstone, "Queen's Household," Tout, *Chapters*, v, 251.

174. Stagg, *CNFD*, i, nos. 95, 99, 111, 117, 201–12, 219, and index p. 257 s.v. "Bisterne, John de." John was forest steward 1254–55 (before Eleanor's time), but was Kancia's "under-steward" (*CNFD*, nos. 84, 99, 101, 104, 106, 122, 130, 179–85, 190, 211). Fl. Jan. 1280 but d. bef. the Q (*CNFD*, no. 290; JUST 1/1014 *mm.* 8, 9, where his widow appears).

175. Prob. Kancia's deputy. See *CPR 1272–1281*, 182; Stagg, *CNFD*, i, nos. 142–43, 172, 201; in 1291 William de Mynsted' and Margaret de Budesthorn' pr. Hugh ejected them from land in the forest fifteen years earlier (JUST 1/1014 *m.* 8). Const. of Orford castle Apr. 1275 (C 62/51 *m.* 9); collector of chevage on the Jewry Oct. 1277 (C 62/53 *m.* 1). See also *CCIR 1279–1288*, 350–51.

176. Prob. steward by Oct. 1277 (*CCIR 1272–1279*, 405); certainly 5 May 1278 (E 327/551). Sacked Feb. 1291 after many complaints; restored Apr. 1291 (*CPR 1281–1292*, 413, 487). For his accting, S.C. 1/1089/22 *mm.* 1–2; accused 1291 of detaining a sum gtd by the Q for a tenant's daus, he cl. it was not allowed in his accts (JUST 1/1014 *m.* 10).

177. Denholm-Young, *Seignorial Administration*, 66–73; Oschinsky, ed., *Walter of Henley*, 3–4.

178. JUST 1/1149 *m.* 6 cites a meeting with Q and council at Macclesfield. In 1279 Geoffrey de Leukenore wrote John de Kirkby that he had sent the Q information "de consilio speciali Walteri de Kancia" (see Chapter Three). For Maylle, JUST 1/836 *m.* 5; below, Chapter Three, Appendix I no. 149; *CHEC*, 64–65. The taking of extents is discussed further below. For dowers, *Seneschaucie*, Chapter One, in Oschinsky, ed., *Walter of Henley*, 266–67; Albreda's complaint is JUST 1/542 *m.* 1d, Joan's JUST 1/542 *m.* 9 (below, Chapter Three, Appendix I nos. 62, 179a). On Piccheford, respectively *DC*, i, 8; D.L. 27/185; JUST 1/1014 *m.* 4; below, Chapter Three, Appendix I nos. 7, 99, 177. For Cressingham, E 159/60 *m.* 2 (M15 Edw.: three have a day "versus A. Reginam Anglie consortem Regis de placito Quo Warranto per Hugonem de Carsingeham seneschallum eiusdem Regine"); *RP*, i, 30–32, 69; *CHEC*, 21, 93; JUST 1/542 *m.* 12d (see Chapter Three, Appendix I no. 238). For commns, e.g., *CPR 1272–1281*, 471–72, 475; *CPR 1281–1292*, 76, 89, 207, 210, 406 bis. Complaints dismissed incl. JUST 1/542 *m.* 1; JUST 1/1014 *mm.* 7, 9d; JUST 1/1149 *mm.* 9d (Combermere Abbey sought pasture rights at Macclesfield), 10 (Hugh de Dutton sought a third part of a messuage at Bollington). Bfs had complaints similarly dismissed, as noted below.

179. *Seneschaucie*, Chapter One, in Oschinsky, ed., *Walter of Henley*, 266–67. Dr. Brand thinks John was yr son of Roger de Lovetot (d. 1274; Sanders, *Baronies*, 80–81; Foss, *Judges*, iii, 132; Moor, *Knights*, iii, 74). JUST 1/1014 *m.* 1d, in H1291, notes an extent of the New Forest taken with John's help seventeen years earlier. The Q's bf Adam Basset was to acct bef. Lovetot and others at the morrow of St. John Baptist 1280 (E 13/8 *m.* 23d); John attested or presided for Chapter Three, Appendix II nos. 2a, 5, 6a–b, 8, 10, 14–16, 26–29, 30a–b, 33–34, 36a, 37; the Q's council is discussed further below. See also *CPR 1272–1281*, 263; *CPR 1281–1292*, 105, 207; J. C. Parsons, "English Administration in Ponthieu," 374–76, 392; Stagg, *CNFD*, i, nos. 186, 336. John recd her accts viewed at the Exch. on debts to Luccans, May 1287 (E 159/60 *m.* 7; *Records 1286–1289*, no. 3143); to audit abbot of Westm.'s accts Feb. 1288 (Westm. Abbey, muniments 9492).

178. JUST 1/836 *m.* 1d (Lovetot paid Mauteby £10 for release of all rancor); accused of withholding the K's writ of right, a subbf cl. that on the day the writ was to be pleaded in

the Q's court at Cawston, he was absent in London by Lovetot's order (JUST 1/836 m. 1). On auditors as outsiders to the lord's service, Denholm-Young, *Seignorial Administration*, 140–41; Plucknett, *Legislation of Edward I*, 155–56; *Seneschaucie*, chaps. 70–76, in Oschinsky, ed., *Walter of Henley*, 288–91.

181. Lovetot's s. John, Q's squire 1284, was kntd Easter 1287 (Moor, *Knights*, iii, 74–75; E 101/351/9 m. 9; *Records 1286–1289*, index p. 610 s.v. "Lovetot;" *CHEC*, 81). A yr s. Nicholas was rector at the Q's manor at Bowden (Stocks and Bragg, eds., *Harborough Parish Records*, 19–20; Hill, ed., *Rolls and Reg. Sutton*, iii, 50–51; *Fasti 1066–1300*, i, 54–55); below, Chapter Three, Appendix I no. 110. John sr "per extentam approbauit" a rent Kancia exacted from a salt–pan in the New Forest, and plowings or grain offered the foresters as acts of kindness, now exacted as customary services (JUST 1/1014 *mm.* 1d, 8). He disallowed the lesser tithe in bfs' accts at Burgh and raised the rent for a flock of fowl at Cawston from 1d. to 1½d. per bird (JUST 1/836 *mm.* 2, 6d). On his lands, *CIPM*, iii, no. 207; *EFF*, ii, index 283 s.v. "Lovetot (Lovetoft), John"; most charges agst him in 1289–90 involved Essex, where he had acq. much land (Tout and Johnstone, *State Trials*, 236–39; Brand, "Edward I and the Justices," 31–40).

182. The prior of Exning failed to pr. Maurice stole a cow and calf; inq. pr. he ejected a couple from their house at Newmarket and imprisoned them for breaking and entering the bldg (JUST 1/836 *mm.* 4, 5d). On Burgh, JUST 1/826 m. 2 (below, Chapter Three, Appendix I no. 151a); compare *Seneschaucie*, chaps. 9, 22, in Oschinsky, ed., *Walter of Henley*, 266–67, 270–71. In 15 Edw. reeves at Stogursey and Camel acctd with John de Horstede; those at Torpel, Upton and Nocton with Roger de Walecote (S.C. 6/1089/22 m. 1).

183. In general, Plucknett, *Medieval Bailiff; Seneschaucie*, chaps. 9, 22, in Oschinsky, ed., *Walter of Henley*, 266–67, 270–71. On provision for the bfs, *CPR 1272–1281*, 471–72; *CPR 1281–1292*, 76; Stewart-Brown, ed., *Rolls of Chester*, 232–33, 237; Ormerod, *Chester*, iii, 63. JUST 1/1149 m. 7d shows tenants fed the bf at Hope, m. 3 that men of Kynarton fed him when he visited. Though stewards usually presided at her courts, bfs also did so (Robert de Bures at Overton, JUST 1/1149 m. 5d *bis*; Thomas de Macclesfeld' at Hope, JUST 1/1140 m. 5); a subbf did so at Overton (JUST 1/1149 m. 5).

184. For Macclesfeld', Stewart-Brown, ed., *Rolls of Chester*, 212; Tait, ed., *Chartulary of St. Werburgh's*, ii, no. 574, and below (he was *uxoratus*); for Waleden, *DNB*, s.v. "Waleden, Humphrey de (d. 1330?)"; on Ponte, apparently also *laicus*, see below. William Burnell, bf in Gartree 14 Edw., was not certainly the clk Eleanor pres. to Westerham bef. 1289 (as above, note 162).

185. *RP*, i, 279, *CChyW*, 11, and *CPR 1313–1317*, 686-87, show Cretyng bf at Overton, 1283; JUST 1/1149 m. 9 says her first bf there held office for about a year and Cretyng was a knt by autumn 1284 (E 101/352/12 m. 7; *GEC*, iii, 532; Moor, *Knights*, i, 249). On Bures, *Knights*, i, 159; N. M. Fryde, "Royal Enquiry," 367 (where wrongly bf at Macclesfield), 368–69, 373–74. Johnstone, "Queen's Exchequer," 145, makes Robert not Richard the Q's *garderobarius* (discussed above). Robert, Q's squire June 1283 (E 101/351/9 m. 8), was bf "apud Sessoneyk in Wallia" M1286 (Westm. Abbey, muniments 23627); see *CChyV*, 264, 313; *Manners*, 96, 98; *DC*, i, 492, 518, 563.

186. Ponte showed John de Antingham had a writ of novel disseisin in the K's court touching land at Wichingham (JUST 1/836 m. 1); Macclesfeld' did likewise when Adam fitz Richard complained of ejection at Hope (JUST 1/1149 m. 5). Adam, bf of the bp of Salisbury, cl. to be his atty; Waleden pr. he was not so attorned and got the complaint dismissed, even though inq. pr. Adam's complaint (JUST 1/1014 m. 1).

187. Prob. from Bridgwater, Soms. (Brand, "Early History of the Legal Profession," 28). Bef. 11 June 1270 Kancia and Ponte entered Richard de Seez' manor at Tothill (JUST 1/542 m. 5). In Soms. ca 1270 (below, Chapter Three, Appendix I no. 196; *CCIR 1279–1288*, 88); in Hants., 1270s (Stagg, *CNFD*, i, nos. 95, 212, 249); in Norf. ca. 1278 (*RP*, i, 299 [see *MA*, iii, 64; Chapter Three, Appendix I no. 148]; *RO*, i, 47; *Manners*, 98; E 101/505/19

m. 2). On Kent, *CPR 1281–1292,* 21; const. at Leeds 1285–90 (*KW,* 695; Martin, ed., *Reg. Peckham,* iii, 924–25; *CClR 1288–1296,* 82, 113; E 101/351/20 *m.* 3). See *CClR 1272–1279,* 349; *CClR 1288–1296,* 299; *EFF,* ii, 63; *Records 1286–1289,* no. 3109; *CHEC,* 98, 123. ?John "de Bruges," K's clk 1285, 1288 (*CPR 1281–1292,* 197, 302, references I owe to Dr. Brand). As Kancia's exor Ponte insisted "quod nichil sciret dicere, nec vellet, nec onus testamenti predicti Walteri sibi assumere" 1291 (JUST 1/1014 *m.* 8d; *Manners,* 109). His prominence (or notoriety) is seen in refs to him as "steward" on the Q's East Anglian lands (JUST 1/836 *m.* 5), and Cressingham's understeward (*Oxenden,* 273); he is otherwise called only bf.

188. *CHEC,* 104; *CPR 1272–1281,* 462; *CClR 1288–1296,* 167; *Records 1286–1289,* index p. 637 s.v. "Silverstrode, John de"; *Manners,* 97; *CPR 1281–1292,* 351, 361, 406. John Gule of Feckenham cl. 1291 fitz Thomas jailed him for trespass of venison without indictment (JUST 1/542 *m.* 7d); fitz Thomas heard pleas there Mar. 1290 but the Q was gtd them only in June (*CPR 1281–1292,* 361, 398). John "de Goule," prob. the 1291 querent, fined for such trespasses at Feckenham, Apr. 1290 (*CPR 1281–1292,* 350). On local recruitment, Oschinsky, ed., *Walter of Henley,* 316–17.

189. JUST 1/836 *mm.* 1 (Petra), 2d (Horeshegh). Jurors said Woderowe was made bf when Didmarton came to the Q's hands (JUST 1/542 *m.* 2d [in 1280: below, Chapter Three, Appendix I no. 81]). JUST 1/1149 *m.* 9 says Streche was at Hope for a year or so after the land was gtd her (Feb. 1283: Chapter Three, Appendix I no. 67); for the dispossession, *CIM,* ii, no. 1555; *CClR 1279–1288,* 455; *CIPM,* i, nos. 524, 770; *VCH Worcs.,* iii, 376. On Chidecroft, *CClR 1288–1296,* 225; JUST 1/542 *m.* 13d (acquitted of breaking down a wall at a mill in Brenchley); he seized lands settled for life on a Crevequer bastard (Chapter Three, Appendix I nos. 116h–j). Walecote acctd for lands in Lincs., Northants., Leics., and Ruts. from 1287 (S.C. 6/1089/22 *m.* 1); see also Mellows, ed., *Pytchley's Book of Fees,* 65. Macclesfeld' acctd for that bailiwick from 14 Edw. (S.C. 1/1089/22 *m.* 2); Ormerod, *Chester,* iii, 63, 748–49, shows Thomas' dau. m. Thomas s. of Roger de Daveneport for whom *CPR 1272–1281,* 471–72; *CPR 1281–1292,* 76; Stewart-Brown, ed., *Rolls of Chester,* 232–33, 237; a sister m. Hugh de Hoppele, Q's free tenant at Hope (JUST 1/1149 *m.* 7). On Cretingham, JUST 1/836 *m.* 6 (Sybilla widow of Hugh de Doddeneys and Theobald de Bellus recover dower in Dodnash detained by Cretingham); compare Geoffrey de Piccheford as a possible protégé of Robert Burnell, above, note 170. William Godwin and John Cok' of Soham, and Henry Juwet of Fordham, were perhaps attached to Cressingham (JUST 1/836 *m.* 4d). In Flints., Bleddyn ap Neuner and David ap Ythel were subbfs (JUST 1/1149 *mm.* 2d, 3d, 7).

190. One of this name witn. Alice de Grymstede's 1291 ackn. of payment for grain at Compton, Wilts., usurped by the Q's bfs to the use of the Q's cousin James de la Plaunche while ward of a manor at Compton was in the Q's hands, 1274 × 1289 (Chapter Three, Appendix I no. 229 and note 149). John le Botiller acq. 3 messuages and 2½ virgates at Compton, 1281 (Pugh, ed., *Feet of Fines relating to Wilts.,* no. 41). Botiller's actions at Woodrow, 1280, are noted in detail below, Chapter Three; on Essex and Hants., Chapter Three, Appendix I nos. 60, 88. ?The John le Botiller whose s. h. John, of Compton (fl. 1316), m. Joan (b. ca. 1282), dau. h. of Sir John le Fauconer (d. 1305) of Hants. (*VCH Hants.,* i, 124, 131).

191. For Ponte, above. Waleden was bf in N. Erpingham prob. before Ponte's tenure ca. 1278 (JUST 1/836 *m.* 2d; above, note 187); accused of ejecting John de Newburgh from Hurcott after 1276 (JUST 1/1014 *m.* 6; *RP,* i, 21–22; below, Chapter Three, Appendix I no. 197a–b). Bf at Lavington after 1288 (JUST 1/1014 *m.* 1; Chapter Three, Appendix I no. 232). Forester as Ponte's sub-bf detained fishing rights from the parson and the vill at Aylsham (JUST 1/836 *m.* 1d *bis*); accused of stealing sheep in Barstable in Sept. 1290 (JUST 1/542 *m.* 1).

192. The acct is S.C. 1/1089/22 *m.* 1. Horstede seized goods of Giles de Fysseburn' at Williton bef. 1280 (below, Chapter Three, Appendix I no. 190 note 139); accused of

seizing fees from John de Newburgh after 1276 (JUST 1/1014 *m.* 6d; Chapter Three, Appendix I no. 197a–b); acctd for lands in Soms. from 14 Edw.; to attend inq. at Somerton, 13 Edw. (Bates, ed., *Cartularies of Muchelney and Athelney,* 128–29; Chapter Three, Appendix I no. 187c note 138).

193. Below, Chapter Three, Appendix I note 87. Welsh lands gtd the Q in wardship in 1289 (Chapter Three, Appendix I no. 2) were admin. for the Q in 1290 by the K's chamberlain in N. Wales (see above, note 123). Cressingham and Bures settled the Q's admin. at Haverfordwest from 1288 (*RP,* i, 84; Chapter Three, Appendix I no. 177); no complaints heard at Chester in 1291 involve Haverfordwest (but see *RP,* i, 30–33). On Washingley, Chapter Three, Appendix I no. 110; S.C. 1/1089/25 *m.* I has Washingley in sequence with Nocton, Torpel, Gartree, Upton, Kingsthorpe, Spelhoe, and Market Harborough. As bf in East Anglia, Ponte had subbfs Robert de Petra and Robert de Eggemere at Burgh, Cawston and Erpingham (JUST 1/836 *m.* 4d), Walter Bukskyn at Scottow, Hautbois, Horstead, Bentley Dodnash, and Tattingstone (*m.* 4d *bis*), and at Aylsham, John le Forester and David (*m.* 1); bef. Ponte's time, Waleden had subbfs William atte Mare and Alexander de Horeshege in S. Erpingham (*m.* 2d). All complaints from Kent are on JUST 1/542.

194. Below, Chapter Three, Appendix I, respectively nos. 134–35, 77a, 80, 149, 238, 199, 1–2.

195. Stagg, *CNFD,* i, 20–22; S.C. 1/1089/25 *m.* 2 (18 Edw.) has reeves at Lockerley, Swainston, Thorness, Brighstone, Ringwood, and manors pertinent to wardship of Patrick de Chaworth's lands.

196. With what follows compare *Manners,* 98 and below, Chapter Three, Appendix I nos. 25, 67, 69, 85, 105, 115, 124, 187, 239. Except for Macclesfield, Burgh, and Leeds, these manors were the Q's earliest tenures in their respective bailiwicks.

197. For Lyndhurst, JUST 1/1014 *m.* 12d; Somerton, Ches., Staffs., and Derbs. are discussed above. JUST 1/1149 *mm.* 5, 7, show Robert de Bures bf at Hope with David ap Ythel subbf and Roger le Fykeis *als* le Porter at Hope; Bures at Overton had a subbf Thomas le Taverner whose subord. was Bleddyn ap Neuner (JUST 1/1149 *mm.* 1, 3, 3d, 5). On Fykeis, below, Chapter Three, Appendix I no. 73 note 107; for Taverner, *CChR,* ii, 410, 422; *DC,* i, 518. For Harborough, S.C. 6/1089/25 *m.* I has Roger de Walecote accting thus; see *Manners,* 98. For Langley, JUST 1/542 *m.* 3; S.C. 1/1089/25 *m.* 1. From ca. 1285 the principal bf at Leeds was Ponte (above, note 187).

198. On the Glos. wardship, below, chap. 3; compare also *CHEC,* 128, and below, Chapter Three, Appendix I no. 5. See *Records 1286–1289,* no. 3229, and Chapter Three, Appendix I no. 110. Cressingham's letters to Upton, quoting the Q's mandate *in extenso,* are E 40/87.

199. On extents, Oschinsky, ed., *Walter of Henley,* 264–65, 312. JUST 1/836 *m.* 1 and *Manners,* 119, show Adam de Fallynge won 5 marks for a rent at Wichingam raised by Lovetot; JUST 1/1014 *m.* 1d and *Manners,* 106, show Richard Buc of Hordley got £10 for rent raised on a salt-pan; the payments to men of Dibden, Sawley, Cadland, and Horbury (*Manners,* 106, 108 *ter*) refer to JUST 1/1014 *mm.* 8–9. Another consequence of the Q's acq. of new lands is evident: on such lands she was not held to respect privileges coming to be claimed by tenants of the ancient demesne, so her officials could raise rents and services (Hoyt, *Royal Demesne,* 171–207; McIntosh, *Autonomy and Community,* 1–49). Alice Follet lost 60s. (JUST 1/1014 *m.* 9; Stagg, *CNFD,* i, index p. 276 s.v. "Follet, Alice, of Exbury"; *VCH Hants.,* iii, 290 [has two daus; the complaint says three]). A carpenter at Hope was paid 30s. of £10 agreed upon for works there; the bf said Lovetot disallowed it but Lovetot pr. the bf never asked (JUST 1/1149 *m.* 6). The other cases cited are respectively JUST 1/1014 *m.* 4; JUST 1/1149 *mm.* 7d, 6d, 3; JUST 1/1014 *m.* 1.

200. For Barwick, below, Chapter Three, Appendix I no. 188; *CIM,* i, no. 575; for the relief, E 13/6 *m.* 9. On Sandwich, Chapter Three, Appendix I no. 120; *CChR,* ii, 368; Canterbury, Dean and chapter library, Reg. I fol. 197v *bis* (bf unnamed; the mayor was

warned "ke nus nen oums autre feez pleinte de co par vostre defaute"). By Nov. 1290, £20 were spent on works there (E 372/143 m. 36); *Manners*, 95, 97, 100, 104, 113, 116, 121, 129, show £440 spent by Aug. 1293.

201. Below, chap. 3., Appx I nos. 27, 28, 177. On Haverfordwest, *CPR 1281–1292*, 330–31; Edwards, ed., *Anct Correspondence*, 170. The Valences petitioned in parlt H1290, when inq. was ordered for 8 Mar. (*RP*, i, 30–31; *CPR 1281–1292*, 398); Q's letters to Cressingham on 6 Mar. prob. concerned that inq. (*CHEC*, 93). Joan did not appear in parlt in June; the Q won judgment by default, prob. the gist of her letters to Cressingham 19 June (*RP*, i, 31; *CHEC*, 108). See also Phillips, *Aymer de Valence*, 246, 251–52; *RP*, i, 68–69, 84; *CPR 1292–1301*, 49, 114.

202. Basset was former bf in Soms. and Dors. E1280, when mainperned to be bef. justices to acct on 25 June; he then ackn. £30:15:8 owing (E 13/8 m. 23d; E 159/55 m. 10). See Stagg, *CNFD*, i, no. 95; *CCIR 1279–1288*, 425; *CCIR 1288–1296*, 146. Acquitted of seizing ten librates at Williton from Giles de Fysseburn' (JUST 1/1014 m. 7), though *Manners*, 99, shows Giles had £7:15:0 for goods taken at Williton by Basset and John de Horstede, perhaps the judgment from a lost complaint (compare, Chapter Three, Appendix I no. 190 note 139). Geoffrey de Southorpe, lessee of Torpel and Upton, went to prison owing some £84 for the farm of those manors (E. King, *Peterborough Abbey*, 43). For Boyville, Chapter Three, Appendix I no. 125.

203. In 1291 the abbot of Cerne cl. that the vill and port of Melcombe Regis, conveyed to the Q in 1280, were worth 100s. (JUST 1/542 m. 7d; below, Chapter Three, Appendix I no. 50) but this amount was prob. inflated: issues from Melcombe were 63s.2¾d. in 15 Edw. (with arrears of 74s.8½d.), and in 1296–97 issues were 63s. (S.C. 6/1090/4).

204. For Langley, *CCIR 1279–1288*, 80–81; S.C. 6/1089/22 m. 1; S.C. 6/1089/25 m. 1. For Soms. and Scottow, *CCIR 1279–1288*, 80–81; S.C. 6/1089/25 m. 1 bis. For Somerton, *BF*, 1265; S.C. 6/1089/25 mm. 1–2 shows two payments of £30 each in 18 Edw. For Gartree, *RH*, i, 237; S.C. 6/1089/22 mm. 1, 2; S.C. 1/1089/25 m. 1. The value of Uphill and Christon is stated in William de Pateneye's complaint to recover the lands in 1291 (JUST 1/542 m. 8; below, Chapter Three, Appendix I no. 199); S.C. 6/1089/22 m. 2, S.C. 6/1089/25 m. 2. For Nocton, *CCIR 1279–1288*, 80–81; Westm. Abbey, muniments 23627 (in two payments). For the forest, Stagg, *CNFD*, i, nos. 352–69; S.C. 6/1089/22 mm. 1–2; S.C. 6/1089/25 m. 1.

205. JUST 1/1149 mm. 3d, 4–4d, 7, 10; JUST 1/1014 m. 8d; E. B. Fryde, *Welsh Entries*, no. 144.

206. For Bokland, JUST 1/1014 m. 6d, where "la Fernycrofte" is surely "la Ferthingcrofte" held by Roger at 2s. rent, May 1291 (Stagg, *CNFD*, i, no. 354; eighteen years before would put Kancia's actions ca. 1273, when the forest was extended [JUST 1/1014 m. 1d]). On Burele, Chapter Three, Appendix I no. 101; JUST 1/1014 m. 6d; *CNFD*, i, no. 388. On Beaulieu, JUST 1/1014 m. 10d (see *Manners*, 105; *CNFD*, i, index p. 281 s.v. "Gras, Robert s. of Geoffrey le"). For St. Benet Hulme, JUST 1/836 m. 4, and on the Bruyns, *RG*, ii, nos. 1569–70.

207. For Clive, Mandeville, and Southwark, respectively JUST 1/1014 m. 9 (Cressingham ackn. Kancia ordered the rent detained eight years earlier), and *Manners*, 110, 126, 129. For St. Albans, Cornwall, Peterborough, St. Benet Hulme, and Amesbury, respectively JUST 1/542 mm. 1 (sum illegible), 11, 12d (*Manners*, 117); JUST 1/836 m. 4d; *RP*, i, 50 bis, 310. Peterborough paid Cressingham and Berewyk' money fees to "secure a certain amount of mutual understanding" (E. King, *Peterborough Abbey*, 133–34).

208. For Pipard and Uplambourne, respectively JUST 1/542 m. 4d and JUST 1/836 m. 4, the Uplambourne detention perhaps perpetrated ca. 1274 when the Q was exor of Bathe's widow (*CFR 1272–1307*, 26; *CIPM*, ii, no. 145). On Peterborough, St. Asaph, and Winchester, respectively *RP*, i, 310; JUST 1/1149 m. 6d (the bp cl. English tenants, "volentes in hiis et aliis altiorem statum habere," withheld suit, tithes and other dues); JUST 1/1014 m. 1 (men of Lavington misinformed the steward when he extended the manor in 1288). For Norfolk, St. Benet Hulme, and Canterbury, respectively JUST 1/836

m. 6; *RP,* i, 299; *CCIR 1279–1288,* 16. William Burnell was accused of usurping the sher.'s tourn in Gartree hundred (above, note 153).

209. For Antingham and Gryndel, JUST 1/836 *mm.* 2d, 4. For Baldwin and Cole, JUST 1/542 *m.* 4; Stagg, *CNFD,* i, nos. 101, 117, 184–85, 190, 212, 249. The other cases cited are respectively JUST 1/1149 *mm.* 1, 2d *bis,* 3d, 6d *bis.*

210. For Winchester, JUST 1/1014 *m.* 6; Stagg, *CNFD,* i, nos. 214, 223; *Manners,* 119, 137, 138. On Cawston, JUST 1/836 *m.* 1. For Imber, JUST 1/1014 *m.* 1; J. C. Parsons, "Towards a Social History," 54–55, 61–62, 68–69. On Kancia, JUST 1/1014 *m.* 8d; Stagg, *CNFD,* i, nos. 179–85, 190, 192, 193, 249.

211. Querents at Hope cl. Roger de Montalt as bf detained them from an inheritance at Peny-wern (JUST 1/1149 *m.* 1d); in the New Forest, Henry Toluse cl. ejection by Eustace Fucher (JUST 1/1014 *m.* 8; Fucher was Kancia's crony but not his bf [JUST 1/1014 *m.* 7d]). Refs to bfs' misconduct in the Q's lifetime are, e.g., *CCIR 1272–1279,* 70; *CIPM,* ii, no. 619; *CPR 1281–1292,* 330–31; see also above, Chapter One, note 3.

212. Denholm-Young, *Seignorial Administration,* 32–86, 99–108. Pecham also urged the e. of Surrey to improve conditions for his tenants, "ad augmentum honoris et famae vestrae cum eisdem subditis, ad salutem animae vestrae misericorditer et humiliter componendo, advertentes quod per hujusmodi quasi vobis inutilia non decet vestros subjectos affligere; ad quorum protectionem et regiminem tenemimi. . . . " (Martin, ed., *Reg. Peckham,* i, 38–39; compare ii, 619–20).

213. Plucknett, *Legislation of Edward I,* 150–56; there is no reason to think that the Q's admin. adopted the experimental re-organization of the K's demesne manors initiated in 1275 (Maddicott, "Edward I and the Lessons of Reform," 21–23; Prestwich, *Edward I,* 102–3). On commns and inqs, above, Chapter Two, note 6; Bates, ed., *Cartularies of Muchelney and Athelney,* 128–29; *CIPM,* ii, no. 619; *CCIR 1279–1288,* 108, 337; *CChyV,* 313; *CFR 1272–1307,* 275; Johnstone, "Queen's Household," Tout, *Chapters,* v, 282, and *English Government,* i, 289–90.

214. On Henry III, Coss, *Lordship, Knighthood, and Locality,* 275–76. Southampton resented Castilian merchants (Childs, *Anglo-Castilian Trade,* 14); perhaps to protect them the Q was gtd custody of the castle, 1276 (below, Chapter Three, Appendix I no. 86), and in Nov. 1283 inq. was to see if rights and franchises pertinent to that tenure were subtracted (*CPR 1281–1292,* 105). Goods of her merchant Gonzalo de Sagaurz' were seized (S.C. 1/19/46 is Burnell's order to restore them, 13 Nov. s.a.), the townsmen tried to exact toll from her men (as above, note 6), and in 1286 they refused to pay murage the K gtd to repair the castle (as above, Chapter One).

215. JUST 1/836 *m.* 5d (reeve adjudged to prison); JUST 1/1149 *m.* 1d (Thomas convicted); JUST 1/836 *m.* 5d (Joan la Converse's charms were not disputed, but Bolytoute failed to prosecute).

216. For dismissal for misconduct, *RH,* ii, 288 (compare *CIM,* i, no. 1184, and Ormerod, *Chester,* iii, 746 note "b"). Fitz Thomas seized land and a wardship in the New Forest (*CCIR 1272–1279,* 405; *CIPM,* ii, no. 529), but held office until 1291; implicated in a 1285 Norf. disseisin, Walter Bukskyn d. in office 17 Edw. (*CPR 1281–1292,* 207; JUST 1/836 *mm.* 4d, 6). Kancia's offenses in the New Forest cost him that stewardship ca. 1277 (Stagg, *CNFD,* i, nos. 117, 179–85, 190, 212, 249), but he remained goldkpr and steward of the Q's lands until he d. 1283. The 1285 commn is *CPR 1281–1292,* 210.

217. For 1279–80, S.C. 1/11/11 and S.C. 1/19/190 (see Chapter Three). The letter quoted is S.C. 1/11/46, s.d (see Chapter Three, Appendix I no. 27).

218. Cole, ed., *Documents illustrative of English History,* xix; JUST 1/1014 *m.* 9. Cressingham remarked that the matter was settled years before; Margaret admitted this, saying she sought the justices' decision for greater security. See also Sayles, ed., *Select Cases,* i, 103, and below, Chapter Three, Appendix I no. 201.

219. On Cauz and Lyndon, JUST 1/542 *m.* 9, JUST 1/1014 *m.* 8, both brought as nothing was done in pursuance of the Q's orders (on Cauz, Stagg, *CNFD,* i, no. 403). For the Welsh

ward, *CHEC,* 20–21, and N. M. Fryde, "Royal Enquiry into Abuses," 374; on Margaret, JUST 1/1149 *m.* 5d. For the 1290 meetings with Upton and the men of Overton, JUST 1/1149 *mm.* 10, 6 (for the date, *CHEC,* 150–51); the Q's death impeded measures she ordered in both cases. For Welsh tenants, E. B. Fryde, ed., *Welsh Entries,* no. 144. Pecham's letter is Martin, ed., *Reg. Peckham,* ii, 619; no complaint touching Westcliffe appears in the extant 1291 proceedings.

220. Johnstone, "Queen's Household," Tout, *Chapters,* v, does not find a thirteenth-century council; compare idem, "Queen's Household," *English Government,* i, 292–94. Seez was to pay part of the ransom on 11 June 1270 (JUST 1/542 *m.* 5; below, Chapter Three, Appendix I nos. 134–35). Botiller's letter is quoted in Chapter Three; see also Chapter Three, Appendix I no. 61b, and *CCIR 1279–1288,* 52 (compare *CHEC,* 48–50). For Wauton's meeting, JUST 1/542 *m.* 4d; on the date (ca. 1286), Chapter Three, Appendix I no. 215.

221. For Giffard, above, Chapter One note 88; S.C. 1/11/11 (s.d.) reads in part: "Dunc ma dame si le conseil nostre seignour le rei et le vostre vus loe, procures sil vus ples les brefs nostre seignour le rei. . . . "

222. Below, Chapter Three, Appendix II. She nom. him arbitrator in an exch. of lands with the e. of Essex, May 1286 (D.L. 27/185). The Grey letter is S.C. 1/30/47 (s.d.). A letter from Burnell to Kirkby, 25 Mar. 1283, forwards the Q's letter enclosing a petition Kirkby will expedite (S.C. 1/9/34 [at Caernarvon]); her letter is perhaps S.C. 1/10/51 (Aberconway, 17 Mar.), on a widow defrauded of houses in London. See also *Records 1286–1289,* nos. 3229 *bis,* 3230, 3235; S.C. 6/1089/25 *m.* 3 shows letters sent him in autumn 1290.

223. Shirley, ed., *Royal Letters,* no. 647; S.C. 1/11/51 (discussed below, in chap. 3). Of 47 of her letters identified 13 are to Chancery clks, 10 of them to Kirkby (S.C. 1/10/39, 48–56; E 159/61 *m.* 1d is to him as Treas.). That quoted here is S.C. 1/10/53; the result was apparently the K's gt to her of the Maelor Saesneg, June X Aug. 1283 (Chapter Three, Appendix I no. 69).

224. Content of letters is specified in *Records 1286–1289,* no. 3229 (compare *CCIR 1288–1292,* 373), and *CHEC,* 93, 108, 114. For 1278, E 327/551, S.C. 1/30/54; on Sandwich, see above. For letters on Haverfordwest, above, note 201, and for 1286, *CChR,* ii, 353.

225. John de Upton', the men of Overton, Margaret de Budesthorn' and Margaret de Bromfeld' are cited above; compare reduction of tenants' rent in Anglesey because of their poverty, and provision for a Welsh ward in 1290, also noted above. An exception also remarked earlier was Sybilla, widow of Hugh de Doddeneys, who vainly sought dower from Q and stewards. See also Riley, ed., *Gesta Abbatum Sancti Albani,* 411–12.

226. Above, Chapter One note 129; below, Chapter Three, Appendix I nos. 61a, 67 (with N. M. Fryde, "Royal Enquiry," 375), 117, 171, 202.

CHAPTER THREE

1. *Guisborough,* 216; *Dunstable,* 363; Martin, ed., *Reg. Peckham,* ii, 619–20, 767–68 (English text, used here), and iii, 937–38 (English text partly in Johnstone, "Queen's Household," Tout, *Chapters,* v, 270–71, and partly the author's translation).

2. *CCIR 1279–1288,* 80–81. Transactions omitted are below, Appx I nos. 60, 62 (only the reversion was conveyed; the Q did not hold the manor in 1281), 81, 116a, 117 (reversion), 135a (gtd away by 1281), 171 (gtd away), 199 (tentatively dated ca. 1280, but perhaps later), 210a. The omission of no. 172 (July 1281) might offer a *terminus ante quem* for the schedule.

3. Sanders and Treharne, eds., *Documents of the Baronial Movement,* 86–87; E. King, "Large and small landowners," 33–34, and idem, *Peterborough Abbey,* 134; Richardson, *English Jewry,* 107; H. P. Stokes, "Relationship," 167–68; Douie, *Pecham,* 328.

4. McFarlane, "Had Edward I a `Policy'?" Hoyt, *Royal Demesne,* chap. 5, and Wolffe, *Royal Demesne,* 45–46, 52–55, 65–66, concentrate on Edward's larger addns, but he acq. much land on a lesser scale (*Kalendars,* i, 34–70; Hall, ed., *Red Book,* i, lxxii–lxxiii, cxxiii–cxxxii); Prestwich, *Edward I,* 237.

5. Jewish debts are discussed in Chapter Two; Roth, *Jews in England,* 64–73; Richardson, *English Jewry,* 106–7. Johnstone, "Queen's Household," Tout, *Chapters,* v, 270, notes "the large share Edward assigned his wife in his exploitation of the Jews." For cases of Edward's cooperation, see *CCIR 1279–1288,* 80–81; for his gifts, *CPR 1272–1281,* 193, and J. C. Parsons, "English Administration in Ponthieu," 383. Financing the Q's purchases is discussed further below. Details of payment, hard to come by, can be contradictory (Raban, "Land market and the aristocracy," 240 note 5)—e.g., below, Appendex I no. 118, where in 1280 Gilbert Pecche is paid either 200 or 1000 marks for a manor in Kent. Compare arrangements for Pecche's later conveyance, Appendix I no. 21.

6. For Margaret's assignment, *CPR 1292–1301,* 451–53; fourteenth-century assignments are in Wolffe, *Royal Demesne,* 230–31, 237, 238–39. On the twelfth-century assignment, see Chapter Two. Summary accounts for *terre Regine* in 1296–97 are on the Pipe roll for 29 Edw. I, E 372/146 mm. 25d, 29–29d, 42–46; S.C. 6/1090/4 is a bundle of detailed accts for them in 1295–96.

7. For what follows, Treharne, "Knights in the Period of Reform"; E. King, "Large and Small Landowners"; Postan, *Medieval Economy and Society,* 159–65; Coss, "Geoffrey de Langley"; Carpenter, "A crisis of the Knightly Class?"; Raban, "Land Market and the Aristocracy"; Stacey, *Politics, Policy and Finance,* 9, 155–56, 216–17; Coss, *Lordship, Knighthood and Locality,* 159–209, 264–304; Prestwich, *English Politics,* 62–63; Harding, *England in the Thirteenth Century,* 194–203.

8. J. C. Parsons, "English Administration in Ponthieu," 382–84. In docts for those Ponthevin purchases, such phrases as "nimia necessitate urgente" appear often but do not specify debts of any kind; for similar language in English docts referring to Jewish debts (not in connection with the Q's purchases), Fowler, ed., *Cartulary of Old Wardon,* 360–64, esp. 363–64.

9. Holt, *The Northerners,* 85–86; Stubbs, ed., *Select Charters,* 289, 294, 377; Stacey, *Politics, Policy, and Finance,* 9, 155–56, 216–17; on Southorpe, E. King, "Large and Small Landowners," 36.

10. For the 1264–65 gts in Derbs., below, Appendix I nos. 35, 37, 38, 129, 134, and prob. also no. 39; on the Soms. lands, nos. 186, 187a–b; for Leics. and Northants., nos. 124a–c, 125, 157a–c; on the New Forest, nos. 84–85, 187b–c; for Aylsham, no. 147a–b; for Macclesfield, no. 25. As noted above, Chapter Two, these manors later appear as centers for the Q's lands in Norfolk, Northants., Hants., and Soms. The 1270 gt is *CChR,* ii, 133. S. D. Lloyd, *English Society and the Crusade,* 171 and note, remarks that other crusaders obtained similar gts at this time, but (as Lloyd seems to imply) the gt to Eleanor cannot be exactly compared to others' precautions; it may have been intended to safeguard reversion to the Crown should she not survive the expedition. The inalienability of lands she held by Crown gt is discussed below.

11. For fitz William, *CIR 1264–1268,* 449, and *CPEJ,* i, 289. On Ernham, below, Appendix I no. 250. For Welham, no. 127; on Benedict, *CPR 1266–1272,* 401; for his appt as the Q's goldkpr at the Exchequer of the Jews, above, Chapter Two., and for his membership in a limited circle of moneylenders associated with the Q's transactions, below; on Fyliol, *CHEC,* 53.

12. For 1274, *CCIR 1272–1279,* 70. For the 1275 dower, see intr. to Appendix I, below. Two manors she acq. in Lincs. ca. 1270, not near Stamford or Grantham, were gtd away in the autumn of 1274 (Appendix I no. 135a).

13. For Redlee, *CPEJ,* ii, 311. On Darcy, Appendix I no. 136; for Cheyndut, no. 105a, and on Redham, no. 152a. For Sadekin, *CPEJ,* ii, 203 (about the feast of St. John Baptist 1275, though the gt seems to have been made earlier). On Hagin, *CPEJ,* ii, 310, and Rigg, ed.,

Select Pleas, Starrs, 87–88; for Crevequer, Appendix I no. 116a and *CPEJ,* iii, 110–11; on Cheyndut, Burgh, and Leyburn, nos. 151a, 115, 105a.

14. Financing the Q's acquisitions is discussed below. On Burgh, see intr. to Appendix I, and Powicke, *King Henry III,* 704; E 101/350/5 *m.* 2, shows 3s. to a messenger sent from the new K in Paris to John de Burgh, and in late June or early July 1273, eight marks paid to Chancery clks going to extend and take seisin of de Burgh's lands. The Burgh lands the Q acq. 1278 are Appendix I nos. 151a, 152a, 146, 148; the K in June 1278 also gtd the Q Camel (Soms.), another of Burgh's former estates incl. in her dower assignment (no. 191c), not far from Somerton, which she had held since 1265 (no. 187). For Redham, no. 152a; on the Kent group, nos. 114–16a.

15. For Bristol, Appendix I no. 80; on Woodrow, no. 233. The letter is S.C. 1/11/11, s.d.; see Appendix I no. 81.

16. S.C. 1/11/107, s.d., anon. ("ma dame Jo suy tut concern pur quey ke la terre seyt pris en la main nostre seynur le re," with a remark that "pur le despit ke il vus a fet le chevalier vus rendra le terre mut leement"). The brief salutation suggests the writer was the Q's steward Walter de Kancia; compare his 1279 letter to her, quoted below. The letter quoted here is S.C. 1/29/190, s.d.; the dates of the Didmarton transaction and the gt of the Oldbury wardship (Appendix I nos. 76, 81) mean that Burdon d. 29 August 1280.

17. Appendix I nos. 76, 81, 230. Nicholas was in Edward of Caernarvon's household, 1289–90 (C 47/3/22); see also *CHEC,* 112.

18. On fitz Alan, Appendix I nos. 77a, 78; for fitz John, nos. 82, 235; (as Matthew survived until 1309, the Q never entered these manors). The Walerand wardship is discussed below; see also Appendix I no. 232.

19. The 1281 schedule of the Q's purchases (*CCIR 1279–1288,* 80–81), neatly groups the manors by shire: Burgh and Scottow (Norf.), Quendon, Fobbing and Shenfield (Essex), Westerham, Teston, Farleigh, Leeds Castle, and Westcliffe (Kent), Langley (Herts.), Dulverton (Soms.), Nocton (Lincs.), Torpel and Upton (Northants.). The schedule isolates lands at Somerton (Soms.) and in the New Forest (Hants.) the Q recovered at law, and the lands she acq. from Henry de Newburgh (Soms., Dors). The advs that end the schedule are arranged like the manors: Burgh and Scottow (Norf.), Shenfield, Fobbing, Stanford, Little Laver, and High Ongar (Essex), Westerham and Westcliffe (Kent), Langley (Herts.), Ringwood (Hants.), Curry Rivel (Soms.), Quendon (Essex), Torpel (Northants.). As noted, the schedule omits purchases in Glos. and Wilts. discussed above.

20. Discussed in Chapter Two.

21. Appendix I no. 159a; the lease is mentioned in the abbot of Peterborough's complaint in 1291 to recover arrears and services due from Torpel and Upton (JUST 1/542 *m.* 12d). Southorpe's M1280 recogn. is E 159/54 *m.* 1d; that in E1285, not incl. the M1280 sum, is E 159/58 *m.* 6. In M1284 he had quittance from Aaron f. Vives for £50 (E 9/45 *m.* 1d), but it does not appear that his dealings with the Q involved this or other such debts. In T1286 the sher. of Northants returned that Geoffrey had insufficient goods in that bailiwick to distr. him (E 9/47 *m.* 8; but here the Q's clk Berewyk' was acting with the exors of John de Bayfeud and it is not certain this concerned the Q). The notice that Geoffrey was taken to Fleet is E 159/60 *m.* 3, where he owes the Q £160 "for arrears of the farm of Torpel." The acct here is from Mellows, ed., *Pytchley's Book of Fees,* 64. Bekingham held some land in Southorpe (*VCH Northants.,* ii, 466), and had lic. to convey to Peterborough Abbey to endow an anniversary service for the Q, 1291 (*CPR 1281–1292,* 414). On Lolham, Appendix I no. 160. Southorpe d. one day after the Q, apparently as a Carmelite at Stamford (*CIPM,* iii, no. 38; E. King, "Large and Small Landowners," 36–37); his wife inh. lands in Hunts. (Dewindt and Dewindt, eds., *Royal Justice,* i, no. 220, and ii, 628–31, 653).

22. Holmes, *Estates of the Higher Nobility,* 19–20, 113–14; Dyer, *Lords and Peasants,* 55–58; Hassall, ed., *Cartulary of St. Mary Clerkenwell,* ix and note 2; Miller, *Abbey and Bishopric of Ely,* 75–112; M. Morgan, *English Lands of Bec,* 38–52; D. Knowles, *Religious Orders in*

England, i, 37–40; Altschul, *Baronial Family,* 210–13; Raban, "Land Market and the Aristocracy," 250, 252–53; Coss, "Geoffrey de Langley," 19–22, and idem, *Lordship, Knighthood and Locality,* 93–119. The Q's acq. of advs is discussed in Chapter Two.

23. On Drayton and Ashford, below, Appendix I nos. 40, 219; For Kent, nos. 116b–j; for Herts., no. 105b–d; on Macclesfield, no. 29a–b; for Burgh, no. 151b; for Banstead, no. 212 note 144.

24. On Witchingham, Appendix I nos. 152b, 154; for Bockingfold, nos. 116d–e; for Macclesfield, nos. 26, 29a–b. Hurcott, the Maelor, and Hope are respectively nos. 48a–b, 28, 27, 70.

25. For Garkevylle, Appendix I no. 105d; the New Forest ejections are nos. 92, 93, 96; Wotton and Thorney are nos. 23c, 159b.

26. On Darcy, Appendix I no. 136. For Camoys, no. 159a; compare his conveyance of Wood Ditton (nos. 20, 23a). On Cheyndut, Appendix I, no. 105a; on Seez, no. 135a–b. On Pecche, nos. 21–22, 64, 118, 211; possibly the Q acq. these debts independently of the K's gt, but the language of the records will not allow this to be stated with certainty.

27. Appendix I nos. 61a–b, 117, 171. Camville detained rents from other houses (Churchill, *et al.,* eds., *Kent Fines,* 206). On advs' importance to thirteenth-century lords and their efforts to recover those alienated to religious houses, Coss, *Lordship, Knighthood, and Locality,* 204, 268–69.

28. For unsuccessful agreements, *CCIR 1279–1288,* 53, and Appendix I notes 92, 99. The 1291 allegations are nos. 97, 100, 128; for Botiller, nos. 60, 88. Householders were evidently involved in nos. 15a, 80, 100, 105c, 215. The Q may also have practiced collusion with Jewish moneylenders (nos. 105a, 215). On Venables, no. 67; on Montchensy, nos. 5, 19, 58–60, 63, 104, 209.

29. Pecche had at least 200 marks for Westcliffe, perhaps 1000 marks; Leyburn had 500 marks for Leeds, Camoys 600 marks for Torpel and Upton, Cheyndut 200 marks for Langley (Appendix I nos. 115, 159a, 105a). Compare pardons of sums owed the Jewry, *CCIR 1279–1288,* 80–81. On Crevequer, Appendix I nos. 23b, 24, 69, 116a; Camville, nos. 61a–b, 106, 117, 171; Pecche, nos. 21, 64, 118, 128, 211. These are cases only of vendors whose debts to the Jewry led to conveyance of their lands to the Q; additional examples of life tenure allowed vendors can be found in Appendix I.

30. On Crevequer and Besilles, *CHEC,* 154. For Camville, *Records 1286–1289,* no. 3114; on his widow and family, Appendix I no. 117 notes 129–30. On Loveday's son, no. 113; for Eleanor's promise to promote the children of another vendor, no. 202. Her generosity to vendors' families recalls the problems many knts faced in providing for their children. On Leyburn, see no. 115.

31. Fifteen knts were involved if the incomplete acq. from Adam de Neofmarche is counted (Appendix I no. 139). The others were Thomas Basset (no. 127), Burgh (no. 151a), Camoys (no. 159a), Camville (nos. 61a–b, 117, 171), Cheyndut (nos. 31a, 105, 137, 246a), Crevequer (no. 116a), Darcy (no. 136), Ernham (no. 250), Leyburn (no. 115), Montchensy (no. 63), Pecche (nos. 21, 22, 64, 118), Redham (no. 152a), Seez (no. 135b), and Wauton (no. 215), whose 1291 complaint is discussed below. Some heirs tried to recover lands much later—Camville's and Pecche's with questionable claims (noted in Chapter Four). In 1291 Camville's son did try to recover lands conveyed by reason of Jewish debts, but cl. only that the Q did not promote Camville's children as she promised; Richard de Seez cl. only that Walter de Kancia refused payment of the ransom for Seez' land (no. 135a). Given the circumstances under which Montchensy lost no. 63 to the Q, he may not have been a willing vendor, but in 1291 he was in the Tower and in no position to bring a complaint (see nos. 5, 19, 58, 59, 60, 104, 209).

32. GEC, x, 552–53; *VCH Hants.,* iv, 512; Moor, *Knights,* v, 147–48; *CIPM,* ii, nos. 6–7, 89. On the complexities involved, compare *CIPM,* v, no. 148.

33. *VCH Hants.,* iii, 254–55, does not notice the Q's tenure; see Appendix I nos. 47, 79, 91, 102, 195, 232, 238 (the 1296–97 accts are S.C. 6/1090/4, those for 1300–1, E 372/146

m. 43d). The bp of Salisbury recovered in 1291 suit owed at his hundred by the tithing of Fyfhide Verdon (JUST 1/1014 *m.* 1). Compare S.C. 1/23/51 (Q to the Chancellor [Beeleigh, 10 Sept. (1289)]): "monstre nous est de par le Den e Le Chapitre de Salesbir' ke akuns de noz genz ont pris en nostre meyn le maner de Herst' par le reson de la mort Dame maut waleran' ki terres nostre segnor le Rey nous ad graunte si come ben savez. . . ." Gts to the Q enrolled 1286–89 are *RG,* ii, nos. 1130–31, 1279; *CCIR 1288–1296,* 373. For indications of the Q's interest in the estates, Appendix I nos. 12, 45, 77a–b, 192, 195 note 141; *CPR 1281–1292,* 301. On the nephews in 1274, Johnstone, "Wardrobe and Household of Henry," 390.

34. The Q did not hold all lands of Maud's dower; Pottington (Devon) is not in her accts to 1290, but is in the 1296–97 accts 1296–97 (S.C. 6/1090/4). For Langford, Winterbourne, and Compton, Appendix I nos. 229, 232; for Broughton, Tytherley, Sparsholt, and Meonstoke, nos. 86, 87, 89, 91, 100; for Axbridge, Cheddar, Congresbury, Somerton, and Cannington, nos. 182–84, 187, 195; for Moreton, Poorstock, Winterbourne, and Woodsford, nos. 47, 48b.

35. *CCIR 1272–1279,* 221 (= *CPEJ,* iii, 78–79, and iv, 82–83); *CCIR 1279–1288,* 28–29 (= E 159/54 *m.* 1).

36. For Castile, Hillgarth, *Spanish Kingdoms 1250–1516,* i, 220–21; Baer, *History of the Jews in Spain,* i, 120; Friedenwald, *The Jews and Medicine,* ii, 635–38. On England, Stacey, *Politics, Policy and Finance,* 155–56; Dobson, "Decline and Expulsion"; Moore, *Persecuting Society,* 27–45. On the 1255 Lincoln murder, Paris, *CM,* v, 516–18; *CPR 1247–1258,* 453.

37. *CPR 1272–1281,* 76; *Bury,* 61; *Waverley,* 409. Eleanor of Provence acq. little land encumbered by debts to the Jewry (and held it only as long as needed to recover what she paid to relieve the Christian lord's debts to the Jews); but she once took 10,000 gold marks from Aaron of York, convicted of forging a charter (Paris, *CM,* v, 136). See also Coss, "Geoffrey de Langley," 173–74. I am grateful to Margaret Howell for her thoughts on the influence of Eleanor's Franciscan advisors.

38. For the friars' animosity to the Jews, Cohen, *Friars and the Jews* is the extreme statement; the view here is from Hyams, "Jewish Minority," 274–75. On usury, Le Goff, *Your Money or Your Life,* 71–82; McLaughlin, "Teaching of the Canonists," (1939), 125–47 (esp. 125–26); Noonan, *Scholastic Analysis,* 100–32; B. Nelson, *Idea of Usury,* 16, 23–24; Helmholz, "Usury and the Medieval English Church Courts," 373–75. Reduction of amounts owed is discussed below; see also Appendix I nos. 105a, 136.

39. For Edward, Hyams, "Jewish Minority," 276, 288; W. C. Jordan, *Louis IX,* 154–55. One of the Q's daus sponsored a converted Jewess who took the name Eleanor de St. Paulo (*CCIR 1288–1296,* 27; *m.* A. E. Green, *Princesses,* ii, 304–5); she was perhaps living in the *Domus conversorum* in 1308 (Adler, "'Domus Conversorum,'" 53–54). On Alphonso X, Baer, *History of the Jews in Spain,* i, 112–30; Bagby, "Jew in the *Cántigas,*" 670–88. On Christian attitudes toward individual Jews and the Jewish community in general, Schatzmiller, *Shylock Reconsidered.*

40. For Hagin f. Moses, *Foedera,* i.2, 192 (attrib. to Eleanor of Provence by Roth, *Jews in England,* 80); H. P. Stokes, "Relationship," 165–66, 169. Manser f. Aaron was to have 600 marks in debts owed other Jews after the Q was gtd John de Burgh's debts to Manser (*CPEJ,* iii, 64–65). She helped the abbot of Stanford pay £100 of £350 owed Elias f. Moses and in 1276 got the K to pardon the remaining £250; Elias was to have £250 in debts of condemned Jews (*CPEJ,* iii, 285–86). When Aaron f. Vives in 1280 gave the Q Gilbert Pecche's debts worth 1360 marks, the K ordered that Aaron have that sum in confiscated debts, less £36 he owed the K (*CCIR 1279–1288,* 5). In 1275 Jacob f. Moses was allowed 280 marks in a tallage after giving the Q debts to that amount owed by Bartholomew de Redham, and 200 marks for Norman Darcy's debts (*CPEJ,* iv, 87); Moses of Clare was also allowed equivalents for Darcy's debts (*CCIR 1272–1279,* 182). On Jacob of Oxford, Roth, *Jews of Medieval Oxford,* 76–78.

41. For the family, Roth, *Jews of Medieval Oxford,* 72. In H1275 the Q owed Elias 350 marks, but as he owed the K the same amount on a tallage, she was quit of the debt, the origin of which is not stated (E 159/49 *m.* 7d). See also *CPEJ,* iii, 285–86. In 1284 it was shown by the Q's attys that after the death of his br. Hagin in 1279, Elias doctored charters for debts owed Hagin by Nicholas de Cantilupe, but Nicholas still had to pay the Q what he owed Elias (E 9/45 *m.* 4d). Debts owed Elias by the Foliot family of Yorks., and Richard de Tany of Essex, came to the Q by writ (E 9/44 *m.* 6d; E 9/45 *m.* 5); she also took a £1000 fine from Elias' widow, to have his concealed goods (*CPR 1281–1292,* 193). On a third br., Benedict f. Moses, see Appendix I no. 127.
42. Henry III gtd Aaron to Edmund bef. Jan. 1271 (*CPEJ,* ii, 170–71). See Appendix I nos. 118, 121, 215. See also *CCIR 1288–1296,* 11, 99 (compare with Appendix I no. 121).
43. *CPR 1266–1272,* 360, 401; *CPEJ,* iii, 57; *CCIR 1272–1279,* 221, 296.
44. E.g., creditors of Burgh and Redham (*CPEJ,* iv, 82, and ii, 310). A number of debts owed one Manser f. Aaron were incl. in transactions summarized in the 1281 schedule (*CCIR 1279–1288,* 80–81), but apart from these refs Manser does not appear in connection with the Q's business.
45. Compare H. P. Stokes, "Relationship," 165–66, 169.
46. On intellectual activity, Hyams, "Jewish Minority"; Roth, *Intellectual Activities,* and "Some notes on pre-Expulsion scholars," 56–61. For the unique reference to a Jew, *CHEC,* 98. Her letter is E 9/36 *m.* 7 (Westm., 6 June 8 Edw.), ordering Aaron f. Vives to acquit Gilbert Pecche, who has satisfied her for debts Aaron lately gave her; the letter uses "tu" to address Aaron, the only example of that usage among the forty-seven letters found for this study. Comparison to the "vos" the Q used to address Burnell or Kirkby suggests this "tu" is not a sign of intimacy, but rather the patronizing "tu" that would be used to address a child.
47. Meetings with Jews are suggested by, e.g., Appendix I nos. 105a, 215. In E1280 Kancia pr. that Hagin f. Moses, in prison, unlawfully took money owed by Adam de Neofmarche (E 9/35 *m.* 4d). In T1281 Kancia won judgment for the Q for £41 agst William de Fauelore, undersher. of Soms., who after hearing the K's writ would issue for levying 300 marks Walter de Furneaux owed Hagin f. Moses (whose debts were the Q's), induced Furneaux to sell him a third the manor of Hinton St. George, and paid Hagin £41 for that portion of the debt. Fauelore cl. he had the K's writ that Hagin had fined to have his goods, and that he paid Furneaux not Hagin; but Furneaux showed a charter between Hagin and Fauelore. Fauelore then cl. the transaction took place bef. the Q was gtd Hagin's debts, but Kancia showed this contradicted Fauelore's first story (E9/38 *m.* 10). In M1284, the Q's attys saw quittances from Jacob f. Moses proffered by William de Cantilupe, and said they could pr. on the spot that the records were altered after Jacob's death by his br. Elias; Cantilupe paid (E9/45 *m.* 4d). On the clks' persistence compare *CCIR 1279–1288,* 38, 269, and *CCIR 1323–1327,* 79–80.
48. Westm. Abbey, muniments 23627 (= Appendix I nos. 13a, 14, 97, 174); S.C. 6/1089/25 *m.* 4 (= nos. 99, 236); *Records 1286–1289,* nos. 3138, 3194, 3201 (= nos. 24, 99, 236); *CHEC,* 86, 88 (= nos. 251, 202). Some cash still reached her treas. by payment of Jewish debts in the 1280s (see below, note 50).
49. In chronological order, the Q's acqs involving the Jewry were: in 1275, Appendix I nos. 105a (Cheyndut), 135b (Seez), 136 (Darcy); in 1276, 127 (Basset); in 1278, 115 (Leyburn), 116a (Crevequer), 151 (Burgh); in 1279, 61a, 117, 171 (Camville); in 1280, 118 (Pecche), 159a (Camoys); between 1277 and 1280, 137 (Cheyndut again); ca. 1280, 63 (Montchensy); between 1275 and 1281, 152c (Redham); in 1284, 21–22, 64, 118, 211 (Pecche again); in 1286, 13a (Cheyndut again); ca. 1286, 215 (Wauton); in 1290, 139 (Neofmarche). Nos. 20 and 23a (1281, 1285) were conveyed by Camoys, the same lord as 159a, but are not said to have involved the Jewry. It cannot be stated with certainty that nos. 128 (1281) and 210a (ca. 1274?) involved the vendors' Jewish debts.

50. Her last gt of all the debts owed an individual Jew was of Hagin f. Moses' debts, Nov. 1279 (*CCIR 1272–1279*, 547). In 1284 she was gtd debts owed the late Elias f. Moses of London by Richard Foliot of Yorks. and his s. Jordan, and by Richard de Tany of Essex (E 9/45 m. 6d), but this was not a wholesale gt as the Foliots were also bound to Benedict of Lincoln and Aaron f. Vives [E 9/44 m. 8d *bis*]. For debts that came to her through the Exch. of the Jews in the later 1280s, see *Records 1286–1289*, nos. 3056–3104; compare the sums discussed in Chapter Two. There appears to be no record of an Oct. 1285 search for debts taken from the Jews' chests in Cambridge and Bedford in 1263–65, which were to be given the Q (*CPR 1281–1292*, 212). Profits from the 1283 gt of goods and chattels are discussed in Chapter Two. On the steadily smaller sums the K collected from the Jewry in this period, Prestwich, *Edward I*, 344.

51. This is not to say that the vendors were not necessarily in difficulties; only that their conveyances do not appear to have involved the Jewry. Nor did Eleanor profit greatly from other problems knts faced: she retained only one manor gtd her after Evesham (Appendix I, intr. and nos. 38, 39, 134–35a, 237; C. H. Knowles, "Resettlement," 35–36). Her presence on the Crusade of 1270 likely informed her of any who incurred debts on the expedition, but it does not seem that any who conveyed lands to her were so indebted (S. D. Lloyd, "Crusader Knights and the Land Market," 119–36). It may also be noted that the Q rarely acq. portions of fees except where such fragments were incl. with other undivided fees; it is unwise to insist this proves she (and by extension the K) were aware of problems in administering smaller holdings and so avoided them, but it does suggest she was not victimizing the most desperately troubled knts.

52. For Nov. 1275, Appendix I nos. 105a, 115, 136, 151a; for 1278, nos. 114–16a, 148, 151a–b; for Nov. 1280, nos. 7, 77a, and *CCIR 1279–1288*, 67–68; for July 1281, nos. 51, 128, 172; for Feb. 1284, nos. 18, 21, 22, 57, 64, 78, 90(?), 149, 152a, 180, 193, 211, 217, 218, 231; for June–July 1285, nos. 159a, 226a, 247, 179a, 23a–b; for Feb. 1286, nos. 13a, 14, 97, 174. Compare J. C. Parsons, "English Administration in Ponthieu," 379–80.

53. For parlts of Henry III (from 1264) and Edward I (to 1290), E. B. Fryde *et al.*, eds., *Br. Chronology*, 542–48. It is easier to find such coincidences for the K's gts to the Q, as with the 1275 dower assignment (*CChR*, ii, 192–93); see also Appendix I nos. 5, 6, 19, 44, 104, 124a, 168, 188, 209 (less certain: nos. 86, 87, 147a, 148). For the Q's trans-actions (those enacted during parlts in her absence from England 1286–89 marked with an asterisk [*]), nos. 13a, 14, 20, *42, *82, 97, *98, 127, 128, 196a, 197a, 198, 202, *235 (less certain: nos. 48a, 61a, 61b, 65, *99, 114, 135b, 136, 151a, 171a, 174, 233).

54. For Eleanor of Provence, e.g., *CChR*, ii, 86, 160, 189, 204, 216, 227, 409–10; *CPR 1266–1272*, 358, 383–84 (more formal, as involving her rights in the Agenais); *CPR 1281–1292*, 189, 484. For the Q's acts, Appendix II; compare discussion of her house-hold in Chapter Two, where it is noted that the Q's household knts rarely witn. her acts. John de Lovetot was both a justice and the Q's auditor; it is impossible to attribute his presence as a witn. to a number of her acts exclusively to one of those capacities or the other. On bps as witn. to her acts, see below.

55. *Records 1286–1289*, nos. 3243–3246; *CHEC*, 138–52. The manors noted are respectively Appendix I nos. 115, 151a, 85, 239, 66, 152, 159a, 25.

56. For Seez, Appendix I no. 135a; for Camville, *CCIR 1272–1279*, 577–78; for Montfort, *CCIR 1279–1288*, 52. John Botiler's 1280 letter, quoted above, shows the Q dealt with the K's council concerning her lands on what must have been a regular basis.

57. JUST 1/542 m. 4d; for the date (ca. 1286), Appendix I no. 215, and for cases in which the Q assisted others see nos. 127, 136, and Chapter Two, note 76.

58. Appendix I no. 125, the letters respectively S.C. 1/11/51 (s.d.), and S.C. 1/30/135 (s.d.).

59. S.C. 1/10/50; see also intr. to Appendix I.

60. On Clifford, *CDI*, i, nos. 2055–56. The letter to Kirkby, S.C. 1/10/53, is quoted in Chapter Two. On the swiftness with which the Q acted, compare her Feb. 1289 letters from Gascony on a wardship in Hunts. gtd her the previous day (*CCIR 1288–1292*, 373

[Appendix I no. 110]; *Records 1286–1289*, no. 3229), and the letters of 24 and 25 Nov. 1280 from Eleanor and her steward on her gt to Adam de Stratton of land at Upton, remarked in Chapter Two.

61. S.C. 1/11/25 (= Shirley, ed., *Royal Letters*, no. 647; English trans. at ii, 647, used here with modern place names); see Appendix I no. 188. Note "our lord" (Henry III) gtd her the wardship, but "my lord" (presumably Edward) gave it to another. She was gtd Haselbury at pleasure for her maintenance 30 Sept., but it was regtd in fee to Alan Plogenet, 19 Oct. Just at this time, however, Eleanor began to receive Montfortians' forfeited lands and perhaps agreed to surrender Haselbury in exchange for those gts (Appendix I, intr. and nos. 38, 39, 134, 237).

62. GEC, vii, 629–37; Moor, *Knights*, iii, 35–36; cont. Gervase of Canterbury, ii, 220–21; *CPR 1266–1272*, 727; Lewis, "Roger de Leyburn," 193–214. The pardons the Q obtained for Roger's s. William in 1278–79 must surely be seen in relation to her earlier relations with Roger (Appendix I no. 115).

63. W. Brown, ed., *Reg. Walter Giffard*, 101; the family is discussed in Chapter One. Walter d. as abp of York.

64. *DNB*, s.v. "Kirkby, John (d. 1290)," and Tout, *Chapters*, vi, 303 s.v. "Kirkby, John." His relations with the Q, and John de Loundres' career, are discussed in Chapter Two.

65. His career is discussed in detail above, Chapter Two. For 1275, *CPEJ*, ii, 310, iii, 78–79, and iv, 82; for 1280, E 9/33 m. 6–6d. Note that the Q's most prominent bf in Kent and Norfolk was Kancia's unsavory underling John de Ponte (for whom see above, Chapter Two). For the debts in 1280, E 9/35 m. 4; Appendix I nos. 118, 139, 159a (see also nos. 124–25, 128). On the financing of Eleanor's acquisitions through Jewish debts at first and later from the revenues of her estates as a determining factor on the pace of the additions to her lands, see above.

66. On Kirkby, above, note 64. On Burnell, Roth, *Jews of Medieval Oxford*, 77. As Chancellor, Burnell's name is rarely missing among those who attested the Q's acts (see Appendix II). Kancia's research to augment revenue is remarked above, Chapter Two.

67. On the knts as particularly antagonistic to the Jews, Hyams, "Jewish Minority," 275–76, 291.

68. Craster and Thornton, eds., *Chronicle of St. Mary's*, 21 (the abbot cl. the charter for the debt was forged but agreed to pay £300); for other religious houses thus indebted to the Q, see Chapter Two. Queen-gold accts show the Q in 1286–89 collecting money from Christians indebted to Jews whose debts had come to her, but do not specify whether the sums collected were principal or interest (*Records 1286–1289*, nos. 3056–3104; E 101/505/19–20).

69. Harding, *England in the Thirteenth Century*, 198; Roth, *Jews in England*, 61–65; Richardson, *English Jewry*, 106–7; Coss, "Geoffrey de Langley," 28–34.

70. Casagrande, "The Protected Woman," 78–79; Martin, ed., *Reg. Peckham*, ii, 555. On the sincerity of Pecham's feelings, Douie, *Pecham*, 51–52.

71. Watt, "The English Episcopate," 144, 146; J. C. Parsons, "Piety, Power," 112–14. Of her surviving acts with witnesses, listed in Appendix II, Burnell witn. nos. 2a–b, 3, 7, 10, 12, 13, 14, 17, 19, 20, 23, 24a–b, 25, 31, 32, 33, 35, 37, 38a–b—prob. as often in his capacity as Chancellor as bp. William de Middelton of Norwich witn. nos. 5, 6a–b, 7, 13, 35. As K's clk, John de Kirkby witn. nos. 4, 6a–b, 10, 12, 13, 14, 19, 20, 26; after he became bp of Ely, only nos. 34, 35. As K's clk, Antony Bek witn. nos. 3, 4, 12, 13; as bp of Durham, only nos. 33, 38a–b. Thomas de Cantilupe of Hereford witn. nos. 3, 5, 6a–b, Walter de Merton of Rochester nos. 2a, 3, Godfrey Giffard of Worcester no. 19. The bp of Chichester who witn. no. 32 cannot be identified with certainty as the witn. lists to two documents seem to be conflated.

72. Raban, "Land Market and the Aristocracy," 243–44, 252–54, 260–61; R. A. L. Smith, *Canterbury Cathedral Priory*, 116–18, 135–38; Stacey, *Politics, Policy and Finance*, 155–56, 216–17. Examples of the speed with which the Q's clks operated are the cases of Darcy

(Appendix I no. 136) Pecche (no. 118), Camville (no. 61a–b), Montchensy (no. 63), and Cheyndut (no. 105a). Richard de Tany's debt of £53:13:4, gtd the Q in 1279, was exacted and paid immediately [E 9/45 *mm.* 8d, 5]). Prosecution for Jewish debts is also discussed above, Chapter Two.

73. Appendix I no. 29a.

74. Stafford, *QCD*, 29, and "Portrayal of Royal Women," 154–55, 158; Le Goff, *Your Money or Your Life*, 82–86; McLaughlin, "Teaching of the Canonists," (1940), 8–9; Farmer, "Persuasive Voices," 531–38. The Scriptural citations are identical in the Vulgate and King James versions. On the few intercessions noted for the Q as compared to other women in Edward's family, J. C. Parsons, "Piety, Power," 122–23; Qs' opportunistic approach to intercession is noted in idem, "The Queen's Intercession." The Q's known intercessions with Henry III and Edward total thirty-six over as many years. The calendared rolls show Margaret, in the seven and one-half years of her marriage, interceding with Edward fifty times; her dated letters add eighteen instances, and any of her several undated letters that originated bef. 1307 would add to the number.

75. *CPR 1272–1281*, 265 (= *CFR*, i, 97); *CChyV*, 291–92; *CPR 1281–1292*, 180. Compare Henry III's 1270 gt above, note 10, and see Prestwich, *Edward I*, 12–13. The only gts the Q made from lands held of the K's gt were wardships (Appendix I nos. 7, 149, 190 note 139, 191c note 140). On inalienability in Edward I's reign, Richardson and Sayles, eds., *Fleta*, Bk. iii, chap. 6 (iii, 12); on inalienability in France, with reference to Philip V's gts to his wife in the fourteenth century, E. A. R. Brown, "Royal Marriage, Royal Property."

76. *CPR 1272–1281*, 332–33, 436; *CChR*, ii, 234, 248–49, 256, 261, 357, 411; *CDI*, i, nos. 2100–1; *RG*, ii, no. 1571; *CPR 1281–1292*, 114, 175, 180, 376, 417. For her gts of wards from lands she acq., Appendix I no. 116a; life bequests, nos. 14, 23a; gts in fee, nos. 65, 94, 119, 134–135a, 138, 171, 250; life gts, nos. 114, 128; gts of an adv., no. 153, and other gts to religious houses, nos. 158, 220, 236; gts of city property, nos. 142–44, 170, 173, 220, 246, 249; exchs for other property, nos. 61a, 63, 114, 118, 219; on her use of wardships and marriages, nos. 7, 11, and *CHEC*, 41–55. It may be noted that the wife of the K who issued *Quia Emptores* in 1290 specified that her gtees hold the lands of the chief lords for services due (*CChR*, ii, 188, 248, 256, 267; *CPR 1281–1292*, 175, 180; compare J. C. Parsons, "English Administration in Ponthieu," 384).

77. Earlier Ks may have acq. land pledged to the Jews (Fowler, ed., *Cartulary of Old Wardon*, 363), but Edward appears not to have done so save through the Q's transactions. He gtd her the goods and chattels of condemned Jews, but took for himself two-thirds of the money she thus collected—another way to profit from the Jewry while appearing to keep his distance (above, Chapter Two)?

78. MacFarlane, "Had Edward I a 'Policy'?", 252–53, 266–67; Powicke, *Thirteenth Century*, 518–19; Prestwich, *Edward I*, 105.

79. On Qs as liminal figures, Fradenburg, "Rethinking Queenship," 5; on women as liminal figures, Bynum, "Women's Stories, Women's Symbols," 49. On freedom from institutionalized restrictions, J. C. Parsons, "Of Queens, Courts, and Books," and for Marian imagery and intercession, idem, "The Queen's Intercession."

80. Johnstone, *A Hundred Years of History*, 153.

81. On complaints of extortionate demands, above, Chapter Two. Compare her willingness to restore Handsworth (Appendix I no. 201; Sayles, ed., *Select Cases*, i, 103), with Sybil de Doddeneys' efforts to secure dower at Bentley Dodnash (no. 210a). See also nos. 23c, 27–29b, 48a–c (with 197a–b), 70–1, 81, 92–3, 95–6, 101, 107a–b, 116d–j, 152b–c, 154, 159b, 179a–b, 226b, 234.

82. Below, Appendix I nos. 23c (pr. but not determined), 27 (recovered), 29b (dismissed as like action pending), 48a–c and 197a–b (partly recovered, 1305), 50 (dismissed as not pr.), 62 (undetermined as querent d.), 70 (recovered), 71 (recovered), 72 (not pr.), 64 (dispr.), 80 note 172 (Q's gtee retained lands), 81 (pr. but not determined; remained

with K), 92 (recovered), 93 (recovered), 95 (pr., damages paid but ?if recovered), 96 (recovered), 97 (dismissed as claim not put in), 99 (not pr.; qu. retained for life), 100 (not pr.), 100 (dispr.), 101 (recovered), 105d (membrane illeg.), 107a (pr., undetermined *rege inconsulto*), 107b (pr. but qu. did not prosecute), 116d (qu. did not prosecute), 116f (recovered), 116g (recovered), 116h (recovered), 116i (recovered), 117 (not pr.), 125 (undetermined), 135a (not pr.), 152b–c (recovered 1301), 154 (dismissed as like action pending), 159b (undetermined *rege inconsulto*), 179b (recovered), 199 (disputed acq. not pr.), 202 (disputed acq. undetermined), 210a (pr., damages paid), 210b (recovered), 215 (remained with K's gtee), 226a (undetermined 1291; qu. sought 1297 and later), 226b (recovered 1292), 238 (ejection during term pr., damages awarded but qu. did not seek to recover). No. 28, evidently not sought in 1291, was recovered *temp.* Edw. II.

83. On Stokepord', see Chapter One, note 129; Burnell's handling of the Q is noted in Chapter One.

84. Christiana (ca. 1235–1312), dau. h. of Robert de Mareis of Ossurys, by a dau. coh. of Walter de Riddelsford of Castledermot, m. ca. 1248 Eleanor of Provence's cousin Ebles de Geneure who d. *s.p.* 1259 (Giraldus Cambrensis, *De Expugnatione Hibernica*, 266, 305–6; Watson, "The families of Lacy, Geneva, Joinville and La Marche," 9–11). On her dealings with the K and Q, *CPR 1272–1281*, 276; *CCIR 1279–1288*, 111–12; Hall, ed., *Red Book*, i, cxxx, cxxxi; *CDI*, i, no. 189, and ii, no. 15; *RO*, i, 46; *RP*, i, 466; *CPR 1282–1292*, 415–16, 431.

85. Hunter, ed., *Rotuli Selecti*, 249. Hugh d. 1241; the ref. to him in this list is apparently an error for his s. h. Baldwin, whose manor of Chesterfield was gtd Eleanor, Dec. 1265 (Appendix I no. 39).

86. The principal Paynel lands were at Drax (Yorks.) and West Rasen (Lincs.); see GEC, iv, 317; Farrer, *EYC*, vi, 9–13; Sanders, *Baronies*, 55–56. Andrew le Blund held in Ginge (Buttsbury), Essex (*CIPM*, i, no. 447), Wilts., and Staffs. (*BF*, 593, 724, 727, 732, 970).

87. Nos. 1–3, in cos. Anglesey, Arvon, Denbigh, Merioneth, and Salop., were known to the Q's clks as "terre Regine in Angleseye et Snaudon" (S.C.6/1089/22 *m.* 1; *CHEC*, 63). N. M. Fryde, "Royal Enquiry," 367–68, citing Jones, ed., *Flints. Ministers' Accounts*, thinks all the Q's lands in N. Wales were admin. from Macclesfield (no. 25); this is true only for Hope and the Maelor Saesneg (nos. 67, 69). S.C. 6/1089/22 *m.* 2 and S.C. 6/1089/25 *m.* 2 show two bailiwicks in N. Wales: the Maelor-Hope group, under the bf at Macclesfield though admin. from the Maelor, and the present Anglesey-Snowdon group.

88. Q's squire 1289–90 (*Records 1286–1289*, no. 3197; *CHEC*, 89, 114, 121). He had cash for expns Feb. and Aug. 1290, and in Oct. and Nov. was in Kent "quadam extenta facienda" for "negociis sancte Trinitatis," prob. for Appendix I no. 120 below (S.C. 1/1089/25 *mm.* 3–4).

89. On Gilbert Fraunceys' lands, see intr. to Appendix I.

90. Bef. Mar. 1289 the Q gtd Robert Burnell the marr. of John, s. h. of John fitz Alan of Wolverton (*CCIR 1288–1296*, 36; Sanders, *Baronies*, 100). The ward and marr. had been gtd, June 1275, to the K's cousin Maurice de Craon (*CPR 1272–1281*, 93). It is unclear how or when the marr. came to the Q; but the debts owing Hagin f. Moses, gtd her 15 Nov. 1279, incl. £240 from John fitz Alan of Wolverton (E 9/33 *m.* 6); see above, Chapter Two.

91. Robert was preb. of Preston, dioc. Hereford, ca. 1277 (le Neve, *Fasti*, i, 520); Adam (d. 1287), K's clk. 1260, was archdcn of Salop. ca. 1281–87 (Emden, *Oxford*, ii, 683–84).

92. On 30 May 1280 the Q agreed to help William de Knovill recover right in lands late of Joan de Saunford (d. ca. 29 Mar. 1278), of which he would enfeoff the Q for 250 marks, or less if all the lands were not recovered. These incl. a manor at Trenant (*CCIR 1279–1288*, 53 reads the surname "Clovill"; *CFR*, i, 95 ["Knovill"]; *CIPM*, ii, no. 248 ["Clovill"]; *CIPM*, ii, no. 327). Joan's lands were to be delivered to Knovill and a coh. 2 June 1281 (*CFR*, i, 149), but the Q's agreement with Knovill seems not to have succeeded. For the other lands involved see below, cos. Essex, Oxford, and Suffolk.

93. On Gilbert Fraunceys' lands, perhaps gtd Eleanor after Evesham, see intr. to Appendix I.

94. The Q disposed of the marr. of Joan, dau. h. of Stephen de Grendon of Leaveland, Kent, and Boylestone, Derbs. (*CCIR 1288–1296*, 305, 469–70; *CIPM*, i, no. 359, ii, nos. 356, 375, and viii, no. 214; *CFR*, i, 124–25, 233; Ashton, *The Fleet*, 233–36). It is unclear how or why she obtained the marr.; it does not appear that she held any lands of the inh.

95. *CPR 1281–1292*, 52, states the Q was gtd, 3 Dec. 1282, wardship of the English lands of William de Mohun in minority of his h., and that on 11 Dec. the marr. of the h. was gtd the queen-mother. It may be doubted if the Q obtained this wardship; neither her accts nor the 1291 inquest refers to any estates involved, though some were near lands she already held (*CIPM*, ii, no. 436). The h. d. Aug. 1284; the marrs of his sisters coh. were gtd the queen-mother (*CPR 1281–1292*, 128), and when one pr. her age 1297, it was said the wardship of her lands was demised not by the Q but by the queen-mother (*CIPM*, iii, no. 430; *CPR 1281–1292*, 468). Has the enrollment of 3 Dec. 1282 confused English and Irish lands, and was the Q really gtd wardship of the latter? Or did she later convey the wardship to the queen-mother?

96. In 1291 Joan de Ulewelle cl. that for 40 marks she sold the Q, through Richard de Bosco, 2 messuages, 48½ acres land, 2 acres meadow, ½ of a mill and 40s. rent in Ulwell and Whitecliff; Bosco, who cl. to act in the Q's name, occupied the land himself and paid Joan only 10s. The justices wished to consult the K "quia timetur de collusione" (JUST 1/1014 m. 4). No lands at Ulwell or Whitecliff appear in the Q's accts. Richard de Bosco, K's marshal 1279 (Tout, *Chapters*, i, 158), witn. five acts touching the Q's lands in the early 1280s (below, Appendix II nos. 11, 12, 17, 19, 22).

97. The Q's exors paid £24 damages to Alice de Tynten' for a stew at Lyme (*Manners*, 135); Alice attorned in 1291 (JUST 1/542 m. 12), but the extant rolls have no other notice of her complaint. The rolls are also silent on a tithing at Lyme detained from John de Mandeville, who had £11:10:11 in damages from the Q's exors (*Manners*, 126).

98. The Q Eleanor who held Havering (McIntosh, *Autonomy and Community*, 57–58) was Eleanor of Provence (*CPR 1266–1272*, 107).

99. On 11 Feb. 1281 the Q agreed to help William de Applegar recover right in Sibil Hedingham agst William de Montchensy; Applegar would then enfeoff her thereof (*CCIR 1279–1288*, 115). There is no reason to think this agreement succeeded.

100. In May 1289 the K pardoned Richard de Suthchirche £1000 for a false oath bef. the Bench, in cons. of Suthchirche's release to the K and Q of a manor at Hatfield Peverel; but in July 1292 it was doubted that such release had been made (*CCIR 1288–1296*, 10, 237). Nothing in the Q's accts or in the 1291 inq. suggests she held Hatfield Peverel. Nor is it clear that Suthchirche held at Hatfield Peverel bef. 1289 (Moor, *Knights*, iv, 267–68; *CIPM*, iii, no. 185).

101. In 1337 Gilbert Pecche jr. sought to recover a manor at Birdbrook agst the abbot of Westm., to whom the K in 1292 gtd the manor for the Q's anniversary service. Either Gilbert or the abbot cl. the Q had acq. Birdbrook in fee from Gilbert Pecche sr and that muniments touching the matter might be in Chancery (*CCIR 1337–1339*, 256). Certainly the Pecche family held at Birdbrook; the manor was apparently held in dower by Gilbert Pecche sr's mother, Eve, living 1266 (*AP*, 126; *GEC*, x, 335), and Gilbert conveyed land there in 1280 (*EFF*, i, 147 [no. 780], 186 [no. 1066], and ii, 28 [no. 147]). Morant, *History and Antiquities of Essex*, ii, 344, citing a charter "penes P. Le Neve," states that Birdbrook was conveyed to the K and Q with Gilbert Pecche's other estates in 1283/4, but there is no reason to think she held it in her lifetime. The published records for the lands Gilbert conveyed to the Q do not refer to Birdbrook; the summary accts for her manorial issues 1286–89 do not mention the manor, nor do any complaints before the 1291 inq. involve it. Birdbrook was in the K's hands by Jan. 1292 when he endowed the Westm. service, and it may be significant that Gilbert Pecche sr had d. 25 May 1291 (*GEC*, x, 336); was only the reversion to Birdbrook conveyed to the Q, so that the K entered it at Gilbert's death?

102. The Q's agreement of 30 May 1280 with William de Knovill to recover his right in Joan de Saunford's lands incl. a manor at Shelley, but seems not to have achieved its object. See above, note 92.

103. William de Montchensy of Edwardstone withheld suit owed at William and Gundred Giffard's Barstable hundred; in 1276 they quit him and his hs of the suit and remitted all damages (*EFF*, ii, 10; on Montchensy see nos. 5, 19, 58, 59, 63, 104, 209).

104. Richard de Ewelle sr was gtd Edmund de Hemmegrave's marr. Sept. 1265 (*CPR 1258–1266*, 451). In 1291 Hemmegrave cl. that when he refused to m. Ewelle's dau. Eleanor, the Q exacted £200 from him as the value of his marr. This was deposited with Italian bankers to Eleanor de Ewelle's use, but the Q later had it "arrested"; Eleanor de Ewelle recovered it in 1291 (*CPR 1281–1292*, 417–18), and Hemmegrave quitcl. it to her Feb. 1292 (JUST 1/836 m. 3r). Philip de Beauvais m. a London hss in 1280 (*CPR 1272–1281*, 361, 403–4; *CCIR 1279–1288*, 112; G. A. Williams, *Medieval London*, 333; Talbot and Hammond, *Medical Practitioners*, 254–56). If Eleanor de Ewelle refused to m. Philip, the Q did no more than seize the £200. Eleanor de Ewelle d. unm. ca. Mar. 1349 (*EFF*, ii, 73, 122, and iii, 80; *CPR 1301–1307*, 291; *CPR 1313–1317*, 337; *CPR 1317–1321*, 600; *DC*, i, 483, 510, and ii, 527; *CPR 1345–1348*, 426; *CFR*, vi, 111; *CIPM*, ix, no. 315).

105. See note no. 28 for lands in co. Chester seized as appurt. to no. 69.

106. W. Rees, *Anct. Petitions*, 98–99, gives a petition of ca. 1316 touching lands in the Maelor, late of David ab Ednyfed and Neuner Voel, that the Q gtd her bf Thomas de Macclesfeld'; Rees states Thomas confiscated the land and the Q then gtd it to him. Stewart-Brown, ed., *Rolls of Chester*, 212, shows that bef. Jan. 1285 the Q by letters patent committed to Macclesfeld' twelve acres of the K's land that Thomas had assarted, but otherwise Rees' refs do not suggest that Macclesfeld' confiscated the land.

107. The conveyers incl. Roger le Fykeis, whose wife Hunitha was a coparcener (*Kalendars*, i, 120 [no. 46]). Fykeis occ. on the Q's business 1279 (*CCIR 1272–1279*, 536); her squire 1282–83 (E 101/351/9 m. 8; Lysons, ed., "Roll of Expenses," 42), 1284 (E 101/350/12 m. 3), and 1284–85 (E 101/351/17 m. 3). A 1291 complaint by Roger Tymber agst Roger Fykays calls him janitor (porter) at Hope, and a Roger "le Porter" was a sub-bf at Hope (JUST 1/1149 mm. 5, 7). Qy if Roger le Fykeis, sher. of Worcs. 1290, 1298 (*List of Sheriffs*, 157), who d. by 3 Feb. 1309 (R. A. Wilson, ed., *Reg. Reynolds*, 161–62, 165, 166).

108. On Montrevel (d. 1279), Moor, *Knights*, iii, 197. At Q's inst. named bf of Entre-deux-Mers in Gascony, 8 July 1281 (*RG*, ii, no. 490, and iii, 2067); witn. her charter 22 Feb. 1281 (*CChR*, ii, 248). On the same day as the present surr. to her, he had an *inspeximus* of Henry III's charter (20 Dec. 1261) gting him a Gascon wardship (*CPR 1272–1281*, 193).

109. In 1291 Margery widow of Roger Cantok and Joan widow of John de Lydiard sought these tens, cl. that the Q at the urging of Thomas her marshal caused inq. to be taken on Christiana's right, but neither Cantok nor Lydiard was summ. to the inq. where they could have shown muniments to pr. their right (JUST 1/1014 m. 5d is damaged; any determination cannot be read, but Bardeney certainly kept the lands). That inq. appears to be the one ordered 29 Mar. 1278; see also *CIPM*, ii, no. 334, the writ for which (22 Apr. 1279) states that the K (not the Q) had gtd some of the tens to Bardeney.

110. *CPR 1272–1281*, 8, does not pr. the Q in 1273 held Totton as of the ward of lands of George de Cantilupe. The gt of the Cantilupe ward to her in Sept. 1265 was quickly defeated (no. 188); she did not secure a second gt of it until Nov. 1274 (nos. 190, 208, 224).

111. *CCIR 1279–1288*, 81, states that by 1281 the Q recovered agst the foresters of the New Forest rents and other services worth £20; these remain unidentified. The same ref. states that she had acq. the adv. of the ch of Ringwood, but this appears to be a case like that of a moor at Somerton (no. 187c): the K in fact won judgment on the adv. agst John fitz John in 1273 and allowed her to hold it as appurt. to Ringwood (*VCH Hants.*, iv, 612); she had pres. to Ringwood by 1283 (above, Chapter Two, note 162).

112. The Q who disputed wardenship of God's House, Southampton, with the bp of Winchester was Eleanor of Provence, who held the town in dower (Deedes, ed., *Reg. Pontissara*, i, xvi–ii; Blake, ed., *Cartulary of St. Denys*, nos. 24–25; Kaye, ed., *Cartulary of God's House*, i, xli–xlv; Platt, *Medieval Southampton*, 58).

113. This John le Botiller is more likely the Q's bf than John le Botiller, lord of Wem as implied by *VCH Hants.*, iv, 608, citing *CIPM*, ii, no. 641, which really does not identify the Botiller of the Ringwood transaction as the lord of Wem. As that family did hold land in Hants. (no. 234), the bf might have been a kinsman. John le Botiller (or Boteler) of Wem was b. 17 July in 1266 or 1267 (GEC, ii, 231–32) and cannot possibly have served as early as 1280 as the Q's bf, on whom see above, chap 2, note 190. The case may be analogous to that of the honor of Aumâle: Edward recognized a fictitious heir or alienee who then surr. the lands to him (MacFarlane, "Had Edward I a `Policy'?", 256–57).

114. The Q's exors' accts show 20s. damages paid tenants of Beaulieu Abbey (no location stated), and 66s.10d. to Beaulieu's cellarer for damages at Exbury (*Manners*, 105 bis). It is unclear whether these payments relate to disseisins or ejections; no actions corresponding to them are found in the surviving rolls of the 1291–92 inquest.

115. The Q's 1286 gt of land near Godshill to the K's yeoman William le Brun and Iseult his wife (the Q's woman) was conf. by the K (*RG*, ii, nos. 1569–71). Details are lacking, but the Bruyns were said in 1301 and 1307 to have held land in this vicinity as of the Q's manor of Camel, Soms. (no. 191; compare *CIPM*, iv, no. 34, and v, no, 36, with *VCH Hants.*, iv, 572, none of which refers to the Q's 1286 gt).

116. See also below, Appendix I nos. 250–51.

117. Joan de Tracy cl. 1291 that she demised Whitfield to Hardington for £100, but he was compelled to convey it to the Q before he paid Joan anything; she cl. £100 damages. Piccheford failed to appear at Westm. on the day given (JUST 1/1014 *m.* 4d). Hardington cl. he acq. the manor from Joan by fine, paying her 100 marks beforehand and promising 20 marks yrly for life, and that he had a quitcl. from her s. John (JUST 1/1014 *m.* 4–4d). Joan was h. of John de Wyville (d. 1263), who ejected Quarr Abbey from Whitefield, gtd the abbey in 1158 by Hugh de Wyville; for the abbey's efforts to recover the manor as late as 1401, Hockey, *Quarr Abbey*, 126–29.

118. Maud de Columbars in 1285 surr. to John de Cobham her dower in three of Matthew de Columbars' manors (not incl. Lockerley or Avon) which Michael de Columbars had gtd Cobham in fee saving Maud's dower (*CPR 1281–1292*, 178). One of this name was among the Q's women, 6 Edw. (C 47/4/1 f. 30v).

119. An Alice de Burely was coh. of Eustace Fucher, a forester in fee charged with many offenses Nov. 1276, and perhaps ejected from his lands at that time (nos. 93, 96); was she wife of William Burely and mother of the 1291 querent?

120. In Dec. 1285–Jan. 1286 a clk of Chancery took seisin on the Q's behalf of the manor of Marcle, of which Edmund Mortimer was to enfeoff his wife, the Q's cousin (*Records 1285–1286*, nos. 29, 167; *CHEC*, 44–46, 53–54). The Q's accts do not mention Marcle. Perhaps it was assigned her for a time to repay money advanced for a dowry (compare Maud de Fiennes' dowry, 1275: *CChR*, ii, 190–92), but no such agreement has surfaced. Perhaps the Q was merely making sure her cousin was enfeoffed of Marcle.

121. In July 1274 a John de Reda was clk of the Q's son Alphonso (C 62/50 *m.* 5); in Nov. 1279, usher of the K's wardrobe (Tout, *Chapters*, ii, 160, 163). On the date of this transaction, see below, Appendix II no. 11 and note 156.

122. The Q disposed of the marr. of Joan de Grendon, h. of the manor of Leaveland, but does not appear to have held the manor. See above, note 94.

123. The 1311 reference to Queen Eleanor's tenure at Dartford (*CIM*, ii, no. 106) concerns Eleanor of Provence (*CCIR 1279–1288*, 441).

124. The Q's exors paid £6:13:4 damages to Alexander de Baliol and Isabella his wife for a fishery taken at Luddenham (*Manners*, 107), member of Isabella's barony of Chilham

(Sanders, *Baronies*, 111–12; *BF*, 661, 675). The couple's 1291 complaint is JUST 1/542 m. 8, but the membrane is damaged and it is unclear why the fishery was seized. John de Faversham was paid 5 marks' unspecified damages (*Manners*, 105); no complaint by him in 1291 is found and the reason for the payment is unknown.

125. Also appurt. to Chatham was wardship of a manor at Shrinkling in minority of the h. of Richard de Shrinkling (*BF*, 655, 672), gtd by the Q to Ebles de Montibus two months before she d., as testified to the Chancellor by Hugh de Cressingham (S.C. 1/22/183, s.d.). Her exors gtd the marr. to Thomas de Sandwyz', seneschal of Ponthieu, Feb. 1292 (*CPR 1281–1292*, 411, 478).

126. One of this name was clk of the K's marshalsea Nov. 1279 (Tout, *Chapters*, ii, 160).

127. Walter de Chidcroft had £10 damages from the Q's exors (*Manners*, 105), prob. after a complaint touching Bockingfold known only from *CCIR 1288–1296*, 225. Chidcroft is prob. the Q's bf of that name impleaded 1291 by Michael de Elhurst, who had £20 damages for a wall Walter pulled down, changing the course of a stream that fed Elhurst's mill (JUST 1/542 m. 13d).

128. The Q was gtd wardship of lands and ten. at Brenchley only in 1289 (Appendix I no. 113); the circumstances recited in Appendix I nos. 116g–j, however, pr. that seizures and detentions from the Ayllards were perpetrated after she acq. the Crevequer lands in 1278.

129. The Q brought Robert's s. Thomas into her daus' household (C 47/4/5 f. 3r; *Manners*, 133). In Aug. 1301 Thomas held Bockingfold for life (Appendix I no. 114d–f; *CPR 1292–1301*, 604). Robert's daus Joan and Isabella recd dowries (*Manners*, 106, 112, 117, 120, 125, 128, 129, 130, 131); qy if the Joan and Isabella de Camville in Sussex, Surrey, Notts. and Derbs., 1297 (*Parl. Writs*, i, 288, 294). For a 1341 attempt by Thomas' daus to recover Westerham, see Chapter Four.

130. Joan held Westerham in dower at a rent of £16 (*CCIR 1288–1296*, 165–66; *CPR 1281–1292*, 467, 484); by Apr. 1300 she m. John Duvedale, K's yeoman, and surr. Westerham for lands at Layton, Sussex (*CPR 1292–1301*, 513). Anne, widow of Robert de Camville's s. Robert, had a yrly fee of £20 from the Q (S.C. 6/1089/25 m. 4; *Manners*, 103). In Jan. 1292 Anne was gtd Bockingfold for life (Appendix I no. 114d–f) at a rent of 100s. (*CPR 1282–1292*, 466; *CCIR 1288–1296*, 225); she held it Oct. 1295 (*CCIR 1288–1296*, 435), but by Aug. 1301 Joan's son Thomas held it (*CPR 1292–1301*, 604).

131. Boyville was in the admin. of the Q's Northants. lands, 1275 (*CCIR 1272–1279*, 115), and was named to a comm. on poaching at Great Bowden, 1282 (Appendix I no. 124; *CPR 1281–1292*, 48). Is he the William de Beyvill' of Northants. who pledged Walter de Beyville, forester of the New Forest, 1280 (Stagg, *CNFD*, i, no. 219)? He escaped conviction during the "state trials" of 1289–93 (Tout and Johnstone, eds., *State Trials*, 114–17).

132. The Q disposed of the marr. of Joan, dau. h. of Stephen de Grendon, hereditary kpr of Westm. Palace and Fleet prison. Those sjties incl. property in London and Westm. (*CIPM*, viii, no. 214), but there is no proof the Q held lands or ten. of Joan's inh. (see above, note 94).

133. On 3 Mar. 1279 the Q was gtd wardship of the manor of Wyke Dive (in Wicken) in minority of the h. of Henry Dyve (*CFR*, i, 109; *CIPM*, ii, nos. 234, 415; *RO*, i, 33). The gt was apparently ineffective; Dyve's widow later fined to have the wardship, and in Nov. 1281 the K gtd custody of Wyke Dive to the Q's yeoman John de Shelvestrode (*CPR 1272–1281*, 314, 462).

134. *CChyW*, 201; *CIM*, i, no. 1922; and *CCIR 1302–1307*, 36, allege purchase by the Q "at her own cost" of a messuage in Northampton, gtd to the friars of the Sack. Inq. pr. this was untrue.

135. The gt of the wardship of lands of Henry Dyve (Mar. 1279) would have given the Q Deddington and Ducklington, but this gt does not seem to have taken effect. See note 133.

136. The Q's agreement of 30 May 1280 with William de Knovill concerning recovery of his right in lands late of Joan de Saunford incl. a manor at Lashbrook, but the agreement seems not to have succeeded (above, note 92).

137. On Sampson, Emden, *Cambridge*, cols. 504–5. In 1293 he founded a chantry for the souls of the Q and his parents in the chapel at Easton (*CPR 1292–1301*, 54); S.C. 1/28/153, s.d., from Walter de Winterborne OP, the K's confessor, certifies the Chancellor that the K has ordered inq. on lands to support the chantry. See also Hill, ed., *Rolls and Reg. Sutton*, ii, 120.

138. Bef. 1281 the Q recovered lands at Somerton worth £25 yrly (*CCIR 1279–1288*, 81), perhaps the pasture called Kingsmore by Ilchester, which the K in fact recovered and allowed the Q to hold as appurt. to Somerton. In 13 Edw. the men of Ilchester, the abbot of Athelney, and Henry de Urtiaco cl. the Q depr. them of pasture when the moor came to her (Bates, ed., *Cartularies of Muchelney and Athelney*, 128–29; *RH*, ii, 128). In 1291 Urtiaco and the men of Ilchester pr. their right and won damages (JUST 1/1014 m. 6; *Manners*, 111, 135). On Urtiaco see also note 142 below.

139. Appurt. to Barwick was the ward of lands at Watchet and Williton late of Ralph fitz John fitz Urse, gtd by the Q to John Picard who in M1281 conveyed to Andrew Loterel (E 159/55 m. 7). This wardship fell in bef. 1280: in 1291 Giles de Fysseburn' cl. that when the ward came to the Q's hands, her bf Adam Basset disseized Giles of lands in Williton (JUST 1/1014 m. 7); Basset left office by 1280, when he owed the Q arrears in his accts (E 13/8 m. 23d).

140. Appurt. to Camel was the wardship of Charlton Musgrove, which the Q gtd John de Vescy after Robert de Muscegros' death, Dec. 1280 (*CIPM*, ii, no. 404; *Feudal Aids*, iv, 287; for the Q's long prosecution of Muscegros for debts owed through the Jewry, above, Chapter Two). Inq. in Aug. 1287 showed that lands of John s. h. of Ralph Huscarl at Bruton and Eastrip were in the hands of Henry de Carevill by the Q's commission (*CIPM*, ii, no. 650).

141. A fragm. letter (S.C. 1/10/154 [Stogursey, 5 id. March s.a.]) appears to connect the Q with the respite of Maud Walerand's debts to the K. The letter did not originate with the Q; her clks rarely dated in Roman fashion, and the letter mentions her in the third person. If she did obtain such respite for Maud, perhaps paying the debts herself, Maud might have leased the manors to her to repay the money (compare Appendix I nos. 196b, 214; intr. to Appendix I).

142. *CCIR 1279–1288*, 81, indicates that the Q by 1281 acq. the adv. of the ch of Curry Rivel. But the lord of Curry Rivel, the Henry de Urtiaco whom the Q depr. of pasture on lands appurt. to Somerton (note 138), d. 1322 holding manor and adv. at Curry Rivel (GEC, x, 180 [s.v "Orty"]; *CIPM*, i, no. 315, and vi, no. 319).

143. The Q's agreement of 30 May 1280 with William de Knovill on his right in lands of Joan de Saunford incl. "all her lands in co. Suffolk," evidently her interests at Old Newton, of which she enfeoffed Reginald de Cretinge for life, with reversion to herself and her hs. Neither Knovill nor the kinswoman with whom he divided Joan's other lands was identified as Joan's h. for Old Newton by the Suffolk jurors, who said the h. was one John de Munteny. The agreement with Knovill seems not to have succeeded (see note 92).

144. Transactions in *Kalendars*, i, 44 (no. 80), 45 (no. 86), and 47 (no. 101) were prob. to clear the manor of competing rights in anticipation of its inclusion in the 1275 dower assignment; see also *VCH Surrey*, iii, 254–55.

145. Wauton's widow Joan recd 40s. dower in Betchworth (*CIPM*, v, no. 397) and sought dower in his manor at Frant (Sussex) in 1314–15 (see Appendix I no. 221).

146. The evidently ineffective grant to the Q of the wardship of the lands of Henry Dyve, 23 Mar. 1279 (above, note 133) would have given the Q wardship of the manor of Wonworth in Graffham.

147. Thomas de Bykenhulle was paid £4 by the Q's exors for a yrly rent of 20s. at Knowle (presumably detained or overburdened); John de la Launde of Longdon had £16:13:4

for unspecified damages (*Manners*, 132, 135, 138–39). Their complaints are not found on extant rolls of the 1291 inquest.

148. The gt recited in *CCIR 1302–1307*, 285, as from Edward I to "the late Q," concerns Eleanor of Provence (*CPR 1272–1281*, 425, 438; *CPR 1281–1292*, 137; *RO*, i, 38; Fry, ed., *Wilts. Inqs. Post Mortem*, 312).

149. In 1291 Alice de Grymstede, widow and co-exor of John de Grymstede of Compton, brought two complaints (JUST 1/1014 m. 9d, badly damaged). One seems to involve a wardship seized by the Q but it is not clear whether in Hants. or Wilts. The second action involved seizure of grain at Compton to the use of the Q's kinsman James de la Plaunche who m. the Haversham h., 1289 (*CHEC*, 50 note 182); E 40/14548 (29 Sept. 1291) is Alice de Grymstede's ackn. for herself and her co-exors of receipt of ten marks in final payment of twenty marks James ackn. for grain and rents at Compton taken to his use by the Q's bfs. These are the Grymstedes who cl. right in lands acq. by the Q in Hants. (see Appendix I no. 97); they and the Havershams descended from earlier lords of Compton (Meekings, ed., *Crown Pleas of the Wilts. Eyre*, 132–40; Wrottesley, *Pedigrees*, 88).

150. Henry fitz Auger or Aucher (d. 1303), nephew of Bp Giffard of Worcs. (*CIPM*, iv, no. 172; *VCH Hants.*, iv, 568; Bund, ed., *Reg. Gainsborough*, 58). In June 1295 Henry had lic. to alienate 1½ acres in Fisherton to the OP of Salisbury (*CPR 1292–1301*, 136).

151. The dispossession of foresters at Feckenham (*CIM*, ii, no. 1555, and *VCH Worcs.*, iii, 376) was perpetrated during Eleanor of Provence's tenure (*CCIR 1279–1299*, 455; *CIPM*, i, nos. 524, 770).

152. On Gilbert Fraunceys' lands, perhaps gtd Eleanor after Evesham, see intr. to Appendix I.

153. The surname is omitted in the enrollment.

154. Almost certainly s. of John de Weston, Eleanor's steward in 1264, John de Weston was a minor living with her children, 1274 (Johnstone, "Wardrobe and Household of Henry," 390, 400); her squire, 1278 (C 47/4/1 fol. 40). This act is the earliest evidence for his marr. to Christiana, later the Q's woman. He was certainly the Q's knt and steward at a later date (above, Chapter Two, notes 97–99), but there is no proof of his status at the time of this act or of other of her acts he witn. (below, Appendix II nos. 11, 18).

155. Husband of the Q's woman Ermentrude de Sakeville, Andrew was prob. a knt of Eleanor's household at this period, but no certain proof can be offered. See Chapter Two, notes 98, 103. Andrew also witn. Appendix II no. 18.

156. The K's steward Hugh fitz Otes d. shortly bef. 11 Apr. 1283, prob. on or ca. 10 Feb. when his obit was kept by the OP, Guildford (E. B. Fryde et al., eds., *Br. Chronology*, 74; Palmer, "Friars Preachers of Guildford," 9, 12). The presence of John de Weston indicates a date later than ca. 1280 (see Appendix II no. 9 and note 154).

157. Knt of the Q's household in 1289–90, perhaps for some time bef. that, but not certainly so early as 1281 (he witn. Appendix II no. 17, also in 1281); see above, Chapter Two, notes 98, 100.

158. Q's bf at Overton in Flints. Aug. 1283; she was gtd Overton after 5 June that yr (Appendix I no. 28). A knt by autumn 1284 (E 101/351/12 m. 7), when prob. no longer a bf (Appendix I no. 72), but not certainly the Q's knt until later (*CHEC*, 154; above, Chapter Two, note 97).

159. On Oweyn, see Appendix I no. 170, and Appendix II no. 8.

160. Geoffrey de Aspale, kpr of the Q's wardrobe, appears as a witn. to the 1290 conf. but certainly d. 1287 (*CIPM*, ii, no. 635). For this reason the bp of Chichester is undentifiable, but was either Stephen Bersted (d. 1287) or Gilbert de St. Leofardo, elected 1288.

CHAPTER FOUR

1. Hope, "On the Funeral Effigies," 521–25. On Henry III's heart, *CPR 1281–1292*, 463; Paris, *CM*, v, 475; Wander, "Westminster Abbey," 30–31; Boase, "Fontevrault and the

Plantagenets." On Richard of Cornwall, Denholm-Young, *Richard of Cornwall*, 152 (but compare J. K. Fowler, *Beaulieu Abbey*, 198–21). For Eleanor of Provence's heart (1291), London, 100; on young Alphonso, above, Chapter One; Rishanger, 108; Haydon, ed., *Eulogium*, 147. On the Feb. 1290 payment, *CHEC*, 88. The Lincoln tomb is discussed below.

2. Alexander and Binski, *Age of Chivalry*, nos. 377–78; A. Gardner, *English Sculpture*, 214–16; Stone, *Sculpture in Britain*, 142–43; KW, 481–83. Arguments for the effigy's value as portraiture (e.g., Howgrave-Graham, "Earlier Royal Funeral Effigies," 168–69) are unconvincing. Two fourteenth-century statues on the façade of Lincoln cathedral were restored after 1851 as Edward I and Eleanor of Castile (with modern heads), but it is doubtful that the original statues were intended to represent them (A. Gardner, *English Sculpture*, 148).

3. Panofsky, *Tomb Sculpture*, 39–66. On the Q's image and that of the Virgin, Lindley, "Romanticizing Reality," 73, and A. Gardner, *English Sculpture*, 167–69, 214; striking in their resemblance to Eleanor's tomb effigy are wall paintings of the Virgin and female saints in South Newington Church, ca. 1330–40 (Tristram, *English Wall Painting*, 70–73, pl. 16a–b). On Diana, Camille, *Gothic Idol*, 111 and pl. 60; Monroe, "Two Medieval Genealogical Roll Chronicles," 220. The tiles are noted in Chapter One.

4. It is arguable that the Ponthevin shields appear as Eleanor was ctss in her own right, but they also appear in the "Planché" or "Heralds'" roll of arms, which prob. predates her accession in Ponthieu and has been assoc. with her interest in heraldry (Denholm-Young, *History and Heraldry*, 45–47). The tomb's personal nature may be inferred from evidence suggesting the Q commissioned the chest before her death: her treas. acct for M1290 has a payment to an abbot (title illegible) for marble stones laid to the Q's use (S.C. 6/1089/25 m. 4). The effigy was certainly cast after her death.

5. For the mantle cord, A. Gardner, *English Sculpture*, pl. 250. I am grateful to Nicola Coldstream for pointing out the derivation from Reims.

6. Brieger, *English Art 1216–1307*, 203, questioned by Lindley, "Romanticizing Reality," 74 and note 36. On coronation robes, L. G. W. Legg, ed., *English Coronation Records*, 100; on timelessness in royal attire, Hayden, *Symbol and Privilege*, 62–70 (compare remarks on royal transport by Cannadine, "Context, Performance, and Meaning of Ritual," 111–12, 123–24). For combinative functions of royal tombs, Kantorowicz, *King's Two Bodies*, 419–37. On the effigy's implied frontality as a standing image, below, note 13. See also Geertz, "Centers, Kings and Charisma," esp. 16–20; as "exports," compare the images of St. Edward and St. George the K and Q placed on Becket's shrine at Canterbury, 1285, noted in Chapter One.

7. KW, 481 and pl. 35; Kendrick, *Cathedral Church of Lincoln*, 129–31; Cook, *Chantries*, 134; Galloway, *Eleanor of Castile*, 68–69; Alexander and Binski, *Age of Chivalry*, no. 379.

8. *CHEC*, 88, and *Manners*, 103, show the chapel was new (compare Hinnebusch, *Early English Friars Preachers*, 45); for materials, *Manners*, 128, 131. I am grateful for thoughts from Dr. Phillip Lindley, who provided the plate of Bp Aymer's heart tomb. Bony, *English Decorated Style*, 20 and pl. 117, thinks the London tomb resembled that of Thibaut V of Champagne at Provins, which lacks metal figures; wall-paintings figured in the London tomb (as below) but could not easily have been part of the Provins composition, and the accts do not bear out Bony's idea that the London tomb had sculpted weepers.

9. The gilt effigy became the most esteemed in England as a sign of status (Lindley, "'Una Grande opera . . . '," 113).

10. KW, 479–85; Martin, ed., *Reg. Peckham*, i, 33–34; *CCIR 1288–1296*, 352. The *montjoies* were not the first French examples; at least one cross was put up to mark Philip II's funeral procession in 1223 (Baldwin, *Government of Philip Augustus*, 391).

11. J. Evans, "Prototype of the Eleanor Crosses," 96–99; Branner, "Montjoies of St. Denis," 13–16; Bony, *English Decorated Style*, pl. 166; Hallam, "Eleanor Crosses and Royal Burial Customs," 14–15. Brieger, *English Art 1216–1307*, 201, distinguishes the Eleanor crosses

as a chivalric king's gesture to his wife from the *montjoies* as a kingdom's tribute to a saintly monarch, but both series of monuments were primarily statements of royal eminence and authority.

12. Lovell, "Queen Eleanor's Crosses"; Alexander and Binski, *Age of Chivalry*, nos. 369–76; *KW*, 483–85; A. Gardner, *English Sculpture*, 167–69; Coldstream, "Commissioning and Design of the Eleanor Crosses"; Lindley, "Romanticizing Reality." The Waltham cross was much restored in the nineteenth century (Winters, *The Queen Eleanor Memorial*); a sketch made bef. restoration is in Bony, *English Decorated Style*, pl. 120. The Waltham statues of the Q are now in the Victoria and Albert Museum, London; the Hardingstone statues, conserved in the 1980s, were returned to the monument. The Geddington cross is the best preserved (N. Smith, "Conservation of the Geddington Cross").

13. On distancing image from reality, Lindley, "Romanticizing Reality," 83; on the scepter, J. C. Parsons, "Ritual and Symbol," 65, and on ritual construction of queenship, idem, "Queen's Intercession." On using royal statues to create impressions of the individual, E. A. R. Brown, "Persona et Gesta, 3," 223–27; for frontality as evoking the sacred or transcendent, Schapiro, *Words and Pictures*, 37–49, esp. 38–41 (a reference I owe to Claire Sherman), where it is associated with divine or royal beings and linked to what Schapiro calls "the theme of state."

14. Edmund's tomb was prob. finished by Apr. 1300 when his body was moved from the London Minoresses to Westm. (*Liber quotidianus*, 33). The same artisans perhaps worked on the tomb of Abp Pecham (d. 1292), and at St. Etheldreda's, Holborn (Coldstream, "Commissioning and Design of the Eleanor Crosses," 63–64; Lindley, "Romanticising Reality," 80–81). See also Bony, *English Decorated Style*, 20–23. Binski, "The Cosmati at Westminster," 5–6, sees in the "depersonalized imagery of official attributes" of the tombs of Henry III and Eleanor a rejection of the elaborate ornamentation of the later tombs in this series; Lindley, note 25, points out, however, that as the Westm. tombs of Edmund, Aveline, and William and Aymer de Valence postdate those of Henry III and Eleanor, the latter in fact reject the austerity of the former.

15. Lindley, "Romanticizing Reality," 83.

16. J. Evans, "Prototype of the Eleanor Crosses," 99; Binski, "Cosmati at Westminster," 26–28. But compare Branner, "Montjoies of St. Louis"; for the "miracle," Rishanger, 98. See also Kantorowicz, *King's Two Bodies*, 419–37; Hallam, "Royal Burial," 359–80.

17. W. Brown, ed., *Reg. le Romeyn*, i, 34 (= Raine, ed., *Letters from Northern Registers*, 91–92), and ii, 3; Hill, ed., *Rolls and Reg. Sutton*, iii, 166–67, and iv, 81 (Eleanor of Provence d. 24/25 June 1291); for the 1294 list, *Manners*, 137.

18. Guisborough, 227–28 (the Q d. on a Tuesday); Stubbs, ed., *Ann. Paulini*, 225; *Dunstable*, 366; *Worcester*, 506; *Manners*, 98. Services were also held in 1291 at the manors that served as administrative centers for the Q's estates—Harborough, Burgh, Somerton, Lyndhurst, Leeds, Langley, and Haverfordwest (*Manners*, 98).

19. *CChR*, ii, 411, 424–26; further lands were gtd in Oct. 1295 to supply £5 lacking (ibid., 461), and in 1316 Edward II gave lic. for the abbey to acq. another ten librates in mortmain (*CPR 1313–1317*, 521–22); full text of the Jan. 1292 letters patent in translation in Lathbury, Denham, 79–83, from the surviving original exemplar, long preserved at Denham and auctioned in London in 1976 (*Catalogue of Western Manuscripts and Miniatures. . . which will be sold by auction by Sotheby Parke Bernet. . . 13th December 1976*, lot 14). See also Cook, Chantries, 8 (where "twenty-two manors" is in error; the accts for the lands and the yrly service, preserved at Westm. Abbey, note only the manors named above); *CPR 1281–1292*, 466; *CCIR 1288–1296*, 224, 436; *Kalendars*, i, 110–11 (no. 6).

20. Maidenheath was f. by M1293 (Cook, Chantries, 8); *CCIR 1288–1296*, 288, and *Manners*, 117, imply that this foundation was entrusted to mr Ralph de Ivingho, one of the justices comm. in Jan. 1291 to hear and determine complaints against the late Q and her ministers. On the Harby (later Lincoln) chantry, *CPR 1281–1292*, 487; *CCIR 1288–1296*, 178; *Manners*, 118; Cook, Chantries, 7–8, 134.

21. For Peterborough, *CPR 1281–1292*, 414, Mellows, ed., *Pytchley's Book of Fees*, 71–72, *Kalendars*, i, 110 (no. 5); for Easton, above chap. 3, appx no. 179a note 137 (the priest was to celebrate daily, with "Placebo," "Dirige," and commendatory prayers [Hill, ed., *Rolls and Reg. Sutton*, ii, 120]); for St. Albans, *Kalendars*, i, 111 (no. 9); compare *CPR 1292–1301*, 11; on Harby, W. Brown, ed., *Reg. le Romeyn*, i, 323.

22. For Coventry, C 146/2982 (s.d. but *temp*. Prior Thomas who d. by 1294 [*Fasti 1300–1541*, x, 4]); on London, *CPR 1301–1307*, 316–17; for Bath, Historical MSS Commission, *Cal. of the MSS of the Dean and Chapter of Wells*, i, 204–5, and ii, 583–84; on Lincoln, Hall, ed., *Red Book*, i, lxxxiii–iv. See also *CPR 1292–1301*, 26; *CPR 1321–1324*, 324.

23. On Longespee, *MA*, vi part 1, 501; Malden, "Will of Nicholas Longespee," 524. For the impact of royal chantries, Cook, *Mediaeval Chantries*, 7–8; Blackley, "Isabella of France," 36–45, esp. 43 notes 109–10.

24. The passages quoted are respectively Riley, ed., *Opus chronicorum*, 26, 47–48, and 49–50.

25. Bak, "Roles and Functions of Queens in Árpádian and Angevin Hungary," 14–15; Stafford, "Portrayal of Royal Women," 166. On historical writing at Westminster and St. Albans, Gransden, "Continuation of the *Flores Historiarum*," 472–92; Alexander and Binski, *Age of Chivalry*, no. 346.

26. The Q's travels and her health in 1289–90 as influencing her relationship with her s. are discussed in Chapter One; Johnstone, *Edward of Carnarvon*, 25, 28–31. For the Q's iter in 1289–90, *CHEC*, 138–52; her son's may be traced in C 47/3/22 (*Edward of Carnarvon*, 24, refers only to a brief period in Aug.–Sept. 1290 when the households of the K and Q and their s. were together).

27. Johnstone, *Letters*, 115–16. Is this the John de Langele who had £5 of the gift of the Q's exors, H1292, and whose wife had £5 for services to the Q, M1293 (*Manners*, 108, 135)?

28. Respectively above, Chapter Three, Appendix I nos. 15a, 152b–c, 48a–c, 100, 219, 226a, 106; on Birdbrook, Chapter Three, Appendix I, note 101.

29. Westm. Abbey, muniments 5144; above, Chapter Three, Appendix I no. 117.

30. *CHEC*, 48.

31. GEC, vi, 402. *CIPM*, vi, no. 316 shows Robert de Haustede sr d. shortly bef. 3 Jan. 1322, so the obit of a Robert de Haustede on 18 Dec. in the "Alphonso" psalter is prob. his (BL, Add. 24686, fol. 10v); the psalter's obit of a William de Haustede on 28 Sept. (fol. 9) is prob. that of Robert sr and Margerie's s., a rector of Rolvenden (Kent), who d. shortly bef. 6 Oct. 1322 (Graham, ed., *Reg. Winchelsey*, ii, 712–13, 909, 913; *CPR 1281–1292*, 410; *CPR 1292–1301*, 136, 226; *CFR*, iii, 31, 180; Lambeth Palace, MS Reg. of Abp Reynolds, fol. 305). Margerie d. shortly bef. 18 Jan. 1338; her s. Robert jr. was said to have d. seven years earlier (*CIPM*, viii, no. 150).

32. Respectively above, Chapter Three, Appendix I note 104; GEC, ii, 355–56.

33. *Rishanger*, 120–21; Riley, ed., *Gesta abbatum sancti Albani*, 411–12; Walsingham, *Historia Anglicana*, i, 32.

34. Mannyng, *Peter Langtoft's Chronicle*, ii, 252 (spelling modernized); compare Piers Langtoft, *Chronicle*, ii, 194: "Pus ke sa femme à Deu est comaundé,/ De trestuz ses fiz est nul demoré,/ Fors soul sir Eduuard, ke Deus l'ad reservé [Since his wife was commanded to God,/ Of all his sons none remained,/ Except Lord Edward alone,/ Whom God left him]." The possibility exists that he worked from a Langtoft MS that included lines that had dropped out of other copies, but Langtoft's modern editor does not suggest that this happened in any of the MSS with which he worked. Mannyng is better known as the translator of *Handlyng Synne*.

35. *RP*, iv, 268. The e. of Norfolk, descendant of Edward I's second marr., cl. precedence over the e. of Warwick who had no royal blood. Warwick retorted that royal blood did not settle precedence: the e. of Devon followed Warwick, though Devon as a

descendant of Edward and the "rayr" Eleanor was related to Henry IV by the full blood—whereas Norfolk was related to Henry only by the half blood, and hence had even less right on that ground to precedence over Warwick than Devon might be presumed to have.

36. R. A. Griffiths, "Sense of Dynasty in the Reign of Henry VI,' 13–16; Allen, "Yorkist Propaganda," 171–92. On interest in noble descents from Plantagenet women in this period, Parsons, "Mothers, Daughters," 72; compare the resort to such descents in 1425, as noted above.

37. Serjeantson, *History of Delapré Abbey,* 23; Galloway, *Eleanor of Castile,* 25, 28. On Stony Stratford, see Gibson's 1695 edition of Camden's *Britannia* (originally 1586), col. 202, where the cross is mentioned in the present tense though most of the crosses, incl. Stony Stratford, had been demolished by 1695.

38. Leland, *Itinerary,* i, 8, and ii, 23.

39. Worcestre, *Itineraries;* Leland, *Itinerary,* i, 8, 310–11, and v, 201; Wheatley, ed., *Stow's Survey of London,* 238–39; Galloway, *Eleanor of Castile,* 27–30.

40. Brie, ed., *Brut,* i, 178, 185; Holinshed, *Chronicles,* ii, 431, 435, 439; Grafton, *Chronicle,* i, 255, 282, 283, 289; Hardyng, *Chronicle from the Firste Begynnyng,* fol. clv; Fabyan, *New Chronicles,* 393; Vergil, *Urbinitatis Anglicae Historiae,* 310, 345. The original Latin of the verses and the (sixteenth-century?) English version quoted here are in Crull, *Antiquities of St. Peter's,* 299–300. That the Latin text was perhaps already displayed in the fourteenth century is suggested by the queen's reference to "A county of land I have, in Spain," in Trounce, ed., *Athelston,* 78, a reference I owe Patricia Eberle. The display of the Ponthevin arms on the Q's tombs and the crosses could have contributed to such a misunderstanding. See Chapter One, note 23.

41. Levin, "John Foxe and the Responsibilities of Queenship," 118–22. Foxe pays virtually no attention to other medieval English queens.

42. Martienssen, *Queen Katherine Parr.*

43. Holinshed, *Chronicles of England,* ii, 431, 435, 439. On Parker's edn of the *Historia Anglicana,* see Riley's intr. to the RS edn (28.i, vol. i, ix–x).

44. Camden, *Britannia,* i, 390–91 (the English translation given here is that from Edmund Gibson's 1695 edn of *Britannia,* cols. 320–21). Dunn's edn of Camden's *Remains* (as in following note) shows that Camden took the story from Arévalo in Bel's *Rerum hispaniarum scriptores* (1579), i, 297. A churchman who often traveled in Italy, Arévalo presumably saw Fiadoni's work there; see Tate, "Rodrigo Sánchez de Arévalo (1404–1470) and his *Compendiosa Historica Hispania,*" 58–80. On Camden's edn of Walsingham, incl. in his *Anglica, Normannica, Hibernica, a veteribus scripta* (Frankfurt, 1603), see intr. to Walsingham, *Historia Anglicana,* i, ix–x).

45. Camden, *Remains,* 236–37.

46. Peele, *The Famous Chronicle of king Edward the first,* ed. Hook.

47. Hook (*Edward the First,* 186), glosses this as "probably the high cork-soled overshoes worn to keep the feet out of the mud," which accords oddly with Eleanor's complaint about heat and dust in the speech quoted. But perhaps added at the time of revision to prepare Eleanor's haughty rejection of Welsh soil as too base for her foot, which follows in her next speech.

48. *Sic,* prob. for "Clare," Gloucester's family name.

49. Peele, *Edward the First,* sc. 6 (ll. 1115–49), 10 (ll. 1487–90; compare l. 1687).

50. Hook, intr. to Peele, *Edward the First,* 19–34, 57–60; on Greene's work, Assarsson-Rizzi, *Friar Bacon and Friar Bungay,* 43 (on Holinshed), 147–49 (for the date). *Friar Bacon* represents Edward's crusade as long past when he m. Eleanor. A lost Tudor play perhaps about Eleanor of Castile was *The Story of Queene Elenor, with the Rearing of London Bridge upon Wool-Sackes* (L. B. Wright, *Middle-Class Culture in Elizabethan England,* 617 note 1). The identity of the Q of this title is unclear; the Eleanor linked with London bridge was the wife of Henry III (*CPR 1266–1272,* 459; *RH,* i, 405; Stapleton, ed., *Antiquis Legibus,*

141–42), but the ref. to wool-sacks might reflect the tradition that Eleanor of Castile brought Merino sheep to England (above, Chapter One). Possibly two Eleanors were elided, as *Edward the First* mingled the Eleanor of Aquitaine of the "The Queen's Confession" with the Eleanor of Castile of "The Lamentable Fall," as discussed below.

51. Above, Chapter One; Peele, *Edward the First,* sc. vi (ll. 1030–39). On Parker's edn of Matthew Paris, see *CM,* i, ix.

52. In the text reconstructed from broadsides by Hook (in Peele, *Edward the First,* 211-16), this line reads "Her guilty hand did staine."

53. The earliest extant text of "The Lamentable Fall" was perhaps printed 1586 X 1625 (Peele, *Edward the First,* ed. Hook, 19–20), but was prob. transmitted orally before publication. The text given here is from T. Evans, *Old Ballads,* i, 238–43. On the theory that it dates from Mary I's reign, Peele, *Edward the First,* ed. Hook, 211–12, and Evans, *Old Ballads,* i, 239–40, where the ballad has the title "Warning-piece to England, against Pride and Wickednesse; being the fall of Queen Eleanor, Wife to Edward the First King of England, who for her pride and God's Judgments, sunk into the Ground at Charing-cross, and rose at Queen-hith" (compare J. L. L. Crawford, *Catalogue of a Collection of English Ballads,* ii, 467 [no. 1292], a version printed ca. 1690). That the ballad's queen is "her grace" (not "her majesty") suggests a fairly early date. The printer's intr. to a text printed ca. 1720 (in Evans, *Old Ballads,* i, 237–38) is substantially quoted in Peele, *Edward the First,* ed. Hook, 211–12, but ends with the following, which Hook omitted: "Probably, [the ballad's author] chose out this pious queen, that people might easily see, tho' it was said, it could not be meant of her; and, perhaps, he was glad to mention one so good and virtuous, that people might look back upon her history, and see the difference between her and the bigotted queen, who then sway'd the English sceptre" (on the date, Peele, *Edward the First,* ed. Hook, 206, 211).

54. Percy, *Reliques of Ancient English Poetry,* ii, 145; see discussion in Owen, *Eleanor of Aquitaine,* 158–60. Child, *English and Scottish Popular Ballads,* vi, 257–64 (no. 156, giving several variants), believes that while the "Confession" was printed only in the seventeenth century, it was in oral circulation long bef. that; it was obviously used for *Edward The First* as early as 1590–92. It is clearer in Child's variants (esp. "V," at 262–63) than in Percy's text that the Q is the mother of both sons, one fathered by the e. marshal and the other, whom she hates, by the king; in "V," a Scottish variant, she also admits that her dau. playing nearby was fathered by a French friar. Another variant makes her the mother of seven sons, only the youngest of them the K's.

55. Axton, *Queen's Two Bodies,* 27–29, 31–33, 101–5; Braunmuller, *George Peele,* 96–97.

56. On Peele's particular animosity toward Spain among contemporary English playwrights, Peele, *Battle of Alcazar,* ed. Yoklavich, 220.

57. Axton, *Queen's Two Bodies,* 101–5 (not mentioning the revision theory or that *Edward the First* incorporates preexisting material).

58. Greene, *Frier Bacon and frier Bongay,* ed. Grosart, II. 1267–1337 (Hercules), 1799–1803 (Edward's portrait), 1849 ("not very coy"); Axton, *Queen's Two Bodies,* 101–5. On Eleanor's "unladylike" behavior in *Friar Bacon,* Hook, intr. to Peele, *Edward The First,* 58.

59. Axton, *Queen's Two Bodies,* 23, 91–97. "Robert Doleman" is usually accepted as an alias of Robert Parsons, SJ.

60. L. B. Wright, *Middle-Class Culture in Elizabethan England,* 465–507; Rogers, *Troublesome Helpmate,* 100–34, 140–51; Woodbridge, *Women and the English Renaissance.*

61. Peele, *Edward the First,* ed. Hook, sc. 10 (Edward of Caernarvon's birth; l. 1644 is quoted), 12 (his christening), 15 (mayoress' death). On childbirth and queens' intercession, Parsons, "Ritual and Symbol," 67; compare Strohm, "Queens as Intercessors," 101–2.

62. Peele, *Edward the First,* ed. Hook, sc. 15 (ll. 2071–2108); on Cleopatra, Woodbridge, *Women and the English Renaissance,* 15, 71, 119, 128, 305.

63. Peele, *Edward the First,* ed. Hook, sc. 10 (ll. 1631–86). On Amazons, Woodbridge, *Women and the English Renaissance,* 15, 38–39, 69, 117, 128, 142, 158, 160, 164–65, 181,

315. On sixteenth- and seventeenth-century views on the contagion of marital insub-
ordination and the need to control it, Woodbridge, 18, 197–98; Rogers, *Troublesome
Helpmate*, 140–51. See also N. Z. Davis, "Women on Top."

64. Henderson, "Elizabeth's Watchful Eye," with which compare C. Jordan, "Woman's rule
in sixteenth-century British political thought," esp. 428. It is tempting to think of the
contrast between the *Arraignment* and *Edward the First* in terms of the corrective relationship suggested by Einstein, *Mozart*, 207, for *Ein Musikalischer Spass* (K. 522) and *Eine
Kleine Nachtmusik* (K. 525).

65. On royal lineage and the realm's self-image, Nelson, "Inauguration Rituals," 71.

66. Greenblatt, *Renaissance Self-Fashioning*, 167–68. Compare the comment by John
Harrington, as Elizabeth lay dying in 1603, that she was "this state's natural mother"
(quoted in Levin, "Power, Politics and Sexuality," 108).

67. The Marian imagery applied to Elizabeth is too complex to be considered here; on the
aspects suggested, see J. Wilson, *Entertainments for Elizabeth I*, 21–22; Wells, *Spenser's
Faerie Queene and the Cult of Elizabeth*, 14–21. See also Levin, "Power, Politics, and
Sexuality," 95–100; J. N. King, "The Godly Woman in Elizabethan Iconography," 41–84,
and idem, "Queen Elizabeth I," 30–74.

68. L. B. Wright, *Middle-Class Culture*, 506; Rogers, *Troublesome Helpmate*, 135–59;
Thompson, *Women in Stuart England and America*, 8–15, 161–81; Masek, "Women in an
Age of Transition," esp. 146–62; E. C. Williams, *Anne of Denmark*, 109–11, 143–47,
158–59, 200–1; Oman, *Henrietta Maria*; Davidson, *Catherine of Bragança*; Hopkirk,
Queen over the Water; Zook, "History's Mary," 170–91.

69. Owen, *Eleanor of Aquitaine*, 156–61; Peele, *Edward the First*, ed. Hook, 206–12. The
Lincoln cross vanished by the eighteenth century but the year of its destruction is uncertain; nor is there reliable information on demolition at Dunstable. The Stamford cross
was perhaps still standing in 1717, though some accounts date its downfall to the Civil
War; see Galloway, *Eleanor of Castile*, 68–78.

70. R. Baker, *History of the Kings of England*, 94; on the work, Sambrook, *James Thomson*,
192. Gibson's edn of *Britannia* is cited above, note 44. For the printer's preface to "The
Lamentable Fall," above, note 53.

71. N. Smith, "Conservation of the Geddington Cross," 93–94; George, *Catalogue of
Political and Personal Satires*, no. 8972.

72. Arkell, *Caroline of Ansbach*; Walters, *Royal Griffin*, 121, 127, 161.

73. M. J. W. Scott, *James Thomson*, 229–31; Sambrook, *James Thomson*, 192–98.

74. Scott, *James Thomson*, 229–31; L. Stone, *Family, Sex and Marriage*, esp. 282–87 (emphasizing novels rather than dramas).

75. Hunter, "On the Death of Eleanor of Castile," 167–91. Sánchez de Arévalo's version
of the Acre legend had been resuscitated in 1826 by Blore, *Monumental Remains*, 2, but
did not much influence Hunter.

76. In general, Pope-Hennessy, *Agnes Strickland*. "Strickland" is used here in singular and
plural to refer to both sisters and to the *Queens*, "Agnes" when it is certain she was
responsible for material under discussion. Other Strickland sisters were Susanna
Moodie (1803–85), known for *Roughing It in the Bush*, a memoir of life in Upper Canada,
and Catherine Traill (1802–99), a children's writer; see Moodie, *Letters of a Lifetime* and
Letters of Love and Duty; Blain, Grundy, and Clements, eds., *Feminist Companion*, s. vv.
"Moodie, Susanna (Strickland)," and "Traill, Catherine Parr (Strickland)."

77. Strickland, *Queens* (1872), i, xiv; Pope-Hennessy, *Agnes Strickland*, 232.

78. Ibid., i, x; on earlier women historical writers, N. Z. Davis, "Gender and Genre," 153–
82.

79. Ibid., i, x, xi.

80. Pope-Hennessy, *Agnes Strickland*, 85–86, 149, 160–61, 232, 267, 280–81, 284, 303–4.

81. Ibid., 49–58; Strickland, *Queens*, i, xvi.

82. Strickland, *Queens*, i, 430–31.

83. Ibid., i, 3, 65 note 1.
84. Compare remarks on Christine de Pizan by Poulet, "Capetian Women and the Regency," 96; on Agnes' refusal to work for women's rights, Pope-Hennessy, *Agnes Strickland*, 243–44.
85. Pope-Hennessy, *Agnes Strickland*, 189–90.
86. The sources edited in Strickland's day are summarized at the beginning of Chapter One; Strickland, *Queens*, i, 449–50, cites *RP*, i, 475, 477, badly misrepresenting the former.
87. For use of Green's details, J. C. Parsons, "Mothers, Daughters," 71 and note 14. Dau. of a Methodist pastor who taught her privately, M. A. E. Wood (1818–95) m. 1846 the artist G. P. Green, whose studies on the Continent allowed her to work in foreign archives. Inspired by *Queens,* she undertook *Princesses* in 1843 but delayed publication until *Queens* was done; in the interim she ed. *Letters of Royal and Illustrious Ladies* (1846), used by Strickland in later edns of *Queens*. But Strickland made little if any use of *Princesses*; Pope-Hennessy's *Agnes Strickland* never refers to Green, odd given Agnes' usual cultivation of those who might provide new information from original sources. Green ed. 41 vols of Tudor and Stuart State Papers for the PRO, 1853–93. The only acct of her life is *DNB*, s.v. "Wood, Mary Anne Everett"; Blain, Grundy, and Clements, eds., *Feminist Companion*, notes her dau., a novelist and children's writer, s.v. "Everett-Green, Evelyn, 'Cecil Adair,' 1856–1932."
88. For examples, J. C. Parsons, "Eleanor of Castile," 44 and note 86. The only edns of *Flores* available were Abp Parker's texts (1567 and 1570, the former reliable, the latter less so [*Flores,* i, xliii]); it is unclear which of them Strickland used.
89. Strickland, *Lives,* i, 439.
90. E.g., Howitt, *Biographical Sketches* (1866). The anonymous *Crown Jewels of England* (London, 1897), is inarguably a low point.
91. Cannadine, "Context, Performance and Meaning of Ritual," 101–64 (esp. 131–32); on interest in the abbey, the classic work is Stanley, *Westminster Abbey*. See also N. Smith, "Conservation of the Geddington Cross," 94; G. Scott, *The National Memorial,* 16, 35–36. Credit for suggesting the crosses to Scott as a model for the Albert Memorial was cl. by Abel, *Memorials of Queen Eleanor,* unpaginated preface (Mr. John Shrive drew this work to my attention and kindly allowed me to consult his copy); but if Scott had used them for the Martyrs' Memorial in 1841, it is unlikely he needed much urging to use them again two decades later. Reproduction of the Lincoln tomb is noted above. Evoking medieval royalty by comparing individuals to their nineteenth-century counterparts was common (e.g., M. A. E. Green, *Princesses,* ii, 413, likens Eleanor of Provence as queen-dowager to William IV's widow.)
92. Only in later edns, implying that Strickland was not initially aware of the ballad; *Queens* (1864 edn), ii, 308: "The common people have not dealt so justly by her; the name of this virtuous woman and excellent queen is only known by them to be slandered by means of a popular ballad, called 'The Fall of Queen Eleanora. . . .'"
93. Child, *English and Scottish Popular Ballads,* vi, 257; *DNB,* s.v. "Eleanor of Castile (d. 1290) queen of Edward I"; Patmore, *Seven Edwards,* 24; Costain, *Three Edwards,* 17.
94. D. Parsons, ed., *Eleanor of Castile,* is the proceedings of a commemorative conference sponsored by the University of Leicester in June 1990. Dr. Janet Nelson and Mrs. Jean Powrie kindly supplied information about memorial services held at Westminster and Lincoln, and observances elsewhere.
95. W. C. Jordan, *Louis IX,* 5–6.
96. Parsons, "Queen's Intercession"; Trounce, ed., *Athelston,* 76–78.
97. Johnstone, *Edward of Carnarvon,* 23. The contrast between the two Eleanors is also emphasized by A. Crawford, *Letters of the Queens of England,* 54–75.
98. J. C. Parsons, "Mothers, Daughters," 63–78, and idem, "Of Queens, Courts and Books."

Bibliography

PUBLISHED SOURCES

Note: Full citations for abbreviations of chronicles and other sources appearing here can be found in Title Abbreviations *(see pp. xvi–xix).*

d'Achéry, L., ed. *Spicilegium sive Collectio Veterum Aliquot Scriptorum,* 3 vols. (Paris, 1723).

Adams N., and Donohue, C., Jr., eds. *Select Cases from the Ecclesiastical Courts of the Province of Canterbury,* c. 1200–1301. Selden Society, 95 (London, 1981).

Agobard of Lyons. *S. Agobardi Episcopi Lugdunensis Liber apologeticus pro filiis Ludovici Pii adversus Patrem. PL* 104, cols 307–320.

Alcuin of York. *Alcuini Epistolae,* ed. E. Dümmler. *MGH* Epistolae, iv, 1–481 (Berlin, 1895).

anonymous, ed. "Testamento del Rey Don Alonso [sic] X otorgado en Sevilla à 8 de Noviembre de 1283." *Memorial Histórico Español,* 2 (1851), 110–22.

Aungier, G., ed. *The French Chronicle of London.* Camden Society (1844).

Baker, R. *A Chronicle of the Kings of England from the Time of the Romans Government unto the Death of King Iames. . . . Where vnto is now added ye reigne of King Charles ye I. And the first Thirteen years of the Reign of King Charles the II* (London, 1674).

Barnes, P. M. "The Anstey Case," in P. M. Barnes and C. F. Slade, eds., *A Medieval Miscellany for Doris Mary Stenton.* PRS, N.S. 36 (1962), 1–23.

Bates, E. H., ed. *Two Cartularies of the Benedictine Abbeys of Muchelney and Athelney in the County of Somerset.* Somerset Record Society, 14 (1899).

Beardwood, A., ed. *Records of the Trial of Walter Langeton, Bishop of Coventry and Lichfield 1307–1312.* Camden Society, 4th ser. 6 (1969).

Bel, R., ed. *Rerum Hispaniarum Scriptores,* 2 vols. (Frankfurt, 1579).

Berger, E., ed. *Registres d'Innocent IV,* 4 vols. (Paris, 1884–1920).

Bernardus Guidonis. *De fundatione et prioribus conventuum provinciarum Tolosanae et Provinciae ordinis Praedicatorum,* ed. P. A. Amargier (Rome, 1961).

Blackley, F. D., and Hermansen, G., eds. *The Household Book of Queen Isabella of England for the Fifth Regnal Year of Edward II* (Edmonton, 1971).

Blake, E. O., ed. *The Cartulary of the Priory of St. Denys near Southampton,* 2 vols. (Southampton, 1981).

Bonazzi, G., ed. *Chron. Parmense,* in L. A. Muratori, *Rerum Italicarum Scriptores* (new ser., Bologna 1900ff) 9.ix (1902), 3–259.

Bouquet, M. *Recueil des Historiens des Gaules et de la France,* 24 vols. (Paris, 1869–1904).

Brie, F. W. D., ed. *The Brut, or the Chronicles of England,* 2 vols. Early English Text Society, O.S. 131, 136 (London, 1906–1908); facsimile of the Westminster, 1480 ed. (Amsterdam, 1973).

Brown, W., ed. *The Register of Walter Giffard, Lord Archbishop of York 1266–1279.* Surtees Society, 109 (Durham, 1904).

———, ed. *The Register of John le Romeyn, lord Archbishop of York 1279–1285,* 2 vols. Surtees Society, 124 (Durham, 1916–17).

Brownbill, J., ed. *The Ledger-Book of Vale Royal Abbey.* Lancashire and Cheshire Record Society, 68 (1914).

Brunel, C., ed. *Recueil des actes des comtes de Pontieu (1026–1279)* (Paris, 1930).

Bund, J. W. W., ed. *The Register of Bishop Godfrey Giffard, 1268–1302.* Worcester Historical Society (1898).

———, ed. *The Register of Bishop William Gainsborough, 1303 to 1307.* Worcester Historical Society (1907).

Calendar of Memoranda Rolls (Exchequer), Michaelmas 1326–27 (PRO, London, 1969).
Calendarium Genealogicum, 2 vols. (PRO, London, 1865).
Camden, W. *Britannia, sive Florentissimorum Regnorum Agnliae, Scotiae, Hiberniae, et Insularum adjacentium ex intimâ antiquitate Chorographica Descriptio* (London, 1586); English trans. and ed. by E. Gibson (London, 1695).
———. *Anglica, Normannica, Hibernica a Veteribus Scripta* (Frankfurt, 1630).
———. *Remains of a Greater Work Concerning Britain,* ed. R. D. Dunn (Toronto, 1984).
Chaplais, P., ed. *Treaty Rolls Preserved in the Public Record Office, I. 1234–1325* (PRO, London, 1955).
———, ed. "Some Private Letters of Edward I." *EHR* 77 (1962), 79–86.
———, ed. *Diplomatic Documents I. 1101–1272* (PRO, London, 1964).
Cheney, C. R., and M. G. Cheney, eds. *The Letters of Pope Innocent III (1198–1216) concerning England and Wales* (Oxford, 1967).
Churchill, I. J., et al., eds. *Calendar of Kent Feet of Fines to the end of Henry III's Reign.* Kent Archeological Society Records Branch, 15 (1956).
Cole, H., ed. *Documents Illustrative of English History in the Thirteenth and Fourteenth Centuries* (London, 1844).
Craster, H., and M. E. Thornton, eds. *The Chronicle of St. Mary's Abbey, York.* Surtees Society (1934).
Cuttino, G. P., ed. *Gascon Register A (Series of 1318–1319),* 3 vols. (Oxford, 1975–76)
Daumet, G. "Les testaments d'Alphonse X le Savant." *Bibliothèque de l'Ecôle des Chartes,* 67 (1906), 70–99.
Davies, J. C., ed. *Cartae Antiquae Rolls, Rolls 11–20.* PRS, N.S. 33 (1960).
Davis, F., ed. *Rotuli Ricardi Gravesend Diocesis Lincolniensis.* CYS 31 (Oxford, 1925).
Deedes, C., ed. *Registrum Johannis de Pontissara Episcopi Wintoniensis (1282–1304),* 2 vols. CYS 19 (Oxford, 1915–24).
Delisle, L., and E. Berger, eds. *Recueil des actes de Henry II,* roi d'Angleterre et duc de Normandie, 4 vols. (Paris, 1909–27).
Dewindt, A. R., and E. B. Dewindt, E. B., eds. *Royal Justice and the Medieval English countryside,* 2 vols. (Toronto, 1981).
Douie, D. D., ed. *The Register of John Pecham, Archbishop of Canterbury,* 2 vols. CYS, 64–65 (Torquay, 1968).
Douie, D. D., and H. Farmer, eds. *Magna Vita Sancti Hugonis. The Life of S. Hugh of Lincoln,* 2 vols. (London, 1961).
Edwards, J. G., ed. *Calendar of Ancient Correspondence concerning Wales* (Board of Celtic Studies, 1935).
———, ed. *Littere Wallie* (Cardiff, 1940).
L'Estoire de Eracles Empereur et la Conqueste de la terre d'Outremer. Acàdémie des inscriptions et belles-lettres, *Recueil des historiens des croisades,* Occidentaux iii (Paris, 1849).
Fabyan, Robert. *The New Chronicles of England and France* (London, 1516; ed. H. Ellis, London, 1811).
Fauroux, M., ed. *Recueil des actes des ducs de Normandie de 911 à 1066* (Caen, 1961).
Feudal Aids, 6 vols. (PRO, London, 1899–1921).
Fiadoni, Bartolomeo (Ptolemaeus Luccensis). *Historia Ecclesiastica,* ed. L. A. Muratori in *Rerum Italicarum Scriptores,* xi (1727).
———. *Ptolomaei Luccensis Brevis Annales,* ed. B. Schmiedler. *MGH SS,* N.S. 8 (1955).
Florez, H. *España sagrada,* 51 vols. (Madrid, 1747–1879).
Forster, J. trans. *The Chronicle of James I, King of Aragon, surnamed the Conqueror,* 2 vols. (London, 1883).
Fowler, G. H., ed. *The Cartulary of the Cistercian Abbey of Old Wardon, Bedfordshire* (Manchester, 1931).
Frati, L., and A. Sorbelli, eds. *Memoriale historicum Matthaei de Griffonibus,* in L. A. Muratori, *Rerum Italicarum Scriptores* (new ser., Bologna 1900ff), 18.ii (1902), pp. 3–111.

Fry, E. A., ed. *Abstracts of Wiltshire Inquisitiones Post Mortem A.D. 1242–1326*. Index Library/British Record Society, 37 (London, 1908; rpt Liechtenstein, 1968).

Fry, E. A., and G. S. Fry, eds. *Dorset Feet of Fines, Richard I-Richard III*, 2 vols. Dorset Records, 5, 10 (Aberdeen, 1896-1910).

Fryde, E. B., ed. *A Book of Prests of the King's Wardrobe for 1294–95* (Oxford, 1962).

———, ed. *List of Welsh Entries in the Memoranda Rolls, 1282–1343* (Cardiff, 1974).

Gapes, W. W., ed. *Registrum Ricardi de Swinfield Episcopi Herefordensis*. CYS 6 (London, 1909).

Gibbs, M., ed. *Early Charters of the Cathedral Church of St. Paul's, London*. Camden Society, 3rd. ser. 58 (1959).

Gibson, S., ed. *Statuta Antiqua Universitatis Oxoniensis* (Oxford, 1931).

Giraldus Cambrensis. *De Expugnatione Hibernica*, ed. A. B. Scott and F. X. Martin (Dublin, 1978).

Grafton, R. *Grafton's Chronicle; or, History of England*, 2 vols. (London, 1809).

Graham, R., ed. *Registrum Roberti Winchelsey Cantuariensis Archiepiscopi*, 2 vols. CYS 51 (Oxford, 1952–56).

Green, E., ed. *Pedes finium for the County of Somerset, Richard I to Edward I (1196–1307)*. Somerset Record Society, 7 (1892).

Green, M. A. E., ed. *Letters of Royal and Illustrious Ladies of Great Britain*, 3 vols. (London, 1846).

Greene, R. *The Honorable Historie of frier Bacon, and frier Bongay*, ed. A. B. Grosart in *The Life and Complete Works in Prose and Verse of Robert Greene, M.A.*, 15 vols. (New York, 1881–86, reissued 1964), xiii, 1–109.

Greenstreet, J. "Kent Fines, Edward II." *Archaeologia Cantiana* 13 (1880), 289–320.

Griffiths, R. G., ed. *Registrum Thome de Cantilupo Episcopi Herefordensis*. CYS 2 (1907).

Hackett, M. B., ed. *The Original Statutes of Cambridge University* (Cambridge, 1970).

Hall, H., ed. *The Red Book of the Exchequer*, 3 vols. RS 99 (London, 1897).

Halliwell, J. O., ed. *The Chronicle of William de Rishanger, of the Barons' Wars. The Miracles of Simon de Montfort*. Camden Society, 15 (1840).

Hardyng, John. *The Chronicle from the Firste Begynnyng of Englande. 2 Parts* (facsimile of the London 1543 ed., Amsterdam, 1976).

Harvey, B. F., ed. *Documents illustrating the rule of of Walter de Wenlok, Abbot of Westminster*. Camden Society, 4th ser. 2 (1965).

Hassall, W. O., ed. *Cartulary of St. Mary Clerkenwell*. Camden Society, 3rd ser. 71 (1949).

Haydon, F. S., ed. *Eulogium, sive temporis chronicon ab Orbe Condito usque ad Annum Domini, 1366*, 3 vols. RS 9 (London, 1858–63).

Hill, R. M. T., ed. *The Rolls and Register of Bishop Oliver Sutton*, 8 vols. to date. Lincoln Record Society (1948f).

Hincmar of Reims. *De Ordine Palatii*, ed. T. Gross and R. Schieffer, MGH Fontes 3 (Hannover, 1980).

Hockey, S. F., ed. *The Account Book of Beaulieu Abbey*. Camden Society, 4th ser. 16 (1975).

Holder-Egger, O., ed. *Chronica Monasterii Sancti Bertini auctore Johanne Longo*. MGH SS 25 (Hannover, 1880).

———, ed. *Cronica Salimbene de'Adam*. MGH SS 32 (Berlin, 1905–13).

Holinshed, R. *Chronicles of England, Scotland and Ireland* (London, 1577; reissued in 6 vols, London, 1807–8, rpt New York, 1965).

Huici Miranda, A., and M. S. Cabanes Pecourt, eds. *Documentos de Jaime I de Aragon*, 4 vols. (Valencia, 1976–82).

Hunter, J., ed. *Rotuli selecti ad res Anglicas et Hibernicas Spectantes* (London, 1834).

Imperiale, C., ed. *Otberti Stanconi . . . Annales Ianuensis Ann. MCCLXX–MCCLXXIX*, in *Fonti per la storia d'Italia*, 102 vols. (Rome, Istituto storico Italiano per il medio evo, 1887–1933), xiv, 129–87.

Johnson, C., ed. *Dialogus de Scaccario* (London, 1950).

Johnstone, H., ed. "The Wardrobe and Household of Henry, Son of Edward I." *BJRL* 7 (1923), 384–420.

————, ed. *Letters of Edward Prince of Wales, 1304–1305.* Roxburghe Club (Cambridge, 1931).

Joinville, J. de. *The History of St. Louis by Jean Sire de Joinville,* trans. R. Hague (London, 1955).

Kaye, J. M., ed. *The Cartulary of God's House, Southampton,* 2 vols. (Southampton, 1976).

Kemp, B. R., ed. *Reading Abbey Cartularies,* 2 vols. Camden Society, 4th ser. 31, 33 (1986–88).

Lambert of Ardres. *Lamberti Ardensis Historia Comitum Ghisnensium,* ed. J. Heller. *MGH SS* xxiv (Hannover, 1879), 550–642

Landon, L., ed. *Cartae Antiquae Rolls, Rolls 1–10.* PRS, N.S. 17 (1939).

Langtoft, Piers. *The Chronicle of Pierre de Langtoft, in French verse from the earliest period to the death of Edward I,* ed. T. Wright, 2 vols. RS 47 (London, 1866–68).

Legg, J., ed. *Three Coronation Orders.* Bradshaw Society, 13 (London, 1900).

Legg, L. G. W., ed. *English Coronation Records* (Westminster, 1901).

Lehmann-Brockhaus, O., ed. *Lateinische Schriftquellen zur Kunst in England, Schottland und Wales,* 5 vols. (Munich 1955–60).

Leland, J. *The Itinerary of John Leland in or about the years 1535–1543,* ed. L. T. Smith, 5 vols. (London, 1907–10).

Lhomel, G. de, ed. *Cartulaire de la ville de Montreuil-sur-Mer* (Montreuil, 1904).

Luard, H., ed. *Roberti Grosseteste episcopi quondam Lincolniensis Epistolae.* RS 25 (London, 1861).

Lysons, S., ed. "Copy of a Roll of the Expenses of King Edward the First at Rhuddlan Castle in the Tenth and Eleventh Years of his Reign," *Archaeologia,* 16 [1812], 32–79.

————, ed. "Copy of a Roll of Purchases made for the Tournament of Windsor Park in the sixth year of King Edward the First." *Archaeologia,* 17 (1814), 297–310.

Maitland, F. W., ed. *Memoranda de Parliamento, 1305.* RS 98 (London, 1893).

Malden, A. R. "The Will of Nicholas Longespee, Bishop of Salisbury." *EHR,* 15 (1900), 523–28.

Mannyng, Robert (of Brunne). *Peter Langtoft's Chronicle (as illustrated and improv'd by Robert of Brunne) from the Death of Cadwalder to the end of K. Edward the First's Reign,* ed. T. Hearne, 2 vols. (Oxford, 1725).

de Manuel Rodríguez, M., ed. *Memorias para la Vida del Santo Rey Don Fernando III* (Madrid, 1800; rpt Barcelona, 1974).

Martin, C. T., ed. *Registrum Epistolarum Fratris Johannis Peckham Archiepiscopi Cantuariensis,* 3 vols. RS 77 (London, 1882–85).

Meekings, C. A. F., ed. *Crown Pleas of the Wiltshire Eyre, 1249.* Wiltshire Archaeological and Natural History Society Records Branch, 16 (Devizes, 1961).

Mellows, W. T., ed. *Henry of Pytchley's Book of Fees.* Northamptonshire Record Society, 2 (1927).

Menendez Pidal, R., ed. *Primera Crónica General de España,* 2nd ed., 2 vols. (Madrid, 1955).

Michelant, J., ed. *Der Roman von Escanor von Gerard von Amiens* (Tübingen, 1886).

Muratori, L. A., ed. *Rerum Italicarum Scriptores,* 25 vols. in 28 folios (Milan, 1723–51).

————, ed. *Annali d'Italia,* 12 vols. (Milan, 1744–49)

Musset, L., ed. *Les actes de Guillaume le Conquérant et de la reine Mathilde pour les abbayes Caennaises* (Caen, 1967).

Myers, A. R. "The Household of Queen Margaret of Anjou, 1452–3," *BJRL,* 40 (1957–58), 1–75.

————. "The Jewels of Queen Margaret of Anjou," *BJRL,* 42 (1959), 113–31.

————. "The Household of Queen Elizabeth Woodville, 1466–7," *BJRL,* 50 (1967), 207–35, and 51 (1968), 443–81.

Nichols, J. A., ed. "The History and Cartulary of the Cistercian Nuns of Marham Abbey" (Ph.D. Diss., Kent State University, 1974).

Oschinsky, D., ed. *Walter of Henley and other Treatises on Estate Management and Accounting* (Oxford, 1971).

Parsons, J. C., ed. "The Beginnings of English Administration in Ponthieu." *Mediaeval Studies,* 50 (1988), 371–403.

Peele, G. *The Famous Chronicle of king Edward the first, sirnamed Edward Longshankes, with his returne from the holy land,* ed. F. S. Hook in C. T. Prouty, general ed., *The Life and Works of George Peele,* 3 vols. (New Haven, 1952–70), ii, 69–170.

———. *The Battell of Alcazar, fought in Barbarie, betweene Sebastian king of Portugall, and Abdelmelec king of Marocco,* ed. J. Yoklavich in C. T. Prouty, general ed., *The Life and Works of George Peele,* 3 vols. (New Haven, 1952–70), ii, 293–347.

Pertz, G. H., ed. *Chronicon Colmariense, MGH SS* 17 (Hannover, 1861).

Phillimore, W. P., ed. *Coram Rege Roll for Trinity term 25 Edward I, A.D. 1297* (London, 1897).

Prarond, E., ed. *Le Cartulaire du comté de Ponthieu* (Abbeville, 1897).

Pugh, R. B., ed. *Abstracts of Feet of Fines relating to Wiltshire for the Reigns of Edward I and Edward II.* Wiltshire Archeological and Natural History Society, Records Branch (1939).

Raine, J., ed. *Letters from Northern Registers.* RS 61 (London, 1873).

Real Academia de la Historia, ed. *Las Siete Partidas,* 3 vols. (Madrid, 1807).

Rees, W. *Calendar of Ancient Petitions relating to Wales* (Cardiff, 1975).

Richardson, H. G., and G. O. Sayles, eds. "The Provisions of Oxford: a forgotten document and some comments." *BJRL* 17 [1933] 291–321.

———, eds. *Fleta,* 3 vols. Selden Society, 72, 89, 99 (London, 1955–84).

Rigg, J. M., ed. *Select Pleas, Starrs and other Records from the Rolls of the Exchequer of the Jews.* Selden Society, 15 (1902).

Riley, H. T., ed. *Opus chronicorum.* RS 28.iii (London, 1865).

———, ed. *Gesta Abbatum Sancti Albani,* 3 vols. RS 28.iv (London, 1867–69)

Rishanger, W. *Willelmi Rishanger Chronica et Annales,* ed. H. T. Riley. RS 28.ii (London, 1865).

Round, J. H., ed. *The Great Roll of the Pipe for the Thirty-Third Year of the Reign of King Henry the Second. A.D. 1186–1187.* PRS 37 (London, 1915).

Rutherford, A., ed. "The Anglo-Norman Chronicle of Nicholas Trivet" (Ph.D. Diss., University of London, 1932).

Rye, W., ed. *A Calendar of the Feet of Fines for Suffolk* (Ipswich, 1900).

Salter, E., ed. *The Feet of Fines for Oxfordshire, 1195–1291.* Oxfordshire Record Society (1930).

Sayles, G. O., ed. *Select Cases in the Court of King's Bench under Edward I,* i. Selden Society, 55 (1936).

———, ed. *Select Cases in the Court of King's Bench under Edward I,* ii. Selden Society, 57 (1938).

———, ed. *Select Cases in the Court of King's Bench under Edward I,* iii. Selden Society, 58 (1939).

Shadwell, C. L., and H. E. Salter, eds. *Oriel College Records* (Oxford, 1926).

Sharpe, R. S., ed. *Calendar of Wills Proved and Enrolled in the Court of Husting, London, A.D. 1258–A.D. 1688, I: 1258–1358* (London, 1889).

———, ed. *Calendar of Letter-Books of the City of London at the Guildhall: Letter-book A (ca 1275–1298)* (London, 1899).

Shirley, W. W., ed. *Royal and other Historical Letters illustrative of the Reign of Henry III,* 2 vols. RS 27 (London, 1862–66).

Stapleton, T., ed. *Liber de Antiquis Legibus.* Camden Society, 34 (1846).

Stenton, D. M., ed. *The Great Roll of the Pipe for the Ninth Year of the Reign of King Richard the First. Michaelmas 1197 (Pipe Roll 43).* PRS, N.S. 8 (London, 1931).

———, ed. *The Great Roll of the Pipe for the Tenth Year of the Reign of King Richard the First. Michaelmas 1198 (Pipe Roll 44).* PRS, N.S. 9 (London, 1932).

———, ed. *The Great Roll of the Pipe for the Fourth Year of the Reign of King John.* PRS, N.S. 15 (London, 1937).

———, ed. *The Memoranda Roll for the Michaelmas Term of the First Year of King John (1199–1200).* PRS, N.S. 21 (London, 1943).

Stewart-Brown, R., ed. *Calendar of County Court, City Court and Eyre Rolls of Chester 1259–1297.* Chetham Society, N.S. 84 (Manchester, 1925).

Stocks, J. E., and W. B. Braggs, eds. *Market Harborough Records to A.D. 1530* (London, 1890).

Stokes, E., ed. *Warkwickshire Feet of Fines, I* (London, 1932).
Stones, E. L. G., and G. G. Simpson, eds. *Edward I and the Throne of Scotland, 1290–1296,* 2 vols. (Oxford, 1978).
Stow, J. *Stow's Survey of London,* intr. by H. B. Wheatley (London, 1956).
le Strange, H., ed. *Le Strange Records* (London, 1916).
Stubbs, W., ed. *Gesta Regis Henrici Secundi Benedicti Abbatis,* 2 vols. RS 49 (London, 1867).
———, ed. *Chronicles of the Reigns of Edward I and Edward II,* 2 vols. RS 76 (London, 1882–83).
———, ed. *Select Charters and other illustrations of English constitutional history, from the earliest times to the reign of Edward the First.* 9th ed., rev. H. W. C. Davis (Oxford, 1913).
Symonds, T., ed. and trans. *Regularis Concordia Anglicae Nationis Monachorum Sanctimonialiumque* (London 1953).
Tait, J., ed. *The Chartulary or Register of St. Werburg, Chester.* Chetham Society, N.S. 79, 82 (Manchester, 1920–23).
Tanqueray, F. J. "Lettres du Roi Edward I à Robert de Bavent, King's Yeoman sur des questions de venerie." *BJRL* 23 (1939), 487–503.
Teulet, J. B., ed. *Layettes du Trésor des Chartes,* 6 vols. (Paris, 1863–1909).
Timson, R. T., ed. *The Cartulary of Blyth Priory* (London, 1973).
Torrace, F. ed. *Chronicon Petri Cantinelli,* in L. A. Muratori, *Rerum Italicarum Scriptores* (new ser., Bologna 1900ff), 28.ii (1902).
Tout, T. F., and H. Johnstone, eds. *State Trials of the Reign of Edward I.* Camden Society, 3rd ser. 9 (1906).
Treharne, R., and I. J. Sanders, eds. *Documents of the Baronial Platform of Reform and Rebellion, 1258–1267* (Oxford, 1973).
Trevet, Nicholas. *Nicholai Trevet Annales,* ed. T. Hog (London, 1845).
Trounce, A. McI., ed. *Athelston. A Middle English Romance.* Early English Text Society, O.S. 224 (Oxford, 1951)
Turner, T. "The Will of Humphrey de Bohun, Earl of Hereford and Essex, with extracts from the inventory of his effects, 1319–1322." *Archaeological Journal,* 2 (1846), 339–49.
Ullmann, W., ed. *Liber Regie Capelle. A Manuscript in the Biblioteca Publica, Evora.* Henry Bradshaw Society, 92 (London, 1961).
Vergil, Polydore. *Urbinitatis Anglicae Historiae* (Basel 155, rpt Menston, 1972).
Vincent of Beauvais, *De Eruditione Filiorum Nobilium,* ed. A. Steiner (Cambridge, MA, 1938).
Ximenez de Rada, R. *De Rebus Hispaniae Libri IX,* ed. F. Lorenzano in *Roderici Toletani Opera* (Madrid, 1793, rpt Valencia, 1970).
Wadding, L. *Annales Minorum seu trium ordinum a s. Francisco institutorum, auctore A. R. P. Luca Waddingo Hiberno,* 28 vols. (Quaracchi, 1931–47).
Walsingham, T. *Thomae Walsingham Historia Anglicana,* ed. H. T. Riley, 2 vols. RS 28.i (London, 1863–64).
White, F. P., et al., eds. *Chertsey Abbey Cartularies,* 5 vols. Surrey Record Society (London, 1915–32).
Whitelock, D., ed. *English Historical Documents c. 500–1042,* 2nd ed. (London, 1979).
Wilson, R. A., ed. *The Register of Walter Reynolds, Bishop of Worcester 1308–1313.* Dugdale Society, 9 (London, 1928).
Wood, M. A. E., ed. and trans. *Letters of Royal and Illustrious Ladies of Great Britain,* 3 vols. (London, 1846).
Woodbine, G. E., ed., S. E. Thorne, rev. and trans. *Bracton De Legibus et Consuetudinibus Angliae,* 4 vols. (Cambridge, MA, 1968–77).
Worcestre, W. *Itineraries,* ed. J. H. Harvey (Oxford, 1969).
Wright, T., ed. *Political Songs of England.* Camden Society (1839).
Wrottesley, G. "Calendar of the Final Concords or Penes [sic] Finium, Staffordshire. Edward I and Edward II, 1272–1307." *Collections for a History of Staffordhire.* William Salt Archaeological Society, N.S. 14 (London, 1911), 28–111.

AUTHORITIES

Note: anthologies and collections of articles are given separate citations only when more than one essay from the book is cited; otherwise full information for the anthology is given under the sole article cited.

Abel, J. *Memorials of Queen Eleanor, Illustrated by Photography; with a Short Account of their History and Present Condition* (London, 1864).

Adair, P. "Countess Clemence: Her Power and its Foundation," in T. Vann, ed., *Queens, Regents and Potentates,* 63–72.

Adler, M. "History of the 'Domus conversorum'." *TJHSE,* 4 (1899–1901), 16–75.

Alexander, J. J. G., and P. Binski, eds. *Age of Chivalry. Art in Plantagenet England 1200–1400* (London, 1987).

Alexander, J. W. "A Historiographical Survey: Norman and Plantagenet Kings since World War II." *Journal of British Studies,* 24 (1985), 94–109.

Allen, A. "Yorkist Propaganda: Pedigree, Prophecy and the 'British History' in the Reign of Edward IV," in C. Ross, ed., *Patronage, Pedigree and Power,* 171–92.

Altschul, M. *A Baronial Family in Medieval England. The Clares, 1217–1314* (Baltimore, 1965).

Anonymous. *The Crown Jewels of England* ([London?], 1897).

Appleby, J. T. *The Troubled Reign of King Stephen* (London, 1969).

Arkell, R. L. *Caroline of Ansbach* (Oxford, 1939).

Armstrong, C. A. J. "The Piety of Cicely, Duchess of York: A Study in Late Mediaeval Culture," in idem, *England, France and Burgundy in the Fifteenth Century* (Ronceverte, 1983), 135–56.

Assarsson-Rizzi, K. *Friar Bacon and Friar Bungay. A Structural and Thematic Analysis of Robert Greene's Play* (Lund, 1972).

Ashton, J. *The Fleet* (London, 1889).

Aston, T. H., and Faith, R. "University and College Endowments to ca. 1348," in J. Catto, ed., *The History of the University of Oxford, I,* 265–310.

Axton, M. *The Queen's Two Bodies. Drama and the Elizabethan Succession* (London, 1977).

Baer, A. *A History of the Jews in Spain,* 2 vols. Trans. L. Schoffman. (Philadelphia 1961–66).

Bagby, A. I., Jr. "The Jew in the *Cántigas* of Alfonso X, el Sabio." *Speculum,* 46 (1971), 670–88.

Bak, J. "The Roles and Functions of Queens in Arpádian and Angevin Hungary," in J. C. Parsons, ed., *Medieval Queenship,* pp. 13–24.

Baker, D., ed. *Medieval Women. Dedicated and Presented to Professor Rosalind M. T. Hill on the Occasion of her Seventieth Birthday.* Studies in Church History subsidia, I (Oxford, 1978).

Baldwin, J. *The Government of Philip Augustus: Foundations of French Royal Power in the Middle Ages* (Berkeley, CA, 1986).

Ballesteros Beretta, A. *Sevilla en el siglo XIII* (Madrid, 1913).

———. *Alfonso X el sabio* (Barcelona, 1963).

Banks, T. *The Dormant and Extinct Baronage of England,* 4 vols. and supplement (London, 1807–26).

Barker, J. R. V. *The Tournament in England, 1100–1400* (Woodbridge, 1986).

Barlow, F. *Edward the Confessor* (London, 1970).

———. "The King's Evil." *EHR,* 95 (1980), 3–27.

———. *Thomas Becket* (Berkeley CA, 1986).

Barron, C. M., and C. Harper-Bill, eds. *The Church in Pre-Reformation Society: Essays in Honour of C. F. R. Du Boulay* (Woodbridge, 1985).

Baylen, J. O. "John Maunsel and the Castilian Treaty of 1254: A Study of the Clerical Diplomat." *Traditio,* 17 (1961), 482–91.

Beaune, C. "Mourir noblement à la fin du moyen âge," in *La mort au moyen âge* (Colloque des médiévistes français, Strasbourg, 1977), 125–43.

Bedos-Rezak, B. "Women, Seals and Power in Medieval France, 1150–1350," in M. Erler and M. Kowaleski, eds., *Women and Power in the Middle Ages*, 61–82.

Beebe, B. "The English Baronage and the Crusade of 1270." *BIHR*, 48 (1975), 127–47.

Bell, S. G. "Medieval Women Book Owners: Arbiters of Lay Piety and Ambassadors of Culture," in M. Erler and M. Kowaleski, eds., *Women and Power in the Middle Ages*, 149–87.

Bémont, C. *Simon de Montfort, Earl of Leicester 1208–1265.* Trans. E. F. Jacob (Oxford, 1930).

Binski, P. "Reflections on *La estoire de Seint Aedward le rei*: Hagiography and Kingship in Thirteenth-century England." *JMH*, 16 (1990), 333–50.

———. "The Cosmati at Westminster and the English Court Style," *Art Bulletin*, 72 (1990), 5–34.

Blaauw, W. H. *The Barons' Wars*, 2nd ed. (London, 1871).

Blackley, F. D. "Isabella of France, Queen of England (1308–1358) and the Late Medieval Cult of the Dead." *CJH*, 15 (1980), 23–47.

Blackstone, W. *Commentaries on the Laws of England*, 4 vols. (London, 1765–1769; facsimile ed., Chicago, 1979).

Blain, V., I. Grundy, and P. Clements, eds. *The Feminist Companion to Literature in English. Women Writers from the Middle Ages to the Present* (New Haven, 1990).

Blore, E. *The Monumental Remains of Noble and Eminent Persons: Comprising the Sepulchral Antiquities of Great Britain. . . .* (London, 1826).

Boase, T. S. R. "Fontevraut and the Plantagenets." *Journal of the British Archaeological Association*, 3rd ser. 34 (1971), 1–10.

Bond, E. A. "Notices of the Last Days of Isabella, Queen of Edward the Second, Drawn from an Account of the Expenses of her Household." *Archaeologia*, 35 (1854), 462–63.

Bony, J. *The English Decorated Style. Gothic Architecture Transformed, 1250–1350* (Oxford, 1979).

Brand, P. "Edward I and the Justices: The 'State Trials' of 1289–93," in P. Coss and S. Lloyd, eds., *Thirteenth Century England I*, 31–40.

———. "The Early History of the Legal Profession of the Lordship of Ireland, 1250–1350," in D. Hogan and W. N. Osborough, eds., *Brehons, Serjeants and Attorneys* (Dublin, 1990), 15–50.

Branner, R. "The Montjoies of St. Louis," in E. Fraser, ed., *Essays in the History of Architecture Presented to Rudolph Wittkower* (London, 1967), 13–16.

Brault, G. "Arthurian Heraldry and the Date of *Escanor*." *Bulletin bibliographique de la société internationale arthurienne*, 11 (1959), 81–88.

Braunmuller, A. R. *George Peele* (Boston, 1983).

Brett, M. *The English Church Under Henry I* (Oxford, 1975).

Brieger, P. *English Art 1216–1307*, Oxford History of English Art, 4 (Oxford, 1957).

Brieger, P., and Verdier, P. *Art and the Courts: France and England from 1259 to 1328*, 2 vols. (Ottawa, 1972).

Brown, E. A. R. "Eleanor of Aquitaine: Parent, Queen and Duchess," in W. W. Kibler, ed., *Eleanor of Aquitaine*, 9–34.

———. "Royal Salvation and Needs of State in Early Fourteenth- Century France," originally in W. C. Jordan, B. McNab, and T. F. Ruiz, eds., *Order and Innovation in the Middle Ages*, pp. 365–83, 541–61; rev. in E. A. R. Brown, *The Monarchy of Capetian France and Royal Ceremonial* (Aldershot, 1991), no. IV.

———. "Death and the Human Body in the Later Middle Ages: The Legislation of Boniface VIII on the Division of the Corpse." *Viator*, 12 (1981), 221–70.

———. "Royal Marriage, Royal Property, and the Patrimony of the Crown: Inalienability and the Prerogative in Fourteenth—Century France." California Institute of Technology Humanities and Social Sciences Working Paper, 70 (Pasadena, 1982).

———. "Burying and Unburying the Kings of France," in C. R. Trexler, ed., *Persons in Groups. Social Behavior as Identity Formation in Medieval and Renaissance Europe* (Binghampton, 1985), pp. 241–66.

————. "The Prince is Father of the King: The Character and Childhood of Philip the Fair of France." *Mediaeval Studies*, 49 (1987), 282–384.

————. "*Persona et Gesta*, 3. The Case of Philip the Fair." *Viator*, 19 (1988), 219–46.

————. "The Political Repercussions of Family Ties in the Early Fourteenth Century: The Marriage of Edward II of England and Isabelle of France." *Speculum* 63 (1988), 573–95.

————. "Authority, the Family and the Dead in Late Medieval France." *French Historical Studies* 16 (1990), 803–32.

Brown, R. A. *The Origins of English Feudalism* (London, 1973).

Bruce, J. C. *The Evolution of Arthurian Romance from the Beginnings down to the Year 1300*, 2nd ed., 2 vols. (Baltimore-Göttingen, 1928).

Brückmann, J. J. "English Coronations, 1216–1308: the Edition of the Coronation Ordines" (Ph.D. Diss., University of Toronto, 1964).

Brühl, C. "Les auto-couronnements d'empereurs et de rois (XIIIe–XIXe siècles). Remarques sur la fonction sacramentelle de la royauté au moyen âge et à l'époque moderne," in idem, *Aus Mittelalter und Diplomatik*. Gesammelte Aufsätze, 2 vols. (Munich, 1989), i, 444–60

Burns, R. I., SJ, ed. *The Worlds of Alfonso the Learned and James the Conqueror. Intellect and Force in the Middle Ages* (Princeton, 1985).

Bynum, C. W. "Women's Stories, Women's Symbols: a Critique of Victor Turner's Theory of Liminality," in idem, *Fragmentation and Redemption. Essays on Gender and the Human Body in Medieval Religion* (New York, 1991), 27–51.

Cam, H. M. *The Hundred and the Hundred Rolls* (London, 1930).

————. "Cases of Novel Disseisin in the Eyre of London, 1321", in idem, *Law-Finders and Law-Makers in Medieval England. Collected Studies in Legal and Constitutional History* (New York, 1965), 95–105.

Camille, M. *The Gothic Idol. Ideology and Image Making in Medieval Art* (Cambridge, 1989).

Cannadine, D. "The Context, Performance and Meaning of Ritual: The British Monarchy and the 'Invention of Tradition,' c. 1820–1977," in E. Hobsbawm and T. Ranger, eds., *The Invention of Tradition* (Cambridge, 1983), 101–64.

Carpenter, D. A. "Was There a Crisis of the Knightly Class in the Thirteenth Century? The Oxfordshire Evidence." *EHR*, 95 (1980), 721–52.

————. "What Happened in 1258?" in J. Gillingham, and J. C. Holt, eds., *War and Government in the Middle Ages*, 106–19.

————. *The Minority of Henry III* (London, 1990).

Cartwright, F. F. *Disease and History* (New York, 1972).

Casagrande, C. "The Protected Woman," in C. Klapisch-Zuber, ed., *A History of Women in the West, II*, 70–104.

Catto, J., ed. *The History of the University of Oxford, I: the Early Oxford Schools* (Oxford, 1984).

Cerulli, E. *Il libro della scala e la questione delle fonti arabo-spagnole della Divina Commedia* (Vatican City, 1949).

Chaplais, P. *Piers Gaveston: Edward II's Adoptive Brother* (Oxford, 1994).

Cheney, C. R. *Notaries Public in England in the Thirteenth and Fourteenth Centuries* (Oxford, 1972).

Cheney, M. G. "Mr. Geoffrey de Lucy, an Early Chancellor of the University of Oxford." *EHR*, 82 (1967), 750–63.

Cherry, J. "Heraldry as Decoration in the Thirteenth Century," in W. M. Ormrod, ed., *England in the Thirteenth Century*, 123–34.

Child, F. J. *The English and Scottish Popular Ballads*, 10 vols. (Boston, 1882–98).

Childs, W. R. *Anglo-Castilian Trade in the Later Middle Ages* (Manchester, 1978).

Clanchy, M. T. "The franchise of return of writs." *TRHS*, 5th ser. 17 (1967), 59–82.

Clapham, A. W. "On the topography of the Dominican priory of London." *Archaeologia*, 63 (1911–12), 57–84.

Clay, R. M. *The Medieval Hospitals of England* (London, 1909).

Clifford, E. R. *A Knight of Great Renown* (Chicago, 1961).

Cohen, J. *The Friars and the Jews. The Evolution of Medieval Anti-Judaism* (Ithaca NY, 1982).

Cokayne, G. E. *The Complete Peerage*, 2nd ed., 12 vols. in 13 folios (London, 1910–40).

Coldstream. N. "The Commissioning and Design of the Eleanor Crosses," in D. Parsons, ed., *Eleanor of Castile 1290–1990*, 55–67.

Collier, J. F. "Women in Politics," in M. Z. Rosaldo and L. Lamphere, eds., *Woman, Culture and Society*, 89–96.

Cook, G. H. *Medieval Chantries and Chantry Chapels*. 2nd ed. (London, 1963).

Corcos, A. "Extracts from the Close Rolls, 1279–1288." *TJHSE*, 4 (1899–1901), 202–19.

Coss, P. R. "Sir Geoffrey de Langley and the Crisis of the Knightly Class in Thirteenth-Century England." *Past and Present*, 68 (1975), 3–37.

———. *Lordship, Knighthood and Locality. A Study in English Society c. 1180–c.1280* (Cambridge, 1991).

Coss, P. R., and S. D. Lloyd, eds. *Thirteenth Century England I. Proceedings of the Newcastle Upon Tyne Conference 1985* (Woodbridge, 1986).

———. *Thirteenth-Century England II. Proceedings of the Newcastle upon Tyne Conference 1987* (Woodbridge, 1988).

Costain, T. *The Magnificent Century* (Garden City, NY, 1958).

———. *The Three Edwards* (Garden City, NY, 1958).

Councer, C. R. "Heraldic Painted Glass in the Church of St. Lawrence, Mereworth." *Archaeologia Cantiana* 77 (1962), 48–62.

Cox, E. L. *The Eagles of Savoy: The House of Savoy in Thirteenth-Century Europe* (Princeton, 1974).

Cox, J. C. "Catalogue of the Muniments and Manuscript Books Pertaining to the Dean and chapter of Lichfield." *Collections for a History of Staffordshire*, vi.2 (1886), 199–221.

Crawford, A. "The King's Burden?—The Consequences of Royal Marriage in Fifteenth-century England," in R. A. Griffiths, ed., *Patronage, the Crown and the Provinces in Later Medieval England* (Gloucester, 1981), 33–56.

———. "The Piety of Late Medieval English Queens," in C. M. Barron and C. Harper-Bill, eds., *The Church in Pre-Reformation Society*, 48–57.

———. *Letters of the Queens of England, 1100–1547* (Stroud, 1994).

Crawford, J. L. L. *Catalogue of a Collection of English Ballads of the XVIIth and XVIIIth Centuries*, 2 vols. (Aberdeen, 1890).

Crook, D. "The Last Days of Eleanor of Castile: The Death of a Queen in Nottinghamshire, November 1290." *Transactions of the Thoroton Society*, 94 (1990), 17–28.

Crull, J. *Antiquities of St. Peter's, or the Abbey Church of Westminster* (London, 1711).

Cummins, J. *The Hound and the Hawk. The Art of Medieval Hunting* (New York, 1988).

Cuttino, G. P. *English Medieval Diplomacy* (Bloomington, 1985).

Daumet, G. *Mémoire sur les relations de la France et de la Castille de 1255 à 1320* (Paris, 1913).

Davidson, L. C. *Catherine of Bragança* (London, 1908).

Davies, J. C. *The Baronial Opposition to Edward II* (London, 1918).

Davis, N. Z. "Women on Top: Symbolic Sexual Inversion and Political Disorder in Early Modern Europe," in B. Babcock, ed., *The Reversible World. Symbolic Inversion in Art and Society* (Ithaca, NY, 1978), 147–90.

———. "Gender and Genre: Women as Historical Writers, 1400–1820," in P. H. Labalme, ed., *Beyond Their Sex. Learned Women of the European Past* (New York-London, 1984), 153–82.

Davis, R. H. C. *King Stephen, 1135–1154* (London, 1967).

Dean, R. J. "Nicholas Trevet, Historian," in J. J. G. Alexander and M. T. Gibson, eds., *Medieval Learning and Literature: Essays Presented to Richard William Hunt* (Oxford, 1976), 339–49.

Dedieu, H. "Quelques traces de religion populaire autour des frères mineurs de la province d'Aquitaine," in M. H. Vicaire, ed., *La religion populaire en Languedoc du XIIIᵉ siècle à la moitié du XIVᵉ siècle.* Cahiers de Fanjeaux, 11 (Toulouse, 1976), 227–50.

Delaborde, H. F. "Une oeuvre nouvelle de Guillaume de St-Pathus." *BEC*, 63 (1902), 263–88.

DeMolen, R. L. "The Birth of Edward VI and the Death of Queen Jane: The Arguments For and Against Caesarean Section." *Renaissance Studies*, 4 (1990), 359–91.

Denholm-Young, N. *Seignorial Administration in England* (Oxford, 1937).

———. *Richard of Cornwall* (New York, 1947).

———. "The Tournament in the Thirteenth Century," in R. W. Hunt, ed., *Studies in Medieval History*, 252–63.

———. *History and Heraldry, 1254 to 1310* (Oxford, 1965).

———. *Collected Papers* (Cardiff, 1969).

Dobson, R. B. "The Decline and Expulsion of the Medieval Jews of York." *TJHSE*, 26 (1979), 34–52.

Doherty, P. C. "The Date of the Birth of Isabella, Queen of England (1308–1358)." *BIHR*, 48 (1975), 246–48.

Dondaine, A. "Guillaume Peyraut: vie et oeuvres." *Archivum Fratrum Praedicatorum*, 18 (1948), 162–236.

Douie, D. *Archbishop Pecham* (Oxford, 1952).

Dupront, A. "Sacre, autorité, pouvoir: profil d'anthropologie historique," in J. Sainsaulieu, ed., *Le sacre des rois.* Actes du colloque internationale d'histoire sur les sacres et couronnements royaux (Reims 1975) (Paris, 1985), 315–42.

Dyer, C. *Lords and Peasants in a Changing Society: The Estates of the Bishopric of Winchester, 680–1540* (Cambridge, 1980).

Eales, R. "The Game of Chess: An Aspect of Medieval Knightly Culture," in C. Harper-Bill, ed., *The Ideals and Practice of Medieval Knighthood, I,* 12–34.

Ehrlich, L. *Proceedings against the Crown (1216–1377)* (Oxford, 1921).

Einstein, A. *Mozart. His Character, His Work.* Trans. A. Mendel and N. Broder (Oxford, 1945).

Elliott, D. *Spiritual Marriage: Sexual Abstinence in Medieval Wedlock* (Princeton, 1993).

Ellis, E. *A General Introduction to Domesday,* 2 vols. (London, 1833).

Emden, A. B. *A Biographical Register of the University of Oxford to 1500,* 3 vols. (Oxford, 1957–59).

Enright, M. J. "Lady with a Mead-cup. Ritual, Group Cohesion and Hierarchy in the Germanic Warband." *Frühmittelalterliche Studien*, 22 (1988), 170–203.

Entwhistle, W. J. *The Arthurian Legend in the Literatures of the Spanish Peninsula* (London, 1925).

Erler, M., and Kowaleski, M., eds. *Women and Power in the Middle Ages* (Athens, GA, 1988).

Evans, J. "A Prototype of the Eleanor Crosses." *Burlington Magazine*, 91 (1949), 96–99.

Evans, T. *Old Ballads, Historical and Narrative, with Some of Modern Date. . . .,* 2nd ed., 2 vols. (London, 1784).

Eyton, R. W. *Court, Household and Itinerary of King Henry II, instancing also the Chief Agents and Adversaries of the King in His Government, Diplomacy, and Strategy* (London, 1878).

Facinger, M. "A Study of Medieval Queenship: Capetian France." *Studies in Medieval and Renaissance History*, 5 (1968), 1–47.

Farmer, S. "Persuasive Voices: Clerical Images of Medieval Wives." *Speculum*, 61 (1986), 517–43.

Farrer, W. *Honours and Knights' Fees,* 3 vols. (London, 1923–25).

Fenwick, M. E. "The Inquiry into Complaints Against the Ministers of Eleanor of Castile, 1291–92" (M.A. thesis, University of London, 1931).

Fernandez de Retana, L. *Albores del Imperio: San Fernando III y su epoca* (Madrid, 1941).

Finucane, R. C. "Sacred Corpse, Profane Carrion: Social Ideals and Death Rituals in the Later Middle Ages," in J. Whaley, ed., *Mirrors of Mortality: Studies in the Social History of Death* (New York, 1981), 40–60.

Folda, J. *Crusader Manuscript Illumination at Saint-Jean d'Acre, 1275–1291* (Princeton, 1976).

Foss, E. *The Judges of England,* 9 vols. (London, 1848–64).

Fowler, G. H. "Montchensy of Edwardstone and Some Kinsmen." *Miscellanea Heraldica et Genealogica,* 5th ser. 10 (1938), 1–10.

Fowler, J. K. *A History of Beaulieu Abbey A.D. 1204–1539* (London, 1911).

Fradenburg, L. O. "Rethinking Queenship," in idem, ed. *Women and Sovereignty,* 1–13.

———, ed. *Women and Sovereignty* (Edinburgh, 1992 = *Cosmos,* 7 [for 1991]).

du Fresne du Cange, C. *Histoire des comtes de Ponthieu,* ed. A. le Sueur (Abbeville, 1917).

Friedenwald, H. *The Jews and Medicine: Essays,* 2 vols. (Baltimore, 1944; rpt 1967).

Fryde, N. M. "A Royal Enquiry into Abuses: Queen Eleanor's Ministers in North-east Wales, 1291–92." *Welsh History Review,* 5 (1970–71), 366–76.

Galbraith, V. "Good Kings and Bad Kings in Medieval English History." *History,* 30 (1945), 119–32.

———. "The Literacy of the English Medieval Kings." *Proceedings of the British Academy,* 21 (1935), 201–35.

Galloway, J. *Eleanor of Castile, Queen of England, and the Monuments Erected in her Memory* (London, 1909).

Gardner, A. *English Medieval Sculpture.* 2nd ed. (Cambridge, 1951).

Gardner, E. G. *The Arthurian Legend in Italian Literature* (London, 1930).

Geertz, C. "Centers, Kings and Charisma: Reflections on the Symbolics of Power," in S. Wilentz, ed., *Rites of Power,* 13–39.

George, M. D. *Catalogue of Political and Personal Satires Preserved in the Department of Prints and Drawings in the British Museum, vol. VII: 1793–1800* (London, 1942).

Giesey, R. "Models of Rulership in French Royal Ceremonial," in S. Wilentz, ed., *Rites of Power,* 41–64.

Giles, P., and F. Wormald, eds. *A Descriptive Catalogue of the Additional Illuminated Manuscripts in the Fitzwilliam Museum Acquired between 1895 and 1979,* 2 vols. (Cambridge, 1981).

Gillingham, J. "Richard I and Berengaria of Navarre." *BIHR,* (1980), 157–73.

Gillingham, J., and J. C. Holt, eds. *War and Government in the Middle Ages. Essays in Honour of J. O. Prestwich* (Woodbridge, 1984).

Giménez y Martínez de Carvajal, J. "San Raimundo de Peñafort y las Partidas de Alfonso X el Sabio." *Anthologica Annua: Publicaciones del Instituto español de estudios eclesiasticos,* 3 (1955), 201–338.

Given-Wilson, C. "The Merger of Edward III's and Queen Philippa's Households, 1360–69," *Bulletin of the Institute of Historical Research,* 51 (1978), 183–87.

———. *The Royal Household and the King's Affinities: Service, Politics and Finance in England, 1360–1413* (New Haven, 1986).

Given-Wilson, C., and A. Curteis. *The Royal Bastards of Medieval England* (London, 1984).

Gonzàlez, J. *El reino de Castilla en la época de Alfonso VIII,* 3 vols. (Madrid, 1960).

———. *Reinado y Diplomas de Fernando III,* 3 vols. (Córdoba, 1980–86).

Gonzalo, J. *Las conquistas de Fernando III en Andalucía* (Madrid, 1946).

Goodman, A. "Alfonso X and the English Crown," in J. C. de Miguel Rodríguez, A. Muñoz Fernandez, and C. Seguro Graiño, eds., *Alfonso el Sabio,* 39–54.

Gough, R. *Sepulchral Monuments of Great Britain,* 2 vols. in 5 folios (London, 1786–96).

Gransden, A. "The Continuation of the *Flores Historiarum* from 1265 to 1327." *Mediaeval Studies,* 36 (1974), 472–92.

Green, M. A. E. *Lives of the Princesses of England from the Norman Conquest,* 6 vols. (London, 1849–55).

Greenblatt, *Renaissance Self-Fashioning: More to Shakespeare* (Chicago, 1980).

Griffiths, R. A. "The Crown and the Royal Family in Later Medieval England," in idem and J. Sherborne, eds., *Kings and Nobles in the Later Middle Ages: A Tribute to Charles Ross* (New York, 1986), 15–26.

———. "The Sense of Dynasty in the Reign of Henry VI," in C. Ross, ed., *Patronage, Pedigree and Power,* 13–36.

Guilloreau, L. "Marie de Woodstock, une fille d'Édouard I moniale à Amesbury." *Revue Mabillon*, 9 (1914), 341–59.

Hallam, E. M. "Royal Burial and the Cult of Kingship in France and England, 1060–1330." *JMH*, 8 (1982), 359–80.

———. "The Eleanor Crosses and Royal Burial Customs," in D. Parsons, ed., *Eleanor of Castile 1290–1990*, 1–22.

Hanawalt, B. A. "Golden Ages for the History of English Medieval Women," in S. M. Stuard, ed., *Women in Medieval History and Historiography*, 1–24.

———. "Lady Honor Lisle's Networks of Influence," in M. Erler and M. Kowaleski, eds., *Women and Power in the Middle Ages*, 188–212.

Harding, A. *England in the Thirteenth Century* (Cambridge, 1993).

Harmer, F. E. *Anglo-Saxon Writs* (Manchester, 1952).

Harper-Bill, C., ed. *The Ideals and Practice of Medieval Knighthood, I. Papers from the First and Second Strawberry Hill Conferences* (Woodbridge, 1986).

Harvey, B. F. *Westminster Abbey and its estates in the Middle Ages* (Oxford, 1977).

———. *Living and Dying in England 1100–1540. The Monastic Experience* (Oxford, 1993).

Hasted, E. *The History and Topographical Survey of the County of Kent.* 2nd ed., 12 vols. (Canterbury, 1797–1801; rpt London, 1972).

Hayden, I. *Symbol and Privilege. The Ritual Context of British Monarchy* (Tucson, 1987).

Helmholz, R. H. "Usury and the medieval English church courts." *Speculum*, 61 (1986), 364–80.

Henderson, D. "Elizabeth's Watchful Eye and George Peele's Gaze: Examining Female Power Beyond the Individual," in L. O. Fradenburg, ed., *Women and Sovereignty*, 150–69.

Herriott, J. H. "A Thirteenth-Century Manuscript of the Primera Partida." *Speculum*, 43 (1968), 278–94.

Highfield, J. R. L. "The Early Colleges," in J. Catto, ed., *The History of the University of Oxford*, I, 225–64.

Hillgarth, J. N. *The Spanish Kingdoms 1250–1516, I: 1250–1410* (Oxford, 1976).

Hilpert, H. E. "Richard of Cornwall's Candidature for the German Throne and the Christmas 1256 Parliament at Westminster." *JMH*, 6 (1980), 185–98.

Hilton, R. H. *A Medieval Society: The West Midlands at the End of the Thirteenth Century* (London, 1966).

Hinnebusch, W., OP. *The Early English Friars Preachers* (Rome, 1951).

———. *The History of the Dominican Order*, 2 vols. (New York, 1965–73).

Historical Manuscripts Commission. *Calendar of the Manuscripts of the Dean and Chapter of Wells*, 2 vols. (London, 1907–14).

Hockey, S. F. *Quarr Abbey and Its Lands, 1132–1631* (Leicester, 1970).

Hollister, C. W. "The Viceregal Court of Henry I," in B. S. Bachrach and D. Nicholas, eds., *Law, Custom and the Social Fabric in Medieval Europe: Essays in Honor of Bryce Lyon* (Kalamazoo, 1990), 131–44.

Holmes, G. A. *The Estates of the Higher Nobility in Fourteenth-Century England* (Cambridge, 1957).

Holt, J. C. *The Northerners: A Study in the Reign of King John* (Oxford, 1961).

———. "Feudal Society and the Family in Early Medieval England: iv. The Heiress and the Alien." *TRHS*, 5th ser. 35 (1985), 1–28.

Hope, W. H. St. J. "On the Funeral Effigies of the Kings and Queens of England." *Archaeologia*, 60 (1907), 520–29.

Hopkirk, M. *Queen over the Water. Mary Beatrice of Modena, Queen of James II* (London, 1953).

Howell, M. "The resources of Eleanor of Provence as queen consort." *EHR*, 102 (1987), 372–93.

Howgrave-Graham, R. P. "The Earlier Royal Funeral Effigies: New Light on Portraiture in Westminster Abbey." *Archaeologia*, 98 (1961), 159–69.

Howitt, M. *Biographical Sketches of the Queens of England* (London, 1866).

Hoyt, R. S. *The Royal Demesne in English Constitutional History: 1066–1272* (Ithaca, NY, 1950).

Hughes, D. O. "Regulating Women's Fashion," in C. Klapisch-Zuber, ed., *A History of Women in the West, II*, 136–58.

Huneycutt, L. L. "Female Succession and the Language of Power in the Writings of Twelfth-Century Churchmen," in J. C. Parsons, ed., *Medieval Queenship*, 187–99.

Hunt, R. W., ed. *Studies in Medieval History presented to Frederick Maurice Powicke* (Oxford, 1948).

Hunter, J. "On the Death of Eleanor of Castile, Consort of King Edward the First, and the Honours Paid to her Memory." *Archaeologia*, 29 (1842), 167–91.

Hutchinson, G. E. "Attitudes Toward Nature in Medieval England: The Alphonso and Bird Psalters." *Isis*, 65 (1974), 5–37.

Hyams, P. "The Jewish Minority in Mediaeval England, 1066–1290." *Journal of Jewish Studies*, 25 (1974), 270–93.

Isenburg-Büdingen, W. K. von, and F. Freytag von Loringhoven. *Stammtafeln zur Geschichte der Europäischen Staaten*, 3rd ed., 4 vols. in 3 folios (Marburg, 1953).

James, M. R. *The Apocalypse in Latin and French (Bodleian, MS Douce 180)* (Oxford, 1922).

John, B. *Pembrokeshire* (London, 1976).

Johnson, C. "The System of Account in the Wardrobe of Edward I." *TRHS*, 4th ser. 6 (1923), 50–72.

Johnstone, H. *A Hundred Years of History from Record and Chronicle, 1216–1327* (London, 1912).

———. "The County of Ponthieu, 1279–1307." *EHR* 29 (1914), 435–52.

———. "Archbishop Pecham and the Council of Lambeth of 1281," in A. G. Little and F. M. Powicke, eds., *Essays in Mediaeval History presented to Thomas Frederick Tout* (Manchester, 1925), 171–88.

———. "Poor-relief in the Royal Households of Thirteenth-century England." *Speculum*, 4 (1929), 149–67.

———. "The Queen's Household," in Tout, *Chapters*, v, 231–89.

———. "The Queen's Exchequer under the Three Edwards," in J. G. Edwards, ed., *Historical Essays in Honour of James Tait* (Manchester, 1933) 143–53.

———. *Edward of Carnarvon* (Manchester, 1944).

———. "The Queen's Household," in J. F. Willard and W. A. Morris, eds., *The English Government at Work 1327–1336*, 3 vols. (Cambridge, MA, 1940–1950), i, 250–99.

Jones, A. *Flintshire Ministers' Accounts, 1301–1328* (Prestatyn, 1913).

Jordan, C. "Woman's Rule in Sixteenth-century British Political Thought." *Renaissance Quarterly*, 40 (1987), 421–51.

Jordan, W. C. *Louis IX and the Challenge of the Crusades. A Study in Rulership* (Princeton, 1979).

———. "*Persona et gesta*, 2: the images and deeds of the thirteenth- century Capetians, ii. The case of Saint Louis." *Viator*, 19 (1988), 209–17.

Jordan, W. C., B. McNab, and T. F. Ruiz, eds. *Order and Innovation in the Middle Ages: Essays in Honor of Joseph R. Strayer* (Princeton, 1976).

Kanner, B., ed. *The Women of England from Anglo-Saxon Times to the Present: Interpretive Bibliographical Essays* (Hamden, CT, 1979).

Kantorowicz, E. H. *The King's Two Bodies: A Study in Medieval Political Theology* (Princeton, 1957).

———. "Kingship Under the Impact of Scientific Jurisprudence," in M. Clagett et al., eds., *Twelfth-Century Europe and the Foundations of Modern Society* (Madison, WI, 1961), 89–109.

Keen, M. *Chivalry* (New Haven, 1984).

Keller, J. E. *Alfonso X el Sabio* (New York, 1967).

———, ed. *El Libro de los Engaños e Asayamientos de las Mugeres*, 2nd ed. (Chapel Hill, 1959).

———, trans. *The Book of the Wiles of Women* (Chapel Hill, 1956).

Kendrick, A. F. *English Embroidery* (London, 1905).
———. *The Cathedral Church of Lincoln* (London, 1917).
Kertzer, D. I. *Ritual, Politics, and Power* (New Haven, 1988).
Keynes, S., and M. Lapidge. *Alfred the Great* (Harmondsworth, 1983).
Kibler, W. W., ed., *Eleanor of Aquitaine: Patron and Politician* (Austin, TX, 1976).
King, E. "Large and Small Landowners in Thirteenth-century England: The Case of Peterborough Abbey." *Past and Present,* 47 (1970), 26–50.
———. *Peterborough Abbey 1086–1310: A Study in the Land Market* (Cambridge, 1973).
King, J. N. "The Godly Woman in Elizabethan Iconography." *Renaissance Quarterly,* 38 (1985), 41–84.
———. "Queen Elizabeth I: Representations of the Virgin Queen." *Renaissance Quarterly,* 43 (1990), 30–74.
Kirshner, J., and S. F. Wemple, eds. *Women of the Medieval World. Essays in Honor of John H. Mundy* (Oxford, 1985).
Klaniczay, G. "From Sacral Kingship to Self-Representation: Hungarian and European Royal Saints," originally in E. Vestergaard. ed., *Continuity and Change: Political Institutions and Literary Monuments in the Middle Ages* (Odense, 1986), 61–86; rev. in G. Klaniczay, *The Uses of Supernatural Power: The Transformation of Popular Religion in Medieval and Early-Modern Europe* (Princeton, 1990), 79–94.
Klapisch-Zuber, C., ed. *A History of Women in the West, II: Silences of the Middle Ages,* general eds. G. Duby and M. Perrot; various trans. (Cambridge, MA, 1992).
Klinck, A. L. "Anglo-Saxon Women and the Law." *JMH,* 8 (1982), 107–34.
Knowles, C. H. "The Resettlement of England after the Barons' Wars." *TRHS,* 5th ser. 32 (1982), 25–41.
Knowles, D. *The Religious Orders in England,* 3 vols. (Cambridge, 1948).
Lachaud, F. "Embroidery for the Court of Edward I." *Nottingham Medieval Studies* 37 (1993), 33–52.
Lamphere, L. "Strategies, Cooperation and Conflict Among Women in Domestic Groups," in M. Z. Rosaldo and L. Lamphere, eds., *Woman, Culture and Society,* 97–112.
Lane, H. M. *The Royal Daughters of England,* 2 vols. (London, 1910).
Langlois, Ch.-V. *Le règne de Philippe III le Hardi* (Paris, 1887).
Lasater, A. E. *Spain to England: A Comparative Study of Arabic, European and English literature of the Middle Ages* (Jackson, MI, 1974).
Lathbury, R. H. *The History of Denham, Bucks.* (Uxbridge, 1904).
Lawlor, H. J. *The Fasti of St. Patrick's, Dublin* (Dundalk, 1930).
Lee, P. A. "Reflections of Power: Margaret of Anjou and the Dark Side of Queenship." *Renaissance Quarterly,* 29 (1986), 183–217.
Legge, M. D. *Anglo-Norman in the Cloisters: The Influence of the Orders upon Anglo-Norman Literature* (Edinburgh, 1950).
———. "The Lord Edward's Vegetius." *Scriptorium,* 7 (1953), 262–65.
———. *Anglo-Norman Literature and its Background* (Oxford, 1963).
Le Goff, J. *Your Money or Your Life: Economy and Religion in the Middle Ages.* Trans. P. Ranum (New York, 1988).
le Neve, J. *Fasti Ecclesiae Anglicanae: Or A Calendar of the Principal Ecclesiastical Dignitaries in England,* 2nd ed., 3 vols. (Oxford, 1854).
Levin, C. "Power, Politics, and Sexuality: Images of Elizabeth I," in J. R. Brink, A. P. Coudert, and M. C. Horowitz, eds., *Sixteenth Century Essays and Studies, XII: The Politics of Gender in Early Modern Europe* (1989), 95–110.
———. "John Foxe and the Responsibilities of Queenship," in M. R. Rose, ed., *Women in the Middle Ages and the Renaissance. Literary and Historical Perspectives* (Syracuse, NY, 1986), 113-33.
Lewis, A. "Roger de Leyburn and the Pacification of England, 1265–7." *EHR,* 54 (1939), 193–214.

Leyser, K. J. *Rule and Conflict in an Early Medieval Society. Ottonian Saxony* (Oxford, 1979).
Lindley, P. G. "'Una Grande opera al mio Re': Gilt-Bronze Effigies in England from the Middle Ages to the Renaissance." *Journal of the British Archaeological Association,* 143 (1990), 112–130.
———. "Romanticizing Reality: The Sculptural Memorials of Queen Eleanor and their Context," in D. Parsons, ed., *Eleanor of Castile 1290–1990,* 69–92.
List of Sheriffs for England and Wales, from the Earliest Times down to A.D. 1831, Compiled from Records in the Public Record Office. PRO Lists and Indexes, ix (London, 1898).
Lloyd, L. D., and D. M. Stenton, eds. *Sir Christopher Hatton's Book of Seals* (Oxford, 1950).
Lloyd, S. D. "The Lord Edward's Crusade, 1270–72: Its Setting and Significance," in J. Gillingham and J. C. Holt, eds., *War and Government in the Middle Ages,* 120–33.
———. *English Society and the Crusade, 1216–1307* (Oxford, 1988).
———. "Crusader Knights and the Land Market in the Thirteenth Century," in P. R. Coss and S. D. Lloyd, eds., *Thirteenth-Century England II,* 119–36.
Lodge, E. C. *Gascony Under English Rule* (London, 1926).
Loengard, J. S. "Of the Gift of her Husband: English Dower and its Consequences in the Year 1200," in J. Kirshner and S. F. Wemple, eds., *Women of the Medieval World,* 215–55.
Loomis, R. S., ed. *Arthurian Literature in the Middle Ages: A Collaborative History* (Oxford, 1959).
Lourie, E. "A Society Organized for War: Medieval Spain." *Past and Present* 35 (1966), 54–76.
Lovell, W. "Queen Eleanor's Crosses." *Archaeological Journal,* 49 (1892), 17–43.
McFarlane, K. B. "Had Edward I a 'Policy' Towards the Earls?" *History,* I (1965), 145–59, rpt in idem, *The Nobility in Later Medieval England. The Ford Lectures for 1953 and Related Studies* (Oxford, 1973), 248–67.
MacDonald, R. A. "Law and Politics: Alfonso's Program of Political Reform," in R. I. Burns, ed., *The Worlds of Alfonso the Learned and James the Conqueror,* 192–97.
———. "Alfonso the Learned and Succession: A Father's Dilemma." *Speculum,* 40 (1965), 647–53.
Macrae, E. "Geoffrey of Aspall's Commentaries on Aristotle." *Mediaeval and Renaissance Studies,* 6 (1968), 94–134.
Maddicott, J. R. "Edward I and the Lessons of Baronial Reform: Local Government, 1258–80," in P. R. Coss and S. D. Lloyd, eds.,. *Thirteenth Century England I,* 1–30.
Madox, T. *The History and Antiquities of the Exchequer of the Kings of England* (London, 1711).
Maitland, F. W. *Domesday Book and Beyond* (Cambridge, 1907).
Malkiel, M. L. de. "Arthurian Literature in Spain and Portugal," in R. S. Loomis, ed., *Arthurian Literature in the Middle Ages,* 406–18.
Marsh, F. B. *English Rule in Gascony, 1199–1259* (Ann Arbor, 1912).
Martienssen, A. *Queen Katherine Parr* (London, 1973).
Masek, R. "Women in an Age of Transition, 1485–1714," in B. Kanner, ed., *The Women of England,* 138–82.
Mason, E. "'Pro Statu et Incolumitate regni mei': Royal Monastic Patronage, 1066–1154," in S. Mews, ed., *Religion and National Identity,* 99–117.
Mayer, E. *História de las instituciones sociales y politicos de España, siglos V–XIV,* 2 vols. (Madrid, 1935).
McIntosh, M. K. *Autonomy and Community. The Royal Manor of Havering, 1200–1500* (Cambridge, 1986).
McLaughlin, T. P. "The Teaching of the Canonists on Usury." *Mediaeval Studies,* I (1939), 81–147, and 2 (1940), 1–22.
Menache, S. "Isabelle of France, Queen of England: A Reconsideration," *JMH,* 10 (1984), 107–24.
Mertes, K. *The English Noble Household 1250–1600* (Oxford, 1988).
Mews, S. ed. *Religion and National Identity.* Studies in Church History 18 (Oxford, 1982).

Meyer, M. A. "Women and the tenth-century English monastic reform." *Revue bénédictine,* 87 (1977), 34–61.

———. "Land Charters and the Legal Position of Anglo-Saxon Women," in B. Kanner, ed., *The Women of England,* 57–82.

———. "The Queen's 'Demesne' in Later Anglo-Saxon England," in idem, ed., *The Culture of Christendom. Essays in Medieval History in Commemoration of Denis L. T. Bethell* (London, 1993), 75–113.

Miguel Rodríguez, J. C. de, A. Muñoz Fernandez, and C. Segura Graiño, eds. *Alfonso X el Sabio, Vida, Obra y Epoca, I.* Sociedad Española de Estudios Medievales (Madrid, 1990).

Miller, E. *The Abbey and Bishopric of Ely* (Cambridge, 1971).

Monroe, W. H. "Two Medieval Genealogical Roll Chronicles in the Bodleian Library," *The Bodleian Library Record,* 10 (1979–82), 215–21.

Moodie, S. *Letters of a Lifetime,* ed. C. Ballstadt, E. Hopkins, and M. Peterman (Toronto, 1985).

———. *Roughing it in the Bush,* intr. by Margaret Atwood (London, 1986).

———. *Letters of Love and Duty,* ed. C. Ballstadt, E. Hopkins, and M. Peterman (Toronto, 1993).

Moor, C. *Knights of Edward I: Notices Collected by the Rev. C. Moor,* 5 vols. Selden Society, 80–84 (London, 1919–32).

Moore, R. I. *The Formation of a Persecuting Society* (Oxford, 1987).

Morgan, M. *The English Lands of the Abbey of Bec* (Oxford, 1946).

Morgan, N. *Early Gothic Manuscripts, II: 1250–1285* (London, 1988).

Mugnier, F. *Les Savoyards en Angleterre au XIIIᵉ siècle et Pierre d'Aigueblanche Évêque d'Héreford* (Chambéry, 1890).

Muñoz Sendino, J., ed. *La Escala de Mahoma* (Madrid, 1949).

Murray, H. J. R. "The Medieval Games of Tables." *Medium Aevum,* 10 (1941), 57–69.

Musto, R. "Queen Sancia of Naples (1286–1345) and the Spiritual Fanciscans," in J. Kirshner and S. F. Wemple, eds., *Women of the Medieval World,* 179–214.

Nelson, B. *The Idea of Usury. From Tribal Brotherhood to Universal Otherhood,* 2nd ed. (Chicago, 1969)

Nelson, J. L. "Queens as Jezebels: the Careers of Brunhild and Balthild in Merovingian History," in D. Baker, ed., *Medieval Women,* 31–77.

———. "Inauguration Rituals," in idem, *Politics and Ritual in Early Medieval Europe* (London, 1986), 283–307.

Nichols, J. *The History and Antiquities of the County of Leicester,* 4 vols. in 8 folios (London, 1795–1815, rpt Wakefield, 1971).

Noonan, J. T., Jr. *The Scholastic Analysis of Usury* (Cambridge, 1957).

O'Callaghan, J. F. *A History of Medieval Spain* (Ithaca, 1975).

Oman, C. *Henrietta Maria* (London, 1936).

Ormerod, G. *The History of the County Palatine and City of Chester, compiled from original evidences,* 2nd ed. rev. and enlarged by T. Helsby, 3 vols. (London, 1875–82, rpt Manchester, 1980).

Ormrod, W. M. "The Personal Religion of Edward III." *Speculum,* 64 (1989), 849–77.

———, ed. *England in the Thirteenth Century. Proceedings of the 1989 Harlaxton Symposium.* Harlaxton Medieval Studies, 1 (Stamford, 1991).

Owen, D. D. R. *Eleanor of Aquitaine. Queen and Legend* (Oxford, 1993).

Painter, S. *Studies in the History of the English Feudal Barony* (Baltimore 1943).

Palmer, C. "The Friar-Preachers, or Blackfriars, of Guildford." *The Reliquary and Illustrated Archaeologist,* N.S. 1 (1887), 7–20.

Panofsky, E. *Tomb Sculpture: Four Lectures on Its Changing Aspects from Ancient Egypt to Bernini* (New York, 1964).

Parsons, D., ed. *Eleanor of Castile 1290–1990: Essays to Commemorate the 700th Anniversary of her death* (Stamford, 1991).

Parsons, J. C. "The Year of Eleanor of Castile's Birth and Her Children by Edward I." *Mediaeval Studies,* 46 (1984), 245–65.

——. "Eleanor of Castile and the Countess Margaret of Ulster." *Genealogists' Magazine,* 20 (1984), 335–40.

——. "Towards a Social History of the English Royal Court: The Senches of London, 1246–1350." *Medieval Prosopography,* 9 (1988), 51–71.

——. "The Beginnings of English Administration in Ponthieu." *Mediaeval Studies,* 50 (1988), 371–403.

——. "Eleanor of Castile and the Viscountess Jeanne of Châtelleraut." *Genealogists' Magazine,* 23 (1989), 141–44.

——. "Eleanor of Castile: Legend and Reality through Seven Centuries," in D. Parsons, ed., *Eleanor of Castile,* 23–54.

——. "Ritual and Symbol in the English Queenship to 1500," in L. O. Fradenburg, ed., *Women and Sovereignty,* 60–77.

——. "Piety, Power and the Reputations of Two Thirteenth-century English Queens," in T. Vann, ed., *Queens, Regents and Potentates,* 107–23.

——. "Mothers, Daughters, Marriage, Power: Some Plantagenet Evidence, 1150–1500," in J. C. Parsons, ed., *Medieval Queenship,* 63–78.

——. "Of Queens, Courts and Books: Reflections on the Literary Patronage of Thirteenth-Century Plantagenet Queens", forthcoming in J. H. McCash, ed., *The Literary and Artistic Patronage of Medieval Women* (Athens, GA, 1995).

——, ed. *Medieval Queenship* (New York, 1993).

Patmore, K. A. *The Seven Edwards of England* (London, 1911).

Percy, T. *Reliques of Ancient English Poetry: Consisting of Old Heroic Ballads, Songs, and other Pieces of our earlier Poets.* . . *Together with some few of later Date,* 3 vols. (London, 1765).

Phillips, J. R. S. *Aymer de Valence, Earl of Pembroke 1307–1324* (Oxford, 1972).

——. "Edward II and the Prophets," in W. M. Ormrod, ed., *England in the Fourteenth Century. Proceedings of the 1985 Harlaxton College Symposium* (Woodbridge, 1986), 189–201.

Phythian-Adams, C. "Rutland Reconsidered," in A. Dornier, ed., *Mercian Studies* (Leicester, 1977), 63–84.

Picciotto, C. "The Legal Position of the Jews in Pre-expulsion England, as Shown by the Plea Rolls of the Jewish Exchequer." *TJHSE,* 9 (1918–20), 67–84.

Pickford, C. E. "Miscellaneous French Prose Romances," in R. S. Loomis, ed., *Arthurian Literature in the Middle Ages,* 348–57.

Platt, C. *Medieval Southampton* (London, 1973).

Plucknett, T. F. T. *Legislation of Edward I. The Ford Lectures delivered in the University of Oxford in Hilary Term 1947* (Oxford, 1949).

——. *The Medieval Bailiff* (London, 1954).

Pollock, F., and Maitland, F. W. *The History of English Law Before the Time of Edward I,* 2nd ed., 2 vols. (Cambridge, 1898, rpt 1968).

Pope-Hennessy, U. *Agnes Strickland 1796–1874: Biographer of the Queens of England* (London, 1940).

Post, G. "*Status, id est, magistratus; l'Etat, c'est moi,* and *Status regis:* the `Estate Royal' (1100–1322)." *Studies in Medieval and Renaissance History,* 1 (1964), 3–103.

Postan, M. M. *The Medieval Economy and Society* (London, 1972).

Powers, J. F. "Two Warrior-Kings and their Municipal Militias: The Townsman- Soldier in Law and Life," in R. I. Burns, ed., *The Worlds of Alfonso the Learned and James the Conqueror,* 95–129.

Powicke, F. M. *King Henry III and the Lord Edward* (Oxford, 1947).

——. *The Thirteenth Century, 1216–1307* (Oxford, 1953).

——. "King Edward I in Fact and Fiction," in D. J. Gordon, ed., *Fritz Saxl (1890–1948): A Volume of Memorial Essays* (London, 1957), pp. 129–32.

Powley, E. B. *The House of de la Pomeray* (Liverpool, 1944).

Prarond, E. *Histoire d'Abbeville avant la guerre de Cent Ans* (Abbeville, 1891).

Prestwich, M. "Royal Patronage under Edward I," in P. R. Coss and S. D. Lloyd, eds., *Thirteenth Century England I*, 41–52.
———. "The Piety of Edward I," in W. M. Ormrod, ed., *England in the Thirteenth Century. Proceedings of the 1984 Harlaxton Symposium* (Woodbridge, 1985), 120–28.
———. *Edward I* (Berkeley, CA, 1988).
———. *English Politics in the Thirteenth Century* (New York, 1990).
Procter, E. S. "Materials for a Study of the Reign of Alphonso X of Castile." *TRHS* 4th ser. 14 [1931], 39–64.
———. *Alphonso X of Castile: Patron of Literature and Learning* (Oxford, 1951).
Prynne, W. *Aurum Reginae* (London, 1668).
Raban, S. "The Land Market and the Aristocracy in the Thirteenth Century," in D. Greenaway, C. Holdsworth, and J. Sayers, eds., *Tradition and Change: Essays in Honour of Marjorie Chibnall* (Cambridge, 1985), 239–61.
Ramsay, J. H. *The Dawn of the Constitution* (Oxford, 1908).
Rannie, D. W. *Oriel College* (London, 1900).
Rees, W. *South Wales and the March* (Oxford, 1924).
Rhodes, W. E. "Edmund, Earl of Lancaster." *EHR*, 10 (1895), 19–40, 209–37.
Richard, J. *Saint Louis* (Paris, 1983).
Richardson, H. G. "The Letters and Charters of Eleanor of Aquitaine," *EHR*, 74 (1959), 193–213.
———. *The English Jewry Under the Angevin Kings* (London, 1960).
———. "The Coronation in Medieval England: the Evolution of the Office and the Oath." *Traditio*, 16 (1960), 111–202.
Richardson, H. G., and Sayles, G. O. *The Governance of Medieval England from the Conquest to Magna Carta* (Edinburgh, 1963).
Ridgeway, H. "The Lord Edward and the Provisions of Oxford (1258): A Study in Faction," in P. R. Coss and S. D. LLoyd, eds., *Thirteenth Century England I*, 89–99.
———. "Foreign Favorites and Henry III's Problems of Patronage, 1247–1258." *EHR*, 104 (1989), 590–616.
———. "King Henry III and the `Aliens', 1236–1272," in P. R. Coss and S. D. Lloyd, eds., *Thirteenth-Century England II*, 81–92.
Robo, E. *Mediaeval Farnham* (Farnham, 1935).
Rogers, K. M. *The Troublesome Helpmate. A History of Misogyny in Literature* (London, 1966).
Rosaldo, M. Z. "Woman, Culture and Society: A Theoretical Overview," in idem and L. Lamphere, eds., *Woman, Culture and Society*, 17–42.
Rosaldo, M. Z., and L. Lamphere, eds. *Woman, Culture and Society* (Stanford, 1974).
Ross, C., ed. *Patronage, Pedigree and Power in Later Medieval England* (Gloucester, 1979).
Roth, C. *The Jews of Medieval Oxford.* Oxford Historical Society, N.S. 9 (Oxford, 1951).
———. "Some Notes on Pre-Expulsion Scholars." *Journal of Jewish Studies*, 3 (1952), 56–61.
———. *Intellectual Activities of Medieval English Jewry.* British Academy Supplemental Papers, 8 (London, 1953).
———. *A History of the Jews in England*, 3rd. ed. (Oxford, 1964).
Ruíz, T. F. "Castilian Merchants in England, 1248–1350," in W. C. Jordan, B. McNab, and T. F. Ruiz, eds., *Order and Innovation in the Middle Ages*, 173–85.
———. "Unsacred Monarchy: The Kings of Castile in the Late Middle Ages," in S. Wilentz, ed., *Rites of Power*, 109–44.
Russell, J. C. *Dictionary of Writers of Thirteenth-Century England* (London, 1936).
Salter, E. *English and International: Studies in the Literature, Art and Patronage of Medieval England* (Cambridge, 1988).
Salzman, L. F. "Tregoz." *Sussex Archaeological Collections*, 93 (1955), 34–58.
———. *Edward I* (London, 1968).
Sambrook, S. *James Thomson 1700–1748: A Life* (Oxford, 1991).
Sánchez de la Cuesta y Gutierrez, G. *Dos Reyes enfermos del corazón: los conquistadores de Sevilla* (Seville, 1948).

Sanders, I. J. *English Baronies. A Study of Their Origin and Descent, 1086–1327* (Oxford, 1960).

Sandler, L. F. *Gothic Manuscripts 1285–1385: A Survey of Manuscripts Illuminated in the British Isles, v,* 2 vols. (London, 1986).

Sayles, G. O. *The Medieval Foundations of England,* 2nd ed. (London, 1950).

———. *The King's Parliament of England* (London, 1975).

Schapiro, M. *Words and Pictures.* Approaches to Semiotics, paperback series, 11 (1973).

Schatzmiller, J. *Shylock Revisited: Jews, Moneylending and Medieval Society* (Los Angeles, 1990).

Schramm, P. E. *A History of the English Coronation.* Trans. L. G. W. Legg (Oxford, 1937).

Scott, G. *The National Memorial to the Prince Consort* (London, 1873).

Scott, M. J. W. *James Thomson, Anglo-Scot* (Athens, GA, 1988).

Segura Graiño, C. "Semblanza Humana de Alfonso el Sabio," in J. C. de Miguel Rodríguez, A. Muñoz Fernandez, and C. Segura Graiño, eds. *Alfonso X el Sabio,* 11–29.

Serjeantson, R. M. *History of Delapré Abbey* (Northampton, 1909).

Sivéry, G. *Marguerite de Provence. Une reine au temps des cathédrales* (Paris, 1984).

Smith, N. "A Note on the Conservation of the Geddington Cross," in D. Parsons, ed., *Eleanor of Castile 1290–1990,* 93–95.

Smith, R. A. L. *Canterbury Cathedral Priory* (Cambridge, 1943).

Snellgrove, H. S. *The Lusignans in England, 1247–1258* (Albuquerque, NM, 1950).

Socarras, C. *Alphonso X of Castile.* A Study on Imperialistic Frustration (Barcelona, 1976).

Society of Antiquaries of London. *Vetusta Monumenta quae ad rerum Britannicarum memoriam conservandam Societas antiquariorum Londini sumptu suo edenda curavit,* 3 vols. (London, 1747–1835).

Soulsby, I. *The Towns of Medieval Wales: A Study of their History, Archaeology and Early Topography* (Chichester, 1983).

Spiegel, G. "The *Reditus Regni ad Stirpem Karoli Magni:* A New Look." *French Historical Studies,* 7 (1971), 145–71.

———. "Pseudo-Turpin, The Crisis of the Aristocracy and the Beginnings of Vernacular Historiography in France," *JMH,* 12 (1986), 207–223.

Stacey, R. C. "Agricultural Investment and the Management of the Royal Demesne Manors, 1236–1240." *Journal of Economic History,* 46 (1986), 928–32.

———. *Politics, Policy and Finance under Henry III, 1216–1245* (Oxford, 1987).

Stafford, P. "Sons and Mothers: Family Politics in the Early Middle Ages," in D. Baker, ed., *Medieval Women,* 79–100.

———. "The King's Wife in Wessex, 800–1066." *Past and Present,* 91 (1981), 3–27.

———. *Queens, Concubines and Dowagers: The King's Wife in the Early Middle Ages* (Athens, GA, 1985).

———. "The Portrayal of Royal Women in England, Mid-Tenth to Mid- Twelfth Centuries," in J. C. Parsons, ed., *Medieval Queenship,* 141–65.

Staines, D. "Havelok the Dane: A Thirteenth-Century Handbook for Princes," *Speculum,* 51 (1976), 602–23.

Staniland, K. "Welcome, Royal Babe! The Birth of Thomas of Brotherton in 1300." *Costume,* 19 (1985), 1–13.

———. "Royal Entry into the World," in D. Williams, ed., *England in the Fifteenth Century. Proceedings of the 1986 Harlaxton Symposium* (Woodbridge, 1987), 297–313.

Stanley, A. P. *Memorials of Westminster Abbey* (London, 1867).

Steiner, A. "Guillaume Perrault and Vincent of Beauvais." *Speculum,* 8 (1933), 51–58.

———. "New Light on Guillaume Perrault." *Speculum,* 17 (1942) 519–48.

Stenton, D. M. *English Society in the Early Middle Ages,* 4th edn (Harmondsworth, 1965).

Stokes, H. P. "The Relationship Between the Jews and the Royal Family of England in the thirteenth century." *TJHSE,* 8 (1918), 153–70.

Stone, L. "Jean de Howden, poète anglo-normand du XIIIe siècle." *Romania,* 69 (1946–47), 496–519.

Stone, L. *Sculpture in Britain: The Middle Ages* (Harmondsworth, 1955).

Stone, L. *The Family, Sex and Marriage in England, 1500–1800* (London, 1977).
Strayer, J. R. "The Laicisation of French and English Society in the Thirteenth Century," in
    S. Thrupp, ed., *Change in Medieval Society* (London, 1965), 103–15.
———. "The Crusades of Louis IX," in K. M. Setton *et al.*, eds. *A History of the Crusades*,
    5 vols. (Philadelphia, 1969–1985), ii: *The Later Crusades, 1189–1311* (1969), 514–18.
Strickland, A. *Lives of the Queens of England from the Norman Conquest*, 2nd ed., 8 vols.
    (London, 1851, reissued 1854).
Strohm, P. "Queens as Intercessors," in idem, *Hochon's Arrow. The Social Imagination of
    Fourteenth-Century Texts* (Princeton, 1992), 95–119.
Stuard, S. M. "Fashion's Captives: Medieval Women in French Historiography," in S. M.
    Stuard, ed., *Women in Medieval History and Historiography*, 59–80.
———, ed. *Women in Medieval History and Historiography* (Philadelphia, 1987).
Studd, J. R. "Henry III and the Lord Edward." *BIHR*, 50 (1977), 4–19.
Swanson, R. N. "Medieval Liturgy as Theatre: The Props," in D. Wood, ed., *The Church and
    the Arts*. Studies in Church History 28 (Oxford, 1992), 239–53.
Talbot, C. H., and E. A. Hammond. *The Medical Practitioners in Medieval England: A Biographical
    Register* (London, 1965).
Tate, R. B. "Rodrigo Sánchez de Arévalo (1404–1470) and his *Compendiosa Historica
    Hispanica*." *Nottingham Medieval Studies*, 4 (1960), 58–80.
Taylor, A. "Royal Alms and Oblations in the later Thirteenth Century. An Analysis of the
    Alms Roll of 12 Edward I (1283–4)," in F. Emmison and R. Stephens, eds., *Tribute
    to an Antiquary: Essays presented to Marc Fitch by Some of his Friends* (London, 1976),
    93–125.
Taylor, A. J. "Edward I and the Shrine of St. Thomas of Canterbury." *Journal of the British
    Archaeological Association*, 132 (1979), 22–28.
Taylor, J. M. *Eva Perón: The Myths of a Woman* (Chicago, 1979).
Thomson, J. *Edward and Eleanora: A Tragedy* (London, 1739).
Thompson, R. *Women in Stuart England and America: A Comparative Study* (London, 1974).
Thoroton, R. *The Antiquities of Nottinghamshire, Edited and Enlarged by John Throsby*, 3 vols.
    (Nottingham, 1790–96, rpt Wakefield, 1972).
Thorpe, L. "Mastre Richard, a Thirteenth Century Translator of the `De Re Militari' of
    Vegetius." *Scriptorium*, 6 (1952), 39–50.
———. "Mastre Richard at the Skirmish of Kenilworth?" *Scriptorium*, 7 (1953), 120–21.
Tolley, T. "Eleanor of Castile and the `Spanish' Style in England," in W. M. Ormrod, ed.,
    England in the Thirteenth Century, 167–92.
Tout, T. F. *Chapters in the Administrative History of Medieval England*, 6 vols. (Manchester,
    1929–33).
Trabut-Cussac, J. P. "Itinéraire d'Édouard Ier en France, 1286–1289." *Bulletin of the Institute
    of Historical Research*, 25 (1952), 160–203.
———. "Le financement de la croisade anglaise de 1270." *Bibliothèque de l'Ecôle des Chartes*,
    119 (1961), 113–40.
———. "Don Enrique de Castille en Angleterre, 1256–1259." *Mélanges de la casa de
    Velázquez*, 2 (1966), 51–58.
———. *L'administration anglaise en Gascogne* (Geneva, 1972).
Treharne, R. F. *The Baronial Plan of Reform, 1258–1263* (Manchester, 1932).
———. "The Knights in the Period of Reform and Revolution." *BIHR*, 21 (1946), 1–12.
Tristram, E. W. *English Wall Painting of the Fourteenth Century* (London, 1955).
Turner, R. V. "Eleanor of Aquitaine and Her Children: An Inquiry into Medieval Family
    Attachment." *JMH*, 14 (1988), 321–35.
Tyerman, C. *England and the Crusades, 1095–1588* (Chicago, 1988).
Vale, J. *Edward III and Chivalry* (Woodbridge, 1983).
Vann, T. "The Theory and Practice of Medieval Castilian Queenship," in idem, ed., *Queens,
    Regents and Potentates*, 125–47.

————, ed. *Queens, Regents and Potentates.* Women of Power, I (Cambridge, 1993).
Vauchez, A. *Les laïcs au moyen age: Pratiques et expériences religieuses* (Paris, 1987).
————. "Lay Peoples' Sanctity in Western Europe (Twelfth and Thirteenth Centuries)," in R. Blumenfeld-Kosinski and T. Szell, eds., *Images of Sainthood in Medieval Europe* (Ithaca, 1991), 21–32.
Vaughan, P. *Matthew Paris* (London, 1958).
Wagner, A. *Heralds of England* (London, 1967).
————. *English Genealogy*, 2nd ed. (Oxford, 1972).
Walters, J. *The Royal Griffin. Frederick Prince of Wales* (London, 1972).
Wander, S. H. "Westminster Abbey: a case study in the meaning of medieval architecture" (Ph.D. Diss., Stanford, 1975).
Ward, E. "Caesar's Wife: The Career of the Empress Judith (819–829)," in P. Godman and R. Collins, eds., *Charlemagne's Heir. New Perspectives on the Reign of Louis the Pious (814–840)* (Oxford, 1990), 205–27.
Warren, W. L. *Henry II* (Berkeley, CA, 1973).
Watson, B. "The Artists of the Tiptoft Missal and the Court Style: Perspectives from the Techniques of the Book." *Scriptorium*, 33 (1979), 25–39.
Watson, G. W. "The Families of Lacy, Geneva, Joinville and la Marche." *The Genealogist*, N.S. 5 (1905), 1–16, 73–82, 163–72, 234–43.
Watt, J. A. "The English Episcopate, the State and the Jews: The Evidence of the Thirteenth-Century Conciliar Degrees," in P. R. Coss and S. D. Lloyd, eds., *Thirteenth-Century England II*, 137–48.
Waugh, S. L. "Marriage, Class and Royal Lordship in England under Henry III." *Viator*, 16 (1985), 181–207.
————. *The Lordship of England: Royal Wardships and Marriages in English Society and Politics 1217–1327* (Princeton, 1988).
Wells, R. H. *Spenser's Faerie Queen and the Cult of Elizabeth* (Totowa, NJ, 1983).
Weinstein, D., and R. M. Bell. *Saints and Society: The Two Worlds of Western Christendom, 1000–1700* (Chicago, 1986).
Wilentz, S., ed. *Rites of Power: Symbolism, Ritual and Politics since the Middle Ages* (Philadelphia, 1985).
Wilkinson, B. "The Household Ordinance of 1279." *History*, 12 (1927), 46–47.
Williams, G. A. *Medieval London: From Commune to Capital* (London, 1963).
Williams, E. C. *Anne of Denmark* (London, 1970).
Wilson, J. *Entertainments for Elizabeth I* (Woodbridge, 1980).
Winters, W. *The Queen Eleanor Memorial, Waltham Cross* (Waltham Abbey, 1885).
Wolff, R. L. "Morgage and Redemption of an Emperor's Son: Castile and the Latin Empire of Constantinople." *Speculum*, 29 (1954), 45–84.
Wolffe, B. P. *The Royal Demesne in English History: The Crown Estate in the Government of the Realm from the Conquest to 1509* (Athens, OH, 1971).
Woodbridge, L. *Women and the English Renaissance: Literature and the Nature of Womankind* (Urbana, 1984).
Wright, L. B. *Middle-Class Culture in Elizabethan England* (Chapel Hill, 1935).
Wrottesley, G. *Pedigrees from the Plea Rolls, Collected from the Pleadings in the Various Courts of Law, A.D. 1200 to 1500.* Reprinted from *The Genealogist*, N.S. 5–21 (1887–1903) (London, s.d.).
Yapp, W. B. "The Birds of English Medieval Manuscripts," *JMH*, 5 (1979), 315–49.
Young, C. R. *The Royal Forests of Medieval England* (Philadelphia, 1979).
Zanger, A. "Fashioning the Body Politic: Imagining the Queen in the Marriage of Louis XIV," in L. O. Fradenburg, ed., *Women and Sovereignty*, 101–20.
Zook, M. "History's Mary," in L. O. Fradenburg, ed., *Women and Sovereignty*, 170–91.
Zweig, S. *Marie Antoinette: Portrait of an Average Woman.* Trans. E. Paul and C. Paul (New York, 1933).

❀ Index ❀

services for 213-216
tombs and monuments 205-13
travel 32-33, 56, 63, 144
resources of
dower 13-15, 19, 26, 76, 122, 127, 157
extant accounts analyzed 75, 81-84
income and expenses estimated 25-26, 84
Jews and 78-80
exacts usery 150
landed revenue 76-77, 83-84
loans to 85-86
money gifts to 80-81
prerogative revenue 77-81
queen-gold 26, 72, 77, 83-84
revenue outside England 81
Ellesworth, Simon de 160
Elmdon (Warks.) 194
Eltham (Kent) 178
England, kings of
Charles I 236
Charles II 236
Edward the Confessor, Saint, cult of 15, 17, 25,
55-56, 213
Edward I 2, 7, 10, 12-16, 36, 55, 59, 60, 91,
101-02, 129
attempt on life of (1272) 29
Barons' Wars and 21-25
children of 38-39, 41
chivalry and 29, 55-56
Crusade of 1270 and 29-30
Eleanor of Castile and 43-50, 65-66, 101,
153-54, 220-21, 250-52
lands and 20-24, 33, 74-76, 127, 136-38
Jews and 140
legislation of 112-13
monumental program and services for E
206-15
his relatives and 36-37
succession to the throne 38, 45
Edward II 2, 5, 34, 40, 41, 91, 278n.197
Edward III 2
Edward VI 223
Ethelwulf 37
George II 237
Henry I 2 76 86, 206
Matilda the Empress, dau of 222, 236
Henry II 4, 7, 20, 32, 73, 77
Henry III 2, 4, 8, 10-15, 17-27, 30, 34, 35-36,

37, 39, 73, 76, 79, 86, 97, 101, 113, 122,
124, 126-27, 136, 138, 147, 170, 206, 208,
209, 213, 232, 251
Lusignan siblings of 21-22, 37, 46, 113;
see also Lusignan, Geoffrey de; Valence,
Aymer and William de; Winchester,
Aymer de Valence bp of.
Henry VI 5
Henry VIII 223
James I (VI of Scotland) 233, 235-36
James II 236
John 7, 11, 12, 15, 72, 75-76, 206
Richard I 15, 72, 206
Stephen 2, 20, 76, 86
Eustace, s. of 20
William III 236
England, queens of
Adelicia of Louvain 86
Anne Boleyn 223
Anne of Cleves 223, 236
Anne of Denmark 236
Berengaria of Navarre 72-73, 76
Caroline of Ansbach 237
Catherine of Braganza 236
Edith-Matilda of Scotland 2, 86
Eleanor of Aquitaine 4, 5, 7, 72, 74, 75, 77,
86, 93, 222, 236, 244
Eleanor of Provence 2, 4, 8, 17, 20, 22, 25, 32,
34, 35-36, 37-38, 39, 45, 57, 73, 74, 76,
86, 87, 97, 110, 114, 122, 139, 143, 147,
153, 158, 196, 209, 230, 249
Savoyard relatives of 21-22, 34, 36, 37,
46-47
Elizabeth I 222-36
Elizabeth Woodville 37
Henrietta Maria of France 236
Isabella of Angoulême 47, 72, 73, 75-76, 86
Isabella of France (wife of Edward II) 2, 5, 222,
236, 244, 291n.103
Jane Seymour 223
Katherine of Aragon 236
Katherine Howard 223
Katherine Parr 223
Margaret of Anjou 5, 37, 222, 236, 249
Margaret of France 153
dower lands of 123
s. of 64
Mary I 226, 233